1008276428

# EXPLORATIONS IN LATIN LITERATURE

Denis Feeney is one of the most distinguished scholars of Latin literature and Roman culture in the world of the last half-century. These two volumes conveniently collect and present afresh all his major papers, covering a wide range of topics and interests. Ancient epic is a major focus, followed by Latin lyric, historiography and elegy. Ancient literary criticism and the technology of the book are recurrent themes. Many papers address the problems of literary responses to religion and ritual, with an interdisciplinary methodology drawing on comparative anthropology and religion. The transition from Republic to Empire and the emergence of the Augustan Principate form the background to the majority of the papers, and the question of how literary texts are to be read in historical context is addressed throughout. All quotations from ancient and modern languages have now been translated, and Stephen Hinds has contributed a Foreword.

DENIS FEENEY is Giger Professor of Latin in the Department of Classics at Princeton University. His publications include *The Gods in Epic* (1991), *Literature and Religion at Rome* (1998), *Caesar's Calendar* (2007) and *Beyond Greek* (2016). He was also a Series Editor, with Stephen Hinds, of *Roman Literature and its Contexts* for Cambridge University Press. He is a Fellow of the British Academy and Member of the American Academy of Arts and Sciences and has held Fellowships from the Guggenheim Foundation and the American Council of Learned Societies.

# EXPLORATIONS IN LATIN LITERATURE

*Volume 1*

*Epic, Historiography, Religion*

DENIS FEENEY
*Princeton University*

WITH FOREWORD BY
STEPHEN HINDS
*University of Washington*

# CAMBRIDGE
## UNIVERSITY PRESS

University Printing House, Cambridge CB2 8BS, United Kingdom

One Liberty Plaza, 20th Floor, New York, NY 10006, USA

477 Williamstown Road, Port Melbourne, VIC 3207, Australia

314–321, 3rd Floor, Plot 3, Splendor Forum, Jasola District Centre,
New Delhi – 110025, India

103 Penang Road, #05–06/07, Visioncrest Commercial, Singapore 238467

Cambridge University Press is part of the University of Cambridge.

It furthers the University's mission by disseminating knowledge in the pursuit of education, learning, and research at the highest international levels of excellence.

www.cambridge.org
Information on this title: www.cambridge.org/9781108481861
DOI: 10.1017/9781108680226

© Denis Feeney 2021

This publication is in copyright. Subject to statutory exception and to the provisions of relevant collective licensing agreements, no reproduction of any part may take place without the written permission of Cambridge University Press.

First published 2021

*A catalogue record for this publication is available from the British Library.*

*Library of Congress Cataloging-in-Publication Data*
NAMES: Feeney, D. C., author.
TITLE: Explorations in Latin literature / Denis Feeney.
DESCRIPTION: New York : Cambridge University Press, 2021. | Includes bibliographical references and index.
IDENTIFIERS: LCCN 2020041267 (print) | LCCN 2020041268 (ebook) | ISBN 9781108481861 (v.1 : hardback) | ISBN 9781108481854 (v.2 : hardback) | ISBN 9781108668200 (ebook)
SUBJECTS: LCSH: Latin literature – History and criticism.
CLASSIFICATION: LCC PA6003 .F44 2021 (print) | LCC PA6003 (ebook) | DDC 870.9–dc23
LC record available at https://lccn.loc.gov/2020041267
LC ebook record available at https://lccn.loc.gov/2020041268

2 volume set ISBN 978-1-108-66820-0 Hardback
Volume 1 ISBN 978-1-108-48186-1 Hardback
Volume 2 ISBN 978-1-108-48185-4 Hardback

Cambridge University Press has no responsibility for the persistence or accuracy of URLs for external or third-party internet websites referred to in this publication and does not guarantee that any content on such websites is, or will remain, accurate or appropriate.

*In memory of my teachers*
*Mike Farrell and Ken Trembath*
*(Auckland Grammar School)*
*Pat Lacey (Auckland University)*
*Robin Nisbet (Oxford University)*

# Contents

| | | |
|---|---|---|
| Foreword by Stephen Hinds | | page ix |
| List of Acknowledgements and Original Places of Publication | | xx |
| | Introduction | 1 |
| 1. | The Taciturnity of Aeneas | 15 |
| 2. | The Reconciliations of Juno | 39 |
| 3. | Epic Hero and Epic Fable | 62 |
| 4. | *Stat magni nominis umbra*: Lucan on the Greatness of Pompeius Magnus | 83 |
| 5. | History and Revelation in Virgil's Underworld | 91 |
| 6. | Following after Hercules, in Virgil and Apollonius | 117 |
| 7. | Beginning Sallust's *Catiline* | 141 |
| 8. | Leaving Dido: The Appearance(s) of Mercury and the Motivations of Aeneas | 148 |
| 9. | Epic Violence, Epic Order: Killings, Catalogues, and the Role of the Reader in *Aeneid* 10 | 168 |
| 10. | *Mea tempora*: Patterning of Time in Ovid's *Metamorphoses* | 183 |
| 11. | Interpreting Sacrificial Ritual in Roman Poetry: Disciplines and their Models | 204 |
| 12. | *Tenui . . . latens discrimine*: Spotting the Differences in Statius' *Achilleid* | 228 |

13. On Not Forgetting the 'Literatur' in 'Literatur und Religion':
    Representing the Mythic and the Divine in Roman
    Historiography                                                247

14. Virgil's Tale of Four Cities: Troy, Carthage, Alexandria
    and Rome                                                      271

15. First Similes in Epic                                         286

16. Fictions of Citizenship in Livy's *History*                   322

*Published Works of Denis Feeney*                                 365
*Bibliography*                                                    374
*Index Locorum*                                                   402
*General Index*                                                   412

# *Foreword*

*Stephen Hinds*

When I was approached about the idea of writing a preface to Denis Feeney's collected papers, my immediate reaction was that Denis is too young to collect his papers, and that I myself am too young for reminiscences about my years of reading Denis' papers. After all, our early encounters in pubs along the river Cam did not see us in still-new civvies at the end of World War Two; the actual year was 1984, all but two of the Cambridge men's colleges had by then admitted women, and none of the undergraduates swarming the streets between Magdalene and St. John's Colleges at closing time had seen any action in the European theatre. Denis writes powerfully in his Introduction, below, of the things that made the early 1980s a formative time to arrive as a Latinist in Cambridge; we were lucky to be there. As it happens, however, it was not one of the Cambridge Wednesday seminar sessions that first cemented our friendship but a cross-country rail excursion from Cambridge to the Liverpool Latin Seminar, another place in Britain in which vital arguments about Roman poetry (many of them with roots in the Edinburgh University of the 1960s) were happening in those years. This was not a world of reimbursed hotel bookings, conference badges, and the like: a rag-tag army of Latinists converged from all corners of the British Isles and beyond via what was then British Rail, and bundled into Francis and Sandra Cairns's capacious house in Birkenhead. After the business of the gathering was done, we partook of giant pots of homemade pasta, after which the more junior among us slept off the still-famous *vino della casa* in improvised bedding on floors and under tables. In those days the Classical Association did not stage APA-type conferences, the European research *réseau* was not yet a thing, and Thatcher-era higher education policies had just begun to drive a generation of Classics PhDs to become acquainted with the actual APA in search of an academic living.

This was all thirty-five years ago, and many things have changed, so I suppose it really is time for collected papers after all. However, it is clear to me, and I hope it is clear to Denis, that these two volumes are an interim stocktaking only: an (almost) four-decade retrospect, to be sure, but with plenty more in prospect.

Denis has organised the essays chronologically but has split them between two volumes ('Epic, Historiography, Religion' in Volume 1, 'Elegy, Lyric and Other Topics' in Volume 2). There are many ways besides these in which one might organise and group them: by the individual ancient author treated; by the side of the Atlantic on which they were written (Q: in which city did Denis buy the same house twice, four years apart? A: Madison, Wisconsin); by their chronological proximity to one or other of the epoch-making books which have defined different phases of Denis' intellectual career as a literary critic, a historian of religion, and increasingly, in recent years, as a historian *tout court* (albeit a highly unusual and original kind of historian).

Let me attempt to list some characteristics of the Denis to be encountered here, which reach across the diversity of his output in books and articles alike. The first thing that can be said to anyone who has picked up this collection is that it will be a very good read indeed, one that can be recommended not just for dipping but for end-to-end immersion. Denis is a fine prose stylist, and a constructor of arguments which combine wit, clarity and nuance. Those of us who have heard him as visiting lecturer or conference panellist over the years know that he almost invariably performs without a script (as most of us do in the classroom but not in our 'papers' at the podium); and we have noted with undisguised envy how he lectures in perfect periods with perfectly structured arguments. He writes very much as he speaks, so that one typically has the sense in these pages not of a thesis served cold but of an argument developing even as the prose unfolds. Every point is delivered with the freshness and authenticity of an oral performance—if one can offer such a compliment to a scholar so invested in the non-privileging of the authenticity of the oral over the written.

Denis is, then, good to read; and this is what one would expect from a critic as sensitive as he to the unfolding dynamics of a literary text. In the heady days of that Cambridge Wednesday Latin seminar in the mid-1980s, reading was everything. These were 'jam sessions' in which extended presentations were eschewed, and in which commentatorial analysis and critical close reading were tested, and rendered sharper, more precise and less safe, by a range of reflections, both imported and locally sourced, upon contemporary 'theory'—which likewise were worked out in the detailed exegesis of particular Latin texts, not presented as *a priori* grids or superstructures. Like many who took part in those seminars, Denis and I have spent much of the rest of our careers trying to recreate, in different kinds of classroom and conference room, that pivotal moment when interpretation would move from the expected to the unexpected, more often than not catalysed by a pause followed by a 'well, seems to me ... ' intervention from John Henderson. I remember renewing the feel of those Wednesdays on a visit to Madison circa 1990 in which I sat in on a graduate seminar class on ancient and Renaissance epic co-taught by Denis and Susanne Wofford to a mixed Classical and Early Modern group.

Among the essays collected here, one that gives an excellent sense of what it is like to sit in a classroom with our author is Vol. 1.9 on '... Killings, Catalogues, and the Role of the Reader in *Aeneid* 10' (1999), from *Reading Vergil's Aeneid: An Interpretive Guide*, ed. Christine Perkell, a collection originating (to quote the *CR* review) 'in a summer school for American college and university teachers which aimed to encourage non-specialists to read the *Aeneid* in courses where it might otherwise not have been included'. The piece is a master class in teaching, in reading and in teaching reading; it reminds me of all the times I have watched Denis take a group through a text, opening it up in detailed and spacious ways alike.

If Denis is an exceptional reader, he is also (although he seeks to deny it) an exceptional thinker. An idea long on his back burner is a book on Cicero as an intellectual model for the Augustan poets. Despite one teaser article, Vol. 2.17 'Ovid's Ciceronian Literary History' (2015), and a Petrarchan sense of Ciceronianism running all the way through his *oeuvre*, we have been denied such a book because Denis claims (Introduction) to be 'unable to think like a philosopher'. Well, 'philosopher' or not, to an extent uncommon among critics of Latin poetry Denis shows a sustained and energetic commitment to the investigation of ideas that, for most of us, will eminently qualify him as a serious thinker, and a serious historian of thought. I think, for example, of the tough-mindedness of Vol. 1.11 'Interpreting Sacrificial Ritual' (2004), which takes on some heavyweight positions and shows Denis' characteristic rigour in always seeking to test theory, and to adjudicate *between* theories, by argument; although not usually a polemical writer, he is in this case prepared to spill a little (sacrificial) blood in his quest for resolution.

Never one to be drawn into abstraction for its own sake, however, he will characteristically build from a telling example or vignette. Witness these opening moves in Vol. 2.3 'Towards an Account of the Ancient World's Concepts of Fictive Belief' (1993): 'What do we mean when we say "Evander, or Chloe, or Little Dorrit, did this or that", and how are these utterances different from saying "Hitler, or Caesar, or John Major, did this or that"? ... The very existence of a *Blue Guide to Literary Britain and Ireland* is a thought-provoking phenomenon.' Thought-provoking, and anything but evidence of inability to nail a thought.

Staying with Vol. 2.3, let me say something about Denis as a master of bibliography, inside and outside the field. Another quote, late in that same essay: 'Classicists have long been accustomed to cite the ancients' distinction between the modes of belief proper to poetry and to the law-court; Victor Sage's study of the relationship between the Gothic horror novel and changing attitudes to legal testimony suggests that this conventional antithesis could be re-examined in a much more dynamic fashion.' That's Victor Sage, *Horror Fiction in the Protestant Tradition* (1988): one stands in awe of the fishing expedition that found this point of comparison. Denis' bibliography is never just a matter of rounding up the 'usual suspects', and the search is never done: 'Only at the last minute before submission did I see the extremely interesting book of B. Harrison (1991); he has his own ways of ... ', etc. (2.3 again, at n.20).

Even or especially within his own areas of specialisation, his engagement with the prior literature is always active and attentive: not for him the routine or apotropaic 'see also'. Denis seems ever receptive to the idea that the next academic piece he reads may be a game-changer; and, in general, there is an open generosity in the way he credits the scholars he cites, whether friends or strangers, whether emergent or established. Take this early set-up in Vol. 2.1 '*Si licet et fas est*: ... ' (1992) (on which more in a moment), problematising unexamined elements in the common antithesis 'poetry for and against Augustus': 'With one marvellously acute question C.R. Phillips opens up many of the cracks in the edifice: "Literary critics have usually not attended closely to the protean character of the principate—about what, precisely, were the authors ambivalent?".' As noted above, it is never too late to acknowledge an eye-opening publication: e.g., in Vol. 1.13 'On Not Forgetting the "Literatur" ... ' (2007), 'only after sending the final draft ... did I see the important paper on Greek "sacred history" by Dillery (2005). ... it is clear that ... ' In line with this, Denis is readier than most of us to walk back a previously published position of his own: he makes sure that we do not miss his editorial addendum to Vol. 1.14, at n.22: 'For up-to-date discussion [of Carthaginian cultural developments], see the papers in Prag and Quinn (2013), which touch upon Carthaginian participation in the cultural exchanges of the western Mediterranean. Accordingly, I retract the ignorant comments at this point in the current paper', a correction first issued in *Beyond Greek* (2016) and repeated here.

A Denis on view everywhere in this collection is the Latinist who is also a far from faint-hearted Hellenist. Already Vol. 1.1, 'The Taciturnity of Aeneas' (1983), is an essay equally invested in and responsive to Homeric 'model' and Virgilian 'imitation', at a time when Hellenists and Romanists usually saw comparison between the two as a great-books competition in which either the Greek epic poet or the Latin one had to be presented as the loser. A discussion of the *Aeneid*'s 'small share of dialogue or conversation' triggers a contrastive survey of the question in Homer, which, Denis says (n.49), he 'might dispense with ... if there were an appropriate discussion to which I could refer; but I do not know of one'. We are the winners as he embarks on a sensitive and sympathetic reading of 'the healing and unifying power of dialogue' in the Homeric poems, with its own momentum, before returning to the very different power of the 'stifled, unconsummated' conversations so characteristic of Virgil's Aeneas, in the truncated *Italiam non sponte sequor* of *Aen.* 4.361 and elsewhere. As in *The Gods in Epic* (1991), a book which transformed the comparative study of Greco-Roman epic, it is not just that Denis becomes a better reader of Virgil by reading Greek (many Latinists aspire to that), but that he becomes a better reader of Homer by reading Latin (few Hellenists see the point in that). Our vocabulary of poetic biculturality continues to evolve; but the relationship between Greece and Rome is as ever a high-maintenance one, and few critics have worked as hard at it over the years as has Denis, most recently in the tour-de-force archaeology of Roman literature and culture in *Beyond Greek* (2016). Because or although he himself transcends such 'brain-balkanisation' (to use a Feeneyan term), Denis knows just what kinds of academic inertia are involved in 'thinking like a Latinist' or 'thinking like a Hellenist': witness the telling anecdote just ahead in his Introduction about a group of Oxford undergraduates responding in very different ways, according to their conditioning, to exam questions on a Latin poetic paper and on a Greek one.

As suggested at the outset, an available plotline in these volumes is the one that tracks Denis' growing authority as a historian. A key article here, for me, is Vol. 2.1 '*Si licet et fas est*: Ovid's *Fasti* and the Problem of Free Speech Under the Principate' (1992), which (as already noted) begins with a tour-de-force meditation on the reductive historical thinking which is a vulnerability of much work on 'poetry for and against Augustus'. This piece's contribution to the new-wave *Fasti* criticism of the time gives early notice of the Feeney who has always been ahead of most critics of Roman verse in his understanding of how a historical argument works, and ahead of most Roman historians in his understanding of how a poetic argument works. Long before Denis began to write books which are embodiments of historical scholarship in their own right, he was always one of the few Latin poetry people to whom 'real' historians (and of course Denis would be the first to question the underpinnings of that category) paid attention.

Fifteen years on, consider (again) Vol. 1.13 'On Not Forgetting the "Literatur" in "Literatur und Religion" ... ' (2007). The title (besides tweaking the title of the Basel conference where it originated) promises a belated coda to Denis' *Literature and Religion at Rome* (1998). But actually the paper, in its opening problematisation of 'history as text', is more generally reflective of Denis' work on history and historiography in and around the time of *Caesar's Calendar* (also 2007), and works throughout with scholarship, notably Tony Woodman's and John Marincola's, at the literary end of historical studies. When the piece pivots towards the representation of human access to the gods, an earlier book of Denis' comes to mind: in effect, the other shoe drops here from the 'epic of history' chapter in *The Gods in Epic* (1991), as a nuanced account of the boundaries of historiography as a genre unfolds under the sign of the divine. After a great section on Herodotus (fully inhabiting its Hellenism), the second half of the paper offers mutually illuminating investigations of Livy Book 1, a book on which Denis once contemplated writing a commentary, and of Dionysius of Halicarnassus. Back to the present, and Denis is not yet done with Livy's opening pentad: the brand-new Vol. 1.16 'Fictions of Citizenship in Livy's *History*' has arrived as a bonus 20,000-word offering for the present collection just before deadline, outside the bounds of my retrospective survey but adding a fresh chapter to the *oeuvre* of Feeney *Historicus*.

The range of inquiry on display in his four sole-authored books makes it abundantly clear that Denis has never been a recycler. One reason why a near-complete reprint of his article *oeuvre* can stand as a collection, without any need to edit out duplicates, is that each piece does in fact do something different and distinctive—even when the editors of yet another volume of essays on Horace come knocking on his door. In this sentence in Vol. 2.10 'Becoming an Authority: Horace on his Own Reception' (2009), as he registers Horace's disinclination to get trapped in a single genre, Denis could be writing of himself: 'This is what I think of as the "Picasso dilemma", one faced by all creative people; their fans want more of what made them fans in the first place, whereas real artists like Horace want to keep remaking themselves and doing something new.' Like Horace, Denis on Horace always finds a way to avoid the expected.

While Denis was penning those words, as it happens, the articles in progress on his desk were an especially unexpected bunch. The following year (2010) sees him taking (and giving) instruction in economics and mathematics: in Vol. 2.13, a post-Market-Crash meditation on tropes of financial credit in Plautus' *Pseudolus*, undertaken after 'many tutorials on Roman money' from Brent Shaw (n. 1); and in Vol. 2.12, a reception piece on *Antony and Cleopatra*, whose discussion of the number-crunching *topoi* of Roman civil war (triumvirate, divided pair, rule of one) achieves escape velocity when Denis draws on R. Kaplan, *The Nothing That Is*, to elicit (n.49) the crucial mathematical ingredient available to Shakespeare but not to his ancient sources: 'naught', or zero. And the year after this brings Vol. 2.14 '*Hic finis fandi*' (2011), an extended exploration of the absent demarcations of direct speech in Latin poetic texts, with the added bonus for the reader of a rough guide to the history of ancient and modern punctuation practices worldwide.

Obvious novelties aside, however, Denis' articles do allow his *recurrent* habits of reading to be seen. Whereas the balance of attention in the books increasingly lies elsewhere, the papers continue to centre upon the major writers of the mid-first century BCE to the mid-first century CE. Denis himself hints just below, in the Introduction, at the potential to find his critical evolution played out in changing treatments of the *Aeneid*. And also, as just remarked, but to an extent that took me by surprise, one takeaway of these essays, seen together, is how much Horace there is. In effect, nested within Volume 2 is the core of a virtual book on Horace, perhaps Denis' most sustained homage to his DPhil supervisor Robin Nisbet. It is to the article format that Denis turns, then, for sustained problem-solving in the Latin literary canon: besides Virgil and Horace, much Ovid and Catullus in these volumes; some Lucan, some Livy, and, as noted earlier, a persistent seam of Cicero. The lean in such pieces towards the reading list (both undergraduate and graduate) owes something to the symbiosis of writing and teaching which Denis himself will advertise below: M. Porcius Iasuchthan may feature in a footnote in the splendid Vol. 2.8 'Two Virgilian Acrostics . . . ' (joint with Damien Nelis, 2005), n.3, but he is not about to get an article of his own.

As a tail-piece to this brief inventory of Feeneyan traits, and at the risk of getting unhelpfully inside the head of the author of future articles, I take a moment here to celebrate one of Denis' trademark stylistic mannerisms: viz the use of expository metaphors from ballistics, ordnance and war-craft.

I have commented on the energy of Denis' writing; one might have a drinking game based on the discovery of flying and detonating projectiles in his critical prose (Vol. 1.6 'a shattering collision of human and divine perspectives'; 1.8 'to understand its impact as the explosion of a certain kind of knowledge and power'; 2.16 'the ricocheting power of the double simile'). As many who have been with him at conferences in the mid-Atlantic states or in continental Europe will have witnessed, Denis has a secret identity as a military history buff (glimpses of actual battlefield tourism in the opening footnotes to 2.6 and 2.18).

Not so secret, even. Coming up shortly (Introduction, again) is the following set-up: 'I am reminded of the metaphor used by the Confederate chief of staff during the second day of the battle of Shiloh … ' Indeed. Witness too, in Vol. 2.3, the slyly demotic use of Len Deighton's *Bomber* (in an essay which only a few pages earlier had been quoting Sidney's *Defence of Poesie*) to illustrate what happens when a writer overplays his hand in attempting to create the 'reality effect':

> The rearmost shell of this salvo exploded seventy-one feet from Löwenherz's port engine. The theoretical lethal radius of an exploding 10.5 cm. shell was fifty feet. This one fragmented into 4,573 pieces of which … 3,036 were fragments of less than a fiftieth of an ounce … etc.

Denis borrows the *Bomber* quotation, we are told, from Anthony Snodgrass; but the use of the airport bookstall to make a literary theoretical point is also (in period terms) pure Morris Zapp.

Denis has done an excellent job below of setting the stage for most of his individual essays, with deft touches of autobiography and anecdote; so I shall do no more in closing than to flag a few personal favourites of my own among the earlier-dated pieces, less likely to have been encountered by younger readers in real time and in their original contexts. (One unintended consequence of a collection like this is that decades of intellectual stratigraphy may be obscured in future books and articles by levelling references to Feeney (2021)!)

Among the early *Aeneid* articles, Vol. 1.2 'The Reconciliations of Juno' (1984) is a fine example of Denis' way with argument: the reading is precise and penetrating, almost forensic, and shows the rigour of thought that would soon mark *The Gods in Epic* (1991) as a major achievement of literary criticism and literary history alike. Speaking of the courtroom, no one is harder on Denis than Denis in revisiting the argumentative framing of Vol. 1.1 'The Taciturnity of Aeneas' (1983)—'I ended up arguing the case for Aeneas as his defense attorney'—so let the record show that, a good two decades before the present retrospect, the opening page of Vol. 1.8 'Leaving Dido' (1998) had already subjected 1.1 to searching reexamination. In 2021 there is only one 'mansplainer' still in the dock, and that is Aeneas himself.

Vol. 1.4 '*Stat magni nominis umbra . . .*' (1986), alone and in its juxtaposition with Virgil's and Lucan's underworlds in the final section of 1.5 'History and Revelation . . . ' (also 1986), takes us back to the Lucanian boom of the late 1980s and early 1990s. There were perhaps others in those years whose criticism could better channel the anger and nihilism of Lucan (Henderson, Johnson), or his impetuous youth and cosmic ambition (Masters). But the argumentative and representational rigour (that word again) of this Lucanian anger and ambition is nowhere better parsed than in the above-cited articles by Feeney, as also in the laser-guided explosiveness (if I may) of the sections of *The Gods in Epic* devoted to *De Bello Civili*. 1.4, by the way, will strike us now as remarkable in its brevity, given what an influential article it is: five short journal pages, not a single line wasted, and several implications left for the reader to pursue on his or her own. Such a piece would nowadays be inflated into a forty-pager or even a full monograph: but back then (at least in British Latin), too much 'sharing' was regarded with suspicion, careless talk cost lives, and an article in a journal like *Classical Quarterly* was expected to innovate in as few words as possible.

For unparalleled ability to recapture the sheer strangeness of Rome's poetic interaction with Greece, an earlyish highlight for me is Vol. 2.4 'Horace and the Greek Lyric Poets' (1993). Watch and wonder as Denis builds his literary historical commentary upon *Odes* 1.1.35 *quodsi me lyricis uatibus inseres . . .* (I give about one quotation per page): 'How extraordinary, then, that this list should ever be thought capable of extension, with the addition of a tenth name . . . '; 'Horace will achieve this in the teeth of the invincible chauvinism of the Greeks, virtually every one of whom had a practically pathological inability to appreciate the other literary culture . . . '; 'The Greek lyricist who was closest to him in time, Pindar, had still died over 400 years earlier (438 BCE)—as far from Horace as Sidney or Marlowe are from us . . . '; 'Between Horace and this remote world was interposed yet another culture, that of Hellenistic Greece, of Alexandria—at first sight another barrier, but also a corridor . . . '; 'The very urge to reach back five and six hundred years for inspiration and a standard of judgement is itself a classicising urge. Like all successful classicising initiatives, it looks wholly natural after the event, but it cannot have seemed so at the time.' All this in a section which also finds Denis attempting to reconstruct exactly how many modern OCT volumes would be filled by the now-lost Greek lyric poetry available to Horace.

Vol. 2.2 'Shall I Compare Thee ... ' (1992) may be my all-time favourite among Denis' papers, on the extraordinary Catullus 68, a finely paced piece which dramatises with perfection the adventure of reading that not-quite narrative elegy. As his own *in nuce* reality-check has it: 'What actually *happens* in 68? A man provides a house, a woman arrives—the rest is analogy and reflection, nested within the expression of thanks to Allius. The poem confronts us urgently with the problem of what similes are, what kind of significance they construct.' A historian of early Feeney will note the aptness to occasion: this essay was for a volume in honour of David West (p. 40), whose own articles on the Virgilian multiple-correspondence simile were a major landmark in the long 1970s of Roman poetic criticism. Back to Denis in 1992: 'Here Catullus ... highlights the dilemmas in which he has caught the scrupulous reader, as he deftly mocks (or gently sympathises with) the weighing and judging in which we have become involved in trying to descry the degrees and shades of similitude.' What is on offer here is not just a new reading of the elegy, but a new theorisation, appropriately deft and disarming, of the poetics of Latin simile. An incidental pleasure of the piece, for insiders, will have been to imagine how the soon-to-be author of the Classical Association's 1995 presidential address 'Cast out theory' reacted to the statement, two pages from the end, that 'The beloved herself is a gap, a vacancy to be filled with analogies.' The Barthesian smile lingers, still in those days an irritant to some.

On its twenty-first birthday, this iconic paper was to find a kind of sequel in Vol. 2.16 'Catullus 61: Epithalamium and Comparison' (2013), spacious in its opening moves, generous in its cultural sweep, and capable of unlocking a productive reread of the earlier piece. Its only flaw was that the author's modesty inhibited him from flagging in his footnotes just how central 'Shall I Compare Thee ... ' had become to the field of Catullan simile—and hence from exploiting the potential to measure the new essay against the earlier one quite as fully as he might. The position of the two as near-bookends in Volume 2 of the present collection will now invite that cross-referential reading.

And so back to the present (and the future). As noted earlier, I had already framed my preface when a bonus item snuck in under the wire, Vol. 1.16 'Fictions of Citizenship in Livy's *History*', giving firm notice that Denis is by no means done with publication. One other essay besides this has given me the pleasure here of a first-time read. I end, then, by drawing attention to Vol. 1.14 'Virgil's Tale of Four Cities' (2009), the Ninth Syme Memorial Lecture at Victoria University of Wellington. A lovely paper (newly available here to a readership in the northern hemisphere) on 'the complexity of the always changing Roman identity', effortlessly deploying half a lifetime of exploration in a fresh and engaging read of the *Aeneid* as a poem of literature and of history, reported back to the homeland in an act of *pietas* by a Kiwi whose own identity continues to be constructed, personally, familially and academically, between three continents, by land, sea and air. Enjoy this collection.

# List of Acknowledgements and Original Places of Publication

1. 'The taciturnity of Aeneas', *Classical Quarterly* 33 (1983), 204–19.
2. 'The reconciliations of Juno', *Classical Quarterly* 34 (1984), 179–94.
3. 'Epic hero and epic fable', *Comparative Literature* 38 (1986), 137–58.
4. '*Stat magni nominis umbra*: Lucan on the greatness of Pompeius Magnus', *Classical Quarterly* 36 (1986), 239–43.
5. 'History and revelation in Vergil's underworld', *Proceedings of the Cambridge Philological Society* 32 (1986), 1–24.
6. 'Following after Hercules, in Virgil and Apollonius', *Proceedings of the Virgil Society* 18 (1986), 47–83.
7. 'Beginning Sallust's *Catiline*', in *Nile, Ilissos and Tiber: Essays in Honour of Walter Kirkpatrick Lacey*, ed. V.J. Gray (Auckland: University of Auckland, 1994), 139–46.
8. 'Leaving Dido: the appearance(s) of Mercury and the motivations of Aeneas', in *A Woman Scorn'd: Responses to the Dido Myth*, ed. M. Burden (London: Faber & Faber, 1998), 105–27.
9. 'Epic violence, epic order: killings, catalogues, and the role of the reader in *Aeneid* 10', in *Reading Vergil's Aeneid: An Interpretive Guide*, ed. Christine Perkell (Norman, OK: Oklahoma University Press, 1999), 178–94.
10. '*Mea tempora*: patterning of time in Ovid's *Metamorphoses*', in *Ovidian Transformations: Essays on Ovid's* Metamorphoses *and its Reception*, eds. P. Hardie, A. Barchiesi and S. Hinds (Cambridge Philological Society, Supplementary vol. 23; Cambridge: Cambridge University Press, 1999), 13–30.
11. 'Interpreting sacrificial ritual in Roman poetry: disciplines and their models', in *Rituals in Ink: A Conference on Religion and Literary Production in Ancient Rome held at Stanford University in February 2002*, eds. A. Barchiesi, J. Rüpke and S. Stephens (Stuttgart: Franz Steiner Verlag, 2004), 9–29.

12. '*Tenui … latens discrimine*: spotting the differences in Statius' *Achilleid*', *Materiali e Discussioni* 52 (2004) (*Re-Presenting Virgil: Special Issue in Honor of Michael C.J. Putnam*, eds. G.W. Most and S. Spence), 85–105.
13. 'On not forgetting the "Literatur" in "Literatur und Religion": Representing the Mythic and the Divine in Roman Historiography', in A. Bierl, R. Lämmle and K. Wesselmann (eds.), *Literatur und Religion: Wege zu einer mythisch-rituellen Poetik bei den Griechen*, vol. 2 (Berlin: de Gruyter, 2007), 173–202.
14. 'Virgil's tale of four cities: Troy, Carthage, Alexandria and Rome', The Ninth Syme Memorial Lecture (Victoria University of Wellington, 2009; 18 pp.).
15. 'First similes in epic', *Transactions and Proceedings of the American Philological Association* 144 (2014), 189–228.
16. 'Fictions of citizenship in Livy's *History*', first published here.

*Introduction*

These two volumes bring together virtually all of the articles and chapters I have written, omitting an early essay and a number of pieces for Companions. There is one noteworthy gap in the record, as I published nothing but some book reviews in the four years from 1987 to 1990. I was frustrated at being unable to make progress on my first book, *The Gods in Epic*, since I kept being distracted by writing articles, especially in response to invitations to lectures and conferences. When I complained about this to my wife, a veterinary surgeon, she said, 'Well, just say no to everything till you've finished your book.' This was excellent advice, which I followed. Although I was not consciously aware of it at the time, I have come to realise that what mainly drew me into academic life (apart from the usual factors that draw anyone into anything, such as accident and inertia) were the conditions of freedom and autonomy it offered.[1] It would be suicidal nowadays to take my wife's advice.

In preparing these pieces, I have regularised the citation and reference system throughout, keeping to the conventions of *L'Année philologique* and the *Oxford Classical Dictionary*.[2] I have tried to correct all errors in the original papers, whether my own or those of editors: no doubt errors still remain, but at least they are now all mine. I have updated references where necessary, citing the fragments of Ennius' *Annales*, for example, from the edition of Skutsch rather than Vahlen. I have made a few additions, marked with square brackets. This is sometimes to correct errors (as in Vol. 1.14 n.22), or else to supplement bibliography. I have given further secondary references in a rather ad hoc way, because systematically updating on every topic, going back often over thirty years, would have added

---

[1] The best case for pure or 'basic' research remains the 1939 essay, 'The usefulness of useless knowledge', by the founding Director of the Institute for Advanced Study at Princeton, now reprinted with a companion essay by Robbert Dijkgraaf, the current Director: Flexner (2017).
[2] I have also translated into English all main quotations from Latin, Greek, German, French and Italian.

greatly to the bulk. Instead, I have mentioned items that I should have been aware of at the time, and also items of special significance that have appeared since initial publication, especially when filling gaps that I called attention to in the original publication (e.g. Vol. 1.6 n.4). This is not a terribly scientific procedure overall, but there it is.

I have not rewritten the papers to make them look as they would if I were writing them now, appealing as that idea sometimes was. The first paper in particular, 'The Taciturnity of Aeneas', now looks hair-raisingly bluff in its sidelining of Dido's perspective and its advocacy on behalf of Aeneas. Ironically, in a paper that denounced one-sided rhetoric when enlisted in a partisan cause, I fell victim to the phenomenon I was exposing, so that I ended up arguing the case for Aeneas as his defense attorney; Philip Hardie's exposure of these and other blind spots in the article is recommended reading.[3] I have refrained even from improving the style, tempted though I was to hack out all the 'thus's and 'thereby's and other faux-archaisms that I was for some reason given to in the 1980s, and that I have been red-lining in my students' writing for years. Some of the papers were delivered as invited lectures, and I have let that comparatively informal atmosphere stand (as in Vol. 1.9, originally the basis of a presentation to an NEH summer seminar organised by Christine Perkell, or Vol. 1.14, the Syme Memorial Lecture at Victoria University of Wellington). Many of the papers have a dialogic atmosphere as a result of being initially delivered at conferences. A big change in publication for our generation was the growth in conference proceedings as a venue, and many of the papers were kick-started by having to give a paper at a conference, with most of the rest of them being in response to an editor's invitation.[4] As a result, I see that I submitted nothing to a refereed journal between 1986 and 2011 apart from a note in *Classical Quarterly* in 2005, jointly written with Damien Nelis: all the journal articles between those dates were for specially commissioned occasions of one kind or another.

The trajectory of these publications is easier to plot in the earlier stages. My DPhil dissertation (1982) was a commentary on the first book of Silius Italicus' *Punica*, supervised by Robin Nisbet. He was an ideal supervisor: patient, encouraging, rapid in response to any written work and omniscient on anything to do with Latin scholarship (and much else besides). I was not, however, born to be a commentator, and even though I learnt an enormous amount about Latin literature as a result of working through 694 lines of hexameter with Robin Nisbet over a five-year period, I felt the need

---

[3] P. Hardie (2012), 130–6.   [4] Remarked on also by D. Fowler (2000), vii, xi.

to add two excursuses to the commentary. One treated the problem of the epic hero, and was published in *Comparative Literature* as 'Epic Hero and Epic Fable' (Vol. 1.3); the other addressed the problem of the participation of the gods in historical epic, and was the germ of my first book, *The Gods in Epic* (1991). As a result of this background, all of my publications were on epic until 1992, when I published my first paper on another genre—on Ovid's *Fasti* (Vol. 2.1), in direct response to an inspirational lecture on Ovid and the calendar delivered by Andrew Wallace-Hadrill at Edinburgh in 1987 (now Wallace-Hadrill (1987)). I had never read more than random snippets of the *Fasti* before this lecture made me sit down and read the poem properly: the experience led not only to a second paper on that poem (Vol. 1.11), but also more indirectly to the book I eventually wrote on Roman time, *Caesar's Calendar* (2007).

Andrew's lecture stands out in my memory partly because it is an exception, since almost all of these papers had their starting point pretty directly in teaching. It is good to have time off for research from teaching and administration, but I find it hard to imagine thinking about Classics without regular engagement with students' responses to the texts and issues. I have been extremely fortunate in my pupils, undergraduate and graduate, over the last forty years, and the experience of working with them has always prodded me to keep thinking after the class has ended. The first two papers in Volume 1 were the result of teaching Virgil's *Aeneid* for Honour Moderations for four years at Balliol and Merton colleges, and I can now see in retrospect that 'The Taciturnity of Aeneas' was a kind of distillation of everything I felt about the *Aeneid* at that point. The paper on similes in Catullus 68 (Vol. 2.2) came out of reading that poem with a brilliant group at Merton, who kept asking, as we made our way through the text, 'Why are there so many similes in this poem?'—a question it had, embarrassingly, never before occurred to me to ask. The paper on Plautus' *Pseudolus* (Vol. 2.13) ultimately came from lectures on that play at Bristol in 1991; my only venture into post-classical literature (Vol. 2.12) was the result of reading *Antony and Cleopatra* with a small group of Princeton undergraduates in my first semester there, in Fall 2000; two papers on Catullus grew out of close readings of his corpus in a graduate seminar at Princeton in Spring 2009 (Vol. 2.15 and 16). My first paper on Horace (Vol. 2.4) was the product of a graduate seminar at the University of Wisconsin-Madison in 1988, together with a class on Greek lyric that I taught at Bristol in 1991, which led Niall Rudd to ask me to contribute a paper on 'Horace and the Greek Lyric Poets' to his volume *Horace 2000: A Celebration*. The only complaint I could possibly make about my idyllic working conditions at

Princeton would be that, thanks to the strict demarcation lines in American Classics, I have very seldom taught Greek since 2000, and I am sure that this has had an effect on what I have written about.[5]

I have kept circling back to certain topics that will not let go of my interest, such as similes (Vol. 1.15; Vol. 2.2 and 16), or Aeneas' desertion of Dido (Vol. 1.1 and 8), or fictive belief (Vol. 1.13 and 16; Vol. 2.2, 3 and 13), or the importance of Cicero as an intellectual model for the Augustan poets (Vol. 2.6, 7 and 13). In the case of Cicero, this recurrent interest was a result of the fact that I planned for a long time to write a book on this subject. I had to give up the idea, very reluctantly, after repeatedly coming up against the intractable and embarrassing fact that I am unable to think like a philosopher. This was brought home to me very vividly when I was assigned Aristotle's *Nicomachean Ethics* as one of my lecture topics in the team-taught Humanities Sequence at Princeton in Fall 2010. I was able to prepare a lecture, partly with the help of my oldest son, Matthew, who was then studying Philosophy at Reading University; I was able to deliver it, since after all I was able to talk for fifty minutes without hesitation, deviation or repetition. But ten minutes into the tutorial discussion with the undergraduates afterwards I was out of my depth, as one eighteen-year-old after another pointed to a page and started probing away at exactly what Aristotle meant when he said this, or that. It was remarkable to see how students who had never before read a word of Aristotle could get on his wave-length in a way I had never been able to do. It was a sobering experience. Clearly, there was no point in writing about Cicero's achievement and the poets' response to it if I could not do justice to this crucial dimension of his work.

A key abiding fascination, one that comes up one way or another in most of these papers, and that was also the main focus of my first book, *The Gods in Epic*, is the bundle of issues to do with fiction and representation. In the face of these problems I was led to my first attempt to come to grips with contemporary theoretical approaches, and I was soon afterwards led into anthropology and comparative religion as I moved on to the interface between Roman religion and Latin literature. This double engagement requires some deeper context—so far as I can recover it, at least: I have always known that I have less access to any conscious motivation in my ways of doing things than a more methodologically self-aware person, such as Don Fowler or Stephen Hinds.

---

[5] The exceptions are two highly enjoyable graduate seminars that I co-taught with my friend Andrew Ford, on Hellenistic Literature (Spring, 2001) and Ancient Literary Criticism (Spring, 2012).

## Introduction

I have been very lucky to be one of a cohort of Latinists born roughly between 1950 and 1960. This cohort has developed a certain sense of shared identity over the years. I do not name them, for fear of causing *invidia* (well, I do not name any more of them: I have just named two). And I do not at all mean to imply that we, or I, have not been inspired by the cohorts ahead of us and behind us.[6] The reason I mention this particular group in this context is because it seems to me that all of us had a more or less similar experience as we entered the profession: having received a virtually theory-free training we then tried to supplement it as best we could by our own reading and brain-storming, in the period before dedicated conferences and workshops got under way, let alone graduate seminars on theory and method. At Auckland and Oxford, for example, I was trained with essentially the same toolkit that I would have been trained with twenty-five years earlier. It was a very good toolkit, one that demanded knowledge of non-Anglophone (especially German) scholarship, and above all command of the original sources. When I first asked Robin Nisbet about how to approach the problem of ancient allegorical composition and interpretation, he got up and walked to his shelf and handed me his copy of Félix Buffière's Budé edition of pseudo-Heraclitus' *Homerika Problemata*.[7] This was the right thing to do, and I would do the same with a student now; but neither of us thought to follow up with a modern bibliography.[8] I remember Nicholas Richardson, my mentor at Merton College, giving me a clipping of a *Times Literary Supplement* review of the English translation of Gérard Genette's *Narrative Discourse*, but this kind of intervention was rare. It was only when I arrived for a Post-Doctoral Fellowship at Harvard in 1982 that the other Junior Fellows introduced me for the first time to the names of Vidal-Naquet, Vernant, Derrida and Foucault.

My haphazard self-education picked up apace when I moved to Cambridge (1984–5) and started attending the extraordinarily rewarding weekly literature seminars, where John Henderson and Simon Goldhill in particular were test-driving all manner of approaches. It was a polarised atmosphere at the time, not just in Cambridge but across the UK, and this may perhaps explain why I found myself occupying some sort of common ground in the middle with Stephen Hinds, who was then finishing his

---

[6] Let me just acknowledge here Tony Woodman, a mentor and frequent collaborator, born ten years before me.
[7] Buffière (1962).
[8] Times have certainly changed: when I returned to Oxford in the late 1990s, I had a very enjoyable term co-teaching a graduate seminar on 'Classics and modern literary theory' with Angus Bowie.

PhD, which became *The Metamorphosis of Persephone*.⁹ The Cambridge University Press series that Stephen and I edited together from 1993 to 2016, *Roman Literature and its Contexts*, was specifically designed to provide a venue for a variety of theoretical approaches to Latin texts.¹⁰ Editing the series was, in a sense, a large project of self-education, since we had a ring-side seat while a number of highly gifted scholars displayed the possibilities of a range of theoretical and critical approaches.

At this stage my particular theoretical interests, as I said earlier, were in *mimesis* or representation, and in models—especially anthropological models—of comparative religion. I had always been fascinated, even as an undergraduate, by how conventional black marks on a white background can be so powerful in their impact and so apparently evocative of experience, and many, maybe even most, of the papers in these volumes are involved somehow with this question.¹¹ I responded eagerly to theories of fiction, narratology and discourse, since they seemed to offer some ways of understanding, for example, how the representation of a god in a poem differs from the representation of a god in a temple or in a work of philosophy. This dovetailed with my interests in religion. As a result, I ended up with a bipolar focus, fascinated with textual representation on the micro level and with social structures of religion on the macro—and fascinated with how these two perspectives interacted with each other.

This dual commitment perhaps goes some way to explaining why I have never grasped the force of the common antithesis between formalism and historicism. I remember seizing with delight on a typically svelte aphorism on this topic from Roland Barthes when I first encountered it: 'a little formalism turns one away from History, but ... a lot brings one back to it'.¹² A superficial formalism takes you away from history, to be sure, but a deeply felt formalism, one that responds to the particularity of a specific artefact and to the ways that it works in connection with other artefacts and other genres and discourses, can only be part of a historical project. Texts are as concrete as you want. Texts have a history and they are a part of

---

⁹ Hinds (1987). I don't know if Stephen felt this way, but I sometimes felt rather as Frank Kermode did, from his far more exposed position: 'There is a war on, and he who ventures into no-man's-land brandishing cigarettes and singing carols must expect to be shot at' (Kermode (1983), 7).
¹⁰ It is a real pleasure to acknowledge the strong support we always received from Cambridge University Press, and from the Classics editors, first Pauline Hire and then Michael Sharp.
¹¹ As a specific example of how much I learnt from co-editing *Roman Literature and its Contexts*, I may point to the first chapter of D.F. Kennedy (1993), a discussion of 'Representation and the rhetoric of reality' that I found particularly stimulating and informative.
¹² Barthes (1972), 111 = Barthes (1957), 184: 'Parodiant un mot connu, je dirai qu'un peu de formalisme éloigne de l'histoire, mais que beaucoup y ramène.'

history, and the forms of expression that make them possible have a finely grained cultural specificity that we have to attune ourselves to even if our objective in reading texts happens to be 'historical' and not aesthetic.

I always saw my projects as 'historical', in some sense, as working to recover the larger networks in which literary texts operated, and that is no doubt partly a result of my experience as an undergraduate and graduate with scholars like Pat Lacey and Robin Nisbet, who combined historical and literary interests. I was, however, eventually more receptive than they would have been to the idea that any category of the 'non-literary' was itself radically textual, only apprehensible through specific discourses, so that an opposition between literature and 'raw facts' was unreal.[13] The point was put memorably by Hayden White in *Tropics of Discourse*, which I think I first read around 1985:

> Nor is it unusual for literary theorists, when they are speaking about the context of a literary work, to suppose that this context—the 'historical milieu'—has a concreteness and an accessibility that the work itself can never have, as if it were easier to perceive the reality of a past world put together from a thousand historical documents than it is to probe the depths of a single literary work that is present to the critic studying it.[14]

Underlying much historicist work is 'the assumption that when literature engages with ritual or anything else it is participating in an identifiable larger system of meaning in which the terms are always set in advance by conditions which are more primary or authentic or real', that texts are 'parasitic upon something quintessentially more substantial and really there, and recoverable in that substantiality and reality'.[15] This is an assumption I have never been tempted to share.

From this perspective the antithesis between 'formalism' and 'historicism' also collapses, as Don Fowler so vividly argued, in essays that put the case better than I could and that crystallised the issues for me as I read them. We need, as he said, 'to broaden the notion of text and in doing so to seek to integrate work on intertextuality with the various forms of cultural criticism, and ... the first step here is to deconstruct oppositions like "formalism" vs. "historicism"'.[16] As he showed, supposedly hard-edged

---

[13] My first systematic thoughts on these issues were, if memory serves, particularly influenced by White (1978); Kramer (1989); Conte (1994b), 109–10; D.F. Kennedy (1993), esp. 7–8; Barchiesi (1997a), esp. 'Introduction'.
[14] White (1978), 89. Note that White's language almost subliminally allows for the possibility of perceiving that 'reality of a past world'.
[15] From the paper 'Interpreting Sacrificial Ritual in Roman Poetry ... ', Vol. 1.11, 225, 226.
[16] D. Fowler (2000), 131.

sociological or political models are themselves textual constructs, so that, for example, '"Roman social relations" consist in a set of texts, not in an impossible mystic reality outside textuality.'[17]

I was never, then, quite won over by New Historicism. First of all, I could never follow what New Historicists were actually trying to claim about the relationships between texts and contexts. In particular, I responded with instant assent to the scepticism expressed by David Perkins about the explanatory power of the New Historicist models (or the Old Historicist models for that matter).[18] I discussed these problems in the paper on Horace's *Epistle to Augustus* (Vol. 2.7), following Perkins and other scholars in being unpersuaded that we can 'explain (in any rigorous sense of the word) the way any given literary text is shaped by its contexts, because it is impossible to know what kind of causal relationship we might be talking about: the nexus of cause and effect is irrecoverable, and the number of contextualisations to be taken into account is insuperably large'.[19] I have always been very impressed by how difficult it is to tease out meaningful connections between intellectual or artistic developments and their nesting societal or technological conditions. To a certain extent, this is just an issue of evidence, which partly explains why New Historicism flourished in studies on the Early Modern period. In this period, there is enough evidence to make the project's implied causative stories seem plausible, whereas the modern period has far too much evidence, and the ancient world not nearly enough. A second major difficulty I had with New Historicism was the totalising nature of its constructions—a result of the intellectual debt it owes to a certain kind of symbolic anthropology. The models almost inevitably posit a totalising synchronic structure: a culture turns out to be like a massive text, and through some variety of synecdoche, any literary or cultural instantiation will be a fragmentary manifestation of that original overarching text.[20]

At a certain level, preferences of this kind are as much a matter of temperament as anything else, and for reasons that I cannot recover I have always been antipathetic to holistic and communitarian ways of doing things in any sphere: this is why the pointilliste and contrarian Jonathan Z. Smith has been one of my favourite scholars of religion.[21]

---

[17] D. Fowler (2000), 112; cf. 111: '"Intertextuality" is often associated with a formalist approach to literature, and contrasted with forms of cultural criticism that go outside the text. This seems to me to embody a narrow view of text and a naivety about the way the things supposedly "outside" the text are always already textualized.'

[18] Perkins (1992), chapter 6. [19] Vol. 2.7, 124.

[20] Discussed in 'Interpreting Sacrificial Ritual ... ', Vol. 1.11; see now the wide-ranging discussion of formalism and historicism in Hinds (2010).

[21] Witness his splendid banalisation of animal sacrifice in J.Z. Smith (1987), discussed in Vol. 1.11.

Anything I have ever learnt about the Greeks and Romans has made me feel yet more keenly how various and diverse and contentious their societies were, no matter how strenuously they might have tried at different times for different reasons to project uniformity and adherence to tradition. Literary texts can be put to all kinds of uses, but the idea that what we label as 'literature' could not disturb and refashion its society has never seemed to me to fit well with the self-consciously disruptive nature of the texts I spend my time reading with my students. For this reason, the scholarly construction of the ideal original reader is a model that has real problems: as I discussed in the paper on 'Criticism Ancient and Modern' (Vol. 2.5), most of the original readers must have found a first encounter with revolutionary texts such as Cicero's *philosophica* or Horace's *Odes* extremely disorientating.

Ever since the Romantics, with their fetishising of the primary, communal, organic, and oral, Greek studies have been more given to communitarian models than Latin or Roman studies. I have had a rather complicated relationship with the methodologies of Greek studies, and with their applicability to Roman studies. When Stephen Hinds and I launched *Roman Literature and its Contexts* our manifesto explicitly praised the way that 'students of Greek literature, in the best traditions of Classical scholarship, have been strengthening their contacts with cognate fields such as social history, anthropology, history of thought, linguistics and literary theory'; we went on to say that 'the study of Roman literature has just as much to gain from engaging with these other contexts and intellectual traditions'. I stand by those words, written almost thirty years ago, and I have always done my best to learn from my colleagues in Greek. But I have resisted—at first instinctively, and then more self-consciously—an inertial tendency in Greek studies to privilege the supposedly oral and communal dimensions of literary texts, which regularly get flattened out to the status of a social reflex in the process.

To give some examples to support this very large generalisation, I can refer to the paper on 'Horace and the Greek Lyric Poets' (Vol. 2.4), and to my second book, *Literature and Religion at Rome*, which turned out—rather to my surprise, because this was not at all what I had in mind when I started the book—to be a kind of polemic against Greek models of literature and ritual, and against their transplantation into Latin Studies.[22] One salient recent example of such transplantation has been the use by Latinists of models of archaic and classical Greek orality and

---

[22] Feeney (1998). The work of John Scheid was very important to me here, especially his masterpiece, Scheid (1990), as was the major review of that book in Beard (1991).

performance as part of an attempt to retrieve some social power for the texts of Latin literature, which would supposedly otherwise be shut off in an arid reading environment: the same strategy has been used for Hellenistic poetry.[23] Against such a move, I would point out, first of all, that the merits of these models in their own Greek context are open to debate. The focus on the organic social context of the original performance in Greek studies has often led to a disregard for the power that textual circulation must have had from an early stage in the alphabetic revolution: as Robert Fowler points out, 'By the late sixth century there were something like 200,000 epic and lyric verses, and early works of prose, circulating in writing.'[24] Further, it is not proven that textual circulation through schools, booksellers, and public and private libraries is devoid of social power, however one would want to define that: Latinists have been very alive to the importance of such contexts of reception, and to the intimately linked questions of the literary entailments of the technologies of the ancient book roll.[25]

The experience of reviewing *Matrices of Genre*, edited by Mary Depew and Dirk Obbink, gave me an opportunity to reflect on these general differences between Hellenists and Romanists through the specific case study of the problem of genre. As I put it in that review,

> Genre in pre-hellenistic Greece tends to be seen in quasi-sociological terms as a reflex of social practice, to be explained by its performative function in a social setting ... Such an approach drains the power away from the concept of genre, which might be seen not as indissoluble from real praxis but, in a Contean way, as a mediator which enables cultural perceptions to become part of literary perceptions.[26]

The approach of the Latinists in this volume strikes me as bearing out once more the force of Barthes' aphorism about a lot of formalism taking one back to history:

---

[23] Habinek (2005); Wiseman (2015); Cameron (1995) on Alexandria.
[24] R.L. Fowler (2012); cf. R.L. Fowler (2004), 225. On the kinetic impact of the new alphabetic technology, see Powell (2002); Yunis (2003).
[25] My papers in Vol. 2.8, 14 and 15, together with Feeney (2017), are some contribution to the debates; from a very large bibliography on books, reading practices and libraries in Greece and Rome, I pick out Roman (2001) and (2006); Hutchinson (2008); Lowrie (2009); Johnson and Parker (2009); König, Oikonomopoulou and Woolf (2013); Houston (2014); Jansen (2014). Spelman (2019) now takes the story of the use of standard texts in Greek education back to at least the fifth century BCE. The account in Langdon (2015) of over 1200 herders' graffiti from southern Attica, dating to before 500 BCE, will enforce rethinking of literacy rates and education in Archaic Greece.
[26] Feeney (2003), 338. The outstanding papers in that volume by Mary Depew and Alessandro Barchiesi on the relation between performance and text in Greek hymns and Horace's *Odes* respectively together provide a promising line for investigations into poetry's situation in time.

*Introduction* 11

The powerful Roman papers by Don Fowler and Stephen Hinds show that the most apparently esoteric issues of genre-bending loop back into culturally-grounded readings, of Roman constructions of gender (Hinds) and of parental–filial relationships (Fowler). It may seem that the way to make genres and their instantiations powerful is to tie them as closely as possible to the 'real', but the main impression I derive from this book is that giving genre its own power is the best way to do justice to the social frame and the literary productions together.[27]

I have the impression, in any case, that the orthodoxies that have held sway in Greek studies for so long now must be overdue for wholesale revision. I am reminded of the metaphor used by the Confederate chief of staff during the second day of the battle of Shiloh, who asked his commander, General Beauregard, 'General, do you not think our troops are very much in the condition of a lump of sugar thoroughly soaked in water—preserving its original shape, though ready to dissolve?'[28] It is heartening to see real signs of dissolving in some recent collections that are putting searching questions to the communitarian orthodoxies, and the introduction to their collection on *Textual Events* by Felix Budelmann and Tom Phillips is an excellent essay on the history of organicist paradigms for the study of Greek poetry, with a road map forward.[29]

I wish that Don Fowler had been able to carry out his plan of trying out his intertextuality project on Greek texs, for we need more active dialogue across these two halves of the contemporary Classics brain.[30] The depth and rigidity of the divide came home to me very forcibly when I was examining in the Final Honour School at Oxford in the summer of 2000. No one expects to learn anything very substantial when examining, but this experience gave me a remarkable insight into how early on Classicists are acculturated into their bicameral mind, when they are still twenty-one or twenty-two years old.

Michael Winterbottom and I were responsible for the paper on Ovid, and Nicholas Richardson and I had the Fifth-Century Greek literature paper. We had to give the candidates passages to comment on, and one of the passages that Michael Winterbottom and I gave the Ovid candidates came from *Tristia* 1.3, culminating in a comparison between the misery in Ovid's house on the night of his departure from Rome and the last night of Troy: *si licet exemplis in paruo grandibus uti,/haec facies Troiae, cum caperetur, erat* ('if it is allowed to use mighty examples in a little case, this was the

---

[27] Feeney (2003), 339.    [28] Foote (1958–74), 1.347.
[29] Budelmann and Phillips (2018), 1–15; cf. Hunter and Uhlig (2017); Kelly and Spelman (forthcoming).
[30] D. Fowler (2000), 131–4.

appearance of Troy when it was being sacked', *Tr.* 1.3.25–6). This self-referential marking of the use of a literary example (Book 2 of Virgil's *Aeneid*) was far too easy a target, as we ruefully acknowledged to each other afterwards. They gave us 'self-referential marker', they gave us 'allusive signal' and 'Alexandrian footnote'; they referred to Gian Biagio Conte and Stephen Hinds, they referred to John Miller.[31]

For the Greek paper, Nicholas Richardson and I chose a passage from Sophocles' *Ajax* (1266–89). Here Teucer, standing by his brother's corpse, is upbraiding Agamemnon for not remembering any of Ajax's great exploits, referring to his defence of the Achaean ships in *Iliad* 15 (1273–9) and his single combat with Hector in *Iliad* 7 (1283–7), using explicit language of 'remembrance' (μνῆστιν, 1269) and 'remembering' ('Do you no longer remember anything?', οὐ μνημονεύεις οὐκέτ' οὐδέν . . ., 1273). Now, the great majority of these candidates were the same ones who took the Ovid paper; yet out of ninety exam papers not one picked up on this language of 'memory' and only four or five even so much as mentioned the words '*Iliad*' or 'Homer'. Instead, seizing on the last line of the passage, where Teucer mentions his status as a bastard, they gave us their essay on Pericles' citizenship law. Ideally, we would have had essays that did not just document the allusions to Homer but addressed the interaction between tragedy and epic at many levels: how this new genre of tragedy is still working itself out against epic, redefining the norms of closeness and difference with each performance; they could have juxtaposed the kind of memory we see in tragedy and in ritual against the kind of memory of Ajax preserved in epic, asking whether Ajax's memory will now be preserved in Homer's *Iliad* or in Sophocles' *Ajax*; they could have asked what work the memory of Homer is doing in Athens in other contexts as well. After all, they were taking Greats fourteen years after the publication of Simon Goldhill's *Reading Greek Tragedy*, with its splendid chapter on the dynamic presence of Homer and Hesiod in Attic tragedy.[32] All in all, it was a rather depressing experience, but it was still fascinating to see what totally different halves of their brains the same candidates were using when they read their Greek and their Latin texts, and how completely they had absorbed the splits in the field by the age of twenty-two.[33]

---

[31] Conte (1986); Miller (1993); Hinds (1998).
[32] Goldhill (1986), chapter 6 ('Text and tradition'). After Garner (1990), on Homer and tragedy, dedicated works on intertextuality in pre-Hellenistic Greek literature were rare, but now we see a new interest: Currie (2016) on Homer and the Near East; Rawles (2018) on Simonides; Spelman (2018) on Pindar; Kelly and Spelman (forthcoming).
[33] For an excellent discussion of the old war between concepts of performance and text, see Lowrie (2009), part 1 ('Writing, performance, and performativity').

'Nobody likes the Romans', observes Tim Cornell in a memorable footnote.[34] I have to confess that I always have liked the Romans, and I continue to find them fascinating, with their energy and creativity and their eerie proximity to the modern. Certainly, I have had to overcome as best I could the normal Romantic prejudices that haunt our discipline, and that reach into us before we are even aware of them. At the age of fifteen I came second in the Auckland high schools' Latin reading competition, and Pat Lacey gave me my prize (the first time we met). It was a copy of Stewart Perowne's book, *Roman Mythology*.[35] I remember turning to my friend Graham Hunt, who had come first, and saying to him, 'But the Romans didn't have a mythology.' No one had ever told me this in as many words. I had been learning Latin for only four years, and had not yet started Greek. But the Romans' lack of a mythology was just one of those things you picked up from the drinking water at school, and it would be another twenty-five years before I made any kind of systematic attempt to work out what was at stake in saying that the Romans did or did not have a mythology.

I used to wonder why I had not ended up writing on Greek literature, given that if I had to choose ten books to take to the desert island, Virgil and Horace would come in at third and fourth after Homer and Sophocles. On reflection, I think I can see that it probably had something to do with the atmosphere in Greek studies when I was an undergraduate. It seemed to my amateurish teenaged eye that the main signal I was picking up from the scholarship I was reading on Greek literature (not from my teachers at Auckland University, I must add) was a negative one: 'You can't say this, you can't say that.' Oral theory, for example, was a remarkable intellectual achievement with its own genuine fascination, but the main result in practical criticism seemed to be a fence of prohibitions on reading. The obsession with an original performance context that came upon Greek studies shortly after my time as an undergraduate was an intensification of this same restrictiveness, and its malign effects have been well described by Mark Payne, who has given us a searching critique of

> the 'anthropological paradigm' . . . which has dominated the study of this poetry [Greek lyric poetry] over the last couple of decades, an umbrella term for the blend of New Historicism and cultural poetics whose characteristic hermeneutic position I take to be the assumption that the discursive ambitions of Greek lyric poetry were so radically constrained by their original

---

[34] Cornell (1995), 460 n.68.  [35] Perowne (1968).

performance context that valid interpretation consists solely in relating them to that context.[36]

When Alice Oswald gave a poetry reading at Princeton in October 2017 I was pleased to hear her describe her experience as a Classics undergraduate in ways that very much chimed in with my own, as her passion for Homer kept getting squashed by the interdict, 'You can't say that; it's an oral poem.' As a truly strong and creative person, Alice Oswald was able to make her own way into Homer nonetheless; by the time I had started to realise that there were in fact many fine templates available for reading Homer with a literary-critical eye, the moment had passed, and I was on my Roman road.

---

[36] Payne (2018), 257. Again, the kind of scholarship represented in Budelmann and Phillips (2018) and Kelly and Spelman (forthcoming) is a very welcome correction to this fundamentally unhistorical project.

CHAPTER I

# The Taciturnity of Aeneas[1]

AENEAS: Good, good, my lord; the secrets of nature have not more gift in taciturnity.

(Shakespeare, *Troilus and Cressida*, Act IV scene iii)

## I

Aeneas' speech of defence before Dido (*Aen.* 4.333–61) is the longest and most controversial he delivers. Although by no means typical, it can open up some revealing perspectives over the rest of the poem.

The exchange between the two, having as its kernel a dispute over obligations and responsibilities, requires some words of context. The early part of the book describes the establishment of a liaison between the refugee leaders, while revealing amongst the poem's characters a wide discrepancy of opinion over the nature of that liaison. Juno announces that she will arrange the marriage of the couple (125–7); after the ensuing marriage-parody of the cave-scene (165–8), Dido also calls what now exists a 'marriage': *coniugium uocat, hoc praetexit nomine culpam* ('she calls it a marriage, and gives a protective fringe to her fault with this name', 172). Fama too, moving around Libya, speaks as if Dido has taken Aeneas for a husband (192). But the local King Iarbas regards Aeneas as a pirate who has carried off a successful job of plunder (217), while Jupiter looks down from heaven and sees 'lovers', *amantis* (221). Mercury is able to address Aeneas as *uxorius* (266).

Some scholars would have it that there is a genuine ambiguity of fact here.[2] As they point out, Roman marriage was a matter of cohabitation and

---

[1] A first draft of this paper was written while I was a guest at the Fondation Hardt in Geneva, during the summer of 1981; I am very pleased to be able to thank the Fondation for their hospitality, together with the British Academy for the financial assistance that made my stay possible. I also owe a debt of thanks to Professor R.G.M. Nisbet, Professor H.D. Jocelyn and Dr. N.J. Richardson, for their helpful criticisms and comments.
[2] G.W. Williams (1968), 378–83 may fairly be taken as representative; cf. Beaujeu (1954). Monti (1981), 45–8 goes even further, arguing that there is no ambiguity, and that Aeneas is indubitably married.

intent: any accompanying ceremonies had no legal status and were, strictly, irrelevant to the inception of the marriage.[3] Dido, by this view, is quite justified in regarding their liaison as a real marriage: Aeneas is living with her and cooperating with her as consort, in building the new city of Carthage.

There are serious obstacles, however, to believing that Virgil can have intended his audience to regard it as a possibility that this 'marriage' might be an established fact.[4] Elaborate ceremonies may not have been a legal necessity, but individuals of status and importance lived a public life in which such connections were formally marked and openly advertised. The ancient commentators have it right, when they elaborate upon Aeneas' later denial that a marriage exists between them, showing that for persons of this rank there is more to a marriage than mere cohabitation. Ti. Claudius Donatus paraphrases Aeneas' words thus (on line 339):

> iunctus sum, inquit, tibi, sed illud non potest coniugium uocari; non enim semper mulieris ac uiri conuentio matrimonium facit. aliud uocatur quod gessimus. quale enim matrimonium est ubi nullus testis interfuit, nulla ex more sollemnitas, nulla pactio, faces nullae, nulla ipsius foederis consecratio?
>
> I am joined to you, he says, but that cannot be called a marriage; for the coming together of a woman and a man does not always make a wedding. What we have done is called something else. For what kind of wedding is it when there was no witness, no ceremony according to custom, no pledge, no wedding torches, no consecration of the compact itself?[5]

The ambiguity here is not one of fact—are they really married or not?—because in real terms it is plain enough that they are not married. The ambiguity resides in the characters' own interpretation. Aeneas is, by the Roman view, behaving in such a way as to give Dido (and various other characters) some justification for imagining that his intention involves marriage. By directing his focus away from Aeneas until the intervention of Mercury (259–78), Virgil is able to maintain a silence over his hero's own beliefs on this score.[6]

Mercury's message reduces Aeneas to panic. He tells his men to conceal their preparations for departure: he will wait for the right opportunity to inform the Queen (287–94). Dido senses the deception and seeks Aeneas

---

[3] Cf., e.g., Balsdon (1962), 181–2.
[4] Objections of various kinds given by Klingner (1967), 443–4; Sparrow (1973), 5–7.
[5] On 339: Servius Auctus has similar comments. On the scale and cost of marriage ceremonies in the upper classes, see Friedlaender (1919), 1.274–5.
[6] For the direction of the narrative away from Aeneas here, see Klingner (1967), 444–6; Grimm (1969).

out. The speech which she then delivers (305–30) is conventionally described as being in the 'high tragic-rhetorical tradition',[7] the most important paradigms being the speeches of Euripides' and Apollonius' Medea.[8] Austin feels obliged to assert that 'the strength of Dido's personality towers above all the rhetoric',[9] but we do not drain her speech of its emotion or individuality if we recognise its rhetorical organisation and impetus. Virgil has given her an ideal rhetorical animus. She has a good case and she argues it all the way and from every side, with rage (305–11), close logic (311–13) and appeals to pity (320–30).[10] Above all, two crucial points that admit of some doubt are transformed by her words into plain fact: the nature of his leaving and the nature of their relation to each other. To Dido, there is no question about these matters, he is simply in the wrong. Servius Auctus has the tone of it: *hic quasi reus Aeneas a Didone accusatur* ('here Aeneas is accused by Dido like a defendant in court', on line 305).[11]

Aeneas' opening words in reply give the first sign of the distinction between the two in their use of speech, and of Aeneas' recognition of that difference. To begin with *pro re pauca loquar* (337). *pauca* of course is odd, since this is his longest speech in the poem; but the word betrays Aeneas' intuition that anything he might say will be inadequate after a speech such as Dido's. The comment of Conington on the earlier use of *pauca* (*tandem pauca refert*, 333) is equally applicable to this one: '"pauca" ... seems to express Virg.'s feeling that the words come slowly and with effort, and bear no comparison to what the lover would have said had he given way to his emotion'.[12]

---

[7] Austin (1955), 98.
[8] Eur. *Med.* 465–519, Ap. Rhod. *Argon.* 4.335–90. For detailed comparisons, see, besides the commentators, Heinze (1915), 134 n.1 and Highet (1972), 220–3.
[9] Austin (1955), 98.
[10] Cf. the brief remarks of Clarke (1949), 21: 'the rhetorical system of eliciting all the arguments inherent in a situation lies behind Dido's speech in Virgil as it lies behind Ovid's letter [*Her.* 7]'; also 26.
[11] If my discussion of Dido's speeches, here and below, appears harsh, let me say that I do not consider we are ever intended to lose our sympathy for the Queen (here I cannot agree with Quinn (1963), 48–50 on a 'shift' in attitude as the book goes on). It is not a matter of 'judging', still less of deciding which 'side' we favour: cf. the sensible remarks of Douglas (1961–2), 17, in his excellent address to the Vergilian Society: 'What Vergil has done is to present an unpartisan view of all the issues. He has told the truth.'
[12] Conington (1881–4), 2.284. George Eliot (1967), 839 catches the sensation in a passage extensively modelled on this scene, when Daniel Deronda attempts to address the shattered Gwendolyn Harleth: 'he paused a little between his sentences, feeling a weight of anxiety on all his words'. Deronda's attempts at self-control remind one irresistibly of Aeneas: 'Deronda, too, felt a crushing pain; but imminent consequences were visible to him, and urged him to the utmost exertion of conscience' (ibid.).

The meaning of *pro re* is a matter of dispute: 'the urgency of the case admits only a brief reply'; 'I shall speak only briefly, in view of the situation'; 'I will now briefly deal with the charge'; 'let me speak a few words to meet the case'.[13] Austin and Page come closest to the mark. Servius (ad loc.) understood *res* thus, in the meaning 'a matter at issue (in a dispute, esp. in a court of law)':[14] *remoto ingrati crimine descendit ad causam* ('having got rid of the charge of ingratitude he gets down to the matter at issue'). Seneca took the phrase the same way, if we may judge by his imitation (which provides a parallel for the use of *pro*): *pauca pro causa loquar/nostra* (*HF* 401–2).

There is also present a very important subsidiary connotation of 'fact as opposed to words': cf. Matius to Cicero, *te rogo ut rem potiorem oratione ducas* ('I ask you to consider the facts more powerful than style', Cic. *Fam.* 11.28.5—'the facts of Matius' present situation and past record', as Shackleton Bailey (1977) paraphrases in his commentary ad loc.); Cic. *Tusc.* 5.32, *rem opinor spectari oportere, non uerba* ('I think the fact should be considered, not words'); Quint. *Inst.* 3.8.32, *quod nos honestum, illi uanum ... uerbis quam re probabilius uocant* ('what we call honourable, they call empty ... and finer in words than in fact').[15] Euripides exploits a similar two-sidedness in πρᾶγμα, when Hippolytus begins to answer the charges of his father: τὸ μέντοι πρᾶγμ' ἔχον καλοὺς λόγους,/εἴ τις διαπτύξειεν, οὐ καλὸν τόδε ('your *case*, your *charge*[16] affords the opportunity for fine words, but if one should open it up, the *facts of the matter* are not at all fine', 984–5). In Hippolytus' speech, the λόγος/ἔργον antithesis is explicit in the collocation of πρᾶγμα and λόγους; in Aeneas', the antithesis is more diffuse, looking forward to *ne finge* (338), and referring back to *quae plurima fando/enumerare uales* (333–4).

It has been argued[17] that Aeneas is insulting Dido with these words, *quae plurima fando/enumerare uales*. But since Dido has in fact referred to her kindness to Aeneas only very briefly in her first speech (*si bene quid de te merui*, 317), it is more sensible to follow the interpretation of Servius Auctus (on 335), which refers the meaning to the future.[18] If the words

---

[13] Conington (1881–4) ad loc.; Highet (1972), 76; T.E. Page (1893), 417; and Austin (1955) ad loc., respectively.

[14] *Oxford Latin Dictionary* s.v. *res* 11a.

[15] Virgil has capitalised upon the antithesis twice in the preceding section: *heu quid agat? quo nunc reginam ambire furentem/audeat adfatu?* (283–4); *temptaturum aditus et quae mollissima fandi/tempora, quis rebus dexter modus* (293–4).

[16] W.S. Barrett (1964) ad loc. compares Arist. *Rhet.* 1415b22, οἱ πονερὸν τὸ πρᾶγμα ἔχοντες, 'those speakers with a bad case to argue': see LSJ s.v. πρᾶγμα III 4 for this meaning.

[17] See Pease (1935) on 333.

[18] *quantacumque enumerare potueris in me tuo beneficio conlata, eorum tibi debere gratiam non repugno* ('however great the benefits you will have been able to list as conferred on me by your kindness, I do not refuse to owe you gratitude for them').

refer to the future, we look to the future, and we find there, in Dido's second speech, a list of precisely the sort which Aeneas here tells her is superfluous: *eiectum litore, egentem/excepi et regni demens in parte locaui./amissam classem, socios a morte reduxi* ('when you were thrown out on the shore, in need, I took you in and like a fool I gave you a share in my kingdom. I brought back your fleet and your companions from death', 373–5).

What is the force of Aeneas' language in this clause? *enumerare* has aroused no comment, but it is an odd word to find in an epic. Virgil uses it once elsewhere, in its basic sense of 'numbering off', when Anchises in the underworld announces that he will 'count off' his future progeny: *hanc prolem cupio enumerare meorum* (6.717). What Virgil intends here is quite different. He uses the word in its technical rhetorical sense of making an *enumeratio*, συναθροισμός, a list of conclusions, complaints, etc., which could be used in various parts of the speech.[19] Apart from Virgil, the only poets who exhibit the verb in this specialised rhetorical sense are those two most 'rhetorical' poets, Ovid[20] and Statius.[21] Aeneas' words are, more specifically, part of the 'long enumeration' motif, which stresses the undesirability or impossibility of making a long or complete list.[22]

Aeneas here is at once conceding the value of all that she has done for him and defensively anticipating that she can make up a fine list if she wants to. But it will do no good. *pro re pauca loquar* is a plea for both of them to eschew a parade of words, to face the facts, to stick to the point. Of course, to Dido (and to many readers), the services she has done for him *are* the point, and she returns to them in her next speech (373–5), listing them over until she is mad with pain (*heu furiis incensa feror!*, 376), unable to believe that to Aeneas they are not everything as well.

Aeneas moves on to the two matters at issue, his 'flight' and their 'marriage': *neque ego hanc abscondere furto/speraui (ne finge) fugam, nec coniugis umquam/praetendi taedas aut haec in foedera ueni* ('nor did I hope to sneak away furtively in flight, nor did I ever hold forth the marriage torches of a husband or enter into *these* covenants', 337–9). These two and

---

[19] See Martin (1974), 307; for many examples of the technical use of the verb, see *TLL* s.v. 618.44ff., *sensu technico rhet.*
[20] Twice: *Met.* 1.215; *Ars Am.* 1.254–6, *quid tibi femineos coetus uenatibus aptos/enumerem . . . ?/quid referam Baias?*
[21] Seven times: e.g. *Achil.* 1.140, *sed longum cuncta enumerare*; *Silv.* 3.1.102, *uix opera enumerem.*
[22] Cf. Nep. *Lys.* 2.1, *ne de eodem plura enumerando defatigemus lectores*; Cic. *Planc.* 74, *omnes [gratias] enumerare nullo modo possent.*

a half lines are all he has to say on the two counts. The two items are linked; moreover, it is important to realise that the linking is not a matter of economy: they are viewed under the same aspect. The problem of the marriage was discussed above: I turn to that of the departure.

When, after Mercury's visitation, Aeneas orders his men to prepare to leave, he tells them *classem aptent taciti sociosque ad litora cogant,/arma parent et quae rebus sit causa nouandis/dissimulent* ('to fit out the fleet *in silence* and get the companions to the shore, get the equipment ready and *cover up* what the reason is for everything changing', 289–91). When Dido's first sentence of attack only fourteen lines later picks up these very words (*dissimulare etiam sperasti, perfide, tantum/posse nefas tacitusque mea decedere terra?*, 'did you hope, traitor, to *cover up* such a great wrong and get away from my territory *in silence*?', 305–6), the correspondence is seized upon by Highet as a sure means of exposing the shabbiness which Aeneas displays when he denies that he was attempting to run away without telling her: 'to his hearer, and to nearly all readers, this must appear to be a barefaced lie'.[23] Virgil, however, takes four lines (291–4) to tell us that Aeneas fully intends to speak to the Queen before going; so that when Aeneas replies that he had not planned to run away without speaking to her, we have no option but to believe him.

The correspondence between Aeneas' words and Dido's serves to establish in the question of the departure the same ambiguity and the same atmosphere of partial justification which Virgil had set up in the question of the marriage. Dido has feared all along that Aeneas would run away from her,[24] and she is now entitled to believe that it is happening, because Virgil has created a ready illusion that this is what Aeneas is in fact doing. Aeneas *is* deceiving her, but she does not know that he is deceiving her only for a time.[25] She pounces on his actions and treats them as plain in fact and motive, with the (partial) justification for her interpretation made plain to Aeneas and the audience by her use of his very words. This is the quagmire which the poet, by a sleight of hand, reveals before his hero, as Aeneas hears his own words being, as it were, quoted back at him.

Aeneas digs his heels in and doggedly insists that she is mistaken. Faced with a tangle of right and wrong, of motive and justification, with an opponent, not an interlocutor, so single-mindedly insistent on her interpretation alone, he is

---

[23] Highet (1972), 75; cf. 289. It is surprising that, so far as I discover, Highet is the only writer on the problem to attempt to explain this striking and significant correspondence.
[24] Cf. 298, *omnia tuta timens*; 419–20, *hunc ego si potui tantum sperare dolorem,/et perferre, soror, potero.*
[25] Nor, of course, does she know why he is going.

blunt in disillusioning her.[26] The terse defensiveness of his speech, so notoriously chastised by Page and others,[27] corresponds to the familiar silence or strained taciturnity of more modern heroes, when faced with an uncompromising attack from wife or lover.[28] Thus Vronsky before Anna, towards the end: 'And standing before her he brought out slowly: "Why do you try my patience?" He looked as if he could have said a good deal more but was holding himself in.'[29] Governing all these reactions is the same sense of incapacity before an insistent pressure of words.

Dido's determinedly one-sided view both of his departure and of their 'marriage' is rejected as if in one breath, for the same irresolvable problems of appearance and half-truth apply to both questions. *hanc fugam* and *haec foedera* are parallel, and some of the force of *ne finge* carries over into the second clause: 'this running away you speak of, those relations you speak of, they do not in reality exist: do not mould things so that it looks as if they do' (*neque ego hanc abscondere furto/speraui (ne finge) fugam, nec ... haec in foedera ueni*, 337–9).

With *ne finge*, Aeneas' criticism of her speech comes into the open. The words are perhaps weary, or even plaintive, rather than brutal, but the force of the rebuke becomes apparent in the context of Virgil's use of *fingere* elsewhere. The verb occurs in relation to speech in four other places. When Fama moves about Libya, she is described as *tam ficti prauique tenax quam nuntia ueri* ('as much an aficionado of the fictive and depraved as a messenger of the truth', 4.188). Turnus tells off the disguised Allecto for trying to alarm him about the Trojans: *ne tantos mihi finge metus* ('don't invent such great fears and foist them upon me', 7.438). Finally, in the great clash of words between Drances and Turnus in Book 11, each man throws the word at the other. First Drances, *inuisum quem tu tibi fingis (et esse/nil moror)* ('I whom you misrepresent as being hostile to you—and I waste no time denying that', 11.364–5). Then Turnus, *uel cum se pauidum contra mea iurgia fingit,/artificis scelus* ('he makes out that he is panicky in the face of

---

[26] Though it does not seem to be recognised that when Aeneas says *nec coniugis umquam/praetendi taedas* ('nor did I ever hold forth the marriage torches of a husband') he is in fact admitting a grave moral failing. If a man of Aeneas' (even compromised) integrity says that he did not use promises of marriage as a pretext, he is not simply telling the woman she has nothing to complain about.
[27] See, conveniently, Pease (1935), 45–6; Austin (1955), 105.
[28] Such is the preconception behind the bluff appraisal of Aeneas' predicament in Speaight (1958), 8: 'There are situations in which there is practically nothing a man can say.'
[29] Tolstoy (1954), 776. Simone de Beauvoir (1960), 464 catches the predicament acutely, with a mother facing her daughter: 'She had a talent for jumbling the true and the false with such skill that I was overwhelmed by the effort I'd have to make to contradict her. Weakly, I said, "You've got everything all twisted."'

my verbal assaults—a professional's trick', 11. 406–7). Aeneas' use of the word is not savage as in the Turnus–Drances exchange—nor is it as indulgent as Turnus' reproach to Allecto. What Aeneas tells her is that she should not 'mould' the facts into her own view; English perhaps says 'twist'. Virgil puts into his mouth, to convey the criticism, a word that pinpoints with some precision the moulding and misrepresentation which is part of the orator's stock-in-trade: cf., e.g., Cic. *Flac.* 51, *tota enim conuertet atque alia finget* ('he will turn everything around and make it different').[30] Hence the mutual charges of distortion and pretence that pass between Turnus and Drances; hence Aeneas' protest against Dido's use of apparent 'fact' in her presentation of her charge on the matters of the departure and the marriage.[31]

Aeneas now attempts to make Dido understand the pressures upon him. The comment of R.D. Williams upon this central section is extreme, but not unrepresentative of modern views: 'His effort to minimise the pain of the situation by avoiding emotion makes his speech seem hard and unfeeling.'[32] This desiccation of Aeneas' words is a result of the false point of view from which his conflict is normally regarded: love for Dido on the one hand, dry duty on the other.[33] Monti has sympathetically demonstrated that the issue is a clash between two 'loves':[34] his obligations to his son, his men, his father's memory, his gods, these are emotional commitments, the force of which he expounds with urgency to Dido, trying to enable her to see why he must act as he does.

At the end of his exposition of the human and divine pressures upon him, Aeneas once more addresses Dido personally, saying *desine meque tuis incendere teque querelis* ('stop burning up yourself and me with your laments/expostulations', 360). *querelis* has been described as 'one of the few words in the episode that are characteristic of the erotic elegy',[35] but such is not the tone here. Only once elsewhere does Virgil use the word of an articulate creature, when he puts it in the mouth of Juno, who rounds

---

[30] Further examples in *TLL* s.v. IIb of *fingere* as the hallmark of oratorical or impassioned speech.
[31] For the antithesis present here between *res* and *fingere*, cf. Cic. *Brut.* 149, *uereor ne fingi uideantur haec, ut dicantur a me quodam modo: res se tamen sic habet.*
[32] R.D. Williams (1971), 423.
[33] A convenient collection of the views of the consensus in Monti (1981), 104 n.11. Austin (1955) is aware of the emotional force of Aeneas' words at some points in this central portion: see his remarks on 351ff. Similarly Lefèvre (1974), 111–12.
[34] Monti (1981), 42–3; cf. 104 n.10: 'Aeneas tells Dido not only that his obligations prevent him from remaining with her, but also that he faces the choice between love for her and love for his own people and that he does not decide in her favor. This is not to deny that Aeneas loves Dido; it is a question of choices.'
[35] De Witt (1907), 78.

off her speech against Venus in Book 10 by pouring scorn on the other goddess' remonstrations: *nunc sera querelis/haud iustis adsurgis et inrita iurgia iactas* ('now too late you rise up with your unjust expostulations and hurl about pointless abuse', 10.94–5). In Juno's mouth the word carries its technical rhetorical meaning of 'expostulation' or 'protest'. Cicero gives as an example of the *communes* of earlier orators *uitiorum et peccatorum acrem quamdam cum amplificatione incusationem aut querelam* ('a certain harsh and ramped-up attack on and protest against vices and sins', *De or.* 3.106); and in the *Topica* he lists *querelae* in the subheading 'practical questions relating to emotion': *quo ex genere sunt querelae, incitationes, miserationesque flebiles* (86).[36]

The rhetorical reference of *querelis* is brought out by the rhetorical reference of *meque ... incendere teque*. *incendere* is commonly used to describe the inflammatory effect of speech, whether on a crowd or an individual,[37] and Virgil has this usage often: *inceditque animum dictis* (4.197); *talibus incensa est iuuenum sententia dictis* (12.238).[38] More specifically, *incendere* attains the status of a semi-technical term in Cicero's oratorical writings, to describe the effect of the emotional weapons of which he was so fond—*hae dicendi faces*, as he calls them ('these torches of oratory', *De or.* 2.205). The orator will use his words to set his audience ablaze with emotion. Thus Demosthenes in the *De Corona*, though beginning calmly, *post sensim incendens iudices, ut uidit ardentis, in reliquis exultauit audacius* ('next gradually setting the jury on fire, when he saw them ablaze, he vaulted more boldly in the remainder of the speech', *Orat.* 26).[39]

Aeneas' words, however, are more pointed than this: *both* of them are being set on fire by her remonstrations (*meque ... teque*). Such is the power of her words that the more she tries to set Aeneas on fire the more inflamed she herself becomes, and the more inflamed she becomes the more she tries to set him on fire. This mutual conflagration is the effect which Cicero, and after him Quintilian,[40] describe as the aim of the orator who wishes to achieve the most effective *pathos*. No orator, says Antonius, can set his listeners alight unless he himself is on fire: *ut enim nulla materies tam facilis ad exardescendum est, quae nisi admoto igni ignem concipere possit, sic nulla*

---

[36] Cf. *Part. or.* 121, *Brut.* 88; in speeches, *Lig.* 23, *Scaur.* 39, *Flac.* 55, 87.
[37] Plaut. *Pseud.* 201, *sermone huius ira incendor*; Liv. 1.59.11, *his ... memoratis incensam multitudinem perpulit ut ...*
[38] Cf. 1.50, *talia flammato secum dea corde uolutans*; 11.376, *talibus exarsit dictis uiolentia Turni.*
[39] Cf. *De or.* 3.23; Quint. *Inst.* 4.2.75, *peroratio incendit et plenos irae [iudices] reliquit*; ibid. 114.
[40] *Inst.* 6.2.26–8.

*mens est tam ad comprehendendam uim oratoris parata, quae possit incendi, nisi ipse inflammatus ad eam et ardens accesserit* ('just as no material is so prone to bursting into flame that it can catch fire unless fire is moved up to it, so no mind is so ready to take in the force of the orator that it may be kindled unless he himself has approached it in flame himself, and ablaze', *De or.* 2.190). Antonius singles out Crassus as supreme here: so powerful, he says, is Crassus' repertory, *ut mihi non solum tu incendere iudicem, sed ipse ardere uidearis* ('that you seem not only to set the judge on fire but to be ablaze yourself', 188).[41]

What Aeneas is telling Dido here is that her words are a reckless incitement of passion, by which both of them are being made to suffer for no purpose: with remonstration and passionate protest alone nothing can be achieved but torture. She is, by a different metaphor, 'intoxicated' by her language. The effect he fears continues in her next speech. She uses her words to stoke her passion, until she feels herself ablaze with indignation and hurt—*heu furiis incensa feror!* ('alas I am carried along on fire with passion!', 376).

Aeneas' criticism here is of a piece with his criticism at the beginning of his speech. No solution or reconciliation is possible if her words are only vehicles of a one-sided offensive which, by its very nature, precludes compromise or understanding. We note, too, that his criticism is couched in specific, even technical language, which relates precisely to the use (or misuse) of language as employed by the orators: I return later to the significance of this fact.

It is impossible to tell how Virgil would have finished the speech had he lived to complete the poem. All we have is a truncated reference—the only one—to Aeneas' emotions: *Italiam non sponte sequor* ('I am not following after Italy of my own accord', 361). But Aeneas is interrupted (*bene 'dicentem' non 'postquam dixit'*, 'Virgil well says "as he spoke" not "after he spoke"', Servius Auctus on 362)[42] by a Dido who expresses only contempt for his explanations: *scilicet is superis labor est . . .* etc. ('oh sure, this is something the gods are taking trouble over', 379). Of his father, his son, his people, she makes no mention. Her second speech (362–87)

---

[41] Speaking of his own prowess in the *Orator*, Cicero claims *nulla me ingeni sed magna uis animi inflammat, ut me ipse non teneam; nec umquam is qui audiret incenderetur, nisi ardens ad eum perueniret oratio* ('no great force of intelligence inflames me, but rather that of spirit, to the extent that I can't restrain myself; nor would the listener be inflamed, unless the speech came to him on fire', 132).

[42] Whenever Virgil has *dicens* (2.550; 10.744, 856; 12.950) or *dicente* (10.101), he means 'even as X spoke'.

abandons any attempt at persuasion, and develops passionately the attack which had formed only part of her first speech.[43]

She interrupts herself by fleeing his presence (388–90). And he is left, *multa metu cunctantem et multa uolentem/dicere* ('hesitating in fear over many things and wanting to say many things', 390–1). After the gulf that has opened between them, the enjambment and isolation of *dicere* harshly expose the inadequacy of mere speech. Thus was Orpheus left standing by his wife, *prensantem nequiquam umbras et multa uolentem/dicere* ('grabbing at the shades in vain and wanting to say many things', *G.* 4.500–1); thus, more appositely, was Aeneas left by the shade of his wife Creusa in Book 2, *lacrimantem et multa uolentem/dicere deseruit* ('she left him in tears and wanting to say many things', 790–1). The comfort he wishes to give Dido he cannot provide (393–6): any hope of solace or reconciliation is denied.

## II

If we look at this block of speeches with our attention centred on the character Aeneas, two points stand out. First, the distinction, patent in the speeches themselves and picked out by Aeneas, between Dido's use of speech and Aeneas'. Second, the ineffective and unnaturally truncated nature of the dialogue, with the denial to Aeneas of the opportunity to speak the words he wishes to speak.

We saw that Virgil marks the breaking-off of the dialogue with words that recall Aeneas' enforced silence in Book 2, when the shade of his wife vanishes before he can reply to the speech it has delivered. With his mother Venus the same frustration of speech is to be observed. Near the beginning of Book 1 Aeneas has a long and important conversation containing much information and instruction (321–401); but he does not know he is speaking with his mother, for she is in disguise. As she turns away he recognises her; he follows while she flees from him (*fugientem*, 406), calling out, *cur dextrae iungere dextram/non datur ac ueras audire et reddere uoces?* ('why is it not granted to join right hand to right hand and to hear and exchange genuine conversation?', 408–9). Their conversation has not in fact been genuine, and contact between them is deliberately broken off by the mother before the son may speak and hear *ueras uoces*. 'The distance between god and man remains irremoveable, even between mother and son', remarks A. Wlosok on the passage, with a degree of truth;[44] but it is

---

[43] My description of this second speech is only a precis of R.D. Williams (1971).
[44] Wlosok (1967), 87.

not simply because Venus is divine that Virgil has represented her as inaccessible to her son's speech.[45] Aeneas also suffers one such broken exchange with his father, at the end of Book 5 (722–42), when Anchises' shade flees at the approach of dawn. *iamque uale*, says Anchises ('and now farewell', 738): the same phrase in the same position is spoken to Aeneas by Creusa's ghost (2.789).[46] Aeneas speaks as the shade vanishes, *quo deinde ruis? quo proripis? ... /quem fugis? aut quis te nostris complexibus arcet?* ('where are you rushing to so soon? To where are you snatching yourself away? Whom are you fleeing? Or who keeps you away from my embraces?', 741–2). As the silent shade of Dido turns away from him, Aeneas likewise calls out, *quem fugis?* ('whom are you fleeing?', 6.466); he follows his mother as she runs away from him, *fugientem* ('fleeing', 1.406).

These episodes are examples of a feature of the *Aeneid* which has often been commented upon, namely, the poem's small share of dialogue or conversation. Heinze chose this observation as the starting point for his discussion of the speeches, taking Homer as the standard of comparison;[47] Highet provides statistics, with some further discussion.[48] Some picture of the Homeric model is necessary in order to establish the background.[49] The aspect I wish to concentrate on is the efficacy, the potency of Homeric speech and dialogue, the way in which speech is used by Homer's men and women to approach each other, to attain an end, to achieve a solution.

The councils of the Achaean chiefs in the *Iliad* reveal progress and development as the words spoken work their way upon the minds of the hearers. Book 9 has two fine examples. At the beginning of the book there is a lengthy debate, in which we hear speeches from Agamemnon, Diomedes, Nestor, Agamemnon, and finally Nestor again. Agamemnon had at first been in despair, suggesting that they all go home to Greece (13–28); as one speech follows another, the men move away from this disastrous proposal and eventually arrive at a solution: ambassadors will go and plead with Achilles to abandon his wrath and be reconciled. The ambassadors do not succeed in their aim, but the various effects of their various styles of oratory work progressively upon Achilles, turning him to modify his stand.[50] At first he is threatening to sail home the next day

---

[45] Further discussion of the lack of intimacy between Aeneas and Venus in Highet (1972), 37–8.
[46] And to Orpheus by Eurydice's ghost (*G.* 4.497).   [47] Heinze (1915), 404.
[48] Highet (1972), 22–5.
[49] I might dispense with this section if there were an appropriate discussion to which I could refer; but I do not know of one. Indeed, there is surprisingly little written on the subject altogether, as Latacz (1975), 395 remarks in the introduction to his useful survey on direct speech in Homer.
[50] The modification of Achilles' position is well traced by Whitman (1958), 190; cf. Lesky (1968), 790–1.

(356–63). After Phoenix's long speech (434–605) he relents so far as to say that he will decide on the next day whether to sail home or not (618–19). But it is the blunt rebuke of Ajax which crowns the weakening process (624–42), for his words prompt instinctive agreement from Achilles: πάντα τί μοι κατὰ θυμὸν ἐείσαο μυθήσασθαι ('you appear to have spoken entirely in accordance with my mind', 645). All thought of leaving is now gone, and Achilles will fight if Hector comes to the ships of the Myrmidons (650–5).

The most accomplished exponent of speech in the Homeric poems is, of course, Odysseus, who is kept alive by his wits and tongue in his wanderings,[51] talking his way home through a world which is 'menacing ... with the mysteriousness of undeclared motives, inscrutable people, liars and cheats',[52] and, once he is arrived, talking his way into a position where he can kill his enemies and regain his standing. The use of words between Odysseus and Penelope in their reunion scene (23.85–240) has been well described by Stanford, who traces the modulation of their reactions as they speak to each other, feeling their way until recognition and reconciliation are achieved.[53] Twenty years of separation still divide them, and Athene gives them a double night (241–6). τὼ δ' ἐπεὶ οὖν φιλότητος ἐταρπήτην ἐρατεινῆς,/τερπέσθην μύθοισι, πρὸς ἀλλήλους ἐνέποντε ('and when the pair had taken their pleasure in delightful love-making, they took pleasure in words, conversing with each other', 300–1); as they speak to each other, sharing what each has suffered alone, their reunion is made complete: husband and wife reestablish their intimacy and heal their private hurt.

The healing and unifying power of dialogue is a constant feature of the Homeric poems. In *Odyssey* 4, for example, we see Menelaus greeting Telemachus and Peisistratus, the son of Nestor. In speaking of his lost friends, Menelaus mentions Odysseus, so that Telemachus is moved to tears (113–16). Helen enters and guesses his identity (141–4), so that first Peisistratus may openly speak of Telemachus' troubles (156–67), and then Menelaus may speak again of his own grief for his old friend (169–82). Their words bring the purging tears to all four (183–7); Peisistratus is moved to commemorate his brother Antilochus (190–202), and Menelaus graciously puts the seal on their weeping (212). Their open talk of their pain, and the resulting tears which they shed together, provide some measure of solace.

The Odyssean scene is a more humble statement of the theme which dominates the last book of the *Iliad*.[54] The gods have ordered Achilles to

---

[51] Walcot (1977); Stanford (1963), 13–15.  [52] Griffin (1980), 80.  [53] Stanford (1963), 56–9.
[54] Griffin (1980), 69.

surrender Hector's body, and he has said that he will give it to any Trojan who may come (134–40). The arrival of Priam himself is completely unexpected, and stuns Achilles and his friends (480–4). Achilles' reaction is left in suspense, and the factor that determines his response is, quite simply, Priam's speech. Priam establishes between them the strongest link there can be, by reminding Achilles of his own father (486–506). They weep together, Priam for Hector, Achilles for Patroclus and for his father Peleus (509–12). Griffin's comment on this scene is characteristically just: 'as the great enemies . . . meet and weep together, we see the community of suffering which links all men'.[55] So from the audience's point of view. For the two men, the 'community of suffering' is not an awareness that comes spontaneously upon them; it is a truth established by the words of Priam, a truth recognised and acknowledged by Achilles when he too compares the lot of his father with that of Priam (534–48), thus putting into new perspective the pity for his father which has been a cloud on his mind ever since he accepted the inevitability of his own early death.[56]

The link established is still fragile. Priam overplays his hand when he asks for the exchange to be made immediately, and provokes an angry outburst from Achilles (560–70); but it is Achilles who makes the next overture, by inviting Priam to eat and drink (599–620). After the meal, in a famous scene, they look at and admire each other (628–32). Priam marvels at Achilles, ὅσσος ἔην οἷός τε ('at how big he was, and what he was like', 630); it passes oddly unremarked that the marvelling on Achilles' side is not simply parallel: εἰσορόων ὄψίν τ' ἀγαθὴν καὶ μῦθον ἀκούων ('seeing his goodly appearance and *listening to his words*', 632). Achilles marvels at Priam's power of speech: this is his ἀρετή, his 'excellence'.[57]

In this way does Homer portray the palliation of a grief apparently beyond resource. The shared tears and the shared meal represent to us the stages in their reconciliation; but the reconciliation is made possible by the power of speech to draw men together and establish connections between them.[58]

---

[55] Ibid., 69.    [56] Cf. *Il.* 18.330–1; 19.334–7; 23. 144–51.

[57] The allusion to Priam's speech must, as Macleod (1982) puts it in his commentary, refer to things said while they ate; it cannot refer to the moment, because as they look at each other they are silent. This is plain from the lines immediately following: 'when they had had their fill of *looking at each other*, then god-like Priam was the first one to speak' (632–4).

[58] The observation of Griffin (1980), 69 n.36 is too bleak: 'No Egyptian drug can obliterate the sufferings of the *Iliad*, for which there is no alleviation and the gods can only recommend endurance.' Men *can* do better than this in the *Iliad*, even if their sufferings are not 'obliterated'. Contrast Priam's mad grief before the reconciliation scene (24.162–5) with his self-possession afterwards (713–17; 777–81), a self-possession which is itself in strong contrast with the unrestrained passion of the mourning women.

It is a shock to return to the *Aeneid* after the world of Homer.[59] 'In the Homeric poems it is unusual for one character to address another without receiving a spoken reply, and conversations in which three or four people join are common. In Vergil, the reverse ... [O]f the 333 speeches in the *Aeneid*, 135 are single utterances which receive no reply in words.'[60] Heinze's discussion of Virgil's restrictions is still very valuable, especially on the subjects of Virgil's concern for compression and narrative pace;[61] but a more thorough-going curtailment is at work. The world of the *Aeneid* is lacking in the Homeric style of open, cooperative and sustaining speech. Virgil consistently excludes from his poem the intimacy, companionship and shared suffering which Homer's men and women hold out to each other through speech.

In Book 3, for example, Aeneas arrives at Buthrotum in Epirus, where he finds Andromache mourning Hector on the shore. We think of such scenes as that from *Odyssey* 4 where shared memory and tears brought some relief to the bereaved and isolated. Such a solution is not to be looked for in Virgil. Andromache's tears are in vain (*incassum*, 345). Aeneas makes no reply to her long speech, nor to all the questions she asks him (337–43), since Helenus arrives and leads him off (345–8). We are not told what happens to Andromache, whether she follows, or whether she stays, weeping by the tumulus of Hector where Aeneas found her. When the Trojans leave, her obsessive misery is precisely the same as when they arrived (486–91).[62]

The *Aeneid* is rigidly undomestic. We hear no human conversation between husband and wife,[63] father and son,[64] mother and child.[65] Viewed as a tableau, the single 'homely' scene in the poem is the sinister

---

[59] In attempting to put Virgil's speeches in perspective, I am afraid I may have put Homer's speeches out of perspective. There is certainly unsuccessful speech in Homer; the first exchanges of words in the *Iliad* are disasters. But it is Homer's norm which is important (if I may borrow the terminology of Johnson (1976), chapter II).

[60] Highet (1972), 23–4. Of these 135, as Highet notes, eight are soliloquies, and there are a few more deductions to be made.

[61] Heinze (1915), 405–8.

[62] Cf. Grimm (1967). Grimm analyses well the lack of contact between the two, although I cannot accept his conclusions.

[63] No speech between Helenus and Andromache in Book 3. Amata speaks once to Latinus (7.359–72), but he does not answer; at 12.10–80 Latinus and Amata are both present, with Turnus and Lavinia, but do not address each other.

[64] Aeneas and Anchises only *converse* in the underworld. Evander speaks once to his son alive (*dum te, care puer, mea sola et sera uoluptas,/complexu teneo* ... etc., 8.581–2), and once to his corpse (11.152–3). Pallas never speaks to his father.

[65] Apart from the 'unreal' conversation between Aeneas and the disguised goddess in Book 1 (321–401). At 8.612–14 she speaks briefly to Aeneas, but he makes no reply.

moment when Ascanius/Cupid hangs in an embrace from his 'father's' neck, and then goes to sit in Dido's lap and infect her with love (1.715–22). The gods, to whom everything is easy, are a foil. The delightful scene between Venus and Vulcan in Book 8 (370–406), with the homely simile following (407–15), is unimaginable in the human action. Jupiter and Juno reach a reconciliation in Book 12 (791–842) in a way that no human characters do. Virgil has pruned back Homer's gods, but there remains a freeness and domesticity in the scenes in heaven (e.g. 1.227–60; 4.90–128) which is never seen on earth. W.R. Johnson is right to stress the importance in the poem of 'the rarity of conversations and debates between the actors (which ease the sense of isolated anxiety, bad solitude, which is a Vergilian hallmark)'.[66] The most intense expression of this anxious solitude is Dido's dream (4.465–8):

> agit ipse furentem
> in somnis ferus Aeneas, semperque relinqui
> sola sibi, semper longam incomitata uidetur
> ire uiam et Tyrios deserta quaerere terra.
>
> He himself, bestial Aeneas, harries her in her frenzy in sleep, and she seems to herself to be always left alone, always going on a long path without her entourage, looking for her Tyrians in a deserted landscape.

From the beginning to the end of the poem Virgil keeps the character of Aeneas before our eyes as the principal exemplar of this unhomeric isolation. His lack of contact with mother and wife has already been noted.[67] Of his affair with Dido only the formal beginning and the wretched ending are represented.[68] We hear no conversation between Aeneas and his father Anchises, at least while Anchises is alive and upon the earth. In Book 2 there are four unconnected utterances between father and son:[69] from Aeneas, an outburst of angry grief when his father refuses to be carried from home (657–70), and an instruction to pick up the household gods and mount on his back (707–20); from Anchises, a line of acquiescence (704), and a line and a half of panic as the pair make their way out of the city (753–4). More remarkably, during the course of Book 3, when father

---

[66] Johnson (1976), 179. See also Lieberg (1971).
[67] Earlier in Book 2, when Aeneas and Creusa are together in Anchises' house, she speaks once to him, without receiving a reply (657–8).
[68] Highet (1972), 35: '[Aeneas] is never heard saying any special words of love to Dido, as Paris does to Helen (*Il.* 3.438–46); nor is he ever seen embracing her, like Odysseus with Penelope (*Od.* 23.231–40).'
[69] 'Nicht Rede und Gegenrede' ('not speech and reply'), says Heinze (1915), 410, of the bursts of speech in Anchises' house.

and son cooperate in steering the Trojans' fortunes, Virgil does not once show us Aeneas addressing his father,[70] while Anchises speaks to his son on one occasion only, seven lines acknowledging the Penates' instructions to Aeneas to make for Italy (182–8). In the underworld there is the form of a conversation, but there is something more than disquieting about the fact that Virgil allows his hero such indulgence only in this unreal place. Even here, although Anchises has held forth the hope *notas audire et reddere uoces* ('to hear and exchange familiar conversation', 6.689), the conversation between them is strangely formal and unintimate; Aeneas' questions are a naturalistic way of directing and organising Anchises' exposition.[71]

To his son Ascanius, heir of all his hopes[72] and companion throughout his travels,[73] Aeneas speaks once only: *disce, puer, uirtutem ex me uerumque laborem,/fortunam ex aliis* . . . etc. ('learn, boy, manly virtue from me and true hard work, good luck from others', 12.435–40). This single address is a farewell, and it has the adumbrations of being a final farewell. Its models are Hector's prayer for Astyanax (*Il.* 6.476–81) and Ajax's words to his son.[74] In each of these models the father never sees his son again, although Hector only suspects this fact (cf. 6.448–9), while Ajax is determined upon it.[75] Ascanius, in his turn, never speaks to his father in the course of the poem.

If Aeneas' only words to his son are in the guise of a final farewell, his only words to Pallas, his 'Patroclus', are such in fact. As the Trojans arrive at Pallanteum, Pallas rushes to interrogate them (8.110–14). Aeneas does not know him when he replies, *Troiugenas ac tela uides inimica Latinis* ('It is Trojans you see, and weapons hostile to the Latins', 117); he goes on to speak in the plural, *ferte haec et dicite* . . . etc. ('take these things and say . . .', 119). Pallas welcomes him, and takes his right hand (122–4), but Aeneas makes no reply. From that moment until Pallas is killed, Aeneas does not address him; it is only to his corpse that Virgil represents him speaking, in a lament (11.42–58), and a short farewell: *'salue aeternum mihi, maxime Palla,/aeter-numque uale'. nec plura effatus ad altos/tendebat muros* ('"hail for ever, mighty Pallas, and for ever farewell". Saying no more he made his way to the high walls', 11.96–8). His terseness at such crises is most poignant, as are his

---

[70] One line of reported speech, pared and bald: *Anchisen facio certum remque ordine pando* (3.179).
[71] Cf. the introductory remarks of Austin (1977) on 6.679–702; Highet (1972), 34. Lieberg (1971), 189, has some good comments on the emptiness of contact between Aeneas and Anchises at this point.
[72] See esp. 1.646; 4.234, 274–6, 354–5; 12.436–7.
[73] Except for Books 8 and 9, when Aeneas is at Pallanteum without Ascanius.
[74] Soph. *Aj.* 550–1, or Accius, *Armorum iudicium*, fr. 10 Ribbeck.
[75] This is so even if we accept the relocation of Ajax's speech in Accius, as suggested by Jocelyn (1965), 128.

appalled and resourceless silences before scenes of great pity or terror (3.47–8, at Polydorus' *tumulus*; 6.331–2, seeing the souls of the unburied), or his strange reticence when we expect speech from him (8.617–19, 729–31, looking at his shield).

Aeneas is distant from his men also.[76] He moves in solitude through a world which yields him no intimacy or comfort, which progressively severs his ties with those who are close to him, and to whom he wishes to be close.[77] His conversations are stifled, unconsummated. Here he is at his most unhomeric, particularly in Book 3, when he is following in the footsteps of his voluble Greek predecessor, Odysseus, conspicuously failing to engage in the whole range of discourse of which the more versatile hero is master. But even if Aeneas is cut off from the converse which enriches and supports the human life of the Homeric poems, much of his speech is effective, although not reciprocal or personal. He offers prayer to win the goodwill of the gods for the common enterprise,[78] and confidently interprets the signs they send (e.g., 7.120–34, 8.532–40). He encourages his men after disaster (1.198–207), and orders them to decisive action. He is shown at the moment of decision ordering Anchises to get on his back and to pick up the household goods, telling his *famuli* to follow on (2.707–20). We hear him inaugurate the funeral games of his father, in a long[79] and formal oration which is the first stage in reestablishing the group's confidence and trust, weakened by the sojourn in Carthage (5.45–71).[80] He orders his army to the crucial step of marching on the city of Latinus, speaking in the harsh and authentic tone of the Roman commander (12.565–73). He speaks as the representative of his people in diplomacy, most notably when he seals the vital alliance with Evander (8.127–51).[81] He does not make the initial alliance with Latinus in Book 7; one of the many reasons for this is that the alliance is broken, and whenever Aeneas makes a diplomatic arrangement it sticks (with the disastrous exception of his pact with Dido in Book 1): note his promise of friendship with the descendants of Helenus (3.500–5), and the ties he establishes as he founds the city for Acestes (5.749–61).

The effectiveness of Aeneas' public speech, either civil or military, is put into perspective when seen beside the speech of the other characters in the

---

[76] Highet (1972), 41–2.
[77] On Aeneas' solitude, see Lieberg (1971), 176–9; Elftmann (1979); especially Liebing (1953), 22, 95, 110, 152.
[78] Highet (1972), 39.  [79] The second longest he makes.
[80] Cf. Quinn (1963), 48: 'One of the functions of Book V is to heal this alienation of commander from his men.'
[81] His third longest speech in the poem.

## The Taciturnity of Aeneas 33

poem. We look in vain in the *Aeneid* for examples of the Homeric type of many-sided debates leading to a worthwhile result. On the few occasions in the *Aeneid* when more than four speeches from three or more speakers come together in a cluster, the atmosphere is panic-ridden and hysterical. The 'Homeric' consultation scene in Book 9, with speeches from Nisus, Aletes, Ascanius, Euryalus and Ascanius again (234–302), is an undisciplined and excited shambles, which issues in disaster: Aeneas, of course, is absent from his army. The set-piece debate in the Latin Senate in Book 11 is a mere shouting match; Latinus' proposals for peace are buried in the exchange of words between Drances and Turnus (225–461). The bedlam is shown for what it is by an interruption: *illi haec inter se dubiis de rebus agebant/certantes: castra Aeneas aciemque mouebat* ('they were carrying on like this among themselves, wrangling over uncertain matters: Aeneas was moving his camp and his battle-line', 445–6). As they tussle away Aeneas acts.[82] Perhaps here lies some part of the explanation for the avoidance of conversation between Aeneas and Anchises in Book 3. Virgil may have been afraid that, by representing constant consultation instead of implying it, he would produce an impression, not of harmony, but of dither. Such an impression would undermine the image he wanted of an effective leadership, as opposed to the disorder of unstructured debate.

A more profound distinction is that which we saw at work in the private sphere, in the opposed speeches of Aeneas and Dido. Speech is not available as a palliative or a private bond in the *Aeneid*: worse, men and women use speech against each other and against their own interests, deceiving or bludgeoning with words to produce disastrous results. The most spectacular example is Sinon's speech in Book 2;[83] but virtually all the major emotional speeches of persuasion or coercion contain falsehood and misrepresentation, generate and are generated by passion, and lead to calamity: so the speeches of Amata in Book 7 (359–72), Turnus and Drances in Book 11 (343–444), and Tolumnius in Book 12 (259–65).[84] Highet's conclusion is substantially correct: 'Vergil, it seems, held that powerful oratory was incompatible with pure truth, and that every speaker presented his or her own case by misrepresenting the facts.'[85]

---

[82] A similar perfervid atmosphere prevails at the beginning of Book 12 (10–80), when we hear speeches from Turnus, Latinus, Turnus, Amata, Turnus. The appeals of Latinus and Amata, so far from inducing Turnus to give up the war, drive him into an even greater frenzy.

[83] *talibus insidiis periurique arte Sinonis/credita res, captique dolis lacrimisque coactis/quos neque Tydides nec Larisaeus Achilles,/non anni domuere decem, non mille carinae* (2.195–8).

[84] See Heinze (1915), 421–4; Highet (1972), 285–90. On Anna's speech in Book 4 (31–53), see G.S. West (1979), 10–13.

[85] Highet (1972), 289.

It is as well to be precise about this, for there is little profit in bandying about the word 'rhetorical' as an indiscriminate term of abuse. Much of Highet's discussion is vitiated by the stance he adopts on the *Vergilius poeta an orator* question,[86] a stance which is little more than 'poetry good, rhetoric bad'. Rhetorical elements in the organisation of the speeches in the *Aeneid* are simply an observable fact,[87] and if we describe any particular speech as 'rhetorical' we do not commit ourselves to a necessary value judgement. What does emerge from the *Aeneid* is a mistrust of powerful language that divides into two aspects, corresponding to the two heads under which Aeneas criticises Dido's speech: powerful language distorts reality, or the truth, in its singleminded pursuit of its particular aim; and it exploits ungovernably the emotions of speaker and audience. The power of words in a private and a public context is thus suspect in analogous ways.

The rhetoricians themselves were fully alive to the force of such criticisms (Quint. *Inst.* 2.16.1–2):

> quidam uehementer in eam [rhetoricam] inuehi solent ... : eloquentiam esse quae poenis eripiat scelestos, cuius fraude damnentur interim boni, consilia ducantur in peius, nec seditiones modo turbaeque populares sed bella etiam inexpiabilia excitentur, cuius denique tum maximus sit usus cum pro falsis contra ueritatem ualet.[88]
>
> Some habitually make strong attacks against rhetoric, saying that it is speech which saves the wicked from punishment, and that by its deception good men are sometimes condemned, deliberations are led in the wrong direction, and not only popular seditions and riots but also irremediable wars are roused, and finally that its use is greatest when it prevails for falsehood against truth.

But when they are praising high-powered oratory, and giving advice on its use, the oratorical writers are almost disarmingly candid about their aims and methods:

> ubi uero animis iudicum uis adferenda est et ab ipsa ueri contemplatione abducenda mens, ibi proprium oratoris opus est ... sicut amantes de forma iudicare non possunt quia sensum oculorum praecipit animus, ita omnem ueritatis inquirendae rationem iudex omittit occupatus adfectibus.
>
> But when force is to be applied to the minds of the jury, and when their mind must be distracted from the bare contemplation of the truth, that is the proper task of the orator ... Just as lovers are no judges of beauty because excitement removes their power of sight, so a juryman leaves behind every

---

[86] Ibid., 277–90.   [87] See G.A. Kennedy (1972), 390–2; Russell (1981), 126–8.
[88] These words should be read with *Aeneid* 7, 11 and 12 in mind.

mode of inquiring into the truth when seized with emotion. (Quint. *Inst.* 6.2.5–6)

nihil est enim in dicendo ... maius, quam ut faueat oratori is, qui audiet, utque ipse sic moueatur, ut impetu quodam animi et perturbatione, magis quam iudicio aut consilio regatur. plura enim multo homines iudicant odio aut amore aut cupiditate aut iracundia aut dolore aut laetitia aut spe aut timore aut errore aut aliqua permotione mentis, quam ueritate aut praescripto aut iuris norma aliqua aut iudicii formula aut legibus.

Nothing is more important in oratory than that the listener should sympathise with the speaker, and be moved himself in such a way that he is ruled by mental excitement and disturbance rather than by prudence and judgement. For men make judgements in more cases through hate, love, desire, anger, joy, hope, fear, error, or some excitement of the mind, than through truth or prescription or any rule of the court, or formula of judgement, or laws. (Cic. *De or.* 2.178)

illud autem genus orationis [sc. uehemens] non cognitionem iudicis, sed magis perturbationem requirit.

That [powerful] type of oratory does not have as its target the judging capacity of a juryman, but rather his disturbance. (Cic. *De or.* 2. 214)

High rhetoric does not admit of dubiety: it is concerned in the first and last resort, not with any objective establishment of a truth, but with getting its way; and it gets its way by whirling speaker and audience up in a grip of passion in which judgement and discrimination are deliberately expunged, in which partial justification, half-truth, uncertainty are nothing but irrelevancies. Criticisms of such language as an evil have a long history, of which the *Aeneid* is a part.[89]

Aeneas stands out prominently against this background. He does not lie when he speaks:[90] often he speaks with great emotion, but he does not use words to win his way by overpowering one emotion with another. The lassitude which so many readers sense in Aeneas' speeches[91] is in fact

---

[89] See von Arnim (1898), 4–114 ('Sophistik, Rhetorik, Philosophie in ihrem Kampf um die Jugendbildung'); Vicaire (1960), 276–80; G.A. Kennedy (1963), 14–17; Hellwig (1973), 304–7.

[90] Despite the claims of Highet (1972), 287–9 that Aeneas distorts the truth like other speakers. His examples are ill founded. At, e.g., 1.200–1, Aeneas tells his men *uos et Scyllaeam rabiem penitusque sonantis/accestis scopulos*. 'Aeneas speaks as though he and his men had actually braved the dangers of Scylla and Charybdis, whereas the narrative shows that they avoided them by sailing southward along the Sicilian coast...' (Highet (1972), 288). Aeneas in fact tells his men that they *went close to* Scylla and Charybdis (*accestis*, 1.201), and this is precisely what happened: *laeuam cuncta cohors remis uentisque petiuit./tollimur in caelum curuato gurgite, et idem/subducta ad Manis imos desedimus unda* (3. 563–5.).

[91] E.g. 5.45–71, 8.127–51, 11.108–19.

a restrained disavowal of the fervour which animates the language of the other characters when they seek to influence their listeners. The restraint tightens progressively into terseness as the tension of the last third of the poem increases, as Aeneas' role is restricted to the business of leading armies and killing Latins.[92]

We are left with a discrepancy, blunt but not distorting, between Aeneas' private and public speech. In the private realm, he is the poem's most consistent and prominent paradigm of the weak and insubstantial nature of human interchange; in the public realm, he is increasingly successful through the course of the poem as the leader of the Trojan enterprise, whether as diplomat or general, with exhortation, encouragement and direction, free from the manipulation and distortion which controls the words of the other outstanding orators of the poem. Highet sketched out the right area for an understanding of the problem when he attempted to refer it to Virgil's observation of Augustus, but his analysis is rather confused.[93] A more satisfying discussion is that of D.J. Stewart, who writes with the assumption that 'one of the tasks ... Virgil set for himself in the *Aeneid* was to write literature about institutions and the political vocation'.[94] He catches well, though one might quarrel with some of his expression, the truth about Aeneas' position:

> All those flat, dull speeches of encouragement, all that weariness, that general hangover quality which Aeneas both experiences and communicates when he looks out over the world, are the politician's special burden. He must pretend to enthusiasms he does not feel, repress emotions he does feel, and generally behave not as a free individual but as the incorporation of a society's needs, a trust-officer for other people's future.[95]

Again, on Dido: 'The Dido story is a metaphor for what any politician must be prepared to do: to sacrifice every last personal tie, if necessary, to help keep the political enterprise going.'[96] The same design guides the denial to Aeneas of free interchange with all those closest to him.

---

[92] See Highet (1972), 39–40.

[93] He concludes: 'For Vergil both Augustus and his prototype Aeneas were more godlike than human; and a god, as we know from Aristotle, cannot have human friends' (Highet (1972), 43). But his consequent remarks are more valuable: 'Did he not also wish to show him as one who, after almost unendurable losses and sufferings, had grown into the melancholy of middle age and the grave contemplation of approaching death?' (ibid.). [For my later retraction of this uncomprehending criticism, see Vol. 1.6, n.60.]

[94] D.J. Stewart (1972–3), 650.

[95] Ibid., 659–60. A fine example is the worthy but flat oration with which Aeneas inaugurates the funeral games (5.45–71); this is the ancient equivalent of the cabinet minister's speech at the opening of a bridge or factory.

[96] D.J. Stewart (1972–3), 660.

It is not a matter of Virgil looking at Augustus and writing down what he saw. Here is Highet's baulk, for, as he says, 'Augustus was far more sociable and less lonely then Aeneas.'[97] When we consider Aeneas, aloof, repressed in speech, devoid of close friends, the public servant without control over his own destiny and attachments, it is not Augustus who comes to mind: it is Tiberius. What other Julio-Claudian could have spoken with more feeling the words of Aeneas, *me si fata meis paterentur ducere uitam/auspiciis et sponte mea componere curas* ... ('if the fates allowed me to lead my life under my own command and to organise my cares of my own accord', 4.340–1)? Douglas was not being facetious when he compared Aeneas' last sight of Dido (*prosequitur lacrimis longe et miseratur euntem*, 'he follows after her with tears and takes pity on her from a distance as she goes', 6.476) with Suetonius' melancholy description of Tiberius' last encounter with the wife Augustus had forced him to divorce:[98] *sed Agrippinam et abegisse post diuortium doluit, et semel omnino ex occursu uisam adeo contentis et [t]umentibus oculis prosecutus est, ut custoditum sit ne umquam in conspectum ei posthac ueniret* ('but after their divorce he grieved that he had driven Agrippina away, and on the one occasion when he happened to see her as a result of a chance encounter he followed her with such strained and swollen eyes that precautions were taken that she should never thereafter come into his sight', *Tib.* 7.3).[99]

I am not suggesting that Virgil was attempting to foresee events;[100] nor was he looking back, as McKay argues when he proposes Julius Caesar as the model for Aeneas.[101] Aeneas is not a *portrait* of Augustus or of any other individual. He represents generally the extreme case of the pressures and cruelties inflicted upon the individual who embodies in his own person the aspirations and future of a whole nation.[102] Augustus was the only man Virgil knew who was such a 'man of destiny'; while it is impossible to believe that Augustus was not a major influence on Virgil's conception of his hero, it is likewise impossible to make any precise suggestions as to the

---

[97] Highet (1972), 42. One suspects that it was the early part of Augustus' Principate, when Virgil knew him, that provided the material for the conventional assessment of his *comitas* (Suet. *Aug.* 53.2–3; 66.1–3; 74). Virgil did not see the Augustus who lived through the deaths of all his early friends, and of Gaius and Lucius, who saw the disgrace of daughter and granddaughter, and survived into 'the atmosphere of gloom and repression that clouded the last decade of the reign' (Syme (1978), 205).
[98] Douglas (1961–2), 21. [99] Following Ihm's Teubner text for *[t]umentibus*.
[100] Cf. Douglas (1961–2), 21: 'Virgil was dead before these events, but he knew all about dynastic marriages of convenience.'
[101] McKay (1963).
[102] Cf. D.J. Stewart (1972–3), 651: 'The *Aeneid* is a study of the preternatural strains and anxieties a political vocation brings to mere natural man.'

nature of that influence.[103] The character of Aeneas stands essentially in its own right, the representative of a predicament which his creator did not see as unique.

As Stewart observes, in the passage quoted above, '[t]he Dido story is a metaphor for what any politician must be prepared to do'.[104] It is in his confrontation with Dido that the tensions inherent in Aeneas' role become most acute. In Dido he faces the most impassioned and eloquent speaker in the poem. He feels the justice and the injustice of her speech, but he does not answer her in the same tenor. With hard-won self-control he tells her that the way she uses words is profitless and cruel, and he attempts to give an explanation, to reach some understanding. His words do not achieve their aim: but there is nothing in the poem to give us reason to believe that any other words would have been more effective.

---

[103] But I cannot resist quoting the following passage from Suetonius, to which Prof. Nisbet referred me as being illustrative of Augustus' constrained and inhibited use of speech: *sermones quoque cum singulis atque etiam cum Liuia sua grauiores non nisi scriptos et e libello habebat, ne plus minusue loqueretur ex tempore* ('He did not conduct his more important conversations with individuals and even with his wife Livia unless he had them written down, from a notebook, so that he wouldn't say too much or too little off the cuff,' *Aug.* 84. 2).

[104] D.J. Stewart (1972–3), 660.

CHAPTER 2

# *The Reconciliations of Juno*[1]

I

The reconciliation between Juno and Jupiter at the end of the *Aeneid* (12.791–842) forms the cap to the divine action of the poem. The scene is conventionally regarded as the resolution of the heavenly discord that has prevailed since the first book; in particular, it is normal to see here a definitive transformation of Juno, as she abandons her enmity once and for all, committing herself wholeheartedly to the Roman cause. So G. Lieberg, for example: 'The two hemispheres of Jupiter and Juno meet at the end of the poem in the totality of the divine universe, guarantee of the glorious future of Rome';[2] or W. Kühn: 'The divine conversation ends in a full and brilliant final accord.'[3]

The comments of Servius give rise to second thoughts. As Juno accedes to Jupiter's requests (*mentem laetata retorsit*, 'rejoicing, she twists her mind back', 841), he observes: *iste quidem hoc dicit; sed constat bello Punico secundo exoratam Iunonem, tertio uero bello a Scipione sacris quibusdam etiam Romam esse translatam* ('that's what he says; but it is agreed that it was in the Second Punic War that Juno was won over, and that it was in the Third War that she was brought across to Rome by Scipio by means of certain rites'). The reconciliation during the Hannibalic War is part of the Ennian tradition, as Servius informs us on *Aen.* 1.281, *consilia in melius referet* ('Juno will turn her counsels to the better'): *quia bello Punico secundo, ut*

---

[1] For their help and criticism I thank Professor R.G.M. Nisbet and Dr. N. Horsfall, also my colleagues in the Harvard University Society of Fellows, Professor Herbert Bloch, Nita Krevans, and Richard Garner, together with the participants in Professor Richard F. Thomas' seminar at Harvard University, who heard a draft of this paper in February 1983.
[2] Lieberg (1966), 165.
[3] Kühn (1971), 165 (general discussion, 162–7, 169). Cf. Boyancé (1963), 27: 'L'évolution qui conduit Junon de son hostilité du debout à son acquiescement de la fin est une des données capitales de la religion de l'*Énéide*'; Buchheit (1963), 133–50, esp. 147; Buchheit (1974); Thornton (1976), 144–5, 152–4; C.H. Wilson (1979), 365–6; G.W. Williams (1983), 76–7.

*ait Ennius, placata Iuno coepit fauere Romanis* ('because in the Second Punic War, as Ennius says, Juno was placated and began to favour the Romans', Enn. *Ann.* VIII.xvi Sk.). If Juno was placated, she had been hostile: Ennius' *Annales* will have shown her ranged against the Romans on the side of Carthage.[4] Now, Ennius was not canonical, and Virgil was not bound to be committed to this Ennian picture of Juno's involvement in the Carthaginian wars; he was free to have his Juno become a supporter of Rome some nine hundred years before Ennius'. At various points in the poem, however, it is plain that Virgil does indeed adhere to this Ennian tradition: by referring back to his predecessor's *Annales* he looks forward to the time when Juno will once again take up arms against the Aeneadae, on behalf of her favoured city Carthage.

The cardinal passage is the *concilium deorum* at the beginning of Book 10.[5] Jupiter chides the gods for causing war between the Trojans and Latins, and for taking sides in that war (6–10). But a proper time for them to fight will come, he tells them (11–14):

> adueniet iustum pugnae (ne arcessite) tempus
> cum fera Karthago Romanis arcibus olim
> exitium magnum atque Alpis immittet apertas:
> tum certare odiis, tum res rapuisse licebit.

> A proper time for fighting will come (don't hasten it on), when savage Carthage at some point in the future will unleash great destruction and the opened-up Alps on the Roman citadels: then you will have permission to struggle with hatreds, then you will have permission to cause havoc.

This is a promise of a divine conflict to mirror the human one,[6] and it is directed principally at Juno, as Servius observes in his note on *ne arcessite* (11): *nolite bellorum tempora praeoccupare. et bene satis facit uxori cum prohibitione. significat autem bellum Punicum secundum* ('Don't anticipate the period of war. And he does a good job of giving satisfaction to his wife with the prohibition. For what he is referring to is the Second Punic War').

---

[4] Buchheit (1963), 54: 'Juno was inimically disposed to the Romans up to this point, until the Second Punic War. Since she gives up her enmity only with the end of the Punic War, she must have been depicted as the great opponent of Rome on the Carthaginian side.' See, too, Häussler (1978), 195–8. Silius Italicus in the *Punica* is following Ennius as well as Virgil in his use of Juno as Rome's divine antagonist in the Hannibalic War: see Woodruff (1910), 403–6.

[5] Norden (1915), 43–6 contended that the whole setting here was Ennian, based on a putative council in *Annales* 7, at the beginning of the Second Punic War. But his case has been undone by Friedrich (1941), 114–15, Timpanaro (1948), 37–40 and Wigodsky (1972), 65–6.

[6] It is not simply a promise of a future war between men, as interpreted by Simpson (1975), 26: see Norden (1915), 51; Häussler (1978), 190.

Necessarily, these words of Jupiter will have had far more resonance for their original audience, with school-acquired knowledge of *Annales Quinti Enni* in their head, than they can for us; Jupiter is foretelling the role Juno will play on the side of Carthage in the *Annales* of Ennius.

If Jupiter prophesies Juno's support of Hannibal, he also prophesies her reconciliation in the *Annales*. He does so in his major speech to Venus in Book 1: *quin aspera Iuno,/quae mare nunc terrasque metu caelumque fatigat,/ consilia in melius referet, mecumque fouebit/Romanos* ('indeed rough Juno, who now wearies out the sea and the earth with fear, and the sky, will turn her counsels to the better, and along with me will nurture the Romans', 279–82). The positioning of these lines causes chronological problems if one takes them to refer explicitly to the scene in Book 12, as is generally done,[7] since they come after the death of Aeneas, after the founding of the city of Rome. As Halter puts it:

> We may briefly ask the first question which emerges, namely from what point Juno actually ceases her rage. Since she already abandons her hate in the twelfth book (818), her change of mind should have been mentioned between the fighting and the reign of Aeneas, i.e., between lines 264 and 265. Why does Virgil not follow strict chronology in this important point?[8]

The answer to Halter's question is that Virgil does follow the chronology here, the Ennian chronology, as Servius comments (on 281), when he locates Juno's change of heart: *quia bello Punico secundo, ut ait Ennius, placata Iuno coepit fauere Romanis* ('because in the Second Punic War, as Ennius says, Juno was placated and began to favour the Romans', Enn. Ann. VIII.xvi Sk.). N. Horsfall has drawn the right conclusion, observing that Juno's reconciliation belongs at this point in the prophecy because it was 'a necessary prelude to the defeat of Carthage, the first great obstacle to *imperium sine fine* encountered by Rome overseas and to the great wave of foreign conquests she undertook in the sixty years after the second Punic war—including, of course, *Pthiam clarasque Mycenas*'.[9] After Juno's reconciliation she will acquiesce in the conquest of Greece, seeing her favoured cities of Mycenae and Argos go under, in poetic fulfilment of the pledge she had made to Zeus in the *Iliad* (4.51–4):[10]

---

[7] E.g. by Austin (1971), on 281: 'Iuno will amend her design ... For her yielding see 12. 841.'
[8] Halter (1963), 14.   [9] Horsfall (1973–4), 3.
[10] Ovid follows a similar line in *Fast.* 6, where he has Juno boast of the sacrifices she made for the Romans' sake: he is more systematic, including Homer's three towns plus Samos, mentioned in Virgil's proem as Juno's second favourite city (*Aen.* 1.16); *paeniteat Sparten Argosque measque Mycenas/et ueterem Latio supposuisse Samon* (6.47–8).

ἤτοι ἐμοὶ τρεῖς μὲν πολὺ φίλταταί εἰσι πόληες,
Ἄργός τε Σπάρτη τε καὶ εὐρυάγυια Μυκήνη·
τὰς διαπέρσαι, ὅτ᾽ ἄν τοι ἀπέχθωνται περὶ κῆρι·
τάων οὔ τοι ἐγὼ πρόσθ᾽ ἵσταμαι οὐδὲ μεγαίρω.

Three cities there are by far most dear to me, Argo and Sparta and Mycenae of the wide ways; sack them, when they vex you in your heart—I shall not stand before them, nor grudge it you.

Consider, too, the Homeric paradigm for Jupiter's promise to Venus. In *Odyssey* 1, Zeus comforts Athene over her suffering protégé, promising that Poseidon will eventually lay aside his anger against Odysseus: Ποσειδάων δὲ μεθήσει/ὃν χόλον ('Poseidon will relax his anger', 77–8). Poseidon's relenting is not an action described in the poem itself: Teiresias tells Odysseus how to placate the god (11.121–34), and as the poem ends Odysseus' atonement is still in the future. Similarly, in the *Aeneid*, the final reconciliation of Juno which Jupiter prophesies is not represented in the narrative, but lies beyond the poem's close.

A third and final passage. In the poem's introduction, Virgil describes Juno's love for Carthage (1.15–18), saying *hoc regnum dea gentibus esse,/si qua fata sinant, iam tum tenditque fouetque* ('that this should be the place to rule over the peoples—if somehow the fates would allow it—even then this is what the goddess strives for and cherishes', 17–18). *iam tum* is crucial—'even then she was planning for Carthage to rule the peoples of the earth', anticipating the aid she would give Carthage later on, when the issue of who should rule the world was to be decided. It is as good as certain that the motif referred to in *regnum . . . gentibus* is an Ennian one. Lucretius and Livy, in related language, both represent the Punic Wars as a contest for world dominion,[11] and Kenney observes that 'no doubt Ennius was their common model'.[12] Certainly in the case of Lucretius, we may point to clear imitation

---

[11] Lucr. 3.833–7, *ad confligendum uenientibus undique Poenis,/omnia cum belli trepido concussa tumultu/ horrida contremuere sub altis aetheris oris/in dubioque fuere utrorum ad regna cadendum/omnibus humanis esset terraque marique* ('when the Carthaginians came from all sides to the fray, when all things shook and trembled under the lofty expanses of the sky, shivering with the panicky tumult of war, and *were in doubt* as to whose sway of the two *all men* should fall by land and sea'); Liv. 29.17.6 (quoted by Kenney (1971), on 832–42), *in discrimine est nunc humanum omne genus, utrum uos an Carthaginienses principes orbis terrarum uideat* ('*the whole human race* has now reached *the critical point* which will decide whether it will see you or the Carthaginians as lords of the world'); Liv. 30.32.2, *Roma an Carthago iura gentibus daret ante crastinam noctem scituros* ('they would know before tomorrow nightfall whether Rome or Carthage would administer laws to the peoples of the earth').

[12] Kenney (1971), on 832–42. One sees a sign of the same formulation in Polybius, who refers to Carthage and Rome as τὰ πολιτεύματα τὰ περὶ τῆς τῶν ὅλων ἀρχῆς ἀμφισβητήσαντα ('the states who would dispute the supremacy of the whole', 1.3.7). But Polybius generally speaks of a solely

of an Ennian line, which looks as if it belongs in a description of the final struggle between Scipio and Hannibal: *Africa terribili tremit horrida terra tumultu* ('the land of Africa shivers and trembles with the terrible tumult', 309 Sk.); cf. Lucr. 3.834–5, *omnia cum belli trepido concussa tumultu/horrida contremuere* ('when all things shook and trembled, shivering with the panicky tumult of war').[13] The Virgilian *regnum . . . gentibus* employs a word that appears in Lucretius' use of the motif (*utrorum ad regna cadendum*, 836), and a word that appears in Livy's (*iura gentibus daret*, 30.32.2).[14] The rivalry for supremacy posited by the topos is caught by Virgil with the opposition of *regnum* (17), applied to Carthage, and *regem* (21), applied to Rome. Virgil, then, in *iam tum* looks forward to Juno's helping Carthage at a much later date; in *hoc regnum dea gentibus esse/ . . . tenditque fouetque* he refers to a commonplace about the world hegemony of Carthage which is almost certainly Ennian in origin, applied to the Punic Wars; and in *regnum . . . gentibus* he may even be using language from that Ennian context. The likelihood of allusion to Ennius here is increased if we accord weight to Servius' comment on the next lines (*progeniem sed enim Troiano a sanguine duci/audierat Tyrias olim quae uerteret arces*, 'but indeed she had heard that a breed was being traced from Trojan blood that would one day overturn the Tyrian citadels', 19–20): *et perite 'audierat'; in Ennio enim inducitur Iuppiter promittens Romanis excidium Carthaginis* ('and it is skilful to say "she had heard"; for in Ennius Jupiter is brought in promising to the Romans the destruction of Carthage', VIII.xv Sk.). The whole context 'anticipates' the *Annales*.

Ennius had Juno fighting for Carthage against Rome, and so, it seems, does Virgil. What then to make of the reconciliation between Juno and Jupiter in Book 12? Some scholars disregard the Virgilian evidence for Juno's activities in the Punic Wars, and will have the reconciliation in Book 12 as quite complete.[15] Others regard the scene in Book 12 in the same way, but are aware of the force of the 'Ennian' passages and conclude, with varying degrees of discomfort, that Virgil has fallen into self-contradiction. Thus B.C. Fenik, discussing Jupiter's words in Book 10 (*adueniet iustum pugnae (ne arcessite) tempus . . .* etc., 11–14): 'This squares poorly with the

Roman bid for supremacy (see the passages in Walbank (1957–79) on 1.3.4), while for the Roman literary tradition Ennius will have been the true parent.
[13] See Bailey (1947), on 3.835; Kenney (1971), on 834–5.
[14] Horsfall (1973–4), 3 draws attention to the force of the words.
[15] E.g. Buchheit (1963), 147: 'While Ennius at first chose for it the Second Punic War, and Horace the death of Romulus, i.e., the period after the founding of Rome, Virgil shifts the reconciliation back into the earliest days of Rome [I return to Horace below] . . . Juno is, so to speak, the friend of Rome from the beginning of Roman history.' See the works cited in nn.2 and 3 above.

end of the *Aeneid* where Juno's reconciliation lapses into an anticlimax if we are to believe that she again fought against Rome at a later time. We must recognise an inconcinnity here, which may be the result of Virgil's attempting to combine an earlier tradition with a version he wished to create himself."[16]

A few commentators face and accept the implications,[17] but W.R. Johnson is the only writer on the reconciliation scene in Book 12 to expound at length the case that there is something fundamentally qualified about Juno's acquiescence to Jupiter.[18] His discussion is most valuable and important; my remarks may stand as a supplement.

Exactly what do Juno and Jupiter agree to in Book 12? All the talk is of Troy. Juno pleads that the vile race of Teucer alter nothing of her Latins' *mores*, not name or dress or nationality or language; the hated name which she wishes to be obliterated is the last word we hear from her lips (819–28):

> illud te ...
> pro Latio obtestor ...
> ne uetus indigenas nomen mutare Latinos
> neu Troas fieri iubeas Teucrosque uocari
> aut uocem mutare uiros aut uertere uestem.
> sit Latium, sint Albani per saecula reges,
> sit Romana potens Itala uirtute propago:
> occidit, occideritque sinas cum nomine Troia.

> On behalf of Latium ..., this point I beg of you .... Do not order the indigenous Latins to change their old name, or to become Trojans and be called Teucrians, or that the men alter their language or change their costume. Let there be Latium, let there be Alban kings through the centuries, let there be a Roman progeny, powerful with Italian virtue: the city has fallen, let it stay fallen along along with its name, Troy.

Jupiter readily concedes: *commixti corpore tantum/subsident Teucri* ('the Trojans will fade away, mingling in their physical bodies only', 835–6). This is a great victory for Juno. It settles the point of grievance between her

---

[16] Fenik (1960), 236 (cf. 237, 'discrepancies' and 'contradictions'); cf. Moseley (1926), 38–9; Häussler (1978), 189–93 (189: 'these tell-tale inconsistencies'). Häussler sees the references back to the Ennian tradition as an untidy and unwholesome element ('And immediately it seems to us to have become clear that only an *Aeneid* without this look backwards and with an unconditional and definitive reconciliation as its conclusion could have achieved unity of motivation and religious motivation', 193).

[17] Büchner (1958), 1457: 'The battle and with it the plot only ends when Juno gives up (12.841). But not for ever: for she is still promised by Fate in the future a great opportunity to fight for Carthage (10.11ff.).' Cf. Conway (1935) on 1.281 (see n.23 below).

[18] Johnson (1976), 123–7.

and Venus, as expressed in their speeches in Book 10, where Venus begs Jupiter to allow Troy to be reestablished,[19] and Juno will not have it. Above all, it satisfies the vast resentment against the Trojans which the proem of Book 1 had set out as part of Juno's motivation for persecuting Aeneas and his men (1.23-8).

The crucial point is the obvious one, that Juno's hatred of Troy is only half her motivation. As Horsfall points out, she has a 'mythological' motive for her hatred of the *Aeneadae*—the judgement of Paris and all the Homeric matter connected with the name of Troy (1.23-8)—and she has a 'historical' motive, her predilection for Carthage and fear of the fate that awaits the city at the hands of Aeneas' descendants (1.12-22).[20] (Bluntly, for the purposes of the first motive she is regarded as 'Argive Hera', while for the purposes of the second she is viewed under the aspect of the Carthaginian Tanit.)[21] This second, historical, motive is the engine that supplies the momentum of the narrative of Books 1 and 4,[22] which culminates in Dido's curse and the evocation of Hannibal, to engage Rome and Carthage irrevocably in future warfare (4.622-9). In Book 12 only Juno's 'mythological' grievance is removed;[23] the other remains potent, its consequences already irresistibly in train. Juno knows it, and Jupiter knows it: *es germana Iouis Saturnique altera proles,/irarum tantos uoluis sub pectore fluctus* ('you really are the sister of Jupiter, a second offspring of Saturn—so great are the waves of anger that you roll beneath your breast', 830-1). I should follow Servius here,[24] who explains in these words:

---

[19] *Xanthum et Simoenta/redde, oro, miseris iterumque reuoluere casus/da, pater, Iliacos Teucris* (*Aen.* 10.60-2). On the important theme of *Pergama recidiua* in the *Aeneid*, see W.S. Anderson (1957); Knauer (1964), 351-4; Suerbaum (1967).

[20] Horsfall (1973-4), 2. Cf. Büchner (1958), 1339.

[21] On this identification, see Preisendanz (1932), 2184; Pease (1935), on *Aen.* 4.91; Lieberg (1966), 153 n.37; Picard (1954), 65, 109. Bailey (1935), 131-2 confuses the two faces of Juno here: 'out of this hatred of the Trojans arises the special position which Juno holds in the *Aeneid* of the patron-goddess of the newly founded Carthage'.

[22] See especially Horsfall (1973-4) on the crucial importance of the Carthaginian theme in the early books; cf. Pöschl (1962), 13-16, esp. 15: 'Juno ... is first mythical personification of the historical power of Carthage'; W.W. Fowler (1916), 40: 'At the outset of his poem, with all the emphasis he can use, Virgil associates [Juno] in interest—an interest perverse in the eyes of all Romans—with the most deadly enemy Rome ever had to meet, and with the mythical queen of Carthage, the Cleopatra of his poetic fancy.' Wigodsky (1972), 29 is quite mistaken to assert that 'Vergil is not interested in the Punic Wars as such'; while Coleman (1982), 168 n.53 plays down Juno's association with Carthage, as a result of taking Juno's reconciliation in Book 12 as complete.

[23] As seen by Conway (1935), in his note on Jupiter's promise of Juno's reconciliation (1.281, *in melius referet*): 'The time of this final acquiescence of Juno in the greatness of Rome is left unspecified both here and in 12.841, where she desists merely from persecuting Aeneas on condition that the language, religion and government of Rome shall be Italian, not Asiatic.'

[24] The result is very close to Johnson (1976), 126, esp. n.106. The passage is much discussed: bibliography in Kühn (1971), 164 n.9; add Wigodsky (1972), 67-9 on 'Saturnia'.

> 'soror Iouis es, id est Saturni filia.' unde non mirum est tantam te iracundiam retinere sub pectore. nam scimus unumquemque pro generis qualitate in iram moueri: nobiles enim etsi ad praesens uidentur ignoscere, tamen in posterum iram reseruant. quod nunc Iunoni uidetur obicere: nam cum se concedere diceret, petiit tamen quod grauiter posset obesse Troianis.

> 'You are the sister of Jupiter, that is daughter of Saturn.' Hence it is no surprise that you keep such anger in your heart. For we know that each person is moved to anger in accordance with the rank of his birth: for nobles, although they seem to forgive for the present, nevertheless reserve their anger for a future point. This is what he now seems to accuse Juno of; for though she claims that she is conceding, she has nevertheless requested something that could be seriously prejudicial to the Trojans [he means the loss of their name].[25]

My only difference is that Juno is reserving her anger far longer into the future than Servius suggests—until she reappears in her old role in the *Annales*. As we read the scene in Book 12, we must have always in mind the Ennian Juno, of whose actions Virgil has regularly reminded us.

Does this mean, as Fenik complains, that 'Juno's reconciliation lapses into an anticlimax if we are to believe that she again fought against Rome at a later time'?[26] We should rather think of the anticlimax that is attendant upon the traditional account of the scene, whereby the daemonic power that has generated the action so far evaporates with an order, a request, and a smile. It is a question of emphases. Johnson's eloquent account lays its principal stress on what the scene holds of the sinister and baleful. While acknowledging the essential accuracy of his reading, we must recognise that none the less there *is* a resolution of sorts here, that something *is* accomplished which is not wholly shabby or a fraud.[27] This much is guaranteed even by the elaborate formal correspondences between the Jupiter-scene in 12 and the Jupiter-scene in 1:[28] the relief which Jupiter promises Venus may not be unalloyed when it comes at the end of the poem, but in some measure it does come. Another formal sign to mark Juno's acquiescence is seen in the frame of the scene with Jupiter. At the beginning, Jupiter addresses her as she is looking down on the fighting from a cloud (*fulua*

---

[25] Servius' interpretation is similar to the comments of the bT scholia on *Il.* 15.212, where Poseidon stops supporting the Greeks—for the moment: εὐσχήμονα τὴν ἀπαλλαγὴν ὁρίζεται, ἐπανατείνων τὴν ὀργὴν εἰς ὕστερον ('he sets out his departure in fair words, stretching his anger out into the future'). On such shared themes in the Greek and Latin commentators see Fraenkel (1949), 151–4.

[26] Fenik (1960), 236, cited n.16 above.

[27] I find some of Johnson's (1976) comments on the evil of Jupiter disconcerting (126 and n.110); also his suggested interpretation of *his mentem retorsit* (127).

[28] On these correspondences see Halter (1963), 14–16, 78–9; Buchheit (1963), 499–501; Knauer (1964), 324–6; Kühn (1971), 164–5.

*pugnas de nube tuentem*, 792). *de aere, de elemento suo*, comments Servius ad loc. ('from the air, from her own element'): the identification is based on the allegorists' equation of Ἥρα ('Hera') and ἀήρ ('air').²⁹ Jupiter chides her: *aut qua spe gelidis in nubibus haeres?* ('on the basis of what hope are you clinging on *in the cold clouds*', 796). At the end of the dialogue, won over by Jupiter, Juno gives a token of her agreement by leaving her element: *interea excedit caelo nubemque relinquit* ('in the meantime she withdraws from the sky and leaves the cloud', 842). The device is perhaps rather mechanical, but it signals an accommodation.³⁰

What the scene in 12 resolves is the question of Aeneas' settlement in Latium, and the final passing away of Troy; it does not resolve any more of Juno's grudges. The divine reconciliation is qualified to the extent that it reflects only so much of the Roman endeavour as has been accomplished so far: it leaves open what historically remains open. The great anxieties that surround the first beginnings of the Roman state are not dispelled at a stroke; the momentum of empire continues, and the energies of the poem's forward movement are held in suspense, not checked. Ahead lie centuries of strain, with Carthage as the highest crisis, and with Juno's hate once more to face.

In a recent paper on 'The judgement of Paris and *Iliad* Book XXIV', M. Davies has well described the way in which Homer's final book establishes a contrast between the ability of men to achieve reconciliation with each other and the relentless nature of the gods' animosities. He goes on to detect a Virgilian reversal of this Homeric pattern:

> [I]n *Aen.* xii 791 ff. Jupiter bids [Juno] set aside her resentment and loathing of the Trojans and she consents with surprising speed and readiness. Jupiter smiles, and reconciliation and peace are restored on Olympus. On earth, however, there is no such happy resolution: Turnus begs for mercy but Aeneas is overwhelmed by hatred and anger and kills the suppliant. The whole poem ends not as the *Iliad* does on a note of mortal reconciliation and reintegration, but surprisingly and distressingly on a note of continued hatred, hostility and rage.³¹

---

²⁹ See Servius on *Aen.* 7.300; Heinze (1915), 299; Pease (1955–8), 716–7; Buffière (1956), 107–8. Note Juno's *aeria ... sede* in 12.810.

³⁰ *excedit caelo* is puzzling to me. What does it mean to say that Juno 'withdraws from the *caelum*', and what is the relation between this phrase and *nubemque relinquit*? In the scheme that saw Juno as *aer*, Jupiter was the *caelum* (Pease (1955–8), 715–16; Buffière (1956), 106). Hence I have sometimes been tempted to read *cedit* (in the sense of 'deferring' or 'yielding to', *Oxford Latin Dictionary* s.v. 8 and 10): 'she deferred to the Jupiter-element and left her own'. I am by no means confident of this; but note the parallelism between *cedit caelo nubemque relinquit* and the words spoken earlier in the scene by Juno: *et nunc cedo equidem pugnasque exosa relinquo* (818).

³¹ M. Davies (1981), 61.

This is fine comment on the distinction between the attempts of Homer's men and Virgil's men, but I would suggest that in the *Aeneid* even the immortal sphere is unreconciled within itself at the close, just as in the *Iliad*. The significant contrast at the end of the poem is that between the deadly weakness of men's efforts and the ease with which the gods can make an arrangement while still unreconciled in full: this is their essential invulnerability, their power ῥεῖα μάλ' ὥς τε θεός ('quite easily, as befits a god').[32] Homer's gods reach a momentary accommodation without their grievances being abnegated;[33] Juno does the same with Jupiter, winning a point, losing a point, and deferring a third.

## II

The discussion so far has involved many incidental references to the figure of Juno in Ennius' *Annales*. It is time to turn directly to Ennius, in an attempt to discover what aspects of Ennius' goddess and her activities lie behind the reconciliation scene in *Aeneid* 12. Further evidence will come from Ovid, and above all from Horace, whose third 'Roman Ode' exhibits, like Virgil's closing episode, an angry Juno making an accommodation concerning the incipient Roman power. In Horace, too, the talk is all of the passing away of Troy; if we must try to ascertain what Ennian sanction there may be for the common talk of Troy, we must also express some opinion on the notorious topic of why this subject received such emphasis from these poets at this time.[34]

Even in saying so much I have run ahead of the argument, because it is by no means agreed that the common elements between Virgil and Horace are in fact Ennian, or that the Juno whom we see and hear in Horace's ode bears any relation to the Juno of Ennius' *Annales*. The Ennian episode which is the focus of the problem is the Council of the Gods in the first book (I.xxx–iv Sk.). On the agenda of the meeting was the apotheosis of Romulus. We do not rely solely on Horace for this knowledge. Ovid twice tells the story of

---

[32] *Il.* 3.381, 20.444. Johnson (1976), 124 is good here. Griffin (1980), 189 has convincing observations on the gods' 'ease' in Homer, and on the Euripidean 'contrast between human misery and the radiant unconcern of the gods'. Virgil's passionately involved deities are, in this regard, rather closer to Homer's than to Euripides'.

[33] Besides M. Davies (1981), see Macleod (1982) on *Il.* 24.25–30 ('the judgement of Paris'): 'Homer heightens and extends his tragedy by taking us back to where it started. This reminds us that even if for the moment "the gods" are to unite in allowing the ransom of Hector's body, the gods hostile to Troy still have reason to be as angry as ever; and the city they hate must fall.'

[34] Discussion tends to resolve itself into deciding either for or against the proposition that a real project of moving the capital lies behind the insistence on Troy's total disappearance: Fraenkel (1957), 267–9 has a history of the dispute (a dispute which also involves Liv. 5.51–4, on transferring the capital to Veii). See further n.74 below.

Mars asking Jupiter for permission to fetch his son Romulus to heaven, reminding Jupiter of an earlier occasion when a promise had been given that this elevation would one day take place (*Fast.* 2.481–8; *Met.* 14.806–15). In the *Metamorphoses* passage, Mars refers explicitly to a *concilium deorum* as the setting for the giving of the promise (*concilio quondam praesente deorum*, 812), and in both passages he quotes an identical line as the exact words of Jupiter's promise: *unus erit quem tu tolles in caerula caeli* ('one there will be whom you will raise up into the blue of heaven', *Met.* 14.814 = *Fast.* 2.487). This line is quoted by Varro as his first example of poetic diction,[35] and is virtually certain to be a line of Ennius.[36] Mars tells Jupiter that he has memorised the words and stored them up in his retentive mind. The verse which conveys this claim refers just as happily to the cultivated poet who has retained from childhood bits of hairy Ennius in his head: *tu mihi concilio quondam praesente deorum/(nam memoro memorique animo pia uerba notaui)/'unus erit quem tu tolles in caerula caeli/dixisti* ('you said to me once in the presence of the council of the gods (for I recall it, and noted down your holy words in my mindful heart), "One there will be whom you will raise up into the blue of heaven"', *Met.* 14.812–15).[37]

It is in fact generally reckoned that Horace's poem recalls Ennius' council in *Annales* 1.[38] The last stanza of Horace's poem declares virtually outright that he has just been 'quoting' epic matter: *desine peruicax/referre sermones deorum et/magna modis tenuare paruis* ('stop being pushy and relating conversations of the gods and slimming down great matters to small measures', *C.* 3.3.70–2). Ovid refers to Ennius' *concilium* explicitly (*concilio ... deorum*, *Met.* 14.812),[39] while Horace's reference characteristically avoids that degree of precision: *consiliantibus ... diuis* (17–18). But although Ennius is not just

---

[35] *Ling.* 7.5–6, *Dicam in hoc libro de uerbis quae a poetis sunt posita ... incipiam hinc: 'unus erit quem tu tolles in caerula caeli/templa.'*

[36] Cf. Vahlen (1928), clx: 'That this is a piece of Ennius is not said by Ovid; but Varro *Ling.* 7.6, though he does not inform one openly, nevertheless indicates this in a manner not obscure to those who know Varro's way of doing things.'

[37] After the interview with Jupiter, Mars descends and snatches up Romulus in his chariot (*Met.* 14.818–26; *Fast.* 2.496—as befitting the genre, a much more elliptical version). The line from the *Fasti* (*rex patriis astra petebat equis*) resembles Horace's reference to Romulus' 'death' (*Martis equis Acheronta fugit*, *Carm.* 3. 3. 16): it is natural to assume a common Ennian model (indeed, Horace's *Martis* has been emended to *patris* on analogy with Ovid's line: see Bentley (1711) ad loc.).

[38] Cf. Vahlen (1928), clix; Pasquali (1964), 687; Oksala (1973), 102, 156. It seems to be taken for granted that Horace sets the council after Romulus has been snatched away by Mars (exceptions include Häussler (1978), 195 n.23). But this snatching away is part of what the council is there to decide. Ovid gives us naturally to understand that the gods decided in advance that Mars would be allowed to rescue his son for immortality, and I see nothing in Horace's poem that is at odds with this picture.

[39] As does Lucilius, in his parody: *uellem concilio uestrum, quod dicitis olim,/caelicolae, hic habitum, uellem adfuissemus priore/concilio* (frr. 20–2 W.).

the formal model (that is, for the basic idea of a *concilium deorum*), but also the model for the *occasion* (to discuss the apotheosis of Romulus), there are few scholars who claim that the content of Juno's speech in Horace is based on anything Juno might have said in Ennius. Some commentators say nothing on the subject.[40] Many deny the notion outright, or express serious doubt,[41] while Heinze, Steuart, Wilkinson, Waszink and Commager represent the small group who consider that the words of Horace's Juno are drawn originally from the mouth of Ennius'.[42] Heinze and Commager point to the strong correspondences between Horace's scene and Virgil's in *Aeneid* 12, with their common insistence on the disappearance of Troy, and conclude that Ennius is the joint source,[43] thus by-passing the argument over whether Horace followed Virgil or Virgil followed Horace.[44]

I think it is fair to say that the *natural* conclusion to draw from Horace's poem and its connection with *Aeneid* 12 is that both go back to Ennius and depend on Juno's voicing of similar sentiments in the council in *Annales* 1.[45] I think it is also fair to say that the *only* reason for declining to draw this conclusion is the belief that Ennius' Juno was not reconciled to Rome until the Hannibalic War, and therefore could not have made any agreement favourable to the Roman state at any earlier stage.[46] The general tendency of my argument will by now be plain. Virgil could depict Juno, at a very early stage of Roman history, making a deal with Jupiter (agreeing to Aeneas' settlement but winning the final annihilation of Troy), while still remaining full of menace until finally placated during the Punic Wars. With such a pattern before our eyes, we need not allow the knowledge that Ennius' Juno was likewise not fully reconciled to Rome before Hannibal's time to

---

[40] No comment, for instance, from G.W. Williams (1969) ad loc., who rather views the speech as 'a sort of answer to a problem raised by the contemporary epic, the *Aeneid*: how and when did Juno's hostility to Rome cease?' Fraenkel (1957), 267 and Kiessling and Heinze (1908–21), vol. 2, on *Carm.* 3.3.15, only refer to Horace's taking from Ennius the motif of a *concilium deorum*: in his discussion of the speech itself, Fraenkel does not mention Ennius.

[41] Cf., e.g., Vahlen (1928), clix; Oksala (1973), 156 (both doubting); Buchheit (1963), 146; Pasquali (1964), 687; Häussler (1978), 195 n.23 (all denying: 'but above all, there was hardly talk of Troy in this *concilium deorum*', Buchheit (1963), 146 n.626).

[42] Steuart (1925), 176; Heinze (1928), 230–3; Wilkinson (1946), 73–4; Waszink (1957), 325; Commager (1962), 222 n.122.

[43] Wigodsky (1972), 147 draws the same conclusion, but refers to *Ann.* 8, not *Ann.* 1.

[44] Bibliography on the priority question in Buchheit (1963), 146 n.626; Wigodsky (1972), 147.

[45] Though one may speculate about one poet being 'put on to' the subject by the other.

[46] Cf. Vahlen (1928), clix denying that Juno spoke in Ennius as Horace's Juno does: 'For the goddess, having been hostile to the Romans of old, mitigated her anger at last in the Second Punic War. Cf. Servius on *Aen.* 1.281, "in the Second Punic War, according to Ennius, Juno was placated and began to favour the Romans" ... But why should she begin to favour them then, when she had already permitted the Romans to extend the bounds of their dominion far and wide?' Identical reasoning in Buchheit (1963), 146.

prevent us from concluding that in *Annales* 1 she may have come to some qualified agreement, the prototype of Virgil's, agreeing to the apotheosis of Romulus on condition that Troy vanish for ever.

The details of the case remain to be worked out, but first it is worth bringing to bear another argument to show that there is likely to have been some sort of reconciliation with Juno involved in Ennius' account of the decision to grant godhead to Romulus. In describing (or inventing)[47] the apotheosis of Romulus, Ennius took over many essential details from the traditional accounts of the apotheosis of Heracles.[48] He is unlikely to have been original in this. As J.K. Newman points out, Theocritus 17 is good evidence for the existence of Hellenistic epics which treated Heracles as paradigm for the deification of Alexander and later monarchs.[49] In that poem we see Alexander and the first Ptolemy enjoying immortality in heaven (16–25). They sit opposite Heracles, and escort him to Hebe's chamber after the feast. Their immortality is explicitly said to be a result of their descent from Heracles (22–7):

ἔνθα σὺν ἄλλοισιν θαλίας ἔχει Οὐρανίδῃσι,
χαίρων υἱωνῶν περιώσιον υἱωνοῖσιν,
ὅττί σφεων Κρονίδης μελέων ἐξείλετο γῆρας,
ἀθάνατοι δὲ καλεῦνται ἑοὶ νέποδες γεγαῶτες.
ἄμφω γὰρ πρόγονός σφιν ὁ καρτερὸς Ἡρακλείδας,
ἀμφότεροι δ' ἀριθμεῦνται ἐς ἔσχατον Ἡρακλῆα.

There he holds feasts with the other heavenly ones, rejoicing mightily in the sons of his sons, that Zeus has taken old age from their limbs, and that they are called immortal, being his descendants. For to them both the mighty son of Heracles is ancestor, and both are numbered finally back to Heracles.

Various items of the Romulus story recall the Heracles legend. Each was the mightier twin;[50] the 'death' of each involves a storm, the disappearance of the body, and the inference amongst those left behind that their leader must have become a god.[51] An Ennian fragment (*Romulus in caelo cum dis*

---

[47] In favour of Ennius' originality, see, e.g., Wilamowitz (1932), 2.422 n.2; Elter (1907), 31–2, 40; against, e.g., Ogilvie (1965), 84.
[48] See especially Elter (1907); also Newman (1967), 68–71.
[49] Newman (1967), 71: cf. n.2, 'The coincidence of Theocritus and Ennius here (cf. the same phenomenon in Horace, *Odes*, IV, 8) shows that they were both drawing on common Hellenistic material, not that Ennius knew the work of Theocritus.'
[50] A.R. Anderson (1928), 31: 'The identification of Romulus as a successor of Hercules was further helped by the fact that each was the mightier twin'; see generally A.R. Anderson (1928), 29–31.
[51] *subito coorta tempestas cum magno fragore tonitribusque tam denso regem operuit nimbo ut conspectum eius contioni abstulerit; nec deinde in terris Romulus fuit. Romana pubes sedato tandem pauore postquam ex tam turbido die serena et tranquilla lux rediit, ubi uacuam sedem regiam uidit, etsi satis credebat*

*genitalibus aeuum/degit*, 'Romulus in the sky leads his life with the gods who gave birth to him', 110–11 Sk.) echoes the conventional phraseology describing Heracles' new life in heaven: cf. Hom. *Od.* 11.602–3, αὐτὸς δὲ μετ' ἀθανάτοισι θεοῖσι/τέρπεται ἐν θαλίης ('and he takes joys in the feasts with the immortal gods'); Hes. *Theog.* 954–5, ὃς μέγα ἔργον ἐν ἀθανάτοισιν ἀνύσσας/ναίει ἀπήμαντος καὶ ἀγήραος ('who, having achieved a great work amongst gods lives free from pain and old age');[52] id. fr. 25.27–8, ζώει δ' ἔνθα περ ἄλλοι Ὀλύμπια δώματ' ἔχοντες/ἀθάνατος καὶ ἄγηρος ('and he lives where the others live who inhabit the halls of Olympus, deathless and ageless'); Hom. *Hymn Dem.* 15.7–8; Theoc. 17.22. Of particular concern for our purposes is the fact that a stock element of the Heracles tradition dealt with the problem of how Hera gave over the notorious anger which she had exercised against the hero since his birth.[53] The tradition is unanimous in linking together the enrolment of Heracles amongst the gods, the abandonment by Hera of her anger against him, and the marriage of Heracles to Hebe as a token of the reconciliation. Hesiod gives the details (fr. 25.26–33):

νῦν δ' ἤδη θεός ἐστι, κακῶν δ' ἐξήλυθε πάντων,
ζώει δ' ἔνθά περ ἄλλοι Ὀλύμπια δώματ' ἔχοντες
ἀθάνατος καὶ ἄγηρος, ἔχων καλλίσφυρον Ἥβην
παῖδα Διὸς μεγάλοιο καὶ Ἥρης χρυσοπεδίλου·
τὸν πρὶν μέν ῥ' ἤχθηρε θεὰ λευκώλενος Ἥρη
ἔκ τε θεῶν μακάρων ἔκ τε θνητῶν ἀνθρώπων,

---

*patribus qui proximi steterant sublimem raptum procella, tamen uelut orbitatis metu icta maestum aliquamdiu silentium obtinuit. deinde a paucis initio facto, deum deo natum, regem parentemque urbis Romanae saluere uniuersi Romulum iubent* ('a storm which suddenly arose with great crashing and thunder covered the king with so dense a cloud as to prevent the gathering from seeing him; and after that Romulus was no longer on earth. When the Roman youth, their fear finally calmed once a serene and tranquil light had returned after so disturbed a day, saw that the royal throne was empty, although they were sufficiently convinced by the story of the senators who had stood nearby that Romulus had been snatched up to heaven by a storm-wind, they nevertheless kept sad silence for a while, as if struck by the fear of being bereft. Then, after a few of them had initiated it, they all hailed Romulus as a god, born of a god, the king and father of the city of Rome'), Liv. 1.16.1–3; cf. Diod. Sic. 4.38.4–5 on the end of Heracles: 'and at once with thunderbolts falling from the surrounding sky, the whole pyre was burnt up. Afterwards when those who accompanied Iolaus to collect the bones found nothing at all, they supposed that Heracles, in accordance with the oracles, had passed from the world of men to that of gods.' As Ogilvie (1965), 84 notes, this is all typical of the passing of Greek heroes.

[52] M.L. West (1971) ad loc. says that taking ἐν ἀθανάτοισιν with ναίει produces a very awkward hyperbaton; but the parallel passages incline one to accepting it.

[53] The rage of Hera is famous since Homer; cf. *Il.* 18.119, ἀλλά ἑ Μοῖρ' ἐδάμασσε καὶ ἀργαλέος χόλος Ἥρης ('but Fate subdued him and the violent rage of Hera'); Hes. *Theog.* 314–15, [Ὕδρην] Λερναίην, ἣν θρέψε θεὰ λευκώλενος Ἥρη/ἄπλητον κοτέουσα βίῃ Ἡρακληείῃ ('the Lernean [Hydra], which the white-armed goddess Hera nourished, insatiably wrathful with the might of Heracles').

νῦν δ' ἤδη πεφίληκε, τίει δέ μιν ἔξοχον ἄλλων
ἀθανάτων μετά γ' αὐτὸν ἐρισθενέα Κρονίωνα.

And now already he is a god, and has emerged from all his sufferings, and he lives where the others live who inhabit the halls of Olympus, deathless and ageless, possessing fair-ankled Hebe, daughter of great Zeus and gold-sandalled Hera. Before, the white-armed goddess Hera hated him above all the blessed gods and mortal men; but now she feels love for him, and honours him above all the immortals after the mighty son of Kronos himself.

Apollodorus has a précis: ἐκεῖθεν δὲ τυχὼν ἀθανασίας καὶ διαλλαγεὶς Ἥρᾳ τὴν ἐκείνης θυγατέρα Ἥβην ἔγημεν ('thence winning immortality and being reconciled with Hera, he married her daughter Hebe', 2.7.7). For a fuller account, see Diodorus Siculus.[54] A late Etruscan mirror survives, which gives a pictorial representation of the tradition.[55] Jupiter is presiding over the reconciliation between Hercules and Juno: fertility symbols suggest that what we are seeing is Hercules 'being presented as son-in-law'.[56]

It has been claimed that Heracles' marriage to Hebe was reflected by Ennius in Romulus' marriage to 'Hora' (his earthly wife Hersilia, who became, like Hebe, a goddess of youth).[57] This interpretation is based upon a vexed fragment: *teque Quirine pater ueneror Horamque Quirini* ('and I venerate you, father Quirinus, and the Hora of Quirinus', 100 Sk.). It has been long denied—most recently and vigorously by Skutsch—that Ennius knew of the identification of Romulus and Quirinus, and Skutsch asserts accordingly that the fragment can have nothing to do with the transformation of Hersilia into Hora;[58] the line concerns another god and another consort. Let the verse pass before such disagreement. There is, however, an Ovidian passage which may give some support to the presupposition that Juno's reconciliation in *Ann.* 1 might have involved her playing some part in the marriage of the newly enrolled god. Ovid tells the story of the assumption of Hersilia in *Met.* 14, straight after the heavily Ennian episode

---

[54] 4.39.2–3: 'and it must be added to what we have said that after his apotheosis Zeus persuaded Hera to make Heracles her son, and in future for the whole of time to show him a mother's consideration . . . and they say in myths that after the adoption Hera settled Hebe with Heracles'.
[55] Roscher, *Lex.* 1.2.2259.
[56] Winter (1910), 179 n.2; cf. Bayet (1926), 380–3, esp. 381: 'The scene is thus strictly analysed as the reconciliation of Hercules and Juno on the threshold of the divine dwellings—it is a variant on the apotheosis of the hero.'
[57] Cf. Elter (1907), 33, 40; A.R. Anderson (1928), 31; Newman (1967), 68.
[58] Skutsch (1968), 132–7 (with introductory bibliography on the discussion, 132). Of course, the apotheosis of Romulus and the identification with Quirinus are two separate issues.

of the interview of Mars and Jupiter and the taking up of Romulus into heaven (805–28): note that it is *Juno* who takes the initiative in bringing Hersilia to join her husband: *flebat ut amissum coniunx, cum regia Iuno/Irin ad Hersilien descendere limite curuo/imperat* ('his wife was bewailing him as lost to her, when Queen Juno ordered Iris to descend to Hersilie on her curved path', *Met.* 14.829–31).

Besides the heavenly marriage, the other 'Herculean' elements of Romulus' deification are to be seen condensed in Horace, where Juno says that she will give over her anger, and allow Romulus to be enrolled amongst the gods (*Carm.* 3.3.30–6):

> protinus et grauis
> *iras* et inuisum nepotem,
>  Troica quem peperit sacerdos,
>
> Marti redonabo; illum ego lucidas
> inire sedes, ducere nectaris
>  sucos et *adscribi quietis*
>   *ordinibus patiar deorum.*
>
> forthwith I will yield to Mars my fierce *anger* and my grandson that I have hated, the son borne by the Trojan priestess; him I will allow to enter the realms of light, to drink draughts of nectar and *to be admitted to the peaceful orders of the gods.*[59]

This material is not Horatian. It goes back to Ennius, who had it from Greek epic, nationalistic, encomiastic, mythological.

So far from a reconciliation of Juno being out of place in Ennius' council in *Annales* 1, it appears that the goddess' relenting is an indispensable part of the conception of Romulus' apotheosis.[60] There is no reason to resist this conclusion on the grounds that Juno later fought against Rome for Carthage. It is not a circular argument to bring in the qualified reconciliation of Virgil's *Aen.* 12 as evidence of a qualified reconciliation in *Ann.* 1, because in the first part of the paper the reasons for this interpretation of *Aen.* 12 were self-sufficient and did not depend for their validity on any hypothesis about the content of *Ann.* 1. Further, one may look to Horace's

---

[59] Note that Horace has Hercules prominently on display as a paradigm for the deification of Augustus: *hac arte Pollux et uagus Hercules/enisus arces attigit igneas,/quos inter Augustus recumbens/ purpureo bibet ore nectar* ('by this technique Pollux and wandering Hercules strove and reached the fiery citadels; amongst them Augustus will recline and drink nectar with crimson lips', 3.3.9–12). On such paradigms in Horace and Virgil, see Pietrusinski (1978).

[60] The one obvious difference between Ennius' Romulus story and the Greek Heracles legend is that in Ennius the accommodations are made before Romulus' 'death', while with Heracles it seems that it was regular to have them settled after Mt. Oeta. See n.72 below.

ode, to see there a Juno who is not yet an enthusiastic partisan of the Roman state: 'her promise deals with the deification only, and, so far from indicating the direct protection implied by *fauere* [i.e. in Serv. *Aen.* 1.281, *placata Iuno coepit fauere Romanis*], holds out a clear threat of reprisals should there be any attempt to restore Troy'.[61] As Steuart sums up: 'In Bk I Juno so far relents as to agree to the deification of Romulus; but active cooperation does not begin till the period of the Second Punic War.'[62]

One paragraph of more speculative matter before returning to Virgil. The congruence between Horace and Virgil in their emphasis on Troy leads one to regard it as likely that when Juno spoke in *Ann.* 1, she stipulated the final end of Troy as a condition of her agreeing to Romulus' apotheosis (Ennius will have had ample room to deploy the theme of Juno's hatred of Troy in the early part of the book, which dealt with the fall of Troy and the wanderings of Aeneas). She may have demanded that the Troy of Priam remain waste for ever. She may have insisted, like Virgil's Juno, on the matter of the *name*. The *concilium deorum* is usually located by scholars either at the time when the twins are exposed[63] or else just before the actual foundation of Rome.[64] In either case, but particularly in the latter, the gods may well have wanted to settle the crucial question of what would be the name of the new city and the new people.[65] In Ennius' version, Romulus and Remus were the sons of a woman with the conspicuously Trojan name of Ilia,[66] the very

---

[61] Steuart (1925), 176. Cf. T.E. Page (1896) on 3.3.38 *exules*: 'the word is employed however with a certain amount of contempt; with all her magnanimity Juno is not above the feminine weakness of saying something unpleasant (cf. the sneer implied in "peperit sacerdos", l. 32 ...)'. I should not make too much of Juno's 'magnanimity' in this poem.

[62] Steuart (1925), 176.

[63] Vahlen (1928), clxi; Skutsch (1968), 131; E.H. Warmington (1935) on fr. 57 W.

[64] Rosenberg (1914a), 1097–8; Waszink (1957), 325. This location seems more likely, as being of far greater moment: now is decided the beginning of the state whose achievements are the subject of the whole work. In the *Fasti*, Ovid has Juno tell of how Mars helped placate her by promising that she would be powerful in the city of her grandson: *ipse mihi Mauors 'commendo moenia' dixit/'haec tibi. tu pollens urbe nepotis eris'* ('Mars himself said to me, "I entrust these walls to you. You will be mighty in the city of your grandson"', 6.53–4). Mars 'bribes' Juno as Virgil's Jupiter does (*Aen.* 12.838–40); if both scenes go back to Ennius' *concilium deorum*, Mars' words are very apt as spoken to mollify his mother when the city of Rome is on the point of being established: *commendo moenia haec tibi ...*

[65] In favour of the city's name as a topic of debate in Ennius, I find only L. Mueller (1884), 178 and Valmaggi (1947), 18–19.

[66] 'Ilia' is the original name in the myth, where she was the daughter of Aeneas (see next note). 'R(h)ea Silvia' was invented as part of the scheme that devised the Alban king lists: see Rosenberg (1914b); Bömer (1957–8) on Ov. *Fast.* 2.383. As Bömer observes on the significance of the name 'Ilia': 'This version emphasizes Trojan origin, and particularly the descent from Aeneas.' This is the version to which Horace alludes, <u>Troica</u> *quem peperit sacerdos* (*Carm.* 3.3.32).

grandsons of Aeneas.[67] Aeneas' first settlement in Latium had been called simply—'Troia':[68] did Juno demand as her price for acquiescence that the new city of his grandsons *not* receive what might have seemed an obvious name?[69] Ennius was grappling with divergent and incompatible myths: it would not have been out of place for him to explain how the Trojans came and did not leave their name.[70] The question of the city's name was very important to Ennius. As Romulus and Remus take up their posts for the decisive contest in augury at the foundation of the city, the poet tells us: *certabant urbem Romam Remoramue uocarent* ('they were competing over whether to call the city "Roma" or "Remora"', 77 Sk.). In the *concilium deorum* Jupiter had informed Mars that only one of his twin sons would gain immortality.[71] If Juno won her point about the city's not having 'Troy' for title, Jupiter may have told Mars that the city would be named after one of his sons: the winner would receive the prize of godhead.[72]

Hypotheses about 'what must have been in Ennius' become dear to their architects, but to few others. To return to Virgil's last book. The salient elements of his Ennian model which stand out more certainly are the insistence on the passing away of Troy, the limited or qualified nature of

---

[67] Cf. Serv. Auct. on *Aen.* 1.273, *Naeuius et Ennius Aeneae ex filia nepotem Romulum conditorem urbis tradunt*; cf. Serv. *Aen.* 6.777, *dicit . . . Iliam fuisse filiam Aeneae*.

[68] Cf., e.g., Serv. *Aen.* 1.5, *Troiam autem dici, quam primum fecit Aeneas, et Liuius in primo [1.1.4] et Cato in Originibus testantur*. Extensive parallel passages, bibliography and discussion in Schröder (1971), 95–6. As Schröder says (96), 'Almost all ancient authors concur in calling the first Trojan settlement in Latium "Troy".' It must be stressed that there is no *direct* evidence that Ennius utilised this tradition. But the tradition is virtually unanimous in saying that the Trojans arrived at an area called the *ager Laurens*, and *there forthwith founded 'Troia'* (cf. passages listed in Schröder (1971), 95–6. A line of Ennius gives the first half of this version: *quos homines quondam Laurentis terra recepit* (30 Sk.). I do not see it as unlikely that he gave the second.

[69] Cf. Waszink (1957), 325, who argues, on the basis of Lucil. fr. 31 W, that Neptune in Ennius may have objected to the foundation of a *noua Troia*.

[70] Schröder (1971), 102–8 conveniently collects the various historical and poetic accounts of the name changes and adoptions involved in the Trojan immigrants' losing their proper title.

[71] Cf. Ov. *Fast.* 2.485–8 (Mars is speaking): *redde patri natum. quamuis intercidit alter,/pro se proque Remo, qui mihi restat, erit./'unus erit, quem tu tolles in caerula caeli/tu mihi dixisti: sint rata dicta Iouis* ('return the son to his father. Though one of the two has perished, the one which remains will serve for himself and for Remus. You said to me, "there will be one whom you will raise up to the blue of heaven": let Jupiter's words be ratified'). Is there a contrast with Castor and Pollux, twins who were both deified?

[72] Here would be the explanation of Ennius' placing of the reconciliation of Juno before Romulus' death, rather than after it, as the strict example of Heracles required: cf. n.60 above. I realise that in Horace Juno speaks only of Romulus as a candidate for immortality, but it is reasonable to allow ground for Horace's tact in recasting the story of how Augustus' model joined the gods. After all, by any reconstruction of the council, there must have been *some* mention of the embarrassing Remus, if we follow the evidence of Ovid that Jupiter spoke of both twins, promising immortality for only one of them (*unus erit quem tu tolles . . .* etc.; '"unus" is clearly said in contradistinction to "ambo"', Skutsch (1968), 131). Horace is suppressing *some* talk of Remus: it is only a question of how much.

the goddess' acquiescence, and the mention of the deification of a god's son. If one has the Ennian archetype in mind, one sees why the dialogue between Jupiter and Juno *starts off* as if it is going to be a discussion on the apotheosis of Aeneas: *quae iam finis erit, coniunx? quid denique restat?/ indigetem Aenean scis ipsa et scire fateris/deberi caelo fatisque ad sidera tolli./ quid struis?* ('What will the end be now, wife? What finally is left? You yourself know, and you admit that you know, that Aeneas is owed to heaven as a deified hero and is being raised by the fates to the stars. What are you up to?', *Aen.* 12.793–6).[73] Juno's harping on the name of Troy may (more tentatively) be seen as an allusion to the words of the same goddess in Ennius *Ann.* 1. There she may have demanded that the city should not be called 'Troia' but, if needs be, 'Roma' or 'Remora'; in Virgil, one name crowds in upon another as she ends her speech, pleading that the new race should not be Trojans or Teucri—Latin, Alban, Roman, Italian, anything but Trojan (12.819–28):

> illud te . . .
> pro Latio obtestor . . .
> ne uetus indigenas nomen mutare Latinos
> neu Troas fieri iubeas Teucrosque uocari
> aut uocem mutare uiros aut uertere uestem.
> sit Latium, sint Albani per saecula reges,
> sit Romana potens Itala uirtute propago:
> occidit, occideritque sinas cum nomine Troia.

> On behalf of Latium ..., this point I beg of you .... Do not order the indigenous Latins to change their old name, or to become Trojans and be called Teucrians, or that the men alter their language or change their costume. Let there be Latium, let there be Alban kings through the centuries, let there be a Roman progeny, powerful with Italian virtue: Troy has fallen, let it stay fallen along with its name.

*cum nomine Troia* . . . To Virgil and Horace the lapsing of Troy was a part of their poetic heritage, but one feels compelled to ask what charged the topic with such urgency for them. A tradition of this kind is simply available, and unrigorous: it is up to the inheritors to make something or nothing of it. Fraenkel contests the old idea that the poets are directly disparaging an actual political proposal, as reported in Suetonius, that the

---

[73] Cf. De Witt (1920), 66 on the 'similarity of treatment' in *Aen.* 12 and Hor. *Carm.* 3.3: 'Juno is reminded that Aeneas is to become a deity under the title "Aeneas indiges", and to this she tacitly consents, just as she assented to the assumption of Romulus, but she again makes stipulations.' Cf. Commager (1962), 222. This is not to say that Aeneas was elevated to heaven in Ennius, a notion argued against by Skutsch (1968), 131.

capital should be transferred from Rome to Troy.[74] But Fraenkel is also representative of a reluctance to see anything of more moment in the words of Horace's Juno than 'a matter of ordinary feeling and therefore of poetry, with no political implication whatever'.[75] The implied opposition between poetry and significance is unnatural, while a directly political reference is not the only one which the poems' surfaces may yield.

It seems plain that in both Horace and Virgil Troy represents, at the least, degeneracy and moral shabbiness.[76] The historical setting for each poet is a remote one, fixed at the time when the nation is being established; while many commentators are content to accept the possibility in Horace of an 'allegorical' reference to the present,[77] it is rare for the same approach to be applied to those portions of the *Aeneid* where Troy and Trojans are the subject. By its nature, the ode can stand in a more direct significative relation to the present than can the overtly 'historical' epic. Horace may generate and exploit a symbolic reference in 'Troy' within his small compass, loading it with the ills of the past and promising *bonus euentus* to the state if that inheritance is forsworn.[78] Virgil, on the other hand, is more tightly bound to his setting, and the significance of Troy is likely to be of a more aetiological character. Such is the approach of R.F. Thomas, who sees the dubious moral character and civilised corruption of the Trojans as being 'a flawed element which will be transmitted to the present, and realized in the moral degeneracy which is a part (and only a part) of modern Roman civilization'.[79]

It is important also to bear in mind that the Trojan past dwindles while the epic progresses, as Aeneas and his men escape from the dream of founding simply another Troy, in the manner of Helenus.[80] Especially, the final dialogue between Jupiter and Juno purports to jettison so much of the Trojan background that only their *corpora* are to contribute to the new race (*commixti corpore tantum/subsident Teucri*, 'the Trojans will fade away,

---

[74] The Suetonius passage is *Iul.* 79.3; see Fraenkel (1957), 267–9. Professor Nisbet suggests to me that the notion of a literal rebuilding of Ilium is perhaps too lightly rejected; there was no question of moving the capital, but the site was of high strategic value, especially for a Parthian campaign, and might have been built up as a base of the type Agrippa maintained in Lesbos. We must await the commentary. [See now Nisbet-Rudd (2004), 36–8.]

[75] Fraenkel (1957), 269; cf. the works cited in Commager (1962), 222 n.121. Oksala (1973), 102 is also cautious about possible 'Allegorie'.

[76] For Horace, note especially the first lines of Juno's speech (*C.* 3.3.18–24). On the degeneracy of Troy in the *Aeneid*, see now R.F. Thomas (1982), 98–100 (taking the speech of Numanus Remulus as his text, *Aen.* 9.598–620).

[77] On various allegorical interpretations of Troy in the ode, see Commager (1962), 215–20.

[78] Thus Commager (1962), 216–18. My approach owes a great deal to his discussion.

[79] R.F. Thomas (1982), 99.     [80] On this development, see the works cited in n.19 above.

mingling in their physical bodies only', 835–6). Alone, these promises are not powerful and unequivocal enough altogether to annul the effect of the earlier fears of Trojan contamination; the Trojans' *corpora* may be sufficient infection. Yet Jupiter's words go some way towards dampening these fears, and it is possible that some hope of escape is to be read here. The 'Trojanness' of Rome is not inevitably effective, and may be outgrown.

This is difficult, and uncertain. At least what may be established is the fact that Virgil is using Troy in the same way as he had in the *Georgics* (*satis iam pridem sanguine nostro/Laomedonteae luimus periuria Troiae*, 'it is a long time now since we paid enough with our blood for the perjuries of Laomedon's Troy', 1.501–2), and in the same way as Horace had used the murder of Remus in *Epode* 7: the effect is to embody a radical anxiety about the integrity of the state by pushing far back into the past the original springs of Roman corruption. What is different in the closing stages of the *Aeneid* is the hope expressed of the possibility of rehabilitation: this much is in common with Horace's third Roman ode. The passing of Troy, a 'historical fact' in Ennius, is susceptible to treatment, in the differing textures of ode and epic, as a possible release from 'the weight of all the evil elements in the past'.[81]

Anxiety about the validity of the state may be expressed, in the conventions of epic or lyric, as an apprehension concerning the goodwill of heaven, the divine sanction. This uncertainty is incorporated by the poets in the perennial and potent shape of Juno. As Fowler says of her part in the *Aeneid*:

> this use of Juno ... was perhaps made easier and more natural because, as goddess, she belonged rather to Rome's early enemies than to Rome herself. She was a familiar figure in many or most of the cities mentioned in the pageant [*Aen.* 7.647–817]—on the Aventine, at Tibur, Praeneste and Falerii, in southern Etruria (as Uni), and in Campania. But at Rome, strange to say, she had no great local name and fame in early times, and thus no feelings could be hurt if a Roman poet made her the deadly enemy of Rome.[82]

One of Juno's towns above all we must add to Fowler's list—Carthage. The identification of Italian Juno with the chief goddess of the Carthaginians was no fiction of the poets.[83] The Pyrgi inscription appears to show the grouping as early as c. 500 BCE.[84] Hannibal himself, in

---

[81] The phrase of Commager (1962), 221.
[82] W.W. Fowler (1916), 40. On this disparity between Juno's cult in Rome and the other local towns, see Wissowa (1912), 187–9. She was, of course, part of the Capitoline triad from Etruscan times, but dramatically inferior to Jupiter in cult.
[83] On this identification, see n.21 above.   [84] Dumézil (1974), 665–7.

honouring Juno Lacinia, linked the goddesses together,[85] as did the Roman government, by some mode of thought or other, when they strenuously honoured Juno during the war to which Hannibal gave his name:

> During the Second Punic War, the Juno Regina of the Aventine and the Juno of Lanuvium received numerous and important signs of devotion and respect (Liv. 21.62.8; 22.1.17), and this betrayed the worry of the Romans, who felt that their Punic enemies were protected by a goddess eminently dangerous to Rome, just as Hera had been for Aeneas and his Trojans.[86]

From both a historical and literary point of view, the most significant supplication to Juno was that of 207.[87] Here was sung a *carmen* by Livius Andronicus, and it may have been this ceremony which Ennius selected as the occasion for the long-awaited final reconciliation of Juno.[88]

Juno's position as Rome's most respected divine antagonist is reflected in the disproportionate number of *euocationes* which the tradition accords to her. Four cases of *euocatio* are reported, and in three of them Juno is the deity concerned.[89] One of these (at Carthage) is very problematical as a historical event,[90] and Ogilvie is certainly right to say that there 'were many other "euocationes" now unknown to us (Plin., *HN* 28.18), and the ratio of three Junos to one (Vertumnus) may be perfectly coincidental'.[91] What is probably not coincidental is the evidence, implied in the sample, that the *euocationes* involving Juno were the ones dwelt upon and retained.

Buchheit would trace the origin of Juno's role in Latin poetry back to Naevius.[92] However that may be, she embodies antipathy to Rome in Ennius, Virgil, Horace, Ovid and Silius. Each of these poets shows her being reconciled, and on different occasions. 'Consistency is not necessary with these legends', observe Nisbet and Hubbard, remarking on the various dates.[93] The dates vary, but the paradigms of vindictiveness and conditional tolerance are remarkably consistent, a tribute to the power of the goddess. For poets writing even about their own times, it is natural to treat her as unmanageable and disquieting. In a major key, there is

---

[85] Liv. 28.46.16 (cf. Cic. *Div.* 1.48); cf. Dumézil (1974), 465; R. Bloch (1972), 388; Basanoff (1947), 63–6.
[86] R. Bloch (1972), 394. What most Romans of this era knew about Aeneas and the Trojans is a controversy best left untouched here.
[87] Liv. 27.37.7; cf. Horsfall (1973–4), 2.
[88] As suggested by Steuart (1925), 175–7 and Buchheit (1963), 144–5, esp. n.620. Other suggestions include a *concilium deorum* after Cannae (Vahlen (1928), clxxxix); a dialogue between Jupiter and Juno at the same date (Norden (1915), 168–9); a divine discussion upon Hannibal's appearance before the walls of Rome (on the basis of Sil. *Pun.* 12: Fürstenau (1916), 61, 63).
[89] At Veii, Falerii Veteres, Carthage (the fourth is Vertumnus at Volsinii); see Ogilvie (1965), 674.
[90] A comprehensive discussion by Rawson (1991), 93–101.   [91] Ogilvie (1965), 674.
[92] Buchheit (1963), 54–8.   [93] Nisbet and Hubbard (1978), on Hor. *Carm.* 2.1.25.

Horace's picture of Carthaginian Juno still active in the civil wars, avenging her people's defeats: *Iuno et deorum quisquis amicior/Afris inulta cesserat inpotens/tellure, uictorum nepotes/rettulit inferias Iugurthae* ('Juno, and whichever of the gods, more friendly to the Africans, had left in powerlessness that unavenged land, brought the victors' grandsons as funeral offerings to Jugurtha', *Carm.* 2.1.25–8). In a minor key, there is Ovid's Juno in the *Fasti*, asserting her claim in queenly fashion to be the bestower of the name for the month of June (6.21–64). Strife supervenes when her claim is contested by Iuventas (67–88), and even Concord's arrival fails of a resolution, as that goddess too joins in the bickering (91–6). The poet bows his way out, with a bland allusion to the issue of an earlier quarrel of Juno's: *perierunt iudice formae/Pergama* ('Troy was destroyed by a judge in a beauty contest', 99–100).

In the *Aeneid* Juno moves some considerable distance from her original stance of total opposition to Rome. At the end of the epic the forces represented by Juno nudge closer to those of Jupiter, and rest there for the while, in tension. One thinks perhaps of Plutarch's good and evil divine principles, which hold the universe in shifting balance;[94] the lines of Euripides which he quotes as his leitmotif[95] are in harmony with the poem's close:

οὐκ ἂν γένοιτο χωρὶς ἐσθλὰ καὶ κακά,
ἀλλ' ἔστι τις σύγκρασις ὥστ' ἔχειν καλῶς.

Good and evil would not occur apart, but there is a certain blending that leads to a good result.

---

[94] *De Is. et Os.* 369a–b.  [95] 369b (fr. 21 Nauck).

CHAPTER 3

# *Epic Hero and Epic Fable*[1]

The epic hero occupies a secure niche in modern criticism. His reassuring presence guarantees the unity of an epic poem and directs our scrutiny when we search for theme. If he is not easy to pick out, there ensues a quarrel over his identity, with a list of candidates for the post; the poem in question, especially if it is an ancient epic, is either disparaged as formless and episodic, or else praised for bold independence, held together on other and more interesting principles. Modern critics evidently see it as the norm for ancient and modern epics alike to be organised around an individual, who will embody the meaning of the poem. Robert Scholes and Robert Kellogg describe the nucleus of the epic as 'the chronicle of the deeds of the hero'; by their account, 'the epic plot is to a certain extent bespoken by epic characterization. The plot is inherent in the concept of the protagonist.'[2] According to Northrop Frye, '[i]n literary fictions the plot consists of somebody doing something. The somebody, if an individual, is the hero ... Fictions ... may be classified, not morally, but by the hero's power of action, which may be greater than ours, less, or roughly the same.'[3] Of Frye's five classifications, the epic hero belongs to number three, the hero of the 'high mimetic mode', 'superior in degree to other men but not to his natural environment'.[4] Morton W. Bloomfield, after a careful discussion of the meaning of the word 'hero', asserts: 'Whatever term be used for the major personage or personages of narrative or drama, that these genres have always been presented around such figures cannot be doubted.'[5] Classical scholars concur: the same preconceptions underlie C.M. Bowra's discussion, for example, of the characteristics of 'literary epic'.[6] It must be said, however, that among Classical scholars, for various reasons, there is little

---

[1] I have benefitted from the help and criticisms of Dr. N.J. Richardson, Professor R.J. Tarrant, Mr. D.A. Russell, Dr. John Kerrigan, Professor Helen Vendler, Professor Jan Ziolkowski, and an anonymous member of the editorial board of *Comparative Literature*. Especially I should like to thank Professor John Creaser for his aid to a novice in the area in which he is so expert.
[2] Scholes and Kellogg (1966), 209.   [3] Frye (1957), 33.   [4] Ibid., 33–4.
[5] Bloomfield (1975), 29.   [6] Bowra (1945), chapter 1, 'Some characteristics of literary epic'.

discussion in broad terms of the generic question of epic and its hero, much less than among scholars of literature from the Renaissance on.

The general orthodoxy still obtains, despite the voices of a few dissenters.[7] To test its value, what is needed is not only a discussion of the practice and theory of ancient epic, but also an investigation into the birth and nurture of the epic hero who occupies the attention of the modern critics. He will be seen to be, in essence, a child of the Renaissance, a demanding child, but not universally successful in pressing his claims. In England he was given title and dominion by the Neoclassicists, and it is by virtue of that authority that he still exercises his power.

A convenient starting point is afforded by the reflection that neither Greek nor Latin has a word to describe the epic hero: ἥρως and *heros* have no literary reference, but describe individuals, normally held to be descended from gods, whose tombs received quasi-divine honours. Nor does any other word, such as πρωταγωνιστής ('protagonist') discharge this service. This is not so decisive an observation as it may appear at first. As we shall see, the literary-critical meaning of 'hero' was not domesticated into English until 1673, and yet D.W. Lucas justly remarks that 'the Elizabethans had indubitable heroes, though they had no word for them'.[8] Still, the modern reader who comes to ancient epics expecting to find a hero should pause at the realisation that the object of his search is without so much as a name, that an ancient poet could not say, in as many words, 'Who is the hero of my poem?' nor an ancient critic pose a like question of the texts he had before him. The critical authority which this figure exercises over our expectations should suffer its first weakening at this point.

Another approach is needed into the epics, to look for their true centre of gravity. The example of John Jones's work, and the express recommendation of R.J. Getty, refer us to Aristotle's *Poetics*.[9] It is at least understandable that critics have found a tragic hero when they have turned to the *Poetics*. What is puzzling about the conventional assessment of the nature of epic is that it overlooks not only the positive side of what Aristotle has to say—his presentation of the epic model as being, in the Homeric type, a self-sufficient and complete action (1459a19–22)—but also the explicit

---

[7] Discussion of Lucan's *Bellum Civile* has called forth doubts on the necessity of having a hero: see, above all, the trenchant observations of Getty (1940), xxiv–ix. Greene (1963), 18 has more general qualifications. Although Jones (1962) does not discuss the hero of epic, I should mention here the powerful impulse given to this paper by the argument of his valuable book.
[8] Lucas (1968), 140.    [9] Jones (1962); Getty (1940).

and repeated rejection of the idea that the organisation of an epic depends on an individual character (1451a16–22, 1459a37). For Aristotle, this is a misconception to be put quite on a par with organising an epic around one period of time. When Homer undertook the *Iliad*, according to Aristotle, he selected one part of the war as his 'one action', and incorporated other parts as episodes (1459a35–8). Aristotle sees no single character as the centre of the *Iliad*, as becomes plain when he goes on to contrast Homer's practice with that of lesser poets: 'But the others make a poem about one man or one period of time' (1459a37–b1). To Aristotle the *Iliad* is 'the imitation of a single action' (1462b11), and this is no irrelevant formalism. As Getty puts it, 'the centre round which the *Iliad* revolves is not Achilles but the wrath of Achilles'.[10] Even within the proem, when the subject of the wrath of Achilles has been announced, the wrath (μῆνις) develops a bold syntactical autonomy, controlling the first five lines in an extraordinary way, governing three verbs in three successive lines (2–4).[11] Achilles' wrath is indeed his, but the kindling, course, and assuaging of the wrath comprehend many people and many interests; the poet's focus on the wrath provides him with a structural and a thematic plenitude which would have been denied him if he had sung 'about one man'. James Redfield has written well on the impoverishment of the poem that comes from various influential modern readings which see the poem as centring on 'Achilles' inner experience'. In Redfield's fine book Hector receives the full attention he deserves, and we come to see that indeed, as he puts it, 'in some sense the story of the *Iliad* is the story of the relation between these two heroes'.[12]

Aristotle sets off the *Odyssey* also as distinct from poems 'about one man' (1451a16–30). This may appear paradoxical, until one realises that what Aristotle was looking for in this poem as well as in the *Iliad* was the outline of a cohesive and 'epic' action. That the action might be described as that of one man is a matter of complete indifference to Aristotle: it might be of one, or seven, or thousands, so long as it exhibited those structural features which he saw as the characteristic form of the genre. We will return to the *Odyssey*, and to those poems 'about one man'. For the moment let us remain with Aristotle's prototype, a poem whose unity and structure are organic, and do not depend on an individual, since 'one man's actions are

---

[10] Getty (1940), xxvi.
[11] Redfield (1979), 101 speaks of the 'personification' of the μῆνις ('wrath') with the adjective 'destructive', and continues, discussing line 2, 'the relative clause reinforces our sense of the μῆνις as a numinous agent'.
[12] Redfield (1975), 27.

numerous and do not make up a single action' (1451a18–19). If we look for a more or less 'Aristotelian' pattern, a pattern which is not monocentric, in other ancient epics, where the controversy over the hero is alive and keen, it will not be on the assumption that Aristotle was a legislator for later practice, but rather because his insights into Homer ring true, and invite us to discover whether the epic paradigm that provided those insights may not prove valuable elsewhere.

Nowhere is there more debate than in the area of Silver Latin epic, where the *Bellum Civile*, *Thebaid* and *Punica* occasion a diversity of opinion through having no one central character to take on the role of 'hero'. In connection with Lucan, Getty has declared the problem to be a mirage;[13] but other discussions of the *Bellum Civile* continue to take it for granted that Lucan regarded the norm of epic as being a poem about a hero,[14] just as other discussions of the *Thebaid* attribute a similar preconception to Statius, and either blame him for failing to follow the norm, or praise him for a self-conscious abandoning of the strait-jacket.[15] With Silius it is the matter of identity alone that exercises the commentators: is the hero Hannibal? Or Scipio? Or Rome?[16]

Silius' poem most straightforwardly reveals the irrelevance of this approach. His declared subject is *arma*, 'arms' (line 1), and he asks the Muse to allow him to record *quantos . . . ad bella crearit/et quot Roma uiros* ('what great men and *how many men* Rome created for war', 1.3–4). With such a programme, concentration on one man is not compatible. Certainly Hannibal figures prominently: this corresponds to historical fact. It is more important to realise that Hannibal is particularly prominent in the first ten books as a result of a *structural* decision taken by Silius. In an attempt to superimpose some form on the mass of material before him, Silius has selected the battle of Cannae as the crescendo of the poem. With seven books before and after, the three 'Cannae' books, 8–10, occupy the centre of the epic; the historical proportion of events is radically dislocated so that this nadir of Roman fortunes may become, by a paradoxical turn, the high point of a poem celebrating Rome's resilience and fortitude.[17] Hannibal's run of successes up to this point—Ticinus, Trebia, Trasimene—is important as preparation; the early books are not there to tell us about Hannibal, but to establish a cumulatively disastrous progress towards the structural and thematic kernel of the epic. If Hannibal is the main agent in the

---

[13] Getty (1940), xxiv–ix.   [14] See Ahl (1976), 150–6.
[15] Blame from Legras (1905), 147–9, 207. Praise from Vessey (1973), 55–8, 317–28.
[16] Discussion, with bibliography, in Bassett (1966); add von Albrecht (1964), 55.
[17] On the pivotal importance of Cannae, see Schetter (1978), 73–4.

progress, so be it. Silius may exploit his presence in the interests of cohesion and in furtherance of his themes of Carthaginian turpitude, but to say that these books are directed towards the character Hannibal is to confuse effect with cause.

Silius' stock is so low that his poem alone will perhaps not serve as a sufficient example of a pattern where the absence of a hero, so far from being a failing, is not even an anomaly. His predecessor and model, Lucan, has less shape to his poem, but in the *Bellum Civile* it is just as plain as in the *Punica* that the action is greater than any of the actors. The action is civil war, the catastrophe is corporate, the protagonists are numerous and diverse. Speculation on the structure of an unfinished poem is dangerous, but enough is intact for us to see at least that Lucan did not present the death throes of the Republic as the disaster of an individual. After the general and anonymous program (1.1–7), when Lucan comes to discuss the causes of the war he expresses the problem as one of explaining *quid in arma furentem/inpulerit populum, quid pacem excusserit orbi* ('what drove a frenzied *people* to arms, what knocked peace out of the world', 1.68–9). The leaders, Caesar and Pompey, are catalysts, and their differences demand analysis (1.98–157); but, says Lucan, greater causes are operative: *hae ducibus causae; suberant sed publica belli/semina, quae populos semper mersere potentis* ('Such were the motives for the leaders; but underlying these were seeds of war on a national scale, of the sort which always bring down powerful nations', 1.158–9). The selection of a single man as fulcrum suits Lucan's pessimistic theme as little as it suits Silius' optimistic one.

Statius' *Thebaid*, surviving intact, provides a clearer case of self-sufficient shape, where the action imitated has its own independence, and the choosing of a hero is beside the point.[18] The poet states the scope of his action as *fraternas acies alternaque regna profanis/decertata odiis* ('the battle lines of brothers, and alternate kingships fought over with unholy hatred'); subjoined is the theme of the guilt of a whole city (1.1–2). In his exordium he marks his starting point as the moment when the secret of Oedipus was revealed and his sons came into the kingdom (1.16–17). Above all the episodes and meanderings of the poem, it is the course of this fraternal strife which acts as a framework. We see the development of the initial falling out, an expansively deployed multiple motivation, with Oedipus' summoning of the Fury (1.46–96), her infection of the brothers (123–30),

---

[18] Recent discussions dispense with 'action' and beg the question of where to turn to if the characters fail us. Thus Vessey (1973), 57: 'Integration of narrative is achieved more by the philosophical and psychological basis on which the epic is built *than by the characters themselves*' (my emphasis).

and the council of the gods (197–303). The second book displays the irrevocable estrangement, with the visitation to Eteocles of his grandfather's ghost (1–133), and the rejection of Tydeus' embassy (389–477). The preparations for war, alternating from one brother's camp to the other's, the march, and the digression of Hypsipyle and Archemorus, take us to Book 6. At this halfway stage, before the war actually begins, Statius reintroduces the rivalry of the brothers. Jocasta pleads with Polynices to reconcile himself to Eteocles (7.508–10), but the wavering Polynices is swept away by events, and the two brothers are committed.

The chiefs of the invading armies are picked off one by one, until at the beginning of Book 11 the Fury Tisiphone decides to round off the war with a combat between Eteocles and Polynices. The preparation and enactment of the duel take up most of the book (57–579), but the energies of the brothers' enmity are not exhausted by their mutual murder. Even in death the brothers are irreconcilable, as their bizarre funeral shows, with the flames of their joint pyre dividing (12.429–33). The 'profane hatreds' of the exordium are still at work: *uiuunt odia improba, uiuunt* ('they are alive, their shameless hatreds, they are alive', 12.441). Thebes is still ailing, as the watching women observe, addressing the divided fires: *nil actum bello; miseri, sic dum arma mouetis,/uicit nempe Creon* ('nothing has been achieved by the war; you unhappy pair, while you fight thus, Creon has been the victor after all', 12.442–3). In a manner which is more familiar from tragedy (one thinks, for example, of Sophocles' *Ajax*), a substantial coda is required to lay to rest the momentum of evil generated by the divisive forces that have been let loose (just as a substantial introduction was required to build them up). Oedipus' softening comes first, as he repents of his role in instigating his sons' quarrel (11.605–26), but the rottenness of the city of Thebes requires excision from outside, with Theseus for agent.

What of the *Odyssey* and *Aeneid*, that offer in their first lines ἄνδρα, *uirum*, 'man'?[19] As a preliminary observation, against those who desire a hero for his value as a structural tool, we may note that the *Odyssey* and *Aeneid* do not rely on Odysseus and Aeneas for their structural integrity. So much Aristotle stated for the *Odyssey*, as we saw above, when he brought in its unified structure against the authors of *Theseids* and *Heracleids*. Homer did not shape his poem around the *man*, says Aristotle; 'rather, he composed the

---

[19] Note that neither the Greek nor the Latin *Argonautica* refers to Jason as its subject, but to 'the deeds of *men*' (Ap. Rhod. *Argon* 1.1), and to 'straits sailed through by the *sons* of gods, and their *ship*' (V. Fl. 1.1–2). On Apollonius, see Carspecken (1952), 110–11.

*Odyssey* around one action of the sort I mean, and the *Iliad* similarly' (1451a28–30). We can only agree with Aristotle that the unity of the *Odyssey* resides in its action, its description of a νόστος, a 'homecoming', with the master of the household returning home to reestablish the proper order there (1455b16–23). It is this action that accommodates the Telemachy and the final scenes, after the reunion with Penelope. Readers tend to have their eyes fixed upon the solitary figure of Odysseus, and the passages in the poem which concern the relations of the family, from Laertes to Telemachus, are often felt to be more or less extraneous.[20] In Virgil's case, the self-sufficiency of the poem's action is even more evident, although the same instinct which leads to a search for the unifying hero in the Silver Epic complacently identifies Aeneas as the guarantor of the unity of the *Aeneid*. Richard Heinze most economically states the real position: 'In the centre of his poem stands the hero from whom it takes his name, but it is not he who creates unity, but an action: the migration of the Trojans or the carrying-over of the Penates from Troy to Latium.'[21]

Such an emphasis as Heinze's redresses the balance for more than structural considerations, since it is important to treat with circumspection the almost automatic assumption that the *Aeneid* is 'about' Aeneas, that the poem exists as a vehicle for the character. The poem's first words appear to satisfy this expectation, but we have a corrective in the note of the ancient commentary known as Servius 'Auctus' (an 'expanded' version of Servius). According to this commentary, the beginning of an epic will have the announcement of the subject (*professiuum*), the invocation of the Muse (*inuocatiuum*) and the start of the narrative (*narratiuum*). He continues: 'And Virgil takes up the announcement of the subject in four ways: from the leader ("I sing of arms and the man", 1.1), from the journey ("who first from the shores of Troy", 1.1), from the war ("he suffered also much in war", 1.5), and from the establishment of the race ("whence comes the Latin race", 1.6).' The tradition of ancient scholarship represented in these crabbed notes did not see in the *Aeneid*'s exordium the announcement of a poem about a *man*; the subject is greater and the man serves the subject. As Getty puts it, 'the central theme of [the] *Aeneid* was not the life of Aeneas, but the fulfilment by Aeneas of his own destiny in founding the nation which was to become Rome'.[22] This perspective is the truer and the more valuable, for it allows due importance to the main agent without allowing him to crowd out the action: Aeneas is there for the story, not vice

---

[20] See Wender (1978), 68–71 for the importance of seeing three generations at Ithaca.
[21] Heinze (1915), 436.    [22] Getty (1940), xxvi.

versa. Certainly important elements of what the *Aeneid* has to say reside in the character Aeneas, most obviously the demands of the political vocation. But Aeneas does not embody *the* meaning of the poem;[23] such a myopic focus attenuates the extensive power of the *Aeneid*.[24] Major sections of the work are strangely flat and unfruitful if we refer them to Aeneas, regarding them from a standpoint that looks to Aeneas for significance. The Roman pageant of Book 6, for example, is there for the reader; Aeneas is the nominal audience, but however closely we search to find what it all means for the character, here or later in the poem, the text yields no more to us than the bald line, '[his father] inflamed his spirit with a passion for the fame to come' (6.889). A.K. Michels has well criticised the recent attempts, most thoroughly developed by Brooks Otis, 'to see the visit to the underworld as the turning point in Aeneas's career, the moment at which he abandons the past, and confidently faces the future, prepared to labour for the greatness of his race which lies centuries ahead'.[25] As she says, 'One would expect that this vision of the future glory of his race would have some effect on Aeneas, but we may ask whether in fact it does ... [A]t no point after he returns to the land of the living does Aeneas ever show any recollection of what his father has revealed to him.'[26]

Otis' idea of a developing Aeneas, with his eventual triumph over *furor* ('madness'), has come in for some rough handling, and the current critical tendency is rather to concentrate upon his inability to master his passions. His enraged killing of Turnus in the final scene has become the central text of the 'pessimistic school', who see the act as a negation of the poem's earlier celebrations of victorious order and empire.[27] Boyle's words are representative:

> Aeneas's final act and words in the poem are intended to be seen as unequivocal acts of *furor* ... and the effect of this is to focus the reader's attention once more upon the non-fulfilment of the imperial ideology and to elicit a final condemnation (and a condemnation prefigured many times in the poem) of the forces of empire and history which Aeneas represents. The death of Turnus may signify the victory of Aeneas, Rome and her empire, but it is Virgil's concern to emphasise that it is a victory for the forces of non-reason and the triumph not of *pietas* but of *furor*.[28]

---

[23] Otis (1963), 219–23 is representative of the approach which sees the ideas of the *Aeneid* concentrated in the figure of Aeneas.
[24] On the 'polysemous' nature of the *Aeneid*, see Johnson (1976), 16–22.   [25] Michels (1981), 141.
[26] Ibid., 140.
[27] Especially influential (but often interpreted too simplistically by later writers) has been Putnam (1965), chapter 4, esp. 200–1. For bibliography, see Boyle (1972), 90 n.90.
[28] Boyle (1972), 85.

Whatever we decide about the culpability of Aeneas' act,[29] Boyle here shares with Otis the misconception that Aeneas *is* what the poem means, that in the portrayal of Aeneas is to be found Virgil's whole meaning of empire. We must resist the centripetal attraction of the chief character and contemplate his last action as one element of what the poem says. Jupiter's speech in Book 1 is not obliterated, the significance of the shield in Book 8 is still potent; the countervailing elements in the *Aeneid* coexist and we have to account for them all, not plump for one and shut out the rest.[30]

The *Odyssey* is a rather different matter, for in that poem the medium for the thematic content, overwhelmingly, is the man himself; in a way that is not true of the other epics so far discussed, the *Odyssey* is indeed 'about' its principal character. Discussions of this aspect of the *Odyssey* prepared the ground for the post-classical development of the 'epic hero', as the critics, allegorisers and moralists got to work on the 'Everyman' that they discovered in the poem. This path will lead from the ancient to the medieval world; before following it, we must review those traditions of ancient epic which deliberately took one individual as the focus of composition. These are, broadly, the mythological and the encomiastic.

The first group is now substantially represented only by the unfinished *Achilleid* of Statius, and by Nonnus' *Dionysiaca*. Aristotle found fault with the writers of *Heracleids* and *Theseids* for narrating a life from beginning to end without selection (*Poet.* 1451a19–22), but lives of mythological figures were a popular type of poem in many different periods. Although a single episode might form the subject, the usual practice, so far as may now be judged, was to celebrate more generally the deeds of the god or hero. We know of such poems from Pisander in the seventh century BCE, Panyassis in the fifth, Rhianus and Neoptolemus of Parium in the third, Musaeus in the second,[31] while in Latin, there is a *Perseis* by 'a Sicilian', a *Heracleid* by Carus and a *Diomedia* by Iullus Antonius.[32] It would be easy to dismiss these lost epics as following an inferior line of endeavour, but their subject matter alone is not enough to permit us to judge whether any of them rose above a sequential narrative of diverse feats. A paraphrase of the action of the *Aeneid*, along the lines of Aristotle's paraphrase of the action of the *Odyssey* (1455b16–23), could easily obscure the poem's integrity of structure; similarly, a 'poem about Perseus, Diomedes or Theseus' might have possessed some unity of structure beyond that provided by the eponymous

---

[29] It is possible to be a good deal less condemnatory: see Camps (1969), 29.
[30] I refer once more to the most illuminating argument of Johnson (1976), 8–16.
[31] On these poets, see Trypanis (1981).
[32] Ov. *Pont.* 4.16.7–8, 25; 4.13.11–12, and Ps.-Acro on Hor. *Carm.* 4.2.33.

hero. As things stand, it is possible only to observe that this strong minority tradition did not extend its influence beyond the scope of its own particular subject matter, and did not lead other poets, such as those who wrote the surviving epics discussed above, to forsake the πρᾶξις ('action') of epic.

The encomiastic tradition is more vigorous; in the twilight of the ancient epic, it intertwined with its parent, historical epic, to prevail more or less completely. Indeed, we first hear of encomiastic epic around the turn of the fifth century BCE, in connection with the *inuentor* of historical epic, Choerilus of Samos, cultivated by Lysander and by Archelaus of Macedon in the hope of gaining immortality. Choerilus may well have produced something in compliance with this hope; certainly his great contemporary, Antimachus, competed at Lysander's festival with a poem on the Spartan regent—and lost.[33] Eulogistic epic poems, performed either at such festivals (which might be recurrent or one-time affairs) or else on the regular games circuit, remained a standard field of Greek poetic endeavour until well into the Empire; their subjects were generally provided by the local monarch and, in Roman times, the emperor.[34] One imagines that such festival encomia were relatively short: Claudian's late examples are perhaps a guideline.[35] There existed simultaneously a (related) flourishing tradition of panegyrical epics of more substantial length.[36] Alexander's deeds were written up by Agis and a second Choerilus; together they provided for posterity a sort of yardstick for poetic inadequacy.[37] Fragments survive of a poem treating of the campaigns of Alexander's father.[38] Antiochus the Great was celebrated in an epic written by Simonides of Magnesia, Eumenes I and Attalus I of Pergamum in epics from Musaeus of Ephesus.[39] The fashion caught on in Rome. The poet Archias came to Rome to find famous men to praise: in the speech defending him, Cicero tells of epics on Marius, Catulus and Lucullus (*Arch.* 19–21). Julius Caesar found his celebrators.[40] His successor, too, was entitled to believe that his great deeds deserved enshrinement in epic as much as the actions of a Catulus. When the Augustan poets wrote *recusationes*—apologising for not praising the emperor, and justifying their

---

[33] See Plut. *Lys.* 18.4. On Choerilus' connections with these great men, see Bethe (1899), 2359–60.
[34] A. Hardie (1983), 85–91.
[35] *Stilicho's Consulate* is in three parts of 385, 476, and 369 lines; *Manilius' Consulate* is 340 lines long; *Honorius' Fourth* and *Sixth*, 656 and 660 respectively.
[36] See Ziegler (1966), 16–18; A. Hardie (1983), 86–91.
[37] On Choerilus, see Crusius (1899); on Agis, Wissowa (1899).     [38] *POxy* 30.2520.
[39] See under the poets' names in the *Suda*.
[40] Varro Atacinus wrote a *Bellum Sequanicum* on Caesar's campaign of 58 BCE; Furius wrote *Annales Belli Gallici* (on both poets, see Conte (1994a), 141).

alternative poetic forms—they must, to some degree, have been responding to an actual expectation.[41]

By Late Antiquity encomiastic and historical epic are virtually indistinguishable. T. Nissen and A. Cameron have observed the blend in Claudian and, later, Corippus and the Byzantine writers such as George of Pisidia.[42] The popularity of this poetry is attested to by the numerous papyrus fragments of Greek epics on the deeds of Roman commanders, from around the fifth century.[43] Handicapped as we are by the disappearance of the 'classical' encomiastic epic, it is still reasonable to assume that in such works the whole focus was on the *laudandus*, 'the subject for praise', even if a single war was the arena in which the subject's virtues were to be displayed.[44] It is here that we come closest to the 'hero'. If the *laudandus* was excluded for so long from the main tradition of historical epic, and if nonhistorical epic did not embrace him, this is testimony to the ancient poets' allegiance to their forms, even within the subdivisions of a genre. Many men wrote epics to praise an individual, but this was not the general purpose of epic.

This is not to deny the importance of the critical tradition that took its start in the detection of encomiastic elements in Homer's poetry.[45] It is understandable that Isocrates, pioneering the new prose eulogy of a contemporary with his *Evagoras*, should allude to Homer as an encomiast (190ab). Plato earlier shows the same attitude; his Protagoras maintains that in the epics of Homer and other poets there are to be found 'many stories, eulogies and encomia of the good men of the old days' (*Prt.* 326a). Similarly, in the *Hippias Minor*, a character says of the *Iliad* and the *Odyssey* that they were, literally, 'composed in the direction of, or with a tendency towards, Achilles and Odysseus' (363b). The phrasing has an encomiastic colour. A similar preoccupation lies behind the ancient scholiasts' discussions of why the *Iliad* was not called the *Achilleias*.[46] It also lies behind the way in which the Late Antique Latin commentator Tiberius Claudius Donatus looks at the *Aeneid*. Donatus' analysis of the *Aeneid* as *laudatiuum*, 'encomiastic', goes far beyond Servius' description of Virgil's aims in his Preface to the *Aeneid* commentary, 'to imitate Homer and to praise Augustus on the basis of his ancestry'. For Donatus, everything in the poem is there for Aeneas:

---

[41] Griffin (1985), 29.  [42] T. Nissen (1940); Cameron (1970), 260–2.
[43] See D.L. Page (1941), nos. 141–4.
[44] Corippus announces that he will use the war as a vehicle for the praise of John (*Praefatio*, line 3). The leader is the subject, not the war: note the recurrence of the key words *ductor, dux*: 1.7, 3.1, 5.9, 7.1, 8.1.
[45] See Koster (1970), 83–4.  [46] bT scholia on *Il.* 1.1.

Certainly it is encomiastic, but this fact is unrecognized and hidden, because, while going through the deeds of Aeneas, Virgil is evidently also assimilating, in an extraordinary variation upon the form of encomium, incidental forms of different subject matter—forms which are nonetheless not alien to the job of encomium; for they are taken up in order to contribute to the praise of Aeneas.[47]

By this time the monocentric view of epos is well on its way to victory.

For the establishment of that victory in the post-classical world, no single influence was more important than the central character of the *Odyssey*: *quid uirtus et quid sapientia possit/utile proposuit nobis exemplar Vlixen* ('[Homer] has placed Ulysses before us as a useful example of what virtue and wisdom can achieve', Hor., *Epist.* 1.2.17–18). Horace's characterisation of Homer's purpose finds an echo in Maximus of Tyre, who describes the *Odyssey* as 'an image of the worthy life and of exact virtue' (26.6b). Such language goes back to the sophist Alcidamas, an older contemporary of Plato, who described the *Odyssey* as 'a fair mirror of human life' (quoted by Aristotle, *Rh.* 1406b12). The allegoriser 'Heraclitus' sees Odysseus as the model of all the virtues, systematically exemplified one by one.[48] The Christian fathers' view of the *Odyssey* as an 'encomium of virtue' is rooted in the same tradition, as Hugo Rahner has shown.[49] The *Odyssey*, to these readers, is an allegory of man's journey through life; as Odysseus encounters and subdues the range of temptations and threats personified in the Sirens, the Lotus-Eaters, and Circe, he shows us the triumph of wisdom and courage over vice, indolence and resignation.[50] Here was a fertile field for growth: in this Odysseus we see already the shadowy lineaments of the medieval and Renaissance hero.

His fortunes are linked with those of his erstwhile Trojan adversary, Aeneas. Virgil incorporated aspects of current philosophical interpretations of Odysseus into his portrait of Aeneas,[51] but the Virgilian critics took the process further, treating the *Aeneid* as an *Odyssey*. In the post-classical world, after men had been deprived (through ignorance of Greek) of direct knowledge of the *Odyssey*, the moral importance of the Latin poem's central character grew ever greater. As Don Cameron Allen puts it, according to this tradition, 'in the character of Aeneas [Virgil] had created an epic figure who wandered more surely and wisely than Odysseus along the symbolic path of mortal existence. At each stage in his progress the

---

[47] Georgii (1905–6), 1.2.9–12; cf. 1.3.18–21.
[48] Buffière (1962), 75–6. On this strand of criticism, see Buffière (1956), 365–91.
[49] Rahner (1963), 332.   [50] Cf. ibid., 281–5, 328–86; Allen (1970), 90–4.
[51] Norden (1934), 154–5.

grave hero exemplified both the decisions and the actions wise men should imitate.'[52] The expression of Vegius, in his standard *De Educatione Liberorum* (Milan, 1491), is typical: 'In the character of Aeneas, Virgil wished to show a man endowed with every virtue, and to show this man both in adverse and in favourable circumstances.'[53] This is a sentiment which Tiberius Claudius Donatus would have read with satisfaction.

The paradigmatic Aeneas that Renaissance readers found in Virgil's poem exercised a powerful influence over their assumptions on the question of the role of the chief actor in epic. This was partly because the exemplary Aeneas of their tradition fitted in so well with their image of the moral purpose of poetry. Equally important for the critics who began, around the 1540s, to address themselves to the problem of defining epic was the fact that Aristotle's *Poetics*, their main text, was rather thin on epic and full on tragedy; perforce, they turned to 'the poet', as Joel E. Spingarn explains: 'The incompleteness of the treatment accorded to epic poetry in Aristotle's *Poetics* led the Renaissance to deduce the laws of heroic poetry and of poetic artifice in general from the practice of Virgil.'[54]

The *Poetics* had become the main text in the 1540s, in spectacular fashion: Tillyard speaks of 'the irruption of Aristotle's *Poetics* into the critical consciousness of the age'.[55] Significant results followed for the theory of epic, since there was an understandable tendency to try to fill out Aristotle's comparatively exiguous comments on epic with his fuller treatment of tragedy. The central *tragic* figure that men descried in Aristotle was assumed to be equally at home in epic, and Aristotle's comments on the necessity of tragic figures being 'morally good' and 'suitable' (1454a16–18) were assumed to apply to the characters of epic. Castelvetro, for example, in his *Poetica* of 1570, first misunderstands Aristotle at this point to be saying that only noble or kingly characters should be represented in tragedy, and then goes on to convert this misapprehension into a generalisation about epic as well: 'The plot of the two genres of poetry, epic and tragedy, should not contain simply human action, but indeed magnificent action, and regal.'[56]

Against such a background something like a 'doctrine' of the epic hero begins to emerge: the word 'eroe' or 'heroe' itself now appears in its familiar modern connotation for the first time. The noble character of paradigmatic moral significance, the focus of the poem, may be seen in the pages of

---

[52] Allen (1970), 135. See also Tillyard (1954), 134–6.  [53] In Fanning (1933), 87.
[54] Spingarn (1938), 108.  [55] Tillyard (1954), 222.  [56] Castelvetro (1570), 188.

Castelvetro, Pigna, Minturno and Beni.[57] Especially influential was Castelvetro's misguided assertion (prefigured by Pigna), that the Aristotelian 'form' of epic was the single action of a single person: 'The epic ought to comprise one action of one person, not from necessity, but for a demonstration of the excellence of the poet.'[58] This era is the one in which the hero as we know him today first stands forth. To some degree a response to medieval and early Renaissance poems, this critical consensus begins in its turn to exert its own influence over the creations of the poets themselves.

There was a difficulty, however, for the conscientious critic who brought his Aristotle to bear on the heroic poem, namely, that one of Aristotle's very few extended discussions of epic comes in the passage which occupied us at the beginning of this essay, where he proclaims the need for unity in epic, and asserts that it does not come from an individual, or from a period of time, but from the presentation of a single whole or complete action. This assertion was hard to reconcile with the hero-centred poem, and hard to reconcile with the multiplex structure of the great romances, such as Ariosto's *Orlando Furioso*, which also had a claim to the title 'poema eroico'. The dilemma was a real one, despite the fact that the long-lived controversy which it bred is easily derided as tedious and unfruitful.

One important party in the discussion, best represented by the robust Giraldi Cinzio, refused to bow to Aristotle. While conceding that Aristotle's prescriptions applied to one type of poem, Giraldi Cinzio defended the manifold action of romance, together with the 'biographical' epic, as being viable alternative forms of the heroic poem.[59] His pupil Pigna took a similar line, and Castelvetro himself said that epic could treat of many actions of one person, one action of a whole race, or many actions of many people—although the highest form was one action of one person.[60] Such flexibility did not suit most critics, who continued to invoke Aristotle's authority, but without, it must be said, achieving much success in applying Aristotle's observations to real poems. 'Favola', 'attione', 'unità' were words much on their lips, but they show no insight into what Aristotle actually means. Paolo Beni, for example, claims that the *Odyssey* and the *Aeneid* escape Aristotle's interdict on 'poems about one man' by virtue of the fact that Odysseus and Aeneas are leaders of groups of

---

[57] Ibid., 179; Pigna (1554), 25; Minturno (1564), 49; Beni (1607), 39.
[58] Castelvetro (1570), 179: I give the translation of R.C. Williams (1917), 18. On the influence of Castelvetro's view, see Finsler (1912), 72.
[59] Giraldi Cinzio (1554), 19–21; see Tillyard (1954), 226–7.
[60] Pigna (1554), 108; Castelvetro (1570), 178–80.

men;[61] this line of defense, bearable for the *Aeneid*, involves Beni in some spectacular special pleading in the case of the *Odyssey*. The hero tugs all analysis, even of action, towards himself.

High above this level of discussion rises Torquato Tasso, who became the focus of the controversy over unity of fable.[62] In his *Discorsi dell'arte poetica* he addresses himself to the problem of the multiple plot of romance and the single plot of Aristotle. He champions strongly the cause of Aristotle, saying that a true epic may contain a variety of incident and episode—'but that the poem should be nonetheless one that contains such a great variety of material, that its form be one, and the fable be one.'[63] He discusses 'unità' and 'favola' at greater length in his *Del giudizio sovra la Gerusalemme di Torquato Tasso, da lui medesimo riformata*, a book about his rewriting of the *Gerusalemme Liberata* into the new *Gerusalemme Conquistata*. Once more he takes Aristotle as his text, but not in a scholastic or uncomprehending spirit. He quotes, and agrees with, Aristotle's contention that the plot should be 'an imitation of one action and that a whole one' (1451a31–2). He goes on to disagree explicitly with Castelvetro's claim that this action should be that of one person: of this 'unity of person', says Tasso, 'there is no mention at all in this section' (IV.160–1). Godfrey in his poem is preeminent but not the sole or exclusive hero: 'Godfrey conquers in the company of many ... But none of them is sufficient on his own for victory' (163). The action of an epic does not depend on an individual for cohesion or form. Tasso has his own understanding of this point: it is not a puzzling piece of dogma from the *Poetics*, but an insight into the nature of epic which his reading of classical epic corroborates. Of his own poem he says, 'the plot is an imitation of an action of many, as is the *Argonautica* of Apollonius, and of Valerius Flaccus, and the *Thebaid* of Statius, and—as some have asserted—as is the *Iliad* of Homer' (163). This is a point he had long maintained. In the early stages of his composition of the *Liberata*, he had opposed the demands of his critic Speroni, insisting that his action should be 'one of many', not 'one of one'.[64] Certainly Tasso still takes it for granted that Godfrey is the principal heroic person in his poem, just as he takes it for granted that Achilles is in the *Iliad*, but he tries to keep the relationship between hero and fable in balance. In a characteristically vivid picture, he compares Achilles' position in the 'body' of the *Iliad* to that of a Persian king's outsize hand: 'and if the Heroic Poem,

---

[61] Beni (1607), 71–3.   [62] See Finsler (1912), 73–7; Brand (1965), 119–22.

[63] Published in 1587 (against his will), but written around 1564–65, as he began seriously to take in hand the composition of his epic. I quote from *Opere di Torquato Tasso* (Florence, 1724), 4.28; hereafter cited in the text by volume and page numbers.

[64] See Brand (1965), 76.

as it appears to Aristotle, resembles the body of an animal, Achilles will be in that body similar to a member that is out of proportion to the other members, as we read in the Histories was the case with the hand of Aria, King of the Persians' (164).

Tasso's views did not prevail into orthodoxy, although critics continued to repeat as if by rote the tag about plot being the soul of poetry.[65] As the momentum of neoclassicism mounted, the hero bulked ever larger. As Tillyard puts it: 'The type of epic the Renaissance *per se* stood for was indeed the heroic, the kind that exhibited a hero who, by doing great deeds, was a pattern of behaviour to the contemporary prince or gentleman.'[66] Some scrupulous readers of Aristotle continued to insist that the unity of an epic did not depend on the hero. So Ben Jonson follows Aristotle in criticising those 'that have thought the Action of one man to be one'. He continues:

> For though the Arguement of an *Epick-Poeme* be farre more diffus'd, and powr'd out, then that of *Tragedy*; yet *Virgil* writing of *Aeneas* hath pretermitted many things. He neither tells how he was borne, how brought up; how he fought with *Achilles*; how he was snatch'd out of the battaile by Venus; but that one thing, *how he came into Italie*, he prosecutes in twelve bookes ... So Homer lai'd by many things of Ulysses and handled no more, then he saw tended to one and the same end.[67]

Similarly, Pope: 'The Unity of the Epic Action, as well as the Unity of the Fable, does not consist either in the Unity of the Heroe, or in the Unity of Time.'[68] But the paramount idea remained that an epic necessarily shows an image of virtue in the figure of the 'heroic person'. So much, indeed, Tasso agreed with, but he did not see this as the *esse* of epic, in the manner represented by the definition of Hobbes, in his 'Answer to Davenant's Preface to *Gondibert*' (1650): 'He therefore that undertakes an Heroick Poem, which is to exhibit a venerable & amiable Image of Heroick vertue ... '[69] The word 'hero' itself, in its current literary-critical meaning, was taken over into English surprisingly late—in 1673, by John Dryden,[70] who expounded on the French critics such as René Le Bossu, and fixed authoritatively the neoclassical dogma that the epic relates a great action of 'some illustrious hero'.[71] In the main tradition of later English genre criticism, this has usually been taken for granted.[72]

---

[65] See Herrick (1946), 69–71 on this motif.   [66] Tillyard (1938), 213. Cf. Steadman (1967), 6–9.
[67] G.B. Harrison (1966), 104.   [68] Pope (1967), 20.   [69] Spingarn (1908), 2.60.
[70] Watson (1962), 2.172.   [71] Yonge (1882), 145.
[72] On neoclassical views of the epic hero, see Swedenberg (1944), 306–7; Hägin (1964), chapter 3.

It was the neoclassical Dryden who originated the controversy over the question of the hero of John Milton's *Paradise Lost*. He claimed that, since the hero (Adam) loses and the villain (Satan) wins, it was no true epic, making his point rather flippantly by saying that Satan was in reality Milton's hero.[73] It would be unhistorical to see in this an anticipation of the positions of William Blake and Percy Bysshe Shelley; Dryden is not talking about Milton's commitment to the character, but about his failure to comply with what Dryden took to be the natural form of epic, a great hero's accomplishment of a great feat.[74] Discussion has gone on ever since, based on the assumption that a hero is demanded by the form, that, as E. Sirluck expresses it, 'a generic approach enforces the question of the identity of the generic hero'.[75]

Yet the present paper is intended to demonstrate that there was available to Milton an idea of the form and nature of epic in which the figure of the 'generic hero' was not paramount. For Milton, looking back to Aristotle and the Aristotelian tradition up to Tasso, it was possible to see the *esse* of epic as being the imitation of an action. The frame of this action might take in any number of agents, and the agents themselves might represent diverse kinds of 'heroism', but the question at the kernel of the genre was not the neoclassical 'What individual is the centre of the poem?' but rather: 'What is the self-sufficient action which the poem represents?' This viewpoint forms the basis for Addison's counter to Dryden's remarks about the hero. Addison discusses *Paradise Lost* according to what he sees as the canons of Aristotle's *Poetics*,[76] and he replies, in consequence, 'I think I have obviated this Objection in my first Paper. The *Paradise Lost* is an Epic, or a Narrative Poem, and he that looks for an Hero in it, searches for that which *Milton* never intended.'[77] Addison's dictum is regularly misunderstood. Hägin would have it that 'for Addison, *Paradise Lost* is an epic "without a hero" in the same sense as for Thackeray, for instance, *Vanity Fair* is "a novel without a hero"'.[78] But Thackeray is writing whimsically or ironically in the knowledge that a novel ought to have a (morally significant) hero, whereas Addison's whole point is that, if you look at *Paradise Lost* as an epic on an Aristotelian pattern, you will see that it requires no hero of the Le Bossu or Dryden order precisely because it is an epic poem.

---

[73] Ker (1900), 2.165.   [74] Salter (1974), 33.
[75] Sirluck (1967), 7. A preliminary guide into the large bibliography on the hero question is provided by Steadman (1975), 192–4.
[76] Cf. Elioseff (1963), 49.
[77] *Spectator* No. 297, 9 February 1712. The earlier paper is No. 267, 5 January 1712, where he discusses *Paradise Lost* as an Aristotelian single, whole, and complete fable.
[78] Hägin (1964), 153.

It is this 'Aristotelian' conception of the genre which provides a resolution of the dilemma confronting modern scholars when they come to discuss the 'generic hero'. The question is no longer as much discussed as it once was, not because it has been resolved but because the whole debate now seems unfruitful and even irrelevant. Nonetheless, when scholars address themselves to the problems of Milton's genre, it is plain that they still regard the norms of the genre in surprisingly strict neoclassical terms: the hero posited is the Dryden type, the great achiever. Very important qualifications to this approach have been made by Steadman—qualifications with which I agree fully. Steadman refers rather to the language of Italian Renaissance poetics, by which 'Adam would be the "primary hero" or "epic person" of *Paradise Lost* since he is 'the man whose "first Disobedience" and "loss of Eden" are specifically cited in the first lines of the proposition and constitute the subject, argument, and principal action of the poem'.[79] In this matter the emphases need to be registered in a similar way as in the *Iliad*. There, as we saw, Achilles' wrath is likewise 'cited in the first lines of the proposition, and constitute[s] the subject, argument, and principal action of the poem', and in this sense Achilles is indeed the 'primary hero' or 'epic person'. But just as it is a distortion of the *Iliad* to see it as Achilles' poem, so it would be a distortion of *Paradise Lost* to see it as Adam's. The relationships of each of these 'epic persons' to their epics are analogous in many ways; the analogies are, as I shall show in a moment, highlighted by Milton in his proem.

The neoclassical bent, on the other hand, is evident in, for example, the recent book of Shawcross. He starts with the assumption that the hero is a 'staple of the epic', and he includes 'the lack of a clear hero who achieves heroic action' as one of Milton's 'variations from the standard epic tradition'.[80] His discussion of the hero, interesting as it is in many respects, is handicapped by the fact that, in positing this archetype for the genre, he is reacting against a norm that is by no means the absolute he takes it to be.

L. Mackinnon, in a review of Shawcross' book, exemplifies an alternative response to the difficulties of regarding *Paradise Lost* in terms of neoclassical genre theory: 'If *Paradise Lost* is an epic, Satan is its hero: *Paradise Lost* cannot be an epic. Rather, epic is one of the many genres this avowedly unique poem subsumes in its progress.'[81] A similar approach may be seen in Alistair Fowler, who puts it thus: 'Milton . . . expects readers to recognise his Satan as hero of the pagan epic that *Paradise Lost* as a whole is not.'[82] The expectations concerning the genre are still neoclassical, but

---

[79] Steadman (1976), 8.  [80] Shawcross (1982), 33, 99.  [81] Mackinnon (1982).
[82] A. Fowler (1982), 68.

their scope is restricted to those portions of the poem in which Satan appears to fulfil the necessary requirements: it is then a matter of 'antigenre'. Fowler correctly identifies as 'pagan' the kind of heroism Milton embodies in Satan, but this does not entail accommodating the poem to an assumed norm of hero-centred epic of achievement. I do not mean to gloss over the importance of the generic mixture in *Paradise Lost*, described by Fowler.[83] The point is that it is not necessary to appeal to this mixture in order to 'save the phenomena'. To say that Satan is the hero of the 'classical epic portion' of *Paradise Lost* is to misunderstand classical epic. Fowler himself, when discussing the titles of epics, refers to Harry Levin's selection of general titles for epics with 'contending heroes' ('the *Iliad*, the *Pharsalia*, the *Lusiads*'),[84] and he cites *Gerusalemme Liberata* and *Paradise Lost* as further examples. The basic framework of *Paradise Lost* is epic, and it can accommodate Satan under the same terms of genre by which the framework of the *Bellum Civile* can accommodate Caesar.

Milton's own pronouncements on epic are few and curt. The only discussion of any extent, written some years before *Paradise Lost* was begun,[85] shows Milton enmeshed in the intricacies of the Italian critics' arguments over single and complex plots, romance and Aristotelian epics.[86] Further, he is at this stage still strongly under the influence of the mainstream Italian critics, with their noble paradigms, for the last item on his list of matters to be settled for a projected epic is 'what K. or knight before the conquest might be chosen in whom to lay the pattern of a Christian *Heroe*'.[87] In time he discarded his plans for an *Arthuriad* or similar poem and turned to the Fall for his subject. In the poem's opening we see the consequent changes in emphasis, as Milton sketches out the span and nature of his epic.

The exordium displays the poet's programme; according to the Argument to the first book, it 'proposes . . . *the whole subject*' (my emphasis, i.e., the action to be imitated), 'man's disobedience, and the loss thereupon of Paradise wherein he was placed'. The general sweep of the exordium's statement is very reminiscent of the *Aeneid*'s opening lines.[88] There is the demarcation of the range of action ('I sing of arms and the man . . . and brought his gods into Latium', *Aen.* 1.1–6; 'Of Man's first disobedience . . . with loss of Eden', *Paradise Lost* 1.1–4). There is the allusion to the historical consequences, not to be imitated in the poem, but rather revealed

---

[83] Ibid., 89–90.   [84] Referring to H. Levin (1977), xxvi–vii.
[85] In *The Reason of Church Government* of 1642, in Wolfe (1953–82), 1.812–14.
[86] It will be plain that I agree broadly with the analysis of this compressed passage in C.S. Lewis (1961), 3–5. On Milton's debt to the Italian critics, see Steadman (1976), chapter 1.
[87] Wolfe (1953–82), 1.813–14.   [88] Cf. A. Barker (1949), 17.

as prophecy ('whence comes the Latin race ... ', *Aen.* 1.6–7; 'till one greater Man ... ', *PL* 1.4–5). But the direct statement of the action ('Of Man's first disobedience ... ') recalls Homer's statement of the action in the first line of the *Iliad*, 'Sing, goddess, of the wrath of Achilles.'[89] Milton's 'Man' is at once general and particular: 'man' in Hebrew is 'Adam', and 'Man' here denotes Adam, just as in line 4 'one greater Man' denotes Christ, the 'second Adam'. In both poems the subject is announced as an action that is proper to a named individual, but the latter is not their structural focus. Milton develops his exordium with a relentless series of nouns that chart out the *event*—'disobedience, fruit, loss'—just as in Homer's exordium Achilles is left while the wrath expands autonomously with its own energy. C. Gildon remarked, 'Milton begins his poem of things, and not of men'[90]—and the same could be said of Homer. Instead of an individual, the poem presents the framework of an act, in its preparation, course, and consequence, comprehending many agents and much incident.

Addison puts it thus: 'We see [the action] contrived in hell, executed upon earth, and punished by Heaven.'[91] As a description of the fable at the core of *Paradise Lost* Addison's formulation may appear flat and unfruitful, but it is scarcely more spare than Milton's own description of the 'action', the 'whole subject', in the Argument to Book 1, where he says that the first book 'proposes, first, in brief, the whole subject, man's disobedience, and the loss thereupon of Paradise wherein he was placed: then touches the prime cause of his fall, the Serpent, or rather Satan in the Serpent'. The very astringency of the poem's central line of movement not only forms a sheet anchor for the manifold superimposed rhythms and counterpoints of structure,[92] but also sets off the issues and events involved in the action, 'the fate of worlds, the revolutions of heaven and of earth'.[93]

The 'hero', Dryden's 'hero', may be a will-o'-the-wisp, but the nature of heroism is a vital element in the poem's meaning. The three principal agents in the action, infernal, terrestrial, and celestial, are Satan, Adam, and Christ. Each of them is used by Milton in various ways as the vehicle of a systematic critique and revaluation of the Renaissance and epic concepts of heroism.[94] Such a procedure is eminently epic; it is a critical commonplace that the

---

[89] Cf. M. Mueller (1969), 293.   [90] Gildon (1721), 260.   [91] *Spectator* No. 297, 9 February 1712.
[92] Sirluck (1967), 13–16 treats well the meshing of the poem's recurrent and eddying movements, anticipating and reflecting, with the direct forward energy of the core fable.
[93] So Samuel Johnson describes the poem's 'subject', in his *Life of Milton* (Hill (1905), 172). See here Steadman (1976), 139.
[94] The important books of Steadman (1959) and (1967) have largely superseded earlier work. See also Blessington (1979), chapter 1.

essence of heroism is put to the test by Homer, Apollonius, Virgil, Lucan, Statius and Tasso.[95] Yet Milton's Aristotelian pattern of a fable enables us to contemplate each of these characters in his place without being obliged to accord any of them the title of '*the* hero'. No one of these pictures of heroism is what the poem is about, and no one of these individuals is meant to stand as the demanding focus of the poem; all have their roles in a comprehensive fable which unites their agencies in a great event.

While it is important, then, to ask what the poem's paradigms of heroism mean, 'Who is the hero of *Paradise Lost*?' is not a significant question within the terms of Milton's generic allegiance and professed intent. It is not a question that the type and nature of the epic invite us to pose. Rather, by cleaving to the fable, by reacting against the conventions of neoclassicism and going beyond even Tasso to the examples of ancient epic, Milton restored the distinctive capaciousness of the form.

---

[95] On Homer, see Nagy (1979); on Apollonius, see Lawall (1966); on Virgil, see Quinn (1968), 1–22; on Lucan, see Ahl (1976), 150–5; on Statius, see Vessey (1973), 196–209, 283–93; on Tasso, see Kates (1974). In general, on the recasting of heroic types in Satanic forms, see Farron (1979–80).

CHAPTER 4

# Stat magni nominis umbra: *Lucan on the Greatness of Pompeius Magnus*[1]

At the age of twenty-five, Gn. Pompeius acquired the spectacular *cognomen* of *Magnus*. According to Plutarch (*Pomp.* 13), the name came either from the acclamation of his army in Africa, or at the instigation of Sulla. According to Livy, the practice began from the toadying of Pompeius' circle (*ab adsentatione familiari*, 30.45.6). The *cognomen* invited play. At the *Ludi Apollinares* of July 59 BCE, Cicero tells us, the actor Diphilus won 'a dozen *encores*' when he pronounced, from a lost tragedy, the line *nostra miseria tu es magnus* ('to our misfortune art thou great').[2] Four or five years later Catullus scored a fine hit, filching Pompeius' *cognomen* and giving it to his zealously competitive father-in-law: *Caesaris uisens monimenta magni* ('seeing the monuments of *Great* Caesar', 11.10). In Lucan's *Bellum Civile* such plays on the *cognomen* are elevated into something of considerable power, testifying to a consistent controlling design, of the sort which many still deny the poem.

When Pompeius first appears he is compared with Caesar, to his detriment: *nec coiere pares* ('nor did they meet as equals', 1.129). So much for Pompeius' vaunted intolerance of an equal, of which we have just been reminded: *nec quemquam iam ferre potest Caesarue priorem/Pompeiusue parem* ('nor any longer can either Caesar endure a superior or Pompeius an equal', 1.125–6).[3] Many of the images in this introductory section have a programmatic power, and will recur. With *nec coiere pares* Lucan presents the two as an ill-matched pair of gladiators. The metaphor is ubiquitous. Note, in particular, 5.1–3, and 6.3, *parque suum uidere dei* ('the gods saw their equally matched pair').[4] We are further told that Pompeius seeks *fama*, is a *popularis*, indulges the people, basks in the applause he receives

---

[1] I am most grateful to Stephen Hinds for his criticism and comments.
[2] *Att.* 2.19.3. The 'dozen *encores*' are from the translation of Shackleton Bailey (1965–68). I thank Dr. J.R. Patterson for the reference.
[3] Getty (1940) ad loc. collects examples of this formulation.
[4] See here Ahl (1976), 82–115, esp. 86–7.

from the mob in his theatre: *famaeque petitor/multa dare in uolgus, totus popularibus auris/impelli plausuque sui gaudere theatri* (131–3). We will return later to this complex of ideas.

The crucial conceit comes next, when Lucan tells us that Pompeius is a paper tiger: *stat magni nominis umbra* (135). He is 'the shadow of a great name'. '"Name" in the sense of "reputation"', observes Getty.[5] Certainly; but, of course, his name *is* '*Magnus*', so that he is the shadow of his own name. In a reversal of the *nomen/omen* figure,[6] Pompeius' destiny is no longer embodied in his name, as it once had been. The allusions are picked up shortly afterwards, when Lucan says of Caesar, *sed non in Caesare tantum/nomen erat* (143–4). Getty feels compelled to choose between taking *tantum* as an adverb or an adjective, between translating, in other words, 'Caesar had more than a mere name', or 'Caesar did not have such a great name.' Yet both interpretations are felt. Caesar did not have a name as *magnum* as *Magnus*, nor was a name from the past all he had to rely on. And history works further tricks for the poet: for Lucan's audience, the greatest name in the world was—Caesar.

Pompeius' name of *Magnus* is an anachronism, a reproach, a promise which he has outlived and can no longer fulfil. Many are deceived (not least Pompeius himself). At the beginning of Book 5, the consul Lentulus Crus urges the Senate *Magnum . . . iubete/esse ducem*, 'order Magnus to be your leader' (46–7). The reader, with hindsight to guide him, will also detect a doomed promise: 'order your leader to be great'. It is the illusory and insubstantial *nomen* to which the Senators react: *laeto nomen clamore senatus/excipit* ('the Senate greets the name with a happy shout', 47–8). Pompeius' case is the same as that of Athens, described half-disparagingly in the list of towns which immediately follows: *fama ueteres laudantur Athenae* ('Athens is praised, ancient in its reputation', 52).[7]

By 49 BCE, inactive as a *dux* for fourteen years, Pompeius Magnus has his pretensions as another Alexander the Great exposed as a thing of the past.[8] And yet, in a finely judged movement, Lucan transforms the values by which he is to be assessed, and reveals to us a process by which Pompeius does live up to his name, becoming in fact *magnus*, outstripping the petty

---

[5] Getty (1940) ad loc.   [6] On this figure, see Pease (1920–3) on Cic. *Div.* 1.102.

[7] Athens is a longstanding target for such gibes. Compare the words of Livy (taken from Polybius, as Briscoe (1973) notes in his commentary ad loc.): *contraxerant autem sibi cum Philippo bellum Athenienses haudquaquam digna causa, dum ex uetere fortuna nihil praeter animos seruant* ('now the Athenians had entered upon war against Philip for no good reason at all, since they retained nothing of their former good fortune except their spirit', 31.14.6).

[8] The true Alexander in the poem is of course Caesar: see Morford (1967), 13–19.

associations of popular *fama*, and achieving a *nomen* which is no mere *umbra*.

The gradual process begins with Pompeius' total defeat at Pharsalus. Now at last it is possible for him to begin to emancipate himself from his past (7.686–9):

> iam pondere fati
> deposito securus abis: nunc tempora laeta
> respexisse uacat. spes numquam inplenda recessit:
> quid fueris nunc scire licet.

> Now you lay aside the burden of fate and go away, free from care; now there is leisure to look back at the happy times; the hope that could never be filled up has gone away; now it is possible to know what you were.

Especially, once Pompeius' part in the civil war is over, he is no longer tainted with the title of *dux factionis*, his *nomen* is no longer at the head of one party, and a new pair of contestants emerges: from now on, the issue in the fighting, says Lucan (7.694–6),

> non iam Pompei nomen populare per orbem
> nec studium belli, sed par quod semper habemus,
> libertas et Caesar, erit.[9]

> will no longer be the name of Pompeius, loved by the people throughout the world, nor devotion to war, but the matched pair we always have—Liberty and Caesar.

Pompeius retires to Larisa. *scilicet inmenso superest ex nomine multum*, observes the poet, with irony, and pathos ('indeed, a lot is left over from his immense name', 717). The laments and tears of the people of Larisa form his escort as he sets out: thereby, for the first time, only in defeat, Pompeius receives true proof and 'enjoyment' of the popularity he had long courted: *nunc tibi uera fides quaesiti, Magne, fauoris/contigit ac fructus* ('now, Magnus, you could really believe in and enjoy the favour you wanted to get', 726–7).

The narrator can see the implications of Pompeius' defeat, but the character has not yet achieved that perspective, and is still dogged by his name, still a victim of its delusion. At the beginning of Book 8, in flight, *cunctis ignotus gentibus esse/mallet et obscuro tutus transire per urbes/nomine* ('he would have preferred to be unknown to all the peoples and to go safely through the cities with no one knowing his name', 19–21). Later in the

---

[9] Cf. Due (1962), 111–14.

book, he speaks to his remaining companions, still hoping for a recovery, keeping his faith in his name (8.274–6):

> sed me uel sola tueri
> fama potest rerum toto quas gessimus orbe
> et nomen quod mundus amat.
>
> but I can be protected just by the fame of the deeds I performed all over the earth and by the name that the world loves.

He is living in the past, and dreams of going east (8.320–1):

> quas magis in terras nostrum felicibus actis
> nomen abit, aut unde redit maiore triumpho?
>
> Into what lands did my name go with more successful outcome, or from what lands did I come back with a greater triumph?

Lentulus dissuades him, and advises him to go to Ptolemy. Yes, he is a king, says Lentulus, but there is no need to fear that empty title. For the reader who remembers Pompeius' first appearance, the words which express this conceit are crammed with irony: *quis nominis umbram/horreat?* ('who would fear the shadow of a name?', 449–50).[10] Who indeed? Not Ptolemy. Barely one hundred lines later, the murder is planned, and Lucan asks, *tanti, Ptolemaee, ruinam/nominis haud metuis ... ?* ('don't you fear, Ptolemy, the ruin of such a great name?', 550–1).

It is only at the moment of death that Pompeius perceives, and begins to achieve, his true *fama*, outgrowing his past and his hunt for a misconceived *fama*. As he sees the sword (8.615–17),

> lumina pressit
> continuitque animam, nequas effundere uoces
> uellet et aeternam fletu corrumpere famam.
>
> he closed his eyes and held his breath, so that he wouldn't blurt out anything and besmirch his eternal fame with weeping.

He addresses himself: *nunc consule famae* ('now take thought for your fame', 624). Dogmatic interpretations of Pompeius as a Stoic *proficiens* are awry,[11] but it is none the less true that his claim to genuine *fama* is

---

[10] The words also convey the notion that Ptolemy is the shadow, not of his *own* name, as is Pompeius, but of his ancestors' great name.

[11] Pompeius as a *proficiens* ('someone making progress in the philosophy') made his appearance in Marti (1945). The idea is conclusively dealt with by Lintott (1971), 504–5. Discussion continues: see Rutz (1984), 164–9.

validated by his acceptance of an attitude to death which corresponds to the values asserted by the narrator. At the beginning of this book Lucan had sketched out an ideal for Pompeius to aim at in his attitude to death, and one of the questions of the murder-narrative is whether he can attain it: *quisquamne secundis/tradere se fatis audet nisi morte parata?* ('does anyone dare to entrust himself to favourable circumstances unless he has made preparations for death?', 8.31–2). Death provides Pompeius with a true perspective for his life (8.629–32):

> spargant lacerentque licebit,
> sum tamen, o superi, felix, nullique potestas
> hoc auferre deo. mutantur prospera uita,
> non fit morte miser.
>
> They can scatter and rip me, but I am still, oh gods, fortunate, and no god has the power to take that away from me. Prosperity in life changes, but death does not make a man wretched.

The greatness of Pompeius Magnus is vindicated in his death.[12] His quaestor Cordus, beside the makeshift pyre he has constructed, addresses him thus: *o maxime … ductor* ('oh greatest leader', 8.759–60). The man first introduced as *famae petitor* ('a seeker after fame', 1.131) gains rather than loses *fama* with his conventionally inglorious death and burial: *nil ista nocebunt/famae busta tuae* ('that tomb will do no harm to your fame', 8.858–9).[13] As so often, Caesar is a foil. In the mighty storm of Book 5, Caesar contemplates suffering the same physical fate as comes to Pompeius, but in his ignorance and egoism lays hold of a brutal and self-obsessed perspective (668–71):

> mihi funere nullo
> est opus, o superi: lacerum retinete cadauer
> fluctibus in mediis, desint mihi busta rogusque,
> dum metuar semper terraque expecter ab omni.
>
> I do not need any funeral, oh gods: keep my torn corpse in the middle of the waves, let me have no tomb or pyre, just so long as I am always feared and awaited in dread by every land.

Note how Lucan, so characteristically, refers back to these words when he describes Cordus rescuing Pompeius' corpse from the waves (8.717–20):

---

[12] Cf. Lintott (1971), 502. Lintott rightly stresses the fact that it is Pompeius' death, not his defeat as such, which provides his amelioration (501).

[13] Lucan's reversals here produce the paradoxes remarked upon by Mayer (1981), 185: 'At one moment Pompey's tomb is a disgrace, at the next a glory; now an object of pilgrimage, now lost to sight.'

> ille per umbras
> ausus ferre gradum uictum pietate timorem
> conpulit ut mediis quaesitum corpus in undis
> duceret ad terram traheretque in litora Magnum.
>
> he dared to tread through the shadows of darkness and forced his fear, conquered by piety, to look for the corpse in the middle of the waves, bring it to land, and drag Magnus to the shore.

Caesar was happy for his corpse to float at sea so long as he was feared; Pompeius' corpse does float at sea, but it is rescued, in a bold usage, by somebody's 'fear', a fear that has been conquered by *pietas*.[14] Again, after Cordus has addressed Pompeius as *maxime*, we must relish the irony when Caesar is subsequently hailed with the same word: by a *satelles* ('henchman') of Ptolemy (9.1014; two lines earlier, this man *colla gerit Magni*, 'carries the head of Magnus'); and—worse—by Cleopatra (10.85).

Lucan reserves for the ninth book his final transformations of the aura of failure and inadequacy which had controlled the first image of Pompeius.[15] *Stat magni nominis umbra*, we read there ('he stands the shadow of a great name', 1.135); but in the second line of this book, Pompeius is *tanta umbra* ('such a great shadow/shade of the dead', 9.2). The conceit thus alluded to is not fully deployed until Cato's encomium later in the book, where we see that only as an *umbra* does Pompeius achieve true *nomen* ('name/reputation'). As Cato begins his speech, it appears at first that his appreciation of Pompeius may not be altogether favourable, for he describes him as *maioribus inpar* (190). *Magnus* is not a match (that image again) for 'those who are greater'. But Pompeius receives his due. To Cato, he is *clarum et uenerabile nomen* ('a famous and venerable name', 202). As Cato ends, Lucan reminds us, for the last time, of his first picture of Pompeius, as one misguidedly seeking popular fame, a shadow of what his name dictates he should be (9.215–17):

> uocibus his maior, quam si Romana sonarent
> rostra ducis laudes, generosam uenit ad umbram
> mortis honos.
>
> with this utterance a greater honouring of his death came to the well-born shade than if the Roman rostra had echoed the leader's praise.

---

[14] The first man to honour Pompeius after his death is motivated by *pietas*, which was the Pompeians' battle-cry at Munda; Pompeius' younger son took the *cognomen* of *pius* (cf. Syme (1939), 157). Another play on this fact at 9.147, where this son is *iusta ... furens pietate* ('raging with righteous devotion').

[15] It is not, then, as commonly asserted, a matter of 'Lucan's increasingly pro-Pompeian attitude' (so put by Holliday (1969), 55): see here Due (1962), 106.

The *umbra* ('shade') is *generosa* ('well-born'): the qualities which Cato salutes are not those which the living man had thought to be his claim to greatness, but rather qualities which are—strictly—innate (9.208–11):

> o felix, cui summa dies fuit obuia uicto
> et cui quaerendos Pharium scelus obtulit enses . . .
> scire mori sors prima uiris, set proxima cogi.

> oh fortunate man, because he was a beaten man when he met his last day, and the Egyptian crime brought in his path a death by the sword that he should have sought out . . . The best fate for men is to know how to die, but the next best is to be forced to die.

It matters a good deal that this final validation comes from the mouth of Cato. He understands at the beginning what Pompeius represents at the beginning, and in his speech to Brutus in Book 2 makes it plain that Pompeius is after mastery (320–2). In this speech, Lucan gives him words which chime in with the range of imagery we have been discussing. As Cato announces that he will join Pompeius despite his misgivings, he says, *tuum . . . /nomen, Libertas, et inanem persequar umbram* ('I shall follow your name, Liberty, and your empty shadow', 303). The *umbra* is that of Libertas here, naturally; but any reader who paused, hesitating whether to attribute it to Pompeius, will be gratified to read, not twenty lines later, *quin publica signa ducemque/Pompeium sequimur?* ('Why shouldn't I follow the standards of the Republic and Pompeius as leader?', 319–20). Pompeius is the played-out leader of a played-out cause: he and Libertas are both *umbrae* ('shadows'), *nomina* ('[mere] names'). In his encomium in Book 9, Cato acknowledges that the death of the one is the death of the other (204–6).

Cato likewise understands after Pompeius' death what was signified by that death, for Pompeius, as a man. Yet he is superior to Pompeius in being able to live in the light of that knowledge, self-sufficient, free of the fears of death and ignominy, free from superficial assessments of achievement. Lucan discloses this truth in Book 9, when he compares Cato's *uirtus* and *nomen* ('virtue' and 'name/fame/reputation') to that of the *maiores* ('ancestors', lit. 'greater ones'), and of Pompeius himself (9.593–600):[16]

> si ueris *magna* paratur
> fama bonis et si successu nuda remoto

---

[16] I am still kicking myself for not noticing until I received off-prints that Lucan here and throughout puns on the *nomen* of 'Pompeius' as well as on his *cognomen*, 'Magnus'. The usual Greek word for the Roman triumph is πομπή (*pompē*), so that 'Pompeius Magnus' is 'Triumph-Man the Great'. In the last sentence of this quotation, then, Lucan punningly says he would rather have a Catonian *triumph* than a *Pompeian* one.

inspicitur uirtus, quidquid laudamus in ullo
*maiorum*, fortuna fuit. quis Marte secundo,
quis *tantum* meruit populorum sanguine *nomen*?
hunc ego per Syrtes Libyaeque extrema *triumphum*
ducere maluerim, quam ter Capitolia curru
scandere *Pompei*, quam frangere colla Iugurthae.

If a *great* fame is in store for truly good men and if unadorned virtue herself is perceived when success is taken away, then whatever we praise in any of the *greater* ones was only luck. Who gained *such a great name* by victory in war or by killing peoples? I would prefer to lead this *triumph* through the Syrtes and the outermost parts of Libya rather than climb the Capitol three times in the chariot of *Pompeius* or snap the neck of Jugurtha.

Yet Cato had never conducted a triumph, to experience the temptations to delusion open to Pompeius. Pompeius' final victory over himself is by so much the more impressive. Emancipating himself from the illusory greatness of his past, Pompeius achieves true greatness by and in death.[17]

---

[17] It is very likely, as Professor M.D. Reeve suggests to me, that Lucan got at least the germ of his presentation from the writings and conversation of his uncle. Seneca has one or two comparatively straightforward plays on Pompeius' *cognomen*: note *Cons. Marc.* 14.3, *Cn. Pompeius non aequo laturus animo quemquam alium esse in re publica magnum* ('Cn. Pompeius, who wasn't about to tolerate happily that anyone else should be great in the state'); cf. *Ben.* 4.30.2, *unius uiri magnitudo tanta quondam* ('the greatness of one man, once so great'). But there is a highly suggestive sequence of allusions in one of the *Epistles*, where Seneca exposes the hollowness of Pompeius' grand title: *Ne Gnaeo quidem Pompeio externa bella ac domestica uirtus aut ratio suadebat, sed insanus amor magnitudinis falsae ... quid illum in Africam, quid in septentrionem ... traxit? infinita scilicet cupido crescendi, cum sibi uni parum magnus uideretur* ('Not even Cn. Pompeius was persuaded to take part in foreign or civil wars by virtue or reason, but by his insane love of a false greatness .... What dragged him off to Africa, to the North ...? A boundless lust for getting bigger, since he was the only person who thought he wasn't big enough', 94.64–5).

CHAPTER 5

# *History and Revelation in Virgil's Underworld*[1]

Virgil's parade of heroes, a panegyric that becomes a threnody, is an odd blend. It is framed by an elaborate quasi-philosophical eschatology, whose relation to the parade is problematical. Much of the passage puts itself forward as high panegyric, yet certain sections are at variance with that tendency. The lament for Marcellus (6.868–86) is most commonly remarked upon; other passages are equally, or more, anomalous.[2] Still, the massive self-assurance of the picture of the underworld has its own imposing conviction, so that although the disparateness of the contributing elements has been documented often enough,[3] few have felt the need to dispute the question of whether the blend coheres as a single statement. One noteworthy reader of Virgil was, however, compelled to give minute attention to the implications of the historical vision in Book 6. Incidentally throughout the *Bellum Civile*, but especially in his own sixth book, with the vision of hell called forth by the agency of the witch Erictho, Lucan provides a provocative reading of *Aeneid* 6. His insights will be exploited in the discussion as a valuable stimulus to reflection and reassessment; an appendix will give a more systematic account of his reinterpretation of Virgil.

In formal terms, Anchises' eulogistic speech is genealogical protreptic, using historical exempla and the promise of glory to steer Aeneas towards virtuous rule.[4] The opportunity for the speech is provided by a substantial and complex eschatology, made up mainly from Plato (especially *Republic*

---

[1] A version of this paper was read to a meeting of the Cambridge Philological Society on 10 October 1985. I thank those present for a valuable discussion. For their help and criticism I am also grateful to N.M. Horsfall, Professor R.G.M. Nisbet, Professor David West, Philip Hardie, R.O.A.M. Lyne, Stephen Hinds, and J.M. Masters.
[2] Cf. Büchner (1958), 1391. Important discussions by Clausen (1964), 145–7; R.D. Williams (1972); Griffin (1985), 168–70; Tarrant (1982); above all, Johnson (1976), 105–11.
[3] Bibliography on this disparateness in Solmsen (1972), 31–3; cf. Horsfall (1981), 145.
[4] 'Genealogical protreptic' is the phrase of Horsfall (1976), 84: bibliography ad loc., n.102; note especially von Albrecht (1967).

10), and from Cicero's *Somnium Scipionis* (itself the last book of a *Republic*, and intimately linked with the myth of Er).[5] The eschatology relates the toils of the soul in its progress between this life and the next (724–51). Too few readers are puzzled by this blend of mysticism and worldly motivation; the stark oddity of nationalistic, glorifying protreptic in such a setting and tradition is perhaps not sufficiently appreciated.[6]

No one systematic picture emerges from Plato's account of the soul's fate after death,[7] but certain basic themes and patterns do emerge. The entire tendency is to encourage the reader to cultivate the life of philosophic virtue. Plato's contempt for the carnal unrealities of actual life, which are irreconcilably inimical to the interests of the soul, leads him to urge us to live in such a way that we may emancipate ourselves totally from earthly concerns, and escape one day from the tomb that is our body into the upper regions.[8] Within the terms of reincarnation, this means that when we come to select our next lot in life, we must choose according to the priorities of the soul, not of the body. The main temptation in our path here is the life of politics, public affairs, tyranny (*Resp.* 619a, *Phd.* 82c–d). Plato allows that there are a very few decent characters amongst the public men (*Grg.* 526a–b, *Phdr.* 248d), but asserts that such a life almost necessarily involves one in the inflicting and the suffering of great evil and pain, since scarcely any can resist the corruption of power (*Leg.* 691 c–d, *Resp.* 494b–c).[9] Thus, in the myth of Er, the soul with the first lot chooses straightaway the life of the greatest tyrant and does not see until too late the destiny that awaits him—παίδων αὑτοῦ βρώσεις καὶ ἄλλα κακά ('eating his own children and other evils', *Resp.* 619c). The last named soul of Plato's catalogue is that of Odysseus, who has learnt through suffering, and abandoned φιλοτιμία ('love of glory'). He hunts out the inconspicuous life of a private citizen who minds his own business (620c).[10]

Such a perspective does not commend itself to Roman sentiment. It is in fact remarkable how much Platonic matter Cicero retains for his adaptations in the *Tusculan Disputations* and the *Somnium Scipionis*. As regards the slighting of renown and achievement, the consul, proconsul and augur

---

[5] The discussion of Norden (1934), 47–8 is still indispensable. See further n.12 below.
[6] It is recognised by Johnson (1976), 105–11.
[7] As is stressed by Annas (1982) (a reference I owe to M.M. Mackenzie, whom I thank for help on these Platonic matters). The main Platonic passages are *Grg.* 523a–27e; *Phd.* 112e–14c; *Resp.* 614b–21d; *Phdr.* 245c–50c.
[8] Although hope of this escape is not actually held out in the myth of Er.
[9] The philosopher-king may be free from this corruption, but Plato seems to have become increasingly pessimistic on this score; see Annas (1981), 106.
[10] For praise of the inconspicuous life in such contexts, cf. *Phd.* 82c–d, *Grg.* 526c.

has some scruples. A brief section of the *Disputations* attempts, not altogether happily, to reconcile a philosopher's disdain for the matters of this life with the patriot and stateman's partiality for the goods of fame (1.109–11). The problem had engaged Cicero more extensively in the *Somnium Scipionis*. There he follows Plato in teaching the inferiority of the body's interests (19), the pettiness of earthly glory (esp. 20–5), and the immortal reward of the virtuous soul (14–16), while at the same time trying to assert that it is the rulers and preservers of states who have the surest title to that immortal reward.[11] Again, the success of the blending is not complete, and the uncertainties of Cicero's presentation highlight the striking incongruities of the amalgam of Platonic and imperial thought. Yet the attempt alone was bold, and a strong impulse on Virgil's imagination.

Virgil's debt to Plato and Cicero is clear, and well documented.[12] Anchises' description of the cycle of purification and rebirth (724–51) has Platonic matter mixed with Stoic, and owes much in expression to the *Somnium Scipionis*.[13] Especially Platonic is the presentation of corporeal existence as entrapment in a sinful prison.[14] If the speech itself puts us in mind of Plato's doctrines, the personal setting recalls the situation of the *Somnium Scipionis*, where a son meets a deceased father and is given a discourse on the role of the statesman.[15]

The reader who has his expectations primed by such reminiscences is going to be considerably puzzled at a number of points where Virgil's drift runs directly counter to his models. It is not the mere fact of inconsistency which should arrest us, for Virgil's eclecticism is by no means always synthetic.[16] At issue here is a fundamental paradox, an eschatology which is expressed and presented within a recognised philosophical tradition, but which appears to champion mundane values disparaged by that tradition, turning our eyes insistently towards this corporeal world, away from the concerns of the soul. Various writers have commented on the difficulties of

---

[11] This is, as it were, a base version of the Platonic problem involved in why the Guardian should go back into the cave after attaining his own enlightenment: Annas (1981), 262–70. On these links between Cicero and Plato, see Boyancé (1936), 147–60. Many writings on Cicero's Platonic debts are discussed by Schmidt (1973), 309–10.
[12] On the Platonic element, see the works cited by Solmsen (1972), 31–3. On the Ciceronian, see Norden (1934), 47; Lamacchia (1964); Klingner (1967), 485–92; Camps (1969), 89–90.
[13] Cf. Austin (1977), 221.
[14] Note 731–4 in particular, and the language of malaise and imprisonment to describe earthly life in 734 (*clausae ... corpore caeco*), 736 (*malum*), 737 (*corporeae pestes*), 739 (*malorum*), 742 (*infectum scelus*). Very Ciceronian language here: cf. esp. *Somn.* 29.
[15] Cf. (besides works in n.12) Boyancé (1936), 39–40; Alfonsi (1955).
[16] As we have recently been well reminded by Horsfall (1981).

the link between the 'philosophical' exposition and the subsequent praise of Rome, but for the most part they accept the independence of the two sections.[17] The paradox is not inert, however, but operative; it is not one which the poet glosses over, or leaves tactfully unstressed, but one to which he regularly directs our attention.

When Aeneas sees the shades gathered at the river of Lethe, he shudders at the sight, and asks what is the reason for what he sees: *causasque requirit/ inscius Aeneas* ('and Aeneas in his ignorance asks for the reasons', 710–11). He is being cast as the ignorant disciple, who wishes to be told *causae* by his mentor. Anchises explains that the souls are ready to return to earth once they drink of the river (713–15). He continues (716–18):

> has equidem memorare tibi atque ostendere coram
> iampridem, hanc prolem cupio enumerare meorum,
> quo magis Italia mecum laetere reperta.
>
> For a long time now I've been wanting to itemise these souls to you and to show them to you face to face, to count off these my descendants, so that you may rejoice all the more with me in the discovery of Italy.

These almost jaunty words might stand in themselves as sufficient introduction to the parade of heroes, but we are interrupted by a shocked question from the enduring hero (719–21):

> o pater, anne aliquas ad caelum hinc ire putandum est
> sublimis animas iterumque ad tarda reuerti
> corpora? quae lucis miseris tam dira cupido?
>
> Oh father, must we think that some souls go from here aloft to the sky, and return once more to sluggish bodies? What is this so appalling desire for the light that the poor things have?

That, as Servius saw, is *the* pertinent philosophical question at this point.[18] Possibly, it may also be that Virgil puts us in mind of the characteristic Platonic mode of composition here, for this is the only occasion in the poem where Virgil uses *dialogue* in this way—Anchises, Aeneas, and again Anchises—without any intervening narrative to introduce the speaker.[19]

The expectations that Aeneas' questions set up are reinforced by Anchises' 'Platonic' account of reincarnation, in which life on earth is

---

[17] Thus Otis (1963), 300–1; Solmsen (1972); R.J. Clark (1979), 182–3.
[18] Note, especially, these words: *miscet philosophiae figmenta poetica et ostendit tam quod est uulgare, quam quod continet ueritas et ratio naturalis* ('he blends poetic fictions into the philosophy and presents as much common lore as what is contained by truth and natural science').
[19] Cf. Lipscomb (1909), 116.

represented as something in its essence antipathetic to the soul. Yet the parade of heroes, when it comes, is a catalogue of earthly achievement, of kings and statesmen, the very category against which Plato warns so strenuously. No Odysseus here, seeking the ordinary life—rather, to go no further, two men whose public position caused them to put their children to death (Brutus, 817–23, and Torquatus, 825). The question of Aeneas is there precisely to point the contrast between this 'earthly' eschatology and the otherworldly direction of the models.

Aeneas' question formally resembles the question put by Africanus Minor to his natural father Paullus in the *Somnium Scipionis*.[20] There Scipio asks Paullus why, if mortal life is so vile, he should not die voluntarily, to escape the prison of the body and reach heaven; he is told that God alone may decide the time of his death (15), and that in the meantime he must serve the state (16). It has been suggested that the Ciceronian model helps to explain the difficulties of Virgil's transition from philosophy to eulogy,[21] but in fact Virgil's treatment looks even more idiosyncratic if set against the *Somnium Scipionis*, despite the numerous general debts. Cicero, in blending Platonic thought with Roman ethics, had two principal devices of accommodation. The prize of immortal beatitude which Plato had held out to the philosopher was promised by Cicero to the statesman (13–16), while at the same time Cicero strove— with what success?—to preserve the integrity of his philosophical position by systematically disparaging earthly *gloria* (20–5). Virgil, on the first point, says, in effect, nothing.[22] On the second point, it is plain that Anchises' panegyric is radically at odds with Cicero's presentation.

Scipio exhorts his grandson again and again to despise *gloria* (20):

> haec caelestia semper spectato, illa humana contemnito. tu enim quam celebritatem sermonis hominum aut quam expetendam consequi gloriam potes?
>
> Keep on always looking at this celestial sphere, keep on despising that human one. For what celebrity from human beings' speech are you able to catch, or what glory that is worth yearning for?

He shows him the petty globe, patchily inhabited, so many people so remote from Rome: *a quibus expectare gloriam certe nullam potestis* ('from whom you can certainly not expect any glory', 20). Could the *nomen* of Scipio, or any

---

[20] Cf. Lamacchia (1964), 263–6; Klingner (1967), 490–1.
[21] Lamacchia (1964), 263–6; Klingner (1967), 490–1.
[22] A few great souls may eventually achieve a pure life in the aether (Austin (1977), 279–80), but most souls do not achieve this, and it is not the basis of the exhortation to statesmanship, as it is in Cicero.

Roman, cross Ganges and Caucasus (22)? Virgil's parade of heroes, on the other hand, begins, continues and ends with personal *gloria* and *nomen*:

> nunc age, Dardaniam prolem quae deinde sequatur
> *gloria*, qui maneant Itala de gente nepotes,
> *inlustris* animas *nostrumque in nomen* ituras,
> expediam dictis
>
> come on now, I shall lay out in words the *glory* that now attends on the Dardanian offspring, the descendants that await from the Italian race, *famous* souls and ones that will inherit *our name* (756–9)
>
> Procas, Troianae *gloria* gentis
>
> Procas, *glory* of the Trojan race (767)
>
> uincet amor patriae *laudumque immensa cupido*
>
> love of the fatherland will win out, and *immeasurable lust for praise* (823)
>
> quae postquam Anchises natum per singula duxit
> incenditque animum *famae* uenientis *amore*
>
> after Anchises led his son through these things, one by one, and fired up his mind with *love of the fame* to come (888–9)

Lucan took the point. His resuscitated corpse in Book 6 looks like a better philosopher than Anchises, and appears to know what the context demands. In a splendid announcement to the young Pompeius, the corpse tells him not to worry about the glory of this brief life: *nec gloria paruae/ sollicitet uitae* (6.805–6). This is exactly what Cicero and Plato would have said. And then the twist: *ueniet quae misceat omnes/hora duces* ('there will come an hour that will mix together all the leaders', 806–7). The grand perspectives and portentous backdrops of Cicero evaporate: mere death, mere failure provide the context for the philosophical aphorism.

The effects of Virgil's deliberate, even blatant, reversals remain to be assessed. First, we must examine in more detail, as well as the setting, the contents—Anchises' speech itself, the parade of heroes. At the beginning I observed that various elements of the speech were at odds with its ostensible role as high panegyric. A consideration of the conventions behind the oration will establish the perspective for the discussion.

The speech becomes something of a history of Rome, by way of providing Aeneas with a series of *exempla* which will incite him to greatness.[23] The

---

[23] On *exempla*, see Litchfield (1914); Pease (1955–8) on Cic. *Nat. D.* 2.165.

*exempla* are given a notional coordination in that the persons figuring in them are taken to be descendants of the speaker and the addressee (756–8). The presumed continuity of the *gens Julia* underpins the whole, but in the second half of the speech the great Republican *gentes* come into their own—Marcii, Bruti, Decii, Drusi and so on (815–86). The emphasis on the *gens* and the continuity of the *gens* is felt throughout:[24] it is one of the features which most markedly links Anchises' speech with the *laudatio funebris* (and a *laudatio funebris* it becomes overtly, with the lament for Marcellus, 868–86).[25] The funereal associations have been well discussed by Skard and Burke.[26] We have a procession of men whose faces Anchises recognises as one would the ancestral *imagines* in the funeral parade of a noble (*omnis longo ordine posset/aduersos legere et uenientum discere uultus*, 'he could pick them out in the long procession as they came towards him, and learn the faces of those approaching', 754–5); Aeneas has the individuals pointed out and explained to him by his father, as would any son in a Roman street, watching the procession go by. We have the praise of the family line. Especially, we receive the impression that representatives of the *gens* from many, many generations are rubbing shoulders together on the same spot, as would the actors wearing the masks at an actual funeral. At various places in the speech there is a rough chronological schema in the groupings, but behind it all is the notion that the members of each *gens* stand together. Thus, when Aeneas sees the Marcellus of the first century BCE standing beside the Marcellus of the third, he can tell the family resemblance, but he does not know whether this is a son, or a more remote descendant (*filius, anne aliquis magna de stirpe nepotum?*, 864); and Anchises sees all the Fabii before him, so that he cannot speak of all of them (*quo fessum rapitis, Fabii?*, 845).

This theme of the continuity of the *gens* is most important. One of its effects is to set up what Ahl has called 'a number of riddles for the reader',[27] for Virgil is often studiedly vague about which members of a family we are meant to see behind the name. Which Drusi does he mean in 824? Which Gracchi, which Scipiones in 842–3? Here we may be helped by the exemplary character of the speech, for by looking at the associations of such names in other exemplary contexts, it is often possible to divine what Virgil is driving at. A proficient exploiter of the exemplary tradition is Lucan; consistently he sheds light on problematic Virgilian passages. Cicero and Seneca are likewise valuable. Another effect of the focus on the continuity

---

[24] Cf. von Albrecht (1967), 176–7; Horsfall (1980) and (1982).
[25] N.M. Horsfall points out to me that there must be links with the *laudatio funebris* which Augustus spoke over Marcellus (fragments in Malcovati (1928), 53–4).
[26] Skard (1965); Burke (1979).   [27] Ahl (1976), 143.

of the *gens* is to put us in mind of a man's descendants when an individual is named, since to a Roman a noble was, in one side of his persona at least, the temporary incarnation of the essence of his family.²⁸

It is this frame of mind which produces and explains the riddles. If Virgil mentions, for example, the *first* Brutus, his audience is readily suggestible to associations with the assassin of Caesar; while mention of Gracchi or Drusi is potentially provoking, as the audience is invited to reflect upon the diverse fates and worth of successive bearers of the same name. Virgil had before him, in Horace *Odes* 1.12, an example of this approach (perhaps a directly inspiring example; although, as we shall see, the *Georgics* already contain one variety of the technique). In Horace's poem, of the many *exempla* from Roman history, some are of distinctly ambiguous reference. In *superbas/Tarquini fasces* ('the proud rods of Tarquin', 34–5), as Nisbet and Hubbard remark, the adjective points to one Tarquin, the noun to the other (although they plump for the younger).²⁹ Which Scaurus is behind the *Scauros* of 37? Of more moment is the ambiguity in *fama Marcelli* (46, where Nisbet and Hubbard see a process of association between two different Marcelli), and *Iulium sidus* (47). In particular, Horace surprises us with *Catonis/nobile letum* ('the noble death of Cato', 35–6), in the same stanza as Romulus, Numa and Tarquin. Why is Cato in the company of the *reges*? Horace may be for the moment graciously giving credence to the dogma of Cato's sect, that the true *rex* is the Stoic *sapiens*: *rectius enim [sapiens] appellabitur rex quam Tarquinius* ('indeed the wise man will more correctly be called king than Tarquin', Cic. *Fin.* 3.75; a doctrine normally ridiculed by Horace, cf. e.g. *Epist.* 1.1.107). More surely: the name of Cato, who resisted the tyranny of Caesar, follows the archetypal tyrant, Tarquin; the name of Brutus, too shocking for panegyric of Caesar's heir, is hinted at by Cato's presence, for resistance to tyranny, whether Tarquin's or Caesar's, is what the first and last Brutus embodied.³⁰

If tact was a principal motive for Horace's ambiguity, in the hands of Virgil these confusions become vehicles for a more sophisticated and profound conception. The riddles will emerge as being part of a process whereby the entire panegyric receives extensive qualification. Whole sections of the speech treat openly of dark and painful matters—the civil wars of Pompey and Caesar (826–35), Brutus' execution of his children (820–3) and Marcellus' funeral (868–86). These larger passages have attracted much comment. We will need to recognise that the glorifying impetus of the

---

²⁸ Cf. MacMullen (1966), 7–8; Griffin (1985), 190.   ²⁹ Nisbet and Hubbard (1970) ad loc.
³⁰ On Cato and the Bruti, see G.W. Williams (1980), 18.

speech as a whole is checked and intermittently retarded by countervailing tendencies of dubiety, mourning, even disparagement. Norden discerned the elements of ψόγος ('disparagement') within the ἐγκώμιον ('praise').³¹ Modern critics will perhaps rather refer to the qualifications that characterise the epic as a whole, or else, if they wish to contain discussion within the terms of genre, they will acknowledge the two-sidedness that is inherent in the bestowal of high praise.³² So in the *laudes Italiae* of *Georgics* 2, as Richard Thomas has shown, apparent praise is shot through with reservation.³³ Between the untroublesome names of the Decii and Camilli, we have the name Marii: *Decios Marios magnosque Camillos* (169). The plurals are riddles. The Decii were father and son, famous for the same glorious act of *deuotio* ('self-sacrifice'): *hi duo fuerunt, qui Mures dicti sunt, pater et filius* ('these were a pair, both called Mus, father and son', Serv. *Aen.* 6.824). The Marii, likewise, were father and son. C. Marius is an ambivalent enough figure in himself, a great general, but a sinister and disquieting character:³⁴ his son had nothing to be said for him. When a pair of exemplary relatives are immediately succeeded by a suspect father and a bad son, the panegyric doubles back upon itself. Again, the Indian whom Caesar keeps away from the citadels of Italy is adorned with the startling and provocative epithet of *imbellis* ('unwarlike', 172). The miniature work of this *Georgics* passage is extended in the speech of Anchises over some 130 verses.

The first problem we encounter is at 773–6, with the listed towns of the *prisci Latini*, 'early Latins':

> hi tibi Nomentum et Gabios urbemque Fidenam,
> hi Collatinas imponent montibus arces,
> Pometios Castrumque Inui Bolamque Coramque;
> haec tum nomina erunt, nunc sunt sine nomine terrae.
>
> these will found Nomentum and Gabii and the city of Fidenae, these will place the citadels of Collatia on their hills, and Pometii, Castrum Inui, Bola and Cora; these will then be their names, now they are lands without a name.

*tum . . . erunt, nunc sunt . . .* ('will then . . . now are'); the words invite us to ask what the towns were in Virgil's day. Look at these places:

*Nomentum* A byword for an out-of-the-way backwater in Seneca and Martial.³⁵

---

³¹ Norden (1934), 314.   ³² Note the interesting remarks of Martindale (1984), 67.
³³ R.F. Thomas (1982), 45–9.
³⁴ On this ambivalent figure, see R.F. Thomas (1982), 64 n.52; Litchfield (1914), 51 n.4.
³⁵ Sen. *Ep.* 104.1; Mart. 6.43, 10.44.3–4, 12.57.1–2.

*Gabii* In Horace, a yardstick of depopulation, together with Fidenae, the next town in Virgil's list (*Epist.* 1.11.7–8). To Cicero and Juvenal it is emblematic of insignificance, while Propertius and Dionysius of Halicarnassus draw a contrast between its former and present condition.[36]

*Fidenae* Strabo has the town in a list of places, τότε μὲν πολίχνια, νῦν δὲ κῶμαι, ἢ κτήσεις ἰδιωτῶν ('once cities, but now countryside, or possessions of private citizens', 5.3.2). Note that Virgil pointedly calls it an *urbs*. The place also figures in a similar list of vanished towns in Pliny (*HN* 3.68–70).

*Collatia* In Strabo's and Pliny's lists.

*Pometia* Likewise in Pliny's list.

*Castrum Inui* Vanished very early in the Republic, a victim to fever.[37]

*Bola* Likewise in Pliny's list.

*Cora* Florus treats the erstwhile power of Cora almost as a joke: *Cora— quis credat?—et Alsium terrori fuerunt* ('Cora—who would believe it?— and Alsium were a source of terror', 1.11.6).[38]

*haec tum nomina erunt, nunc sunt sine nomine terrae* ... The tenses are intriguingly two-sided, depending on whether one's perspective in time is that of Aeneas, or of Virgil's audience. To Aeneas, the words say that these will be famous names after his time, whereas now, in his lifetime, they are areas of land without any title (or else, places that exist but have no fame). To the contemporary audience, the words are saying that the places will be what they are in fact—*mere names*; now, for 'us', they are only *pieces of land*, without the *reputation* they once had (Lucan's adaptation, which follows shortly, plays upon these meanings; Virgil exploits the pathos of *nomen* in a rather different way at *Aen.* 7.411–13: *locus Ardea quondam/dictus auis, et nunc magnum manet Ardea nomen,/sed fortuna fuit*, 'a place once called Ardea by the ancients, and now Ardea remains a great name, but its fortune is finished'). The shifts in tense and reference are unsettling. What is proferred as praise becomes disparagement, or condolence, as it is uttered. The glorious future of the independent states is taken away from them before it has even happened, as the poet nudges his audience into remembering their contemporary eclipse, swallowed into obscurity by the dominance of the metropolis. The fate of these places is embodied, indeed, in

---

[36] Cic. *Planc.* 23; Juv. 6.56–7, 10.100; Prop. 4.1.34, *qui nunc nulli maxima turba Gabi*; Dion. Hal. *Ant. Rom.* 4.53. On this theme of contrast between cities' former and present condition, see Gossage (1955), 72–4.

[37] H. Nissen (1883–1902), 2.579.

[38] On Cora's obscurity see H. Nissen (1883–1902), 2.644. The disappearance of the towns of the Campagna was a general phenomenon: cf. Ashby (1927), 18–19.

the name of the first town in the list: *Nomen-tum*, 'Name-then'.³⁹ In such a context of instability, one is perhaps prompted to ask (as I was by David West) whether Virgil can conceive of a time when even Rome will be only a name. It has not happened yet.

Lucan takes half of what Virgil offers. His imitation condenses the conventional sarcasm concerning the vanished Latin states into a statement of the debility of Roman power (7.391–6):

> tunc omne Latinum
> fabula nomen erit; Gabios Veiosque Coramque
> puluere uix tectae poterunt monstrare ruinae
> Albanosque lares Laurentinosque penates,
> rus uacuum, quod non habitet nisi nocte coacta
> inuitus questusque Numam iussisse senator.

Then the whole of the Latin name will be a fable; ruins covered in dust will scarcely be able to point out Gabii, Veii and Cora, and the household gods of Alba and Laurentum, empty countryside, with no one to inhabit it except an unwilling senator forced to spend the night, grumbling that Numa gave this order.

*Latinum/fabula nomen* ('Latin name/fable', 391–2) is dazzling play on Virgil's use of *nomina*; *rus uacuum* ('empty countryside', 395) takes up, and strips of ambivalence, Virgil's *terrae* ('lands').⁴⁰

Romulus comes next. He is introduced as making himself the 'comrade or associate of his grandfather' (*quin et auo comitem sese Mauortius addet/ Romulus*, 777–8). Virgil refers to the story we see in Livy (1.3.10–6.2). The grandfather of Romulus and Remus was one Numitor (his name occurs earlier at 768, preparing us for this story). He was disinherited and exiled by his younger brother Amulius. Amulius was responsible for the exposure of the twins, but, when grown, Romulus collaborated with his grandfather Numitor to kill the usurper by stealth (Liv. 1.5.6). He and Remus then restored Numitor to the throne of Alba Longa.

The man who began adult life by killing his great-uncle went on to kill his brother. Virgil does not mention the deed here, nor even the brother, but there is a hint, in *huius ... auspiciis* ('under his auspices', 781). The taking of the auspices at the foundation of Rome, Virgil obliquely reminds us, was a *competition*, which Remus lost (Enn. *Ann.* 72–91 Sk.). If an earlier

---

³⁹ As pointed out to me by Simon Goldhill. Norden (1934) and Austin (1977) on 730 are, then, only half right to draw a distinction between the pride of Virgil and the realism of Horace (*Epist.* 1.11.7–8).
⁴⁰ J.R. Patterson informs me that Lucan is far less true to the facts of *his* contemporary reality than is Virgil; the 'facts' of literature count for more.

argument of mine is correct, then line 780 also refers to this competition, and to the prize of divinity which Romulus won at the expense of his brother.[41]

The founder of the city was a genuinely ambiguous figure, never more so than in the years when Virgil was at work on the *Aeneid*. He had an important role in Caesarian and Augustan cult, and in the literature of the time.[42] Dio reports that Octavian wanted the name for himself (53.16.7). In the end, a less controversial title won the day, though one which itself had associations with the *conditor urbis* (Suet. *Aug.* 7.2)—less controversial, because much in the Romulus myth was disquieting (and not only the fratricide).[43] When Anchises speaks of Romulus, his words have a strong and primary panegyrical direction, which I do not mean to shut out—and yet Virgil does not allow us to block Remus from our memory. A very similar operation is to be seen in Jupiter's prophetic speech in Book 1. Jupiter describes the birth of the twins: *geminam partu dabit Ilia prolem* ('Ilia will give birth to twin offspring', 274). The first five feet of the next line allude to the wolf who nursed the twins (*inde lupae fuluo nutricis tegmine*, 'in the tawny protection of the wolf-nurse'), and it is with considerable shock that we reach the final word and discover that it is *singular* (*laetus*, 'happy').[44] We carry on to find Romulus as the subject: *Romulus excipiet gentem* ('Romulus will take over the race', 276). *Remo scilicet interempto*, comments Servius ('i.e., after the removal of Remus'). Just so. We continue: *Mauortia condet/moenia Romanosque suo de nomine dicet* ('he will found the walls of Mars and will call the Romans after his own name', 276–7). It was when Remus jumped over Romulus' *moenia* that he was killed,[45] while the naming of the people after Romulus rather than after Remus was a result of Romulus' victory in the contest of auspices: *certabant urbem Romam Remoramne uocarent* ('they were competing over whether to call the city "Roma" or "Remora"', Enn. *Ann.* 77 Sk.). And yet Virgil does not leave us here, for at the end of the speech, in the vision of hoped-for peace after the civil wars, the brothers are shown as reconciled: *cana Fides et Vesta, Remo cum fratre Quirinus/iura dabunt* ('hoary Faith and Vesta, Quirinus along with his brother Remus, shall give laws', 292–3). It was possible simply to suppress mention of Remus (as

---

[41] Chapter 2 above, 'The Reconciliations of Juno'.
[42] Syme (1939), 305–6; Weinstock (1971), 176–85.
[43] Cf. Syme (1939), 313–14; Fuchs (1938), 85–7; Wagenvoort (1956), 169–83.
[44] 'The position of *laetus* gives the adjective marked emphasis', remarks Austin (1971) ad loc., making a different point.
[45] Enn. *Ann.* 92–4 Sk.; Ov. *Fast.* 4.841–4.

does Cicero, for example, in the *Republic*, 2.4–12); what is striking in Virgil is the way in which we are reminded of Remus even as we hear the praise of Romulus the founder.

To Lucan only one side of Romulus appeals, that to which Horace responded in the dark days of the Triumvirate (*Epod.* 7). The city was unsound from the moment of its foundation (7.437–8):

> uolturis ut primum laeuo fundata uolatu
> Romulus infami compleuit moenia luco . . .

> As soon as Romulus filled up with his disgraceful grove the walls that had been founded by the vulture's flight on the left . . .

The civil wars have their beginning in Rome's beginning (1.95):

> fraterno primi maduerunt sanguine muri.

> The first walls dripped with the blood of a brother.

Once Virgil has dealt with Romulus, there follows a panegyric on Rome (781–7), which develops into the praise of Augustus (791–805). Rome's other kings follow (808–17; note that Augustus, by this arrangement, is one of the *reges*); as the establishment of the Republic approaches, equivocation returns.[46]

Towards the end of the list of kings comes Ancus Marcius, *iactantior Ancus/nunc quoque iam nimium gaudens popularibus auris* ('the more boastful Ancus, even now already rejoicing too much in the breezes of the people', 815–16). If any king had a name for being a *popularis*, it was not Ancus Marcius, but Servius Tullius (Dion. Hal. *Ant. Rom.* 4.8.3). Virgil's licence is explained by his wish to associate the individual with the 'popular' family of the Marcii, who claimed descent from the king.[47] E. Badian, in connection with our passage, refers to one M' Marcius, the first man to distribute grain to the plebs, as well as to another early member of the family, who introduced a law to restrain usury. As he says, 'the later Marcii obviously prided themselves on early *populares* in the family'.[48] Even such a man as L. Marcius Philippus (cos. 91) could exploit the family tradition: as tribune *c.* 104 BCE he acted in an ostentatiously demagogic fashion, and attempted to introduce a *lex agraria*.[49] Another member of the family, Q. Marcius Rex (cos. 68), was outside Rome with his army in 63

---

[46] Cf. Büchner (1958), 1391: 'the second part, which reviews further characters, kings after Romulus and heroes of the republic, beside the pride also displays every dubious element of Roman history'.
[47] Suet. *Iul.* 6.1, *ab Anco Marcio sunt Marcii Reges*. See here Wiseman (1974), 154.
[48] Badian in "Discussion" to Skutsch (1972), 34–5.   [49] Münzer (1930), 1562.

BCE when he received a letter from the rebel Manlius, asking for redress of grievances. In Sallust's account, Manlius appeals to the aristocracy's tradition of giving succour to the plebs—either Manlius or Sallust judged Marcius an appropriate person to whom to address the following words: *saepe maiores uostrum miseriti plebis Romanae decretis suis inopiae eius opitulati sunt* ('often your ancestors took pity on the Roman plebs and came to the succour of their poverty with their decrees', *Cat.* 33.2). Thus, lightly, Virgil touches upon a theme in the political life of his people, identifying a king with a family, and a family with a dubious political tradition.

The tension becomes acute as we turn to the Tarquins, linked with Brutus, who introduce a passage of notorious ambivalence, compounded of awed pride and shock (817–23):

> uis et Tarquinios reges animamque superbam
> ultoris Bruti, fascisque uidere receptos?
> consulis imperium hic primus saeuasque securis
> accipiet, natosque pater noua bella mouentis
> ad poenam pulchra pro libertate uocabit,
> infelix, utcumque ferent ea facta minores:
> uincet amor patriae laudumque immensa cupido.

> Do you want to see the Tarquin kings and the proud spirit of Brutus, the avenger, and the rods taken back? He will be the first to receive the consul's supreme command and savage axes, and when his sons set new wars in motion he as father will summon them to punishment on behalf of fair liberty, unfortunate man, however later people will speak of those actions: love of the fatherland will win out, and immeasurable lust for praise.

Here the theme of the continuity of the *gens* is at its most powerful. Also at its most evident, for the associations made by Virgil's contemporaries between the assassin of Julius Caesar and his supposed ancestor, the first consul, are well-established facts.[50] With a number of touches Virgil draws our attention to the similarities linking the two deeds, at the beginning and the end of the *res publica*. The essential truth was stated by F. Fletcher, in his note on *superbam*:

> Here as applied to the spirit of Brutus it is a reminder that arrogance is not a monopoly of 'tyrants' (*reges*). None of Virgil's readers could fail to think of the descendant, another *ultor Brutus*,[51] whose intellectual arrogance they had known. He had also violated natural ties in the belief that he was serving his country: the killing of Julius Caesar, like the execution of his own sons by

---

[50] Cf. MacMullen (1966), 8–10.   [51] Cf. Luc. 5.207, *ultores Brutos*; 9.17–18.

the elder Brutus, was an act praised by some and blamed by others, and Virgil's comment in 822–3 may be applied equally to either action.[52]

Certainly the tyrannicide was the object of a considerable industry of hagiography, which began soon after his death, and which is exemplified for us in Plutarch's *Life*.[53] Not all approved, however: Brutus was far less popular than Cato as an *exemplum*, and controversy concentrated on the clash between two types of *pietas*, between patriotism and humanity.[54] Valerius Maximus states the case against most forcibly (6.4.5):[55]

> Brutus suarum prius uirtutum quam patriae parentis parricida—uno enim facto et illas in profundum praecipitauit et omnem nominis sui memoriam inexpiabili detestatione perfudit.

> Brutus, rather the murderer of his own virtues than of the parent of the fatherland—for with one deed he both hurled those virtues into the abyss and drenched the entire memory of his name with irredeemable loathing.

Virgil's language enmeshes us in the same dilemma of judgement: *uincet amor patriae laudumque immensa cupido* ('love of the fatherland will win out, and immeasurable lust for praise', 823). The phrasing invites the reader's decision: do we accord or withhold the *laudes* which Brutus wishes to have? A modern reader perhaps starts at the notion of attributing desire for praise to the second Brutus, but even Cicero could grumble on this score, while Appian attributes to Brutus the desire for δόξα ('glory').[56]

Two lines, in which the pressure does not altogether relent, separate us from Caesar and Pompey, and the civil wars (824–5):

> quin Decios Drusosque procul saeuumque securi
> aspice Torquatum et referentem signa Camillum.

> Indeed, look at the Decii and the Drusi, and far off, savage with his axe, Torquatus, and Camillus bringing back the standards.

'These names', observes Horsfall, 'and not Brutus' alone, sandwiched between the great monumental blocks of the Kings and Caesar and Pompey must be of particular importance.'[57] Virgil uses the same device

---

[52] F. Fletcher (1941), 91. Similarly Austin (1977) ad loc.; Jackson Knight (1966), 368; R.D. Williams (1972), 212–13.
[53] Cf. MacMullen (1966), 18.   [54] Cf. Litchfield (1914), 41–2; Wistrand (1981), 5–6.
[55] Cf. [Sen.] *Oct.* 498–9; Sen. *Ben.* 2.20.1–2.
[56] *B Civ.* 2.114; cf. Cic. *Att.* 14.11.1; 12.2; 14.3.5. For evidence of the tyrannicide's *anima superba* see Cic. *Att.* 6.1.7, 14.20.5; Plut. *Brut.* 34.7–8, 45.9. But he was a complex character (Syme (1939), 58; MacMullen (1966), 6), and could be very charming: cf. Cic. *Att.* 14.17A.5.
[57] Horsfall (1982), 12.

as we observed in *Georgics* 2, whereby, in a panegyrical context, a suspect or disquieting name is inserted between two more straightforwardly praiseworthy names. In the *Georgics* passage, the unsettling name had been that of the Marii; here, there are two names, of the Drusi, and of Torquatus, 'savage with his axe'. The parallelism of effect is powerfully marked by the fact that in the *Georgics* and the *Aeneid* it is the *same names* which act as a frame. In the *Aeneid* we have the Decii and Camillus bracketing the Drusi and Torquatus in the middle, and in the *Georgics* the same thing happens: *Decios Marios magnosque Camillos* . . . (2.169).

In the case of the Drusi, Servius saw the link with Augustus' wife Livia, who was one of the Livii Drusi.[58] Such an association may well be felt, while Horsfall's identification of a 'Gallic' connection in the vicinity is also very appealing.[59] But our context, as in the *Georgics*, is one of names listed as *exempla*, and we must look to other similar contexts in order to establish the full tone of the allusion. As Horsfall remarks, 'the alliteration of *Decios Drusosque* is striking. Virgil highlights the strength of the gens.'[60] The juxtaposition is very important, in just the same way as the juxtaposition of *Decios Marios* in *G.* 2.169. The Decii were father and son, with the son following exactly in the footsteps of the father;[61] in Lucan, the corpse sees them together, as here: *uidi Decios, natumque patremque,/lustrales bellis animas* ('I saw the Decii, son and father, spirits that appeased the gods in war', 6.785–6). The Drusi of this exemplary tradition were also father and son. Here, however, the son did not live up to the standard of the father, but fell off disastrously, and became a byword for degeneration. The senior M. Livius Drusus (tr. pl. 122, cos. 112) was the principal enemy of C. Gracchus, and was praised in the optimate tradition.[62] His son (tr. pl. 91) was excoriated, often in direct comparison. Cicero quotes the words of C. Carbo (tr. pl. 90) (*Orat.* 213):

> o M. Druse, patrem appello, tu dicere solebas sacram esse rem publicam, quicumque eam uiolauissent ab omnibus esse ei poenas persolutas. patris dictum sapiens temeritas filii comprobauit.
>
> Oh Marcus Drusus—it is the father I am calling to—you used to say that the republic was sacred, and that whoever had violated her had been

---

[58] Norden (1934) (followed by Austin (1977)) refers us to M. Livius Salinator, victor at the Metaurus in 207 BCE. But this man was not a Drusus, and the distinction was drawn (Suet. *Tib.* 3.1–2). The Horace passage which Norden and Austin cite refers to the other consul of the year, C. Claudius Nero, ancestor of Horace's addressee: *quid debeas, o Roma, Neronibus,/testis Metaurus flumen . . ., Carm.* 4.4.37–8.

[59] Horsfall (1982), 13.   [60] Ibid., 12.

[61] A grandson is occasionally mentioned as having also sacrificed himself in *deuotio* (Cic. *Fin.* 2.61).

[62] Plut. *C. Gracch.* 8.4. The truth will have been less straightforward: see Stockton (1979), 192, 200 n.15.

punished by everybody. The wise saying of the father was verified by the rashness of the son.

The name Drusus does not occur in a laudatory context in lists of *exempla*. The reference is always to the younger Drusus, and it is always condemnatory, linking him with other notorious demagogues, such as the Gracchi, Saturninus, Sulpicius and Cinna (*Rhet. Her.* 4.31, Cic. *Vat.* 23). The force of Virgil's reference is shown by Lucan's adaptation; in the underworld, the corpse had seen *laetantis, popularia nomina, Drusos/legibus immodicos* ('rejoicing *popularis* names, the Drusi, immoderate in their legislation', 6.795–6). This theme of sons falling short of their fathers' standards is one which Virgil will pick up later in the parade, in speaking of the Gracchi (842); it is the theme with which he had first experimented in *Georgics* 2.

There were many things to say about the great Torquatus. Virgil chooses his execution of his son, so that we see Torquatus alone, in the singular, after Decii, father and son, and Drusi, father and son. The language takes us back to Brutus' like deed (*saeuumque securi*, 'savage with his axe', 824; *saeuasque securis*, 'savage axes', 819). When Camillus follows Torquatus, we may feel that Virgil's dubieties are on the ebb; but immediately Anchises shows us the shades of Caesar and Pompey (826–35). Their calamitous wars are too painful to be described directly. Anchises beseeches both of them to abstain (832–3). He prays then to Caesar to relent first (834–5):

> tuque prior, tu parce, genus qui ducis Olympo,
> proice tela manu, sanguis meus!

> And you first, you be sparing, who trace your descent from Olympus, throw away your weapons, my blood offspring!

This plea is sometimes seen as a reference to Caesar's famous *clementia*.[63] Certainly Caesar was *clemens*, but only once he had begun the war; here Anchises is begging his descendant to lay down his arms first, before Pompey does.

If Augustus is the central peak of the first half of the speech, the glimpse of the civil wars is the peak of the second.[64] In a manner by now familiar, Virgil then veers away from these horrors into a celebratory passage (836–46); but it is possible that even here there are traces of civil strife to be recognised.

The victories over Greece come next, with a couple of easy riddles of identity for the reader to answer (*ille* is L. Mummius at 836, L. Aemilius Paullus at 838). At 841 a riddle of more moment may be presented:

---

[63] Thus Austin (1977) ad loc.  [64] Cf. R.D. Williams (1972), 208–9.

> quis te, magne Cato, tacitum aut te, Cosse, relinquat?
>
> Who would leave you, great Cato, unmentioned, or you, Cossus?

The commentators tell us that Cato the Censor is meant here. In Virgil's time he could be called *Cato maior*, 'Cato the elder'.[65] When Anchises addresses someone as '*great* Cato', then the positive form of the adjective, if it prompts thoughts of the comparative, is perhaps disconcerting. Was Cato Censorius then *greater* than Cato Uticensis? Which Cato *was* the greater?[66] When seen from this angle, the question form becomes energised: the question of whether to leave Cato the younger unmentioned was, after all, not untopical.[67]

Following Cato and Cossus comes *Gracchi genus* ('the family of Gracchus', 842). The phrase has caused difficulty,[68] but once again the *gens* is the focus,[69] and once more, as in the case of the Drusi, the exemplary tradition directs our attention to the degeneration of demagogic sons from optimate fathers. Ti. Sempronius Gracchus (cos. 177), father of the tribunes, was a model for later generations.[70] It is noteworthy that although Cicero speaks of him with warm praise, he never includes the name of Gracchus in his frequent lists of exemplary names—except once, and then specifically, in the singular, in strict chronological sequence, so that this representative of the family alone could be understood (*Nat. D.* 2.165). The name was simply too loaded, tied in men's minds to the sons. Thus Cicero, in the *De provinciis consularibus*, mentions Ti. Gracchus, and hastily assures his audience that he did not mean the tribune: *an Ti. Gracchus (patrem dico, cuius utinam filii ne degenerassent a grauitate patria!)* . . . ('Or Ti. Gracchus (I mean the father—and if only his sons had not fallen off from the seriousness of their father!) . . . ', 18). These words illustrate the fixed attitude of the exemplary tradition.[71] Once more, Lucan's adaptation is an aid to understanding. The corpse sees Drusi and Gracchi together (6.795–6):

> uidi ego laetantis, popularia nomina, Drusos
> legibus immodicos ausosque ingentia Gracchos.

---

[65] At least, such was the title Cicero gave his essay on old age (*Att.* 14.21.3; *Amic.* 4; *Off.* 1.151), and there seems to be an allusion to the usage in a punning passage of Lucan (6.789–90). How regular this nomenclature was remains uncertain; Cicero may only have used the title *Cato Maior* to avoid confusion with his *Cato* (on Uticensis). I am grateful to Jonathan Powell for help on this point.

[66] Ahl (1976), 140 first pointed out the problem.

[67] It is typical of Virgil's manner in this section that the unproblematic Cossus should be mentioned in the same breath; cf. esp. 824–5. [But see now Vol. 2, Chapter 1, n.42]

[68] See Ahl (1976), 140–1.   [69] Cf. von Albrecht (1967), 168.

[70] See Norden (1934) on 842; Münzer (1921), 1409.

[71] Cf. Cic. *Off.* 2.43, *Fin.* 4.65, *Har. resp.* 41; [Sen.] *Oct.* 882–9 (this last passage links the Gracchi brothers and the younger Drusus as examples of demagogic degeneration within a family).

I saw *popularis* names rejoicing, the Drusi, immoderate in their legislation, and the Gracchi, who dared huge things.

The mother of the tribunes was the daughter of Scipio Africanus Maior, and the family of the Scipiones is the next to appear (842–3):

> geminos, duo fulmina belli,
> Scipiadas, cladem Libyae.
>
> twin Scipios, two thunderbolts of war, Libyan downfall.

Who are these Scipiones? As we move through the lines, a number of different suggestions present themselves in sequence, so that the extension of the *gens* is once more brought home to us.

When a Roman listener had heard as far as *geminos, duo fulmina belli,/ Scipiadas*, he would have thought he knew who was meant: the two brothers Gn. Cornelius Scipio Calvus (cos. 222), and P. Cornelius Scipio (cos. 218), respectively uncle and father of Africanus Maior (*geminos* would reinforce the expectation that brothers are being spoken of). This is how Servius takes it, and it is plain from the language of Cicero and Silius that Servius' interpretation has some sanction.[72] Generally, when Cicero speaks *tout court* of *duo Scipiones*, he means these two, as is seen most clearly at *Tusc.* 1.110, where in an exemplary list he has *duos Scipiones, duos Africanos*.[73]

It was Ennius who devised the pun in *fulmina*, and he applied it to Africanus Maior as well as to the two brothers.[74] Virgil picks up this reference to Africanus with *cladem Libyae* ('Libyan downfall'), a phrase that cannot apply to the two brothers, who did not campaign in Africa. All at once the reader is forced into some readjustment. It must then be Africanus—no, not just he, but *both* Africani (*duo fulmina*). The second of these, Africanus Minor, the captor of Carthage, was of course not in Ennius: the historical perspective suddenly opens up, as Virgil squeezes another two generations from the Ennian phrase, extending the reference down to 146, with Africanus Minor's sack of Carthage. In seven words we see the family of the Scipiones over four generations.

And for more than four generations. *cladem Libyae* applies to the disasters which the two Africani *inflicted* upon Libya. Exactly a hundred

---

[72] *Gn. et P. Scipiones, duo fulmina nostri imperii*, Cic. *Parad.* 12; *Balb.* 34; Sil. 7.106–7; *geminos... Scipiadas*, 13.382–4; 15.3–4, 16.87.
[73] See Pease (1955–8) on Cic. *Nat. D.* 3.80; cf. Cic. *Planc.* 25, *quis Gn. et P. Scipionibus, quis Africano?*
[74] See Skutsch (1968), 145–50. Austin (1977) on 842 expounds the pun, which depends on the similarity for the Greek words for 'scipio', 'staff' (σκῆπτρον) and *fulmen*, 'thunderbolt' (σκηπτός).

years after Scipio Aemilianus annihilated Carthage, another Scipio, Q. Caecilius Metellus Pius Scipio, *suffered* a disaster in Libya, as commander of the Republican forces against Caesar in the Thapsus campaign of 46. The African fate of the Scipiones was taken seriously by both sides in the Thapsus campaign,[75] and the varying fortune of bearers of the name became something of a topic; the two Senecas have some fine epigrams on the subject.[76] In particular, Lucan represents Scipio's death in Libya as atonement for the victims of his ancestors,[77] and in his underworld the elder Scipio is seen bewailing the fate of his descendant (6.788–9):

> deplorat Libycis perituram Scipio terris
> infaustam subolem.

> Scipio bewails his unlucky descendant who will perish on Libyan lands.

Lucan seems to be drawing out a latent suggestion of Virgil's text: the Scipiones were associated with more than one disaster in Libya.

If the mention of the Scipiones in Africa does contain ambivalence, then it is the last such citation in the speech. Fabricius, Regulus and the Cunctator round off the exempla in noble fashion. Before Anchises closes, he enunciates his celebrated doctrine of empire, fixing for the Romans the nature and the limits of their achievement (847–53):

> excudent alii spirantia mollius aera
> (credo equidem), uiuos ducent de marmore uultus,
> orabunt causas melius, caelique meatus
> describent radio et surgentia sidera dicent;
> tu regere imperio populos, Romane, memento
> (hae tibi erunt artes), pacique imponere morem,
> parcere subiectis et debellare superbos.

> Others will hammer out breathing bronzes more softly (I am convinced of it), and will lead living faces from the marble; they will plead cases better, and they will chart out the movements of heaven with a rod and describe the rising constellations: you, Roman, remember to rule the peoples with empire (these will be your arts), and to fix a settled order on pacification, spare the surrendered and war down the proud.

Griffin has best clarified the way in which these words hold back as much as they offer, deny as much as they assert.[78] Many admirable forms of artistic and intellectual endeavour must be spurned in the cause of political and

---

[75] Suet. *Iul.* 59; Plut. *Caes.* 52.2; Cass. Dio 42.58.    [76] *Suas.* 7.7; *Epist.* 24.10.
[77] 6.309–11, *nec ... Poenorumque umbras placasset sanguine fuso/Scipio.*
[78] Griffin (1985), 169–70, 195–6.

military preeminence. Yet, of course, the irony is not inert, as we hear Anchises proclaim that the Romans must abjure a faith in ideals of artistic attainment, when the very existence of the poem in which he is a character is witness to the power of that faith.[79]

We think we have come to the end, but Anchises resumes, showing us the great Marcellus of the Hannibalic War, leading us into the lament for the young Marcellus who had recently died. There is no question of seeing this lament as a late addition to an existing parade. The melancholy coda was part of the basic conception from the very beginning.[80] Augustus' designated heir receives high praise, but waste and futility are the ruling tones. The formal cast of Anchises' speech throughout has been that of a prophecy, and here at the end that prophesying form becomes activated, as the perspective makes itself, for the poet and his readers, genuinely forward-looking. Marcellus had embodied the future,[81] a future which is painted gloriously (872–81), and then taken away from us, unrealised. As Anchises closes, scattering flowers in his descendant's honour (883–6), the contemporary of Virgil is left suspended, his attention all forward, all expectant: what, then, will follow Marcellus? Will the divine Augustus, as promised, be able to carry us through?

When, shortly afterwards, Aeneas comes to leave the underworld (893–8), his departure is described in terms which recall the philosophical myths introducing the parade. Here we are much indebted to Tarrant, who has clarified the longstanding difficulties of the gates of horn and ivory by setting their imagery in the context of the Platonic doctrines of the soul.[82] Aeneas leaves by the gate of the *falsa insomnia* ('false dreams') because he is still alive, still a prisoner of the body and of the illusions of the 'real' world which the body is doomed to inhabit.[83] Tarrant is completely convincing when he goes on to draw more general conclusions on the effect of such a setting for the view of mortal achievements in the historical vision: 'Virgil seems to have found Plato's view of the physical world as a mere shadow of a purer world a useful structure of thought by which to express his own sense of the evanescence of mortal aspirations.'[84]

We have been led by this framing device back to the unresolved questions which occupied us at the beginning, concerning the paradox

---

[79] Cf. Johnson (1976), 108.
[80] Convincingly argued by Otis (1963), 303–4 and Horsfall (1982), 15–16.
[81] Cf. von Albrecht (1967), 178–9; Tracey (1975), 38.   [82] Tarrant (1982).
[83] Cf. Cic. *Somn.* 14, *immo uero ... hi uiuunt, qui e corporum uinculis tamquam e carcere euolauerunt, uestra uero quae dicitur uita mors est* ('actually in fact those are alive who have flown out of the chains of their bodies as if out of a prison, and your "life", as it is called, is death').
[84] Tarrant (1982), 54.

presented by Virgil's use of the otherworldly myths of philosophy to introduce a show of mundane achievement, and a celebration of *gloria*.

The parade of heroes exhibits mighty national and individual accomplishments. It also covers civil war, *populares* and demagogues, fathers executing sons, the disappearance of once-great cities, the falling-off of families, the stifling of promise, the shunning of art, the hunger for personal glory: in short, the political life's intolerable demands on human nature, together with the 'evanescence' (to use Tarrant's fine phrase) 'of mortal aspirations'. The insistent stress on *gloria* is not only remarkable in this 'philosophical' context; it is altogether striking in a poem that is so preoccupied with the great contemporary ethical shift in attitudes to *gloria*, away from the ruinous competition and egoism that was the essence of traditional *gloria*.[85]

The 'Platonic' setting creates two principal effects (if we may be so blunt in fixing the passage's diffused force). The personal aims and sufferings of the politicians on view are put into a disconcerting perspective once we have been invited to see them as characters in a Platonic myth, once we have been reminded of the moral exhortations for which Plato's myths were a vehicle, turning us away from the vanity of this world, and especially from the vain, hollow harshness of public life. Further, the setting presents the Roman state as the τέλος ('end goal') of the way in which the world is ordered, while making it difficult or impossible for us to decide on a clear response. Rome *is* celebrated by the device, but the reader has been given the perspective of a Platonist, and it is bewildering to be promised an elaborate revelation which ultimately declares that there is in fact nothing more than the mixed uncertainties of actual history. From the standpoint of a moral philosopher, the achievements of the Roman state do not have a self-evident importance. When Virgil leads us to expect a Platonic vision, and deceives our expectation, a complex rearrangement of priorities ensues. He gives us instead something powerful and something of one kind of beauty; but when he denies his poem and his audience the beauty and the consolation of the myths of philosophy, immortality and redemption, this formal and aesthetic exclusion mirrors and recreates the exclusion which is the lot of the chief character in the poem, and of the poem's audience in the world.[86]

---

[85] On this see Earl (1967), 59–97 (a reference I owe to I.M.LeM. Du Quesnay). Note too (as Professor Reeve pointed out in discussion) how the next book opens with the *fama*, *honos*, and *nomen* of Aeneas' nurse Caieta—*si qua est ea gloria* (7.4).

[86] Cf. esp. Griffin (1985), 169–70 and Johnson (1976), 105–11 for an excellent discussion of Virgil's use of perspective here.

This world is indeed what concerns Virgil here. The very elaboration of the picture of the underworld has led many to speculate on the religious sentiment or message to be found there, but as far as the elements of religion or philosophy are concerned, I take the truth to be more or less as Servius stated it: *sectis philosophorum poetae pro qualitate negotiorum semper utuntur* ('poets make use of the schools of the philosophers according to the essential nature of the matter in hand').[87] In the meeting of Aeneas and Anchises, the 'essential nature of the matter in hand' is not a religious revelation, but an image of the nature of Rome and of the political process, an image of the life of the Roman statesman, or of any such statesman.

## Appendix: Lucan's Underworld

Lucan's hell, like Virgil's, has an image of the nature of Rome. Lucan has been a valuable aid in the discussion so far; an investigation of his underworld, interesting and rewarding in itself, will give further support to the reading of Virgil suggested here, by showing that Lucan recognised Virgil's equivocations, and seized upon them as his point of departure.

When scholars compare Lucan's underworld scene with Virgil's, they represent Lucan as the inverse of Virgil, negating the glorious vision of Rome's history with a pessimistic one.[88] Of course, there is a certain amount of solid truth in such a picture, as is well brought out by Bramble's pithy juxtaposition: 'Where ... in Vergil's underworld scene we have the founder of Rome, a venerable Sibyl, and a parade of future heroes, in Lucan's νέκυια ["necromancy"] we find a coward, a witch, and the triumph of Rome's villains. The cycle is at an end: decay replaces birth, discord follows greatness.'[89] By this perspective, Lucan splits up Virgil's succession of great heroes, substituting two opposed camps: the good shades lament, and the wicked shades gloat over, the advent of the civil wars (6.779–99).

Such a reading, however, in glossing over Virgil's qualifications, misrepresents his parade of heroes, and hence inevitably misrepresents Lucan's adaptation. Within the framework of the epics, Virgil's catalogue of heroes looks forward, while Lucan's, more regularly, looks back. This chronological orientation is operative in a more profound sense as well. The direction of Virgil's passage carries our expectation forward to the future,[90] to the uncertain hope that Augustus may be able to overcome the latent flaws in

---

[87] On *Aen.* 10.467; cf. Serv. on *Aen.* 1.227; Ti. Claudius Donatus 1.6.1–5 (Georgii).
[88] Thus Guillemin (1951); Paoletti (1963); Narducci (1979), 54–62.  [89] Bramble (1982), 543.
[90] Cf. von Albrecht (1967), 178–80. Panegyrics naturally look to the future, to the influencing of future events: see Kennedy (1972), 260.

Roman life and history, and restore the state. Lucan's perspective is entirely backward-looking. By taking up and exploiting Virgil's doubts and misgivings, he can represent Virgil's vision as a chimaera, a false dawn. His presentation again and again magnifies the reservations of Virgil to show that the hoped-for achievement has not come off, to show that Virgil was mistaken in believing that in the balance of flawed and sound the scale could possibly incline to the good. All that is positive in Virgil is stifled and suppressed by Lucan, while the discordant notes in his predecessor's piece become the leitmotif of his own arrangement.

The donnée of Lucan's epic is, as it were, Caesar's refusal to listen to the plea of Anchises (*tuque prior, tu parce, genus qui ducis Olympo,/proice tela manu, sanguis meus!*, 'and you first, you be sparing, who trace your descent from Olympus, throw away your weapons, my blood offspring!', Verg. *Aen.* 6.834–5). Within his underworld picture, Lucan ruthlessly forces Virgil's ambiguities into the open and makes them explicit. In Lucan, we have the Decii and Camillus, weeping in the company of the vanquished good (6.785–6). The Drusi, sandwiched between them in Virgil (824), are shunted nine verses off into the company of the *populares* (6.795). Lucan keeps Virgil's plural (*Drusos*): he may be suggesting that the father was no better than the son, despite the talk of the *boni*.[91] Lucan forces the tribunes out from behind Virgil's covering *Gracchi genus* (842), and brackets them with the Drusi: *uidi ego laetantis, popularia nomina, Drusos/legibus immodicos ausosque ingentia Gracchos* ('I saw *popularis* names rejoicing, the Drusi, immoderate in their legislation, and the Gracchi, who dared huge things', 6.796–7). In Lucan, both Drusi and Gracchi are in the company of Catiline (793). This ultimate bogey-man of ruling-class mythology is not named in *Aeneid* 6, but he does appear on the shield in Book 8, in Tartarus (8.668). Lucan is relocating the Drusi and Gracchi, placing them where they should 'really' have been in Virgil—with Catiline.[92]

Virgil's poised ambivalence concerning the first and last Brutus is obliterated. In Lucan's underworld, the first Brutus is the only happy good shade, for he foresees his descendant's assassination of Caesar (6.791–2). In the poem generally, there are no doubts about the sanctity and justice of the tyrannicide's act (5.207–8, 9.17–18), although Lucan is certainly aware of the controversy: as Septimius prepares to kill Pompey, Lucan exclaims, *scelus hoc quo nomine dicent/qui Bruti dixere nefas?* ('what

---

[91] So claims the tradition used by Tacitus: *Gracchi et Saturnini turbatores plebis, nec minor largitor nomine senatus Drusus* ('the Gracchi and Saturnini, stirrers-up of the plebs, and no less lavish in the name of the Senate, Drusus', *Ann.* 3.27).

[92] I thank Stephen Hinds for pointing out the role of Catiline to me.

are they going to call this deed, the people who called Brutus' deed an abomination?', 8.609–10). Lucan has, like Virgil, the great names of Scipio and Cato, but no glorious resonance attaches to them, for their function is merely to mourn the deaths their descendants will suffer in civil war (6.788–90):

> deplorat Libycis perituram Scipio terris
> infaustam subolem; maior Carthaginis hostis
> non seruituri maeret Cato fata nepotis.
>
> Scipio bewails his unlucky descendant who will perish on Libyan lands; Cato, a greater enemy of Carthage, mourns the fate of his descendant who will not be a slave.

Note the characteristic play on *maior*: Cato 'maior' is a 'maior' *hostis* to Carthage than Scipio. And is that Scipio Maior or Minor?[93]

Outside Lucan's underworld vision, this approach persists, as we have already seen. Virgil advances the names of the vanished towns of the Latin League with a poignant blend of antiquarian pride and commiseration (6.773–6); to Lucan, they signify *Italiae solitudo* ('the desolation of Italy') and no more (7.391–6). Romulus is a figure of *almost* undiluted grandeur in Virgil; in Lucan's poem his bloody kingship is emblematic of the Roman urge to fratricide (1.95–7). Finally, the wars between Caesar and Pompey are a fragment only of Virgil's picture, which may possibly be subsumed in the whole, but to Lucan the battle of Pharsalus is the very τέλος ('end goal') of Roman history, not to be outgrown or atoned for (7.638–41):

> maius ab hac acie quam quod sua saecula ferrent
> volnus habent populi; plus est quam uita salusque
> quod perit: in totum mundi prosternimur aeuum.
> uincitur his gladiis omnis quae seruiet aetas.
>
> The peoples of the world have a wound from this battle too great for their own epoch to endure; it is more than life and safety that perishes: we are flattened for the whole lifespan of the world. By these swords is conquered the whole future age, fated to slavery.

The power of Lucan's eloquence need not command our assent. He had the easier case to argue, and, in dealing merely with the end of one political system, he had a smaller scope than Virgil, who dealt with the entirety of

---

[93] Such play appears irresistible. Note Virgil's arrangement in *Georgics* 2.169–70: *magnosque Camillos,/ Scipiadas duros bello et te, maxime Caesar.* That is, *magni, Maior, Minor, maximus*: 'big, bigger, lesser, biggest'.

what Rome stood for, and with the perennial nature of life in the public arena, exposed to the historical process. Nonetheless, it is salutary to recognise the force of some of Lucan's censure of the *Aeneid*. With considerable justification, Lucan saw that the main impetus of Jupiter's prophecy in Book 1, of the parade in Book 6, and of the shield in Book 8—indeed, a principal tendency in the entire work—was to glorify the figure of Augustus, and to justify the submerging of Republican tradition in his person.[94] Lucan deserves our attention when he protests that 'the Republic' cannot simply be appropriated in this way. There was no spirit of the Republic to be extracted. Lucan's poem illustrates the truth of Ennius' dictum, that the Republic was not an essence, but a product of men and institutions (*Ann.* 156 Sk.):

> moribus antiquis stat res Romana uirisque.

> Through ancient customs stands the Roman state, and men.

---

[94] See Horsfall (1976), 89 on this process (of which the *Aeneid* is only one contemporary example).

CHAPTER 6

# *Following after Hercules, in Virgil and Apollonius*[1]

In creating a Hercules for his *Aeneid*, Virgil had a great deal of material to hand, even in the field of epic alone. The archaic period saw many epic poems on Heracles, of varying length, covering his whole life, or episodes from it: we have half a dozen titles, some with fragments, of which the *Heracleia* of Herodotus' uncle Panyassis was the best known.[2] Later times saw little slackening in production. Aristotle refers dismissively to 'those who write an epic about Heracles or about Theseus' (1451a21–2), while the Hellenistic period leaves testimony to the existence of, again, something over half a dozen epic poems on the hero.[3] Doubtless some poems have left no trace at all. Since they are lost virtually in their entirety, we cannot really assess the contribution these poems made to the *Aeneid* (although I shall be making some claims for the so-called *Shield of Hercules*, preserved in the Hesiodic corpus). One epic poem does survive intact, however, in which Heracles figures prominently, and that is the *Argonautica* of Apollonius of Rhodes—the only epic, in fact, that survives entire out of the multitude produced between Homer and Virgil. Even amongst Hellenists, Apollonius has only recently begun to emerge from his unjustifiably underrated position, and students of Virgil, generally speaking, still tend to be insufficiently alive to the pervasive influence exerted upon Virgil by this very fine poet.[4]

As an introduction, and a demonstration of just how far-reaching and systematic Virgil's adaptations of Apollonius can be, let us consider the

---

[1] For their help and criticism I thank Dr. R.L. Hunter, Dr. N.M. Horsfall, Dr. W.S.M. Nicoll, Mr. J.G. Howie, Mr. R.M. Pinkerton and Dr. J.Y. Nadeau.
[2] Huxley (1969), 99–112, 177–88.
[3] Lloyd-Jones and Parsons (1983), nos. 393–4, 669, 715, 948, 1166 (and 1168?).
[4] The words of Knauer (1964), 56 n.2 are still [1986] valid: 'incidentally, despite a number of preparatory works ... the influence of Apollonius is not yet securely understood'. [When I gave a version of this paper to the Virgil Society in 1986 a graduate student introduced himself to me afterwards and informed me that he was in fact writing a dissertation to fill this gap: see now Nelis (2001).]

section of the *Aeneid* which most extensively concerns Hercules: Aeneas' visit to Pallanteum, the site of Rome.

Even as Aeneas' ships make their way up the Tiber, an Apollonian note is immediately sounded (8.91–2). The gleam of the men's shields comes from Apollonius' description of the very first sailing of Argo,[5] while the whole atmosphere recalls Apollonius, through a Catullan filter: this is the first time a ship has ever passed here (cf. *Argon.* 4.316–22: Catull. 64.1–18). One may also be reminded of the end of *Argonautica* 2 (itself adapted from *Odyssey* 5.451–3), where the Argonauts finally arrive at Colchis, and row at night up the river, which makes way before them (1264–6)—a hint magnified by Virgil, who has Tiber cooperate with the Trojans, easing his flow and aiding their passage (8.86–9). Aeneas, like Jason, is arriving at the true 'goal' of the quest, at the τέλος (although, characteristically of Virgil, Aeneas does not know that Pallanteum is Rome: he arrives at his τέλος in ignorance). The allusion to Rome as the true τέλος of the expedition is reinforced at the end of the book, as Aeneas looks at his divine armour. The cuirass is compared to a dark cloud that kindles with the rays of the sun, and gleams far and wide (8.622–3); the simile is taken from Apollonius' description of the golden fleece, as Jason looks at it for the first time (4.125–6).

Aeneas arrives as Evander's people are performing the annual celebration of their deliverance by Hercules from the monster Cacus. King Evander tells Aeneas of how he remembers the visit of Anchises to Arcadia, when Evander was young, when the first stage of manhood was covering his cheeks with the flower of youth (160). He makes a treaty with the Trojans—a *foedus* (169). He invites Aeneas to join in the feasting, and tells him the story of how Hercules liberated them from Cacus, on his return from the far West, with the cattle of Geryon: *attulit et nobis aliquanto optantibus aetas/auxilium aduentumque dei* ('eventually time brought to our prayers the help and the arrival of a god', 200–1). Aeneas is another god-sent deliverer from evil, as Evander recognises further on: *fatis huc te poscentibus adfers* ('you come here at the behest of fate', 477). The people of Evander fight continuous war with the Latins (55, 473–4), and in defeating the Latins, Aeneas will emulate Hercules, performing a similar—indeed, a greater—deed of preservation. King Evander promises to send his son along with Aeneas on the expedition.

At the beginning of *Argonautica* 2, Polydeuces has his celebrated boxing-match with Amycus, brutish king of the brutish Bebryces. Amycus is killed,

---

[5] *Argon.* 1.544–5; cf. Gransden (1976) on *Aen.* 8.91–2; Hügi (1952), 75. Mr. Howie informs me that Apollonius goes back to Homer for the gleam of weapons as a portent of victory: cf. Krischer (1971), 36–8.

and his people shattered in a pitched battle. Some 600 lines further on, the Argonauts arrive in the land of King Lycus and his people, the Mariandyni, the neighbours of the Bebryces. News of the killing has already arrived. Apollonius says (2.755–8):

> ἀλλὰ καὶ ἀρθμὸν ἔθεντο μετὰ σφίσι τοῖο ἕκητι,
> αὐτὸν δ' ὥστε θεὸν Πολυδεύκεα δεξιόωντο,
> πάντοθεν ἀγρόμενοι· ἐπεὶ ἦ μάλα τοίγ' ἐπὶ δηρὸν
> ἀντιβίην Βέβρυξιν ὑπερφιάλοις πολέμιζον.

> The Mariandyni made a treaty with the Argonauts because of their killing of Amycus, and Polydeuces himself they welcomed as a god, flocking in from all around—for they themselves had been waging war for a long time with the overbearing Bebryces.

King Lycus entertains the Argonauts with feasting. He tells them a story of how Heracles delivered his people from troublesome neighbours. Heracles had passed by on his return from the far East, with the girdle of the Amazonian queen, at a time when Lycus was just starting to get the down of manhood on his cheeks (779). Heracles subdued, for Lycus' father, the Mysians, the Phrygians, the Bithynians and the Paphlagonians (786–91). Now Lycus says that it was not without the will of the gods that Polydeuces waged war on the Bebryces.[6] He will set up a temple for Castor and Polydeuces, and dedicate land to them, as to gods (806–10). Finally, Lycus will send his son along with the Argonauts on their expedition.[7]

These are very provocative parallels, and there are others in the area.[8] The extent to which these parallels are embedded in Book 8 of the *Aeneid* is shown by the way Virgil invites the reader, in his characteristic fashion, more familiar to us from his Homeric adaptations, to supplement the text by reference to the model. Most conspicuous and important is the claim to divinity, founded on the basis of emulating Hercules, who won his immortal reward as a benefactor of mankind, an ἀλεξίκακος, a 'warder-off of evil'. This claim is never *explicitly* asserted for Aeneas in Book 8, but the many hints in this direction are strongly reinforced when the reader is invited to read in, from the Apollonian model, the explicit and overt references to the way in which Polydeuces receives divine honours as a result of following the example of Heracles.

---

[6] The text of 796–8 is disputed: *Aen.* 8.200–1 and 477 appear to show that Virgil took the passage as the scholiast does, and I translate what I think Virgil's text would have been. The account of the scholion in Fränkel (1968), 234 is remarkable special pleading.
[7] Noted by the standard commentators.
[8] Note, in particular, the structural similarities between the hymns in *Argon.* 2.700–19 and *Aen.* 8.287–302: see, e.g., Gransden (1976) ad loc.

As always with Virgil, however, recognition of similarity immediately provokes awareness of departure and difference. Both Aeneas and the Argonauts are following in the footsteps of Heracles, but in the *Argonautica* Heracles is personally known to the listeners as well as to the speaker; he was the Argonauts' dear and trusted shipmate, and when they meet King Lycus, not two months have gone by since he was accidentally left ashore on the coast of Mysia. Aeneas has never met Hercules. To him, Hercules is a remote figure, and a Greek—what is more, a Greek who sacked Troy, as we are allusively reminded in Evander's first speech (157–8), and as the Salii commemorate in their hymn (290–1):

> ut bello egregias idem disiecerit urbes,
> Troiamque Oechaliamque.
>
> [they sang] how he also wrecked outstanding cities, both Troy and Oechalia.

Such difference impels us to inquire more closely into what Virgil is making of Apollonius' Heracles. Indeed, the admiring reaction of such an abnormally sensitive and intelligent critic as Virgil should make us wish to inquire more closely into what Apollonius himself is making of Heracles. Heracles was, after all, *the* most ambivalent creature in Greek myth. He was ambivalence itself—*heros–theos*, receiving divine *and* heroic sacrifice in cult,[9] lying, as M.S. Silk well puts it, 'on the margins between human and divine, [occupying] the no-man's-land that is also no-god's-land, ... a marginal, transitional, or, better, *interstitial* figure'.[10] That is, he occupies the interstices, the zones of transition, neither one thing nor the other. He may be the hero in epic, tragedy, or comedy. He is at home in the shared feast,[11] sometimes as a glutton, and he is also famous for violating the holy laws of hospitality. He is the ultimate expression of Greek virility, and spends a year as the slave of a woman, the Asiatic Omphale. He is physical strength incarnate, and also a philosopher's paradigm of intellectual resource and self-control. He is the great civiliser, who wears the skin of an animal. His very name is a paradox: the glory of Hera, the glory of the goddess who persecuted him all his life. It would be surprising if an artist of Apollonius' wit and zest failed to make something of this remarkable figure.[12]

We are not disappointed. Even the very first mention of Heracles, in the catalogue of Argonauts, repays close attention as an index of Apollonius' high craft, and as a marker of certain of his basic preoccupations (1.122–3):

---

[9] Cf. Burkert (1985), 208.   [10] Silk (1985), 6 (original emphasis).   [11] Burkert (1985), 211.
[12] On these aspects of Heracles, see Galinsky (1972), 1–39; Burkert (1985), 208–11.

Οὐδὲ μὲν οὐδὲ βίην κρατερόφρονος Ἡρακλῆος
πευθόμεθ᾽ Αἰσονίδαο λιλαιομένου ἀθερίξαι.

nor, indeed, nor did the force of strong-minded Heracles, so we hear, make light of Jason's earnest desire [that he come on the expedition].

The first line, as so often in Apollonius, is a tissue of Homeric phraseology, and, as so often, the impact of the line in the third century is one that is uniquely unhomeric, conditioned by the intellectual transformations of the intervening years. Homer, in variations on stock phrases, says βίη Ἡρακλείη, 'the force of Heracles' (*Il.* 2.658, etc.), and he says κρατερόφρονα Ἡρακλῆα, 'strong-minded Heracles' (*Il.* 14.324). He never combines the two. By the time of Apollonius, Heracles had become the stock example of the antithesis between βία ('force') and φρόνησις ('practical wisdom'): sometimes, as in Pindar, the supreme embodiment of both qualities; sometimes, as in the comic tradition, held up as the exemplar of physical force alone; while sometimes, as in Isocrates' *Letter to Philip*, or in certain Stoic and Cynic circles, he was praised for his φρόνησις above all, in preference to his physical might.[13] Antisthenes, regarded as the founder of the Cynic school, wrote three works on Heracles, of which one was entitled Ἡρακλῆς, ἢ περὶ φρονήσεως ἢ ἰσχύος ('Heracles, or On practical wisdom or strength', Diog. Laert. 6.16–18). Shortly before him, Herodorus wrote a seventeen-volume work on the hero, and in one allegorising fragment mention is made of his καρτερικῆς ψυχῆς ('strong spirit') and his θρασυτάτου σώφρονος λογισμοῦ ('mighty, wise rationality').[14] Apollonius' collocation of these Homeric phrases makes them do completely new work, provoking the reader into wondering which of these capacities Heracles will embody in this poem—or will he embody both? In Homer, Heracles had stood for, above all, βία ('force'), and the infatuations of βία.[15] Will he do the same in Apollonius? As we ponder these questions, we may note that the men immediately preceding Heracles in the catalogue are the sons of Bias (118).

Also very important in this line is another Homeric reference. The line recalls very closely a verse from Achilles' great speech in *Iliad* 18, when he finally makes his irrevocable choice between glory or a long life. To his mother he says, 'Let me die soon!' (98). 'Not even', he says, 'not even the might of Heracles escaped death'—οὐδὲ γὰρ οὐδὲ βίη Ἡρακλῆος φύγε Κῆρα (117). To Homer, of course, Heracles was mortal: it was a later

---

[13] Cf. Höistad (1948), 22–73; Galinsky (1972), 23–39, 101–8.
[14] *FGrH* I 218, F14. This Herodorus was an important source for Apollonius, as Richard Hunter points out to me: cf. Desideri (1967).
[15] Galinsky (1972), 10–12.

tradition that inserted a reference to his apotheosis into the Homeric *nekyia*. If there is force in the allusion, it may be that we are alerted to the issue of Heracles' immortality: which way is Apollonius going to go?

The Virgilian density of Apollonius' allusions, then, already provokes questions concerning Heracles' status and significance. Before passing on, we must note that Heracles' participation in the expedition is represented as an interruption of his cycle of labours. He has just captured the Arcadian boar, and he joins the expedition ᾗ ἰότητι παρὲκ νόον Εὐρυσθῆος ('on his own initiative, in opposition to the will/purpose of Eurystheus', 1.130). Since the tradition tells us that Heracles was doomed to serve the will of Eurystheus until the cycle of labours was complete, we recognise that his participation is anomalous. Further, Apollonius' poetic and scholarly tradition was virtually unanimous in saying that Heracles did not actually go on the expedition, since Argo spoke, saying that she could not carry his weight.[16] Apollonius hints at this tradition when Heracles steps into Argo before they set off: καί οἱ ἔνερθε/ποσσίν ὑπεκλύσθη νηὸς τρόπις ('the keel sank down underneath his feet' (1.532–3).[17] Only eight lines before, Argo had given a cry, to start the expedition (1.525). As her keel gives way, we must wonder whether she will give another cry, and whether Heracles will have to get out. All is well, and they set off, but Apollonius has left the impression that Heracles should not really be there. In various ways, it will become increasingly and significantly apparent that Heracles does not belong in this company.[18]

There *may* be a hint at the tradition of the oafish Heracles in the stress on his great weight (although we moderns are out of sympathy with the ancients in finding ridiculous their notion that weight was a proper attribute of gods and heroes). There *may* be a hint at this tradition later on in the first book, when Heracles rows so powerfully that he snaps his oar (1168–71). But the remarkable thing about the picture of Heracles in the first book is Apollonius' fixed concentration on the Heracles of the philosophers, the exponent of φρόνησις ('practical wisdom') and σωφροσύνη ('prudent moderation'). We see him high-mindedly refusing to take command of the expedition, selflessly leaving the job to Jason (1.345–9). Above all, we see him on Lemnos virtually as cast in the Parable of Prodicus, steadfastly choosing Virtue rather than Vice, staying at the ship with a few

---

[16] Cf. Vian and Delage (1976), 44 n.2, and comment on 1.123.
[17] Another hint comes when he breaks his oar (1.1168); see Vian and Delage (1976) ad loc.
[18] He is out of place with these *epigoni*. 1.992 says as much, with a reference to the proem of the Cyclic *Epigoni* (a famous text: cf. Ar. *Pax* 1270): 'but there he was left again with *men of a later generation*' (ἀλλὰ γὰρ αὖθι λέλειπτο σὺν ἀνδράσιν ὁπλοτέροισιν).

companions, rather than stewing in the fleshpots with Jason and the others (1.855–60).¹⁹ Since Apollonius may well be the first writer to bring Heracles to Lemnos, it is all the more striking that Heracles conforms to this model here, when he might have succumbed to the wine and the women that provide so many pitfalls for him in the alternative tradition. It is his self-control which salvages the expedition, as he shames the others into reapplying themselves to their task (1.862–78).

Such is the picture we have of Heracles as we approach the moment where he is finally to leave the expedition, which he should never have been on in the first place. And as the events are introduced which will lead to his separation from the Argonauts, Apollonius fills in, tangentially, the first truly direct references to the 'other Heracles', who has so far been suppressed. The result is a passage, and an impression, of one antithesis after another.

Hylas, Heracles' attendant, goes off to fetch water so that he can get everything quickly ready for Heracles, 'in due order' (κατὰ κόσμον, 1.1210). Such, says Apollonius, were the habits in which Heracles was bringing up the boy (1.1211)—the habits of κόσμος. Well and good. We then learn how Heracles acquired Hylas (1.1212–19):

νηπίαχον τὰ πρῶτα δόμων ἐκ πατρὸς ἀπούρας,
δίου Θειοδάμαντος, ὃν ἐν Δρυόπεσσιν ἔπεφνεν
νηλειῶς, βοὸς ἀμφὶ γεωμόρου ἀντιόωντα.
. . . αὐτὰρ ὁ τόνγε
βοῦν ἀρότην ἤνωγε παρασχέμεν, οὐκ ἐθέλοντα.
ἵετο γὰρ πρόφασιν πολέμου Δρυόπεσσι βαλέσθαι
λευγαλέην, ἐπεὶ οὔ τι δίκης ἀλέγοντες ἔναιον.

He first snatched him as a child from his father's house, from god-like Theiodamas, whom he pitilessly killed in the land of the Dryopes, in a quarrel over a ploughing ox . . . Heracles demanded that he provide a ploughing ox, but Theiodamas was unwilling. For Heracles wanted a grievous pretext for war against the Dryopes, since they lived without a thought for justice.

One antithesis after another. In an act of rape, Heracles seized the boy from his father, whom he killed pitilessly, in a dispute over an ox. It is from this squalid incident that he got his title 'Bouthoinas', 'feaster on oxen', as was

---

¹⁹ Cf. Fränkel (1968), 115; Vian and Delage (1976) on 1.856. A further consideration is pointed out to me by Mr. Howie, remarking that Apollonius cannot afford to have Heracles impregnate a Lemnian, for that might cause difficulties with the claims of the kings of Cyrene, descended from Euphemus (Pind. *Pyth.* 4.256–9).

told in Callimachus' *Aetia* (Book 1, fr. 24). Apollonius conflates here two farmer-killing ox-related episodes which were adjacent in the first book of Callimachus' *Aetia*, doing away with the kindly motive of the second Callimachaean story, in which Heracles asked Theiodamas for food for his little son Hyllus.[20] In Apollonius there is nothing of this. Next, however, we learn that Heracles' real motive was to start a war against the people of Theiodamas, because they cared nothing for justice. After Heracles the bully and glutton, we have Heracles the civiliser and upholder of δίκη ('justice') against barbarism. It is all rather disorientating, especially after the one-sidedly elevated picture we have had so far; and the impression is reinforced when we read of Heracles' frenzied reaction to the news of Hylas' disappearance (1.1261–72). We have now seen both ends of the Heraclean spectrum.

Unwittingly, the Argonauts sail off, leaving behind both Heracles and his friend Polyphemus. At this point we move into territory which is more closely tied in situation to the *Aeneid*, for from now on Heracles is not one of the company. He is someone who the Argonauts talk about, and hear about; in a strange sense, as we shall see, they are following in his footsteps, and the question of the distance—physical and otherwise—between the Argonauts and Heracles, comes to be of increasing significance. Likewise, in the *Aeneid*, Hercules is a figure to be spoken of, and followed after, but not encountered.

The first thing we hear about Heracles after he is abandoned is something told us by the poet, some twenty-five lines later, namely, that he will kill two of his erstwhile shipmates, the sons of Boreas, because they stopped Telamon from turning the ship around, to go back and pick him up (1.1299–1309). Heracles' killing of the sons of Boreas was a given 'fact' in legend, but there were various versions of motive and occasion, and Apollonius' version is unique.[21] No mention need have been made at all: it is significant that Valerius Flaccus suppresses the story, just as he had suppressed any mention of Heracles' killing of the father of Hylas. These two grim anecdotes frame the narrative of Heracles' marooning. They are both stories told by the poet in parenthesis: Apollonius is starting to feed in snippets of information which reveal new facets of Heracles, and they are snippets which are not necessarily available to the Argonauts.

One remarkable piece of news the Argonauts do hear. As they quarrel away over whether or not to go back to look for Heracles, the sea-god Glaucus appears from the depths, and says these words (1.1315–20):

---

[20] Cf. Vian and Delage (1976), 46–8.   [21] Cf. Vian and Delage (1976), 122 n.2.

Τίπτε παρὲκ μεγάλοιο Διὸς μενεαίνετε βουλήν
Αἰήτεω πτολίεθρον ἄγειν θρασὺν Ἡρακλῆα;
Ἄργεῖ οἱ μοῖρ᾽ ἐστὶν ἀτασθάλῳ Εὐρυσθῆι
ἐκπλῆσαι μογέοντα δυώδεκα πάντας ἀέθλους,
ναίειν δ᾽ ἀθανάτοισι συνέστιον, εἴ κ᾽ ἔτι παύρους
ἐξανύσῃ.

Why are you eager, contrary to the plan of great Zeus, to take bold Heracles to the city of Aeetes? At Argos it is his fate to toil at fulfilling all his twelve labours, for presumptuous Eurystheus, and to live with the gods, sharing their hearth, if he can fulfil the few labours left.

First of all they hear what the reader has known all along—that Heracles' arrival at Colchis is not part of tradition and not part of the plot. He has to complete his twelve labours—in *Argos*. Ἄργεῖ receives some stress, and I think that the reader at this point is entitled to assume that the Argonauts will not cross Heracles' path again. Most importantly, they hear Glaucus almost offhandedly declare that Heracles is going to become a god—*if* he achieves his few remaining labours successfully. That conditional is crucial. He is not guaranteed immortality—he may even yet not attain it—but he will win it as his reward if he completes the allotted cycle. The phrasing makes the reader concentrate on the tradition that saw Heracles' immortality as a reward for what the labours signified—a reward, that is, for endurance, and for the beneficent cleansing of evils from the world.[22]

Cleansing an evil from the world is precisely what Polydeuces does in the very next episode, when he kills Amycus; this close linking of Polydeuces' deed with Glaucus' speech on Heracles' immortality may owe something to a tradition that Glaucus prophesied to the Argonauts when Heracles and the Dioscuri were all present, promising all three immortality (Diod. Sic. 4.48.6). As we saw at the beginning, to King Lycus and his Mariandyni this is an act worthy of Heracles, and one deserving divine honours. Even as he prepares to fight Amycus, Polydeuces is compared to the star he will later be as a god (2.40–2); his opponent is compared to a giant (2.38–40), a breed which Heracles specialises in exterminating (even in this poem: cf. 1.999–1011). King Lycus, however, sets up a temple, not to Polydeuces alone, but also to his brother Castor. The immortality of the Dioscuri is a very odd thing. Sometimes, they alternate in sequence between Hades and Olympus: sometimes, only one is immortal, and the other for ever

---

[22] Though with συνέστιος ('sharing the hearth'), as Richard Hunter suggests, Apollonius may again be hinting at Heracles' gluttony (see LSJ s.v. for the word's close association with feasting); from Homer on, poets often stress Heracles' *eating* with the gods (itself an oxymoronic concept for a 'human'): cf. Hom. *Od.* 11.603; Theoc. 17.22; Callim. *Hymn* 3.144–61.

dead.[23] Apollonius stresses their shared divinity (cf. 1.150), for Castor receives a share of the reward that his brother has merited as a result of, unwittingly, emulating Heracles. It may be that their immortality is not of the same calibre as Heracles'. Certainly, their association in immortality is markedly different from Heracles' solitary apotheosis; Heracles too, after all, had a twin brother.

King Lycus tells the Argonauts that he had seen Heracles when the hero was returning from the East with the girdle of Hippolyte. As the Argonauts move eastwards up the coast of the Black Sea, they are following the trail Heracles had blazed. They pass by the very spot where he craftily won the girdle, by ambushing Hippolyte's sister and holding her hostage (2.964–9). If they had tarried there, says Apollonius, they would have had to fight the Amazons, and they would have taken casualties (985–8); but Zeus sends favourable winds, and they manage to pass by without incident (993–5). The divine agency extricates the Argonauts from having to cope with a crisis which Heracles had managed to overcome. Shortly before, they likewise fail to avail themselves of the opportunity to follow Heracles' example, when they camp for a number of days at the mouth of the river Acheron (728–45). According to one tradition, this is the place where Heracles descended to the underworld to fetch Cerberus, the hound of Hades.[24] Apollonius, alert as ever to surprise us, refrains from introducing an epic underworld scene here: such an ordeal is not for the Argonauts. It is, of course, within the capacity of Aeneas, who has greater hope of attaining to the standard of Heracles. Jason's steersman dies at this place (854–5); is it fortuitous that Aeneas' steersman Palinurus dies just before Aeneas makes his descent (*Aen.* 5.833–61)?

Heracles can still be an inspiration to the Argonauts, however. They approach the island of Ares, populated by vicious birds, which shoot their feathers at them (2.1030–42). Just like the Stymphalian birds that Heracles had to deal with, thinks the reader. Sure enough, one of the Argonauts had been there with Heracles, and recalls Heracles' trick of scaring the birds with bronze rattles. 'Heracles', he says, 'did not have the strength to drive off the birds with arrows ... We must devise μῆτις ("cunning wisdom") as he did' (1052–8). Heracles is held up here as a paradigm of using skill, or wisdom, to devise a plan when mere strength is not sufficient. This use of μῆτις is one field in which the Argonauts can hope to emulate their former shipmate.

As they make their way up the coast, they encounter visible traces of Heracles' earlier expedition. They pass the tomb of Sthenelus, one of

---

[23] Cf. Burkert (1985), 212–13.   [24] Xen. *An.* 6.2.2; see Frazer (1921) on Apollod. *Bibl.* 2.5.12.

Heracles' companions. In one of the most moving passages in the poem, Sthenelus' shade is granted a brief glimpse of his fellow Greeks, and stands on his barrow, looking at the ship (2.915–20). In following Heracles, he had met death, and piteous isolation. More fortunate are three brothers whom the Argonauts meet on their next stop. They, too, had been on the expedition against the Amazons, and had been separated from Heracles (2.957): the Argonauts give them the companionship and the safe journey home which Heracles had not been able to provide. Heracles' prodigious self-sufficiency has its reverse side. He is a figure of fundamental isolation. We have already seen him losing Hylas and being cut off from the Argonauts; now we have seen four other men who lost touch with him on an earlier journey.

The second book, then, shows the Argonauts, in varying ways, coming close to Heracles, or falling short of him. Polydeuces comes closest of all; in the use of brains, the crew approximate him; but in his invulnerability and isolated self-sufficiency, Heracles remains unique.

Book 3 is the book of Jason's victory, and Heracles is mentioned once only. Apollonius lets us understand, with his tongue in his cheek, why he had disposed of Heracles—because with him there would have been no poem; Heracles could have won the fleece by outright superior force. As Medea's father takes up his mighty spear, Apollonius says (3.1232–4):

> τὸ μὲν οὔ κέ τις ἄλλος ὑπέστη
> ἀνδρῶν ἡρώων, ὅτε κάλλιπον Ἡρακλῆα
> τῆλε παρέξ, ὅ κεν οἷος ἐναντίβιον πτολέμιξεν.
>
> No other of the heroes could have withstood it, once they had left Heracles behind far away, who alone could have fought him, force against force.

Book 4 describes the home leg. At the beginning of the book, Jason and Medea commit the shabby murder of Medea's brother. Eventually they will be ritually purified by Circe, and then married on the island of Phaeacia. On the way, they stop at the city of the Cylleans. Here, after a long lapse, we hear again the name of Heracles, for the people are named after a son of his, called Hyllus. This is not the son of Deianeira, but of another woman, whom Heracles had 'broken in' (ἐδάμασσεν, 4.542). He had met this woman on the island of Phaeacia, where Jason and Medea are headed. What had he been doing on Phaeacia? Being purified for the deadly slaughter of his children (4.541). We have had to wait a long time to hear about this most terrible of Heracles' actions. We hear about it as Jason and Medea head towards *their* purification, for the murder of

Medea's brother—and as they head, beyond the action of the poem, towards Medea's own murder of the children she will have with Jason. Book 4 is very much Medea's book (she is the subject of the book's invocation): Heracles is polyvalent enough to be a paradigm even for her.

Hyllus, the son of Heracles, is already dead when the Argonauts arrive, killed, as befits a son of Heracles, in a dispute over oxen (4.551). These deeds of Heracles lie, then, far in the past. 850 lines later, in Libya, when they are desperate with thirst, at the other end of the Mediterranean from where they had last seen Heracles,[25] the Argonauts, to their great surprise and ours, only just miss Heracles, to find themselves literally in his footsteps—and in no other sense than literally. They come tantalisingly close to meeting him again, for only on the previous day he had passed through this very stretch of desert (4.1436). The Argonauts are in the Garden of the Hesperides: there is the dragon, killed only the day before by Heracles (1400); there is the tree, despoiled of its golden apples (1397); there are the Hesperides, bemoaning their loss (1406–7). One of the Hesperides tells them the story, bitter with anger against the bestial Heracles, whom she calls 'dog-like' (κύντατος, 1433), and compares to a beast of the field, as he fills his great belly from the spring he had caused to flow by kicking a rock (1449). This spring is the salvation of the Argonauts, as one of them observes: 'Friends, even in his absence Heracles has saved his companions, afflicted with thirst' (1458–9). The best-qualified of the Argonauts dash off to find him (1464–7): the sons of Boreas, who can fly; Euphemus, the fastest runner; Lynceus, with the spectacular eyesight, who, as the story went, could see even under the earth (1.153–5). One unmarvellous Argonaut also goes—Canthus, of whom more in a moment. All fail. 'Only Lynceus thought he could see Heracles, far off, on the limitless land, seeing him as you see the moon, or think you see the moon, on the first day of the month, all obscured' (1477–80).[26] Lynceus rejoins his companions, swearing to them that none of the searchers would be able to catch up with Heracles on his route (1481–2).

What does all this mean? Above all, it means that Heracles has managed to fulfil the conditions stated by the sea-god Glaucus at the end of Book 1. He has completed his labours, he has taken the golden apples of eternal life, which represent his final labour, and won his prize of immortality.[27] He has gone virtually all the way down the path towards becoming a god, and

---

[25] Note 1.84–5 on Libya as the far end of the world from Colchis.
[26] Following the text and interpretation of Vian and Delage (1976) ad loc.
[27] On the significance of the apples, see Bond (1981) on Eur. *HF* 394–9.

that is the extraordinary interstitial point which Apollonius captures in that beautiful moment when Lynceus sees him in the far distance, or thinks he sees him. In this last mention of him in the poem, he is passing out of the world of men, and into the world of gods. In saving his companions, even in his absence, he has already begun to fulfil the functions of a god.[28]

At the moment when the Argonauts come closest to him, they are in fact further away from him than they have ever been; as Lynceus says, they will never catch him up. The vast difference between their principal achievement and his is heightened by a systematic series of correspondences.[29] Heracles, in the furthest West, takes golden μῆλα from a tree guarded by a serpent, which he kills. The rationalisers of myth claimed that these μῆλα were really sheep.[30] Jason, in the furthest East, takes the golden fleece of a ram from a tree guarded by a serpent, which is lulled into sleep by the magic of Medea. Jason's unwitting 'anticipation' of Heracles' deed reveals the difference and the distance between them.

In this last scene, Apollonius luxuriates in the paradoxes at his command. Just when Heracles lays his hands on his guarantee of apotheosis, Apollonius casts him at his most brutish, a creature of violence, wearing the raw untanned hide of a beast (1438–9). Heracles causes misery to the Hesperides, but as the ἀλεξίκακος ('warder-off of evil') he saves the Argonauts. Brutish and thirsty, he can still use his wit (or be thought capable of it—cf. 4.1445 with 2.1058–9). We may begin to see here another reason why Heracles does not belong with the Argonauts. He is, certainly, a relic from an earlier generation, both of heroes and poetry. He also approximates all too closely to certain of the more unsettling conceptions of divinity, in his power, his invulnerability, his self-sufficiency, his apartness and otherness.[31] He may be beneficent, but he is so much 'himself' that he moves eventually into total isolation. In the course of the poem he is separated from the Argonauts, from Hylas, from Polyphemus. In the second book we see four of his companions from the Amazonian expedition who were cut off from him in Asia Minor. As Heracles moves out of the poem for good, Canthus tries to follow him, but is prevented from doing so; he is killed by a local shepherd, as he tries to steal his sheep for his fellow Argonauts (1487–9). Unsuccessful in Heracles' métier of rustling, or in stealing μῆλα, Canthus fails to catch up with Heracles in any sense. His death,

---

[28] Cf. Hom. *Od.* 4.444; and compare *Argon.* 4.1436 with *Od.* 2.262. When Virgil adapts the Lynceus simile for Dido in *Aeneid* 6 (451–4), the sense of a vast and unbridgeable gulf is redeployed for a different use.
[29] Cf. Lawall (1966), 129; Beye (1982), 149.
[30] Diod. Sic. 4.26.2: the word μῆλα can mean either 'apples' or 'sheep' in Greek.
[31] His apartness already stressed in the Homeric *nekyia*, *Od.* 11.601–27.

by a ring-pattern, takes us back to the moment when Heracles first disappeared, at the end of the first book, for Canthus is trying to find out where Heracles left Polyphemus, after the two had been stranded together. Heracles did not protect Polyphemus either: Polyphemus followed along the coast of Asia Minor looking for Argo, and died there.[32]

A god, says Aristotle, is self-sufficient,[33] and does not need friends (*Eth. Eud.* 1244b8–10): it is, indeed, not possible to be friends with a god (*Eth. Nic.* 1158b35–59a6). Aristotle also sheds light on what lies behind Apollonius' dramatic polarities of Heracles as god and beast. 'Man is by nature', says Aristotle, 'an animal intended to live in a *polis*. He who is without a *polis*, by reason of his own nature and not of some accident, is either a poor sort of being, or a being higher than man' (*Pol.* 1253a2–4).[34] Heracles does not belong with the Argonauts, or with any human company: he has no fixed polis—does he belong to Tiryns, Argos or Thebes?;[35] he cannot tie in successfully with a family, for he kills his children and is killed by his wife. And when he becomes a god, unlike Polydeuces, he takes no one with him. Aristotle further says, 'The man who is isolated—who is unable to share in the benefits of political association, or has no need to share because he is already self-sufficient—is no part of the polis, and must therefore be either a beast or a god' (*Pol.* 1253a27–9). The *Argonautica* is not a commentary on Aristotle, but some such preconceptions lie behind Apollonius' paradoxes here, as he tells us of the bestial and god-like Heracles striding off alone across the desert, towards divinity.[36]

Virgil's exploitation of the figure is less systematic, and less flamboyant, but scarcely less intriguing.

The first time Hercules is named in the *Aeneid* Virgil is, as it were, picking up where Apollonius left off. Apollonius' Heracles had been moving away into remoteness, and that is how we first encounter

---

[32] Argo makes three consecutive stops on this section of coast in Book 2, all involving comrades left by Heracles: the first is at Sthenelus' tomb; the second is to pick up the three brothers; and the third is the site where Polyphemus later dies (2.1001, 4.1474–5).

[33] The self-sufficiency of the divine is an idea that goes back to Xenophanes (F 171 Kirk, Raven, Schofield (1983)).

[34] For the *Politics* I give the translations of E. Barker (1946).

[35] Apposite here may be the tragic fragment, very likely on Heracles, often quoted by Diogenes the Cynic: (ἄπολις, ἄοικος, πατρίδος ἐστερημένος, 'city-less, family-less, deprived of a fatherland', *TrGF* Adesp. 284).

[36] Those who write on Heracles in Apollonius tend to opt for one Heracles or the other as being solely present. Fränkel (1968) sees only the noble Heracles of the philosophers; most insist on Heracles as the archaic figure of violence: Galinsky (1972), 108–12 (some qualifications at 112–15); Beye (1982), 96; Lawell (1966), 124–8. But everything depends on acknowledging both sides. D.N. Levin (1971) does so, though without any development.

Hercules in the *Aeneid*, as a figure so remote that Aeneas is unsure whether or not to believe what he has heard about him. Just after landing on Italian soil for the first time, the Trojans catch sight of Tarentum (3.551–2):

> hinc sinus Herculei (si uera est fama) Tarenti
> cernitur.
>
> here the bay of Tarentum founded by Hercules (if rumour is true) is picked out.

Aeneas has heard stories about this distant figure, but that is all. It is a brief reference, but it is worth observing that Hercules is described, on first mention, as the founder of a city, as Aeneas hopes to be. It is, however, a Greek city: the Trojans are in Magna Graecia at this point, *Graiugenum ... domos suspectaque ... arua* ('homes of Greeks, plough lands to be wary of', 550). Still, despite their differences of nationality, the context reminds us that Aeneas and Hercules have some things in common. Four lines before Hercules' name occurs, we see the Trojans offering appeasing sacrifice to their bitter enemy, Juno (547). Aeneas, like Hercules, is hounded by this goddess: the language used in the poem's exordium already invites comparison between his lot and Hercules'.[37]

Two books go by, and Aeneas now comes much closer to Hercules, talking to men who had seen him, and walking on the same ground. What is more, for the first time we see someone attempting, as had various of the Argonauts, to measure up to Hercules, to emulate him. And we see that person failing.

The episode concerned is the boxing match in the funeral games of Book 5. The Trojan Dares stands up first (368–9). At Hector's funeral games, we learn, he had finished off a man who had boasted of being one of the tribe of the Bebryces, the tribe of Amycus (371–3). Promising form, in Apollonian terms: this man could be the new Pollux. His opponent is a local man, Entellus, who was taught boxing by King Eryx. Entellus still has Eryx's boxing-gloves, and we learn from his mouth about Eryx's last fight: he was killed by Hercules, on this very spot (410–14).

To Aeneas, this is a disquieting story. As Entellus pointedly reminds him, Eryx was Aeneas' half-brother, the son of Venus and Butes (412; cf. 3.24). We are seeing Hercules 'from the other side', from the point of view of relatives and friends of his victim. To Aeneas, Hercules is still an enemy.

Entellus is, in a way, a toned-down version of King Amycus, and his fight with the Trojan Dares is closely modelled on the fight between Amycus and

---

[37] Henry (1873–92), 1.188–95; Galinsky (1972), 132.

Polydeuces in *Argonautica* 2 (with elements from Theocritus 22).[38] Entellus is the more brutish of the two, while Dares, like Polydeuces, is younger, more nimble, relying on craft, not solely on strength.[39] The climax of the fight is especially close to Apollonius (and to Theocritus). The older man aims a massive blow, which the younger man deftly evades (3.443–5; cf. *Argon.* 2.90–3; Theoc. 22.118–23). At this point, in Apollonius and Theocritus, the younger man puts home the winning blow—but Virgil turns the tables, and has the older man recover from his ignominy to destroy his opponent (453–60). The Trojan Dares, in his literary and mythical pedigree, had had everything on his side. In defeating one of the Bebryces he had followed the example of Polydeuces, who had, in his turn, emulated Heracles. Now Dares is himself directly emulating Hercules, arriving from overseas, like him, standing on the same ground, and squaring up to the successor of the man whom Hercules had defeated.[40] But Dares confounds prediction, and is beaten by the new Amycus. Hercules remains an enemy of Trojan kinfolk: he is too vast a figure to be assimilated by the likes of Dares. Dares, like virtually all the Argonauts, can follow in Hercules' footsteps only literally: Aeneas, as we have already seen, is to be the new Pollux, the new imitator of Hercules, when he goes to the site of Rome.

The next man to follow in Hercules' footsteps is, indeed, Aeneas himself, who follows his path down to the underworld, a feat twice described as a *labor* (6.129, 135; cf. 6.103). No Argonaut ever attempted as much. 'A few descendants of the gods', says the Sibyl, 'have managed to come back up again; those whom impartial Jupiter loved, or whose blazing virtue carried them to heaven' (6.129–131). Hercules is the prime example of this category, and Aeneas will follow him, even to celestial immortality, as Jupiter has promised in Book 1 (259–60). During the parade of heroes, we receive the first intimation that the future Augustus is in this line also. Indeed, he is cast as even superior to Hercules in the range of his might: *nec uero Alcides tantum telluris obiuit* ... ('nor indeed did Hercules cover as much of the earth', 6.801–3). The enormous geographical range of Hercules' labours is drastically pruned back, and three comparatively trivial labours are chosen, involving certain beasts. There is a Lucretian tinge to these lines (compare Lucr. 5.22–44): what difference would it make to

---

[38] Cf. Rütten (1912), 16–19. Entellus, however, as Dr. Nicoll points out to me, goes some way towards clearing himself of the image of a loser by refusing to wear the gloves of Eryx (519).

[39] Note *arte* ('by skill'), *Aen.* 5.442; ἣν διὰ μῆτιν ('through his cunning wisdom'), *Argon.* 2.75; ἰδρείη ('by knowledge'), Theoc. 22.85.

[40] It may also be a good omen that the Bebrycian whom Dares defeated at Troy had the same name as Eryx's father—Butes (3.372).

anyone if the Arcadian boar and Lernaean hydra were still alive? A note of emulous rivalry, not present in the *Argonautica*, begins to emerge: the political achievements of the family of Aeneas are not necessarily inferior to the labours of the Greek hero.[41]

The connections between Hercules, Aeneas and Augustus await their full development in Book 8. Before then, we have another Dares-figure, another character who has Herculean associations, without being able to live up to them. Dares had had good claims to be a follower of Hercules; this man has even better, for he is the second hero mentioned in the catalogue of Italians in Book 7 (655–79), and he is Hercules' son.

He is, it appears, an invention of Virgil's. His name is Aventinus, and the name declares his 'Roman' origin. While Hercules was staying at the site of Rome with the cattle of Geryon, he impregnated a priestess, and she gave birth on the Aventine hill (7.659–63). Aventinus' shield bears the Hydra, an emblem of his father (657–8); he wears his father's distinctive costume, the lion-skin (666). So 'Herculean' is he that he anticipates in various ways Romulus, whom Ennius had made into another Hercules. His mother has the same name as Romulus' mother, Rhea—note the play on the full name, Rhea Silvia, in 659, *silua quem Rhea sacerdos . . .* ('whom *in a wood* Rhea the priestess . . . '). The son, like Romulus, of a priestess, he is also, like Ennius' Romulus, the *pulcher* son of a *pulcher* god (Enn. *Ann.* 38 and 75 Sk.). He is born on Romulus' hill, the Aventine, where Romulus won the auspices contest (72–91 Sk.). This is potentially a very dangerous antagonist, son of the sacker of Troy, who might stop the new Troy rising in Italy. But his threat is totally subsumed by Aeneas, the true new Hercules, who will be at Aventinus' birthplace within 250 lines, to be equipped with his own Herculean shield. There, Aeneas listens as the Salii praise Hercules for his sack of Troy (290–1). The words might have been a threat, but Aeneas, having left Troy to stand on the site of Rome, has drawn their sting. Aventinus is never mentioned again. This pseudo-Hercules is a false alarm, a token of inadequacy in the face of Aeneas' increasing ability to assimilate past symbols of Trojan failure and convert them into future symbols of Roman success.[42]

In Book 8 we get closer still to Hercules. As in Book 5, Aeneas is in exactly the same spot as Hercules had been in some years before, but this time he is, as we saw at the beginning, walking in the footsteps of Hercules in the true sense, conforming to the Apollonian prototype which stamps him as an emulator of Hercules, winning immortality through being

---

[41] Cf. Otis (1963), 302.  [42] On this tendency, see Suerbaum (1967).

a saviour, a warder-off of evil. Aeneas is coming closer to Hercules all the time. In particular, never before have Aeneas and the audience heard about Hercules in any detailed and characterised fashion. In Book 5, we have only the uncharged epithet *magnum* ('great', 414), with no description from Entellus of the *tristis pugna* ('sad fight', 411) of which he had been the eyewitness; in Book 8 we have ninety lines from Evander, with a minute account—for the first and only time in the poem—of Hercules in action (185–275).

What do we see? We receive a picture which, although muted, recalls above all the Heracles of Apollonius' fourth book, in the Garden of the Hesperides. There is a formal correspondence, in that both scenes concern the action by which the hero comes into possession of divine status: but there are more extensive correspondences between what we hear from the nymph and what we hear from Evander. The standpoint of the two speakers is very different, for the nymph loathes the hero, while Evander venerates him. This divergence makes it all the more striking that Evander, like the speaker in Apollonius, concentrates on the frenzy and power of Hercules, while maintaining an extreme distance from him, so that Hercules is as isolated as he had been in the desert of Libya.

Let me develop these two points. It is very remarkable that Evander's speech describes no meeting between Hercules and himself, no hospitality or contact of any sort.[43] Virgil is concentrating on the *exploit*, of course, but the form of the *aetion* ('origin-story') virtually demands a description of hospitality. For Apollonius, Heracles is a figure from an earlier, rougher kind of poetry: for Virgil, Hercules is also a creature of Hellenistic epyllion, and against this background, within his own *aetion*, Virgil's decision to excise the hospitality motif so dear to Callimachus is indeed noteworthy.[44] As in Apollonius' fourth book, Hercules arrives and does his deed without a word spoken.[45]

Virgil's typical concern for compression is partly responsible. Aeneas is now receiving the hospitality that Hercules received (in the 'story', and in the *Aetia*, Virgil's *aetion* model),[46] and Virgil does not want a close doublet. Further, allusion will be made later in the book to the hospitality Evander gave Hercules (8.362–5). Nonetheless, within Evander's speech, Hercules' utter self-sufficiency and remoteness, the sense that he does not

---

[43] Cf. George (1974), 67–8.   [44] Contrast Ov. *Fast.* 1.545, 5.647.
[45] Apollonius is perhaps already turning tradition in a similar way, for the Hesperides normally cooperate with Heracles: see Livrea (1973), 406.
[46] In the Molorchus story, fr. 55–9.

belong among normal men, are certainly striking, and very reminiscent of the impression left by the fourth book of Apollonius.

Likewise very reminiscent of Apollonius is the way in which Virgil has chosen this juncture to emphasise Hercules' physicality and his *furor* ('frenzy'). He does not polarise a whole range of paradoxes, as does Apollonius, even though it was open to him. In Livy, for example, Hercules is drunk when his cattle are stolen (1.7.4); again, Virgil could have alluded once more to the seduced priestess, the mother of Aventinus. Nonetheless, the focus on the madly violent face of the Herculean prism is unmistakable.[47] When Hercules hears the lowing of his stolen cattle, *hic uero Alcidae furiis exarserat atro/felle dolor* ('thereupon indeed Hercules' anguish had flared up in frenzy with black bile', 219–20). He rushes to Cacus' lair: *ecce furens animis aderat Tirynthius . . . /dentibus infrendens* ('look, Hercules was there, frenzied in his spirit, gnashing his teeth', 228–30). He dashes around the hill: *ter totum feruidus ira/lustrat Auentini montem* ('ablaze with rage he goes around the whole hill of the Aventine three times', 230–1). The impression, even more strongly than in Apollonius, is one of terrific, manic, violence. Even when saviour and candidate for apotheosis, Hercules is *uis*, βία, 'force', incarnate. As we contemplate the picture of Aeneas listening to the *exemplum* spoken by Evander, we must wonder what it means for him, whether this is part of the paradigm which he will also emulate. The other aspect of Hercules stressed here, his isolation, may appear not to correspond to Aeneas' situation, as he is being entertained by Evander. Yet the meal which Aeneas shares with Evander is the last one Virgil will narrate in the poem: Aeneas, as we shall see, is moving toward a solitude of a sort which Hercules never knew.

Hercules is not all *uis*. We hear praise of his *ratio* (μῆτις, 'calculating intelligence') in the hymn of the Salii (299), and another facet of the paradigm is offered Aeneas shortly afterwards, when Virgil alludes to the Hercules of the philosophers, as Evander welcomes Aeneas to his poor palace, enjoining self-restraint and self-sufficiency in emulation of Hercules (364–5):

> aude, hospes, contemnere opes et te quoque dignum
> finge deo, rebusque ueni non asper egenis.
>
> dare, my guest, to despise wealth and to make yourself as well worthy of the god, and do not come disdainful of my meagre possessions.

---

[47] Thus Gransden (1976), 20, correctly; ignored by Otis (1963); glossed over by Galinsky (1972), 144–6.

Hercules here is a paradigm for moral victory, over self, and the temptations of the world. The dichotomies are as sharp as anything in Apollonius—sharper, perhaps, since in Virgil the two different Hercules-traditions are in the mouth of the same speaker, within a hundred lines of each other.

Models are there to be outstripped as well as matched. And, inasmuch as he is the embodiment of a historical force, Aeneas does indeed outstrip his model, and himself provides a model for his descendant Augustus, who has inherited control of the historical force first given expression by Aeneas.[48] The moment that shows us most clearly that Aeneas has caught up with Hercules, and overtaken him, comes at the end of Book 8, when he looks at his shield and picks up on his shoulder 'the fame and fate of his descendants' (729–31). The scene is prefigured in miniature at the beginning of Aeneas' mission, in Book 2, when he drapes himself in a lion-skin (721–3), and takes up his father on his shoulders: *ipse subibo umeris nec me labor iste grauabit* ('I myself will put my shoulders beneath you and that *labour* will not weigh me down', 708).[49] At the end of Book 8, the burden he takes up is incomparably greater. He takes up the historical burden that will issue in an *imperium* over the entire world; he is picking up a world, if not *the* world. In this he approximates to his ancestor, Atlas,[50] and outdoes Hercules, who had briefly acted as Atlas' surrogate.[51]

And yet, at this definitive moment, it is, in a way, Hercules' own shield that Aeneas is picking up. The shield of Achilles in *Iliad* 18 is commonly referred to as Virgil's model here, and that shield was undoubtedly the most famous paradigm available. The so-called *Scutum*, '*Shield of Heracles*', however, preserved in the Hesiodic corpus, is also behind Virgil's picture. The Hesiodic shield is itself extensively modelled on the Homeric one, but certain links with Virgil's shield bear mention. In Homer, we see Achilles' shield as it is being made by Hephaestus; but in the *Scutum* we see it, as in Virgil, at the moment the hero picks it up. In the middle of Aeneas' shield is *Discordia* (702); in the middle of Heracles', Ἔρις ('Strife', 148). There is no sea on Achilles' shield, but Aeneas' and Heracles' shields both have sea, and dolphins (*Aen.* 8.671–4; Hes. [*Sc.*], 207–15). The *Scutum* has a harbour, which is like a 'heaving' water (κλυζομένῳ ἴκελος, 209); Virgil's sea is *tumidi* ('swelling', 671). Above all, the shield of Achilles is generalised, without individual characters; but Heracles' shield describes a specific

---

[48] This is brief allusion to a very contentious topic, with a large bibliography: for an account that I would largely agree with, I refer only to Camps (1969), 98–104.
[49] Cf. Galinsky (1972), 133–4.   [50] Cf. Gransden (1976), 17–18.
[51] Cf. Henry (1873–92), 1.191–5 on Aeneas' superiority to Hercules.

battle, with the contestants named (between Centaurs and Lapiths, 178–90).

Now that Aeneas has reached this climactic point, I imagine that no reader of the *Aeneid* would express surprise if Hercules received no further mention in the poem. Virgil, however, continues his closing-in movement, reversing the direction of Apollonius, who had taken the character of Heracles out of the body of the narrative, and turned him into a figure of anecdote and report. In the middle of Book 10, Virgil actually introduces Hercules into the narrative as a character in his own right: Virgil traces Hercules down that path where even Lynceus could not see, and shows him to us at its far end, as a god.

Hercules' reimbodiment in the narrative is flanked by two authorial references to him. Let us take these passages as they occur.

When Aeneas first enters battle, he dispatches four men within eight lines. The third and fourth are brothers, armed with Hercules' weapon, the club (10.319–22):

> nihil illos Herculis arma
> nec ualidae iuuere manus genitorque Melampus,
> Alcidae comes usque grauis dum terra labores
> praebuit.
>
> The weapons of Hercules did them no good, nor their powerful hands, nor the fact that their father was Melampus, a mighty comrade of Hercules for all the time that the earth provided labours for him.

It would seen that these two are, like Aventinus in the catalogue, false aspirants to the status of Hercules: their associations with Hercules are unavailing when they confront the true new Hercules. The passage appears to be, comparatively, unproblematical.

The focus switches to Pallas. After various combats, he is confronted with a certain Halaesus, and prays to Father Tiber for help (421–3). *audiit illa deus* ('the god heard those prayers', 424); Pallas kills the man. Some thirty lines later, he faces a greater enemy, Turnus, and prays to a greater god, Hercules, basing his plea (ominously?) on *hospitium*, 'ties of hospitality/guest-friendship' (460–1):

> per patris hospitium et mensas, quas aduena adisti,
> te precor, Alcide, coeptis ingentibus adsis.
>
> through the guest-friendship of my father and the meals which you attended as a stranger, I pray to you, Hercules, may you be present at my mighty undertakings.

The response is extraordinary: *audiit Alcides iuuenem* ('Hercules heard the youth', 464). Not the way Father Tiber was able to do. Virgil introduces Hercules into the action itself, hearing Pallas, but unable to do anything but weep; he is unable even to speak, so that the poem goes by without our hearing a single word from him (464–5):

> audiit Alcides iuuenem magnumque sub imo
> corde premit gemitum lacrimasque effundit inanis.[52]
>
> Hercules heard the youth and suppressed a great groan at the bottom of his heart and shed empty tears.

We actually see the god who was recently a man, and we see him powerless to honour the ties he established as a man.

Jupiter, however, has never been anything but a god, and he tells the newcomer how a god regards these things (467–9):

> stat sua cuique dies, breue et inreparabile tempus
> omnibus est uitae; sed famam extendere factis,
> hoc uirtutis opus.
>
> Each person has his appointed day. For everyone the time of life is short and cannot be got back; but to stretch out fame by deeds, that is the task of virtue.

A short life for all, but fame for the virtuous. Hercules should know, for he had been one of Anchises' models in Book 6, along with Bacchus (601–5), when Anchises urged Aeneas on to his mission: *et dubitamus adhuc uirtutem extendere factis?* ('and do we still hesitate to stretch out virtue by deeds?', 806). Virgil refers directly to the Homeric model when Jupiter goes on to mention Sarpedon, who was his son, and who nevertheless died at Troy (470–1).[53] In the *Iliad*, however, when Sarpedon was about to die, it was not Zeus who insisted upon the inviolability of Fate, but Hera, acting as an inflexible foil to Zeus's pity and grief (16.439–57). Now the tables are turned, as Hercules is overcome, and Jupiter enunciates—*dictis amicis* ('with friendly words', 406)—the lesson he has learnt from Hera.[54] These few lines represent a shattering collision of human and divine perspectives, as the most human of the gods is told by the father of the gods how to regard the action.

---

[52] The words recall 4.449, where Aeneas is equally powerless before Fate.
[53] We may be meant to think of the usual tradition concerning Pallas, that he was the son of Hercules (Dion. Hal. *Ant. Rom.* 1.32.1): note, then, the effect of Turnus' words, *cuperem ipse parens spectator adesset* ('I wish your father himself were here to watch', 443).
[54] The Iliadic scene is even more systematically reversed at 10.621–7, where Jupiter tells Juno that she cannot, in the long run, save her favourite.

Once again, Aeneas fits into the paradigm offered by Hercules, as he too fails to protect the young man tied to him by the bonds of *hospitium*,[55] repeating Hercules' disastrous propensity to fail those closest to him. When he attempts to avenge Pallas he is likewise very close to βίη Ἡρακλείη, 'the force of Heracles' (as he is, again, when he actually kills Turnus in the end):[56] *furit* ('he is in a frenzy', 545); *desaeuit* ('he rages', 569); *dira frementem* ('he makes an awful roaring', 572); *furens* ('in a frenzy', 604); *feruidus* ('ablaze', 788); *furit* ('he is in a frenzy', 802); *saeuae irae* ('savage rage', 813).

One scene remains, a mirror to the one which began the sequence of references to Hercules in this book. In that first scene, two enemies of Aeneas found their Herculean associations unavailing; in this scene, an ally of Aeneas encounters the same fate (10.777–8). Mezentius throws a spear at Aeneas: it ricochets off the great shield and hits a certain Antores, who is standing some distance away (10.779–82):

> Herculis Antoren comitem, qui missus ab Argis
> haeserat Euandro atque Itala consederat urbe.
> sternitur infelix alieno uulnere, caelumque
> aspicit et dulcis moriens reminiscitur Argos.
>
> Antores, a companion of Hercules, who, sent from Argos, had cleaved to Evander and settled in a city in Italy. He is laid low, unlucky man, by a wound meant for someone else, and he looks at the sky and remembers sweet Argos as he dies.

Once a companion of Hercules, now a companion of Aeneas, Antores dies by the spear that was meant for Aeneas, in a foreign country which he would never have seen if not for Hercules. Aeneas and Hercules are both jointly 'responsible' for his death. Only twenty lines before, Virgil tells us that the gods are spectators of the battle (758–9). Antores is the first subsequent casualty; one assumes that Hercules is with the other gods, still watching, as his comrade dies.

Hercules is a very complex phenomenon, and being a follower of Hercules is a very complex process. As in the *Argonautica*, there is more than one character following after Hercules; and, as in the *Argonautica*, the component paradoxes of Hercules are opened out and displayed in their separate aspects, which it is open to various of the characters to try to emulate. Aeneas, however, is the prime focus, in a way none of the characters is in Apollonius, and Aeneas comes closer to some of

---

[55] Cf. Henry (1873–92), 1.191–2 (a valuable paragraph). [56] Cf. Gransden (1976), 30.

Hercules' aspects than to others. He is quite different from Hercules, for example, in his human responses; he is a far more sympathetic 'character'.[57] He is, after all, a Jason as well as a Hercules, as he shows when he comes to his Lemnos, in Carthage. And although he goes berserk in Book 10, he returns to himself when he kills Lausus (10.820–32). If, then, his nature is not very Herculean, his status and function are much more so. As an ἀλεξίκακος, a victorious saviour, and a wielder of great power, he even outstrips Hercules, and will become, like him, a god. Yet, in adopting a Herculean status, and discharging Herculean functions, he also finds himself being assimilated to some of the more forbidding aspects of his paradigm. In his exercise of *uis* and *furor* ('force' and 'frenzy') and in his frightful solitude, Aeneas comes all too close to another side of Hercules.[58]

It is the historical and political dimension of the *Aeneid* which conditions the major differences between Virgil's use of Hercules and Apollonius'. The way in which the initially hostile Greek Hercules is absorbed and tamed by the growth of Aeneas may be seen as emblematic of the Romans' accretive urge for assimilation. The political perspective of the *Aeneid*, virtually entirely absent in the *Argonautica*,[59] produces new ways of viewing Hercules and his imitators, and generates its own distinctive paradoxes. The isolation of Hercules and Aeneas, for example, is one of their most striking similarities, a function, partly, of their incipiently divine status.[60] Yet Hercules is ἄπολις, 'city-less', while Aeneas lives for the *urbs*; Hercules is alone because he cannot belong with any organisation, while Aeneas is alone because he is wholly identified with an organisation.[61] This historical dimension sets Aeneas and Augustus quite apart from the Greek god-hero; yet their power, function and status place them, even on earth, as close to the boundary of the divine as it is possible to be. And some things about being on the boundary of the divine do not change.

---

[57] Henry (1873–92), 1.188–95 is very good on the differences between Aeneas and Hercules.
[58] On the solitude of Aeneas, see Chapter 1 above.
[59] Although one cannot help seeing, for example, contemporary political practice in the cult offered to Polydeuces in Book 2, while the claimed Heraclean descent of the Ptolemies (Theoc. 17) no doubt has some impact on Apollonius' portrayal of this grand figure, as Mr. Howie points out to me.
[60] I retract, accordingly, my uncomprehending criticism of the remarks on Aeneas and Augustus of Highet (1972), Chapter 1 above, n.93.
[61] See here Stewart (1972–3).

CHAPTER 7

# *Beginning Sallust's* Catiline

'The prooemia of Sallust's three works', observes F.R.D. Goodyear, '... have engendered endless debate',[1] and a person contributing yet another pebble to the pile may well feel obliged to defend his action. My first justification is the wish to honour Patrick Lacey with an essay on an author whom I first read with him. After twenty years I retain a vivid memory of the relish with which he communicated Sallust's energy and wit to a group of undergraduates who were picking their way through W.C. Summers' old Pitt Press edition at a speed that (as I can see in hindsight) he must have found rather exasperating. My other justification is the conviction that very few people read the opening of the *Catiline* with the assumption that Sallust is fully in control of his material.[2] The criticisms of the monograph's beginning are notorious, and they are usually said to reach back to Quintilian's comment that *C. Sallustius in bello Iugurthino et Catilinae nihil ad historiam pertinentibus principiis orsus est* ('Sallust in the *Jugurtha* and *Catiline* started with prooemia not at all relevant to the genre of history', 3.8.9). While Quintilian seems to be observing (without necessarily criticising) a formal departure from conventional historical beginnings,[3] modern scholars concentrate on the prefaces' supposed intellectual confusion and structural incompetence. Two pages of Goodyear's essay offer 'disproportionate bulk', 'a texture of loosely related themes', 'a little ramshackle', 'the thought is not worked out'.[4] If commentators seem satisfied that we are not observing a great thinker at work, let us see if perhaps we may discover a great artist at work. The opening of the *Catiline* has been subjected

---

[1] Goodyear (1982), 270.
[2] Syme, of course, being the exception: 'He knows what he is trying to do, he dominates the subject' (Syme (1964), 67); cf. Woodman (1988), 120–4 on the first paragraph, esp. 122 on how Sallust puts 'an idea into the reader's mind only to return to it later', a technique which 'occurs frequently in the preface and constitutes one of the subtleties of Sallust's style'.
[3] Earl (1966), 5; cf. Earl (1972), 846 arguing that Sallust has opened the work as if it were a philosophical treatise.
[4] Goodyear (1982), 270–1.

to earnest and moral readings; what is offered here might be termed, antithetically, an ironic and literary reading.

We go through two pages of general discussion about *gloria* and *uirtus* before Sallust vouchsafes that writing, and in particular writing about deeds, is his real concern (3.1). Against conventional thinking, he will have it that writing great deeds is practically as glorious as performing them. At last we have the delayed introductory phrase *res gestas scribere* ('to write history'), words which are only allowed to appear once he has elaborately cleared the ground for seeing this activity as being on a par with politics.⁵ His self-consciousness about the novelty of his approach is caught especially with his strange phrase describing the difficulty of writing history, *facta dictis exaequanda sunt* (3.2). 'Deeds have to be made equal to words'—an odd way of saying what his argument requires, that 'words have to be made equal to deeds', that the account has to live up to the event. But then making deeds equal to words—putting doing and writing on an equal footing—is exactly what he has been doing in his discussion so far.

After the phrase *res gestas scribere* has appeared, and its performance justified as an activity, we might expect to be told which *res gestae* are to be narrated for us, but a paragraph of autobiography delays us while we learn of Sallust's reasons for turning from action to writing. We might label this as garrulity, if not for the self-reflexiveness of the language he uses when he finally returns to talk of the deferred topic of *res gestae*: *sed a quo incepto studioque me ambitio mala detinuerat, eodem regressus statui res gestas populi Romani ... perscribere* ('but returning to the undertaking and pursuit from which mischievous ambition had detained me, I decided to write up the history of the Roman people', 4.2). Here he comments self-referentially upon the digression represented by his autobiographical section (3.3–4.1). If *ambitio mala* detained him from his beginning before he decided to return to it in his life, then his little autobiographical digression about *ambitio mala* has done exactly the same thing within his book, detaining him from his beginning of *res gestae* before he decides to return to it. The *regressus* of his autobiography, then, does double duty for the thematic return to his programme.⁶

---

⁵ The appropriateness of these words as a historical beginning is shown by the sentence with which Sallust later opened his *Histories*: *res populi Romani M. Lepido Q. Catulo consulibus ac deinde militiae et domi gestas composui.*

⁶ For a collection of dogged speculations about Sallust's youthful dabbling in historiography, see the commentary of Vretska (1976) ad loc.

He appears, at last, to be back on track with his resumptive announcement *statui res gestas populi Romani*, 'I decided the history of the Roman people ... '—after which splendid words we encounter the destabilising adverb *carptim*, 'selectively', 'in disconnected segments'. What Sallust means by this, of course, is that he will not be following the mainstream tradition of Roman historical writing, which narrated the deeds of the Roman people *un*selectively, from the foundation of the city down to the historian's own time.[7] One explanation for the meandering movement of his beginning is to be found here, for throughout the preface he flaunts his rejection of this prestigious alternative way of recording the past, and he does so by ironically parading snippets of alternative, more imposing, beginnings. The deceptive *res gestas populi Romani* announcement is trumped a page further on, when he reaches back to provide a general context for Catiline's moral depravity, and delivers an imposing sentence of the kind that could have stood as the ornamental opening to a 'proper' account of the deeds of the Roman people: *urbem Romam, sicuti ego accepi, condidere atque habuere initio Troiani* ('the city of Rome, according to my authorities, was founded and occupied in the beginning by Trojans', 6.1). The loaded word *initio* ('beginning') carries a good deal of Sallust's mordant power here, since he had told us earlier that he was going to give us a character sketch of Catiline *before* making his *initium narrandi* ('beginning of narrating', 4.5), and this digressive *initio*, doing no more than providing context for that sketch, is doubly displaced from the proud beginning moment it should have been.[8] He reinforces the point shortly thereafter, when he tells us that he could have narrated the heroic deeds of Roman military history, *ni ea res longius nos ab incepto traheret* ('except that the subject-matter would drag me too far from my undertaking', 7.7). And towards the end of the monograph, between the speeches and the comparison of Caesar and Cato, he reminds us again of the kind of history-writing which his wilful selectivity is suppressing: *sed mihi multa legenti, multa audienti quae populus Romanus domi militiaeque, mari atque terra praeclara facinora fecit* ... ('but as I read many accounts, and listened to many accounts, of the splendid deeds which the Roman people

---

[7] See Wiseman (1979), 18–26 on the various strands of Roman historiography before Sallust, and the dominance in the first century BCE of the *ab ovo* annalistic approach.

[8] Tacitus, famously, does select this beginning moment for the real beginning of his *Annales*, *Urbem Romam a principio reges habuere*. He shows his understanding of Sallust's fracturing technique by combining this sentence from 6.1 with another illusory beginning earlier on in Sallust's preface, *igitur initio reges* (2.1).

performed at home and on campaign, by sea and land ... ', 53.2). He is reading and hearing many such accounts, but he is not writing any.

If Sallust ironically gestures towards the kind of history he is not going to begin writing, since he is writing selectively (*carptim*), we are entitled to ask what his principle of selection will be. *ut quaeque memoria digna uidebantur*, he tells us, 'according to how worthy the episodes appeared to be of being preserved in memory' (4.2). He then announces his particular subject, the conspiracy of Catiline, and tells us what was particularly memorable about it, namely, the novelty of the crime and the peril, *memorabile ... sceleris atque periculi nouitate* (4.4). The whole business of memorability is presented by the movement of the prooemium as being inherently tautological. The historian writes about memorable things, but things become memorable by being written about by the historian.[9] The historian suppresses as well as preserves. The historian, especially one who professes to be writing *carptim*, 'selectively', is aware of the fact that every mention of something is in effect a displacement of something else. There are indeed many omissions and silences in this apparently garrulous and meandering preface: not the glorious annals of the Roman people, but crime and evil instead; not foreign wars, but civil; not Cicero, but Catiline. The monograph is a third of the way through its progress before Cicero is even mentioned, in connection with the story of the conspirators drinking human blood: *nonnulli ficta et haec et multa praeterea existumabant ab eis, qui Ciceronis inuidiam, quae postea orta est, leniri credebant atrocitate sceleris eorum, qui poenas dederant* ('quite a few people thought that this and much else was made up by those who believed that the bad feeling which later arose against Cicero would be alleviated by making the crime of those who had been punished an outrageous one', 22.3). The first time that Cicero is mentioned, then, he is under a posterior cloud of *inuidia* that crowds out the memory of the deed which Sallust has not even described yet.

Sallust's most explicit comment upon the distortion of the historian's representation comes immediately after a particularly conspicuous suppression of *memoria*, when he says that he could commemorate great Roman military exploits (*memorare possum ...*) if not for the fact that

---

[9] Another twist is provided by the idea that the historian becomes memorable himself through the act of writing. The lust for glory is one of the subjects of the monograph; it is also its openly acknowledged motivation. When *memoria* is first mentioned in the work it is 'the memory of ourselves' (*memoriam nostri quam maxume longam efficere*, 1.3), and praise comes both to the performers and the writers of deeds (*et qui fecere et qui facta aliorum scripsere multi laudantur*, 3.1). Much of this paradox can be retrospectively unpacked from a single word in the first sentence of the work, where the fate to shun is that of leading one's life *silentio*—conclusively shown by Woodman (1973) to mean both 'without being talked about' and also 'without saying anything': cf. Baker (1982).

such subject-matter would drag him too far from his undertaking (*ni ea res longius nos ab incepto traheret*, 7.7). After this spectacular smothering he delivers himself of a sentence that turns out to refer as much to historical tradition as to its ostensible subject, *fortuna*: *sed profecto fortuna in omni re dominatur; ea res cunctas ex lubidine magis quam ex uero celebrat obscuratque* ('but fortune certainly is the ruling power in every sphere; fortune celebrates and smothers everything on the basis of whim rather than truth', 8.1).

Such is the starting point for his marvellously ironic reflection upon the power of history (8.2–4):

> Atheniensium res gestae, sicuti ego aestumo, satis amplae magnificaeque fuere, uerum aliquanto minores tamen quam fama feruntur. sed quia prouenere ibi scriptorum magna ingenia, per terrarum orbem Atheniensium facta pro maxumis celebrantur. ita eorum qui fecere uirtus tanta habetur quantum eam uerbis potuere extollere praeclara ingenia.

> The deeds of the Athenians, in my opinion, were perfectly impressive and magnificent; still, they were considerably less grand than they are reported to be by popular tradition. But because historians of great genius sprang up there, the deeds of the Athenians are celebrated over the globe as if they were the greatest ever. So true is it that the estimation of the *uirtus* of men of action is in exact ratio with the capacity of outstanding geniuses to extoll it.

Here Sallust is looking in particular at two closely linked passages in Thucydides' discussion of the size of the Greek expedition to Troy. Thucydides argues first that Mycenae's current state is no evidence for the force it might once have mustered against Troy, and he adduces the case of Sparta and Athens, whose architectural remains after a future devastation would give a quite misleading impression of their actual former power: people would not believe that Sparta had been as great as report (κλέος) had it, and they would judge Athens' power to have been twice as great as it really was (1.10.2). Besides the physical appearance of cities, Thucydides' other case of unreliable witness is of course Homer, whose exaggeration of the Greek expedition has left a misleading impression in everybody's mind (1.11.3). These Thucydidean comments on the discrepancy between appearance and reality in the spheres of poetry and architecture have been rewritten by the Roman historian to devastating effect: Thucydides' history has itself become a monument of the past, like poetry and architecture, equally liable to be incommensurate with reality.

A further explanation for the perturbing movement of the preface is, then, to be sought in Sallust's wish to put his own shaping and controlling power in the forefront, so as to make it impossible for the reader to be lulled into thinking that the facts are speaking for themselves. The ego of the historian, with his abrupt and wilful swerves, with his apparently capricious selection of L. Sergius Catilina out of the whole rogues' gallery of the late Republic, calls attention to the act of will involved in imposing the pattern he wishes on the chaos and flux that presents itself to the observer of human affairs (*quod si regum atque imperatorum animi uirtus in pace ita ut in bello ualeret, aequabilius atque constantius sese res humanae haberent, neque aliud alio ferri neque mutari ac misceri omnia cerneres*, 'and if the mental *uirtus* of kings and commanders were as powerful in peace as in war, then human affairs would be more even and more regular, and you wouldn't see things moving to and fro in different directions, with everything in a state of change and confusion', 2.3; cf. 2.9, *in magna copia rerum*, 'in the great abundance of affairs/subject-matter'). Many apparently 'natural' beginnings are referred to in passing as we go through the preface: the beginning of human government (*igitur initio reges . . .*, 2.1); the beginning of Sallust's career (*sed ego adulescentulus initio . . .*, 3.3); the birth of Catiline (*L. Catilina, nobili genere natus . . .*, 5.1); the foundation of Rome (*urbem Romam . . .*, 6.1).[10] All are subordinated to the strenuous design imposed by the historian.

We may see this signalling of his controlling power at work when he introduces his villainous hero. His first mention of Catiline leads him into a character sketch, which is explicitly stated to be part of the preface, not the narrative (4.5). He then breaks off, claiming that he needs to provide the whole perspective of Roman achievement and decline (5.9). After this lengthy retrogression charting the inversion of Roman *mores*, he finally returns to Catiline in Chapter 14, picking up with further description of his nature. This pattern of organisation, by interweaving our impression of Catiline with a panorama of the wholesale slippage of Roman values, acts out the interweaving of the general and particular which is the whole point of choosing Catiline as a paradigm in the first place. This is not rambling, but high artistic power.

The novelty of Catiline's conspiracy is said by Sallust to be the reason it is particularly memorable (4.4), and it is clearly his self-consciousness concerning the novelty of his own procedure in writing about it which explains many of the apparently objectionable features of the preface: his

---

[10] Not to mention the historiographically correct announcement of the subject (*igitur de Catilinae coniuratione quam uerissume potero paucis absoluam*, 4.3); cf. Earl (1972), 846 on this sentence and *Iug.* 5.1: 'These are first sentences of unimpeachable correctness; but they do not stand first in their works.'

inordinate stress on the value of writing, his oblique dismissal of traditional ways of writing about the past, his parading of his own person and intellect, both in biographical 'digression' and in selection and suppression of subject-matter. Nothing less would have served for the first pages of a man who was setting out to 'conquer a new domain for the literature of the Latins'.[11]

---

[11] Syme (1964), 1.

CHAPTER 8

# Leaving Dido: The Appearance(s) of Mercury and the Motivations of Aeneas[1]

Aeneas needs not one but two visitations from the god Mercury before he will leave Dido and the shores of Carthage. This double divine irruption into a human story of love and conscience is a notorious scandal to interpretation, and generations of readers and scholars have come up with more or less ingenious techniques for writing the disruptive Mercury out of the story. Aeneas' 'impulse to action has a divine origin ascribed to it in a way that strikes us as purely formal', according to one critic; 'what [Mercury] says follows exactly the line of argument that would naturally occur to a man in Aeneas' situation', according to another.[2] I recently attempted to make a case against these various ways of rewriting Virgil's epic narrative into a novelistic piece of naturalism, arguing that the full complexity of Aeneas' dilemma can only be understood if it is read in the light of the vast historical perspectives which Mercury can elicit from his father, Jupiter, and mediate to Aeneas and the reader.[3]

Yet the difficulty of doing justice to Virgil's techniques is shown by the fact that in my own discussion I repeated the suppressions I was protesting against, discussing only the first of Mercury's appearances, in which he speaks to Aeneas in the full light of day (*Aen.* 4.219–78), and ignoring the second, when he appears to the hero in a dream (4.554–80). My aim here is to rectify that telling omission, by looking at the full range of complications which emerge when we look at both visitations, and the interpretations of them given by Aeneas and Dido, against the larger epic backdrop of communication between divine and human. As we shall see, Mercury, archetypally πολύτροπος ('of many turns', 'shifty'), the crosser of boundaries, the patron deity of hermeneutics, presents a severe challenge

---

[1] I have learnt much from E.L. Harrison's generous correspondence with me on Vergil's Mercury, and am indebted throughout to his important article, E.L. Harrison (1984).
[2] Quinn (1968), 317–18; G.W. Williams (1983), 27.   [3] Feeney (1991), 173–5.

to interpretation as he moves continually from one realm and form of manifestation to another.

At the most basic level, Mercury's task is to communicate Jupiter's will, and a fragment of his knowledge, to the human character, Aeneas. Before we can investigate what Virgil makes of this act of mediation, we need to have a picture of the various channels of communication between divine and human in Virgil's epic masters, Homer and Apollonius. The Homeric data have been lucidly summarised by E.L. Harrison. In the *Iliad*, Zeus's particular messenger is not Hermes, but Iris, who repeats his commands to mortals. In addition, Iris once acts on her own initiative when she assumes the guise of a daughter of Priam in order to bring Helen to the wall to watch the combat between Paris and Menelaus (3.121–40); and she once runs the reverse route from her usual one, when she conveys to the house of Winds Achilles' prayer that Boreas and Zephyr should come to blow on Patroclus' pyre (23.192–211). One final isolated incident in the *Iliad* stands out as the most important exception to Iris' usual role as the mouthpiece of Zeus, and that is when Iris tells Achilles to rescue Patroclus' corpse from Hector (18.165–202). Homer tells us that she does this 'without the knowledge of Zeus and the other gods, for Hera sent her forth' (κρύβδα Διὸς ἄλλων τε θεῶν· πρὸ γὰρ ἧκέ μιν Ἥρη, 18.168); and in the subsequent conversation this vital piece of information is stressed again, when Achilles asks Iris who sent her as a messenger, and Iris replies that it was Hera, adding that Zeus does not know about her mission, nor any of the other Olympians (181–6).[4] As we shall see, this unique occurrence of Iris as a messenger of Hera, operating without Zeus's knowledge, assumes great importance in the subsequent tradition.

The last episode of the *Iliad* shows Hermes guiding Priam to the camp of Achilles to ransom Hector's corpse, but, as Harrison stresses, it is a mistake to speak of him as Zeus's *messenger* in this capacity: 'Hermes . . . is brought in to act as escort, and, far from giving him any text to transmit, Zeus actually stresses his role as companion and listener.'[5] In the *Odyssey*, however, we do see just such a decisive shift, for now Hermes completely takes over the role of Zeus's messenger from Iris, who disappears from the pantheon, while Athena assumes Hermes' Iliadic role as an escorter of favoured mortals.[6] Further, as a major Olympian god with his own

---

[4] E.L. Harrison (1984), 11. I leave out of this account *Il.* 5.353–69, since Iris is there not mediating between the divine and human realms, but acting as a herald-character in the divine drama (taking Aphrodite to Olympus after her wounding by Diomedes: Weicker (1916), 2038–9).
[5] E.L. Harrison (1984), 13; cf. N.J. Richardson (1993), on 24.333–48. The reasons why Homer has Hermes here rather than Iris are already spelt out by the bT scholia on 24.333–8.
[6] E.L. Harrison (1984), 15–17.

developed mythic and cultic personality, Hermes is not one to parrot words as Iris had in the *Iliad*. When he relays Zeus's commands to Calypso in *Odyssey* 5, he has his own characterful variations and improvisations, just as Mercury has his own characterful variations and improvisations upon Jupiter's commands in *Aeneid* 4.[7]

The Homeric pattern is, then, reasonably clear. In the *Iliad* Iris acts as the mouthpiece of Zeus, while once acting on her own initiative, once carrying an appeal from a human character to divine, and once acting at the behest of Hera, unknown to Zeus. In the *Odyssey* Iris disappears and Hermes takes over as (a more independent) messenger of Zeus.

What becomes of these patterns in the *Argonautica* of Apollonius, Virgil's second great epic predecessor? Devotees of this witty and iconoclastic poet will be unsurprised to learn that he reverses the reversals of the *Odyssey*, removing Hermes from the cast of characters altogether and returning to the *Iliad* to restore Iris as the divine messenger. Apollonius' revisions are even more remorseless than this summary might indicate, however, for he unerringly homes in on the Homerically atypical and anomalous, seizing on the uncharacteristic Iris episodes of the *Iliad* and making them the norm for his own poem. In the *Argonautica*, Iris never acts as the messenger of Zeus, as she repeatedly had in the *Iliad*, but once acts on her own initiative (as she had once in the *Iliad*), and once at the behest of Hera (again, as she had once in the *Iliad*).

She first appears in Book 2, as the sons of Boreas are pursuing the winged Harpies through the air. The Harpies would have been destroyed, says Apollonius, against the will of the gods, if swift Iris had not seen and leapt down the sky from heaven (284–7); she forbids the sons of Boreas to kill 'the dogs of great Zeus', and they turn back, while the Harpies descend to Crete and Iris returns to Olympus (288–300). Characteristically, much is unstated here, and much is opaque. If we enquire as to Iris's motivation for this intervention, we need to know our Hesiod for the information that Iris is in fact the sister of the imperilled Harpies (*Theog.* 266–9). In particular, Zeus's stake in this transaction is hard to recover. Although Iris is certainly not sent by Zeus, by referring to the Harpies as 'the dogs of great Zeus' she appears to identify them as being under his protection; yet when the Boreads first set out in pursuit of the Harpies, Apollonius tells us that their flight is assisted by Zeus, without whose aid they would never have been able to keep up with their prey (274–7). The inscrutability of Zeus's

---

[7] Ibid., 16–23.

motivation is a paramount Apollonian theme, to which we shall shortly return.

Having followed one pattern of behaviour which is uniquely anomalous in Homer, Iris returns in Book 4 to do the same, for here we see her again acting as she did only once in Homer, this time as Hera's emissary and lackey.[8] At this point it is clear that Apollonius is following the strong post-Homeric tradition of a special relationship between Iris and Hera. The Parthenon frieze, for example, shows Iris standing beside Hera, and she appears memorably and terrifyingly as Hera's servant in Euripides' *Heracles*, sent to announce and instigate the doom of the hero whom Hera so hates (822–57).[9]

Apollonius' adherence to this post-Homeric Iris tradition, and his glee in highlighting how non-Homeric his adherence is, only throws into relief his refusal to have Hermes as a character. Since the *Odyssey*, the representation of Hermes as Zeus's special messenger had become canonical, and had fixed itself as the counterpart to the representation of Iris as Hera's special messenger.[10] It goes without saying that Apollonius is perfectly well aware of this canonical tradition—indeed, he seems to fly directly in the face of it when he first introduces Iris rescuing the Harpies from the sons of Boreas, for the ancient commentators on 2.286 remark that 'others say it was Hermes'. More importantly, Apollonius intersperses his narrative of the search for the golden fleece with numerous references back to Hermes' active role as an emissary of Zeus years before, when the ram first carried the hero Phrixus to the far end of the Black Sea. Hermes it was who turned the ram into gold (2.1144–5), who was sent by Zeus himself to make sure that the suppliant Phrixus received hospitality from the barbarian Aeetes (3.584–8), who met Phrixus in a kindly manner and told him to sacrifice the ram to Zeus in gratitude (2.1146–7, 4.120–1). We can add all of these references up to reconstruct a story rather akin to that of *Iliad* 24, showing the supreme god's concern for morality and the status of the suppliant, mediated to humans through the benign agency of a friendly Hermes.[11]

---

[8] She notices the departure of Jason and Medea from the house of Circe, notifies Hera, and is sent on a tri-partite mission to facilitate the next stage of the Argonauts' journey (4.753–79): see here Hunter (1993), 96 on Apollonius' delight in making extra toils for Iris.
[9] Roscher, *Lex.* 2.330–1, 348; Weicker (1916), 2041; compare the even more sinister representation of Iris' dog-like attendance on a tyrannical Hera in Callimachus' *Hymn to Delos* (216–39).
[10] Roscher, *Lex.* 2.330–1, 348.
[11] Once again, as in the substitution of Iris for Hermes in the episode with the Harpies, Apollonius may be going against earlier tradition in order to highlight his point, for the ancient scholiast on 3.587 says that in the pseudo-Hesiodic *Aegimius* Aeetes took Phrixus in of his own free will because he wanted the fleece, not because of any message from Hermes.

But it is crucial to observe that this elevating story is not part of the poem's actual narrative, and nor is anything like it.

The reason, as I have already intimated, is clear. In Apollonius' poem Zeus is not represented as a character, his motivation is practically inscrutable even to the author, and there is no ready access to his will for readers or characters.[12] The Homeric master-plot has been replaced by an attenuated and diffident form of control. In such a poetic world, the direct participation of the god who mediates between Zeus and humans is unthinkable: where the poet is estranged from the power of participation in Zeus's knowledge, the messenger and interpreter of Zeus has no role to play. The intermittently cited story of Hermes' mediation between Zeus and Phrixus and Aeetes stands as a fragmentary memory of a previous time in poetry and myth, when all the channels of communication were in a comparative state of grace.[13] In the actual time of Apollonius' narrative, the communicating function of Hermes has lost its fullness of presence, leaving a trace only in his parentage of the Argonauts' herald (1.640–9), or in his role as the god of dreams, communicator of enigmas in sleep (4.1733).

In the *Aeneid*, Virgil engages systematically with the Homeric and Apollonian tradition of divine–human communication, together with the elaborate scholarly and allegorical techniques of reading which were for him an indispensable intermediary element of that tradition. As we have just seen, the case of the *Argonautica* highlights how much is at stake after the *Odyssey* in the choice of who is to be the divine intermediary between gods and humans. In the *Aeneid*, where the will, power and knowledge of the supreme god are central to the poem's entire design, it is not surprising to find Hermes/Mercury reinstated into the narrative as Zeus's/Jupiter's emissary for the one crucial episode of Aeneas' abandonment of Dido. Yet Mercury's reinstatement must still be seen within a larger context. First of all, just as in the *Argonautica*, his function must be viewed in antithesis to that of Iris, the special emissary and tool of Hera/Juno.

We may observe a pattern of practically structuralist tidiness in the opposed female/male pairs of Hera/Iris and Zeus/Hermes, translated by Virgil into Juno/Iris and Jupiter/Mercury. The marked gendering of the opposition of Juno and Jupiter has recently been studied by D. Fowler, who analyses the *Aeneid*'s struggle between deferral and closure, emotion

---

[12] Feeney (1991), 58–65.
[13] The story may, then, be yet another reversal of Homer, for in the *Odyssey* the main narrative recounts a successful embassy on Hermes' part (to Calypso, in Book 5), while there is a reference back to a prior *unsuccessful* embassy (to Aegisthus, 1.35–43).

and rationality, error and truth within the terms of the confrontation between the female anarchy of Juno and the male authority of Jupiter.[14] This gendered opposition between the supreme gods is mirrored in the opposition between their respective emissaries. Using their favourite tool of etymological allegory, the ancient critics explain Iris as representing Eris ('Strife'), while Hermes, as the 'hermeneutic' interpreter of Zeus's supreme rationality, is the emblem of '*Logos, Ratio*, the unperverted word'.[15] Servius repeatedly cites these opposed identifications, asserting that Mercury is sent for the purpose of concord, and Iris for the purpose of discord.[16] It is, of course, vital to bear in mind that Jupiter's interpretation of concord, however dominating and successful it may be, and however much the scholarly tradition has identified with it since Servius' times, is still partisan.[17] One god's concord is another woman's discord, as Dido finds out—Mercury's first intervention in the narrative has the function of creating a Concord between Trojans and Carthaginians (1.297–304), but this pact will eventually destroy Dido and Carthage, since Mercury most emphatically does not mediate the speech/rationality/knowledge of Jupiter to Dido, who remains 'ignorant of fate/what Jupiter has said' (*fati nescia*, 1.299). Still, from a Trojan/Roman perspective, Servius' blunt dichotomy is serviceable enough. As far as Jupiter is concerned, it is undeniably an act of concord for Aeneas to continue towards the right future in Italy, and it is undeniably an act of discord for Juno to send Iris to instigate both the burning of the Trojan ships (5.606–63) and the Latin attack on the Trojan camp (9.1–24).[18]

Mercury's restoration to the epic narrative is, then, a token of the power of Jupiter's and Virgil's authoritative knowledge in this poem. Before turning to Mercury's role in the epic narrative in Book 4, we may observe that the power of Jupiter's and Virgil's authoritative knowledge is no less strikingly illustrated by the eventual fate of Mercury's counterpart, Iris. Virgil does not rest with the terms of the post-Homeric consensus, with Iris

---

[14] D. Fowler (2000), chapter 10, esp. 226–8; cf. Quint (1993), chapter 1, esp. 28–9.
[15] P. Hardie (1986), 278; further references in Feeney (1991), 175; on Iris/Eris, see Pease (1935), on *Aen*. 4.694; on this role of Mercury in *Aeneid* 4, see Heinze (1915), 307–10.
[16] *Aen.* 5.606; 9.2; for links in Roman cult between Mercury and Concordia, see Combet-Farnoux (1980), 343–5. Even Iris' (Hesiodic, and non-Homeric) manifestation as the rainbow may reinforce this antithesis, for she is thereby figured as various, deceitful and illusory (*Aen.* 4.700–1; 5.609, 657–8; 9.14–15): see Plut. *Mor.* 765e-f for an interesting discussion of the rainbow's illusory refractions. It is significant that the one time Iris is sent by Jupiter is also the one time that she is not described as the rainbow (9.803–4).
[17] Feeney (1991), 152–5. On concord/discord in the *Aeneid*, see Cairns (1989), esp. chapter 4.
[18] Likewise, Iris has two missions in the *Iliad* to ensure that Hector can attack the Greek ships (11.185–210; 15.158–219).

as the agent of Hera and Hermes as the agent of Zeus, although for most of the poem it looks as if that is what he is doing. Instead, he undoes that consensus and reasserts the authority of Jupiter by having him eventually reestablish his erstwhile Iliadic dominion over the wayward Iris. In Book 5, Juno sends Iris to instigate the Trojan women to set fire to the Trojan ships (5.606–63), and shortly thereafter, in response to Aeneas' prayer, Jupiter causes a storm in order to extinguish the fire and save the ships (685–99). In Book 9, with a repetition of a line from Book 5, Juno once again sends Iris down from heaven (*Irim de caelo misit Saturnia Iuno*, 9.2 = 5.606), this time to instigate Turnus to attack the Trojan camp (9.1–24). Turnus, as the old-fashioned Iliadic hero, thinks that she may well have been sent by Jupiter;[19] but the irony of Turnus' blunder is splendidly capped at the end of the book, when Jupiter does indeed himself send Iris, this time to force her erstwhile mistress, Juno, to abandon the struggling Turnus in the midst of the Trojan camp (9.802–5).[20] Both in Book 5, then, and in Book 9, Jupiter intervenes to stop the action instigated by Juno and Iris; but in Book 9 he reasserts his Homeric hegemony over all the media of communication by himself sending Iris. He can act like the Zeus of the *Iliad* as well as the Zeus of the *Odyssey*, and he deprives Hera/Juno of the independent capacity to manipulate communication which she had fleetingly enjoyed in the *Iliad* and *Argonautica*, and up to this point in the *Aeneid*. Jupiter's power in the *Aeneid* is so massive that he can eventually recall Iris to her long-lost Iliadic role as *his* messenger, to the task of fostering what *he* sees as concord.

Mercury's mission to Carthage must be placed within these larger contexts —of the poem and of the epic tradition—if we are to begin to understand its impact as the explosion of a certain kind of knowledge and power. He is preeminently the god who may communicate from the divine to the human everything which is summed up in the word *logos*—'speech', 'rationality', and 'fate', *fatum*, the speech-act of Jupiter which embodies and enforces his rationality.[21] But Mercury's devastatingly effective and brutally authoritative voicing in Book 4 is not to be viewed as an isolated act. Once more, we must see his role as part of a structured dialogue with another deceptive and disruptive speech-goddess, not Iris this time, but Fama. Further, as the god who mediates between the upper world and the underworld, he discharges a double function for the two heroes of our book: he may bring rationality and salvation of a kind to Aeneas, but he brings death to Dido.

---

[19] Already picked up by Servius (on 9.22); see here Mackie (1990).

[20] On the 'surprise' effect here, see P. Hardie (1994), on 9.803–5. As remarked in n.16 above, note that this is the only time that Iris' passage is described without the illusory rainbow.

[21] On *fatum* as 'that which Jupiter says', see Feeney (1991), 139–40.

Once Dido has been subjected to her passion, her 'concern for what people may say' (*fama*) no longer stands in the way of her frenzy (4.91), and once she has been joined with Aeneas in the cave, she 'is not moved by how things may look' (*neque ... specie ... mouetur*) nor 'by how things may sound' (*fama*, 170). Virgil then presents us with the embodiment of 'what people may say' and 'how things may sound', in the notorious figure of *Fama*, 'Rumour', the winged sister of the monstrous giants, who imitates Homer's Eris ('Strife') by starting off small and then growing as she moves, and who imitates Hesiod's poetic Muses by adhering to the fictive as tenaciously as she announces true things, singing alike what actually happened and what did not (173–90).[22] Here is a massive threat to Virgil's own poetic enterprise and authority, an alternative version of history from the side of the gigantesque, an alternative track for the mission and the epic to digress into and be trapped in.[23] The implications of the threat are vividly spelt out by the spurned lover of Dido, the neighbouring king Iarbas, who hears the rumours of Fama and prays to his father, Jupiter, to intervene. If this version of *Fama*, 'Rumour', should prove to be really true, says Iarbas, then Jupiter's version would prove to be vacuous: in honouring the god, 'we nurture an empty rumour' (*famamque fouemus inanem*, 218).

The prayer of Iarbas to Jupiter motivates the mission of Mercury, for Jupiter now sends *his* god of epic speech to counteract and displace *Fama*;[24] after Jupiter hears the words of Iarbas, he looks to Carthage, and sees 'the lovers, who have forgotten their better reputation/fame' (*oblitos famae melioris amantis*, 221). When Mercury is mobilised against this catastrophic act of forgetfulness, which dictates abandoning a better *Fama* for a worse, Virgil is adding in another tint from his palette of allegorical scholarship, for Hermes had long been seen as the adversary of forgetfulness. In the battle of the gods in the *Iliad*, Hermes is ranged against Leto, the mother of Artemis and Apollo (20.72, 21.497–501); as the allegorist known as 'Heraclitus' helpfully tells us, all you have to do is change one letter and you have 'Letho', which is close enough to 'Lethe', 'Forgetfulness', the inveterate opponent of Hermes as 'Logos' ('speech').[25] Mercury will soon be standing

---

[22] See here the illuminating and comprehensive discussion of P. Hardie (1986), 273–9, to which I am indebted throughout this section. [See now P. Hardie (2012), chapter 3.]

[23] At the end of his narrative in Books 2 and 3, Aeneas acknowledges that his journey to Carthage is a digression (*hinc me digressum uestris deus appulit oris*, 3.715). Dido's story, then, anticipates the collision between epic's teleology and romance's digressiveness which Quint (1993), 33–4, 45–6 describes in Cleopatra's story.

[24] P. Hardie (1986), 276.

[25] *Homeric Problems*, 55.2; see Buffière (1956), 290. Apollonius already plays on this connection, when he tells us that the herald Aethalides received imperishable knowledge from his father, Hermes: not

before Aeneas and upbraiding him for this disastrous forgetfulness of his true future destiny (*heu, regni rerumque oblite tuarum!*, 267).

Mercury's task is to obliterate the forgetfulness of better reputation or fame, and to replace the worse Fama with what Jupiter sees as Aeneas' genuinely epic 'glory' and 'praise' (*gloria, laus*, 232, 233). What this entails is the destruction of Dido and her *fama*, for, as Philip Hardie points out, Dido 'cannot separate her own existence from that of her reputation; both rise or fall together'—Dido will soon tell Aeneas that her shame and reputation (*pudor et fama*) have been extinguished because of him, and that she is as a result doomed (*moribundam*).[26] Jupiter anticipates this obliteration in his address to Mercury, in which Dido is not so much as mentioned.[27]

The duality of Mercury's function here is caught by the apparently otiose detail lavished on the description of Mercury's wand as he leaves Olympus to discharge his father's mission (4.242–4):

> hac animas ille euocat Orco
> pallentis, alias sub Tartara tristia mittit,
> dat somnos adimitque, et lumina morte resignat.
>
> With this wand he summons pale souls from Orcus, and sends others down to gloomy Tartarus, he gives sleep and he takes it away, and he unseals the eyes in death.

The larger description of Mercury's equipment from which these lines are taken follows closely a repeated Homeric prototype (*Il.* 24.339–45 = *Od.* 5.43–9), but in the lines just quoted there is a significant departure. Homer describes Hermes' wand as the instrument by which he charms the eyes of whichever men he wants, and wakes them up again when they are asleep. Virgil, however, by introducing Mercury's power over the dead, alludes to the chthonic dimension of Hermes' personality, as the *Psychopompos* ('Escorter of souls').[28] Metaphorically Mercury will soon wake up Aeneas from his sleep, and literally he will do the same thing in his second visitation (4.571–2). Dido, however, will die as a result of Mercury's mission from Jupiter. When Aeneas wakes up after Mercury's second

---

even now that he has crossed the underworld river of Acheron does forgetfulness overcome his spirit (1.644–5; with further play on the fact that Lethe is likewise also a river of the underworld).

[26] P. Hardie (1986), 279 on *Aen.* 4.321–3.

[27] Finely observed by E.L. Harrison (1984), 20: 'Had Jupiter said "Let him leave that foreign queen behind: she stands in the way of the Roman destiny", that no doubt would have seemed bad enough. But for him to proceed as if Dido did not even exist involves an extra dimension of callousness.'

[28] E.L. Harrison (1984), 26–8, with full references to earlier discussions (note esp. Pöschl (1962), 145–6); P. Hardie (1986), 277.

visitation, he cuts his ties with Dido and Carthage by drawing his sword and cutting through the cables that connect his ship to the land (4.579–80). His sword there is described as being like a thunderbolt (*fulmineum*), and in this way his act of severance, inspired by Jupiter's Mercury, becomes the fulfilment of Dido's prayer at the beginning of the book, in which she had asked that Jupiter consign her to the shades with a thunderbolt if she ever violated her vows to her first husband (*pater omnipotens adigat me fulmine ad umbras/ . . . ante, pudor, quam te uiolo aut tua iura resoluo*, 4.25–7).[29]

Charged with his mission from Jupiter, Mercury now descends to the earth, traversing the opposite direction to that of his opponent, Fama, acting out his function as one who mediates between realms.[30] On his way to Carthage Mercury pauses on Mt. Atlas, an emblem of the unshakable divine order which his mission is set to restore, and simultaneously an emblem of the petrification which afflicts the agents and the victims alike of that divine order (246–53).[31] To Dido, Aeneas' imperviousness to her first speech will make him appear like an offshoot of the crags of the Caucasus (366–7), and Virgil compares Aeneas' ignoring of Anna's intercessions to the steadfastness of an oak stuck in Alpine rocks, its roots stretching down to Tartarus and its peak stretching up to heaven (441–6);[32] in the underworld, the insubstantial and gleaming shade of Dido will reciprocate this imperviousness, being moved by Aeneas' words no more than if she were a fixed piece of hard flint or a crag of marble from Mt. Marpessus (*quam si dura silex aut stet Marpesia cautes*, 6.471).

Since the god Mercury is now about to burst in upon Aeneas' reverie, in a way which many, if not most, readers have found to be repellently artificial and unnatural, we should pause to take stock of the options Virgil had at his command in narrating Aeneas' decision to leave Dido. It is important to remind ourselves that Virgil could easily have anticipated our modern scruples and written the scene in entirely naturalistic terms. After all, when Odysseus has been dallying too long with Circe, his men remind him that it is time to think of home, and they persuade him to leave (*Od.* 10.469–75). When Apollonius imitates this Odyssean scene in the *Argonautica*, as the Argonauts are dallying with the women of Lemnos, he likewise has one of the ship's company, Heracles, shame the heroes into

---

[29] Moles (1987), 159.
[30] As one Latin etymology for 'Mercurius' had it, he is so named because he 'runs in the middle' (*medius currens, Medicurrius*): see Pease (1935) on *Aen.* 4.256.
[31] Thornton (1976), 51–2; Morwood (1985); P. Hardie (1986), 278.
[32] Morwood (1985), 58; P. Hardie (1986), 280–1.

resuming their voyage (1.861–78). The fact that Virgil has these options shows that he is not the hapless victim of a sclerotic and outmoded technique. He is under no compulsion whatever to introduce Mercury, and if he has not given us the naturalistic narrative many of us want, it is not because it is beyond his genre's resources. Let us see what it is that he has gained from his choice.

First of all, it is vital that Mercury departs from his Homeric prototype and speaks to Aeneas. He would have spoken to Dido if he had followed the paradigm of *Odyssey* 5, when Hermes is despatched by Zeus to tell Calypso to release Odysseus; Hermes' mission to Calypso was interpreted by the ancient commentators as being an allegorical representation of Odysseus' own rhetorical persuasive powers.[33] In the *Aeneid*, such a solution would produce bathos instead of tragedy, while it is crucial to the entire drama that Aeneas' rhetoric is a disaster.[34]

As Mercury attacks the unsuspecting Aeneas, then, he is not so much *Peitho*, 'persuasion', as *Logos*, 'rationality'—though 'rationality' of a very particular kind, namely, the rationality and vision of Jupiter as interpreted by a partial and energetic witness.[35] It is the gulf between Jupiter's vision and Aeneas' current obsession which Mercury's unnaturalistically abrupt intrusion spectacularly illuminates, making possible a more profound realism in the process:

> As we watch Aeneas' reaction to Mercury's message, with the words of Jupiter still in our ears, we are forced to see this in the perspective of twelve centuries of history even as the reading itself makes us feel that here and now, Aeneas and Dido, is all that counts. The reader's sense of disjunction, of trying to harmonize these two irreconcilable focuses, catches the bewilderment of the character, Aeneas, who is performing an analogous act of harmonization, juggling his priorities to restore them to their correct balance. Only if we listen to Jupiter and Mercury can we feel this disjunction fully, as we follow Aeneas in trying to inhabit two (mutually incompatible) worlds of significance simultaneously ... We feel only a fraction of any of this if we brush aside Jupiter and Mercury as nothing more than Vergil's oddly roundabout way of revealing to us how Aeneas changed his mind and decided to leave Carthage.[36]

The sequel, however, adds considerable nuance to this conclusion. Simply to assert that we are not dealing with naturalism is too straightforward,

---

[33] Buffière (1956), 291.
[34] For the tragic consequences of Virgil's reversal of the Homeric model, see Knauer (1964), 214.
[35] For Mercury's characterful interpreting of the words of Jupiter, see E.L. Harrison (1984), 18–23.
[36] Feeney (1991), 174–5. I should there have referred to the arguments of Otis (1963), 82–3, 92–3.

because when Dido and Aeneas speak to each other we see that the problem of how to judge between naturalistic and unnaturalistic motivations is hotly contested. Aeneas does not speak only of divine motivations when he tries to account for his decision, while in Dido's reaction to Aeneas' account of his divine motivations, we find that the modern reader's disdainful and dismissive response is already part of the narrative.

When Aeneas defends himself against Dido's rhetorical attack, he himself says that he has naturalistic motivation aplenty. What is striking is the way in which his guilt-stricken thoughts of his father and his son are sandwiched between his descriptions of two divine injunctions, the institutional and distant commands of Apollo, and the personal and recent commands of Mercury, vividly and urgently narrated as the climax (345–59):

> sed nunc Italiam magnam Gryneus Apollo,
> Italiam Lyciae iussere capessere sortes;
> hic amor, haec patria est. si te Karthaginis arces
> Phoenissam Libycaeque aspectus detinet urbis,
> quae tandem Ausonia Teucros considere terra
> inuidia est? et nos fas extera quaerere regna.
> me patris Anchisae, quotiens umentibus umbris
> nox operit terras, quotiens astra ignea surgunt,
> admonet in somnis et turbida terret imago;
> me puer Ascanius capitisque iniuria cari,
> quem regno Hesperiae fraudo et fatalibus aruis.
> nunc etiam interpres diuum Ioue missus ab ipso
> (testor utrumque caput) celeris mandata per auras
> detulit: ipse deum manifesto in lumine uidi
> intrantem muros uocemque his auribus hausi.

But now great Italy is what Apollo of Gryneum has commanded me to make for, Italy is the command of his Lycian lots. If you, despite being a Phoenician, are held by the citadels of Carthage and the sight of a Libyan city, how can you hold it against Trojans to settle in the land of Italy? For us as well it is right and fated to seek dominions that are foreign. Whenever night covers the earth with her damp shadows and whenever the fiery stars rise, the agitated phantom of my father Anchises admonishes me in my sleep and terrifies me. The thought of my son Ascanius and of the injury I am doing to his dear person admonishes me too, for cheating him of rule over Hesperia and of the territory that is his by fate. And now even the interpreter of the gods, sent by Jupiter himself—I swear on my head and yours—has brought commands down through the swift breezes: I have myself seen the god in the clear light of day entering the city walls, and I have drunk in his words with these ears of mine.

It is highly significant that when Dido reacts to these pleas she ignores the human dimension of Aeneas' motivation altogether, omitting Aeneas' father and son to concentrate all the withering power of her sarcasm on the—to her—utterly specious appeals to the divine (376–80):

> nunc augur Apollo,
> nunc Lyciae sortes, nunc et Ioue missus ab ipso
> interpres diuum fert horrida iussa per auras.
> scilicet is superis labor est, ea cura quietos
> sollicitat.

> Now it's Apollo the augur, now it's his Lycian lots, now to cap it all, sent by Jupiter himself, the 'interpreter of the gods' brings horrid orders down through the breezes. Oh yes, of course, this is something the gods exert themselves about, this is an anxiety that disturbs their tranquillity.

Dido's reaction shows that the appeals to divine injunctions are meaningless to her, and her reaction is thus consistent with the generally Epicurean attitude to divinity she exhibits from the start.[37] This attitude to divinity is also, partly, a metaphor for her general tendency to emphasise the individual and the personal at the expense of the supra-personal historical elements represented by the divine plot. The difference between her and Aeneas in this regard is already clearly illustrated by the different ways they refer to Aeneas' adventures before his arrival at Carthage. When, at the end of Book 1, Dido invites Aeneas to tell his story, all the second person pronouns and possessive adjectives are *singular*, and the events are 'accidents' and 'wanderings': 'the accidents of your people, and your wanderings; for you ...' (*casusque tuorum/erroresque tuos; nam te ...*, 1.753–4; compare her first address to Aeneas in Book 1, where it is 'accident' and 'violence' that have brought him into her presence: *casus, uis*, 615–16). When Aeneas has finished his story at the end of Book 3, his last words use a second-person *plural* possessive adjective, and attribute his arrival to divine action: 'god drove me to your shores' (*uestris deus appulit oris*, 3.715).[38]

Dido's dismissive reaction to Aeneas' appeals to divine injunctions is clearly not eccentric, in the sense that hers is a reaction that many readers will have had, and not just modern ones. Aeneas may speak in earnest terms of an actual epiphany, carefully described, and this form of speech may stand for an awareness of an ever-widening backdrop against which the

---

[37] Feeney (1991), 173 n.177.
[38] The narrator's perspective is, of course, even broader than Aeneas': two lines later Virgil sums up Books 2 and 3 as 'the fates of the gods, and progressive movements' (*fata ... diuum cursusque*, 3.717).

individual must contextualise himself. But Aeneas' and Virgil's refusal to use a naturalistic narration or interpretation is contested by Dido (and by many readers). Much more than a narratological choice between representational modes is at issue here. The choice of representational mode brings with it a cluster of ideological consequences, forcing upon characters and readers a choice between competing historical and ethical frameworks, and between different ways of positioning the self within those frameworks.[39] The main point at issue is a willingness or a refusal to see oneself as a certain kind of historical agent. What a choice like this does to a person is to be spelt out soon, when Mercury appears again to Aeneas, in a dream.

Before Aeneas dreams of Mercury, Dido also dreams. From the beginning, one of the many qualities the refugee leaders share is their dreaming capacity. The first thing Aeneas hears about Dido is that she had a dream in which her murdered husband appeared to her and told her to run away (1.353–60); Aeneas himself had such a dream, on the night Troy was taken, when Hector appeared to him and told him to run away (2.270–97).[40] These dreams follow the epic pattern by which a figure appears to the sleeper and speaks; in particular, these dreams both belong to the category of 'oracular dream', 'which serves to guide the founder of a new city towards his or her goal'.[41] Such, precisely, will be the continuing pattern for Aeneas' dream of Mercury. As the crisis approaches, however, Dido's dreams no longer follow this epic pattern of fated progress, but revert to a tragic pattern of nightmare.[42]

Dido dreams of being deserted by her people, and of being harried by a bestial Aeneas (4.465–8), in a state of hallucination like that of heroes of Attic drama, 'as Pentheus in his madness sees the columns of Furies, and sees a twin sun and a double Thebes appear' (*Eumenidum ueluti demens uidet agmina Pentheus/et solem geminum et duplices se ostendere Thebas*, 469–70). At this moment of collapse, one of the many significations of the 'double Thebes' is the splitting of the concord between Tyrians and Trojans of which Dido and her patron goddess, Juno, had dreamed—a spirit of concord fostered precisely by the first mission of Mercury in Book 1 (302–3).

---

[39] My debt to the work of G.B. Conte is great at this point: for the struggle between points of view and their ideological implications in the *Aeneid*, see Conte (1986), 141–84, esp. 150–8. Further, on the ideological implications of choices between different narratological readings, D. Fowler (2000), chapter 2.
[40] Block (1981), 215–16; Krevans (1993), 268–9.
[41] Krevans (1993), 268; her discussion of Dido's and Aeneas' dreams is fundamental here.
[42] Ibid., 270–1. The fact that Ennius' tragic/epic dream of Ilia is now the model is caught by the self-referential language which introduces the dream, as we are told that Dido is terrified by *uatum praedicta priorum*, both 'the predictions of ancient soothsayers' and 'the things said already by earlier bards' (464).

When Dido first speaks in the poem, addressing the Trojan supplicants, she invites them to settle with her own people *on an equal basis* (*uultis et his mecum pariter considere regnis?*), tells them that the city she is founding is theirs (*urbem quam statuo, uestra est*), and says that there will be *no distinction* between Trojan and Tyrian (*nullo discrimine*, 1.572–4). In Book 4, when the Carthaginian goddess Juno approaches Venus to plot the marriage of Aeneas and Dido, she suggests that they rule the new people together as a joint endeavour (*communem populum*, 4.102). Venus shows that she knows exactly what Juno has in mind, when she ironically replies that she isn't sure if Jupiter intends there to be *one city* for the Tyrians and Trojans, or approves of the idea that the citizen bodies should be *mixed together* and treaties *joined* (*sed fatis incerta feror, si Iuppiter unam/esse uelit Tyriis urbem Troiaque profectis,/misceriue probet populos aut foedera iungi*, 110–12). The 'one city', *unam urbem*, of this fantasy is smashed back into its constituent parts when Dido dreams as one who dreams of 'double Thebes', *duplices Thebas*.

Aeneas' dream is very different (556–80):

> huic se forma dei uultu redeuntis eodem
> obtulit in somnis rursusque ita uisa monere est,
> omnia Mercurio similis, uocemque coloremque
> et crinis flauos et membra decora iuuenta:
> 'nate dea, potes hoc sub casu ducere somnos,
> nec quae te circum stent deinde pericula cernis,
> demens, nec Zephyros audis spirare secundos?
> illa dolos dirumque nefas in pectore uersat
> certa mori, uariosque irarum concitat aestus.
> non fugis hinc praeceps, dum praecipitare potestas?
> iam mare turbari trabibus saeuasque uidebis
> conlucere faces, iam feruere litora flammis,
> si te his attigerit terris Aurora morantem.
> heia age, rumpe moras. uarium et mutabile semper
> femina.' sic fatus nocti se immiscuit atrae.
>
> Tum uero Aeneas subitis exterritus umbris
> corripit e somno corpus sociosque fatigat
> praecipitis: 'uigilate, uiri, et considite transtris;
> soluite uela citi. deus aethere missus ab alto
> festinare fugam tortosque incidere funis
> ecce iterum instimulat. sequimur te, sancte deorum,
> quisquis es, imperioque iterum paremus ouantes.
> adsis o placidusque iuues et sidera caelo
> dextra feras.' dixit uaginaque eripit ensem
> fulmineum strictoque ferit retinacula ferro.

To him the form of the god, coming back with the same expression, appeared in sleep, and seemed again to advise him in this way, similar to Mercury in every respect, in voice and complexion and blonde locks and youthfully good-looking limbs: 'Goddess-born, can you carry on sleeping under the threat of this disaster? Don't you see the dangers which surround you now, you madman; don't you hear the favourable west winds blowing? That woman swirls tricks and dreadful wickedness in her heart, resolved to die, and she stirs up all kinds of tides of anger. You're not fleeing from here in a rush while there is still the chance to rush? Soon you will see the sea churned up by ships and savage torches flaring, the shore ablaze with flame, if Dawn's rays light upon you delaying in these lands. Hey, come on! Smash your delays! A variable and changeable thing, always, is woman.' With these words he blended into the black night.

Then indeed Aeneas, terrified by the sudden shadowy vision, snatches his body out of sleep and assails his allies, lashing them into rushing action: 'Wake up, men, and sit down on the rowing benches; quickly, let out the sails. A god sent down from high heaven again, look, spurs us on to hasten our flight and cut the plaited cables. We follow you, blessed one of the gods, whoever you are, and we obey your command again, with a cry of glad triumph. Oh be with us, be on our side and help us, and put favourable stars in the sky.' He spoke and snatched his sword, like a thunderbolt, from its scabbard, and smote the connecting cable with the drawn iron.

The first problem posed by these lines is whether or not the vision is genuine, for readers since Servius have been made suspicious by language such as 'the form of the god', 'similar to Mercury'. Virgil certainly has invested the experience with an atmosphere of mystery and eeriness, but this is appropriate to the awesome nature of epiphany, and Harrison has conclusively shown that, within the terms of epic realism, 'Mercury's second visit is as genuine as the first'.[43] The vital point—once again clearly established by Harrison—is that the elements of uncertainty in the scene all stem from the fact that the second epiphany is focalised through Aeneas, whereas the first epiphany had been focalised through Mercury: 'Earlier he took us inside Mercury, as it were, and let us see Aeneas as he seemed to the god on his arrival at Carthage ... Now he reverses the process and lets us see the god through the eyes of the dreaming Aeneas.'[44]

---

[43] E.L. Harrison (1984), 33. On epiphanies, see Lane Fox (1986), 102–67 and Versnel (1987). Virgil has even picked the ideal time of night—just before the dawn—for such a vision: Lane Fox (1986), 151 (cf. *Aen.* 8.67–8).

[44] E.L. Harrison (1984), 30. Servius 'auctus' already makes this point, commenting on 570 (*nocti se immiscuit atrae*, 'he mingled himself in the black night'): *hoc ad uisum somniantis referendum est* ('we should refer this to the point of view of the sleeper': this is how to say 'focalise' in Latin).

Human knowledge being what it is, a human can never be quite certain that he has made the right identification;[45] and it is Aeneas' apprehension of this which mediates to us the conditional language ('It certainly looks like Mercury, it has all the characteristics I saw the other day . . . '). Hence the prudent way Aeneas addresses the vanishing vision with the words *quisquis es*, 'whoever you are'. This phrase has been taken to show that Aeneas does not know which god it was, but Servius is right to stress instead that although Aeneas thought it was Mercury he had seen, he could not be absolutely sure (*licet uiderit, non tamen re uera nouit esse Mercurium*): 'after all', as Harrison puts it, 'the last deity he had personal experience of looked like Diana (1.229)—yet she soon proved to be that very different deity, his own mother, Venus'.[46] Twice elsewhere in the poem, the phrase *quisquis es* is used in conversation when the speaker wishes politely to say, 'I have no independent means of knowing whether what you say/appear to be is true; but let us assume that you are who you say you are/appear to be.'[47] However cautious Aeneas is in his pagan piety, then, he is sure that this god is coming for the second time (*iterum . . . iterum*, 576–7), and he has as much confidence in what he has seen as any hero could hope to have.

If we consider the words *quisquis es* from outside Aeneas' character, we see that Mercury's manifold and mutable nature is being acknowledged. For Aeneas, Mercury is the one who brings divine commands from high heaven: for Dido, of course, he is bringing a death-warrant, and acting as the *psychopompos*. As so often, Servius has the wrong end of the stick with his reference here to a doctrine that there are three separate Mercuries (in the realms of Heaven, Earth, and Underworld, *superum, terrenum, inferum*); but, as so often, it is the right stick, for the one Mercury does mediate between all these realms, consigning Dido to the Underworld with his descent from Heaven to Earth.

Just as when he first spoke to Aeneas, Mercury improvises with zest upon the initial theme given him by his father, Jupiter. We may write off Mercury's foul words about Dido's female nature as his own improvisatory supplement to Jupiter's initial command, the consequence perhaps of his status as 'the god of athletic youth, of the *palaistrai* and gymnasia', with his

---

[45] Lane Fox (1986), 158; Versnel (1987), 45–8.

[46] *per litteras*. The same conviction that human knowledge of the divine cannot be certain is behind Servius' reference here to the cautious all-embracing language of Roman ritual, whereby the *pontifices* address Jupiter as 'Jupiter Omnipotent, or whatever other name you may wish to be addressed by' (*Iuppiter Omnipotens, uel quo alio te nomine appellari uolueris*).

[47] 1.387 (the disguised Venus to Aeneas); 2.148 (Priam to Sinon).

'homoerotically tinged element'.[48] But that would be to neutralise the boldness Virgil shows in imbuing the communication of 'rationality' with this sprightly misogyny. It is difficult to know which speech-act is more revealing of imperial rationality's crushing subordination of the female to the male—Jupiter's complete suppression of Dido, or Mercury's arch and dexterous contempt. In Mercury's phrasing we see exposed the supposedly disinterested detachment of the ordering rationality being pressed upon Aeneas: 'The word of the father which controls disorder is ... almost by definition arbitrary, a mask for violence; if it had reason on its side, why does it need to speak with *authority*?'[49] The god of *logos* is also the archetypal liar, and as we listen to him speak to Aeneas we are being forced to acknowledge that there is no speech-act, whatever its author and its pretensions to reason, without a bias and a point of view.[50]

Once again, Mercury's point of view has been contested in reception, as R.O.A.M. Lyne remarks, referring to the letter that Ovid later composed for Dido: 'it is pleasant that Ovid makes Dido throw the word "mutabilis" back at Aeneas' (*tu quoque cum uentis utinam mutabilis esses!*, 'Oh that you too had been changeable with the winds!', *Her.* 7. 51).[51] It is also important to see that Mercury's point of view is contested within the *Aeneid*, for only twenty-five lines after Mercury has delivered himself of his notorious aphorism about female changeability, we hear Dido refusing to *change* her fixed resolve to commit suicide despite her initial insane impulse to pursue the fleeing Trojans: *quae mentem insania mutat?* (595).

Aeneas definitively aligns himself with the will of this god when he says, 'We obey your command again, with a cry of glad triumph' (*imperioque iterum paremus ouantes*, 577). Here Aeneas is at last adopting the same attitude to Jupiter's messenger as the messenger had automatically adopted to Jupiter after receiving his orders ('he was getting ready to obey the command of his great father', *ille patris magni parere parabat/imperio*, 238–9); it is the same attitude of automatic glad obedience which his own men had shown him when he first told them, after Mercury's first

---

[48] Burkert (1985), 158 on Hermes. Excellent discussion of the register and force of *uarium et mutabile semper/femina* in R.O.A.M. Lyne (1989), 48–51; cf. 43–8 on the caustic *uxorius* in the first epiphany (4.266).
[49] D. Fowler (2000), 226 (original emphasis).
[50] Cf. Conte (1986), 182 on how Virgil 'wished to display the ideological bias of the epic norm by showing that the truth, which it claimed entirely for itself, was relative, and he did so by setting other points of view alongside its own perspective'.
[51] R.O.A.M. Lyne (1989), 51.

visitation, to get ready to leave Carthage ('they all happily obey the command', *omnes/imperio laeti parent*, 294–5).

These marked verbal overlaps reveal that Aeneas, as a commander and a servant, is in alignment with what the epic and imperial plot demand of him—he is now 'quoting' the narrator. Taken together with Aeneas' focalisation of Mercury, this device shows that Aeneas is now internalising constraints which had formerly been represented as external. This naturalising, psychologising process is an interesting complication of the narrative modes used so far; it has been building since Aeneas spoke to Dido and described his thoughts of his father and son as well as his direct vision of Mercury. This time the visitation of Mercury, although reconstructable as a real event in the *fabula*, has been focalised entirely through Aeneas, and internalised by him, becoming an event on a par with the appearance of his father Anchises in dreams. It is worth observing that this shows how Virgil could have moved in a more naturalistic circuit all the way along. It is more important, however, to go beyond this formalist observation and to see what is entailed by these shifts in narratological technique: the shift in focus is a metaphor for the way the man of destiny becomes an agent of destiny, identifying himself with forces originally conceived of as external. This is no doubt the major explanation for the fact that Mercury never again appears to Aeneas—or, indeed, in the poem at all.[52]

The divine communication that so terrified Aeneas and so revolted Dido has now become an integral part of Aeneas' world. For her part, Dido will not believe in the reality of Mercury and of the apparatus for which he is a mouthpiece, and readers who follow her lead—a majority?—will not want to believe in that reality either. They will be as repelled as she was by the apparent frigidity and inconsequentiality of speaking of Mercury in this way. They will be dominated by the feeling that speaking in this way is beside the point. This entails writing Mercury out, and most readers have instinctively done that too.

I have been arguing against writing Mercury out, because so much of the meaning of the narrative is located in him and in our reaction to him. But we must be aware of the complicity we risk embracing when we insist on acknowledging his power in the fiction. It is vital to give full weight to all the significance in the figure of Mercury in order to appreciate the colossal poetic profit which accrues to Virgil as a result of his investment in the god, but it is equally vital to see that this poetic profit is committed to

---

[52] Here my conclusion is very close to that of Otis (1963), 307, although I depart from him in not seeing the changes in Aeneas as a 'spiritual regeneration'.

discharging an enormous ideological debt. It is clear that the profit and the debt alike have continued to be contested ever since.[53] I have tried to argue that they are already contested even within the poem, and that the intermediary figure of Mercury is the main site on which that struggle over interpretation takes place.

[53] [As demonstrated by the essays in the original home for this chapter, Burden (1998).]

CHAPTER 9

# *Epic Violence, Epic Order: Killings, Catalogues, and the Role of the Reader in* Aeneid 10[1]

By the time we reach Book 10 we have read three quarters of this very long poem and we have still not yet seen what the first words of the epic promised us—*arma uirumque*, 'arms/man', the epic hero in the quintessentially epic action of warfare.[2] As a young poet, in his first poetic work, the *Eclogues*, Virgil had apparently already wanted to compose an epic and sing of 'kings and battles' (*reges et proelia, Ecl.* 6.3) but had found himself derailed by the intervention of Apollo into verse of a nonmartial variety. Now, even when he has taken up again this long-deferred epic project, it appears that he still finds it difficult to deliver the epic apparatus of war. In the first half of the poem we have had a love-story, much wandering, a tale of inglorious sack, some funeral games, a trip to the underworld. As the second half of the poem begins Virgil announces that at last he is moving into a higher gear, with 'a greater order of events, a greater task' (*maior rerum . . . ordo, maius opus*, 7.44–5): at last, he says, he will 'tell of horrid wars' (*dicam horrida bella*, 41). Yet we are still kept waiting, with more preliminaries (Book 7) and yet another detour, to the site of Rome and the future (Book 8).

Of course, none of this is accidental. As epic narrators so often do, Virgil self-consciously comments on the way his story is unfolding, repeatedly calling attention to the deferral of the expected epic action. At the beginning of Book 9, for example, when Iris is sent by Juno to incite Turnus to attack the Trojan camp in Aeneas' absence, she says, 'Why are you hesitating? Smash all delays!' (*quid dubitas? . . . rumpe moras*

---

[1] My warm thanks to Christine Perkell and all the participants in the National Humanities Summer Institute at Emory in July 1994 for their enjoyable and stimulating company. I am much in debt to David Califf: his paper on 'The divine audience in *Aeneid* 10' for my *Aeneid* seminar in Madison in Fall 1992 taught me much, and inspired me to look again at this old problem.

[2] In the *Iliad* there is plenty of martial action from early on, but we are still kept waiting until Book 20 before we see Achilles, the hero named in the poem's first line, in action.

*omnis*, 9.12–13).³ Even this promising impulse to epic carnage fizzles out dismally, with the transformation of the ships into sea-nymphs abruptly stalling Turnus' assault. It is only 300 lines from the end of Book 9 that we finally have an epic invocation of the Muse (525–8) and a narration of the exploits of Turnus. After that tantalising snippet, Book 10 opens with the supreme god, Jupiter, complaining that war has started against his will. Even though the epic slaughter has hardly begun, and even though the epic hero, Aeneas, has still not been seen in action, it appears that Jupiter would rather not witness a continuation or repetition of the *Iliad*: 'Now give over', he tells the assembled gods (*nunc sinite*, 10.15). What Jupiter wants is 'an agreed treaty' (*placitum . . . foedus*).

The last three books of the poem, then, are a frenzy of violence, yet we are repeatedly reminded that none of it need have happened or been narrated: it could have been a very different story. Our reaction as readers is going to be a complex one. Do we really want that 'different story'? As epic readers, would we have been satisfied and pleased if Jupiter's league of peace had been enforced at the beginning of Book 10, with the poem ending 2,500 lines early, Turnus still alive, a wedding-song to round it off? What Virgil's technique does here is reveal to us our complicity in the violence he is narrating, as he acts out his narrative choices, and makes us acknowledge our narrative preferences. One of the most important issues we must address in reading this first book of dedicated epic violence is the kind of pleasure and satisfaction such narratives give. The precious verse artefact here turns to the task of describing how men have their arms chopped off and heads split, their abdomens pierced and their entrails poured out on the ground; and Virgil's commentary on his own deferral of that task has reminded us that we would have felt somehow cheated if he had not delivered on the promise of epic fulfilment. What kind of readers is this poem trying to turn us into?

Book 10, then, is a good place to examine the problem of the aesthetics of violence. It is also a good place to examine the self-referential nature of Virgil's narrative, as he makes his action of narrating and our action of reading part of the text, alluding continually to the choices which he and we are making as we progress. Finally, as we wonder about why epics do the things they do, Book 10 is a good place to examine the conventional nature of epic: why do epics all have to have the same old things—poured-out

---

³ By repeating the phrase *rumpe moras* from an earlier occurrence, Virgil here reminds us that one third of the epic has passed since Mercury said the same thing to Aeneas in order to force him to break free of the poem's first huge delay, the delay in Carthage (4.569).

entrails, invocations, divine councils, catalogues? Are these conventional features of the *Aeneid* simply the inert inheritance of the past, or are they earning their keep in their new surroundings? At the close of the chapter I shall look at what would appear to be the most obviously inert and tired piece of epic baggage in the book—the fifty lines of the catalogue of Etruscan ships and troops.

First, the aesthetics of epic savagery. The colossal violence of this genre is regularly explained away as being the inheritance of tradition. Those writing on the later books of Virgil will often helpfully direct you to the Homeric prototypes for particular physical catastrophes, as if such precedent were sufficient explanation. Yet this procedure does not get us very far, not least because, as we shall see, the problem of how we linger over exquisite artistic representation of unbearable pain is already a problem in Homer anyway. If Virgil is famous for anything it is for the beautiful artistry of his verse, and that beauty does not disappear when the verse starts dealing with vile subject-matter. Even if you have no Latin, you can appreciate some of the care and craft lavished on the evocation of unimaginable suffering in this book.

Take one of many deaths in the book, that of Dryops (345–9):

> Hic Curibus fidens primaeuo corpore Clausus
> aduenit et rigida Dryopem ferit eminus hasta
> sub mentum grauiter pressa, pariterque loquentis
> uocem animamque rapit traiecto gutture; at ille
> fronte ferit terram et crassum uomit ore cruorem.

> Here Clausus from Cures comes up, trusting in his body in its first youth, and from a distance he strikes Dryops with his rigid spear, pushing it with heavy force up under his chin, and as the gullet is pierced he snatches away at one and the same time his voice as he spoke and his spirit; but Dryops strikes the ground with his forehead and vomits thick gore from his mouth.

There is a balanced symmetry here between Clausus' act of violence and its result: Clausus 'strikes'—*ferit*—Dryops in the second line of our extract, and exactly the same word is used when the dying Dryops 'strikes' the ground in the last line. The spear 'is pushed with heavy force up under his chin', and the poet delivers a weighty line to mimic that weighty pressure, alerting us to his procedure with the adverb *grauiter*, 'heavily', which is applicable to the inexorably weighty force both of the thrust and of the verse's heavy spondaic movement at this point. Dryops is saying something as he is hit, and if you read out aloud the words which tell us that Clausus robs Dryops of life and voice at the same time, you will feel the back of your throat labouring to reproduce the cluster of gutturals which imitate Dryops' last sounds: *pariterQUe loQUentis/uoCem animamQUe rapit traieCto Gutture*. Dryops strikes the ground and vomits gore with vivid alliteration of 'f' (*Fronte Ferit*) and 'c' (*Crassum ... Cruorem*). The end of our extract is graced with one of Virgil's frequent assonances in '*or*', O*Re* cru*ORem*. The word *ore* ('mouth') is subsumed in the word *cruorem* ('gore'); since we have just been told that Dryops has no breath or voice any more, this beautifully sounding phrase mimics the hideous fact that his mouth is now indeed nothing but gore.

At the beginning of Book 10 Virgil has a passage which appears to comment rather directly on the dilemmas of such aestheticised moments in the midst of carnage and chaos. As the Latins attack the Trojan camp, the Trojans man the walls, and in the middle of them is Aeneas' son, Ascanius, who is in command during his father's absence (132–8):

> ipse inter medios, Veneris iustissima cura,
> Dardanius caput, ecce, puer detectus honestum,
> qualis gemma micat fuluum quae diuidit aurum,
> aut collo decus aut capiti, uel quale per artem
> inclusum buxo aut Oricia terebintho
> lucet ebur; fusos ceruix cui lactea crinis
> accipit et molli subnectens circulus auro.

> He himself in the middle of the group, the most righteous care of Venus, the Dardanian boy, look, with his noble head uncovered, as a jewel glitters, which divides tawny gold, an adornment for the neck, or for the head, or as ivory gleams, artfully enclosed in boxwood or Orician terebinth; his milk-white neck receives the let-down hair, tied up underneath by a band of soft gold.

In yet another self-referential moment, we see a beautiful object of contemplation set in the middle of the battle-narrative being compared to a beautiful object of jewellery set in the middle of its surround. Ascanius' head is like something enclosed in a piece of art, and it is 'itself', in this eddying moment of the poem, something enclosed in a piece of art (note *per artem*, 'by means of art', in line 135, referring at once to Virgil's and the jeweller's art). This jewel-like moment holds apart the material on either side, 'dividing' it, as Virgil puts it in the third line of our extract (*diuidit*). The precious and beautiful head of Aeneas' son, on which so much depends, commands our aesthetic attention in the middle of the chaos.

In this way, the image discharges a function very similar to that of one of its Iliadic models, an elaborate simile comparing blood from a wound on

Menelaus' thigh to dye on a piece of ivory (4.141–7). In Homer, as Susanne Wofford well puts it, 'this simile ... makes the audience or readers briefly take the point of view from which the war seems painful but beautiful, a figurative move that deflects attention to the epic distance, displacing the violence and transmuting the war scene into a source of aesthetic contemplation'.[4] It is characteristic of Virgil that he should add an important historical dimension to the already rich Homeric effects, for the artefacts described here are of the kind in circulation in the imperial court of his own time: the simile opens up a perspective forward in time, illustrating the cultural and historical results of the narrated action. The simile reminds us that the horrors of the narrative will one day result in a social order which will produce a supremely beautiful work of art to commemorate them.

Wofford's general point about the aesthetic and ideological dilemmas of the *Iliad* is a fruitful starting point for discussion of the same dilemmas in the *Aeneid*: 'The poem ... tells the costs of heroic struggle—and makes apparent the difficulty of giving social or aesthetic meaning to such action—in the very moment in which it transforms that struggle into a work of art that precisely does carry such supplementary value.'[5] The poem describes the establishment of imperial order through violence, becoming a test case for the view recently expressed by the historian of ancient religion, Walter Burkert, that 'all orders and forms of authority in human society are founded on institutionalized violence'.[6] We need to ask whether the poem's art valourises or jeopardises the order that is founded on this violence, for it is precisely this order that makes possible the production of works of art such as the *Aeneid*. The genre of epic makes violence unavoidable, and so does the establishment of empire: as is suggested in the title of David Quint's 1993 work—*Epic and Empire*—for the Romans and their inheritors epic is *the* imperial genre. We have already observed Virgil's authorial reluctance to engage in the violence necessary to carry the epic and the empire through to fulfilment, and there are moments in the poem, such as Jupiter's prophecy of eternal peace to Venus in Book 1, where Virgil appears to hope that the power of empire can contain indefinitely the chaos of Furor. Yet the poem's narrative trajectory runs counter to this hope, enmeshing us more and more in martial rage, so that it appears to many readers that the poem may serve to illustrate the truth of

---

[4] Wofford (1992), 33.  [5] Ibid., 6.
[6] Burkert (1983), 1. [See now Lowrie (2005) for a full exploration of the implications of this insight for the *Aeneid*.]

the dictum of Walter Benjamin: 'There is no document of civilisation which is not at the same time a document of barbarism.'[7]

These are very difficult issues, which are often dealt with too briskly by modern critics on both sides of the debate. All readers of the book should take the opportunity to reflect upon how and why they read these terrible scenes: do we loathe Aeneas as he runs amok (517–601)?—do we loathe ourselves if, even in part, we admire the gladiatorial death of Mezentius (856–908)? In particular, how do we feel about our instinct to keep reading on, our urge to be satisfied by the completion of the reading task? The important studies of Peter Brooks have alerted us to the power of what he calls 'narrative desire', a term he uses to capture the way in which 'the reading of plot' is 'a form of desire that carries us forward, onward, through the text'.[8] Whenever we are reading we have a compulsion to achieve the satisfaction of getting to the end, and when we are reading an epic this compulsion may lead us to tolerate or embrace forms of narrative which are appalling. Aristotle spoke of the particular, characteristic pleasure both of tragedy and epic (*Poetics* 1459a21, 1462b13–14), and it is important as readers of the *Aeneid* to be honest with ourselves about the kind of pleasure we want and get from this kind of poem.[9]

At this point we may turn to the second major topic of the chapter, for Virgil himself, as I remarked at the beginning, keeps commenting upon the way in which his narrative is unfolding, and thereby keeps involving us as readers in being self-aware about our choices and preferences. This feature of narrative has been variously termed metanarrative, metafiction, self-reflexiveness, self-referentiality. All of these more or less ugly labels describe the capacity of fiction to provide 'within itself, a commentary on its own status as fiction and as language, and also on its own processes of production and reception'.[10] This may happen in many different ways. We have already seen, for example, how Virgil informs us that he is delaying the onset of epic warfare. This obsession with 'delay' heightens as the poem goes on. One device after another is deployed to delay the final encounter of Turnus and Aeneas, with each device marked by some self-referential moment. Right at the end, when Turnus' sister Juturna finally has to abandon him, she asks *qua tibi lucem/arte morer?* ('By what art can I delay your light?', 12.873–4)—the poet and the character alike have taken the art of delay as far as it will go. Fifteen lines later, as Aeneas closes

---

[7] Benjamin (1968), 256.    [8] Brooks (1984), 37.
[9] In other words, we need an epic counterpart to Nuttall (1996) on the pleasure of tragedy.
[10] Hutcheon (1980), xii. Latinists have done much important work in this area in recent years, particularly on post-Virgilian narratives: Masters (1992) on Lucan is a tour de force.

in on Turnus at last, Aeneas' taunt caps Juturna's lament: *quae nunc deinde mora est?*, 'What delay is there next?' (12.889).

Studies of self-referentiality in Latin poets have also devoted much attention to 'poet-figures', characters in the text who in some way or another embody some aspect of the master-poet's task, or act as a foil to him. The Sibyl, then, prophesies wars and a replay of Homer's *Iliad* (6.83–94); Vulcan's team works on formless subject-matter and hammers into shape a harmonious representation of imperial and cosmic order (8.445–53); Fama spreads a mixture of fact and fiction, flying over the lips of men (4.173–95). Again, we find pieces of 'ecphrasis', images of artistic creation which call attention to the parallel but distinct kind of artistic creation which is the poem: the simile of Ascanius' head is a clear example in our book. Related both to the poet-figure and to ecphrasis is the remarkable moment when Juno makes a counterfeit image of Aeneas in order to lead Turnus away from the battlefield; here we see a cluster of language which calls attention to the fact that—as an ancient literary critic would have put it—the entire poem is itself an 'imitation', a piece of *mimesis*, something insubstantial which deludes us into thinking it real (10.636–42):

> tum dea nube caua tenuem sine uiribus umbram
> in faciem Aeneae (uisu mirabile monstrum)
> Dardaniis ornat telis, clipeumque iubasque
> diuini adsimulat capitis, dat inania uerba,
> dat sine mente sonum gressusque effingit euntis,
> morte obita qualis fama est uolitare figuras
> aut quae sopitos deludunt somnia sensus.

> Then the goddess from insubstantial cloud makes a slight shade with no power, to look like Aeneas (an amazing freak in appearance), and fits it out with Trojan weapons, and imitates the shield and the crest of his divine head, gives it empty words, gives it sound without intelligence, and moulds its steps as it moves, as rumour says figures fly when death has happened, or dreams that trick the senses in sleep.

As a character, Juno is fabricating something that imitates Aeneas; as a poet, Virgil is fabricating something that imitates Homer, for it is from Homer that he has taken the model for the phantom-Aeneas (*Il.* 5.449–50).[11] Virgil's boldness is very impressive at this point, for he

---

[11] He imitates with variation, as the Latinists put it (*imitatio cum variatione*), for in Homer a god friendly to Aeneas had made a phantom-Aeneas in order to save Aeneas, whereas now the phantom-Aeneas is being made in order to save Turnus, Aeneas' enemy.

reminds us of the fundamentally illusory nature of poetry's mimetic art even as he distances himself from the falsehoods of Juno's competing illusionism. He is striving to invest his own fictions with power and lasting weight, yet acknowledges here that they are fictions, as he conjures up the terrible risks of artistic failure.

Juno's intervention is most unusual for the battle books. Normally, the gods observe and reflect, and we may conclude our discussion of self-referentiality with a consideration of the watching gods' role as a figure for what the author and the readers are doing. Especially, we shall concentrate on the crucial moments of plot-decision, crises of judgement, when gods, poet, and reader are observing the alternative future paths of the plot and deciding which one they want to follow. There are numerous divine scenes in Virgil where gods look down on the action, react to it, and talk about which way it ought to go: these scenes have their origin in Homer, and the metanarrative function of such scenes also goes back to Homer, in whom the 'divine audience' is a supple metaphor for the responses of the human audience.[12]

At the beginning of Book 4 of the *Iliad*, after the apparent victory of Menelaus in his duel with Paris to settle the fate of Helen without general war, Zeus goads the divine enemies of Troy with the prospect that the Greeks may sail peacefully home with Helen (4.13–19, tr. Lattimore (1961)):

> So, the victory now is with warlike Menelaos.
> Let us consider then how these things shall be accomplished,
> whether again to stir up grim warfare and the terrible
> fighting, or cast down love and make them friends with each other.
> If somehow this way could be sweet and pleasing to all of us,
> the city of lord Priam might still be a place men dwell in,
> and Menelaos could take away with him Helen of Argos.

After our earlier discussion of Jupiter's intervention at the beginning of *Aeneid* 10, Homer's evocation of ethical and narrative conflict in the audience will be familiar: do we really want a peaceful and premature end to the epic, or will we be complicit with the goddess Hera's vindictive wish to obliterate the city, in accordance with tradition? At the beginning of *Aeneid* 10, when Jupiter says he wants the fighting to stop, and desires a 'league of peace', the dilemma is even more acute, for we know that the eventual end of the war will indeed be a 'league of peace': the tradition of the Trojan arrival in Italy is not that they devastate the cities of the locals,

---

[12] Griffin (1980), 179–204.

but rather that they intermarry and found their own new city. To choose the path of war is urgently compelling, from a generic and ideological point of view; but Virgil's Homeric technique here lays open the alternatives, and forces us to accept responsibility for acceding to the continuation in the way we do.

*Aeneid* 10 has two crucial scenes in which Jupiter and another god look down at the action together and contemplate possible outcomes. Both these scenes are indebted to an Iliadic diptych, a pair of scenes in which Zeus and a goddess discuss the impending doom of a mortal who is dear to Zeus. In the first of these, in *Iliad* 16, Zeus and Hera watch as Patroclus attacks Sarpedon, the son of Zeus (431–61). Zeus says that he is torn between rescuing Sarpedon and allowing his fated death to take place, whereupon Hera remonstrates with him, pointing out that he cannot overturn fate without ruinous consequences for the future order. Zeus does not disobey her, but weeps tears of blood to honor his doomed son. In the second scene, in *Iliad* 22, all the gods watch as Achilles chases Hector around the walls of Troy (166–87). Zeus acknowledges the piety of Hector, and invites the gods to choose whether to rescue him or allow Achilles to kill him. Athene gives a short version of what Hera had said in Book 16, and Zeus allows her to descend to earth to ensure Hector's death. In both of these related scenes (particularly in the more intense and elaborate Sarpedon scene in Book 16), the open canvassing of options is one way of fixing the audience's terrible reaction to the contemplation of these two men's deaths, for we cannot bear it to happen, yet we know that it must happen and that we will endure its narrating.

Both of these Iliadic scenes are important to bear in mind when we examine the two scenes in *Aeneid* 10 in which Jupiter and another god contemplate possible outcomes as a favourite is endangered. In the first of these scenes, Pallas prays to Hercules as he comes face to face with Turnus.[13] Hercules in response can do nothing but groan and weep (464–5); as a recently enrolled god, only a few years before a human guest of Pallas' father, he suffers the all too human reaction of helpless grief as he watches the young man coming to the premature end of his life. Jupiter, however, has a far more detached view, as he—in effect—quotes to his son Hercules the lesson he had learnt in the *Iliad* from Hera, when he had had to face the death of Sarpedon; his mention of Sarpedon is at once a personal memory and a poetic allusion to the Homeric model (467–72):

---

[13] Fundamentally important analysis of the intertextuality between Homer and Vergil in this scene in Barchiesi (1984/2015), chapter 1.

> stat sua cuique dies, breue et inreparabile tempus
> omnibus est uitae; sed famam extendere factis,
> hoc uirtutis opus. Troiae sub moenibus altis
> tot gnati cecidere deum, quin occidit una
> Sarpedon, mea progenies; etiam sua Turnum
> fata uocant metasque dati peruenit ad aeui.
>
> Each person has his fixed day, for everybody the time of life is short and cannot be got back; but to stretch out fame with deeds, this is the task of virtue. Under the high walls of Troy so many sons of gods fell—indeed, Sarpedon fell also, my offspring; Turnus' own fates call him too and he has come to the turning-posts of his given span.

Once, in his Homeric manifestation, the supreme god was a far more involved reader of the action; now he has a new and newly chilling detachment, a truly 'god's-eye view', which is dramatically highlighted by its juxtaposition to the far more emotional reaction of the novice divinity, Hercules. As I said in an earlier discussion of this scene, 'these few lines represent a shattering collision of human and divine perspectives, as the most human of the gods is told by the father of the gods how to regard the action. Every reader has to try to be open to these two perspectives.'[14]

The Iliadic scene used as a model here is even more systematically reversed less than 150 lines later, when, instead of seeing Hera upbraiding Zeus for wishing to save a favourite, we see Jupiter allowing Juno to rescue Turnus only for a time, warning her that his eventual fate is sealed. If all she wants, says Jupiter, is *mora* ('delay'—that word again), that is one thing; but then he carries on (625–32):

> ' . . . sin altior istis
> sub precibus uenia ulla latet totumque moueri
> mutariue putas bellum, spes pascis inanis.'
> et Iuno adlacrimans: 'quid si, quae uoce grauaris,
> mente dares atque haec Turno rata uita maneret?
> nunc manet insontem grauis exitus, aut ego ueri
> uana feror. quod ut o potius formidine falsa
> ludar, et in melius tua, qui potes, orsa reflectas!'
>
> ' . . . but if any favour lies more deeply beneath those prayers of yours and you think that the sum of the war can be swayed or changed, you are feeding off empty hopes.' And Juno weeping replied: 'What if you gave with your mind what you are saying you are reluctant to do, and Turnus' life could be

---

[14] Feeney (1991), 157.

> ratified and continue? Now a heavy death remains for him although he's innocent, or else I am carried along with no grip on the truth. But I pray I'm being tricked instead by a false fear, and you might turn back your plans into a better path—for you can do that.'

Even though, as first readers, we do not know in detail the outcome of the plot, it appears that the outcome is indeed fixed, at least in the minds of the poet and his double, Jupiter. Juno's devastated acknowledgement of the fact that Turnus must be doomed is coupled with a desperate wish that perhaps, somehow, by some plot-turn or other, he might be saved. And her twistings here act out the way in which, as readers, part of us wants this better outcome also, for we know that she is correct in the last words she says in the extract: 'you [that is, Jupiter and Virgil] can do that'.

Although the similarity is not complete, the gap between the poem's divine and mortal characters is very like the gap between the reader and the poem's characters. Just as the gods are involved, yet ultimately detached by virtue of their immortality and invulnerability, so we as readers are passionately involved in the action, yet ultimately detached by virtue of the fact that we know, in the end, that we are reading a fiction. Virgil crystallises this similarity for us in two lines that describe the way the gods view the epic action of Book 10 (758–9):

> di Iouis in tectis iram miserantur inanem
> amborum et tantos mortalibus esse labores.
>
> The gods in the palace of Jupiter feel pity for the empty rage of both sides and for the mortals' so great toils.

Once again, as in his description of the Aeneas-phantom created by Juno, Virgil uses technical language of literary criticism to reinforce his point. 'Pity', ever since Aristotle's *Poetics*, had been the quintessential aesthetic response to the events of tragedy and epic.[15] Here the gods are emotionally involved in a strange way, feeling pity even though they regard the anger of the mortals as *inanem*, literally 'empty'. S.J. Harrison well points out that, together with the word *mortalibus* ('mortal men'), *inanem* stresses 'the futility in divine eyes of the strivings of mortals'.[16] The gods feel pity even though they regard the objects of their pity as being ineffably distant from

---

[15] Or, we should say, it had been *half* of the Aristotelian response, along with 'fear': is it significant that the gods feel only pity and not fear? [I note that in 11.837 the divine nymph Opis is explicitly said to be *interrita* ('unterrified') as she looks down at the human battle.]
[16] S.J. Harrison (1991) ad loc.

their own status—so far distant that their emotions seem 'pointless', 'empty'.

The gods here are a metaphor for our parallel observation of the epic action, for we too feel pity, even as we know (*at some level*, and *in the end*) that what we are pitying is the poet's fictional construction, and therefore *inanem* in the terms of the *Oxford Latin Dictionary*'s definition §11: 'having appearance without reality or substance, false, illusory'. We are passionately involved (or if we are not we might as well stop reading); yet we are, ultimately, at a remove from the actions of the invented characters. Modern criticism is no closer than ancient criticism to solving the mystery of how fictions move and instruct an audience who are continually being reminded of the fictive status of that which moves and instructs them.

As first readers of the epic, then, we are involved spectators, just like the lesser deities. We know that the text is fixed in advance, and that Jupiter/Virgil will not tell us in advance what the exact form of the text's working-out is going to be. As vital plot-turns come along, we are acting also as critics, judging where the text should go, deciding what it is going to mean, and deciding how willingly we are going to go along with the direction it does in the end take. The massive narratological and ideological power of these moments has a dynamic afterlife, which readers may wish to trace through the very different artistic, social and religious environments of Virgil's successors. One might begin with the opening of Ovid's *Metamorphoses*, where we see a divine council deliberating whether to kill off the human species and the poem before they have really begun; most memorably, Virgil's dialogues over destiny and choice are rewritten by Milton in a Christian frame in the divine debates that open the second, third and eleventh books of *Paradise Lost*.

Let us conclude this discussion of epic norms with an examination of an epic convention that few would rank high on their list of favourite poetic set-pieces: the epic catalogue. All epics appear to need a catalogue. Our epic has two—one at the end of Book 7, describing the Latin enemies of the Trojans, and one near the beginning of Book 10, describing the ships of the Etruscan allies of the Trojans. Introducing and interrupting the chaos of warfare are two little emblems of order, with everyone all lined up and itemised—possibly even to the extent of having some alphabetical order in the line-up.[17] As a provisional first point, then, we might see the epic catalogue as an element in tension with the mayhem that follows when the tidily itemised groups collide and try to annihilate each other; as we have

---

[17] See ibid., 108 for discussion of this possibility.

already seen, the relationship between order and violence is an epic and imperial obsession.

But we want to find out more than this: after all, what is a catalogue really *for*? Harrison points out that 'the original purpose of the epic catalogue of warriors was to identify the major participants in the forthcoming action (thus 125 of the 140 named in the two catalogues of *Iliad* 2 reappear in the poem)'.[18] Homer, then, manages to reproduce 89 per cent of the listed characters somewhere else in his poem; but, as Harrison goes on to say, 'in the *Aeneid* this is true of the Latin Catalogue of book 7 (all but three of the fifteen listed reappear), but not of this Catalogue of Etruscans (only three of the eight listed are heard of again)'. Only three out of eight? Surely a literate poet ought to be able to attain a better statistical coverage than an oral one? This cannot be an accident, for Virgil even jokes about it, hailing two of the men in the Etruscan catalogue with the phrase 'Nor shall I overlook you . . . or you' (*non ego te . . . transierim*, 185–6); it is bad enough that these two (Cunerus and Cupavo, if you want to know their names) are not mentioned in the subsequent narrative, but even in the catalogue Virgil 'overlooks' them, telling a little story about Cupavo's father instead.[19]

The raw figures (three subsequent mentions out of a possible eight) are bad enough, but the case is even worse than this, for two of those three are only mentioned again later in order to be swiftly despatched: Abas survives for a mere 250 lines, while Aulestes remains unmentioned until he is killed by Messapus early in Book 12 (290). One solitary individual is named in the Etruscan catalogue and also plays any part worth considering in the subsequent narrative—Asilas (and we shall return to him in a moment). This is not a catalogue but a not-catalogue: it does not serve to tell us the names of the characters who are going to be important later in the action, because they are not going to be important at all—most of them are not even going to be *there*. Harrison is quite right to observe that 'the Etruscan catalogue is generally composed of nonentities who play no significant part in the *Aeneid*'.[20] So why has Rome's greatest poet devoted fifty lines of Rome's greatest poem to a parade of nonentities?

If only one of the men in the Etruscan catalogue plays any part in the subsequent narrative, let us have a careful look at him (175–8):

---

[18] Ibid., 106.
[19] He has already used this joke in the catalogue of Book 7, telling one Oebalus that he will not be absent from his verses (733)—he is never mentioned again.
[20] S.J. Harrison (1991), 108. Corroboration of this conclusion is offered by the fact that Aeneas' ship is carefully mentioned as coming *first* (157), without actually being technically part of the catalogue itself, which begins *after* the description of Aeneas' progress.

> tertius ille hominum diuumque interpres Asilas,
> cui pecudum fibrae, caeli cui sidera parent
> et linguae uolucrum et praesagi fulminis ignes,
> mille rapit densos acie atque horrentibus hastis.

> Number three is Asilas, who interprets between men and gods, whom animal entrails and the constellations of heaven obey, and the tongues of birds and the prophesying fires of the thunderbolt—he snatches along a thousand close-packed men in battle-line with bristling spears.

What this man does is communicate between gods and men by means of all the various media available in Virgil's own day: he is a master of what was known as 'the Etruscan discipline' (*Etrusca disciplina*). The Etruscan *haruspices* were particular experts in inspecting the insides of sacrificial animals, and were summoned from Etruria for this purpose on special occasions. This individual, Asilas, represents an element of Etruscan culture that survived and was maintained in Virgil's day as a self-consciously non-Roman way of doing things. The character Asilas in the catalogue, in other words, has actually left a resilient and distinct trace in the contemporary world of Virgil and his readers, and that is why he leaves a trace in the subsequent narrative—otherwise (according to Virgil's presentation) Etruscan culture has vanished.

With the exception of their religious lore, the Etruscans' function in the poem and in history is to be swallowed up, along with the other Italians and the Trojans themselves, as part of the process of Romanisation: that is why they are under the command of a foreigner, Aeneas, and that is why their parade turns out to be a narratological damp squib. The continual amalgamation of diverse groups into a ceaselessly evolving Roman *ciuitas* is one of the great themes of Roman history, and therefore one of the great themes of the *Aeneid*. In Asilas we see this process in action—not only in the fact that his skill survives as an element of historical Roman culture, but also in the extraordinary precision with which Virgil organises the company he keeps in his reappearances later in the narrative. It is a remarkable fact that every single time Asilas is mentioned after the catalogue his name is bracketed with Latins and Trojans, as if to give us an emblem of the eventual amalgamation of the three main ethnic groups who clash in this moment of origin—*Latini ... Troes ... Asilas* (11.618–20); *et genus Assaraci Mnestheus et fortis Asilas/et Messapus equum domitor, Neptunia proles* ('and Mnestheus, descendant of Assaracus, and brave Asilas, and Messapus, tamer of horses, offspring of Neptune', 12.127–8: i.e., a Trojan, Asilas, a Latin); most strikingly, at the climax of the final battle, just before Aeneas meets Turnus in single combat, we see swept up together in an anticipation of their future unity all the Latins, all the Trojans, Mnestheus (the same Trojan as in our second passage), Serestus (another Trojan), Messapus (the same Latin as in our second passage), *Asilas and the phalanx of the Etruscans*, and the Arcadian cavalry (12.548–51):

> totae adeo conuersae acies omnesque Latini,
> omnes Dardanidae, Mnestheus acerque Serestus
> et Messapus equum domitor et fortis Asilas
> Tuscorumque phalanx Euandrique Arcades alae.

> Absolutely all the battle-lines wheeled about—all the Latins, all the Trojans, Mnestheus and keen Serestus, and Messapus tamer of horses and brave Asilas, the phalanx of the Etruscans and the Arcadian cavalry squadrons of Evander.

In literary criticism you can often go a long way by saying, if someone brings up a problem, 'Yes, that's the point.' So here, if someone says 'This is a very funny catalogue: the men in it just disappear', we say 'Yes, that's the point.'

If we reread the catalogue, we see that the important theme of amalgamation is already sounded when Virgil mentions the place of origin of one contingent, Mantua. This is where Ocnus comes from (199–203):

> fatidicae Mantus et Tusci filius amnis,
> qui muros matrisque dedit tibi, Mantua, nomen,
> Mantua diues auis, sed non genus omnibus unum:
> gens illi triplex, populi sub gente quaterni,
> ipsa caput populis, Tusco de sanguine uires.

> Ocnus, the son of fate-speaking Manto and the Etruscan river, who gave you, Mantua, walls and the name of his mother—Mantua, rich in ancestors, but they do not all have one race: Mantua has a threefold nation, four peoples under each nation, and she is the head for the peoples, her strength comes from Etruscan blood.

The crucial theme of blending and merging under a dominant capital is here already sounded. If we are alert to moments of self-reference, we might also care to pause over the resonance of a place that is named for prophecy, deriving its name from a 'fate-speaking' (*fatidicae*) woman, someone whose name comes from the Greek word for 'prophet' (*mantis*). Asilas, the sole survivor of the catalogue, is also acquainted with the fates; perhaps another fate-speaking person of Etruscan ancestry needs to be seen in connection with the mention of Mantua, although his actual name has been passed over—Virgil himself, who was born in this place of significant name.

CHAPTER 10

# Mea tempora: *Patterning of Time in Ovid's Metamorphoses*[1]

As he begins the *Metamorphoses*, Ovid invokes the gods and asks them to spin out the poem unbroken from the first origin of the universe down to *mea tempora*. The first person possessive adjective *mea*, although regularly mistranslated as a plural, is vitally singular, as Alessandro Barchiesi has insisted: not, as so often, 'our times', but '*my* times'.[2] And not just 'my times', 'the era I happen to live in', but, as Barchiesi further demonstrates, 'my *Times*', with a capital 'T', i.e., the *Fasti*, whose first word and alternative title is *Tempora*. The arrow of Ovid's hexametric time will carry on down until it hits the circle of his elegiac time.[3]

The power of the adjective *mea* is shown, as Barchiesi also points out,[4] when Ovid rewrites these words in his *Epistle to Augustus*, describing the *Metamorphoses* as being 'the few verses in which, rising from the first origin of the universe, I spun the work down to *your* times, Caesar' (*pauca quibus prima surgens ab origine mundi/in tua deduxi tempora, Caesar, opus*, *Tr.* 2.559–60). The singularity of both of these possessive adjectives is very important: not '*our* times', but either 'mine' or 'yours', Ovid's or Augustus'—depending, partly, on the time of writing, or reading. I shall begin my argument by taking that first person *singular* possessive adjective at the beginning of the *Metamorphoses* very seriously, and exploring how and why Ovid's patterning of time is *his*, and not anyone else's. In conclusion, I shall take up the implications of his rewriting of the adjective in exile, from *mea* to *tua*.

As Ovid sat down to ponder over the problem of how to organise the whole sequence of history, of past time, into some kind of fifteen-book order, he had many possible models, since chronography, the writing of time, the listing of dates and the synchronisation of different dating

---

[1] My warm thanks to the editors (Philip Hardie, Alessandro Barchiesi and Stephen Hinds), and to Niklas Holzberg, for their helpful suggestions and comments.
[2] Barchiesi (1989), 91 and (1991), 6.   [3] Barchiesi (1991), 6–7.   [4] Barchiesi (1989), 91.

systems, had been a serious scholarly pursuit for 250 years, with origins dating back almost another 200 years before that.[5] The first Roman to work in this genre, the first person systematically to bring Roman events within the framework of Greek chronographic scholarship, was Cornelius Nepos.[6] His work was entitled *Chronica*, after the famous works of that title by Eratosthenes and Apollodorus, who will engage our attention shortly. We all know this work from the dedication poem of Catullus, who hails Nepos as the one who 'alone/first of Italians dared to unfold the whole of past time in three rolls, learned ones, by Jupiter, and full of hard work' (*ausus es unus Italorum/omne aeuum tribus explicare cartis/doctis, Iuppiter, et laboriosis*, 1.5–7).

In parenthesis, we may remark how this programmatic poem of Catullus' gives us another angle on the issue of how to conceptualise Ovid's simultaneously *perpetuum* and *deductum carmen*. If we read the Catullan programmatic poem from the viewpoint of Ovid we see that the *Metamorphoses* is *both* Catullus and Nepos. Like Nepos' *Chronica*, it includes *omne aeuum*, with *doctrina* and *labor*; it also has the aesthetically desirable qualities of Catullus' *libellus*, so that like the *libellus* it is *nouum* at the beginning (compare *In noua* as the first words of Ovid's poem) and *perenne* at the end (compare Ovid's claim in his last sentence that he will be carried above the stars *perennis*).

Nepos synchronised events in Greek and Roman history, using Olympiads together with the key fixed point of the foundation of the city of Rome, which he followed Polybius in assigning to the second year of the seventh Olympiad (751/750 BCE). So we know that Nepos gave a date for the *akmē* ('peak flourishing') of Homer, 160 years before the foundation of the city (F1 *FRHist*), and for the *akmē* of Archilochus (in the reign of Tullus Hostilius, F4 *FRHist*). He also ranged into events of 'myth', giving a human time period for the reign of Saturn (F2 *FRHist*).

On the basis of the Catullan evidence, Nepos' work will have been available in the mid-50s BCE. A few years later, by the end of 47 BCE, Nepos' mentor, Cicero's friend T. Pomponius Atticus, also published a chronological work with elements of synchronisation, the *Liber Annalis*.[7] For Ovid, however, as for any educated person of his generation, the canonical Roman chronographic work would have been the *De Gente Populi Romani* of the polymath Varro, completed probably in the year of

---

[5] On the importance of this intellectual context for the *Metamorphoses*, see Ludwig (1965), 80.
[6] Wissowa (1900), 1410; Horsfall (1989), 117–18; in general on the chronographic work of Nepos and Varro, Wiseman (1979), 157–66.
[7] Feger (1956), 520–1.

Ovid's birth, 43 BCE.[8] It was Varro, very probably, who defined the date for the foundation of Rome which became canonical, the third year of the sixth Olympiad, 754/753 BCE. As Rawson points out, Atticus already had this date, 'but although his *Liber Annalis* was earlier than the *De Gente*, it is perhaps unlikely that Varro borrowed from him; he may have put it forward in an earlier work which Atticus used':[9] Varro's interest in chronography is evident in many of his works besides the *De Gente* (*Annales*, *Antiquitates*, *De Scaenicis Originibus*), and, as the prototypical academic, he was not above recycling research material from one book to another.

In the *De Gente* Varro divided the whole of human time into three categories (fr. 3 Peter): the obscure period (ἄδηλον), from the origins of human beings to the first flood; the mythical period (μυθικόν), from the flood to the first Olympiad, which lasted about 1600 years; finally, the historical period (ἱστορικόν). Fascinatingly, Varro, with his astrological interests, also had things to say about future time: 'Evidently Varro's historical works included predictions of the future as well as data about the past. His connection of celestial omens and astrology with history was no doubt meant to find yet more *portenta* that the historians had failed to note, and thus to bring to light the hidden, underlying causes of Roman history, past, present, and future.'[10] Ovid's demarcations are different from Varro's first flood and first Olympiad, but we shall see that he keeps to the broad conception of three temporal categories, and that he has other points in common with Varro's schemes as well.

The proem of Ovid's *Metamorphoses*, then, looks as if it is promising some such work as that of Nepos or Varro—from the origins down to the present time. It looks like the programme for a chronography, and Ludwig is certainly right to suggest that Ovid is working with the conception of providing some kind of poetic counterpart to these monumental pieces of synthesising scholarship.[11]

Such Roman works ultimately go back to the great Hellenistic scholars Eratosthenes and Apollodorus.[12] Eratosthenes, writing in the third century, first gave a canonical date to the fall of Troy, which is then the beginning of history—408 years before the first year of the first Olympiad, what we call 1184/1183 BCE (or what we call 1184/1183 BC: the choice of

---

[8] Dahlmann (1935), 1237–42; Rawson (1985), 244–6.   [9] Rawson (1985), 245.
[10] Grafton and Swerdlow (1985), 461; cf. Peter (1902), esp. 243–51.   [11] Ludwig (1965), 80.
[12] On Eratosthenes, Pfeiffer (1968), 255–7; on Apollodorus, Jacoby (1902); Pfeiffer (1968), 163–4. They too had their pre-Hellenistic predecessors, most importantly Hellanicus of Lesbos (c. 480–395 BCE), whose 'Priestesses of Hera in Argos' used the local dating system of Argos as its point of departure in synchronising panhellenic events from mythical times down to his own age: Gudeman (1912), 144–8.

a dating system, as this example shows, and as I shall be arguing throughout, carries considerable ideological weight). Indeed, Eratosthenes even gave a calendrical date for the sack, the seventh or eighth day before the end of the month Thargelion, a date that Virgil alludes to in *Aen.* 2.255, *tacitae per amica silentia lunae* ('through the friendly silences of the quiet moon').[13] Eratosthenes went on to give dates from the fall of Troy until the first Olympiad, 776/775, from which point he carried on using the Olympiad system that he had laid out in a separate work of Olympian victors, building on the initiative of the fifth-century sophist Hippias, the first person to compile a list of Olympian victors in order to make synchronisation possible across the chaotic range of incompatible Greek time-systems.[14] Eratosthenes stopped with the death of Alexander (an interesting terminus), a century or so before his own time. Apollodorus, in his *Chronica*, actually wrote in verse, in iambics. He too began with the fall of Troy, but, like Hellanicus of Lesbos, he extended his time-frame down to his own time, in his case the end of the second century. And of course Eratosthenes and Apollodorus, and Nepos and Atticus and Varro, did it all in chronological order—that was the whole point.

It goes without saying that these catalogues and series, whether Greek or Roman, are not simply helpful lists of scholarly fact, but frames of exclusion as well as inclusion, with their own strategies and ideologies. I may mention some examples here, although running the risk that by this prolepsis I will reduce the impact of what I have to say concerning Ovid's exclusions and inclusions and strategies. It is a very striking fact, for example, that neither Apollodorus nor Eratosthenes in their respective *Chronica* mentioned, i.e. gave a synchronic date for, the Foundation of Rome. Of course, with lost and fragmentary works it is difficult to be entirely confident about pronouncing that something was *not* in them, but Jacoby's arguments on this score in his *Apollodors Chronik* seem conclusive.[15] Indeed, according to Jacoby, Apollodorus and Eratosthenes only took notice of Roman events when they impinged on Greece, and only *started* to take notice of Roman events *at all* when they got to the invasion of Pyrrhus—when Roman affairs are directly involved with those of mainland Greece, in the person of a descendant of Achilles. From this perspective Nepos' initiative in his new Roman *Chronica* takes on added significance, as Wiseman remarks: 'Nepos remedied the omission, bringing

---

[13] Grafton and Swerdlow (1986).  [14] Pfeiffer (1968), 51, 163.  [15] Jacoby (1902), 26–8.

the events of the Roman tradition into the mainstream of "world history" as created by the Greeks.'[16]

The Roman counterpart of this Greek exclusion is represented—as one might have predicted—by Cato the Censor in his *Origines*, a work that was essentially a Roman *Chronography*-cum-*Aetia*. Dionysius of Halicarnassus uses very significant language when reporting Cato's dating of the Foundation of Rome. Although, says Dionysius, other early Roman historians dated the foundation of the city by the Olympiad system, Cato 'does not make Greek time-divisions' (Ἑλληνικὸν μὲν οὐχ ὁρίζει χρόνον), 'but being as careful as anyone in the compilation of ancient historical data places it 432 years after the Trojan war' (*Ant. Rom.* 1.74.2; fr. 17 Peter). The Trojan war, not a Greek athletic festival, is the reference point for dating the beginning of Rome, since the Trojan war, according to Cato's way of doing things, is an event in universal, or Roman, history, not Greek, an *origo* in a profounder sense than simply marking the start of ascertainable history.

In the hexameter tradition that Ovid was writing in, the preeminent time-writer, of course, was Mr. Time himself, Quintus Ennius, the author of the *Annales*, the books of years. Like Eratosthenes before him, and like Apollodorus after him—Apollodorus was about ten years old when Ennius died in 169 BCE—Ennius began with the fall of Troy; he anticipated Apollodorus in carrying on down to his own times.

Lucretius shows how time is built into Ennius' very name (1.117–19):

> Ennius ut noster cecinit, qui primus amoeno
> detulit ex Helicone perENNI fronde coronam
> per gentis Italas hominum quae clara clueret.
>
> As our Ennius sang, who first from pleasant Helicon brought down a garland of perENNIal leaf to be spoken of as brightly famous through the Italian races of mankind.

It has often been pointed out that Lucretius here puns on the author's name, with its lurking 'years' within, in order to reinforce the claim to immortality through the years; but he is simultaneously punning on the title of the masterpiece which will guarantee that immortality, the *Annales*,

---

[16] Wiseman (1979), 157; on Nepos' originality here cf. Geiger (1985), 69–72. Some thirty years after Nepos, the Greek Dionysius of Halicarnassus 'remedied the omissions' of Eratosthenes and Apollodorus from the Greek side, publishing a *Chronica* or *Chronoi* that adapted Roman time to Greek canons for a Greek audience, as part of his larger project of accommodating the Roman *imperium* to the Greeks: Gabba (1991), 198–9; Schultze (1995).

'The Books of Years'.[17] Ennius was born to sing his way through the Years and to live through the years as a result.

Even in fragments, Ennius is someone who yields a rich harvest of material on time. His narrative began with the canonical chronographer's moment of the fall of Troy: *Quom ueter occubuit Priamus sub Marte Pelasgo* ('When old Priam fell under the war of the Greeks', 14 Sk.). The fall of Troy is not just a starting point for Ennius, however, but becomes an especially significant marker for counting years. As Gratwick has so brilliantly suggested, the original fifteen books of the *Annales* may have spanned exactly 1000 years, from the fall of Troy in 1184/1183 all the way down to the year 184/183. This year was important to Ennius' *first* patron, Cato, for it was the year that Cato was censor, and this year was important also to Ennius' *current* patron, M. Fulvius Nobilior, for, on Gratwick's hypothesis, it was the year that Fulvius dedicated, *ex manubiis* from his triumph over Aetolia in 187, the temple of Hercules Musarum.[18] In this temple Fulvius erected nine statues of the Muses that he had looted from Greece. In a massive piece of ring-composition, the *imperator* introduces the Muses into Roman cult for the very first time at the end of the poem, as the poet had introduced them into Roman poetry for the very first time with the first word of the first line of the first book, *Musae*. And the temple of Hercules Musarum is a time-machine of a different kind as well. It is not just the culmination of 1000 years of Roman imperial and cross-cultural history, but the location of the first sets of Roman Fasti—both kinds of Fasti, a list of the Roman consuls, and a calendar of the Roman year. This was Fulvius' responsibility, but who better to advise him on all this than Mr. Years himself, the expert on Roman time, Quintus Ennius?[19] By bringing a work from the origins to the present, and then linking it to the annual calendar, Ennius himself may be a precursor for Ovid's plotting of the *Metamorphoses*' trajectory into the *Fasti*.[20]

The fragmentary remains of the poem reveal other key moments in the time patterning of the *Annales*: the seven hundred years since the city's foundation (*septingenti sunt, paulo plus aut minus, anni/augusto augurio postquam incluta condita Roma est*, 'it is seven hundred years, plus or minus

---

[17] Ennius *must* have punned on his significant name and title himself: hence the key use of *perennis* in such contexts in Lucretius, Catullus (1.10), Horace (*Carm.* 3.30.1) and Ovid (*Met.* 15.875).
[18] Gratwick (1982), 63–5.
[19] Rüpke (1995), 331–68; on *Annales*, temple, and Fasti, see too Barchiesi (1994), 276–7.
[20] Barchiesi (1991), 6–7.

a little, since famous Rome was founded by august augury', 154–5 Sk.);[21] the cycle of reincarnation, perhaps another cycle of 1000 years, this time of the individual's soul (I.x Sk.); the poet's own age at the time of writing the final book of the poem (he gave his age as sixty-seven, *sed.inc.* lxx Sk.).[22]

Ovid's other great epic precursor, Virgil's *Aeneid*, is likewise rich in meaningful patterns of chronology. The poem's first prophecy shows Jupiter counting off a significant cycle of 3 + 30 + 300 years from the end of the poem down to the birth of Romulus and Remus (1.265–74):[23] in a daring act of authorial self-assertion, the end of the narrative, a moment of no inherent chronological import in relation to other schemes, has hereby become a chronological milestone in its own right. In Virgil's underworld, Anchises presents us with a 1000-year cycle of reincarnation (6.748), and then prophesies the return of the Golden Age under Augustus, alluding specifically to the Secular Games, the rite by which Augustus would inaugurate a new cycle of time for the Roman state (6.792–4).[24] The simultaneously aetiological and teleological conception of historical time that links Aeneas and Augustus is but the latest in a series of Roman attempts to find meaning in the links between the fall of Troy and the present—whenever that present happens to be.[25]

Now, having sketched the chronographic models at Ovid's disposal, I need to say that Ovid ignores, refuses, renounces all such schemes and ideologies, or else subverts the canonical reference points that no account of history could totally ignore.

To begin with, the canonical divisions of the epochs of human history are blurred in Ovid, the rigidity of their outlines smudged: I may be brief here, by referring to the arguments of Barchiesi and Holzberg.[26] More or less everyone is agreed that there is a general and broad division in the poem between the epochs of the gods, of the heroes, and of history.[27] Like all divisions in the poem it is fluid, but just recognisable. The division between gods and heroes comes with the introduction of the city of Athens (6.419–21); that between heroic and historical time comes with

---

[21] It is important to remember that Ennius' date for the city's foundation was much earlier than the later canonical mid-eighth century date, for Romulus was Aeneas' grandson according to Ennius, with a consequent date for the Romulean foundation of c. 1100 BCE: Skutsch (1985), 314.
[22] Following Skutsch (1985), 675 for the final book as the one in which he declared his age.
[23] Virgil would have been able to find in Varro the year, the day and the hour of the birth—indeed, of the conception—of Romulus: Grafton and Swerdlow (1985), 456.
[24] Zetzel (1989), 277–84.  [25] A guide into these dense matters in Zetzel (1997).
[26] Barchiesi (1994), 247–8; Holzberg (1998), 144–5; cf. Croisille (1985), 57–9 on the imperceptible transition from heroic to historical time.
[27] Ludwig (1965), 12–13 on earlier literature; Holzberg (1998), 126–53.

the introduction of the city of Troy (11.194–204). As Barchiesi has shown, these crucial moments of division are linked with distinctively odd geographical features, the Isthmus of Corinth and the Hellespont. Both of these are demarcations, but also provide passage: they are barriers, and transitions.

Troy in particular is an interesting case. We have seen how vital the fall of Troy was as the definitive demarcation of the beginning of history in the great majority of chronographic schemes. Even Varro, who did not begin his historical period with the fall of Troy but with the first Olympiad, still made the fall of Troy a crucial watershed within his 1600-year mythical period, as the last of a series of events staggered at 400-year intervals between Ogygus' flood and the first Olympiad.[28] Varro gave great structural prominence to the fall of Troy in the arrangement of his *De Gente Populi Romani*, for this event closed off his second book (Aug. *De civ. D.* 18.13, fr. 14 Peter). Further, according to the very attractive speculation of Peter, the third of Varro's four books will have covered the time between Troy's sack and the foundation of Rome, marking out a definitive epoch in world history, and trumping those Greek scholars who had made Troy's fall the vital beginning moment without cataloguing the most important event it had given rise to.[29]

Note, then, how when we first see Troy in Ovid it is not falling, but being built, or rebuilt (11.199–201):[30]

> inde nouae primum moliri moenia Troiae
> Laumedonta uidet susceptaque magna labore
> crescere difficili
>
> from here he sees Laomedon first building the walls of a new Troy, and the mighty undertaking growing with difficult labour

There are, in fact, two pre-Homeric sacks of the city mentioned in this immediate context (*bis ... superatae ... Troiae*, 11.215), one involving Hercules, who bursts in from the previous 'mythic' section in a moment described by Ludwig as 'the starkest chronological discrepancy in the architecture of the *Metamorphoses*'.[31] Of course Ovid anticipates the canonical sack of Troy by the Achaeans when he soon mentions the marriage of Peleus and Thetis, the parents of Achilles (11.217–20); and the fall of Troy is

---

[28] Peter (1902), 232.   [29] Ibid., 238, 242; but note the reservations of Dahlmann (1935), 1240.
[30] And the language used here to describe Troy's rebuilding evokes the Virgilian language of the building of Rome (*altae moenia Romae*, *Aen.* 1.8), which is the consequence of the fall.
[31] Ludwig (1965), 60.

certainly of huge importance in the poem as a defining epic and tragic moment. Its value as a chronological anchor, however, is another matter, as we shall now see.

After Troy is mentioned the first time, we have over 530 lines of erotic and conjugal myth before we return to Troy:[32] first, the marriage of Peleus and Thetis, then the introduction of Ceyx, and then various stories linked to him until the main Ceyx and Alcyone story, with their transformation into halcyons. Only then, as he describes people watching the halcyons, does Ovid return to the topic of the city (11.749–58):

> Hos aliquis senior iunctim freta lata uolantes
> spectat et ad finem seruatos laudat amores:
> proximus, aut idem, si fors tulit, 'hic quoque', dixit
> 'quem mare carpentem substrictaque crura gerentem
> adspicis' (ostendens spatiosum in guttura mergum),
> 'regia progenies: sunt, si descendere ad ipsum
> ordine perpetuo quaeris, sunt huius origo
> Ilus et Assaracus raptusque Ioui Ganymedes
> Laomedonque senex Priamusque nouissima Troiae
> tempora sortitus . . . '

> These some old man sees flying joined together over the broad seas, and he praises the love they preserved to the end. Someone standing next to him, or the same man, if that's the way chance had it, said 'This one too, that you see skimming the sea with his legs tucked up' (pointing out the diver with his elongated neck) 'is of kingly stock: his ancestry, if you wish to start at the top and come down to him in an unbroken orderly sequence, consists of Ilus and Assaracus and Ganymede, snatched by Jupiter, and the old man Laomedon and Priam, the one who drew the lot of the last time period of Troy . . . '

Much is destabilised here: after all, even the identity of the speaker is uncertain (was it the same old man who praised the constancy of the halcyons, or was it by pure chance someone standing next to him?). In line 755 *ordine perpetuo* ('unbroken orderly sequence') is, as always in this poem, a certain sign that some serious chronological dislocation is afoot: and, sure enough, as we go through the line of Trojan kings we arrive at 757–8, where Priam is described as 'the one who drew the lot of the last time period of Troy'. Troy has already fallen, in other words, although the last time we saw Troy—the first time we saw Troy—it was described as

---

[32] Although, as Holzberg (1998), 146–7 points out, Ovid's awareness of the fact that we should now be plunging into martial terrain is revealed by his marked deployment of epically martial metaphor and terminology throughout these 530 lines.

being built. From the vantage-point of the birdwatchers on the cliffs, in the here-and-now of ornithology, Troy now is described as already over and done with, before we have actually got to the narration of the war and the fall. The whole of the war's narrative is analepsis: the fall is over before it is narrated. But then, we knew that anyway. Everything is always over before it is narrated.

The fall of Troy, then, is made entirely valueless as a secure foundation for the frame of time in the poem. When the fall of Troy finally occurs in 13.404 it may be assigned a date, 1184/1183 BCE, to be the first of only a handful of dateable events in the poem (along with the foundation of Rome in 753 BCE, the importation of Aesculapius in 291 BCE and the assassination of Julius Caesar in 44 BCE); yet its embedding in retrogression and analepsis has robbed it of its talismanic demarcating power.

If Ovid subverts the chronological value of the fall of Troy, other canonical benchmarks he ignores altogether. The return of the Heracleidae was another important marker for many Greeks: this was the beginning of Ephorus' *History*, for example.[33] Nothing in Ovid. What of the first Olympiad, the great moment for all chronographers, when accurate dating and synchronisation first really become possible? No mention in Ovid of Coroebus of Elis, the first victor in the first footrace, the first man in Eratosthenes' or Hippias' lists. No mention of the Olympic games at all, in fact, until Book 14, when we read this description of the age of Picus at the time of his transformation (324–5):

> nec adhuc spectasse per annos
> quinquennem poterat Graia quater Elide pugnam.[34]

> He could not yet have seen four quinquennial contests at Grecian Elis.

This is the report of Ulysses' former companion, Macareus, describing an account he heard from a nymph in Circe's palace. The notional date of the original conversation, then, is, say, 1180; but mark how the nymph describes the age of Picus: 'He could not yet have seen four quinquennial contests at Grecian Elis'. This is one way of saying that someone is about nineteen years old;[35] but of course in 1180 no one could have seen even one contest at Grecian Elis, because the first Olympiad was still more than four

---

[33] Fornara (1983), 8–9.
[34] The text of 325 is problematic, but I trust that my argument will show why I prefer the reading which gives us a reference to the Olympic games here (and I am pleased to report that Richard Tarrant approves this reading, which has the authority also of Heinsius).
[35] For this interpretation see Bömer (1969–86) ad loc.

hundred years in the future. The single most significant dating device in ancient history has here been dislocated four hundred years out of context. As an anchor for a time scheme the Olympic games have become valueless.

Any great time-counting schemes are missing. We do not have a hallowed 1000-year cycle of history or of individual reincarnation. We do have one 1000-year period mentioned, at 14.136–53; this is no grand scheme, however, but simply the lifespan of the Sibyl, haphazardly equivalent to the number of grains in a pile of sand, a random total randomly split into 700 and 300 years by her contingent meeting with Aeneas.[36] The catabasis of Aeneas is exactly at the point in the narrative when we might expect some genuinely significant historical number-crunching, but instead we get a pile of sand and an individual's life—an individual with a more than passing resemblance to Ovid, as the end of her speech shows, *usque adeo mutata ferar, nullique uidenda,/uoce tamen noscar, uocem mihi fata relinquent* ('all the time I shall be carried in metamorphosis, and visible to no one, I shall still be known by my voice, the fates will leave me my voice', 14.152–3).[37]

Ovid avoids significant synchronisms of the kind cultivated by Eratosthenes, Apollodorus, Nepos, Atticus and Varro. He does not correlate events in the Greek and Roman worlds; with one significant exception, as we shall see, he passes from one to the other, from Greece to Italy.[38] If we are given no synchronisms between Greece and Rome, neither are we given any of the material that chronographers are supposed to provide about the relative dates of important artists, poets, or philosophers; again, with one significant exception, the same exception, Ovid does not mention *any* historical artists, poets, or philosophers. We get Pygmalion, not Phidias; Orpheus, not Homer.

Notoriously, even the very foundation of Rome itself is practically glossed over in passing (14.772–5):

---

[36] Ellsworth (1988), 53 makes an unconvincing attempt to see chronographic significance in the splitting of the Sibyl's span into 700 and 300 years. 700 years do not take us back to any important benchmark, and 300 take us forward, not to the time of Tarquinius Priscus, but to a period still over a century before Romulus. If Ovid had wanted to endow the Sibyl's 1000 years with non-contingent meaning, he could have split her lifetime into, for example, 600 and 400, and thereby brought her neatly into line with Varro's scheme, which allowed for some 400 years between the fall of Troy and the first Olympiad.

[37] Ellsworth (1988), 53. Note, too, how Aeneas sees only his ancestors in the underworld, as one might naturally expect (14.117), with no view of the future/present that in Virgil was inextricably linked with Aeneas' present.

[38] Excellent discussion of this transition from the Greek to the Roman at the end of the poem in Myers (1994), chapter 3.

> Proximus Ausonias iniusti miles Amuli
> rexit opes, Numitorque senex amissa nepotis
> munere regna capit, festisque Palilibus urbis
> moenia conduntur
>
> Next the soldier of unjust Amulius ruled the resources of Ausonia, and old Numitor gains his lost kingdom by the help of his grandson, and on the festival of Palilia the city's walls are founded

There is a date here, but it is not the Varronian date of the foundation, the fulcrum for Roman historical chronography, but a Fasti-type day of the year date (the only one explicitly given in the poem). And the secure significance of this foundation date is practically immediately undermined by the beginning of the next book, when we get a really proper elaborate foundation story, the foundation of... Croton; for Ovid's account of the foundation of Croton leads in turn into the most famous anachronism in the whole poem, indeed, the most famous anachronism in Roman history.[39]

This anachronism is the exception I have just mentioned twice, for we pass back to the Greek world momentarily, and we also meet an actual historical philosopher, as Numa goes to Croton to meet Pythagoras—and Pythagoras, as every modern schoolboy knew, was not born until Numa had been dead for over a hundred years. Here is Livy on the subject of where Numa derived his famous wisdom (1.18.2):

> Auctorem doctrinae eius, quia non exstat alius, falso Samium Pythagoram edunt, quem Seruio Tullio regnante Romae centum amplius post annos in ultima Italiae ora circa Metapontum Heracleamque et Crotona iuuenum aemulantium studia coetus habuisse constat.
>
> People falsely proclaim Pythagoras of Samos as the source of his learning, because there isn't anyone else on record as his teacher, but it is agreed that Pythagoras had his coteries of young men studying his lore while Servius Tullius was on the throne in Rome, more than a hundred years later, right on the very edge of Italy around Metapontus and Heraclea and Croton.

Even more pertinent for Ovid is a lengthy discussion between Scipio and Manilius on the subject of Numa and Pythagoras in Cicero's *De Re Publica* (2.27–9), for here the speakers address the quintessentially Ovidian themes of fictional plausibility and Roman Hellenisation. After hearing Scipio praise the reign of Numa and the chronological accuracy of 'our friend Polybius', who established thirty-nine years as the length of that reign,

---

[39] For other links between these foundations, see P. Hardie (1997), 195–8.

Manilius asks if there can be anything to the tradition that Numa was a student of Pythagoras'. Scipio responds in animated terms:

> Falsum est enim, Manili, ... id totum, neque solum fictum, sed etiam imperite absurdeque fictum; ea sunt enim demum non ferenda in mendacio, quae non solum ficta esse, sed ne fieri quidem potuisse cernimus.

> The whole thing is false, Manilius, and not just a fiction but on top of that a bungled and ludicrous fiction. For that's what's really intolerable in lie-telling, when we can tell that something's not just made up but couldn't even have actually happened.

These words must have been an irresistible challenge to Ovid, a disciple of the man who had once written ψευδοίμην ἀίοντος ἅ κεν πεπίθοιεν ἀκουήν ('If I'm going to lie, let me at least tell lies that are going to persuade the person who hears them', Callim. *Hymn* 1.65). Scipio produces elaborate chronological proofs of the impossibility of the meeting, provoking a fine exclamation from Manilius:

> Di inmortales, inquit Manilius, quantus iste est hominum et quam inueteratus error! ac tamen facile patior non esse nos transmarinis nec inportatis artibus eruditos, sed genuinis domesticisque uirtutibus.

> Ye immortal gods, said Manilius, what a monster of an error, and how long-standing! Still, I can easily live with the fact that we were not educated by arts brought in from overseas, but by virtues that were innate and homebred.

This question of whether or not Roman learning is native or imported is clearly the key. Cicero very much wants to imagine a time of pristine Romanness before foreign influence;[40] Ovid knows full well that it is a great historical mistake to deny that Roman culture is hellenised as far back in time as it is possible to go, and he is prepared to repeat a famous anachronism in order to correct this mistake.

The poem, then, contains one synchronisation of the Nepos/Varro variety between Roman time and Greek intellectual history, yet it is the one synchronisation that all of his readers would have agreed had been exploded by modern research.[41] The chronological uncertainty generated here throws its effect back to the preceding foundation story, of Rome: the Catonian, Varronian and Virgilian overarching connections between Troy's fall and Rome's foundation have been broken.

---

[40] Zetzel (1995), 184–5.
[41] Pythagoras, of course, is an ideal figure to generate chronological uncertainty: he keeps *coming back* (*Met.* 15.160–2).

If the canonical moments of demarcation and origin are missing or destabilised, there are of course passages where Ovid marks a new beginning, a new phase. These, however, are not the standard chronological points of demarcation, but the generic ones that matter to Ovid: *primus amor* . . . ('the first love', 1.452); *primus in his Phineus, belli temerarius auctor* ('first amongst these was Phineus, the rash originator of war', 5.8: note the significant words with which this particular first *auctor* is petrified by Perseus: *quin etiam mansura dabo monimenta per aeuum*, 'indeed I shall give a monument to endure through time', 5.227). Ovid is, in sum, consistently evasive about offering connected rationales for the poem except those artistic ones for which he can claim full credit.[42] A sense of Ovidian time is indeed created in the internal world of the poem, one created by the sheer experience of reading. The clearest example of this sensation is given by the story of Salmacis, which is 'brand new' when we first encounter it quite early on (*nouitate*, 4.284), and known to absolutely everybody when Pythagoras alludes to it in the last book of the poem (15.319).

The canonical and authoritative time structures available to Ovid, then, are put under extreme pressure in his poem.[43] His scheme is ordered in its own ways, but he does not want it to be anyone else's order: he wants it to be *mea tempora*. After all, he knows how arbitrary and constructed any time pattern is, since originally there was no time, no demarcation of night and day, for there was no sun or moon (1.10–11):[44] the first word of the poem's narrative proper, after the proem, is a word of time, *ante*, signalling a time before time (1.5). At the beginning of Book 2, with the help of allusions shuttling back and forth between the *Metamorphoses* and the *Fasti*, Ovid reveals that this primal chaos is lurking at the heart even of established natural time. Here we may glimpse chaos potentially in even the most ordered time presentation of all, the palace of Sol (2.25–30):[45]

> a dextra laeuaque Dies et Mensis et Annus
> saeculaque et positae spatiis aequalibus Horae
> Verque nouum stabat cinctum florente corona,

---

[42] As Raphael Lyne put it to me.
[43] As are, indeed, all manner of authoritative structures: Barkan (1986), 84–5. Compare, in particular, the pressures Ovid's poem puts on the concepts of ordered and controlled space which the new imperial geography was attempting to enshrine (R. Lyne (1999)).
[44] Cf. the discussion of the prologue in Zissos and Gildenhard (1999), with their references to Pl. *Ti.* 37d–e and Macrob. *Sat.* 1.8.7 on the absence of time in the original state (32). Their whole discussion, in particular of the palace of Sol, should be read in tandem with mine.
[45] Cf. R. Brown (1987), 213–14.

stabat nuda Aestas et spicea serta gerebat,
stabat et Autumnus, calcatis sordidus uuis,
et glacialis Hiems, canos hirsuta capillos.

> On right and left there were Day and Month and Year, and the Centuries and, positioned at equal intervals, the Hours; there stood new Spring, crowned with a flowering garland, there stood naked Summer, carrying garlands woven out of ears of corn, there stood Autumn too, stained with trodden grapes, and icy Winter, his white hair all shaggy.

This parade of regularity is most imposing, but the very next line reminds us that this order is all brand new: the character Phaethon may be frightened by the 'novelty' of what he sees (*rerum nouitate*, 2.31), but the reader also knows that the post-Chaos order of time is indeed 'novel', 'new' at the date of Phaethon. The reassuring order is further unsettled if we remember the beginning of the *Fasti*, where Janus first declares himself to be the one whom those of old called Chaos (*me Chaos antiqui (nam sum res prisca) uocabant*, 1.103), and then claims that he presides over the gates of Heaven, along with the Hours (*praesideo foribus caeli cum mitibus Horis*, 1.125)—between lines 26 and 27 of *Metamorphoses* 2, in other words. Sure enough, before the narrative of Book 2 has proceeded much further, we see the chaos unleashed by Phaethon and hear a protest from Earth herself: *in chaos antiquum confundimur* ('we are being poured back into the chaos of old', 299)—here the collocation of *chaos* and *antiquum* is a clear intertextual echo of Janus' words in the *Fasti*, quoted above, *me Chaos antiqui* (1.103).

It is vital to Ovid, then, to make his own time, and to break down the domination of the accepted patterns of time. He wants to create a space for uncertainty, for contingency, for unreality, for a different construction of the individual self in time. Here Helga Nowotny affords us some very thought-provoking ways into the larger issue of time.[46] First of all, she evokes the all-pervasive nature of the time schemes which regulate any aspect of human experience, and the inevitable issues of power involved in the tensions of that regulation: 'Time is made by human beings and has to do with power which they exercise over one another with the aid of strategies of time.'[47] As she says, 'Knowing the right moment is useful;

---

[46] My thanks to Henderson (1999), chapter 5 for alerting me to the importance of Nowotny's work. Henderson is describing there Horace's and the state's use of time to control and regulate: Ovid's *Metamorphoses* is the counterexample.

[47] Nowotny (1994), 143; cf. ibid., 'The strategic use of time as a central aspect in the emergence of power, and for the purpose of maintaining it, runs throughout the whole of social life, from interpersonal relations to the big institutions and their built-in tendencies to persist.'

determining it confers power and promises control.'[48] This regulatory pressure of the canonical forms of time is what Ovid wants to break away from, in favour of what Nowotny calls a different 'search for the moment', one which 'can also point inwards, to the unfolding of one's own, temporal self, to the development of an identity repeatedly reassembled from fragments. Then time is made by the flow of time momentarily stopping to let in the unexpected, to break routine, and to be open to the experience of spontaneity and to the "vicissitudes" of life.'[49]

In the *Metamorphoses*, then, despite the ostensible form of the arrangement, Ovid is interested in an altogether different use of time from the chronographic. And I can think of no clearer proof of Ovid's genius, if we wish to talk in these terms, than the fact that while he was composing the time-machine of the *Metamorphoses* he was simultaneously composing the quite different time-machine of the *Fasti*, which is precisely all about Nowotny's 'strategic use of time as a central aspect in the emergence of power', as Newlands in particular has recently shown.[50] We have already seen above that Ennius may be a precursor in this task of composing two quite different works on time, one that starts at the origin and moves sequentially on to the present, and another that describes the annual round of the calendrical year. Of these two Ennian works, only one, the *Annales*, was in verse; perhaps, then, for a model of how to compose two poems of time, one sequential from the origins, and one annually circular, we may look even further back, to Hesiod. Hesiod's calendrical *Works and Days* is acknowledged as a model by Ovid in the *Fasti*, where he is addressed by Janus and by Mars as 'a bard *work*ing on *days*' (*uates operose dierum*, 1.101, 3.177).[51] Hesiod's *Theogony* begins, as does the *Metamorphoses*, with Chaos, and moves through divine time until the poet reaches the present ordered state of the universe, at which point he bids farewell to the gods and their ordered world, and turns to the heroes (963–8).[52] Although there are only some forty more lines to go in the text of the *Theogony* as we conceive of it (and as Hesiod conceived of it), Ovid would have seen the end of the *Theogony* as a transition to the five books of the *Catalogue of Women* or

---

[48] Ibid., 152.
[49] Ibid., 152: she is speaking generally here, and not—however much it may appear that she is!—about the *Metamorphoses*. This is an apposite place to acknowledge how stimulated I was by a brief paragraph on the *Metamorphoses* in a synopsis of Alessandro Schiesaro's ongoing project on 'Knowledge in Roman poetry'.
[50] Newlands (1995).   [51] P. Hardie (1991), 59.
[52] On the importance of the *Theogony* to Ovid's ideal of a 'Weltgedicht' ('world/universal poem'), see Ludwig (1965), 74–5, 83–6; Myers (1994), 6; Barchiesi (1994), 220–2.

*Ehoiai*, a parade of heroic genealogies and myth.⁵³ From this perspective Ovid is a modern Hesiod in both his works.⁵⁴

If Ovid is determined to maintain a strategic uncertainty in his configurations of time in the *Metamorphoses*, then his plan has, of course, a corollary—Ovid's metamorphic poem must do its best to disavow Augustus' time-constructions, along with Nepos' and Varro's and Apollodorus' and Ennius'.

For a start, the teleology of Augustus' *Aeneid* is severely compromised by Ovid.⁵⁵ Now, at first the *Metamorphoses* does appear to buttress a Virgilian picture of the Roman state being inevitably predestined in the structure of the cosmos and the poem, for the first two books have repeated prophecies or prolepses looking forward to the coming Roman, and Augustan, *imperium*. The first comparisons of the poem look forward from mythical time to the contemporary world of Augustus' Palatine establishment, and to his relations with the Senate (1.175–6, 200–4). The first prophecy of the poem shows Apollo foretelling the laurel's role in Roman triumphal ritual and as an honorific adornment for Augustus' house (1.560–3). The Phaethon episode has two almost casual glances forward to Roman dominion and custom, as if to show that the threatened chaos will not materialise this time: in the list of rivers dried up by Phaethon's careering chariot, we see Tiber, *cui ... fuit rerum promissa potentia* ('to whom power over the world was promised', 2.259); and at the end of the episode we are told that the tears of Phaethon's sisters, transformed into amber, will be carried down the Po to become jewellery to be worn by Roman brides (*electra ..., quae lucidus amnis/excipit et nuribus mittit gestanda Latinis*, 2.365–6). Not long afterwards comes the final such forward reference, an even more offhand allusion, as the former whiteness of the crow is compared to the current whiteness of various birds, including the geese who were to save the Capitol (*nec seruaturis uigili Capitolia uoce/cederet anseribus*, 2.538–9). The opening of Ocyroe's prophecy on Aesculapius (2.642–54) should perhaps be mentioned here too, for it looks forward allusively and inexplicitly to the second to last historical event in the poem, Aesculapius' importation into Rome in Book 15 (compare 2.642 and 15.744). Still, after Book 2 these

---

⁵³ M.L. West (1985), 127–8.
⁵⁴ Although he owes to the chronographers the extra conception of extending the heroic time down into history, and the present: Ludwig (1965), 75–6.
⁵⁵ As eloquently stated by Kenney (1982), 441: 'For him the Augustan settlement was not, as it had been for Virgil, the start of a new world, *nouus saeclorum ordo*, but another sandbank in the shifting stream of eternity.'

forward references stop. This is an interesting and underexamined problem, but for our present purposes it is enough to observe that a teleological reading of the poem as a whole becomes harder and harder to sustain as a result.[56]

The end of the poem multiply defeats our attempts to read it as the end of time, a definitive *telos*.[57] In all kinds of ways the energy of the poem sweeps us on towards the future, past the close. The power of Ennius' *Annales* as a model comes into its own at this point, for the first Roman poem of time was also in fifteen books of hexameters, but it was continued, with a supplement of Books 16–18, as Ennius grappled with the Tristram Shandy problem of having to write more the more he lived.[58] The end of the poem shows how the future cannot be contained or controlled, and it picks up on Virgilian hints in order to do so, especially the death of Marcellus at the end of *Aeneid* 6, where the crisis of succession opens before the readership, as we see the loss of what had been going to be the future.[59] Political succession is a vital concern at the opening and close of the last book of the *Metamorphoses*.[60] Book 15 opens with a problem of succession, after the death of Romulus, using language that must have been current in senatorial and courtly circles towards the end of Augustus' life.[61] At the end of the book we see the problem of succession picked up again, in a double context of futurity, as Jupiter looks into the future to tell Venus how Augustus will attempt to control the unknowable and unmanageable future (834–7):

---

[56] After Book 1 these forward references cluster around Phaethon (even the reference to the Capitoline geese is immediately followed by a reference to the swan, whose metamorphosis is narrated at the end of the Phaethon story). I am not sure of the effect of this, but the place to begin an investigation would be with Zissos and Gildenhard (1999), which shows how fundamental categories of natural and narrative time are broken down in Book 2, despite the hairsbreadth escape from total chaos.

[57] Barchiesi (1994), 243–65. As ever, we must guard against failing to do justice to the complexities of the model when doing justice to the complexities of the text under discussion: see Zetzel (1997) for a bracingly non-reductive approach to Virgilian teleology.

[58] The end of the *Fasti* deploys Ennian allusion to similar effect: see Vol. 2, Chapter 1, 31 n.55.

[59] P. Hardie (1993), 92.

[60] Ibid., 94 rightly stresses Ovid's comparative lack of interest in 'generational continuity', referring to Ovid's preferences for other kinds of continuity than the one provided by 'the biological fact that the only kind of perpetuity lies in the replacement of one generation by the next'. It is striking that all of the successions of Book 15 are specifically non-biological ones, as Romulus is succeeded by Numa, Caesar by Augustus, and Augustus by Tiberius: in this last case Ovid places high stress on the fact that Augustus' successor is the biological product of Augustus' wife, not of Augustus himself, *prolem sancta de coniuge natam*, 836.

[61] Compare *Met*. 15.1–2 (*quis tantae pondera molis/sustineat*) and 5 (*animo . . . capaci*) with the Tacitean language which clusters around the abilities to succeed Augustus of, respectively, Agrippa Postumus (*neque . . . tantae moli parem*, *Ann*. 1.4.3) and Tiberius (*solam diui Augusti mentem tantae molis capacem*, 1.11.1): see Goodyear (1972) ad locc., and cf. P. Hardie (1997), 182–3.

## Mea tempora

inque futuri
temporis aetatem uenturorumque nepotum
prospiciens prolem sancta de coniuge natam
ferre simul nomenque suum curasque iubebit.[62]

and looking forward into the age of future time and of the descendants to come, he will order the offspring born from his chaste wife to take up at the same time his name and his cares.

Here the poet, the readership and the *princeps* are all attempting to foresee 'a future without Augustus';[63] he will, after all, one day be indubitably *absens*, as the last word addressed to him in the poem reminds us (15.870).

Nothing shows the mutability of the poem's time categories more powerfully than the rewritings of the poem from exile, as Stephen Hinds has shown in his 'Booking the return trip', and in his return trip to the issue in this volume.[64] As Ovid's Pythagoras says, times are always new (*tempora . . . noua sunt semper*, 15.183–4). Time will always move on, and become different, and make past times, *tempora*, different as a result of the new perspective. The new *tempora* of exile are divorced irrevocably from the *tempora* of the composition of the *Metamorphoses*.[65]

In view of the passages from exile, in particular, it would be romantic to see the *Metamorphoses*' time and authority patterns as straightforwardly independent of Augustus' time and authority patterns. However strenuously Ovid attempts to keep the *tempora* of the *Metamorphoses mea* and not *tua*, however hard he tries to emancipate his masterpiece from time and power constraints which he wishes to project as external, Ovid's schemes inevitably mesh in with Augustus', and the two define themselves in interaction. As far as the issue of time is concerned, this is most clear when we remember the way that the end of the *Metamorphoses* takes us on a trajectory right into the Roman calendar, the Julian calendar which Augustus and Ovid were both hard at work on rewriting for the new

---

[62] *curas* in the final line of this quotation is another of the quasi-technical words in common with Tacitus' account of Tiberius' succession (*in partem curarum ab illo uocatum*, 1.11.1). Versnel (1994), 202–5 has a fascinating discussion of this attempt by the emperors to control future time as well as present time, and he takes the end of *Metamorphoses* 15 as his text.

[63] Barchiesi (1994), 265.

[64] Hinds (1985), and (1999), 52: '*time itself* is always a loaded term as the *Tristia* get under way, a term which moves between Ovid's lived experience and his verse, negotiating a transition from the world-views of his Roman past to world-views which will inform his Pontic present and future. The poet puts life and art in dialogue not only to construct his exiled self . . ., but to construct the temporal frames which that exiled self must inhabit' (original emphasis).

[65] See here Hinds (1999), 48–9, 54–7 on *Tristia* 1.1.4 and 122, 1.7.4.

times. The temporal links between the two poems have been compellingly analysed in Philip Hardie's discussion of Janus, the patron god of the *Fasti*'s opening, and in Alessandro Barchiesi's discussion of the way in which the second-to-last historical event of the *Metamorphoses*, the importation of Aesculapius, takes us forward to the *Fasti*, where the feast day of Aesculapius is marked in red on the first day of the year, the first of January.[66] Once again, Nowotny offers us some very thought-provoking perspectives, now on the dialogic nature of the construction of time, whether we are considering the issue from the perspective of *Metamorphoses*, *Fasti*, or (most piquantly of all) *Tristia*:

> Paradoxically ... proper time is made possible only through the time of others. Only when a common time is created as a frame of reference, which neither belongs completely to the one or completely to the other nor is occupied by him or her, can the constraint of time at least be loosened, even if it cannot be totally removed. Between two individuals, this presupposes a process of constant development, of negotiation and argument by means of their continued temporal strategies. Many sets of strategies are at the disposal of strategic action in time and through time: accelerating or slowing down; fixing a deadline; promising; waiting and keeping the other waiting; acting at the right moment, deciding or biding one's time.[67]

*Mea tempora*, then, but also, inevitably, at the same time, *tua*.

Still, since I have been arguing that Ovid tries very hard to keep the *Metamorphoses* independent of the dominant patterns of time in his world, let us conclude by acknowledging his chronological superiority to the Caesars at the end of the poem. Julius Caesar had an allotted span of *tempora*, which he filled up in March 44, as Jupiter points out to Venus (*hic sua conpleuit ... /tempora, perfectis, quos terrae debuit, annis*, 15.816–17).[68] His adopted son, Augustus, as Jupiter also prophesies, likewise has a span of years which will one day end (*annos*, 838).[69] Ovid's future, however, is different. A day will come that will mark the boundary of the extent of his contingent lifespan (*illa dies ... incerti spatium mihi finiat aeui*, 15.873–4), but in his better part he will be *perennis* (875). Ovid begins by asking the gods to spin the poem down to 'his own times', but since he will keep going

---

[66] P. Hardie (1991); Barchiesi (1991), 6–7.
[67] Nowotny (1994), 144–5. Once again, I must caution that, despite appearances, she is not talking about Ovid and Augustus.
[68] Only two months (by the Roman reckoning) before Ovid's earthly *tempora* began; as Barchiesi (1999), 122 n.35 points out, Ovid was conceived in the year Caesar died.
[69] The text is corrupt, but *annos* at least is certain.

'through the years' and never die the times are always 'his own'. The word that begins the poem's final paragraph, on Ovid's future fate, is *iam*, 'now'—the 'now' of the poet's act of completion, but always into the future the ongoing and ever-changing 'now' of each new reader's act of coming to the end.[70]

---

[70] Cf. R.A. Smith (1997), 5–6, 194–6.

CHAPTER 11

# *Interpreting Sacrificial Ritual in Roman Poetry: Disciplines and their Models*[1]

The interpretation of sacrificial ritual in Roman poetry is a more pressing and rewarding issue than it might have seemed even twenty years ago, when many would have regarded both Roman ritual and Roman literature as equally formalist and arid. We may now be more prepared to entertain the possibility that Roman poetry and Roman ritual are both capable of doing important cultural work, and to accept that the interaction between the two, in the form of poetic engagement with ritual, might likewise be doing important cultural work. It remains, however, very difficult to analyse this interaction between what we call literature and what we call ritual, just as it remains very difficult to analyse any case of interaction between what we call text and what we call context.

## 1. Disciplines and Models

### *1.1. The Need for Models*

It will be helpful to begin by being as explicit as we can about our models, of ritual, and of literature. I take it that we are always using models of one kind or another, whether we acknowledge it consciously or not. More importantly, we always need models of one kind or another because the mass of data will defeat us otherwise. The lack of explicit models means that we just flounder in the sea of evidence—to prove the point, you have only to read the old Pauly-Wissowa entry under 'Opfer (Sinn)'. And to see

---

[1] I thank the company at the Stanford conference in February 2002 for their extremely helpful responses: I am grateful especially to Alessandro Barchiesi and Susan Stephens. Other versions of this paper were given in Leeds, Oxford and Rutgers, and at Damien Nelis' conference on Ovid in Dublin in March 2002; numerous people gave me plenty to think about, but for their highly helpful remarks I must thank above all Monica Gale and Ann Kuttner. Ann Kuttner generously read a first draft, and made me wish that I knew enough about art history to do justice to her suggestions. Mira Seo also read a first draft, and I owe a great deal to her incisive comments.

that genuine advances have been made since then thanks to the self-conscious importing of models into Classics from other disciplines, principally anthropology, you have only to read Andreas Bendlin's entries in *Der Neue Pauly* under 'Opfer': 'Theorien' and 'Ausblick'. The challenge is to try and clarify what is at stake in the choice of models, and especially what is at stake in the interchange of models from one discipline to another. We are often told that the boundaries between disciplines are falling away, and that history, anthropology, literary criticism and political science are coalescing. However welcome and exciting such developments may be, there is a risk that we will end up in a position analogous to that adopted by people who deny that the distinctions between genres are relevant to the study of Ovid's *Fasti* or *Metamorphoses*. As a number of recent studies have taught us, the creative transgression of boundaries does not annul the categories, but redefines them.[2]

I take the problem of sacrifice as a test case partly by way of *recantatio* for not having talked about sacrifice as an issue in *Literature and Religion at Rome* (1998); I gestured towards the problem in the chapter on 'Ritual' ('To moderns, sacrifice is a vital aspect of ritual', 119), and then went on to say nothing specifically about it. Mainly, however, sacrifice appeals as a test case because the role of sacrifice in literature, specifically in Virgil's *Georgics*, has recently occasioned a debate that is highly illuminating for the current enquiry. Habinek and Thomas, followed in particular by Morgan, have turned a searchlight onto the problem of the sacrificial dimension to the *bugonia* at the climax of the *Georgics*.[3] I advance no new reading of *Georgics* 4, and make no claim to 'solve' any of the issues of interpretation. I choose this starting point because the debate illuminates with particular clarity what is at stake in the confrontation between disciplines and their models. I shall then take up the lead provided by Fantham, and follow the theme of sacrifice from Virgil's *Georgics* into Ovid's *Fasti*, in order to provide another test case of the interaction between ritual and literature.[4]

## 1.2. *Models of Sacrifice*

Before turning directly to Virgil and Ovid I should give an account of the models and working hypotheses I am using in the case of sacrifice and of literature, although I remain aware that the motivations for an individual's

---

[2] Conte (1986), 100–29; Hinds (1987) and (2000); Barchiesi (2001a).
[3] Habinek (1990); R.F. Thomas (1991); and Morgan (1999).  [4] Fantham (1992).

preferences and practices in this regard must, at some level, remain opaque to him or her. Some first principles, then, so far as I have access to them, brusquely presented.[5]

The meaning of sacrifice is not a question of origin. In the debate over this question in Hamerton-Kelly's *Violent Origins* between Walter Burkert, René Girard and Jonathan Z. Smith, it is Smith who clearly emerges triumphant. The meaning of ritual is not to be found in the survival of some prehistoric trace, whether it be neolithic hunting guilt (Burkert) or a Remus/Abel human scapegoat sacrifice (Girard); the meaning of ritual is not, as Smith puts it, 'somehow grounded in "brute fact"', but instead in what he calls 'the work and imagination and intellection of culture'.[6] It is always the current work of ritual that matters, not where it might once have come from. This may appear to be a hard perspective for students of the ancient world to work with, since the antiquarian religious work of the ancients is so overwhelmingly aetiological. The methodology of the ancients, however, gives no ground for modern foundationalist theories of explanation by historical origin, since, as we shall see in this paper, ancient aetiological methods are so often intent on 'muddying the waters of the source' and making the origin of sacrifice a problem.[7]

For all his scepticism about origins, Smith does offer, more or less as a *jeu d'esprit*, an aetiological myth for the origin of animal sacrifice which is far more historically plausible than Burkert's or Girard's, namely, the selective culling of domesticated animals in breeding. The Roman literary evidence certainly fits Smith's myth, as we shall see, linking sacrifice always with the world of the agriculturalist and his domesticated animals, not with hunting wild animals. It is salutary to read the work of Jared Diamond, and to learn how bizarre domestication is, how recent it is as part of our species' history, and how few animal species have ever successfully undergone it.[8] We may think of the wild animal as the numinous and uncanny, but from an evolutionary point of view the really weird freaks are all around us, in the shape of the domesticated animals.

Still, Smith affects not to care if his origin myth is true or not, because for him the meaning and work of ritual are contemporary and ongoing, however apparently fossilised the forms. According to him, and to Catherine Bell,[9] whose work develops his in many respects, ritual is not

---

[5] For a fuller discussion and documentation of a number of these issues, see Feeney (1998).
[6] J.Z. Smith (1987), 198.   [7] To borrow the phrase used of Ovid by Barchiesi (1997a), 218.
[8] Diamond (1997), 157–75, showing that only five species are really significant in the history of domestication (sheep, goat, cow, pig and horse).
[9] Bell (1992) and (1997).

precultural, nor is it foundational. This anti-foundational way of looking at ritual is rather at odds with the traditional assumptions of structuralism or symbolic anthropology, as represented in Classics particularly by such figures as Vernant, Vidal-Naquet, Detienne and, in his rather different way, Burkert.[10] Now, the impact of structuralism and of symbolic anthropology on the study of ancient religion has been extremely valuable, and will certainly leave its traces in any imaginable future synthesis, but its main drawback is the way that it posits an overarching holistic and unifying thought-world for any given society, a *mentalité*. Such an approach almost inevitably ends up seeing ritual as an expression of this overarching *mentalité*, and especially as underpinning it in a foundational sense. But such a supposition is very dubious, and Maurice Bloch in particular has exposed its weaknesses, above all its tendency to obscure the fact that ritual is only one of many *mentalités* or knowledge-systems in any society, and by no means *the* foundational knowledge-system; ritual is, or can be, extremely self-contained, so that it cannot readily be 'read off' as a metaphor for other knowledge-systems or power-structures in the society.[11] Wilkins has recently explored this question in connection with the language of the Iguvine Tablets: 'ritual language inhabits a specialised domain even within the subject culture and within the whole context of the practice and evolution of the social uses of language. Ritual language ... can be seen to have its own domain, and within that domain, its own rules.'[12] According to these approaches, there is no one *mentalité* that fits a whole society, whether that *mentalité* is identified with ritual or anything else.[13] Although Bloch has his eye on anthropology and does not explicitly take account of New Historicism or Cultural Poetics, his criticisms could clearly be extended by analogy to take in these other varieties of anthropologically derived holism; I shall return to these questions at the end of the paper.

A corollary to this scepticism about one great overarching system is that one must expect to find a multiplicity of interpretations of ritual activity.[14] *The* Roman attitude to sacrifice is not a recoverable entity; indeed, sacrifice at Rome is described by Richard Gordon as being 'to a degree a vacant sign'.[15] At this point we must also remind ourselves that ritual is not

---

[10] An overview of the French School in Buxton (1981).   [11] M. Bloch (1989), esp. chapter 1.
[12] Wilkins (1994), 164; my thanks to Ann Kuttner for this reference.
[13] See also Lloyd (1990) for a trenchant criticism of the *mentalité* mentality.
[14] Feeney (1998), 127–9.
[15] Gordon (1990), 206; cf. Rüpke (2008), 495 on the historical circumstances that 'make the search for the "essence" of Roman religion futile'.

a discrete category in ancient thought, and nor is sacrifice exactly a discrete subcategory of it.[16] In Rome there is no Platonic form or idea of sacrifice 'out there', which is then represented or captured more or less imperfectly by an artist. When we conduct a quasi-anthropological search for the meaning of ritual or of sacrifice in ancient texts, our object of enquiry is very much a modern construct, for ancient authors have extremely little in the way of explicit theorising about sacrifice: 'Although modern scholars may construct an explanation of Roman sacrifice by putting into modern words themes and associations which were almost entirely implicit and unspoken for the actors, the system itself produced no theological account of the meaning and purpose of sacrifice.'[17] In fact, as I tried to show earlier in the case of divinity, and as I shall try to argue here in the case of sacrifice, at Rome, just as in Greece, it was primarily what we call literature that did the job of exploring what Gordon calls the 'meaning and purpose' of divinity or sacrifice.

### *1.3. Models of Literature*

The engagement with sacrifice in literary texts adds more layers of complication to this already complicated picture. No literary text offers us a *representation*, in the strict sense, of anything, let alone sacrifice. In making this claim I am of course employing a model from literary criticism or hermeneutics, or, rather, signalling a shared concern from a number of different literary critical or hermeneutic models, whether the Contean generic approach, deconstruction, or even the old New Criticism. The idea that literary texts represent or reflect reality is having an odd comeback, but I think we have to take very seriously the objections to this idea which are posed by such literary-critical or hermeneutic models. At the most basic level, any text or genre has its own priorities, traditions, methodologies. Further, Roman literature is very self-conscious about its own distinctive way of engaging with ritual.[18] Roman authors know perfectly well that ritual in their texts is not a facsimile of ritual in other contexts, just as they know that anything in their texts is not a facsimile of anything in other contexts. The apparently real and concrete and grounded nature of sacrificial ritual is so strongly present to us that we can fall into making

---

[16] Feeney (1998), 117–18. Arguably, ritual is not a discrete category of inquiry at any time or place: such is the main argument of Bell (1997).
[17] Gordon (1990), 206. [18] Feeney (1998), 32–8; Barchiesi (2000) and (2002).

assumptions about the transparency of literature's engagement with sacrifice that would arouse scepticism or derision if we entertained them in the case of, for example, love elegy's engagement with biography or carnality.[19] Again, I return to these issues of representation and textuality at the end of the paper.

## 2. Virgil's *Georgics*

### 2.1. Walter Burkert in the Georgics

Many of the issues I have been discussing so far are visible, or just beneath the surface, in the starkly differing papers on the *bugonia* in the *Georgics* by Thomas Habinek and then, in response, by Richard Thomas. It is clear that Thomas' fundamental objection to Habinek's method is that he sees Habinek as importing from Greek studies a structuralist anthropological model whose modern themes and associations, according to Thomas, may conceivably have something to do with the Greek world but have nothing to do with the Roman world.[20]

In some respects Thomas' criticisms are cogent, especially when he objects to Habinek's use of the standard Greek sacrificial model to dictate a necessarily ameliorative interpretation of the resurrection of the bee community: as Habinek puts it, 'Social interaction and human culture come to be seen in a positive light, and, with them, the institution of sacrifice that makes their existence possible.'[21] Thomas is right to say that this is an overly Procrustean imposition of a particular model, in which the model is driving the interpretation, and he makes some telling points in detail, but his fundamental methodological reservation about Habinek's methodology is ill-founded. In trying to locate the sacral or quasi-sacral passages of the *Georgics* explicitly within some larger interpretative context, Habinek may be on the wrong train but he is on the right track.[22] The friction between the sacrificial patterns inside and outside the poem demands interpretation. To Thomas, however, the very use of an extra-literary sacrificial model is illicit, as becomes clear in a series of rhetorical questions towards the end of his article, in the course of which he quotes Habinek's characterisation of sacrifice:

---

[19] See D.F. Kennedy (1993), esp. chapter 1 and Wyke (2002), esp. part 1 for a discussion of the related issues in elegy.
[20] R.F. Thomas (1991), 216–17.   [21] Habinek (1990), 216.
[22] A line I stole, with full apparel, from Professor Joseph Farrell—whom it is a pleasure to thank for his characteristically generous and helpful correspondence on these problems.

can we ever say of 'the Romans' (or even 'the Greeks' for that matter) that for them 'sacrifice is a means of establishing the relationship between human and divine, of defining the order of society and the universe, and of restoring that order when it has been disrupted' (p.212)—even if we add footnotes referring to Burkert's theories on Greek religion? Would not some Romans find such a proposition as ridiculous and trite as we do? Would not some be as horrified and repulsed at witnessing the slaughter of oxen as we would? Or would they feel that they had thereby affirmed correct relations with the gods—whoever they were?[23]

There were indeed various views on the merits of animal sacrifice both in the Roman and Greek worlds, and we shall be seeing some horror and revulsion expressed by Virgil and especially by Ovid later in the paper. Nonetheless, a good deal of Roman state cult is underpinned precisely by some such view of ritual and sacrifice as maintaining order between the state and its gods, the *pax deorum*, and restoring that order when it has been disrupted.[24] Habinek's Burketian formulae are too vague to serve as determinative guides for the exegesis of an immensely complicated literary text, as Thomas quite rightly points out, but the model itself may have something to offer a literary reading, so long as it is not regarded as homogeneous and unitary, or prescriptive in terms of the literary readings it can enable or disable, but instead as an initial set of intellectual or imaginative possibilities. The ritual and sacrifical underpinning of the *pax deorum* is the view presupposed by many Roman observers of Roman state cult, and it is the view presupposed by Virgil in the *Georgics*: note, in particular, how Cyrene tells Aristaeus to supplicate the nymphs and seek *pacem*, so that they will in return grant pardon in response to his prayers, and cease their anger (*namque dabunt ueniam uotis, irasque remittent*, 4.534–6).[25] Virgil does not take over such a view casually or by default because that is how his society as a whole just naturally saw things, but for his particular purposes: he takes this selective point of view as his starting point not in order to replicate it, but in order to give power to his own departures.

Before investigating these departures of Virgil, we need to consider another important methodological point highlighted by Thomas' criticisms of Habinek. As we have seen, Thomas objects in principle to the

---

[23] R.F. Thomas (1991), 217.　[24] Rüpke (2001).
[25] On the linking of *pax* and *uenia*, see Wissowa (1912), 390–1, and on the remission of divine *ira* in response to human *uota* when the *pax deorum* is breached, see Rüpke (2001), 21. It is interesting that Mynors (1990) ad loc. comments on the 'traditional' language of *pax* and *uenia*, while R.F. Thomas (1988) does not.

application of a Burketian Greek sacrificial model to a Latin literary text, largely on the grounds that the model is not framed in terms that would have been accessible to the original participants: Greeks did not think in these terms about sacrifice, and nor did Romans. This is what Gordon describes, in the words already quoted at the end of 1.2 above, as constructing 'an explanation of Roman sacrifice by putting into modern words themes and associations which were almost entirely implicit and unspoken for the actors'.[26] The difference, of course, is that Gordon sees this hermeneutic conundrum as inevitable, whereas Thomas sees it as illicit and anachronistic. But Gordon is right. Any historical or anthropological project is going to need models or frames of analysis that are incongruent with the experience of the participants. We cannot *be* them, and we must process the data into some kind of shape for it to make any sense to us.[27] The challenge for the historian or anthropologist is to be aware of this inevitable incongruity or disparity between the observer's and participant's experience, and so to avoid two opposite errors: one is to project the model onto the participants, and claim that they really knew this structure, though maybe only subconsciously—Gordon is in fact rather close to this position—the other is to say that the facts speak for themselves and do not need ordering in a structure for an outsider to get a grasp on them. For the purposes of analysis, the participant's perspective is regularly unsatisfying. Dirk Obbink puts the point very well in his discussion of ancient and modern theories of sacrifice: 'I do not want to suggest that ancient theories in the matter have necessarily any greater chance than modern theories of being right. They are often demonstrably wrong: paradoxically, their very proximity in time and cultural context to the phenomena in question puts them at a distinct heuristic disadvantage.'[28]

## 2.2. *Patterns of Sacrifice in the* Georgics

As a result of his hostility to what he sees as a New Historicist imposition of non-literary models, Thomas virtually ends up implying that sacrifice is not important or interesting to Virgil. He points to the catastrophic failure of the one real sacrifice narrated in the poem, during the Noric plague in Book 3 (486–93), as if to suggest that the quest for a meaning to sacrifice in

---

[26] Gordon (1990), 206.
[27] The first chapter of D.F. Kennedy (1993) is indispensable on this topic.
[28] Obbink (1993), 80. For further discussion of this interpretative paradox, see Volume 2, Chapter 5, 100–1.

the *Georgics* is pointless.²⁹ It is certainly true that the catastrophic failure of the recognisably Roman and ritually correct performance of sacrifice in Book 3 highlights the absence of regular and successful sacrificial practice elsewhere in the poem. There is indeed very little reference to normative Roman sacrificial practice in the *Georgics*. In Book 1 Virgil glances at the *felix hostia* of the Cerealia, but does not describe its sacrifice—and his offering of honey, milk and wine together has no Roman parallel (1.343–50); at 2.192–4 he evokes a sacrifice complete with wine and 'steaming entrails' (*fumantia exta*, 194); at 2.380 he gives an aetiology for the sacrifice of the goat to Bacchus (not actually part of Roman cult at all), and follows it up with an evocation of the sacrifice of the goat (2.393–6); at 2.536–8 he alludes to the impious feasting on plough-oxen that marks the end of the golden age, in a manner that is ultimately inextricable from a sacrificial reference, however deliberately inexplicit it remains;³⁰ and at 2.146–8 and 3.23 he alludes to, without narrating, the slaughter of oxen at the Roman triumph.³¹

We never, then, actually see a regular Roman sacrifice in the *Georgics*; if modern students of sacrifice are frustrated by this state of affairs, they should reflect that Virgil is not interested in documentary realism or helpful proleptic collaboration. His interest in sacrifice runs deeper, in fact, than one might gather from the list in the previous paragraph. Monica Gale has made the best and most sustained case for Virgil's ability to use sacrifice as a systematic way of thinking about human beings' relationship with animals, and, by extension, with the natural world as a whole.³² She traces a developing process of disenchantment or reorientation through the poem, with the institution being apparently taken for granted in the first book, and then gradually denaturalised, as empathy for the sacrificial victim increases and the freakish nature of human interaction with the rest of the natural world is systematically unlayered.

In his wish to argue against Habinek's use of external models, Thomas comes very close to saying that we may only read with an eye to sacrificial connotation if the text enacts a sacrifice with punctilious correctness. As I suggested above, however, we should expect that literature will not represent—*re*-present—patterns of action from other spheres. That is not where the *technē* of the poet resides, as Aristotle taught us. We should not be surprised by the fact that Virgil's most sustained engagements with sacrificial patterns come at two highly anomalous moments—the Noric plague and the *bugonia*.

---

²⁹ R.F. Thomas (1991), 215–16.   ³⁰ So, rightly, Dyson (1996), 278–9 and Gale (2000), 107 n.161.
³¹ Cf. 3.160, where sacrifice is one of the reasons for rearing oxen.   ³² Gale (2000), esp. 101–12.

*Interpreting Sacrificial Ritual in Roman Poetry* 213

The final book of the poem ends, before the *sphragis*, with the ritual action performed by Aristaeus to placate the nymphs and the shades of Orpheus and Eurydice, a ritual action which results in the completely unexpected emergence of the bees, nine days later, from the rotting carcasses of the slaughtered oxen (4.534–58).³³ In many respects E.L. Harrison is basically right to say that 'the Aristaeus epyllion is above all an illustration in mythological form of orthodox Roman procedure in a plague context'.³⁴ But it is a strange fantasy, with a strangely refracted relation to the supposedly actual Egyptian practice of *bugonia*, let alone to contemporary Roman practice.³⁵ Virgil tells us what Egyptian *bugonia* is like earlier in Book 4, and it is not at all like what Aristaeus does.³⁶

At this point I must mention the Stanford connection. Susan Stephens and Alessandro Barchiesi are both independently working on *bugonia* and sacrifice in Callimachus' Egypt and Virgil's Italy, and they have both been extremely generous in helping me see the larger parameters for the ritual Virgil narrates at the end of his poem. It is clear from their work that the end of the *Georgics* is part of a Virgilian and Augustan debate with a Callimachean and Ptolemaic debate over cultural norms and centres of gravity. Callimachus had appropriated Greek norms to an Egyptian context (so Stephens); the Aristaeus epyllion in particular combats Callimachus' appropriation of Greek norms to Egypt by appropriating them back to Hellas, and to Italy (so Barchiesi); the Egyptian practice of *bugonia* is barbarised and distanced and made groundless as a base for Greco-Roman sacrificial practice (so Stephens and Barchiesi combined).³⁷

For my present purposes, what is most fruitful about these projects is how much light they shed on the longstanding problem of the bizarre nature of the aetiology at this climactic moment of the poem. The very nature of aetiology is called into question here, even at the level of the bad

---

³³ Mynors (1990), 321, following Servius *ad* 4.553, rightly stresses that the resurrection of the bees from the carcasses is not foreseen by Cyrene.
³⁴ E.L. Harrison (1979), 52 n.6.
³⁵ The ritual of leaving sacrificial victims unburnt and unconsumed is actually not as unheard-of as is often claimed: see Mynors (1990), 321 for references to the *animalis hostia* or *animale sacrificium*, 'in which only the victim's life (*anima*) was offered to the deity' (his reference to Macrobius' *Saturnalia* should be 3.5.1–5). Latte (1960), 379 is no doubt correct to say that this category is a piece of antiquarian casuistry with no consequence for cult practice, but the presence of the category in the tradition offers Virgil enough purchase.
³⁶ R.F. Thomas (1988), on 538–58. Stephen Hinds (*apud* Myers (1994), 155 n.86) points out how the fantastic nature of Virgil's *bugonia* is picked up in the wonderful joke of Ovid's Pythagoras, who refers to *bugonia* as *cognita res usu*, when *libro* would be nearer the mark (*Met.* 15.365).
³⁷ [This paragraph reports work in progress at the original date of publication. See now Stephens (2004), 159–60; Acosta-Hughes and Stephens (2012), 242–3.]

casting as *protos heuretes* of Aristaeus, who has to be told *everything*.[38] What exactly is being explained by its origin in the fourth *Georgic*? *Bugonia*, strictly speaking, but that is really a blind. E.L. Harrison and Habinek are right to suggest that the propitiatory practice of Aristaeus adumbrates contemporary Roman practice, but the links between that past moment and current practice are tenuous, to say the least. Virgil keeps going back and back to 'explain' the present, but there is no ultimate grounding for his explanation. Sacrifice is inextricably enmeshed in contemporary society, but it cannot be given a deep foundation in some determining earlier, extra-cultural moment.[39]

How such a reading meshes with the contemporary self-representation of the *princeps* is an open question. Each reader must still interpret the consequences of the sacrificial possibilities at the climax of the poem being treated in this grotesque and self-consciously fantastic way at a time when the *princeps* himself is already well embarked on his career-long practice of making sacrifice and its representation central to the new Rome and the role of its new leader.[40] Barchiesi well brings out how crucial the power of origins was to the image of the *princeps* as sacrificer: 'One of the reasons for the great importance and diffusion of this visual representation of the sacrifice is that this rite is repeated in time and guarantees its own origins.'[41]

Thomas, in other words, could have made his own 'pessimistic' reading of the end of the *Georgics* more convincing by taking the sacrificial models more seriously. But then so could Habinek have made his own 'optimistic' reading more convincing by looking more carefully at what sacrifice might be represented as doing in Caesar's Rome rather than in archaic Greek texts. Virgil's text needs to be historically contextualised, but not in a way that implies that there is *a* reading of sacrifice 'itself' out there in the world, one unifying interpretation, that will effect closure: Elsner's paper on the Ara Pacis, a powerful exposition of the polysemic resonances of sacrifice in Virgil's society, makes it plain how hard it is to enlist the institution as a closural device.[42] Our reading of sacrifice, in other words, is part of a loop that leads into our reading of the poem and back out again. Don Fowler has acutely shown that what is at stake between Habinek and Thomas is

---

[38] Putnam (1979), 314 n.61: 'He seems throughout the episode to have little or no self-reliance or insight of his own. He does what he is told, not what he himself determines.' My thanks to Mira Seo for pointing this out to me.

[39] My debt to J.Z. Smith (1987) is obvious, and I must also acknowledge my debt to a conversation on this point with David Leitao at the Stanford conference.

[40] Gordon (1990).   [41] Barchiesi (1997a), 219.

[42] Elsner (1991). The general point about the illusory power of extra-textual referents to establish closure is eloquently made by D. Fowler (2000), 173–4, 192.

a mutually self-reinforcing attitude towards closure inside and outside the text: the issue of whether sacrifice is more open or more closed as an institution folds back into the issue of whether *Georgics* 4 is read as a text with more or less closure.[43]

The same issue is fundamental to Llewelyn Morgan's reading of the *bugonia*.[44] He argues, rather as Habinek does, that the ritual at the end of the poem is redemptive, optimistically looking forward to a regeneration, and that it is a model for a redemptive social regeneration out of the impious sacrifices of the civil wars, under the new reign of Caesar Octavian. He acknowledges the transgressive and anomalous dimensions to the sacrificial actions at the end of the poem, but he sees them as part of a virtuous circle—the more impious and bloody the sacrifice, the more powerful and creative the redemption. Morgan uses his reading of sacrifice to elucidate vividly some of the poem's main sources of power, showing in particular how the Virgilian fascination with the creativity of violence and the violence of creativity is illuminated by the generation of life from sacrificial death. Yet, as in the argument of Habinek, there is an instinct to close down the open problems of the text by referring them to a supposedly stable external referent.[45] Morgan, again rather like Habinek, sees the institution of sacrifice as grounded in paradox, but as still bearing a unified (if paradoxical) meaning.[46] Another difficulty with his overall argument is that it cannot pass the Karl Popper test: it is unfalsifiable. The more impiety and horror an opponent adduces against the argument for the redemptive power of sacrifice, the more powerful the argument becomes—the more grotesque and appalling the sacrifice, the more paradoxically powerful the redemption. Some Roman readers may well have read the *bugonia* in this way, but I cannot believe that the poem makes such a reading inevitable.

Morgan's argument also bestows a moral justification on a pattern that Virgil may be representing as merely inevitable. Is all this killing, in sacrifice or in civil war, genuinely redemptive and constructive, or is it only a pattern of action that Romans are locked into?[47] If there is no way in

---

[43] D. Fowler (2000), 286–7.  [44] Morgan (1999).

[45] Feldherr (2002), 70–1, makes a very powerful case against a similar appeal to sacrifice in Morgan (1998); I have found his whole argument very helpful.

[46] Morgan (1999), esp. 113–16.

[47] Putnam (2000), 159 well points out that 'as in the case of Remus' death, the negative energy associated with bugonia begets not some idealizing higher ethical scheme but another set of bees and presumably a renewal of their inherently martial identities'. Cf. Perkell (1989), 76 on how for the ancients '*bougonia* apparently signified an exchange of death for life rather than rebirth or resurrection'.

to sacrifice, no validating ground of origin, then it appears that there is no way out either, no way of getting off the treadmill. A main source of the power of the Romulus and Remus myth, newly significant in the civil wars, is its circularity, most memorably evoked in Horace's *Epode* 7.[48] The killings of the civil war are not necessarily the prologue to a definitive settlement, but may be only a replaying of a prototypical pattern of events. The institution of sacrifice would corroborate the claustrophobic power of this approach, since one of the keys to sacrifice is its repetitiveness: the same thing happens again and again, at the same time, in the same place.[49] If we are looking for redemption, circularity may be counterproductive.

Sacrifice emerges as Gordon's 'vacant sign' indeed. As Catherine Bell puts it, 'the strategies of ritual may well generate the sense of a basic and compelling conflict or opposition in light of which other contrasts are orchestrated'.[50] In Virgil's case, the most important of these contrasts would be between order and entropy, the life of the individual and of society, and between the life of the Golden and the Iron Age. Is sacrifice a normative way of keeping the world going round, a sacred act, or is it itself a symptom, a trace of humanity's denatured state, a sign of impiety, the definitive mark of the civilised imperial power?

## 3. Ovid's *Fasti*

### 3.1. *The Two Faces of Ceres*

In following the theme of sacrifice from the *Georgics* to the *Fasti*, my starting point is Elaine Fantham's important article on Ovid and the *Georgics*, in which she makes an entirely convincing case for Ovid responding thoughtfully and systematically to the *Georgics* throughout the *Fasti* in his treatment of sacrifice and the life of agriculture.[51] Fantham begins by examining Ovid's two principal passages about the goddess Ceres, and giving a detailed account of the evident contradictions between them.

The first passage offers an image of Ceres as the emblem of the Iron Age, as the Agonalia of 9 January give Ovid the opportunity for his first and programmatic account of animal sacrifice (1.335–456). It is important for Ovid to have animal sacrifice early on, not just because he is a Hesiodic poet, but because he is a good neoteric, and he follows the neoteric pattern

---

[48] Compare the hideous repetitious force of *iterum* and *bis* in the description of the civil war battlefields at the end of *Georgics* 1 (490–1).
[49] My thanks to Nicholas Purcell for stressing to me the importance of the repetitiveness of ritual.
[50] Bell (1992), 37. [51] Fantham (1992); cf. Gale 2000, 107–9.

isolated by J.E.G. Zetzel in an important article: Ovid likes to start where Virgil ends.[52] Before navigation and commerce there was simple non-animal sacrifice (337–8), but the goddess of agriculture, once we move into the Iron Age of ploughing and sailing, was the first to demand animal sacrifice in the form of a sow (349); and Ovid goes on to describe how the gods demand and receive animal sacrifice of every kind, cutting a swathe through the animal kingdom. He tells us of the goat (354) and the innocent ox and sheep (362)—and with the ox he introduces his own version of the Aristaeus story (362–80), thereby capitalising on the sleight of hand by which Virgil was able to associate animal sacrifice within the aetiological penumbra of the *bugonia*.[53] The killing of the ploughing ox is the climax of this section (383–4), and the killing of the ploughing ox—regularly, but not invariably, associated with its sacrifice—is the definitive mark of the end of the Golden Age and of man's estrangement from nature in Aratus, the end of *Georgics* 2, and in Pythagoras' speech in *Metamorphoses* 15.[54] After the ox there follow the horse (385), deer (389), dog (390) and ass (391). Later, in Book 4 (681–712), we learn that Ceres also likes burning foxes, and at the end of that same book (941–2) we are told that a dog is sacrificed on 25 April for the purely contingent reason that he shares a name with the dog star. In the Book 1 programmatic passage, after the aetiology of ass-sacrifice, with the story of Priapus and Lotis (391–440), Ovid returns to the catalogue of victims, listing all the birds that are killed (441–56), because they are too communicative, revealing to human diviners what the gods are thinking.

The cruel impiety of life in the post-Golden Age appears to be radical, with greedy, ruthless and competitive gods enforcing upon humans the requirement of treating animals, even their workmates, as helpless and terrified agents in the game of communication played out before the altars. The gods make us treat animals as enemies: Ovid derives the name for sacrificial victim, *hostia*, from conquered enemies (*hostibus a domitis*, 1.336), and he does not mean just the human enemies whose defeat is marked by sacrifice to the gods. And at the very beginning of this long programmatic section we are told that one of the etymologies for *Agonalia*, the first sacrifice, is *agonia*, the agony, *metus* ('fear') of the sacrificial victims as

---

[52] Zetzel (1983).
[53] Gale (2000), 111 remarks that Ovid's move 'offers a perceptive commentary' on Virgil. Lefèvre (1976), 46 and Porte (1985), 45, 444–5 see that Ovid's story of Aristaeus is taken over from Virgil and is not itself an aition for ox-sacrifice, but do not observe that Ovid is cashing in a Virgilian trick in this feint.
[54] Aratus, *Phaen.* 132; Verg. *G.* 2.536–8; Ov. *Met.* 15.120–1; see Gale (2000), 107–8. Note how, as soon as the old man Hyrieus in *Fasti* 5 recognises the disguised Jupiter, the presiding deity of the Iron Age, he sacrifices his plough-ox to him (*cultorem pauperis agri*, 515).

they see the knives in the waterbowls (1.327–8).⁵⁵ This stark picture of current life is corroborated by a glimpse of the Arcadian Golden Age, before the birth of Jupiter (2.289–98); here there is no ploughing, no imperial domination of the land through agriculture, no *usus* made of other animals, the horse or the sheep.

To cap this programmatic section on animal sacrifice, animal sacrifice closes the first book, with pregnant sows being sacrificed to Ceres and Tellus (1.671–2) and oxen at the altar of Pax (720); the so-called Italia relief of the Ara Pacis is therefore presumably identified by Ovid with Ceres, or Tellus, or both (1.709–22).⁵⁶ The Ara Pacis, with its *bucrania* over scenes of animal and vegetable fertility and abundance, is one of the monuments in Ovid's Rome which shows the highest degree of self-consciousness about how much killing has to go on in order to maintain the cycles, as the important article of Elsner demonstrates.⁵⁷

The next Ceres passage comes in Book 4 (393–620). When Ovid discusses the sacrifices appropriate to the Cerealia, we see a completely different emphasis, as Fantham shows in detail. Especially, here we are enjoined to perform bloodless sacrifice, of spelt, salt and incense, and to shun the ox as a sacrificial victim, so as to avoid the impiety of killing our fellow-worker (4.413–16):

> a boue succincti cultros remouete ministri:
>    bos aret; ignauam sacrificate suem.
> apta iugo ceruix non est ferienda securi:
>    uiuat et in dura saepe laboret humo.

> Attendants, with your tucked-up clothing, remove your sacrificial knives from the ox: let the ox plough; sacrifice the slothful sow. The neck fitted for the yoke should not be struck by the ax; let the ox live and often toil in the hard soil.

These lines are only the most dramatic case of a systematic contrast with the atmosphere of the Agonalia in Book 1.⁵⁸ In Book 4 we do not see the bloodthirsty Ceres of Book 1; she is *prima Ceres* in 4.401 as the first deity to boost human diet up the food chain from acorns to corn, not the *prima Ceres* of 1.349, the first deity to demand animal sacrifice as revenge on the

---

⁵⁵ Cf. Fantham (1992), 47: I am indebted throughout to her analysis.
⁵⁶ See Galinsky (1996), 148–9 for the various identifications of the 'Italia' relief.
⁵⁷ Elsner (1991). It is important to realise, as Ann Kuttner points out to me, that the *bucrania* on the Ara Pacis are a continuation of a sacrificial and sculptural programme common in the post-classical Greek world, and in Italy as well: Nilsson (1955), 1.88.
⁵⁸ Again, see Fantham (1992) for a full analysis and discussion.

animal kingdom. Further, Ovid hides the iron of the Iron Age (4.405–6), apparently mitigating Ceres' reign. Finally, the just-quoted prayer that the plough ox should be spared the sacrificial axe is a hoped-for Golden Age survival into the present age, rather reminiscent of the strange chronological disturbances one so regularly encounters in the *Georgics*.

### 3.2. The One Face of Ceres

In terms of ritual and aetiology, however, the whole passage in Book 4 is not, in the end, as divergent as it may seem from the devastating view taken of animal sacrifice in the Agonalia section of Book 1. Fantham argues that the first passage is so bitter and so different from the second one that the difference has to be explained biographically as the result of Ovid's disillusionment with his society and its religion in exile. If the inconsistencies are not so radical, we may be less inclined to fall back on a biographical explanation. To begin with, Ceres is not disassociated from sacrifice even in Book 4. Just as in Book 1, Ceres here continues to receive her proper sacrifice of the sow (4.414). And, as we know from the end of Book 1, the peace she delights in (4.407) is guaranteed by the sacrifices of the white ox at the Ara Pacis of the pacific leader (4.408). Above all, it is very important to keep reading from the end of this ritual prescription section into the immediately following myth of the rape of Proserpina, especially since Ovid himself says that it is very apposite to do so: 'the [common]place itself [in my poem/in the calendar] demands that I make public the rape of the virgin' (*exigit ipse locus raptus ut uirginis edam*, 4.417).[59]

We are not disappointed. When Ceres misses Proserpina and goes searching for her, she is immediately compared to the mother cow in Lucretius who has lost her calf to the operators of the sacrifice mill (Lucr. 2.352–9):

> nam saepe ante deum uitulus delubra decora
> turicremas propter mactatus concidit aras,
> sanguinis expirans calidum de pectore flumen;
> at mater uiridis saltus orbata peragrans
> quaerit humi pedibus uestigia pressa bisulcis,
> omnia conuisens oculis loca si queat usquam
> conspicere amissum fetum, completque querelis
> frondiferum nemus adsistens ...

> For often before the fine shrines of the gods a calf falls, sacrificed beside the incense-burning altars, breathing out a warm stream of blood from its chest;

---

[59] On the manifold wit of this line, see Barchiesi (1997a), 75–6.

but the mother, bereaved, wanders through the green glades and looks on the ground for the tracks made by the cloven hoofs, looking over all the places to see if she may anywhere catch a glimpse of her lost offspring, and stops and fills the leafy grove with her laments …

And here is Ceres (*Fast.* 4.459–62):

> ut uitulo mugit sua mater ab ubere rapto
>     et quaerit fetus per nemus omne suos:
> sic dea nec retinet gemitus et concita cursu
>     fertur et a campis incipit, Henna, tuis.

As a mother moos when her calf has been snatched from her udder and looks for her offspring through every grove, so the goddess does not hold back her groans and is carried along at a run, and starts, Henna, from your plains.

Although in the didactic section before the myth Ceres is not associated with ox-sacrifice, in the myth she is associated by simile with one of the animals who will make the Iron Age work, by working, and by providing fodder for sacrifice. Strictly, Ovid keeps up even here the erasure of explicit mention of sacrifice, since he does not explicitly say, as does his model Lucretius, that the calf has been taken for the purposes of sacrifice; yet the pressure to read this dimension in to Ovid's simile and to forge a link with the programmatic Agonalia passage is irresistible, since the sacrificial motivation for the taking of the calf is so powerful a part of the Lucretian model, which itself is designed to cast a pall over the institution of animal sacrifice.[60] In the *Georgics* Virgil had already used significant diction from the Lucretian simile to colour his presentation of the devastation visited on the nightingale/Philomela when the *durus arator* steals her young, to reinforce his theme of the random cruelty that human intervention can inflict on the animal world (4.511–15).[61] Only twenty lines after the simile of Ceres and the mother cow, Ovid acknowledges Virgil's use of the Lucretian simile by himself alluding to Virgil's allusion, comparing Ceres' laments to the lament of Philomela for Itys, using language that recalls both Lucretius' cow simile and Virgil's adaptation of it for his own *philomela* simile.[62] The compulsion to see the goddess Ceres enmeshed in the dynamics of sacrifice is reinforced even before the Itys simile,

---

[60] Gale (2000), 105 on how in Lucretius the simile works to establish animal sacrifice as 'wantonly cruel' and 'pointless'.

[61] Ibid., 135–6, on the debt of Virgil's *amissos fetus* and *questibus implet* (4.512, 515) to Lucretius' *amissum fetum, completque querelis* (2.358).

[62] Cf. Ovid's *querelis/implet, ut amissum* (4.481–2); see Fantham (1998), 47 on the links between this Ovidian passage and the Virgilian one, and on 481–2 for the links with the Lucretian simile.

immediately after the Lucretian cow simile, when we see a hint at the enmity of Ceres towards her typical sacrificial offering, the pig; here we are told that she would have tracked down her daughter's path there and then if pigs had not disturbed the tracks (463–6). In the Agonalia passage Ovid informs us that Ceres started the pattern of animal sacrifice by taking revenge on the pig for rooting up the new crops (1.349–52). Ceres has got more than one reason for not liking pigs.

If these glances at the issue of sacrifice at the beginning of Ceres' search for Proserpina incline one to look for a prototypical Ceres of the Iron Age in Book 4 as well as in Book 1, then there is further confirmation later in the story, when Ceres, after much wandering in search of her daughter, comes to Eleusis, and is interrupted by Triptolemus' mother as she is giving the boy immortality (549–56). Ceres informs the mother that the gift of agriculture will be a recompense for Triptolemus' mortality (559–60):

> iste quidem mortalis erit: sed primus arabit
> et seret et culta praemia tollet humo.
>
> He *will* be mortal; yet he will be the first to plough and sow and take up rewards from the cultivated earth.

This strong marking of Triptolemus as the first agriculturalist is at odds with other touches in the telling of the Ceres myth in *Fasti* 4, especially the presence of someone already cultivating the fields in Sicily when Ceres initially goes searching for her daughter (*arua colentem*, 487), and the reference at the end of the story, when Ceres is reconciled, to the way the fields gave a huge harvest after their period of being neglected and uncultivated (*largaque prouenit cessatis messis in aruis*, 617).[63] Still, especially in comparison with the version of the Ceres story in *Metamorphoses* 5, where there is no suggestion whatever of Ceres' bereavement being a rupture between life before and after agriculture, we must be struck by the very different emphasis in the *Fasti* on the aetiological dimension of the Ceres myth. The gift of agriculture is linked with mortality, both of humans and of the animals humans live and work with.

In the Ceres episode in Book 4, then, the indirect mythic explanation supplements and corrects the more overt didacticism of the exegesis section, and the overall impression is less at variance with the Ceres we see in Book 1 than we might initially think. In Book 1 the shocking nature of sacrifice is overt, and fully stressed, as Ovid concentrates all his efforts on

---

[63] See Fantham (1998), on 4.559–60.

denaturalising his audience's familiarity with the institution, rather as Virgil activates a latent sense of disgust at the sacrificial evisceration of animals the humans care for.[64] In Book 4 Ovid affects to ignore this perspective and to give another, more ameliorative view of the patron goddess of modern life, exempt from the nexus of killing, but the sacrificial imperative behind the life of civilisation keeps breaking through. It breaks through in the form of the myth, with the Lucretian sacrificial simile for Ceres' bereavement, with the reminder of her hatred of pigs, and with the treatment of the Triptolemus story as an aetiology of agriculture. It also breaks through more explicitly immediately after the end of the section on the Cerealia, when Ovid returns to the association of Ceres with animal sacrifice. Two short interludes totalling eight lines follow the Cerealia before Ovid gives us the Fordicidia of 15 April (4.629–72), when a pregnant cow is sacrificed, ultimately a rite that started when Ceres failed (645). The sacrifice is to Tellus, so regularly linked with Ceres (634, 665). Two lines after the Fordicidia we encounter the final day of the Cerealia, 19 April (679–712), where Ovid tells us of how Ceres is honoured by the burning of foxes.

Using the more open-ended *Georgics* as his point of departure, Ovid accentuates one of Virgil's range of possibilities.[65] In the *Georgics*, animal sacrifice is open to multiple interpretation, but Ovid concentrates, directly or obliquely, on one powerful Virgilian possibility: he represents sacrifice as a token of the loss of the Golden Age, as the life of agriculture involves humans in endlessly dominating the land and the animals that share it with us, and endlessly placating uncertain deities by giving them many varieties of that animal life. Human life is denaturalised, and sacrifice must be endlessly repeated in order to stave off the everpresent threat of having to pay the full consequences of that denaturalisation.

### 3.3. *The Specificities of Generic Preference*

The analysis of the two Ceres passages would obviously only be a beginning for a thorough-going study of sacrifice in the *Fasti*. One would need to follow up John Scheid's fascinating study of the dialogues between the different kinds of sacrificial offerings in the cult of the *Fratres Arvales*

---

[64] Gale (2000), 105–6 on *Georgics* 2.194–6; cf. Ovid's own evocation of this disgust in *Fasti* 4.936, *turpiaque obscenae (uidimus) exta canis*. Ann Kuttner made me aware of the importance of the potential impact of this dimension of sacrifice.

[65] Gale (2000), 108: 'Ovid can be seen as making more explicit the tensions which I have been tracing in Virgil.'

(animals, plants, incense):[66] the standard models are obsessed with animal sacrifice, and in English it sounds more than a little ridiculous to speak of 'sacrificing' cakes or vegetables, but Roman cult, and the *Fasti*, have a high degree of interest in non-animal sacrifice as well. One would also need to follow up Andrew Feldherr's eye-opening discussion of how Ovid in the *Metamorphoses* treats the reader/citizen's identification with the sacrificial victim, and see how his important findings work in the context of the *Fasti*.[67] Nor have I touched on one of the most important aspects of sacrifice for Ovid, namely, as the arena for communication between humans and gods.[68]

Ovid casts his net very wide, but we need to remind ourselves how selectively this poem, or any other poem, treats or can treat the full range of the possible meanings of sacrifice. Richard Thomas, for example, makes much of the fact that we never see in the *Georgics* the full Burketian sacrificial model of sacrifice followed by feasting. Yet different poetic and iconographic traditions vary greatly as to which elements of the full ritual they will represent, and each tradition is itself susceptible to evolution: the plastic arts, for example, show a dramatic change in their selection of the key moment of sacrifice in precisely the Augustan period, choosing the instant before the actual killing in preference to the procession.[69] As far as sacrificial feasting itself is concerned, Gordon points out that representations of feasting are non-existent in public sacrificial sculpture of the Imperial period.[70]

Poetry, likewise, has its own variable preferences and emphases. Whatever they may do in the *Aeneid* and the *Metamorphoses*, where the sacrificial feasting of epic is quite common, Virgil in the *Georgics* and Ovid in the *Fasti* practically never link animal sacrifice and feasting explicitly. In the mention of goat sacrifice in *Georgics* 2 we have a description of the animal standing at the altar (*et ductus cornu stabit sacer hircus ad aram*, 395), and then of its *exta* being roasted on spits of hazel (*pinguiaque in ueribus torrebimus exta colurnis*, 396); but the actual killing is not mentioned, and the entire ritual is evoked in the future tense. As for Ovid in the *Fasti*, he does have one set-piece description of the full length of a sacrificial ritual,

---

[66] Scheid (1990).  [67] Feldherr (1997).  [68] Again, Rüpke (2001) for the general issues.
[69] Ryberg (1955), 196; Kuttner (1995), 131–5. On the importance of this moment in Roman representations from this time, in contrast with its earlier comparative rarity in Greece, see Ryberg (1955), 4–5
[70] Gordon (1990), 204; we may in fact have one depiction of feasting, in an image of the Vestal Virgins: Beard, North and Price (1998), 2.150. Ann Kuttner draws my attention to the painting of a sacrificial banquet commissioned by Ti. Sempronius Gracchus to commemorate the victory of his slave army at Beneventum in 214 BCE: on this painting, see now Koortbojian (2002).

right down to the feast after sacrificial killing, when he describes the festival of the Terminalia in *Fasti* 2 (643–58).⁷¹ I take the point here to be related to the important fact that, according to the best ancient sources, originally this festival did not have blood sacrifice at all.⁷² Ancient authorities have it that Numa set up the institution of the Terminalia, like most of his other cults, as bloodless sacrifices.⁷³ It is just possible that the Numa of the *Metamorphoses* returns from his lessons with Pythagoras to teach the Romans *sacrificos ritus* (15.483) that are bloodless, even though I prefer the more ironic reading whereby Numa hears the learned speech of Pythagoras but does not believe it (*ora docta ... sed non et credita*, 15.73–4).⁷⁴ In the *Fasti*, however, there is no doubt that Numa is a man of blood, who regularly performs blood-sacrifice, and is never seen performing bloodless sacrifice, even if he once averts human sacrifice by substituting an onion (3. 339–40).⁷⁵ By contradicting a dominant tradition in this way, Ovid reinforces his theme that Roman civilisation was normatively bound into Iron Age patterns of behaviour from the start. Or else, if he is suggesting that contemporary practice in the Terminalia is totally different from the original rites ordained by Numa, then we have another example of the disruptions in the continuity of this rite so finely elucidated by Barchiesi.⁷⁶ After all, the entire point of Terminus is now moot both in place and time. The whole of the globe is now without bounds under Roman rule, as Ovid tells us (2.683–4), so that Terminus no longer marks boundaries in space. And in terms of time, the terminal function of the Terminalia is a dead letter under the reformed Julian calendar. In the Republican calendar the Terminalia marked a cut-off point in February, after which the intercalary month was inserted; in the Julian calendar, the Terminalia no longer terminate anything.⁷⁷

---

⁷¹ Cf. Miller (1991), 120 for the unusual fullness of this description. Note the exceptionally full, practically Burketian, description of sacrifice offered by Pythagoras in his didactic denunciation of the institution in *Metamorphoses* 15 (127–39), and the comical disruption of the sacrificial pattern in *Fasti* 2, when Romulus and Remus are called away to fight robbers while they are waiting for their sacrificial meat to cook, and Remus comes back first to finish the barbecue without Romulus (359–76).

⁷² My thanks to Martin Sirois for drawing this to my attention.

⁷³ Plut. *Quaest. Rom.* 267c, *Num.* 8.8, 16.1.

⁷⁴ See P. Hardie (1997), 185 n.14 for the first possibility; Barchiesi (2001b), 65–8 for the ironic reading.

⁷⁵ For Numa's blood sacrifice in the *Fasti*, see 3.300, 4.652, 671; cf. Barchiesi (2001b), 66.

⁷⁶ Barchiesi (1997a), 215–18.

⁷⁷ No coincidence, then, that the next festival Ovid treats after the Terminalia is the Regifugia, which likewise used to mark the end of something, the monarchy, but has now also become a dead letter. Ovid marks the point at the end of the Regifugia, where the last line of the episode, *dies regnis illa suprema fuit*, is immediately followed by *fallimur* (2.852–3): on the importance of reading straight on from line 852 to *fallimur* in line 853, see Reeve (1995), 507.

A final example of sacrificial feasting in the *Fasti* is, once again, highly anomalous, and that is the Ourion myth in Book 5, where Jupiter, Poseidon and Mercury feast with a poor old man, and finally all stand together and urinate on the hide of the plough-ox that has just been sacrificed to them and that they have just consumed (495–536). Note that Ovid, as a poet of *Fasti*, who is only allowed to say *quae licet et fas est*, finds urinating gods unsayable and leaves out the precise details (*pudor est ulteriora loqui*, 532). And even the emphasis on the feasting in this tale is to be explained as a result of its nature as a Callimachean Molorchus or Hecale story, where hospitality is vital.

## 4. Resisting Holism

A weak way of dealing with the problems I have been sketching would be to say that different genres (epic, elegy, didactic, sculpture, and the different genres of ritual in their own right) have distinctive ways of doing things that refract their objects—in our case, sacrifice—in different ways. But this approach would immediately lay itself open to the criticism that it leaves unexamined the idea that there is an object out there to be refracted in the first place, when in fact mediation and representation and encoding are operative all the way down, on both sides of what we represent as the fence between 'life' and 'literature'.[78] This approach would also lay itself open to another criticism, namely, that it leaves unexamined a much larger historicising assumption, the assumption that when literature engages with ritual or anything else it is participating in an identifiable larger system of meaning in which the terms are always set in advance by conditions which are more primary or authentic or real.

Here I return to the problems I noted at the beginning of this paper. As I remarked there, historicising approaches—and this is more true the more they are informed by structuralism and symbolic anthropology— almost inevitably posit a holistic *mentalité*, a global system of meaning in which literature participates. At their most extreme, such historicising approaches will have it that literature expresses the circumstances of its social production. Even when the issue of the cause and effect relationship is finessed, as it regularly is in New Historicism or Cultural Poetics, with their metaphors of 'circulation' or 'negotiation', we are still left with a model which posits a totalising synchronic structure. This is why the governing trope of New Historicism is synecdoche. The power of synecdoche comes through very

---

[78] So Conte (1994b), 105–28.

powerfully in Gallagher and Greenblatt's introductory essay to *Practicing New Historicism*. They give, in effect, a charter for synecdoche, with such telling phrases as these: 'If every trace of a culture is part of a massive text ... '; 'If an entire culture is regarded as a text ... '.[79] Later, when discussing the impact of Clifford Geertz, in an overt acknowledgement of the power of symbolic anthropology, they show how Geertz works out from a fragment to reveal the ramifications throughout the social system of thought: 'Part of Geertz's power was his ability to suggest that the multi-layered cultural meanings by which he was fascinated were present in the fragments themselves.'[80] The part stands for the whole, which is always somehow there, and primary.

Our use of the terms 'text' and 'context' can pitch us into similar holistic traps. The language of 'text' and 'context' can help guard against mere formalism and aestheticism, but it can also keep us thinking of texts as parasitic upon something quintessentially more substantial and really there, and recoverable in that substantiality and reality, while likewise keeping alive the illusion that there is a recoverable cause and effect relationship between the context and the text it is often seen as producing.[81] I am not denying that there is a cause and effect relationship between texts and the conditions of their social production, only that this relationship is recoverable. As David Perkins has shown in his profoundly unsettling book, any act of contextualising is inevitably partial and arbitrary.[82]

Still, we cannot read without contextualising, and the two poems I have been discussing here must be read by us, as by their original audiences, in a series of contexts before they can be interpreted. In their very different ways, the *Georgics* and the *Fasti* give Roman readers tools for thinking about patterns of action that otherwise for the most part they may well have taken for granted. If a Roman did want to speculate on the nature and meaning of sacrifice, these texts would have been indispensable. Romans would have encountered in these poems ways of thinking that would not map directly onto their usual experience of ritual; but I hope I have made a case for suggesting that this is the usual state of affairs for the investigation of ritual. Different experiences and different analytical frames are bound to be incommensurable, to some degree.

And we, too, have lessons to learn from the challenge of reading these poems through the spectacles of a ritualist. If we come to the poems with

---

[79] Gallagher and Greenblatt (2000), 14–15.   [80] Ibid., 26.   [81] Cf. D. Fowler (2000), 129.
[82] Perkins (1992), 121–52.

## Interpreting Sacrificial Ritual in Roman Poetry

no model of sacrifice in our minds at all, we will find it very difficult to see the religious or cultural work they are doing. But if we come to these poems with a full-blown model of sacrifice in our minds, determined to see it exemplified, and convinced that the relationship between the literature and the 'real' category of ritual must be one of synecdoche, we will be disappointed, or, more probably, we will do violence to the poems' specific strategies. We need to acknowledge not only that we cannot read without some kind of contextualising model, but also that the imposition of such a model from another discipline can only be a preliminary heuristic step, for direct imposition of the model will fail to do justice to the way any given text may be working. It is not only literary critics who will be badly served if we jettison the category of the literary.[83]

---

[83] [On the relationship between Geertzian anthropology and historiography, see E.A. Clark (2004), 145–55; and on the relationship with Roman religious studies, Bendlin (2006), 299–311, esp. 299–300.]

CHAPTER 12

# Tenui ... latens discrimine: *Spotting the Differences in Statius'* Achilleid[1]

The quotation in my title, *tenui ... latens discrimine*, 'escaping notice by a fine dividing line', refers to the *ambiguus sexus* of the transformed Achilles, which tricks the onlookers after his mother Thetis has dressed him as a girl to save him from the Trojan expedition: *fallitque tuentes/ ambiguus tenuique latens discrimine sexus* ('those looking are taken in by the ambiguous sex, concealed by a slight line of demarcation', *Achil.* 1.336–7). The dividing line between the sexes is the most conspicuous of the *discrimina* simultaneously violated and reconstituted in Statius' fragment, yet it is only one of many, of which some are more latent than others. I propose to survey the various kinds of *discrimen* in the poem, together with the various kinds of transgression and revaluation they entail; and I shall concentrate especially on the dividing line between Virgil and Ovid in Statius' epic inheritance. A number of outstanding recent studies have brought Ovid into the heart of the fragmentary *Achilleid*, where he belongs;[2] our charge in this volume, to honour Michael Putnam by 'Re-Presenting Virgil', affords the opportunity to re-examine the role of Virgil in the *Achilleid*, and to revisit from this particular angle the rich question of the contested boundaries between Virgilian and Ovidian *epos*.

The first *discrimen* in the poem is the one any poet faces, the one between *this* poem and other poems—for Statius, the *discrimen* between *this* epic poem and all the others, between *this* Achilles and all the others.[3] Statius must make it new (*nouos*, 9) against all the odds, despite the fact that Achilles has been the subject of epic since Homer (3–4). Now, just as

---

[1] It is a pleasure to thank Stephen Hinds and Mira Seo for their comments, and also Alessandro Barchiesi for kindly sending me his paper in progress on the problems of Roman sexuality in the *Achilleid* [now Barchiesi (2005a)]. Note that all line references without book citation are to Book 1 of the *Achilleid*, and that references to 'Dilke' are to the commentary of Dilke (1954).

[2] Koster (1979); Fantham (1979); Rosati (1994), esp. 25–33; Barchiesi (1996); Hinds (1998), 135–44 and (2000).

[3] Koster (1979), 191. Many fine comments on the proem, where Statius especially tackles these issues, in Barchiesi (1996) and Hinds (1998), 95–8.

Virgil had prophesied almost one-hundred-and-fifty years before Statius, great Achilles is being sent to Troy yet again (*iterum ad Troiam magnus mittetur Achilles*, *Ecl.* 4.36). Virgil himself had already in a way fulfilled his own prophecy, by producing another Achilles of his own, in the *Aeneid* (*alius iam partus Achilles*, 6.89); in the *Achilleid*, Thetis later picks up Virgil's language, when she says she wants Achilles to join with Deidamia and have a son so that she can have *alium Achillen*, 'another', as it were, 'another Achilles' (322).

Of course, we expect Imperial epic poets to showcase their sense of belatedness to their tradition,[4] and any lazy reader who did not get the point in the proem is reminded soon afterwards by Thetis, whose first speech, delivered when she sees Paris carrying Helen on his ship back to Troy, contains a battery of language that self-referentially alludes to her own sense of belatedness as a character. Brooding that she has missed her chance to start an epic storm against Paris when he was sailing on the outward leg, she laments that her fears are belated (*seri . . . timores*, 42); couldn't I have done it *then*, she says, at the original moment? (*non potui . . . cum primum*, 43); now too—but, she interrupts herself, quoting Harold Bloom, it's too late (*nunc quoque—sed tardum*, 47); still, I'll do what's left over (*quod superest*, 49), I'll embrace Jupiter Number 2 (*secundi . . . Iouis*, 48–9), not Jupiter Number 1, as I did in the first book of the *Iliad*, or as my imitator Venus did in the first book of the *Aeneid*.[5] Statius' continual mentioning of his secondariness is particularly piquant because there is a genuinely primary subject available for him that he keeps putting off—Domitian (described as *primum*, 14; already deferred in the proem to the *Thebaid*, 1.32–3).[6] And it is also piquant because he is secondary to *himself*, inasmuch as he is starting on his second epic, after the *Thebaid* (10–11). Hinds has well brought out the pun on this dilemma in line 9, where, just after praying for new sources of inspiration (*nouos*), Statius asks Apollo to bind his hair *fronde secunda*—where *secunda* means both 'propitious' and, literally, 'second'.[7] With the key words *nouos* and *secunda* in the same line, Statius highlights the extra difficulty facing him, of achieving originality in relation to himself as well as to his predecessors. It is fitting, then, that two lines later he should signal his allegiance to Ovid, the master of the discourse of the inextricability of novelty and indebtedness, and Latin literature's greatest exponent of self-imitation: when Statius

---

[4] P. Hardie (1993), esp. 114–16; Hershkowitz (1998), 35–104.
[5] On the force of *secundi* in 48, see Hinds (1998), 96.    [6] Ibid., 97.
[7] Ibid., 96; cf. Koster (1979), 196.

says 'my temples [of the head] are not now being augmented with their first priestly fillets' (*nec mea nunc primis augescunt tempora uittis*), the words for 'my temples', *mea . . . tempora*, occupy exactly the same metrical position in the line as they do in the fourth line of Ovid's proem to the *Metamorphoses* (*ad mea perpetuum deducite tempora carmen*), where they also mean 'my temples', in addition to their primary meaning of 'my times'.[8]

The beginning of the poem, then, puts on display his anxiety about whether he can establish a distinctive creative distance between himself and earlier poets, but it also puts on display his anxiety about whether he can measure up to his *Thebaid*, and whether he can establish a distinctive creative distance between his first and second epics. The martial characteristics of the Iliadic sections of the poem would have been the greatest challenge here, but even in our fragment we can see him marking an ironic gap between his two epics. This is why, for example, he introduces the Greek commanders in the way he does at 467–72. First we have twin brothers undertaking wars jointly for a change (*gemini pariter sua bella capessant*, 467), but he still marshals the right number of commanders for a Statian epic: if you add them up (Atridae, the son of Tydeus, Sthenelus, Antilochus, Ajax, and Ulysses) you see that the expedition starts as a 'Seven Against Troy'.[9] But this is a red herring, for the troops, shouting for the absent Achilles, know that the real number in this poem is not seven but one: *in Hectora SOLUS Achilles/poscitur; illum UNUM Teucris Priamoque loquuntur/fatalem* ('against Hector, Achilles *alone* is demanded; they say he is the *single one* to bring doom to the Trojans and to Priam', 474–6).[10]

The *Achilleid*'s heightened awareness of its literary heritage helps explain the choked claustrophobia of the seascapes in this poem, which have been, as we shall see in more detail at the end of the paper, crossed and re-crossed by so many expeditions and their tracking texts. These hallowed waters of the Aegean and Dardanelles have been marked as boundaries for transgression since Io was first plundered by the Phoenicians, according to Herodotus (1.1.1–2.2). When Thetis and her nymphs emerge to the surface at the beginning of the action, the open sea of the first sailing in Catullus 64 is constricted, and has become an Asia–Europe frontier, as the nymphs

---

[8] On this double meaning of *tempora* in Ov. *Met.* 1.4 see Ahl (1985), 289–91. The rest of Ovid's fourth line has already had its key terms recycled programmatically into Statius' seventh, where *tota . . . deducere* captures the same Callimachean/epic oxymoron as Ovid's *perpetuum deducite*: Koster (1979), 191–6; P. Hardie (1993), 63 n.8. On the Ovidian destabilisations in the hyper-epic proem, see Barchiesi (1996).

[9] There are even 'seven kings' mentioned in these lines, misleadingly, for they are *septem . . . armenti reges* who supply the oxhide for Ajax's shield (470–1: a phrase from the *Thebaid*, 11.28).

[10] On the Latin epic obsession with the theme of 'the one and the many', see P. Hardie (1993), 3–10.

crowd out all the available space:'[11] 'the shores of the Dardanelles, as they come together to meet, seethe, and the narrow sea cannot stretch out to allow room for the nymphs' (*feruent coeuntia Phrixi/litora et angustum dominas non explicat aequor*, 28–9). When Thetis foresees the revenge of the Greeks, she sees 'the Ionian and Aegean seas squashed by a thousand keels' (*uideo iam mille carinis/Ionium Aegaeumque premi*, 34–5); 'the sea is not big enough for the fleet' (*ipsum iam puppibus aequor/deficit*, 445–6); 'the whole sea is covered over by the long shadow of their sails' (*omne fretum longa uelorum obtexitur umbra*, 790).[12] All of these passages refer to the challenge facing the poet, who must negotiate his own way through these crowded seas as he follows the (especially Ovidian) metaphor of progressing through his composition as if on a sea-voyage.[13]

To motivate the beginning of this belated re-beginning, Statius calls on Phoebus at the beginning, in line 9, because Phoebus will be there at the end, when he kills Achilles, with Paris, at the Scaean Gate. From the start, Phoebus Apollo has a morbid interest in this subject. The simultaneously destructive and creative god is called upon to begin the process that will carry on until the subject of the poem is dead. It is very odd for an epic poet to invoke as his inspirer the creature who is going to kill off his creation. This gives a sinister tinge to Phoebus' zeal in helping the Greeks to find Achilles later in the book: *meus iste, meus*, 'he is mine, mine', says Calchas, the mouthpiece of Apollo (528).[14] It gives a sinister tinge to the poem's first simile as well, where Achilles is compared to Apollo (159–66):

> ille aderat multo sudore et puluere maior,
> et tamen arma inter festinatosque labores
> dulcis adhuc uisu: niueo natat ignis in ore
> purpureus fuluoque nitet coma gratior auro.
> necdum prima noua lanugine uertitur aetas,
> tranquillaeque faces oculis et plurima uultu
> mater inest: qualis Lycia uenator Apollo
> cum redit et saeuis permutat plectra pharetris.

There he was, larger with much sweat and dust, and yet with all his weapons and rushed hard work still sweet to look at. A purple fire swims on his snowy mouth and his hair shines more pleasingly than tawny gold. Not yet is the

---

[11] As Alessandro Barchiesi expressed it to me, *per litteras*.
[12] This theme helps us decide in favour of *artas*, 'tight-packed', against the boring *altas* in 204: *placet ire per artas/Cycladas*.
[13] Mira Seo reminded me of this favourite trope of Ovid's, on which see Kenney (1958), 205–6.
[14] Cf. 529 and 552 for the Apolline inspiration of Calchas, and 682–3 for Apollo's active help as Ulysses goes to search for Achilles.

first period of his age turning with new down, the torches in his eyes are calm, and his mother is present in his face in force: just as when the hunter Apollo comes back from Lycia and takes the plectrum in exchange for the savage quiver.

Apollo may be exchanging his fierce arrows for the plectrum at this moment in the poem, but he will exchange them back, and those savage arrows would have killed Achilles in Book 12.[15] The initial Apollo simile is doing a lot of work, not least in initiating the crucial blurrings of Achilles' gender status, as we shall see shortly; but one of the main jobs of the simile is to efface a vital boundary, as the invincible hero is identified with his destroyer. This is another way, in addition to the hero's transsexuality, of getting at the vulnerability of the apparently invulnerable hero.

This Apollo simile is the first link in a chain of Apollo and Diana similes that bind together Achilles and Deidamia, a chain that is modelled on the pair of similes that Virgil forges to link Aeneas and Dido, through Apollo (4.142–50) and his sister Diana (1.496–504).[16] Statius' simile-chain will take us into a consideration of his most complex boundary-crossings, as the transvestism of Achilles crosses boundaries of gender and genre, blending Virgilian and Ovidian patterns as it puts the incipiently martial hero into girl's dress and out again.

In the *Aeneid*, Dido is compared to Diana in Book 1, when she is first seen by Aeneas; the answering moment comes in Book 4, when Aeneas performs an act of 'joining' in the narrative (*agmina iungit*, 142) to introduce the simile that joins him to Dido/Diana, as he is compared to Diana's brother, Apollo. In Statius, the Apollo simile comes first, as we have just seen, and the Diana simile occurs when Achilles first sees Deidamia, on the beach of Scyros (thus restoring the situation found in both poets' Homeric parent simile, which describes Nausicaa on the beach of Scheria, *Od.* 6.102–9). As in Homer and Virgil, the heroine is compared to Artemis/Diana as she overtops her companions (*umeris quantum Diana relinquit/Naidas*, 294–5). A sign that something novel is afoot is already present in this Diana simile, however, since it is part of a double simile, as it follows immediately upon a simile comparing Deidamia to Diana's polar opposite, Venus: *quantum uirides pelagi Venus addita Nymphas/obruit* ('as

---

[15] This gives the arrows a more literal role in the later narrative than the ones on the shoulders of Apollo in the model simile, in *Aeneid* 4; here Aeneas, who will be responsible for the death of Dido, is compared to Apollo, whose *tela sonant umeris* (149).

[16] My lead in what follows is the important analysis of the Virgilian and Statian similes in Hinds (2000), 237–8.

much as Venus overwhelms the green Nymphs of the sea when she is added to their company', 293–4).

This overt eroticisation of the latent frisson in the Homeric and Virgilian prototypes receives an extra twist fifty lines later, when we have another Diana simile, as Thetis escorts Achilles to the chorus of girls. This time the character compared to Hecate/Diana is Achilles himself, since he has now crossed over and is wearing girl's clothing, and the transgressive nature of Achilles' shift of roles is highlighted by the way the simile contains references to the male roles Achilles is now abandoning, and to the deity he should 'really' be compared to, Apollo (344–8):

> sic ubi uirgineis Hecate lassata Therapnis
> ad patrem fratremque redit, comes haeret eunti
> mater et ipsa umeros exsertaque bracchia uelat;
> ipsa arcu pharetraque leuat[17] uestemque latentem
> deducit sparsosque tumet conponere crines.

> As when Hecate returns exhausted from virginal Therapne to her father and brother, her mother clings to her as she goes and herself veils her shoulders and uncovered arms; she herself relieves her of the bow and the quiver and leads down the tucked-up garment and swells with pride at arranging the dishevelled hair.

A fine tracery connects this simile to the initial Apollo simile, one immediately signalled by the language of 'returning to the father and brother', which creates a formal link back to the first simile in the chain. In the Hecate/Diana simile, the mother is present in the narrative as well as in the simile, unlike the situation in the Virgilian model, where Latona feels joy in the simile without there being any straightforward correlative for her in the narrative (*Latonae tacitum pertemptant gaudia pectus*, *Aen.* 1.502). On looking back to the context of the simile linking Apollo and Achilles, we see that the mother is present in the narrative there as well (indeed, she is powerfully present even in her son's face, *plurima uultu/ mater inest*, 164–5). Further, the mingled pain and joy Thetis feels on seeing her son is described with language that recalls Latona's reaction to Diana in Virgil's Dido simile: *angunt sua gaudia matrem* ('her joys torture the mother', 183). The transgressive crossover of Achilles figuring as Diana in the later simile, then, is already anticipated here, since in Statius the Apollo simile is followed by a citation of the mother's reaction from the *other* simile.

---

[17] Following the emendation of Schrader for the transmitted *arcum pharetrasque locat*.

The climax of this whole pattern of assimilating Achilles and Deidamia via Diana comes just before the moment when Achilles is revealed by Ulysses' trick, as Achilles dances in the chorus with Deidamia and the other princesses of Scyros. As the relevant passage begins, we see the familiar words *nitet ante alias regina* ('she shines ahead of the others, the queen', 823), but immediately after this reference to Deidamia's outshining of the other dancers we read—'and her companion, the son of Peleus' (*comesque/Pelides*). The two of them, via the singular *qualis*, jointly generate the following simile, which compares them to—inevitably—Diana (825), with Pallas and Persephone following (825–6). An elaborate description of the chorus's various dances comes next (828–33), and Statius exits from this sequence with yet another reference to Diana, in words that hover on the brink of simile, to bring the dance sequence to a circular close (signalled self-reflexively with *orbe*): *quo citat orbe Lacaenas/Delia plaudentesque suis intorquet Amyclis* ('in the circle in which the Delian summons her Laconian girls and twists them, as they clap, in her Amyclae', 833–4). But having entered the simile cluster with Deidamia and Achilles paired, Statius emerges on the other side with Achilles alone as the referent. *tunc uero, tunc praecipue manifestus Achilles* ('then, indeed, then especially was Achilles plain to see', 835), he says—with words that, again, resonate with Diana, since they point back to the description of Artemis as 'easily recognisable' in Homer's original Nausicaa simile (*Od.* 6.108). The difficulty of perceiving Achilles' gender-identification and of tracing his figure in the dances and the doubled series of similes could not be more clearly/confusingly evoked.

For all the rich Virgilian colour to the Apollo and Diana simile chain, the overriding interest in gender ambiguity that governs the sequence is clearly not particularly Virgilian, but Ovidian.[18] Right in the middle of the densely Virgilian simile cluster on the beach, between Achilles seeing and then joining Deidamia, comes a sublimely Ovidian moment of metamorphosis, as Thetis—herself one of the great transformation artists of the *Metamorphoses* (11.241–64)—works like a Pygmalion on transforming her son from an ephebe into a girl (332–4).[19] The whole larger shape of the plot until nearly the end of the first book is profoundly Ovidian, based on the plot-line of the *Amores* and the *Metamorphoses* that the important paper of Nicoll first elucidated, whereby a martial epic is derailed to become a love poem.[20] In *Amores* 1.1 the poet wants to compose martial epic, but Cupid comes along and shoots him so that he becomes a love poet; in the

---

[18] Rosati (1994), 28–33; Hinds (1998), 135–44.   [19] Hinds (1998), 135–6.   [20] Nicoll (1980).

*Metamorphoses*, the cosmogonic and grand epic section culminates in Apollo's shooting of Pytho with a thousand arrows (1.438–51), at which point the poet announces the programmatic shift with *primus amor* (452), and moves into the first of many love stories, with the story of how Cupid shot Apollo to make him fall in love with Daphne. Statius' *Achilleid*, likewise, starts off with a plucky attempt to look like a quintessentially martial epic, 'una sorta di super-epos', as Barchiesi puts it.[21] Already with the Ovidian allusions in the proem there are hints of trouble,[22] as with the failure to deliver on a grand sea-storm to start the epic off, but the real wreck of the grand epic occurs when Thetis is standing on the beach, unsuccessfully trying to talk her son into dressing as a girl (274–82). All seems hopeless, and the narrator intervenes with a question (283–4):

> Quis deus attonitae fraudes astumque parenti
> contulit? indocilem quae mens detraxit Achillem?

> What god provided deceit and cunning to the astonished mother? What frame of mind dislodged stubborn Achilles?

Statius does not explicitly answer his question, and we do not see Cupid intervene as a character, but we certainly see Achilles fall in love with Deidamia as she walks onto the beach, and we see the Ovidian programmatic language of 'first love' embedded in a simile describing Achilles' passion (313–17):

> ut pater armenti quondam ductorque futurus,
> cui nondum toto peraguntur cornua gyro,
> cum sociam pastus niueo candore iuuencam
> aspicit, ardescunt animi *primus*que per ora
> spumat *amor*, spectant hilares obstantque magistri.[23]

> As when the future father and leader of the herd, whose horns have not yet completed their full circle, catches sight of a heifer of snowy whiteness who shares his pasture, his spirit catches fire and *first love* foams over his mouth, and the herdsmen watch happily and block him.

It is highly significant that Statius has mapped the vital crux of this masterplot of Ovid's, together with the intensely Ovidian moment of Thetis' metamorphosis of Achilles, into the centre of the most Virgilian sequence of the poem as we have it, with the dense reworking of the Dido and

---

[21] Barchiesi (1996), 55 ('a sort of super-epic'). [22] Cf. n.8 above.
[23] *spumat* in the last line here is a translingual pun on *Aphro*dite, who has already appeared, as Venus, in the double simile with Diana just over twenty lines earlier (293); on the etymology, see Maltby (1991), s.vv. *Aphrodite* and *Aprilis*.

Aeneas similes. He appears to be engineering a confrontation between conventional martial epic and Ovidian epic, and his interest in transgendered transformation is indeed Ovidian rather than Virgilian; but the choice of the Dido and Aeneas similes as his Virgilian *point d'appui* shows that he knows full well what Hinds has recently brought to our attention, that the *Aeneid* too has its moments of generic fracture, as an epic which is 'surprised by sex', which keeps discovering that women are central to epic, and which is almost totally derailed in Carthage by the intervention of none other than Cupid.[24] Just as in the *Metamorphoses*, which does not continue forever as a series of love stories but returns to wars in due course, especially with the Trojan war, so in the *Achilleid* the plot will eventually retrace its generic steps and take Achilles to Troy, where more generic complications would no doubt have awaited him, as we shall see at the end of the paper.

Statius' Virgilian and Ovidian interest in blurring the generic lines between the poetry of war and sex manifests itself, predictably enough, in a systematic exploitation of the *militia amoris* motif.[25] Achilles' first assaults on Deidamia are conveyed in highly militaristic language (567–76): *nouas... admouet insidias* ('he brings up new ambushes'); *sequiturque premitque* ('he pursues and presses'); *lateri... inhaeret* ('he sticks to her flank'); *ferit* ('he strikes'); *occupat* ('he takes possession'); *ligat* ('he ties up'). The culmination of this concern comes with the rape of Deidamia, which makes him the epic *uirum* at last (562), and is the work of *uis*: *ui potitur uotis* ('by violence he gains what he has been praying for', 642). After having so much in common with his mother throughout the poem so far, at this moment of rape Achilles is exactly like his father, of whom these very words were used by Ovid in the *Metamorphoses*, to describe Peleus' conquest of Thetis (*Met.* 11.265).

The most powerfully destabilising transgression point, however, is the transvestism of Achilles, where multiple *discrimina* of gender and genre are confounded. We now have a number of fine studies of this fascinating issue,[26] so that I shall concentrate only on the discriminating theme of my paper, and consider briefly the way in which Statius focuses his attention on the gender issue through the act of scrutinising, so that spotting the differences becomes a task for characters and readers alike. I shall focus on one female viewer, and one male.

From the moment Achilles is first dressed up, we see how hard it is for those looking at Achilles to spot the *discrimen* between the *sexus*, *fallitque*

---

[24] Hinds (2000), 230–1.  [25] Koster (1979).
[26] Cf. the works cited in n.2, and also Cyrino (1998).

*tuentes/ambiguus tenuique latens discrimine sexus* ('those looking are taken in by the ambiguous sex, concealed by a slight line of demarcation', 336–7), and we have seen how hard it is for the reader to track Achilles' identifications in simile. The characters for whom it matters most to see through the ambiguous differences are Deidamia and Ulysses. Here is Deidamia trying to interpret the signals she is picking up from the disguised Achilles (583–91):

> uocisque sonum pondusque tenentis,
> quodque fugit comites, nimio quod lumine sese
> figat et in uerbis intempestiuus anhelet,
> miratur; iam iamque dolos aperire parantem
> uirginea leuitate fugit prohibetque fateri.
> sic sub matre Rhea iuuenis regnator Olympi
> oscula securae dabat insidiosa sorori
> frater adhuc, medii donec reuerentia cessit
> sanguinis et uersos germana expauit amores.

> She is amazed at the sound of the voice, and his weight when he holds her, and—something that escapes her comrades—the way that he fixes her with an excessive gaze, and randomly catches his breath as he speaks. Regularly, as he is on the verge of getting ready to lay bare his deceit, she shuns him with maidenly frivolity and forbids him to make his confession. In the same way, under their mother Rhea, the young ruler of Olympus used to give sly kisses to his sister, all unanxious, when he was still just a brother to her, until the respect due to their shared blood gave way and the sister panicked at the change in his love.

Now, Deidamia can spot a difference between Achilles and the others, but what exactly is Deidamia seeing through when she suspects the love of Achilles? Can we be certain, as everyone seems to be, that these lines describe a girl suspecting that the girl fixated on her really is a boy? Especially with the transgressive simile comparing her feelings to the recognition of incest, can we be certain that these lines are not describing a girl suspecting that the girl fixated on her is a girl? Although no close verbal similarities emerge, the entire atmosphere of ambiguous sexuality and fluctuating identity is powerfully reminiscent of Ovid's story of Iphis' lesbianism, in particular, and of his Orphic stories of incest as well.[27]

Statius is principally concerned, however, with the male gaze, and especially with the scrutiny of Ulysses. Identifying with Ulysses, and gazing

---

[27] As Mira Seo suggests to me; cf. Rosati (1994), 29–30 on Ovid *Met.* 9.711–13 in particular.

through his eyes as he attempts to spot the difference between Achilles and the 'other' girls, is a revealing, disquieting and rather revolting experience.

The key word here is *pectus*. Achilles is disguised as his 'sister', and Thetis introduces her 'daughter' to King Lycomedes as someone who behaves like an Amazon, wanting weapons and a bow, and shunning marriage in the way of Amazons (*Amazonio conubia pellere ritu*, 349–53). Amazons are so called because they are missing one breast;[28] Achilles, of course, is missing two. When the daughters of Lycomedes enter as Ulysses and Diomedes are being entertained at dinner, they are compared to relaxing Amazons (758–60). Ulysses is looking for someone who is not just Amazonian in temperament, however, and so he intently 'weighs up visually' (*perlibrat uisu*) their faces and breasts (*uultus ac pectora*, 761–2). He is hoping, not that he will catch a glimpse of a breast, as Paris managed to catch a glimpse of Helen's breasts at dinner in Ovid's *Heroides* (16.249–52), but that he will catch a glimpse of the absence of a breast. Shortly afterwards, Deidamia tries desperately to cover up Achilles' breasts so that the secret of his breastlessness will not get out (*nudataque pectora ... in ueste teneret*, 768–9). We almost get a telling glimpse later on, during the dancing, if we continue to focalise through the relentlessly scrutinising Ulysses, for one of the dances the girls perform is the 'Amazonian comb', and the stem of the word for 'comb' offers a misleading flash of 'breast', which is then taken away by the termination and by the breastless adjective that follows it: *pect-ine Amazonio* (833).[29]

When Achilles is finally revealed by Ulysses' trick, the focus is on his revealed male *pectus*: *iam pectus amictu/laxabat* ('already he was freeing his breast from his clothing', 874–5); *illius intactae cecidere a pectore uestes* ('his clothes fell untouched from his breast', 878).[30] The fact that it is his naked *pectora* that finally proclaim his 'true' identity is of course a fulfilment of the Parcae's prophecy in Catullus 64 that he will be *forti pectore notus* ('known by his brave chest', 339). He now appears to join the ranks of real heroes, whose breasts are only ambiguous in a metaphorical sense, as in the case of Diomedes, who ponders *ambiguo sub pectore* ('in his ambiguous/undecided breast') the problem of what Ulysses means with the baubles he is taking to Lycomedes' court (713).

His shedding of ambiguity and his new straightforwardness appear to be definitively signalled as he declares his identity to the king, *sicut erat*, 'just as he

---

[28] Maltby (1991), s.v. *Amazon*, citing, *inter alia*, the scholia on our passage.
[29] An Ovidian trick. As Ovid sets the salacious scene for Priapus' attempted rape of Lotis in *Fasti* 1, he describes the Naiads at the picnic, *effusis aliae sine pect-inis usu* ... (405); three lines later the prurient punchline is delivered (*altera dissuto pectus aperta sinu*, 408).
[30] Cf. 2.5, when Achilles joins the fleet *punicea nudatum pectora palla*.

was' (891). What is that? 'Naked' is one easily available meaning in the context, but, more importantly, after all the poem's hard work so far on destabilising our sense of gender identity, we are invited to wonder, 'What is that thing he really was?' Achilles' gesture of revealing his naked body as if to declare a definitive solution to the problem of his masculinity is less decisive than it looks. The poem, after all, has been working within the parameters of a view of masculinity as 'an achieved state, radically undetermined by anatomical sex'.[31] In this poem, it is women who are somehow 'natural', requiring less work to become themselves than do men, whose gender must be continually worked at, taught and learnt.[32] In contrast to the elegiac view of women as the product of *cultus* and artifice,[33] Statius offers a view of Deidamia and her companions as less formed or worked-up. They have a *cultus*, but it is a uniform overlay (*omnibus idem cultus*, 290); and when they are drawn to look at the trinkets that Ulysses has brought to the court, they go *qua sexus iners naturaque ducit* ('where their sex, lacking in elaboration, and their nature lead', 848). Here *iners* does not just mean 'inactive' or 'unwarlike', but, as regularly in Latin poetry, 'lacking in *ars*'. In this regard, Statius is closer to a tragic or epic view of woman as embodying a principle of nature against the masculine principle of culture or reason.[34]

At the beginning of Book 2 the Greeks see Achilles as if Book 1 had never happened (2.5–11), and this prompts us to ask if the whole Scyros episode can be covered up and forgotten about, dismissed as a transitional phase, as Statius hints here[35]—and as Deidamia fears at the end of Book 1 (947–8):

> ast egomet primae puerilis fabula culpae
> narrabor famulis aut dissimulata latebo.
>
> But I will be narrated to your slaves as a boy's story of a first fault, or else I'll be hushed up and you'll pretend it never happened.

*primae* in 947, coming thirteen lines before the end of the book, is strongly self-referential: Deidamia asks, in effect, 'Is my story going to be stuck in

---

[31] Gleason (1995), 59 on the ancient medical theorists' view of 'an infant's gender [as] not an absolute but a point on a sliding scale'.
[32] On the constant work and training involved in maintaining masculinity, see Gleason (1995), esp. 70–3 ('The molding of men'); on Galen's view of the fixity, lack of variation, and comparatively more animal nature of women as opposed to that of men, see Flemming (2000), 328–9. [See now Orr (2005), 18: '... it is ... now clear that the original state of a human embryo is female. It takes active work by SRY [Sex Determining Region of the Y chromosome] to divert the normal path of development from female to male, a process that, in human beings, starts when the fetus is seven weeks old'.]
[33] Sharrock (1991).   [34] Zeitlin (1996), 112; Quint (1993), 25.
[35] Excellent comments in Hinds (2000), 241–4 on how the second book works 'to put the Scyrian action under erasure' (241).

Book 1?' The announced subject in the proem is Achilles lying hidden in Scyros (*Scyro . . . latentem*, 5), but in the lines just quoted Deidamia says that she will be the one to lie hidden (*dissimulata latebo*), and this is true, for she is never mentioned in Homer. For us, of course, the Scyros episode is practically all of the poem we have got, yet in the planned twelve-book whole, Deidamia's question would have been more pressing: can Achilles' transgressive eroticism be tidily bundled up within the boundaries of the first book, or will this book-boundary also suffer the same buckling as the other boundaries of the poem, with the unepic transgressiveness of the first book continuing to leak out to contaminate the poem's overall ambitions of martial elevation?[36]

This poet is motivated from the start by *amor*, declaring his passion to write with *sic amor est* in his proem ('such is my passion', 5).[37] Achilles at Troy will continue to offer many opportunities for *amor* of a sexual variety,[38] and the force of *amor* could have been broader still. As we have seen, the fragment displays a keen interest in the elegiac militarisation of love, but there is enough evidence even in what survives to show that the poem would have carried on to explore also the flip-side of this motif, the epic eroticisation of war. For if it is true that *militat omnis amans*, it is also true that *amat omnis miles*: 'Not only is sex like battle: battle is like sex.'[39]

Note how Achilles' first erotic blush, when he sees Deidamia on the beach (304–10), is recycled in the intensely narcissistic moment when he sees himself in the blood-covered, blushing-red (*rubebat*, 853) shield that Ulysses has used to trick him into self-revelation: *horruit erubuitque simul* (866). It is exceptionally rare for epic heroes to blush (this hero blushes once more in our fragment: 2.84–5). Only once is a man referred to as blushing in the *Aeneid*—Achilles, who, Priam tells his son Pyrrhus, blushed at the rights and faith of a suppliant (2.542).[40] What Achilles sees in the golden shield is 'himself' (*simili talem se uidit in auro*, 865), and the self-reflexiveness here is very deep. Firstly, Achilles sees his own reflection, blushing-red in blushing-red. Here we have another gender-bending moment at this apparently decisive juncture of masculine self-revelation,

---

[36] On this problem, see Rosati (1994), 10–11; Hinds (2000), 241–4.
[37] Koster (1979), 208; Barchiesi (1996), 58.
[38] Koster (1979), 207; Hinds (2000), 224–5, pointing to Propertius 2.3 and Ovid *Heroides* 3 as models.
[39] D. Fowler (1987), 187.
[40] No men blush in the *Thebaid*, not even Parthenopaeus: I thank Ruth Parkes, who knows the *Thebaid* better than I, for corroborating this hunch. [We missed Theseus, *rubuit Neptunius heros*, 12.588.]

since the most famous character who uses a shield as a mirror is Aphrodite.[41] Secondly, as *talem* shows, in another kind of reflexiveness he is simultaneously seeing himself as the lion in the immediately preceding simile (858–63); this is a bold smudging between simile and context, as if Achilles 'knew' what the narrator's simile had just said about him. Thirdly, he is perhaps also seeing 'himself' represented on the shield. Statius tells us only that the shield is 'engraved with battles' (*caelatum pugnas*, 853), yet the famous Pompeian paintings depicting the revelation scene show Achilles together with Chiron on the shield;[42] it may be significant that Ulysses immediately addresses him as *semiferi Chironis alumnus* ('foster child of the half-beast, Chiron', 868), as if pointing to the talismanic scene on the shield. Achilles' moment of self-recognition and self-revelation is, then, multiply self-reflexive, and his thrill of half-comprehending recognition of what those 'battles' on the shield mean is marked by the same blush that marked his first adult erotic rush, when he saw Deidamia on the beach. No wonder that Statius uses the same word, *calor*, after Ulysses' speech to describe both Achilles' passion for battle (881–2) and his passion for Deidamia (888).

The mutual implication of erotic and marital passion is regularly signalled in the *Achilleid*, right from the beginning, when Statius declares that *amor* is his driving force (*sic amor est*, 5), after calling upon a Muse whom we can identify as Erato, at once the Muse named for erotics and the Muse who motivates the *maius opus* of the martial second half of the *Aeneid* (7.37).[43] The commingling of the registers gathers force as the poem goes on. The urge for revenge against Paris stirs Europe with 'sweet frenzies for arms' (*dulcibus armorum furiis*, 398), and 'the love of war seethes' (*feruet amor belli*, 412); Protesilaus has an 'exceptional lust to wage war' (*bellare cupido/praecipua*, 495–6); all the Greek troops 'ditch their commanders and love Achilles as a divinity of war' (*neglectis ... ductoribus omnes/belligerum ceu numen amant*, 503–4); Achilles tells Ulysses that his youthful training 'accelerated his love of the iron' (*ferri properatus amor*, 2.107).[44]

This last phrase comes from Virgil, *amor ferri* (*Aen.* 7.461); as Horsfall's rich note on the phrase reveals, the whole theme of the 'longing for violence' is a powerfully Virgilian one.[45] This perspective reminds us that Virgil's invocation of Erato, which I adduced in the previous paragraph as

---

[41] See the sources cited in Feeney (1991), 70 n.43.　[42] Trimble (2002), 233–4.
[43] See above, n.37, for the force of *sic amor est*; and Barchiesi (1996), 58–60.
[44] On the sexual aura of the 'adrenaline rush' of combat, see Shay (1994), 92.
[45] Horsfall (2000) ad loc.

a generic marker of high martial epic, is itself radically contaminated with the erotics of the Muse's name.[46] Michael Putnam has elucidated this Virgilian theme in compelling fashion. In the first chapter of *The Poetry of the Aeneid*, he homes in on the *ardor* and *cupido* that motivate the night expedition of Nisus and Euryalus in *Aeneid* 9 (184–5), the excessive lust for slaughter that carries away Euryalus (*nimia caede atque cupidine*, 354), and the rage and insane lust for slaughter by which Turnus is inflamed at the end of the book (*furor ardentem caedisque insana cupido/legit*, 760–1).[47] Elsewhere Putnam has written memorably on the erotic impulses that motivate Juno's interventions and Aeneas' revenge.[48] Other important treatments of this topic in the *Aeneid* include the brief but telling section of Heuzé on 'Violence et sexualité', Gillis' book-length study of eros and death, and Fowler's demonstration of how Virgil interweaves the aesthetics of passivity in defloration and death in battle.[49] Statius, it seems, would not have stopped at turning Achilles into an erotic epic hero, as Apollonius had done with Jason,[50] and as Virgil had fleetingly done with Aeneas, whose encounter with Dido makes the love experience central to Roman identity by making its embracing and rejection the focus of one-sixth of the national epic.[51] Even in the fragment as we have it, we can see that he would have pursued the Virgilian theme of the erotics of killing.

As Achilles stands revealed before Ulysses and the court of Lycomedes, Statius tells us that he is moving the poem up a notch into the territory of Virgilian epic, as he alludes to the spurious four-line preface to the *Aeneid*, which purports to be Virgil's own announcement of his escalation from non-epic to epic. Here is the transition from the 'Preface' to the *Aeneid*:

at nunc *horren*tia *Marti*s
*arma* uirum*que ca*no . . .

And here is Statius' adaptation (881–2):

*arma ca*lor*que*
*Marti*us *horren*da . . .

The future trajectory of the poem would have taken Statius into the Virgilian realm of world-empire, which he was clearly planning to focus

---

[46] On the erotic implications of Virgil's Erato, see Putnam (1985); Horsfall (2000) ad loc.; Nelis (2001), chapter 7, esp. 267–75.
[47] Putnam (1965), 50–62; cf. the note of P. Hardie (1994) on *Aen.* 9.354.  [48] Putnam (1985).
[49] Heuzé (1985), 170–8; Gillis (1983); D. Fowler (1987); see too Pavlock (1990), chapter 2.
[50] Beye (1982).
[51] In general, on the importance of the love themes in the *Aeneid*, see the references in Nelis (2001), 86 n.73.

on through a vital *discrimen*, the last this paper will consider. This is the *discrimen* between Europe and Asia.

The gap between Europe and Asia is a mighty and apparently unbridgeable ideological gulf, which Statius squeezes down to what feels like a geographical hair's breadth. We have already seen that the margin between Europe and Asia, the Hellespont, is choked with divine bodies at the opening of the poem, when Thetis and her nymphs emerge to view the second sailing of Paris' ship (28–9); here the shores of Phrixus are described as *coeuntia*, 'coming together/meeting', not so as actually to meet, but as if they are straining to do so. Later in the book, when describing the geographical extent of Greece as it is marshalled for war, Statius gives us another, equally remarkable, description of this crucial geographical feature, and he links it with the Isthmus of Corinth, the Hellespont's mirror-image, as a narrow strip of land with water on either side, instead of a narrow strip of water with land on either side (406–11):

> coeunt gens omnis et aetas:
> nec tantum exciti, bimari quos Isthmia uallo
> claustra nec undisonae quos circuit umbo Maleae,
> sed procul, admotas Phrixi qua semita iungi
> Europamque Asiamque uetat, quasque ordine gentes
> litore Abydeno maris alligat unda superni.
>
> Every people and age come together. Nor are those alone stirred up whom the confines of the Isthmus with its barrier of the double sea surrounds, together with the promontory of wave-sounding Malea, but far off, where the track of Phrixus forbids Europe and Asia, brought together, to be joined, and those peoples in order which the wave of the upper sea confines with the shore of Abydos.

The Hellespont forbids Europe and Asia to be joined despite their being/at the point at which they are moved towards each other (*admotas*, 409). Lines 410–11 are especially difficult, for Abydos is on the Asian shore, where Leander lived, directly opposite Sestos, on the Chersonese, where Hero lived. Dilke translates *quasque ... superni* with 'And those peoples in succession whom the waves of the upper sea confine with the shores of Abydos', noting: 'We need a reference to European tribes [since this is a description of the forces mustering against Troy], so cannot translate "on the shores of Abydos", which would be in Asia.' Europe, then, is demarcated by the name of the *opposite* shore, the one Europe is straining to touch.

Statius' evocation of Ovid's *Heroides* 18 is fleeting but telling, reminding us of how Hero and Leander are separated *and* given access to each other through the medium of this tantalisingly narrow piece of water. Leander finds himself wishing that the dividing water were broader, so as to be less tantalising (173–4), and guilelessly says that he would almost prefer to be separated by the whole globe (*malim . . . toto procul orbe remotus*, 175), forgetting that the divide between Europe and Asia is a global one, no matter how minuscule.[52] Statius' description is Ovidian also in its evocation of crucial passages in the *Metamorphoses* where Ovid revels in the odd nature of the demarcations afforded by both Hellespont and Isthmus, as he uses them to mark key transition points in the articulation of the *Metamorphoses*' subject matter. Barchiesi has superbly brought out what is at stake in Ovid's deployment of the Isthmus as he moves from 'gods' to 'heroes' (6.419–21), and of the Hellespont as he moves from 'myth' to 'history' (11.194–6).[53] His discussion is too lengthy to quote in full here, but any reader of the *Achilleid* may follow up his Ovidian leads, to see how Statius must have been attracted to Ovid's focus on the bizarre nature of the Hellespont as barrier and access as he came to exactly the same point of transition, namely, to the Trojan war. As Barchiesi remarks, referring to the ending of Herodotus' history, the Hellespont is an irresistible 'strategic narrative site' for clashes between West and East.[54] Herodotus' story ends with the Greeks' capture of Sestos, whose Persian governor is crucified in retaliation for his plundering of the tomb of Protesilaus on the tip of the Dardanelles, opposite Troy (9.116–20); the last Asian outpost in Europe is captured in retribution for Asian sacrilege against the first man from Europe to die in Asia.[55]

Statius must have known very well this Herodotean master-plot, as he knows very well the series of tit-for-tat rapes between West and East that Herodotus tells of in his Introduction to the whole History (1.1.1–5.3). Once Achilles is on board, Ulysses gives him a history lesson and tells him all about these reciprocal acts of violence, mentioning Europa, Medea and Helen (2.72–9). As in Herodotus, the Statian plot escalates from rape to invasion, with the Hellespont as the talismanic boundary of transgression. One imperial conqueror after another has tried to bridge that tiny gap, in the endless to and fro between East and West: the Hellespont is the fine line that the poem's action will cross and obliterate, only to reinforce. For the gods' whole plan, we are told, is to mix Europe and Asia together in conflict (*ratus ordo deis miscere cruentas/Europamque Asiamque manus*, 81–2). The global

---

[52] For the charged language of *orbis* in Statius, see the text to n.56 below.
[53] Barchiesi (1997b), 182–3.    [54] Ibid., 183 n.5.
[55] Lateiner (1989), 46–8; Flower and Marincola (2002), 302–3, 308–9.

dimension to the clash is hinted at in the language Statius uses to describe the mobilisation for war. In a decided outbidding of Virgil's description of Mars raging over the whole globe (*saeuit toto Mars impius orbe*, *G.* 1.511), Statius says that Mars 'rages between one "globe" and then the other' (*alternum Mauors interfurit orbem*, 395). Here Europe and Asia are each an *orbis* in itself, as in the language used by Virgil's Ilioneus to describe the Trojan war as a clash between continents: *quibus actus uterque/Europae atque Asiae fatis concurrerit orbis* ('driven by which fates each globe, of Europe and of Asia, collided', *Aen.* 7.223–4).[56]

The Trojan war as the first clash between Europe and Asia would have been a major theme in the rest of the poem, and no doubt it would have been piquantly complicated for Statius' Roman audience by virtue of the information that Dilke innocently supplies in his comment explaining the first half of *alternum orbem* in 1.395: 'Europe (i.e., Greece . . .)'. The Europe/Asia, West/East confrontation is in this poem set up with the Greeks occupying the European, Western half of the frame, when for Statius' audience the Greek was a paradigm of Eastern effeminacy and garrulity. How this would have been worked out in detail it is now impossible to say, but our surviving text offers some glimpses of the possibilities open to Statius. A particularly interesting moment comes when King Lycomedes laments that he is too old to join the expedition, and Ulysses agrees that he is missing out on something special (785–7):

> quis enim non uisere gentes
> innumeras uariosque duces atque agmina regum
> ardeat?
>
> For who would not be afire to see the innumerable peoples and the various leaders and the columns of the kings?

Are these innumerable peoples and jumbled, variegated leaders and monarchs the Greeks, or the Asians, or both? The immediately following words finally offer the (enjambed) word *Europae* (788) to tilt the balance towards taking Ulysses' words to refer to the Greeks, but the confusion and hesitation are telling: from a first-century Roman perspective the monarchical and discordant *Graeculi* may have more in common with the 'Asians' than with the 'Europeans'.

We may only speculate as to how Statius would have explored the blurring of boundaries between Europe and Asia—both 'old' Europe and

---

[56] See Horsfall (2000) ad loc. for the use of *orbis* to mean 'continent', and also for much poetic and historiographic material on the 'Trojan War as the first conflict between the continents'.

Asia, in the time of the narrative, and the 'new' Europe and Asia of his own time. It is very striking, for example, that Domitian is hailed in the proem as the object of the stupified admiration of the flower of Italy (*Itala uirtus*, 14)—and then, enjambed for surprise, of the flower of Greece as well (*Graiaque*). At the end of the *Thebaid* only the youth of Italy is mentioned as the readership of that epic (12.815); the *Achilleid* envisages a different *imperium*. We may also only speculate as to how Statius would have reacted to Virgil's own distinctive contribution to this debate, with Aeneas outstripping or remaining bound to his Asiatic inheritance, as he becomes the ancestor of the new Europeans, the Romans, who keep balancing on the knife-edge of a return to their Asiatic roots, in Troy, or Alexandria.[57] The first sentence of the *Aeneid* goes from *Troiae* in the first line to *Romae* as the last word, seven lines later; the seventh line of the *Achilleid* has *Troia* as its last word.[58] The new Roman epic circles back beyond Virgil's hoped-for teleological resistance to circularity, yet Rome will still, somehow, have been its focus.

Statius' return to the Trojan origins of Rome and Roman epic will have involved him in a more direct engagement with Homer than even Virgil had contemplated. Statius' Achilles has not yet set foot on Trojan soil when the poem breaks off; the Thetis-plot, however, already adumbrates a major future Homeric concern of Statius' planned epic. In her path-breaking study of the *Achilleid*, Elaine Fantham showed how Statius went to Seneca's *Troades* for a great deal of his inspiration in the depiction of a mother desperately attempting to save her doomed child: Seneca's Andromache and Astyanax become Statius' Thetis and Achilles.[59] This theme must have been one of the dominant ones planned for the Iliadic sections of the poem, and those later sections would no doubt have engaged more explicitly with Homer in the process, since this theme is clearly one of Homer's primary preoccupations. For all the attention paid to the heroic code and the interactions of warriors, parents know that at the centre of the *Iliad* is the appalling intuition, shared by Thetis and Andromache, together with Hecuba and Priam, that you cannot protect your children.

Statius' Homer, however, lies on the other side of the *Achilleid*'s most intractably unnegotiable boundary—between Book 2, line 167 and the rest.

---

[57] Quint (1993), 50–96.
[58] See Barchiesi (1996), 47 for the canonical seven-line openings of *Achilleid*, *Iliad*, *Aeneid*, and *Bellum Ciuile*.
[59] Fantham (1979).

CHAPTER 13

*On Not Forgetting the 'Literatur' in 'Literatur und Religion': Representing the Mythic and the Divine in Roman Historiography*[1]

As one of only two Latinists speaking at a conference on the interaction between literature and religion, I found myself reflecting on the historical differences in practice between the subdisciplines of Hellenists and Latinists. Generalisations on such large topics are difficult and suspect, yet my own attempts as a Latinist in a Hellenists' conference to negotiate between the claims of literature and religion made me very self-conscious about the disciplinary issues. I was left feeling isolated in some kind of middle ground, subject to a pincer movement from both flanks. On one side was Latin Studies, where a historicising reaction against long-dominant formalism has been gathering momentum for some time, with Cultural Studies and anthropologically informed approaches making headway against supposedly solipsistic textual readings; on the other side was Greek studies, where the gravitational pull of sociological and anthropological models of great power has been in effect for so long that formalism is scarcely on the horizon at all, and is no longer perceived as a past threat, let alone as a present or future one. My feeling of being stranded in the middle comes from my belief that formalism and Cultural Studies need each other, and are inextricably involved with each other. My natural allies, then, are those Latinists who agree with Don Fowler in thinking that we need 'to deconstruct oppositions like "formalism" vs. "historicism"'.[2] As Fowler puts it in his wide-ranging discussion

---

[1] My thanks to Toni Bierl for inviting me to Basel and for organising the conference, and to all the participants for generating such an enjoyable and thought-provoking debate. I also thank the participants in the University of Virginia colloquium on Roman religion in April 2005, who heard a version of this paper, and especially Julia Dyson Hejduk for her valuable response. Particular thanks for comments and stimulation are due to Cliff Ando, Wolfgang Braungart, Susanne Gödde, Glenn Most, Renate Schlesier, Katharina Waldner and Tony Woodman. Only after sending the final draft to Toni Bierl did I see the important paper on Greek 'sacred history' by Dillery (2005). I have not been able to respond to it here, but it is clear that proper treatment of the themes of my paper would require a book, taking Dillery (2005) and Marincola (1999) as the points of orientation.
[2] D. Fowler (2000), 131.

of intertextuality: '"Intertextuality" is often associated with a formalist approach to literature, and contrasted with forms of cultural criticism that go outside the text. This seems to me to embody a narrow view of text and a naivety about the way the things supposedly "outside" the text are always already textualized.'[3] As so often, the issue was brilliantly summed up by Roland Barthes: 'a little formalism turns one away from History, but ... a lot brings one back to it'.[4]

The difficulty we all faced at our conference was how to read texts within the penumbra of 'literature and religion' without leaning so far to the formalist end of the scale that we shut out the texts' social and religious ramifications, and without leaning so far to the historicist end of the scale that we allow those other cultural discourses to suffocate the distinctive nature of the texts. The danger with the formalism against which so many Latinists are reacting is that it has in practice made it very difficult to take the religious (or social or cultural) dimensions of literature at all seriously. The danger with an overweening historicism is that it can smudge over important distinguishing features of literary discourses, operating as if literary texts do nothing more than mimic or exemplify or reinforce what we already know anyway from other contexts. Historicism is particularly prone to such tendencies when—as is overwhelmingly the case with studies of ancient religion—it is associated with models indebted to structuralism and symbolic anthropology.[5] Such models (including New Historicism) share the tendency to regard societies as inter-related meaning systems—in effect, as massive texts.[6] An important consequence is that the governing trope of these approaches is synecdoche.[7] The part stands for the whole, which is always somehow already there, and primary. Texts are accorded their own discursive status, but they are nonetheless still regarded as fragments of a larger context 'in which the terms are always set in advance by conditions which are more primary or authentic or real'.[8] When the

---

[3] Ibid., 111; cf. 120: 'the opposition of textuality and history is a meaningless one since history is only accessible in discourse'.

[4] Barthes (1972), 111 = Barthes (1957), 184: 'Parodiant un mot connu, je dirai qu'un peu de formalisme éloigne de l'histoire, mais que beaucoup y ramène.'

[5] Here I summarise points from Chapter 11 in this volume.

[6] Gallagher and Greenblatt (2000), 14–15: 'If every trace of a culture is part of a massive text . . . '; 'if an entire culture is regarded as a text'. Cf. ibid., 26, for the debt of their New Historicism to the symbolic anthropology of Clifford Geertz.

[7] White (1978), 94–5 on synecdoche. Bruster (2003), 27, 33 and 43–4 against synecdoche in historicist models; cf. Bannet (1993), 41–4.

[8] Chapter 11 above, 225; cf. White (1978), 94: 'Nor is it unusual for literary theorists, when they are speaking about the "context" of a literary work, to suppose that this context . . . has a concreteness and an accessibility that the work itself can never have, as if it were easier to perceive the reality of

referent of a literary work is some religious, mythic or ritual feature of the culture, with all the connotations of primacy and foundation traditionally attached to such features both in anthropology and in Classics, then the dominance of the synecdoche model will make it very difficult not to cast the text as at best reflective and at worst parasitic.

One way of avoiding such a predicament is through a return to genre—not to a formalistic pigeon-holing conception of genre, but to a more dynamic Contean model of genre, in which genres mutate and interact, and in which they serve a mediating function, enabling culturally coded perceptions to become part of literary perceptions, and vice versa: 'Genre functions as a mediator, permitting such models of selected reality to enter into the language of literature; it gives them the possibility of being "represented".'[9] It is hard to get this mediating function of genre mobilised from within the subdiscipline of Greek studies, however, given that the dominant tendency there is to see genres as arising from specific social practices and remaining rooted in them: if epinician, for example, is supposedly a reflex of social practice, to be explained by its performative function in an occasional setting, then how can religious genres not likewise be bound in to a preexisting and predetermined cultural context which will dictate the terms of interpretation?[10]

Yet the attempt to give power to literary texts by grounding them in a supposedly real base depends upon an implausible correspondence theory of literature, and it will regularly end up failing to do justice to the texts' actual capacities.[11] For literary texts have a certain autonomy—in the particular sense of 'autonomy' so productively introduced into our conversations and discussion at the conference by Renate Schlesier.[12] 'Autonomous' in this sense does not mean 'entirely in a realm of its own', for it is impossible to know what such an autonomous discourse would look like—a radically autonomous discourse would be incomprehensible. If literature did not have a certain kind of autonomy, however, it

---

a past world put together from a thousand historical documents than it is to probe the depths of a single literary work that is present to the critic studying it.'

[9] Conte (1994b), 125; cf. Bruster (2003), who likewise highlights 'the mediating roles of convention and praxis', particularly genre (61; cf. xvi). See Marincola (1999) for a powerful argument in favour of a more Contean conception of genre in the analysis of historiography.

[10] Here I reprise arguments from Feeney (2003), a review of Depew and Obbink (2000).

[11] For severe reservations about correspondence or reference theories of literature, see Lamarque and Olsen (1994), chapter 5, 107–37.

[12] Cf. Csapo (2000), 128: 'Artistic genres have a processual history of their own and a relative autonomy from other forms of cultural production' (with further references to discussions of the '"semi-autonomy" of art' in n.38).

would be simply tautologous, for its functions would be served by some other discourse. And literature does have functions which are not symmetrical with or reducible to the functions of other discourses, as has been well argued by Lamarque and Olsen: 'Literature is not merely a response to already defined existential problems, nor an expression of already felt and accepted moral and social values. It is one of the ways in which these existential problems, as well as social and moral values, are defined and developed for us.'[13] From this perspective the polarisations between formalism and historicism look more and more suspect, since it is precisely the historically based formal features of texts which make it possible for them to perform within a society the kind of work identified by Lamarque and Olsen. As Glenn Most puts it: 'Linguistics, anthropology, and social theory can cast helpful light on genre conceived not as a recipe from handbooks of poetics but rather as a social phenomenon. Genre is the *langue* that makes possible any literary *parole*.'[14]

Paying serious attention to genre in this larger sense, then, is indispensable if we are to do justice to the texts and to the religious, ideological and cultural work they are doing. In this paper, my test case will be the representation of mythic material and of divine action in Roman historiography, and I shall argue that we must pay attention to the distinctions which ancient historians drew between their procedures for representing myth or divinity and those of other writers, particularly poets. Here I shall be debating with a recent paper by Peter Wiseman, in which he argues that in first-century BCE Rome 'for many readers the distinction between the proper pursuits of poets and historians was far from clear-cut, and certainly not a simple matter of literary genre'.[15] As my argument so far has shown, I do not regard 'literary genre' as a 'simple matter', and it is worth revisiting the question of what was at stake for historians in their engagements with other religious discourses.

Before coming to the texts of the first century BCE which are my prime focus, we must begin with Herodotus, the father of the genre, who initiated procedures for the new discourse which had fundamental consequences.[16]

---

[13] Lamarque and Olsen (1994), 451.
[14] Most (2000), 17. Cf. Feeney (2003), 339 on the papers in Depew and Obbink (2000) by Stephen Hinds and Don Fowler, which 'show that the most apparently esoteric issues of genre-bending loop back into culturally-grounded readings, of Roman constructions of gender (Hinds) and of parental–filial relationships (Fowler)'.
[15] Wiseman (2002), 362.
[16] It was a pleasure to see how much Susanne Gödde and I agreed in our independent approaches to Herodotus' representations of the divine at the conference; I learnt much from her presentation (Gödde (2007)).

One of Herodotus' first moves was to introduce a distinction between—to put it bluntly—history and myth, in terms of subject matter, and between history and epic, in terms of narrative mode. These two categories—of form and content, very roughly—are of course intermingled with each other, and we shall revisit the question of their inextricability. But from the opening pages of Herodotus' history the crucial demarcations are there, between history and epic and between what is going to count as myth or history. The demarcations are grounded in a claim to a new kind of knowledge, and in a forswearing of the kind of knowledge which epic poetry claimed.[17] The opening of Herodotus' history is playing off a Homeric conception of the deep past as one inaccessible to normal human knowledge, a conception most crisply formulated by Homer when he invokes the Muses in *Iliad* 2.484–6. Here Homer says that the Muses do have knowledge (ἴστε) about this heroic past, whereas we hear only report (κλέος οἶον ἀκούομεν), and do not know anything (οὐδέ τι ἴδμεν). Much of the force of this Homeric passage comes from the fact that the Greek word to 'know' is cognate with the word to 'see', while the word κλέος, 'report', is cognate with the word to 'hear'. This is an antithesis of wide importance in Homer, one referred to by characters as well: seeing something and knowing it for yourself is incomparably superior to merely hearing about it from another source.[18] When Herodotus rejects the Persian version of Io and turns to Croesus, he is playing on precisely this Homeric antithesis, for he uses Homer's verb of knowledge, but positively (1.5.3). 'We do not know anything', Homer had said; 'I know myself' (οἶδα αὐτός), says Herodotus, without a negative, of his own sure knowledge, not of his ignorance. Homer cannot know for himself about the distant past, and has to rely on the Muses to tell him; Herodotus cannot know for himself about the distant past either, and so he will tell about the things that he *can* know, and know for *himself*—αὐτός.

Throughout his history Herodotus is extremely scrupulous in marking what he will vouch for and what he will not, on the basis of his claims to knowledge, maintaining systematically the distinction of his second preface 'between the myths that are "said" and what "we can know"'.[19] This point is regularly misunderstood by scholars, especially those who wish to deny Herodotus a developed interest in making novel demarcations

---

[17] Huber (1965) remains fundamental. I discuss Herodotus' new epistemology in more detail in chapter 3 of Feeney (2007).
[18] Clay (1983), 12–20; Ford (1992), 60–1. On the crucial importance of this distinction in the historiographical tradition from Herodotus on, see Marincola (1997a), 63–86.
[19] As Moles (1993), 97 paraphrases 7.20.2–21.1; cf. Gould (1989), 125.

between his new 'history' and the old stories. Thomas Harrison, for example, claims that Herodotus treats 'Minos straightforwardly as a historical figure' in his account of Cretan participation in the Trojan war, without any reference to the fact that the entire section is in reported speech, explaining the reference of a Delphic Oracle.[20] I do not mean to associate myself with the view that reported speech is an automatic sign of personal scepticism, a view well countered by Harrison himself;[21] the issue here is the way in which Herodotus is setting out the terms for the technology of his new form of rhetoric. In general, Harrison's discussion of this topic is vitiated by his failure to pay attention to such fundamental narratological questions as 'Qui parle?', questions which have profound generic and discursive implications.

In the case of Herodotus we can see that his strategies in this sphere are part of a larger strategy for creating a new kind of authorial persona. This persona has many strong affinities with the new personae being moulded by his contemporaries in medicine and science, and much of what Geoffrey Lloyd has taught us about the new rhetorical strategies designed in those new discourses could be copied over directly for Herodotus' history.[22] Lloyd highlights the importance to the new scientific discourses of 'the habit of scrutiny, and ... the expectation of justification—of giving an account—and the premium set on rational methods of doing so';[23] he likewise picks out 'the prominence of the authorial ego, the prizing of innovation both theoretical and practical, the possibility of engaging in explicit criticism of earlier authorities, even in the wholesale rejection (at times) of custom and tradition ... '.[24] The implications for Herodotus and Thucydides are obvious. What Herodotus begins is a project of carving out a new kind of discourse about the past which has powerful affinities in rhetorical method and authorial self-presentation with the new discourses about medicine and nature. His new discourse will enable him to compete not only with the body of inherited mythic story, but also, even more importantly, with the other discourses that had already evolved to compete with myth, above all the rationalising and cataloguing of Hecataeus and the other mythographers. A crucial part of this new project is the ability to stake out credible and authoritative knowledge claims; and a crucial part of

---

[20] T. Harrison (2000), 203, 205 on 7.170–1.  [21] Ibid., 24–30, 82–3; cf. Mikalson (2003), 145.
[22] Lloyd (1979) and (1987); R. Thomas (2000) makes many important connections between the intellectual and performance environments of Herodotus and his peers in medicine and science. [I should have referred to Goldhill (2002), chapter 1.]
[23] Lloyd (1979), 250; cf. Lloyd (1987), 99.  [24] Lloyd (1987), 70.

that ability is the claim—however arbitrarily grounded—to be able to demarcate what can be known in this τέχνη and what can not be known.

The question of what can be known and what can not be known readily spills over into the question of what can be narrated and what can not be narrated. Despite all his enormous debts to Homer in terms of his understanding of how to narrate action, Herodotus marks an irreducible line between his kind of narrative and Homer's in terms of representation of the divine. Fundamentally, once he has created his new authoritative voice by demarcating how far his knowledge claims extend, Herodotus does not lay claim to the privileged insight of a Homer, and he does not introduce gods into his narrative as characters.[25] This is a crucial distinction between his own practice and Homer's, one with many powerful ramifications, but one that many readers overlook. Herodotus does not say that the god Pan appeared to Philippides as he was running over the mountains to Sparta; he says that Philippides said that the god appeared to him (6.105.1–2).[26] This may look like a trivial point, but it is not, for it takes us to the heart of the kind of authority Herodotus is claiming, the kind of human-based knowledge claims he feels entitled to assert, and so it takes us to the heart of the kind of discourse this new form is. If we overlook or downplay the discursive boundaries Herodotus is establishing, we are not just doing him an injustice in formal or 'literary' terms, we are missing the impact of his boldness in creating a new kind of representation of human knowledge and action. At this level, the formal and historicising readings fold into each other, for only a scrupulous formalism will allow us to appreciate fully how Herodotus' new discourse situates itself in the cultural dialogues of its time.

Herodotus is in fact still using a Homeric demarcation when he rules out of court his own merely human ability to narrate the gods' participation in the action. Herodotus adapts an internal mode of epic and puts himself into exactly the position occupied by Odysseus, when Odysseus tells his own story in the *Odyssey*. The inspired poet Homer can say 'Aphrodite did this, or Apollo did that', but the human character Odysseus can not; he consistently says just θεός ('god') or δαίμων ('deity') when he suspects some divine agency, since he is unable to vouch for it in personal terms.[27]

---

[25] Feeney (1991), 261–2; cf. Mikalson (2003), 144–55; Gödde (2007).
[26] For interesting discussion of the way this report of Pan's epiphany is part of the larger narrative of Marathon, see Hornblower (2001), 143–5. Similarly (to give the example used by Hornblower (2001), 136), Thucydides does not say that Athena destroyed the Athenian defensive tower at Lecythus, but that Brasidas thought she did, or at least acted as if he did (4.116).
[27] This was clearly laid out by Jörgensen (1904); cf. Clay (1983), 21–5; Mikalson (1983), 112; Feeney (1991), 85–6.

Herodotus' practice is very close indeed to this Homeric—or rather, Odyssean—norm; in this respect, at least, Herodotus is really not a Homer, but an Odysseus.[28] The kind of distinction we see at work in Herodotus is widely observed in both the Greek and Roman worlds.[29] It is very similar to what Parker, discussing fifth- and fourth-century Athens, calls the contrast between 'the theological opacity of oratory and the transparency of tragedy'.[30] As he puts it:

> Oratory never invites the listeners to believe that they can gaze at Olympus and penetrate the counsels of the gods. The claims it makes about divine motivation are almost invariably vague and general; they concern 'the gods', not named individuals, and it would have been inconceivable for an orator to pretend, for instance, to describe a clash of will between Poseidon and Athena. But insight of just that kind into the workings of Olympus was claimed by tragedy.[31]

Needless to say, observing such generic distinctions does not entail claiming that any one of these genres correlates, to the exclusion of the others, with what the Greeks or the Romans 'really believed'.[32]

Herodotus, then, will not vouch for the material of myth on his own account and he will not give a Homerically mimetic narrative of the gods. This is not to say, however, that he is not interested in divine action or in what we call religion; let it suffice here to cite the two recent studies of Herodotus and religion by Harrison and Mikalson.[33] Still, in any discussion of these issues we must be very scrupulous about the terms we use and about observing the generic distinctions at work. Pelling, for example, claims that the opening sections of Herodotus' history are deliberately misleading in focusing on human actions, giving the impression that the narrative will 'leave the gods out', and that 'this is not, it seems, to be the world of Homer, where gods exercise ... influence over events'; soon enough, according to his argument, references to the gods, patterns of fate and oracular responses make it clear that the 'gods and the supernatural *cannot* be left out, try though author or reader will; and the inevitability of

---

[28] See Moles (1993), 92–8 and Marincola (1997b) for the importance of the persona of Odysseus to Herodotus, as a man who travels widely and observes the customs of different people.

[29] On the general language of 'the gods' or 'god' used by orators and historians, as opposed to poets, see Mikalson (1983), 63–8; cf. Feeney (1998), 81: 'it holds broadly true that the ordinary human in the ordinary course of events, without privileged access to knowledge of divinity's action, must necessarily speak in this general manner'.

[30] Parker (1997), 158.   [31] Ibid., 158; cf. Mikalson (1983), 66–73 and (1991) *passim*.

[32] On the issues, Feeney (1998), 22–5; cf. Parker (1997), 159: 'Tragedy expresses some part of what it was like to believe in the Greek gods no less than prose texts do.'

[33] T. Harrison (2000); Mikalson (2003).

a divine dimension is the clearer for the original attempt to avoid it'.[34] Yet it is crucial that Herodotus' techniques for the representation of the 'divine dimension' are not Homeric. Herodotus can perfectly well think that he can use evidence to find patterns of divine action in recent or contemporary history; this is very different from his thinking that he can get information of the kind he wants from the material of myth, and it is also very different from his using the kind of knowledge claims about specific deities in action that can be advanced by authors in other genres, especially epic. Herodotus keeps his realm of knowledge in the human realm, even though, like any other Greek, he is able to use his own observation and intelligence to make inferences about possible divine agencies.[35] He will report what people say about mythic stories, because he knows that what people say is as important as what they do, but he will not narrate such stories on his own account, nor will he rationalise them, as his predecessor and main rival, Hecataeus, had done. Again, he will express his own surmises about the role of the divine in human history, but he will not give narratives on his own authorial account about characterised deities operating in the Homeric manner. The formal definitions of epic given by the ancient scholarly tradition are a useful reminder of what is at stake. According to Servius 'epic consists of divine and human *characters*' (*constat ex diuinis humanisque personis*), and according to Posidonius poetry contains 'a *mimesis* [i.e. a characterful representation] of things divine and human' (μίμησιν ... θείων καὶ ἀνθρωπείων).[36] History, for all the interest which it can display in the inherited body of myth and in religious concerns, does not have both 'divine and human characters', nor does it have 'characterful representation of things divine as well as human', with gods part of the *mimesis* like humans.

These general issues have to be borne in mind when we are considering historical texts from the Roman period as well. The later historical tradition, including the Roman one, is remarkably faithful to Herodotus' pioneering prescriptions in the field of representing the divine:

> from Herodotus on, the historians ... refrained from following Homer into the narration of divine action on its own plane. Even epiphanies in

---

[34] Pelling (1999), 334–5 (original emphasis).
[35] For a compelling and lucid account of Herodotus' perception of divine forces at work in his historical account, see Munson (2001), 183–206; cf. Cartledge and Greenwood (2002), 357–8: 'Thus Herodotus claims to be able to infer divine involvement in human events, but he achieves these inferences through a process of independent inquiry based on the realm of human knowledge.' Mikalson (2003) is very much in accord with such positions: note esp. 146.
[36] Serv. *Praef.* 1.4.4–6 Thilo/Hagen; Posidonius fr. 44 Edelstein and Kidd (1972–88).

historians are, after all, accounts of human experience. An ancient historian will describe a report of a deity appearing in battle, for example, but he will not narrate the decision of the deity to appear, or transcribe the god's conversation before he sets off for the battle-site.[37]

Similarly, the later historians' approach to the inclusion or exclusion of mythic or miraculous material retains recognisably Herodotean features, although there was certainly more variety of treatment here, as we shall see.[38] Because the origin of this historiographical trope of demarcation from myth was not a technological or methodological advance but a new kind of rhetoric, the distinctions claimed between history and myth could vary considerably. Historians could use chronology, for example, to delimit their subject matter from 'the times of myth', as Dionysius of Halicarnassus calls them, when he says that the Assyrian Empire reaches back εἰς τοὺς μυθικοὺς χρόνους (*Ant. Rom.* 1.2.2). The Trojan war was regularly the chosen cut-off point;[39] but for Ephorus, writing a panhellenic history in the middle of the fourth century, the demarcation line was the return of the Heracleidae, eighty years after the Trojan war. Ephorus deliberately proclaims that he will not begin with the events of myth;[40] in a very Thucydidean passage he says that you cannot give an accurate account of ancient events, as opposed to contemporary ones, since deeds and speeches of the distant past cannot be remembered through such a long time.[41] One of the fullest discussions of this topic comes in Plutarch's Preface to the paired *Lives of Theseus and Romulus*, which has recently been the subject of a fine analysis by Pelling: in working on Theseus, Plutarch says, he has gone through that time 'which can be reached by reasonable inference or where factual history can find a firm foothold', and has now reached a point where he might 'say of those remoter ages, "All that lies beyond are fables and tragic stories ..."'.[42]

Inevitably, these are broad generalisations about a very long, varied and contentious tradition, one including historians who narrated the exploits of Dionysus in India or Heracles in the West as prototypes of later Hellenic arrivals, or who invented charter myths for Greek colonies.[43] The case of Roman history is particularly challenging because it shares the

---

[37] Feeney (1991), 261; cf. Hornblower (2001).
[38] Important discussion in Calame (2003), 1–34; n.b. 26: 'Difference in content forms the division less between myth and history than between historiography and poetry.'
[39] Porter (2004), 320.    [40] *FGrH* 70 T 8 = Diod. Sic. 4.1.3.
[41] *FGrH* 70 F 9 = Harp. s.v. ἀρχαίως.
[42] *Thes.* 1, following the translation of Pelling (2002), 171.
[43] On such histories, see, conveniently, Pearson (1975). We return shortly to the question of how such historians may have reported matters of this kind.

characteristics both of a universal history and also of a local history, which had to account for origin stories of all kinds, including the fabulous: a narrative of the history of Rome from the origins will start off as a local history but end up as a universal history.[44] Still, Marincola is fundamentally correct to say that the historians ended up with three options when dealing with myth: leave it out, rationalise it, or report it noncommittally, leaving judgement up to the reader.[45] Of the first option, Ephorus may stand as a paradigm; of the second, Dionysius of Halicarnassus; of the third, Diodorus Siculus, with his careful sequestration of six books of pre-Trojan war mythic material in a self-contained achronological bracket of their own (1.5.1).

The moments when historians confront the problem of myth can provide some of their most interesting moments of self-definition, as they manoeuvre on the boundaries of poetry, drama or philosophy in order to define their projects in the same way that epic or elegiac poets manoeuvre on *their* inter-generic boundaries in order to define *their* projects.[46] We observe an analogous technique already in Herodotus, as Susanne Gödde notes, referring to the passage in Book 2 where Herodotus pulls himself up short before he transgresses his self-imposed ban on talking about 'divine things' ('which I particularly shun narrating', τὰ ἐγὼ φεύγω μάλιστα ἀπηγέεσθαι, 2.65.2).[47] Livy's Preface is a famous case in point, for it engages throughout with the opposing modes of poetry, most spectacularly at the end, with his wish that he could begin his work, as poets do, with prayers and supplications to the gods and goddesses (*praef.* 13). As Woodman points out, this is 'a device which he explicitly borrows from poetry but which serves only to underline the difference

---

[44] I thank Glenn Most for drawing my attention to this issue: [see Elliott (2013), 239 (my thanks to her for allowing me to cite her then unpublished PhD dissertation in the original chapter)].

[45] Marincola (1997a), 118, part of a very valuable discussion; cf. Wardman (1960), 410–12; Veyne (1988), 71–8 on the options of rationalising and *relata referre*, recounting the tradition, what people say, without necessarily vouching for it. On the important fragment of Theopompus about his strategy concerning myth (*FGrH* 115 F 381), see the decisive arguments of Flower (1994), 34–5, proving that Theopompus claims to be signalling explicitly when he incorporates myth, unlike his predecessors. Some might say that this shows the distinction did not matter, but of course it shows the reverse.

[46] On the generic interface between history and myth/epic, see Woodman (1988), index s.v. 'historiography, ancient, and poetry'; Moles (1993) and (1993/2009). As Hornblower (2001), 146 remarks, in advancing a strong claim for Pan's role in Herodotus 6.105.1–2: 'Generic crossover can be a very arresting device.' For the analogy with epic and elegiac poets, see, conveniently, Hinds (1987), esp. 115–17. Woodman (2003), 213 intriguingly suggests, on the basis of Horace's allusions at the end of *Carm.* 2.1, that Pollio's Preface to his Histories ended with a transitional generic distinction between his former genre of tragedy and his new genre of history.

[47] Gödde (2007), 52–3.

between two genres'.⁴⁸ Earlier in the Preface Livy brushes against history's limits, exploiting the trope of chronological demarcation between history and myth in the process, when he acknowledges that much of the tradition concerning the foundation of the city is 'more appropriate to the myths of poetry than to uncorrupted monuments of achievements' (*poeticis magis decora fabulis quam incorruptis rerum gestarum monumentis, praef.* 6). Here he is following Herodotus and Thucydides in setting up a strategy of skirmishing with opposing genres which will carry on strongly into the first book.⁴⁹

Livy comes close to transgressing into the norms of epic when he carries on from the passage just referred to (*praef.* 7):

> datur haec uenia antiquitati ut miscendo humana diuinis primordia urbium augustiora faciat; et si cui populo licere oportet consecrare origines suas et ad deos referre auctores, ea belli gloria est populo Romano ut cum suum conditorisque sui parentem Martem potissimum ferat, tam et hoc gentes humanae patiantur aequo animo quam imperium patiuntur.

> This indulgence is granted to antiquity that it makes the first stages of cities more august by mixing the human and divine.⁵⁰ And if it ought to be allowed to any people to hallow their origins and make the gods responsible for them, then the glory in war of the Roman people is such that when they say that Mars himself was their father and the father of their founder, the peoples of the earth should put up with this with the same resigned frame of mind with which they put up with the Empire.

Here he is not saying, as Moles claims, that 'it remains a plus if a historical work can include the mingling of human and divine'.⁵¹ Livy will report the myth of Romulus' divine parentage because it is in the tradition and has

---

⁴⁸ Woodman (2003), 213; cf. Feldherr (1998), 78; see Moles (1993/2009), 77–81 for a full exploration of the engagement with poetry at this point in the Preface.

⁴⁹ A classic example of a process referred to by White (1978), 95: 'The implication is that historians *constitute* their subjects as possible objects of narrative representation by the very language they use to *describe* them' (original emphasis). Feldherr (1998), 75–8 well brings out the power of the generic confrontations here. Moles (1993/2009), 64 demonstrates the Herodotean and Thucydidean force of Livy's approach to the distinction between myth and history in his Preface, especially in his Herodotean declarations that he sets no store by how stories of this kind will be judged (*ea nec adfirmare nec refellere in animo est*, §6; *haud in magno equidem ponam discrimine*, §8).

⁵⁰ As Tony Woodman points out to me, the first quoted sentence has a focus on the present that is regularly overlooked: as he puts it, *datur haec uenia antiquitati* etc. means (a) 'we concede it to the ancients that *they* mingle human and divine and thereby make the origins of cities more august' and (b) 'we concede to <the notion of> antiquity that, by mingling human and divine, *we* make the origins ...'

⁵¹ Moles (1993/2009), 65; his footnote 40 ad loc. refers to Cic. *Inv. rhet.* 1.23, where Cicero is making a quite different point, advising the orator to show that his case involves the whole *res publica*, including the immortal gods. I should say that this is practically the only sentence in Moles' important article with which I differ. See, rather, Feldherr (1998), 64–5.

immense consequences, but he is not obliged to vouch for it: this is part of his general policy, carried on from Herodotus' example, of narrating miraculous or supernatural material with distancing formulae of reported speech such as *dicitur*.[52] He acknowledges the power of these myths in bolstering Roman power, just as he understands that the way the peoples of the Empire have to acquiesce in the ideology is independent of the truth of the stories.[53] He knows that these myths are indispensable to the *auctoritas* of the Roman Empire, but he also knows that vouching for them in his own right would undermine his own *auctoritas*: the acceptance of the myths is incumbent upon an indulgent Roman posterity and a compliant group of subjects, and Livy does not wish to identify himself with either category. It matters crucially to him, then, to maintain the differences between his genre and those in which such myths are at home. Otherwise he will not be able to sustain the persona necessary to enforce the practical utility that he hopes will come from his history's didactic and moral power, which he expounds in the following sections (9–10), directly addressing the reader as his fellow-citizen (*te . . . tibi tuaeque reipublicae*).[54] If his history fails to demonstrate in a plausible way what the 'life, customs, and men' were like in the past (*quae uita, qui mores . . ., per quos uiros*, 9), then it will have failed in this objective. His demarcation between the old stories and his own educative project is part of his whole strategy at the beginning of the work.

In his actual narration of the fables surrounding the foundation of the city Livy manages to have his cake and eat it too. He is extremely careful to refrain from endorsing the tradition, but he does not wish to uncouple the beginning of Rome from the myths altogether. He contrives to let the glamour and power of the myths leak in to his narrative to some extent, even if he does not vouch for the details and is regularly rather sardonic in his reportage. A feeling that fate must somehow have been behind the emergence of Rome—the kind of view one can readily imagine a first-century BCE Herodotus expressing—is allowed expression in his narrative of the conception of Romulus and Remus, even as he holds back from endorsing the divine parentage itself (1.4.1–2):

---

[52] Levene (1993), 16–30; Feldherr (1998), 64–78; Forsythe (1999), 87–98.
[53] For the role of the Romulus and Remus story in relations with the Greek East, see the remarkable inscription from Chios (Chios Museum, Inv. No. 1000, from the late third or early second century BCE) which speaks in language close to Livy's of how the story of the twins' parentage might be rightly considered true because of the courage of the Romans (following the interpretation of Derow and Forrest (1982), 86).
[54] Kraus (1997), 55–6; cf. Kraus (1994a), 13–15.

> sed debebatur, ut opinor, fatis tantae origo urbis maximique secundum deorum opes imperii principium. ui compressa Vestalis cum geminum partum edidisset, seu ita rata seu quia deus auctor culpae honestior erat, Martem incertae stirpis patrem nuncupat.
>
> But, so I think, fate made inevitable the origin of such a great city and the beginning of an empire that is the greatest after the power of the gods. When the raped Vestal had given birth to twins, either because she thought so, or else because a god was a more honourable source to put the blame on, she named Mars as the father of the doubtful offspring.

After the birth of the twins, an artful word arrangement makes it look for a moment as if we are going to be offered alternative rationalising and supernatural explanations.[55] *seu ita rata seu quia deus* . . . 'Either because she thought so, or else because a god'—here a supplement such as 'really was responsible' is taken away from us, as we go on to read 'was a more honourable source to put the blame on' (*auctor culpae honestior erat*). Either way, it is only what the priestess said.

The story of the foundation of the Ara Maxima is a related example of this kind of technique. In the Preface Livy said that he would not vouch for mythical events before the foundation of the city, yet early on in Book 1 he does give us a famous aetiological tale from fable, involving the demi-god Hercules, from the time before the foundation, even before the fall of Troy. He artfully inserts it as a flashback in the Romulus narrative, so that it is made into a subset of history. When he comes to discuss Romulus' religious practices, he tells us that Romulus performed sacrifices to the other gods according to the Alban rite, but to Hercules according to the Greek rite, following the way the sacrifices had been established by Evander (1.7.3). At this point Livy introduces the myth with *memorant* ('they relate'), and proceeds to narrate the whole colourful tale over the space of two OCT pages (1.7.4–15), including a quotation of Evander's speech, in which the Arcadian king refers to his mother's prophecy of Hercules' apotheosis and the cult of the Ara Maxima, to be tended by the nation that will in the future be the most powerful on earth (1.7.10).[56] Two considerations in particular, both aetiological in nature, make it important for Livy to bend his generic capacities in order to include this story. Livy is very interested in aetiology and its contemporary uses, particularly in these early sections of his work,

---

[55] As indeed it is taken by Ogilvie (1965), 48, who sees here a 'juxtaposition of a natural and a supernatural explanation'; I agree rather with Forsythe (1999), 92. My thanks to Julia Dyson for discussion of this point.

[56] See Forsythe (1999), 95 for a judicious analysis.

and here he contrives to deliver two telling aetiological messages through the medium of the myth without in the end compromising the overall status of his narrative or his persona. First, he wishes to stress that Greek and Roman culture were intermingled from the start, and he uses the case study of the *Graecus ritus* in cult: even before the city was founded, according to this tale, the cult of the site of Rome involved Greek cult.[57] Second, Livy tangentially suggests at the end of the digression that Romulus' fostering of the cult of Hercules already anticipates the way that Augustus himself would be behaving centuries later, in Livy's own day. The cult of Hercules, says Livy, was the only foreign cult adopted by Romulus, who was 'even then a supporter of the immortality achieved by virtue to which his own destiny was leading him' (*iam tum immortalitatis uirtute partae ad quam eum sua fata ducebant fautor*, 1.7.15). In all kinds of ways Romulus is a prototype of Augustus, and one of the resemblances between the two is precisely this care over the cult of deified heroes as a template for their own eventual apotheoses.[58] The kind of pressure that Augustus is putting on the boundaries of contemporary Roman religious practice finds an echo in the pressure Livy puts here on the norms of his narrative.

Passages such as that in Livy's Preface have recently been reinterpreted by Peter Wiseman in a very different way, as a 'partisan statement of philosophical scepticism': Wiseman sees Livy as being in a minority, and he argues for recovering a historiographical tradition that accepted 'miracle stories and divine epiphanies as a proper part of their subject matter', arguing that the 'issue was not one of literary convention but of theological belief'.[59] 'Even in the sophisticated Rome of the first century BC', he concludes, 'for many readers the distinction between the proper pursuits of poets and historians was far from clear-cut, and certainly not a simple matter of literary genre.'[60] Wiseman certainly presents a rich world of inherited stories about divine interventions and miraculous events, and this world is one with which any student of the period must become familiar; further, he makes an important case for the anomalous position of one historian (although it is not, I think, Livy). Yet the question of genre remains crucial, for the intellectual environment of the first century BCE was one where different discourses were self-consciously competing with each other in pursuing different objectives and addressing different,

---

[57] The fact that this is the *single* such cult maintained by Romulus is part of a larger project of minimising, even while acknowledging, the degree of Greek penetration of Roman culture (*haec tum sacra Romulus una ex omnibus peregrina suscepit*, 1.7.15).
[58] On Livy's parallelisms between Romulus and Augustus, see Miles (1995), 164–6.
[59] Wiseman (2002), 353.   [60] Ibid., 362.

though overlapping, audiences. The debates recovered by Wiseman over credulity and scepticism, rather than making generic analysis redundant, were precisely made possible by creative work with generic expectations: no expression of 'theological belief' was possible outside the context of a 'literary convention', so that these apparently polarised terms are mutually defining, not mutually exclusive.

In regarding 'literary genre' as a 'simple matter', Wiseman can cloud the issues by not taking the discursive differences seriously enough. He adduces evidence from a range of different kinds of texts as if they all worked in the same way, and he can overlook fundamental narratological questions such as 'Qui parle?' in rather the same way as scholars regularly do when they discuss Herodotus. Varro's *De Gente Populi Romani*, cited by Wiseman as the source of miraculous stories such as the Vestal carrying water in a sieve to vindicate her chastity, was not a work of history. Wiseman quotes Münzer's speculation that Varro lay behind the version of the Vestal story to be found in Pliny's *HN* 28.12, yet Münzer sees here a difference between antiquarianism and formal history: 'Here there is without doubt an underlying tradition that is overall more antiquarian than annalistic.'[61] Similarly, whatever Valerius Maximus' *Facta Ac Dicta Memorabilia* was, and however indebted it may have been to historical and especially Livian sources, it was not a work of formal history in the tradition of Herodotus.[62] 'Valerius was writing moral protreptic', comments Wiseman, 'not philosophical argument.'[63] And not history either.[64] Just as for the Atthidographers, who 'did not accept a firm boundary between mythical and historical material, and passed within their works from one to the other',[65] so too for Varro, the material for the antiquarian was the inherited mass of tradition about the city, which it was the job of the scholar to organise and transmit. Valerius similarly sees it as his function to 'repeat what is in the tradition' (*tradita repetuntur*, 1.8.7). These projects have their own merits and their own roles to play within the debate over the past and the divine in the period, but they are not the same merits and roles as those of formal history, with its political

---

[61] 'Es liegt ohne Zweifel hier überall eine mehr antiquarisch als annalistische Überlieferung zugrunde', Münzer (1937), 205, quoted by Wiseman (2002), 337 n.31.
[62] Wiseman (2002), 350–2 well brings out the intertextuality between Valerius' introduction and Livy's Preface, but while he says that 'Valerius uses the idiom of historiography', referring to *omnis aeui gesta* and *historiae series*, these phrases actually refer to what Valerius says he is *not* going to write.
[63] Ibid., 352.    [64] Any more than was the biographer Plutarch, likewise adduced by ibid., 347.
[65] Pelling (2002), 188.

and utilitarian programmes.⁶⁶ It is somewhat misleading to group such disparate authors together as 'other historians' to point a contrast with Livy, as Wiseman does in his concluding paragraph: 'For Livy, divine intervention was not appropriate to "uncorrupted" history—but we know that other historians thought it was.'⁶⁷

Someone who does qualify as 'another historian', and who approaches these questions in a manner significantly different from Livy, is Dionysius of Halicarnassus. Wiseman's discussion is highly instructive, showing how Dionysius repeatedly narrates myths at length and foregrounds issues of how to interpret them.⁶⁸ Dionysius is to some extent drawn into this realm by the whole theme of his work: in order to vindicate the Greek nature of the Romans and to justify their hegemony to the Greek world, he needs to go far back into mythical time in order to reach the point of divergence between Roman and Greek, thus involving himself constantly in adjudicating the merits of the stories in the early mythical tradition.⁶⁹ In this way he bears out the point we remarked on above, that a history of Roman origins will be more involved in the fabulous material of origin narratives than histories of the later periods. Yet Dionysius' accounts of apparently divine or miraculous manifestations and his discussions of how to interpret them extend down into the time of the Republic, and certainly reflect a different set of priorities from Livy's. His closer involvement with the antiquarian tradition is partly responsible for this difference in emphasis, for he can resemble a Varro at times.⁷⁰ It is also helpful to see Dionysius as a self-consciously Herodotean historian: 'Just as Dionysius' model, Herodotus, had been forced to rely on native accounts—some of which would contain the fanciful or marvellous—so too Dionysius needed to collect and preserve epichoric traditions.'⁷¹ His stance as an outsider is important when we compare him to Livy. Livy too must sift through his inherited historiographical tradition, but Dionysius is engaged in a different enterprise,

---

⁶⁶ Marincola (1999), 307–8 well cautions against blunt demarcations between 'antiquarianism' and 'history', yet the differences between Varro's procedures and Livy's are tangible.
⁶⁷ Wiseman (2002), 362.   ⁶⁸ Ibid., 343–7.
⁶⁹ Marincola (1997a), 121–2; cf. Gabba (1991), 117–18 on Dionysius' 'demonstration of the political theory proclaiming Rome's Greekness. This is the basic reason why he could not follow Livy in eliminating the fables of a poetically coloured tradition that predated the foundation of Rome and described that very foundation.'
⁷⁰ Gabba (1991), 97–8.
⁷¹ Marincola (1997a), 123; cf. Gabba (1991), 96: 'he was still subject to the principle elaborated by Herodotus: how could he not report what he found in the Roman sources?' For explicit references to epichoric versions, see 1.55.1, 8.56.4.

reporting and assessing 'what the natives say', from the oblique perspective of the non-native.

Dionysius' techniques, nonetheless, are recognisably responsive to the traditions of formal history, however boldly he pushes the envelope at times. His usual procedures are regularly not accommodating to accepting mythic or miraculous narratives on their own terms. Dionysius' procedure is normally as described by Marincola, consisting of 'the contrast of a "mythic" and "historic" account, the two being separate and distinct, with no commerce between them'.[72] Marincola gives the example of the narrative of Heracles in Book 1 (39–42). Here Dionysius first presents a 'mythic' account, with Geryon's cattle and Cacus, and then follows it with a 'truer' account, 'the one used by many of those who have narrated his deeds in the form of history' (1.41.1); this account rationalises the myth by accommodating it to the norms of likelihood and contemporary plausibility, turning Heracles into a conquering general and Cacus into a thuggish local chief.[73] In addition to this technique of pairing 'mythic' and 'truer/historic' versions, Dionysius repeatedly introduces stories of miracles or divine intervention with distancing devices of one kind or another, just like Livy and Herodotus, maintaining in the process a stance of report, of not vouching directly for the material.[74] Dionysius' use of these techniques differs at times, however, in that it can be coupled with reflections on the material which directly qualify the distancing in interesting ways. One of the most remarkable stories narrated by Dionysius exhibits this complex technique, and may stand as an example of how subtle Dionysius' procedures can be, and how fine can be the distinctions between his techniques and those of his Roman counterpart, Livy.

The story is a famous one, related in many other sources,[75] and it concerns the founding of Alba Longa by Aeneas' son, Ascanius. Dionysius introduces the story by saying that during the foundation 'a very big marvel is said to have occurred' (θαῦμα μέγιστον λέγεται γενέσθαι, 1.67.1), and the narrative proceeds in *oratio obliqua* (1.67.1–4). The Penates brought by Aeneas from Troy and settled in his city of Lavinium now need to be moved to the new city, yet the night after they are transported to Alba Longa they miraculously move back to Lavinium. Once more the images are brought back to Alba Longa, and once more they migrate back to Lavinium. At this point the people leave the Penates

---

[72] Marincola (1997a), 122.   [73] Ibid., 122–3.
[74] Especially when introducing the 'more mythical' of his paired versions of past events (e.g., 1.77.2, 2.56.2).
[75] Wiseman (2002), 352–3.

where they are, in Lavinium, and send six hundred of the men from the new city back to Lavinium to take care of them there. Embedded in this myth we may detect some of the main concerns of the Roman myth of Trojan origins, even though Dionysius' eventual elaboration will move the focus somewhat. The Romans want a link back to Troy, but they do not want it to be too direct: in the developed version of the foundation myth, Aeneas does not simply found Rome, but founds Lavinium, and then from Lavinium is founded Alba Longa, and from Alba Longa is founded Rome. Even this chain of connection feels too strong, it seems, with the result that Alba is obliterated, so that the link in the chain is removed. The Penates cannot be destroyed along with Alba, so they have to stay in Lavinium, after being temporarily housed in Alba.[76] The story of the miraculously migrating Penates is partly meant to 'explain' how the Penates come to be still in Lavinium, but it is really there to help focus on the opposing poles of transience and stability that are so important to the foundation myths: the Penates have to stop moving eventually, and they have to stop before they come to be rooted in Rome itself. The Trojan connection, then, is one that is mediated through the Latins to Rome, not directly from Troy to Rome.[77] This perspective on the myth is further corroboration of the idea that it was the settlement with the Latins in 338 BCE—the year described by De Sanctis as 'the turning point of Roman history'[78]—which generated so much of the work on the Trojan myth in Rome and Latium.[79] At this point in Roman history the Trojan myth is mainly about the relations with the Latins: the Romans and Latins are having to renegotiate their relationship, and the shared cults of the old Latin League are now being redescribed in a new teleological story about Roman primacy.

The work which this myth is enabled to do in Dionysius is part of his larger interest in the way the Romans share parts of their inheritance with other Italians and also evolve towards a unique status as the only true fellow-Hellenes. His own attitude to the Roman links with the Trojan

---

[76] The tradition capitalises on the idea of Alba as a temporary staging post for the Penates in the narrative of the Gallic sack of Rome, by choosing the significant name 'Albinius' for the man who makes his family get out of the cart to transport the Vestals and their cult objects to Caere out of the path of the marauding Gauls (Liv. 5.40.9–10, with Ogilvie (1965) ad loc. for the antiquity of the name).

[77] This interest in the degree to which the Trojan connection is mediated via the Latins provides the context for the ambiguity in Virgil and Livy over whether or not the son of Aeneas, the founder of Alba Longa, had a Trojan or a Latin woman for a mother: see Miles (1995), 39–40 on Liv. 1.3.2 and Edgeworth (2001) on Verg. *Aen.* 1.267–71 and 6.763–6.

[78] So Cornell (1995), 348, translating De Sanctis (1907/1960), 267 ('il momento critico della storia romana').

[79] Gruen (1992), 28–9; Hillen (2003), 52.

*sacra* is subtly different from Livy's, for example. Livy has his Camillus stress that it would have been a religious flaw for the rites of Alba and Lavinium to be transferred to the city of Rome (5.52.8), yet Dionysius follows up his narrative with a lengthy discussion of the images of the Penates which he says can actually be seen in the city of Rome, so that it appears that some representations of the Penates found their way to the city in the end (1.68.1–69.4): characteristically, he wishes these images to be 'really' Greek, images of the Great Gods worshipped on Samothrace (1.69.4). Further, when he is discussing what the images in Lavinium and Rome look like, he blends discourses in a way that Roman historians do not. After reporting what Timaeus said about the images in Lavinium (1.67.4), he uses language of scrupulous piety to declare that 'in the case of those things which it is not lawful for all to see I ought neither to hear about them from those who do see them nor to describe them'; he then goes on to introduce his account of the images in Rome by describing them as 'the things which I myself know by having seen and concerning which no scruple forbids me to write'.[80] This is the self-policing pious language one sees in Pindar, for example, or especially in Herodotus, where language of piety is mingled into language of generic appropriateness.[81] The authority of the author is multiply overdetermined, as someone who knows how to speak right about such things on many grounds. It is not a register one encounters in historians within the Latin tradition.

Similarly, Dionysius is far more engaged than the Latin historians in explicit discussion of the philosophical issues involved in adjudicating whether and how the gods intervene in human affairs.[82] His readiness to engage in such discussions once again marks him off from his counterparts in Latin historiography, as does his directly related interest in using the traditional myths to endorse religious piety. His self-consciousness about his blending of genres in this sphere is very clear, for he regularly breaks off his quasi-philosophical discussions with remarks such as 'this is not an opportune moment to consider the question' (οὔτε καιρὸς ἐν τῷ παρόντι διασκοπεῖν, 1.77.3).[83] His willingness to conduct such debates by no means necessarily entails endorsing the myths. As we saw in the case of Herodotus, there is no necessary contradiction between religious perspectives or expressions of piety and a reluctance to endorse the matter of myth;

---

[80] I give the Loeb translation of 1.67.4–68.1.
[81] On this blending in Pindar's *Olympian* 1, see Köhnken (1974), 203–4; Gerber (1982), 69–70; in Herodotus, see Mikalson (2003), 143–5; Gödde (2007). Dionysius' language here is markedly Herodotean (cf. e.g. Hdt. 2.61.1, 170–171.1, 86.2).
[82] Note especially 1.77.3; 2.20.1–2, 61.3, 68.1–2.   [83] Cf. 2.21.1, 61.3.

indeed, as is shown by Dionysius' famous discussion of the absence in Rome of Greek-style myths about divine misdeeds (2.19.1–2), certain kinds of myth positively demanded disbelief from the pious.[84]

Still, on occasion Dionysius certainly does cross lines which we do not observe other historians crossing. He never gives a narrative in his own voice of a characterised divinity in action, and this represents a crucial continuity with the Herodotean tradition, but twice he does endorse miraculous tales, even if in both cases there is a nod in the direction of his generic allegiances.[85] Both stories involve the piety of Roman women being championed. In perhaps his most dramatic example of endorsing a miraculous tale (that of the statues which spoke to commend the piety of the women of Rome), he opens his narrative by saying that it would be 'fitting to the form of history' (εἴη δ' ἂν ἁρμόττον ἱστορίας σχήματι) and a corrective to the impious to give the account 'as the writings of the pontiffs have it' (ὡς αἱ τῶν ἱεροφαντῶν περιέχουσι γραφαί); he continues by expressing the hope that the pious will be confirmed by the story and the impious confounded (8.56.1). At the end of his narrative of the occurrence, he recalls himself with language reflecting on the appropriateness of his kind of history: 'but concerning this it was not right either to omit the local story (παρελθεῖν τὴν ἐπιχώριον ἱστορίαν) nor to spend too much time on it' (8.56.4). Here the Herodotean duty to report the epichoric accounts is certainly acknowledged, along with a sense of restored appropriateness as he moves out of the miraculous tale, but the powerful impetus of his protreptic purpose has taken historiography into a different area. Similarly, he introduces two miraculous stories about Vestals having their virginity vindicated: again, the fact that the Romans believe the stories and their historians have made much of them is adduced, but subordinated to the strong moral point that the gods are concerned with human goodness and wickedness (2.68.1–2). These stories are the most powerful weapons he deploys in his stated programmatic aim of convincing his Greek audience that the Romans have been from the start a people marked by piety and justice (1.5.3).

Rather than Livy, then, as argued by Wiseman, Dionysius looks more like the odd man out in terms of representing the divine in historiography. The two historians' practices share many distinctive features, as inherited ultimately from Herodotus, but the main explanation for the differences between them is to be sought in their different relationships to the Roman state. As a citizen addressing fellow citizens and narrating to them the past

---

[84] Feeney (1998), 48.  [85] Wiseman (2002), 345–6 on 2.68.1–2 and 8.56.

operations of the Senate and people of Rome, Livy is operating from within the web of Roman religious practices. Dionysius is a resident outsider who is addressing fellow Greeks. Livy's representation of things divine is focalised through the Roman state, whereas Dionysius' is focalised through the eyes of an individual from outside the system. Livy has a well-developed interest in divine manifestations and the possible patterns of fate, but Livy's 'perspective is that of the *human* unfolding of events: the intervention of the gods is no less documented here than it is in other genres and works, such as Virgil's epic. But it is represented from the point of view of the City's interests rather than any individual's, and by deduction rather than explicit identification.'[86] Dionysius' perspective is not the same; he is a latter-day Herodotus rather than a native, giving reports to his peers of foreign traditions and endeavouring to make sense of those foreign traditions with the resources available to him from within his own culture.

In fragmentary authors, such as the Latin annalists, we are almost always reliant on testimonia and indirect citation, and without a full text it is naturally very dangerous to judge how they told such stories as the migration of the Penates from Alba Longa to Lavinium.[87] After all, even in the fully preserved text of Herodotus, his very careful and intelligent procedures continue to be misunderstood by many scholars. Or else, imagine if Livy's first book had not survived in the manuscript tradition, and that all we had was a report of the fact that he had narrated Hercules' visit to the site of Rome and the foundation of the Ara Maxima. We would have no way of reconstructing the carefully ironic techniques he has used in order to incorporate this story into his narrative without compromising the status of his history as a document of political value. Further, in considering the actual or possible use of distancing techniques in reporting a marvellous event, we must remind ourselves that such distancing techniques are themselves by no means transparent to interpretation. In particular, reported speech does not automatically betoken either personal scepticism or the undermining of the credit or power of the reported story.[88]

---

[86] J.P. Davies (2004), 141 (original emphasis). As he goes on to say: 'These are matters of literary genre, not personal belief, or philosophical speculation.' Levene (1993) likewise argues for the crucial artistic power of Livy's subtle representation of divine forces at work in human history: 'He binds together great portions of the history with a religious sub-text working consistently beneath the surface of what is ostensibly a largely secular narrative' (241).

[87] Wiseman (2002), 352–3 collects the sources for the Penates' migration. Note the caution of Marincola (1999), 314 on the question of lumping together in 'unitary tradition' the authors usually referred to as 'the Latin annalists'.

[88] T. Harrison (2000), 24–30; Mikalson (2003), 145; J.P. Davies (2004), 51–61.

The histories of the period, then, engage in serious reflection on the possibilities of divine intersection with human affairs, just as Herodotus did, even if Livy's reflection is more densely embedded in his narrative while Dionysius' is regularly more extrinsic, attached to the first-person voice of the narrator. It is no part of my argument that historical texts had no role to play in the great debates about religion at the transition between Republic and Principate which Wiseman evokes so vividly. Yet we must pay attention to the specific practices of the texts if we are to do justice to the role they play, and we cannot do this without taking their self-conscious generic allegiances seriously: Dionysius' infringements, for example, lose some of their power if we do not register them against some kind of expectation of what historiography can tolerate. The differences between these forms of writing and other forms always potentially matter, and moments when writers talk about points of correspondence with other genres are proof that the issue was alive, not that it was dead. Wiseman adduces Diodorus Siculus' preface as evidence for 'a world in which prophecy, poetry, history and moral exhortation were not always thought of as separate conceptual categories',[89] yet Diodorus is playing up the separateness of the categories as much as softening them when he claims that his form of history is even better equipped to contribute to piety and justice than the poets' fictitious storytelling about things in Hades (1.2.2). As in this particular example, it is regularly the dialogue with alternative possibilities that sharpens the points at issue, just as the dialogue between epic and elegy or history defines what epic is, by confrontation and transgression. Historiography keeps reasserting its tradition and redefining itself as it flirts with the possibility of contamination.[90] In the case of Livy it is possible to imagine why he might be interested in the boundaries of representing the divine in history under the pressure of what Augustus was doing to rewrite the boundaries of representing the divine in Roman religion as he wrote. In the case of Dionysius, his occasional self-conscious daring in bringing philosophical discussion to bear on striking *miracula* gives dramatic power to his rhetoric as he tries to convince his fellow Greeks that the Empire they inhabit is run by a pious people who have the sanction of the gods on their side.

---

[89] Wiseman (2002), 359.
[90] Cf. the dynamic, 'Contean' view of genre espoused for the study of historiography by Marincola (1999), 282: 'genre is not a static concept, functioning as a "recipe" with a fixed set of ingredients that the work must contain, but rather is dynamic and should be seen as a "strategy of literary composition"'.

In a sense my conclusion is a minimalist one: the strongest line of demarcation between formal history and other literary forms is that history does not introduce gods as characters into the narrative, while a strong but less watertight demarcation is to be found in historiography's regular distancing of other 'fabulous' or 'mythical' material. But I have been taking the norms of historiography as one example of a larger claim, that when we are considering any example of the interaction between what we call 'literature' and what we call 'religion', we must always be alert to the formal issues if we are to do justice to the social, political or religious work the texts may be doing. Only by paying careful attention to the creative work of a Dionysius or a Livy with the forms of their genre can we see the distinctions between their kinds of authority and their relationships with their audiences. Generic analysis does not extrapolate these texts into an ethereal formalism, but enables us to recover the distinctive power of their interventions into the debates of the day. As in the case of the founder of the form of historiography, Herodotus, the formal and historicising readings fold into, and reinforce, each other.

CHAPTER 14

## *Virgil's Tale of Four Cities: Troy, Carthage, Alexandria and Rome*[1]

The four cities of my title will organise my investigation into the questions that the *Aeneid* poses about the nature of the Roman people and their Empire. The cities' varied ancestries and fates are intertwined throughout the poem, and they afford an opportunity for asking what kind of people the Romans are, what makes them different from other peoples and other empires in the Mediterranean, and what they have in common with them. The two main alternative traditions which Virgil is attempting to make sense of are the Eastern and the Greek, with Alexandria as a kind of middle term between these two: we shall consider first the Eastern question, and then, in conclusion, the Greek.

The time when Virgil was composing his poem was a particularly fruitful one for Virgil and his audience to explore questions about what the Romans did and did not share with the other major cultures of the Mediterranean. He began writing the *Aeneid*, after all, very soon after the battle of Actium on 2 September 31 BCE, when Imperator Caesar, who was to become Augustus just over three years later, defeated Marcus Antonius and the queen of Egypt, Cleopatra. It is a worthwhile exercise to do some counter-factual history and imagine what would have happened if Antonius and Cleopatra had won the battle, which they could easily have done.[2] What would Roman identity and the Roman Empire have looked like then? One of the great traps of history is to think that what happened

---

[1] My 'tale of four cities' is indebted to 'the tale of two cities'—Rome and Alexandria—with which Robin Nisbet opens his paper on 'Horace's *Epodes* and history', in Nisbet (1995), 161–81. My writing up of this Ninth Syme Memorial Lecture, delivered at Victoria University of Wellington, on 18 July 2006, was overtaken by events in the form of two books focusing on very similar themes: Syed (2005), which I saw as soon as I came back to Princeton from New Zealand, and Reed (2007), which came out shortly afterwards. Rather than engage with their different but complementary perspectives and produce a piece of doxography, I have decided to let the lecture stand as delivered, with no more than basic annotation, as a memento of the occasion, and of the very pleasant week I spent with the department at Victoria.

[2] Highly entertaining and thought-provoking ideas in Ober (2001).

to happen had to happen, but of course this is never the case. Antonius was a superb and highly experienced general, with a huge army and fleet, and he had a lot of backing: in the lead-up to the war, both the consuls of 32 BCE and almost a third of the senators left Italy to join him.[3] But it is always very difficult to remind ourselves that what happened to happen did not have to happen, and it is particularly difficult in the case of the reign of Augustus, not least because of the existence of the *Aeneid*. One of the *Aeneid*'s main objectives is to convince the reader that the course of the battle and of the whole of Roman history was all absolutely inevitable, built into the way the universe is designed by the supreme god of the universe, Jupiter, who is also the supreme god of the Roman state.

Caesar's victory at Actium is represented in the poem as divinely sanctioned, with the crucial turning point provided when the god Apollo intervenes (*Aen.* 8.704–6). Apollo was the young Caesar's favourite god. He had been born on Apollo's festival day, 23 September, and in 36 BCE he had started building a temple for Apollo beside his house on the Palatine hill in Rome in order to commemorate the naval victory he had won over Sextus Pompeius off Naulochus in Sicily on 3 September of that year.[4] That temple in Rome is still unfinished when he comes to Greece five years later to fight Antonius and Cleopatra, and there, on a headland overlooking the bay of Actium and the stretch of sea where the naval battle was fought, is a temple of Apollo. When the temple back in Rome was finally dedicated on 9 October 28 BCE, it was dedicated to the Apollo of Actium, *Apollo Actius*, the title Virgil gives him at his moment of intervention in the battle (*Actius . . . Apollo*, 8.704).[5]

When Virgil describes Caesar's god Apollo taking control of the battle from his temple on the headland, Apollo is acting against a motley collection of Egyptian deities, of the kind—so Virgil implies—that the Romans would have been worshipping if the other side had won, *omnigenum . . . deum monstra et latrator Anubis* ('monstrous gods of all kinds and the barking Anubis', 8.698). This image is part and parcel of an 'orientalism' that pervades Virgil's description of the forces arrayed against Caesar and Agrippa, and it has been superbly analysed by David Quint.[6] Horace, likewise, has his well-known images of Eastern depravity to adorn his picture of Caesar's adversaries, with eunuchs and mosquito-netting to set the tone (*Epod.* 9.11–16; *Carm.* 1.37.9–10). It is easy to dismiss all this as

---

[3] Dio Cass. 50.2.6; Syme (1939), 278.   [4] P. Gros in *LTUR* 1.54 for details.   [5] Gros, loc. cit.
[6] Quint (1993), chapter 1, esp. 24–31. My term 'orientalism' refers of course to the title of the highly influential work of Said (1978).

traces of the foulest kind of base propaganda, trotted out in the months leading up to Actium, but the hysteria should not blind us to what was at stake. Antonius was certainly a shrewd man with a proud sense of being Roman, and it is foolish to imagine that his wife Cleopatra would really have sat on the Capitol and acted the queen in Rome, as fantasised by many at the time.[7] Still, if Antonius had won, then clearly there would have been some kind of shift in the Empire's centre of gravity. Antonius was, after all, married to the queen of Egypt, even if it was not a legal marriage in Roman law; his children with her were princes and princesses of eastern kingdoms, and his personal network of loyalties penetrated all through the Greek and 'barbarian' East. It would have been a very different kind of Roman Empire from the one that Augustus oversaw, one with a far more prominent role for Alexandria and its unique blend of multiculturalism.[8]

It might have been much more like the Byzantine Empire, Hellenophone and facing eastwards. After all, the Empire's centre of gravity did eventually shift powerfully to the east, in a process beginning some 350 years later, when the emperor Constantine founded a new capital in the east, at Constantinople, in 324 CE. Constantinople is some 200 miles from Troy, via the Dardanelles and the sea of Marmora. The Roman story begins in Troy, with a band of refugees fleeing from the East to the West, but that seesaw is always threatening to tip back. Actium is perfectly situated to be the fulcrum of a seesaw, exactly in the middle of the Mediterranean, on the dividing line between the Greek-speaking East and the Latin-speaking West. In 31 BCE the Actium seesaw almost pitched the Romans into being an Eastern, Levantine Empire, based on Alexandria. On that occasion the seesaw stayed tipped to the West, but just over 350 years later the new capital at Constantinople did definitively push the balance in the other direction, making the Greek half of the Empire the dominant and enduring half. As Steven Runciman eloquently puts it: 'Throughout the history of the Roman Empire there had been a latent struggle between East and West. The West had won at Actium; but the East overcame its conquerors ... [A]t last the Emperor Constantine the Great adopted an eastern religion and moved his capital eastward, to Byzantium on the Bosphorus.'[9] This Greek Roman Empire lasted until 1453, and it left a tangible trace in the modern Greek world's term for its own identity, which until very recently was not ἑλληνισμός, 'Hellenism', but ρωμιοσύνη, 'Romanness'.[10]

---

[7] See Nisbet and Hubbard (1978) on Hor. *Carm.* 1.37.6 for sources, esp. Prop. 3.11.45–6.
[8] As suggested by Ober (2001), 45–7.   [9] S. Runciman (1951), 5.
[10] As in the title of Yiannis Ritsos' masterpiece of 1954.

Momigliano has shown how regularly this threat of a reversion to the East recurs in Roman history: 'The Greeks and even more the Orientals who saw the Romans taking over everywhere found refuge in hopes, in prophecies, and even in actual revolutionary movements promising to put history in reverse and to give back to Greece or to the East the world-rule they had lost.'[11] In the same passage Momigliano picks out moments of crisis in the late Republic which generated such hopes and prophecies, culminating in the moment of decision of 31 BCE: '[t]he rebellions of the slaves in Italy, the struggle of Aristonicus in Asia Minor about 132 BC, the wars of King Mithridates of Pontus against Rome for twenty-five years between 88 and 63 BC, and finally Cleopatra's war against Octavian'.

Here, then, is a wonderful example of how deeply Virgil saw into Roman identity and Roman destiny, because in the *Aeneid* we can see this great tug-of-war being played out. The altercation between these different elements of Roman culture is fundamental to the idea of Rome. Aeneas is leaving Troy and the East behind physically, as he moves West to found a new Empire, and one of the great themes of the poem is whether the East can also be left behind metaphorically and spiritually, how much of the Eastern component can be outstripped, and how much will remain.[12] The first half of the poem shows Aeneas thinking in terms of going to Italy to found a new Troy: in his speech to his men in Book 1 he tells them that it is fated for the kingdom of Troy to rise again in Latium (*illic fas regna resurgere Troiae*, 1.206). On his way to Italy he repeatedly bumps into reminders of Troy. In Book 3, in particular, he meets friends from the *Iliad* who are stuck in a time-warp, preserving a little toy Troy, a mimickry of the past (3.349–51). This toy Troy is like a city of the dead, another underworld, locked in the dead past.[13] When Aeneas eventually gets to Latium, the little camp he establishes at the mouth of the Tiber is simply called 'Troy'.[14] When Aeneas speaks to Dido to justify his departure, the potentially endless threat of a regress to Troy is laid open, as he avows that if he had his free choice, he would still be in Troy (4.340–4).

The threat to Roman identity of a reversion eastward is one of the many reasons that Carthage is so important in the *Aeneid*. The Carthaginians and Trojans, and especially their leaders Dido and Aeneas, have a great deal in common, since the Carthaginians are another band of refugees, forced to flee from the East to the West and to make a new future in an alien

---

[11] Momigliano (1987), 43.
[12] Quint (1993), chapter 2 is indispensable here; also Suerbaum (1967).
[13] Bright (1981); Hershkowitz (1991); Quint (1993), 58–60.
[14] *Aen.* 10.214, 378; for extensive parallel passages from Cato and Livy, see Schröder (1971), 95–100.

environment.[15] The two peoples, so the poem insinuates, could so easily have joined, as Juno and Anna dream,[16] even though the dream is shattered in Dido's nightmare, when she is compared to Pentheus seeing a double sun and two cities of Thebes.[17] Carthage's metaphorical resonance as a potential move backwards for the ancestors of the Romans is one of the main reasons why the whole Aeneas and Dido affair recalls that of Antonius and Cleopatra so systematically.[18] Aeneas behaves like Antonius for a time and plunges into an involvement with an alien culture from the East, but unlike Antonius he pulls himself away, as Antonius repeatedly tried to do, although he always failed, and returned. It is fascinating to see in Shakespeare's *Antony and Cleopatra* how carefully he models Antony and Cleopatra back on Aeneas and Dido, so that we get a sort of circle of literary and historical allusion: Aeneas and Dido in Virgil are acting like Antony and Cleopatra, and Antony and Cleopatra in Shakespeare are acting like Aeneas and Dido.[19] Antony spells it out for us towards the end of Shakespeare's play, when he looks forward to their death, and their existence in the underworld (4.14.52–5):

> Where souls do couch on flowers, we'll hand in hand
> And with our sprightly port make the ghosts gaze:
> Dido and her Aeneas shall want troops,
> And all the haunt be ours.

We may ask in passing what kind of reading of the *Aeneid* Antony gives here—and of *Aeneid* 6 in particular. In *Aeneid* 6 Dido will not listen to Aeneas, nor will she keep him company even for a moment, but leaves him to join her first husband, Sychaeus (469–74). But this picture is what Antony 'remembers': this is the kind of choice he retrospectively foists back on Aeneas, the choice he would have made, and, in a way, sometimes, the choice all of us wish Aeneas had made.[20]

Carthage, then, is made to be very reminiscent of the vanished Troy, and of the future Alexandria. But there are great differences between what the Trojans and Carthaginians are doing in the poem. The most crucial is that even though Carthage is the foundation of people who have moved to the West from the East it is still a city of Easterners. Here there is a vital

---

[15] On the similarities, and even more importantly on the differences, see Horsfall (1973–4).
[16] 4.48–9 (Anna); 4.102–3 (Juno).
[17] *Aen.* 4.465–70, where the hypothetical 'one city' sardonically spoken of by Venus earlier in the book (110–11) is broken back into its constituent parts (*duplices . . . Thebas*, 470). For the double sun (*solem geminum*, 470) as a portent of discord in the state, see Cic. *Rep.* 1.15–17.
[18] On the resemblances between Dido and Cleopatra, see Pease (1935), 24–7.
[19] Pelling (1988), 17; Wilders (1995), 66.   [20] Cf. Adelman (1973), 68–9.

difference between the migration of the Phoenicians to Carthage and of the Trojans to Italy. The Phoenicians in their new city of Carthage remain Phoenicians, as shown in the normal Latin word for 'Carthaginians', which made no distinction between them and their ancestors in Tyre, labelling them all as *Poeni*, 'Phoenicians'. The Carthaginians remain a genuine colony, an isolated bubble on the shore of Africa. Dido has refused to marry any of the local kings; in Virgil's version this is because she is loyal to her dead husband, Sychaeus (4.34–8), but it is a historical truth as well, that the Phoenicians in pre-Roman North Africa retained their ancestral culture tenaciously and did not systematically intermarry so as to develop a new culture. The myth of Dido before Virgil said that she committed suicide to avoid having to marry one of the local kings;[21] and this myth says something very insightful about the determinative nature of that particular variety of the colonial experience. B.H. Warmington, for example, after acknowledging occasional Carthaginian Hellenisms in architecture or cult, nonetheless concludes that

> the Carthaginians retained to the end of their days a way of life very different, in spite of superficial similarities, from that of most of the rest of the Mediterranean world. There can be no doubt that their adherence to traditional modes of thought gave them a sense of solidarity and was a source of strength to them . . ., but it also affected their capacity to develop in new ways and to do away with practices belonging to a primitive age. They were always strange to their neighbours.[22]

The fate of the Trojans is to be very different. If the Carthaginians are like the British in India,[23] the Roman experience is to be much more like the American one, of intermingling under the umbrella of citizenship. Aeneas is perhaps starting to understand this new development by the end of the poem, as shown by his description of the treaty terms before the duel in Book 12, where he lays it down that if he wins 'both peoples, unconquered, are to move forward on equal terms of law to eternal treaties' (*paribus se*

---

[21] Timaeus, *FGrH* 566 F82: see Pease (1935), 16–17 for other sources.
[22] B.H. Warmington (1969), 152–3 (with 133 on architecture, 145–7 on cult). [See now Feeney (2016), 318 n.23: 'For up-to-date discussion [of Carthaginian cultural developments], see the papers in Prag and Quinn (2013), which touch upon Carthaginian participation in the cultural exchanges of the western Mediterranean. Accordingly, I retract the ignorant comments' at this point in the current paper, which focalise too faithfully the Roman view.]
[23] I should qualify this by saying that the Carthaginians are like the British in India after the cultural shifts that eventually led to the Mutiny and were consolidated in its aftermath; up until around 1800 a different kind of relationship could obtain between the officials of the British East India Company and their Indian contacts, with frequent intermarriage and religious tolerance. For the earlier *modus vivendi*, see the vivid account of Dalrymple (2002).

*legibus ambae/inuictae gentes aeterna in foedera mittant*, 12.190–1). Certainly Aeneas' mother Venus affects not to get the point, when she describes the events of the war in Latium as nothing but the war of Troy all over again (10.26–30), and describes the goal of the Trojans as 'a replanted Troy' in Latium (*recidiua ... Pergama*, 10.58).[24] Venus' view, however, is bad politics and bad history and bad poetry. It is bad poetry because the *Aeneid* is not simply repeating Homer, in the way that Andromache and Helenus are doing with their toy Troy of Buthrotum in Book 3, where they are just replicating Homer instead of using a Trojan and Homeric base as a launchpad for creative new missions.[25] It is bad history and bad politics because Rome is certainly not going to be a foundation like Carthage, a fragment of foreign identity transplanted to new ground and not intermingling. Rome is going to be an entirely new kind of political entity.

In the second half of the poem Virgil gives us an extraordinary history lesson as he illustrates the Roman genius for amalgamation and adaptation of the citizen body. One group after another will be amalgamated and brought in to the new people: the Trojans, of course, but also the Latins, and the Etruscans, and the Sabines, the Volsci, the Aequi, and all the rest, in very much the same way as we see in Virgil's contemporary Livy as well. They will intermarry and form a new kind of group, one that is always changing and developing, in an entity where what matters above all is not blood or *ethnos* but citizenship.[26] The Roman foundational myths of Troy and of Romulus and Remus are fundamentally geared in this period to concentrate on the way that Rome is peopled by outsiders, with new members always coming in to join the evolving and changing citizen body: these myths function very differently from such autochthonous myths as those of the Athenians, and from the exclusivist myth of Dido committing suicide to avoid intermarriage with a local man.

So far I have been stressing the way in which the Trojans are not pulled back to their roots, but move on to form a new composite people in a new country as they grow out of their Eastern heritage; and I have been arguing that this story, and the counterexample of Carthage, are partly a way of thinking about very recent Roman experience, when they came very close to becoming a new Troy, merging with the Alexandria of

---

[24] On the mistaken attempt of many characters to see the events of Latium as merely a replay of the Trojan war, see W.S. Anderson (1957).
[25] Again, I recommend Quint (1993), chapter 2, on this theme of a healthy and creative retracing which allows you to outstrip the past, as opposed to an unhealthy and retrogressive repetition, that keeps you stuck in the past.
[26] The best introduction to this large theme is now Dench (2005).

Cleopatra.[27] According to Virgil this would have been a catastrophic historical mistake, a disastrous reversion; instead, the victory of Caesar means that Roman history is not going to loop back in a circle, but keep moving forward on the same trajectory it has been on for hundreds of years. While this is a reasonably satisfying conclusion in various ways, one that answers to powerful currents in the poem, it is, however, at the same time a gross oversimplification of how the *Aeneid* treats the Eastern component of the Roman experience, and we need at this point to complicate the picture somewhat. I shall now turn to the question of how the ever-changing Roman identity of Virgil's and Augustus' time copes with the undeniable challenge of its non-Western dimension; in the process, we shall need to take stock of the contribution made to Roman identity by a group of people from the East who are also a pressing part of this contemporary issue, the Greeks.

Let us return to the depiction of the battle of Actium on the shield of Aeneas in Book 8. As we saw, we may readily describe the antithesis between the two sides as an emblematic image of a strong dichotomy between the East and the West, a paradigm of Edward Said's 'orientalism'.[28] On one side are the rational, calm, unified, orderly masculine Western forces and their rational, calm gods, lined up against the motley collection of effeminate Easterners with their hybrid deities.[29] This is very satisfying, until we reflect that the hero who is being given this shield is himself an Easterner, a Trojan, and one who wears 'strange clothes', as we have been reminded in Book 7, when the approach of the Trojan envoys to the city of Latinus is reported by a messenger, who describes them as 'huge men wearing strange clothes' (*ingentis ignota in ueste ... uiros*, 7.167–8). Aeneas, in other words, looking at the shield, sees a group of people dressed like him being routed by people dressed like Turnus and King Latinus. Aeneas' costume had been the subject of remark already in Book 4, when Dido's disappointed suitor, King Iarbas, describes his alien garb in tones of dripping contempt, recycling the anti-Cleopatra line about the Eastern eunuchs in the process: 'And now that Paris with his entourage of half-men, with his Maeonian bonnet on his anointed hair, tied up under his chin ...' (*et nunc ille Paris cum semiuiro comitatu,/Maeonia mentum mitra crinemque madentem/subnexus*, 4.215–17). In Book 9 one of the Italians besieging the Trojan camp, Numanus Remulus, gives vent to the same

---

[27] For the contemporary obsessions with the possible rebirth of Troy, including the projected moving of the capital to Alexandria, see Nisbet and Rudd (2004), 36–8.
[28] Said (1978).
[29] See the illuminating chart of Quint (1993), 25, from which I take these categories.

kind of invective, laughing at the Trojans for their costume, with sleeves on their tunics and strings to their bonnets, and accusing them of being devotees of the Berecyntian mother of Mount Ida (9.614–20).[30]

Numanus Remulus is of course promptly shot through the temples by the son of Aeneas (9.632–4), and at the end of the poem Jupiter promises Juno that the Latins will not change their costume and wear effeminate Trojan gear, but continue to wear the *toga* and to speak Latin (12.823–5, answered by 834–6). But the Eastern component remains part of the Roman identity, even down to Virgil's day, and even in the heart of Augustus' Rome. Remulus taunts the Trojans with being devoted to the goddess Cybele, the Berecyntian mother of Mount Ida in the Troad. Hers was a very strange cult, demanding that its priests castrate themselves, dress in distinctive Eastern clothing, and on ritual occasions process through the city flagellating themselves and banging their tambourines.[31] The cult was introduced to Rome at the end of the Hannibalic War, in 204 BCE. The black stone representing Cybele was brought from Pessinos, in Asia Minor, and the goddess was thought to come from Mount Ida, near Troy, an origin signalled in her official cult title of *Mater Deum Magna Idaea*: the Romans who imported the cult will have been imagining themselves going back to the source of their people for the religious power they needed finally to defeat Hannibal.[32] Now, where was the temple of Cybele in Virgil's Rome? It was right next to the house of Augustus on the Palatine hill, part of his systematically designed architectural ideology programme.[33] On the other side of his house was his own brand-new Temple of Apollo. The virile rational Western god is the apparent antithesis of the female ecstatic Eastern goddess, yet Augustus and the Roman people are linked with both: the divine care of the Eastern mother is powerfully present in the *Aeneid*, especially at the beginning of Book 9, and her concern for her Trojan people carries on down to the present day, to the descendant of a Trojan prince who now rules in Rome, Augustus.[34] Even someone as apparently alien and unRoman as the Eastern mother of the gods can have her role and her place in the city and the Empire.[35]

From this position we have another perspective on how to think about the functions Carthage is discharging in the poem. Carthage is indeed the

---

[30] From the extensive bibliography on this speech, see in particular Horsfall (1971); R.F. Thomas (1982), chapter 4.
[31] On these features of the cult, see Beard, North and Price (1998), 1.96–8, 160.
[32] Following the convincing arguments of Gruen (1990), chapter 1; cf. Erskine (2001), 212–16.
[33] Finely elucidated by Wiseman (1984).
[34] On Augustus' careful cultivation of the goddess, see Wiseman (1984), 126–8; Erskine (2001), 212–13.
[35] Beard, North and Price (1998), 1.160 n.134 on the concept of 'foreign'.

'Other' to the Romans—barbarian, mercantile, untrustworthy, cruel.[36] But this is no simple polarity, for the 'Other' does not represent only alterity, as a collection bag for all of the differences between oneself and the other identity. Rather, the 'Other' can be a screen on which to project the aspects of oneself that one would rather not think about on home ground. Cultural issues that are too vital to ignore but too painful or embarrassing to acknowledge as integral can be displaced onto another object for comparatively safer contemplation.[37] From this perspective, Carthage is a way of thinking about many aspects of Romanness which are disquieting, and which Romans would generally prefer not to recognise as germane to themselves—foreign ancestry, luxury, decadence and barbarism. This orientalist catalogue represents qualities that the Romans spend a lot of time denouncing in the Carthaginians, but they are qualities that are central to Rome, or potentially central.[38] Rome is indeed, as Ovid's Dido calls Aeneas' future foundation, 'a city the equivalent of Carthage' (*instar Carthaginis urbem*, *Her.* 7.19), and a persistent thread in ancient thought links Rome and Carthage together as twin cities, with similar constitutions and entwined destinies.[39] The theme that the fates of Carthage and Troy (and therefore of Rome) are linked is likewise sounded in the *Aeneid*, where the suicide of Dido evokes Homer's reference to the fall of Troy. When Dido collapses on the pyre, the lamentation of the women is marked by a simile that refers to the destruction of Carthage or Tyre, 'just as if the enemy had been let in and all Carthage or ancient Tyre were plunging' (*non aliter quam si immissis ruat hostibus omnis/Karthago aut antiqua Tyros*, *Aen.* 4.669–70). The simile alludes to Homer's simile of the lamentation at the death of Hector (*Il.* 22.410–11). The death of Hector makes the fall of Troy inevitable a few weeks later: the death of Dido makes the fall of Carthage inevitable hundreds of years later—a characteristically different epic-historical span of time for Virgil.

Being a Roman depends intimately on continual reassessment of what the 'non-Roman' is, and is therefore ultimately intextricable from the

---

[36] Horsfall (1973–4).
[37] A fundamental contribution is Zeitlin (1986) on this function of Thebes in the Athenian imaginary; P. Hardie (1990) demonstrated how profitably this model could be transferred to Rome. I am indebted to Cowan's outstanding analysis of the role of Capua in Silius Italicus, where he shows the multiple mirroring role of Capua as *altera Carthago* and *altera Roma*, arguing that Silius' Capua resembles 'Rome so closely that important but dangerous issues can be safely explored within its bounds without openly admitting their presence at Rome' (Cowan (2002), 52–3).
[38] Note here the implications of the astute questions posed by Beard, North and Price (1998), 1.160 n.34 about what it means to describe the cult of the Magna Mater as 'foreign'.
[39] For details see Feeney (2007), 53–4.

category of the non-Roman. This apparently paradoxical conclusion is rather like what Virgil achieves in his depiction of passionate love. His main purpose is to demonstrate that it is radically un-Roman to put love first, and in order to achieve this he devotes one whole book and a major portion of another to demonstrate that to be a good Roman you have to turn your back on love. In the end, then, almost one-sixth of the great Roman national epic has become a love story, and the love experience has become central to Roman identity.

If Virgil demonstrates the impossibility of maintaining radically clean lines of demarcation between West and East, apparently Roman and non-Roman, we may observe him reaching somewhat similar conclusions in his treatment of the other major non-Roman identity in the poem, the Greek. Obviously I can only briefly touch on some leading ideas in dealing with such a very large topic.

In Roman culture the Greeks too are often tarred with an 'Eastern' brush. The non-Attic Greeks in particular can be part of a cluster of ideas which associates the Eastern with the effeminate, the soft, the disorganised, the overcivilised, the unbucolic—the whole bundle of prejudices, in short, that Numanus Remulus talks about in his speech in Book 9. According to this stereotype, the West is virile, tough, taciturn, disciplined, while the East—which for the Romans of Virgil's time can be a category that extends to include the Greeks, especially the Greeks of Asia—is effeminate, irrational, polyglot, disorganised.[40] This is all rather hard on the Greeks, of course, since they created all these prejudices in the first place. Already in Homer, who preserves an astonishing impartiality in regard to the Achaeans and Trojans, we see, as the armies march out against each other at the beginning of *Iliad* 3, the first signs of a stereotype that was to have very long legs:[41]

> When the men of both sides were set in order by their leaders, the Trojans came on with clamour and shouting, like wildfowl, as when the clamour of cranes goes high to the heavens ...
> But the Achaian men went silently, breathing valour ...

For the Greeks, the Persian Wars are the main venue for this kind of construction.[42] Having invented this dichotomy, however, they then fell victim to it, as the goalposts shifted further west, to Rome, and they

---

[40] 'The contrast on which the ancient debate centres is a geographical, not a chronological one: Asia versus Attica. It is the east which is constantly blamed for luxury, immorality and stylistic bad taste': Wallace-Hadrill (1989), 162.
[41] *Il.* 3.1–8, tr. Lattimore (1961)    [42] Still fundamental is Hall (1989).

became susceptible to being cast as the weak and passive Other in their turn. Accordingly, one of the main strands in the *Aeneid* regularly distances the Greek dimension as being somehow unRoman, alien to the tough virtues of public service and military service that the poem strives to establish as fundamental to Roman identity. A crucial and often-quoted passage comes in the underworld, where Aeneas' father Anchises declares to his son the nature of the Romans' public duty, their paradoxical 'arts'. The Greeks are the unnamed 'others', who excel in the unmartial arenas (6.847–53):[43]

> excudent alii spirantia mollius aera
> (credo equidem), uiuos ducent de marmore uultus,
> orabunt causas melius, caelique meatus
> describent radio et surgentia sidera dicent:
> tu regere imperio populos, Romane, memento
> (hae tibi erunt artes), pacique imponere morem,
> parcere subiectis et debellare superbos.

> Others will hammer out breathing bronzes more softly (I am convinced of it), and will lead living faces from the marble; they will plead cases better, and they will chart out the movements of heaven with a rod and describe the rising constellations: you, Roman, remember to rule the peoples with empire (these will be your arts), and to fix a settled order on pacification, spare the surrendered and war down the proud.

The arts of the Greeks named by Anchises include sculpture, in bronze and marble, oratory, and astronomy. He does not explicitly name poetry, the quintessential Greek art, because then the irony would be too naked, and the irony of this passage must be registered without becoming overwhelming.[44] Anchises is telling his son, 'Just be a soldier and a civil servant: forget about Greek art.' But he is making this pronouncement in dactylic hexameters, a Greek metre; the poem in which this declaration is made is 'a work of consummate fine art',[45] a precious cultural artefact of the utmost sophistication, one inconceivable without the parenthood of Greek culture. These words were written by a man who lived most of his adult life in the Greek city of Naples, going by a Greek nickname ('Parthenias'), and who no doubt as a matter of course wore Greek costume there and spoke in Greek.[46]

How closely does the poem, and the Roman culture it describes, engage with the Greek dimension? Every line, of course, recalls Greek literary

---

[43] On the cultural cost acknowledged here, see Griffin (1985), 169–70.
[44] R.O.A.M. Lyne (1987), 214–16.   [45] Ibid., 215.
[46] Suet. *Vita Verg.* 11 (nickname), 13 (residence in Naples).

antecedents: Aeschylus, Apollonius, Aratus—and that is only the letter 'A', while we are still a long way in the alphabet from Homer, whose presence suffuses the entire poem. However hostile the Romans felt to the Greeks—and they did at times feel very hostile, a feeling captured in the poem by the fact that they come from Troy, a city destroyed by the Greeks—their culture was a Hellenic culture through and through. I quote at every opportunity Tim Cornell's wonderful aphorism: 'An independent or autonomous Latin culture never had a chance to emerge.'[47] The Romans of the late Republic themselves had different stories, and were followed in this by modern scholars until quite recently, telling of how a pristine Roman culture was progressively encroached upon by dissolute Hellenism as the Empire expanded out beyond the peninsula of Italy. But the more that scholars investigate the earliest days of civic life on the site of Rome, the more clear it becomes that the city had always been part of the web of Hellenic connections, with Greek artworks, traders, and cult documentable in the city well over a century before the beginning of the Republic.[48]

The inextricability of the Greek and the Roman is allegorised for us in Book 8 when Aeneas travels to the site of future Rome, to what will one day be the heart of the Empire, and he finds living there ... a band of Greeks, the people of Evander, centuries before Rome is founded on that spot by Romulus.[49] Even more: these Greeks of Evander embody the values upon which the Romans prided themselves as having once exemplified, before the fall into luxury and dissolution, the values of frugality, poverty, toughness, self-denial.[50] The people in the poem who best embody and anticipate what the ideal Roman identity will be are not Romans, but Greeks. However far back in time you go, Virgil appears to be saying, Greek and Roman are permeable categories. And, as we have seen, modern historians have recently started to agree with him.

Virgil is enacting for us here a process that the anthropologist Michael Taussig calls 'mimesis and alterity', whereby interacting cultures select from each other characteristic features for disparagement or envy.[51] A process of imitation most economically makes these features available

---

[47] Cornell (1978), 110.   [48] Further discussion and bibliography in Feeney (1998), 25–7.
[49] The Sibyl already prophesies to Aeneas that a big surprise awaits him, in that the first ray of hope in Latium will come from a Greek city: *uia prima salutis/(quod minime reris) Graia pandetur ab urbe*, 6.96–7.
[50] 'Evander ... is the man who really introduces Aeneas to what is best in Roman ancestral values and beliefs', Momigliano (1987), 282. This whole essay, 'How to reconcile Greeks and Trojans' (264–88) is required reading on the topic of the *Aeneid*'s engagement with Greece.
[51] Taussig (1993).

for experimentation and analysis, allowing one to capture and control the strange power of the other culture. As the alien features are brought home, the resulting sense of anxiety or revulsion produces a backlash, in which the imitated characteristics are once again set at a distance. The competing cultures, then, oscillate between concentrating on otherness, by focusing on what is different about their rivals, and concentrating on similarity, by the imitative process which best enables them to define and master what makes up that otherness. The interaction between the Romans and the Greeks is a text-book example of this process, and it can be seen running through the whole *Aeneid*. The entire Trojan myth of Roman origins which undergirds the *Aeneid* is illustrative of how these interactions work: it could help make the Romans look like part of the Greek scheme of things, or it could be activated to cast them as anti-Greek if necessary.[52]

The Roman engagement with Greece, then, can be very hostile and contemptuous even as it is admiring and imitative. Analogies only take one so far, but the Roman attitude to the Greeks can be reminiscent of the way that the English of the older generation regarded the French. English cultural life is inconceivable without the French dimension, from dining to universities to architecture, yet nothing marks the upper-class English person more readily than a contempt for the silly and light-weight French. Conversely, the French have their own jaundiced views of the English, and the faults each nation finds in the other overlap dramatically, in very much the same way as we observed in the case of the Romans' use of the Carthaginians as their 'Other'. Julian Barnes, in a review of a book on the relationship between the French and the British, observes that

> what emerges with depressing strength from the ... book is that ... the fundamental character traits each nation deplores in the other are the same: arrogance, cruelty, and a desire for dominance; selfishness, duplicity, hypocrisy; cowardice and betrayal. Are these authentically observed defects, or merely a reflection of the viewing country's own faults? Or both at the same time?[53]

The way the English are in their turn regarded by the Americans is also a suggestive parallel. Americans can be dismissive of the English as being effete and Old World, but they are envious of their culture in many ways, and even deferential towards it; even as they assimilate BBC dramas, however, they can be touched into revealing a sense of cultural insecurity, so it is not straightforward to say whether Americans admire or despise

---

[52] Gruen (1992), 6–51.  [53] Barnes (2007), 6.

English culture. The flip side of this analogy is that the English attitude to Americans is very like that of the Greeks to the Romans. Their sense of being overtaken and outplayed and outspent finds expression in a snooty and patronising disdainfulness, because, rather like the Greeks under Rome, they cannot bear to admit that these rough upstarts are the ones who now have the power to control world culture, with an energy and creativity of their own.

It is not anomalous, then, that Roman culture should always be oscillating in its attitudes to the Greek component, and any engagement with Greek culture is potentially extremely two-edged. But the engagement with Greek culture in the *Aeneid* is only one example of the complexity of the always changing Roman identity, which eventually becomes a pan-Mediterranean culture, engaging with a host of other cultures in the process, and involved in ceaseless and reciprocal transformations as a result.

CHAPTER 15

# *First Similes in Epic*[1]

Extended similes are particularly at home in heroic epic, so much so that they are surprisingly rare in other genres, such as lyric or elegy; as we shall see below, they are also very rare in archaic didactic, although they later become more common in that genre.[2] If similes are a marked feature of heroic epic, then the first similes in epic are themselves particularly marked. The programmatic nature of the first simile in Virgil's *Aeneid* (1.148–53) has often been commented upon, as an emblem of restoration of order after chaos which generates a set of expectations for the rest of the poem. I shall argue that the iconic nature of the initial simile sequence is a feature of epic that goes back to Homer's *Iliad*, and continues well past Virgil. In general, the first similes in epic are programmatic for the cosmos of the whole poem, for they present an icon of the relationship between human beings and the natural world, which in turn gives us an icon of the poem's relationship between order and disorder, chaos and harmony. These icons are an ideal, like all icons, and there are many ways in which these first programmatic moments turn out to have a degree of slippage and lack of fit, as is characteristic of similes in general.[3] A study of the first similes in an epic can shed light on a range of narrative techniques and thematic concerns that carry through the poem as a whole.

---

[1] I gave a first version of this paper an embarrassingly long time ago, at the Triennial meeting of the Roman and Hellenic Societies in July 1988, and also at the Literature Seminar of the Classics Faculty at Cambridge in that year. Since then the problem has been on my mind, and I was glad to have the opportunity to revisit and rethink for the APA Convention in Chicago in January 2014, and for the Corpus Christi College Classics Society later that month. For feedback and advice of various kinds I thank Philip Hardie, Stephen Harrison, Nicholas Horsfall and Antony Smith, who gave a valuable presentation on the *Aeneid*'s first simile to a seminar in Oxford in Hilary Term, 2014. All translations are my own.

[2] Brunner (1966), 354–5; von Glinski (2012), 83; Feeney Volume 2, Chapter 16, 302. On didactic, see Gale (1994), 102: 'The use of extended "Homeric" similes is ... rare in surviving didactic, with the exception of Lucretius' model Empedocles and his imitators Virgil and Manilius.'

[3] Feeney Volume 2, Chapter 16, 311.

## I. Homer's *Iliad*

We begin with the first first similes in epic, in Homer's *Iliad*. The very first similes in the *Iliad* are not developed, although they generate considerable condensed power. As Apollo comes down Mt. Ida in response to the prayers of his priest, Chryses, in order to shoot his arrows at the Achaean host, 'he went like night' (ὁ δ' ἤϊε νυκτὶ ἐοικώς, *Il.* 1.47): since he has been called Φοῖβος, 'bright/radiant', only four lines before, the oxymoronic power of the comparison to night is chilling.[4] A second undeveloped simile soon follows, in the description of Agamemnon's anger at the speech of Calchas, when 'his eyes were like shining fire' (ὄσσε δέ οἱ πυρὶ λαμπετόωντι ἐΐκτην, *Il.* 1.104); and a third is used to describe Thetis emerging 'quickly from the grey sea like a mist' (καρπαλίμως δ' ἀνέδυ πολιῆς ἁλὸς ἠΰτ' ὀμίχλη, *Il.* 1.359).

It is only in the second book, with the poem's fourth simile, that we meet a developed simile of the classic type, the first one in the poem, as the movement of the Achaeans to Agamemnon's assembly is compared to the movement of bees going out to gather nectar (*Il.* 2.87–93):

> ἠΰτε ἔθνεα εἶσι μελισσάων ἀδινάων
> πέτρης ἐκ γλαφυρῆς αἰεὶ νέον ἐρχομενάων·
> βοτρυδὸν δὲ πέτονται ἐπ' ἄνθεσιν εἰαρινοῖσιν·
> αἱ μέν τ' ἔνθα ἅλις πεποτήαται, αἱ δέ τε ἔνθα·           90
> ὣς τῶν ἔθνεα πολλὰ νεῶν ἄπο καὶ κλισιάων
> ἠϊόνος προπάροιθε βαθείης ἐστιχόωντο
> ἰλαδὸν εἰς ἀγορήν·

> As the tribes of dense-flying bees go from a hollow rock, constantly coming on afresh: they fly in clusters on the spring flowers; some fly in throngs this way, some that; so the many tribes of the Achaeans from the ships and huts, in front of the deep beach, filed in companies to the assembly.

There are many lines of approach into this rich simile, but for the purposes of the present argument we shall concentrate on how the simile may be read as an emblem of social cohesion.[5] Homer creates a meticulous parallelism between the organisation of the bees and of the Achaeans. The simile concentrates on the group organisation of the bees, as the context concentrates on the organised sub-groups which make up the larger mass of the Achaeans. The bees are grouped in ἔθνεα, 'tribes', (87), as are the Achaeans

---

[4] My thanks to Simon Hornblower for not letting me overlook the impact of the half-line similes.
[5] Interesting and full discussion in Polleichtner (2005), 116–21, although I disagree that 'swarming' in the technical sense is at issue, rather than a picture of dense groups leaving the hive and then thinning as they fan out.

themselves (91); they fly βοτρυδόν, 'in clusters' (89), and ἅλις, 'in throngs' (90), while the Achaeans move in στίχοι, 'files' (ἐστιχόωντο, 92) and ἶλαι, 'companies' (ἰλαδόν, 93).[6] Now, the action of the simile may appear to be saying the opposite of the context, in that the bees are leaving a central point and going in diverse directions, while the Achaeans are coming from diverse directions to a central point. In fact, the two actions of simile and context supplement each other to achieve a harmonious reciprocity, which reinforces in narrative terms the thematic import of the comparison. The bees and the Achaeans are sub-groups making up a larger unity as they jointly create a cyclical pattern of leaving the central point and then returning: the narrative shows the Achaeans gathering to a central point, and the simile shows them dispersing from it.

Bees to the ancients were the archetypal social animal, and comparisons between human and bee society were frequently made. Hesiod makes emblematic use of the social paradigm of the bee in the single simile in the *Works and Days*, which compares the lazy man to a drone, sitting at home and doing no work (303–6); in the *Theogony*, there are only three similes, one of which also has a comparison to drones, this time with the woman as the point of comparison (594–601).[7] The ancient world's most striking development of the bee/human analogy is in Virgil's Fourth *Georgic*, which draws on longstanding poetic, philosophical and scientific traditions.[8] The honeybees have remained a multivalent and keenly contested emblem of human society ever since, and I recommend the engaging work of B. Wilson as a fine introduction to the long history of the bees as a microcosm of human society.[9] To her survey of subsequent literary expressions of the image, including especially the Archbishop of Canterbury's speech in Shakespeare's *Henry V* (I.ii.192–208), I would add only two personal favourites: the satirising of the whole conceit of the comparison by the work-shy lawyer Eugene Wrayburn in Charles Dickens' *Our Mutual Friend* (1864–5:

---

[6] Noted by Leinieks (1986), 10.
[7] The *Theogony*'s only other developed simile says that the earth melted like smelted tin or iron as a result of the thunderbolt's fire gushing out of the striken Typhoeus (861–4); a hyperbolic analogy in the war between gods and Titans comes close to simile (700–5: the din of the conflict was 'as when Earth and wide heaven above came into contact', ὡς ὅτε Γαῖα καὶ Οὐρανὸς εὐρὺς ὕπερθε/πίλνατο, 702–3). It is no coincidence that the great battles of the *Theogony* generate quasi-epic moments of simile or analogy: compare the density of similes in the section of the Hesiodic *Aspis* that contains the set-piece combat between Heracles and Cycnus (Hunter (2006), 87, referring to 374–9, 386–92, 402–12, 421–3, 426–32, 436–40). Otherwise, in the *Theogony* there is only one half-line simile (Phaethon is 'a man like the gods', θεοῖς ἐπιείκελον ἄνδρα, 987).
[8] R.F. Thomas (1988), 2.175 and Mynors (1990), 278 provide orientation for Virgil's use of the bee analogy, and its background: note esp. Dahlmann (1954) and Griffin (1985), chapter 8.
[9] B. Wilson (2004).

Book 1, Chapter 8), together with Tolstoy's three-page comparison of the abandoned city of Moscow to a queenless hive in *War and Peace* (1869: Volume 3, Chapter 20). The political force of the analogy is still alive, to judge by the fascinating study of the entomologist T.D. Seeley. Entitled *Honeybee Democracy*, his book explains for the first time the precise means by which swarming honeybees reach a 'decision' about where to find a new site for a hive, and draws explicit lessons from their behaviour for how human beings should reach decisions at all levels of society.

The comment of the ancient scholiasts on our first simile certainly shows a high degree of interest in the social force of the comparison (AbT 2.87):

> ἔθνεα·πρὸς τοὺς εἰκαζομένους "Ελληνας, ἐπεὶ σμήνεα ἔδει. πρώτη δὲ αὕτη παραβολὴ τῷ ποιητῇ. συγγενὲς δὲ ποιητικῇ τὸ ζῷον διὰ τὸν μόχθον καὶ τὸ γλυκὺ καὶ τὴν σύνθεσιν τοῦ κηρίου. ἡ μὲν οὖν φαλαγγηδὸν γινομένη πρόοδος εὖ ἔχει· ὡπλισμέναι τε κέντροις εἰσιν, ὑπήκοοι τε καὶ αὐταί εἰσι καὶ ἐπ' ἔργον ἐξίασιν, οὐχ ὡς αἱ γέρανοι, φιλάλληλοί τέ εἰσι μεταβαίνουσαί τε πολλὰς ἀρχὰς πτήσεως ποιοῦνται.

> *Tribes*: with regard to the Greeks who are the object of comparison, since it should have been 'swarms'. This is the poet's first simile. The creature is at home in poetry through hard work, sweetness and the construction of honeycomb. The way the procession happens in phalanxes is good: for they are armed with stings, they are subjects too [like the Achaeans] and they go out to work, not like the cranes (cf. 3.3–7), they are fond of one another and as they change course they make many starts to their flight.

The scholiast picks up on the way that Homer has accentuated the identification of the tenor and the vehicle by describing the bees with the word ἔθνεα, 'tribes', since this is a human word, not a bee one.[10] After noting that the simile is the first one in the poem and then throwing in some more or less random possible connections between bees and poetry, he homes in on the social organisation aspect of the comparison, finding numerous points of contact between the behaviour of the bees and the Achaeans. He also makes a distinction between the industrious bees to whom the Achaeans are compared and the feckless cranes who illustrate the behaviour of the Trojans and their allies at the beginning of Book 3: the later comment on the bird similes concerning the Trojans and their allies disparagingly claims that 'the similes fill out the gappy/uncoordinated nature of their march' (τὸ μέντοι διάκενον τῆς πορείας ἀναπληροῦσιν αἱ

---

[10] 'Tenor' and 'vehicle', coined by Richards (1936), are not ideal words to describe the terms of a simile or metaphor, but we seem to be stuck with them. In the simile 'Hector is like a lion', for example, 'Hector' is the tenor and 'lion' is the vehicle.

παραβολαί, b 3.2). In fact, in Book 2 the Achaeans are also compared to cranes (and geese and swans, 2.459–65), but our scholiast glosses over this in accordance with his usual philhellene bias, and he presses on, in that same comment at the beginning of Book 3, to mark what he considers as the paradigmatic nature of the initial simile applied to each side: 'Homer fixes the nature of both armies and does not depart from their characterisation right to the end' (ἀμφοτέρας δὲ τὰς στρατιὰς διατυποῖ καὶ μέχρι τέλους οὐκ ἐξίσταται τοῦ ἤθους, b 3.2).

The scholiast, however skewed his perspective, is clearly responding to something important in the bee-simile when he focuses on its programmatic social significance, and his modern counterparts likewise remark on the way that the first simile introduces the concept of the Achaean host as an organised and ordered group, setting up a progress that eventually leads in to the organisation of the Catalogue of the Ships some four-hundred lines later.[11] The markedly iconic nature of the bee-simile is even more apparent on a re-reading of the poem, because it transpires that there is no other bee-simile in the *Iliad*: the initial bee-simile is a programmatic singleton, presenting an ideal picture of the Achaeans' cohesion and order.[12] Given that the massive and disparate Achaean host gathered at Troy represents a scale of organisation completely beyond the actual experience of the poet and his audience, it should not surprise us that the poet stamps this remarkable human gathering with an iconic simile from the archetypal social unit of the natural world.

Nonetheless, you have to have one eye shut to read this initial bee-simile as an entirely satisfying emblem of cohesion among the Achaeans, since the background for the opening assembly is precisely the absence of Achilles and the Myrmidons. The latent failure of the idealised simile to correspond to the social reality is immediately brought out into the open by the host's chaotic response to Agamemnon's 'test', in which he tries out their morale by suggesting that they should all immediately return home, leaving Troy untaken (2.139–41). The pattern of confused and potentially catastrophic action that follows is punctuated by a linked chain of similes taken from the natural world in chaos:

---

[11] Leinieks (1986), 10–11; P. Hardie (2010), 18; Elmer (2013), 86–104.
[12] The closest Homer later comes to a second bee-simile is at *Il.* 12.167–72, when Asios complains that Polypoetes and Leonteus will not give ground, 'like wasps flexible about the middle, *or bees*' (ὥς τε σφῆκες μέσον αἰόλοι ἠὲ μέλισσαι, 167): note that the participle in the simile that describes the insects as 'waiting' (μένοντες, 169) is masculine, like the wasps, not feminine, like the bees.

eventually, order will be restored, but the ability of the organism to preserve its power to function will have been severely tested.[13] This chain of similes has an immense impact on the later epic tradition, particularly on Virgil's *Aeneid*, for the similes depict the turbulent movements of the Achaeans' host in terms of the effect of violent storm-winds on the sea.[14]

As soon as Agamemnon has finished the speech in which he deceitfully suggests that they all return home, there is a double simile comparing the chaos of the Achaeans' response to the turmoil caused by the impact of violent winds on sea and land (2.144–50):

> κινήθη δ' ἀγορὴ φὴ κύματα μακρὰ θαλάσσης,
> πόντου Ἰκαρίοιο, τὰ μέν τ' Εὖρός τε Νότος τε            145
> ὤρορ' ἐπαΐξας πατρὸς Διὸς ἐκ νεφελάων.
> ὡς δ' ὅτε κινήσῃ Ζέφυρος βαθὺ λήϊον ἐλθών,
> λάβρος ἐπαιγίζων, ἐπί τ' ἠμύει ἀσταχύεσσιν,
> ὣς τῶν πᾶσ' ἀγορὴ κινήθη· τοὶ δ' ἀλαλητῷ
> νῆας ἔπ' ἐσσεύοντο . . .                                 150

> The assembly was stirred like the great sea-waves of the Icarian Sea, which the East Wind and the South Wind have set in motion, dashing upon them from the clouds of father Zeus. And as when the West Wind coming stirs a deep field of corn as it rushes on it, blustering, and the field bends to it with its ears of corn, so was their whole assembly stirred. They rushed with a yell to the ships . . .

These five lines of comparison remarkably condense three of the most conspicuous 'crowd symbols' of Elias Canetti's list: 'The Sea', 'Corn', and 'Wind'.[15]

Hera sends Athena to stop the stampede (2.155–65), telling her to 'check each man with your gentle words' (σοῖς δ' ἀγανοῖς ἐπέεσσιν ἐρήτυε φῶτα ἕκαστον, 164); but Athena chooses Odysseus as her surrogate, repeating to him the words Hera had used to her, 'check each man with your gentle words' (180). Odysseus takes Agamemnon's scepter (2.185–6), and he follows Athena's advice for each king or outstanding man he meets (188–9), but each man from the people that he sees and finds yelling he hits with the scepter and upbraids (198–9), saying (203–5):

---

[13] Elmer (2013), 86–104 is an excellent account of how Book 2 as a whole courts chaos in the process of reasserting an overall consensus.
[14] For accounts stressing the importance of seeing the chain of nature similes as a connected sequence, see Moulton (1977), 38–42; Leinieks (1986); Ready (2011), 127; Elmer (2013), 101.
[15] Canetti (1962), 80–1 ('The Sea'), 85 ('Corn'), 86 ('Wind').

> οὐ μέν πως πάντες βασιλεύομεν ἐνθάδ' Ἀχαιοί·
> οὐκ ἀγαθὸν πολυκοιρανίη· εἷς κοίρανος ἔστω,
> εἷς βασιλεύς ... 205

> In no way are we all kings here, we Achaeans: it's not a good thing to have lots of leaders; let there be one leader, one king.

Odysseus' actions and words have their effect, and the Achaeans immediately pour back to the assembly with another simile of a great movement of the sea, in the fourth developed simile of the poem (2.207–10), a simile which matches and responds to the simile of wind and sea that marked their initial chaotic departure from the assembly at 2.144–6:[16]

> ὣς ὅ γε κοιρανέων δίεπε στρατόν· οἱ δ' ἀγορήνδε
> αὖτις ἐπεσσεύοντο νεῶν ἄπο καὶ κλισιάων
> ἠχῇ, ὡς ὅτε κῦμα πολυφλοίσβοιο θαλάσσης
> αἰγιαλῷ μεγάλῳ βρέμεται, σμαραγεῖ δέ τε πόντος. 210

> So he, acting as leader, brought the army into order; and they rushed back again to the assembly from the ships and huts with a noise, as when a wave of the much-resounding sea booms on the long beach, and the sea roars.

It is striking that Odysseus is acting as the κοίρανος here (κοιρανέων, 207), just after he has said that there ought to be only one κοίρανος—by implication, Agamemnon. The ideal of single rule that Odysseus espouses is being subtly undermined by his own action, yet the ideal is to some extent recuperated by the only other use of this verb to describe a human being in the *Iliad*, when it is used of Agamemnon as he inspects the Achaean contingents (ὣς ὅ γε κοιρανέων ἐπεπωλεῖτο στίχας ἀνδρῶν, 'so he, acting as leader, was going through the files of men', 4.250): it is Odysseus' rescuing of the expedition that will eventually make it possible for Agamemnon to act as the κοίρανος whom he failed to embody in Book 2.[17]

After Odysseus and Agamemnon manage to restore cohesion and have the army recommit to the goals of the expedition (2.211–393), the chain of nature-similes is rounded off with another image of sea and wind as the Achaeans shout their approval of Agamemnon's call to battle (2.394–7):[18]

---

[16] For the links between these two similes in particular, see Kirk (1985) on 2.144–46; Ready (2011), 127. Note also the echo in line 208 here, marked by αὖτις, 'again', of the language that described the Achaeans' first movement to the assembly, after the bee-simile (νεῶν ἄπο καὶ κλισιάων, 2.91 and 208).

[17] See Kirk (1985) on 2.207 for the link with 4.250 (he notes that the verb is elsewhere used only of the god Ares, 5.284).

[18] For this simile as rounding off the sequence of wind storm similes depicting the assembly, see Bernadete (1963), 7–8; Moulton (1977), 41 (correctly remarking that Odysseus' and Nestor's very

ὣς ἔφατ', Ἀργεῖοι δὲ μέγ' ἴαχον, ὡς ὅτε κῦμα
ἀκτῇ ἐφ' ὑψηλῇ, ὅτε κινήσῃ Νότος ἐλθών,                                 395
προβλῆτι σκοπέλῳ· τὸν δ' οὔ ποτε κύματα λείπει
παντοίων ἀνέμων, ὅτ' ἂν ἔνθ' ἢ ἔνθα γένωνται.

> So he spoke, and the Argives gave a great shout, like a wave upon a high headland, when the South Wind coming stirs it, upon a projecting rock: the waves never leave it alone, of all the winds, whenever they come from this side or that.

Sound is the ostensible point of comparison here, but we might see a comparison between the rock and Agamemnon—an image of the fixity that Agamemnon wants to have, or that Agamemnon ought to have, or that the host wants to see embodied in Agamemnon.[19] As we shall see, that appears to be how Virgil, at least, read the simile.

Over these three-hundred lines in Book 2, we see a large pattern coming into view. The idealised and hoped-for social order of the Achaeans is captured with the image of the bees; the disruption posed to this social order of animal and human is captured with a chain of similes from the natural world of chaotic storm and sea; the restoration of order by Odysseus and, in a very secondary way, by Agamemnon is a triumph of kingly oratory and power, with the ideal of single rule being held up as the archetype for cohesion. Certainly, the restoration of order is an achievement, and the impression of Achaean harmony is reinforced by the ordered sequence of the ensuing Catalogue;[20] yet Book 9 will remind us that the social cohesion of the Achaean host is still broken, and Book 23 will remind us that it remains fragile even once Achilles has been reintegrated into the society of the Achaean host.[21]

This whole opening template of the *Iliad*, with its reception in scholarship and political philosophy, is going to be of great importance for the opening sequence and first simile of Virgil's *Aeneid*; likewise crucial for Virgil will be the opening sequence and first simile of Lucretius' *De Rerum Natura*, which are themselves in dialogue with Homer's patterns. Yet

---

brief comparisons of the Achaeans to 'unwarlike women and/or children [2.289, 337] ... hardly disrupt the pattern'); Elmer (2013), 101.

[19] Scott (2009), 48 ('The emphasis within the simile seems to be on steadfastness'); cf. Elmer (2013), 101 on how the action of the waves 'is organized around a single point of reference, the jutting headland that seems to figure Agamemnon as the focus of the army's attention'.

[20] So Elmer (2013), 86–104.

[21] N.J. Richardson (1993), 165 on the quarrels surrounding the chariot-race in Book 23, even if they are resolved by Achilles, and 246 on the wrestling match between Ajax and Odysseus, which 'has been seen by some modern scholars as related to the famous [contest] for the armour of Akhilleus at his own funeral games, which led to Aias' suicide'.

Homer's *Odyssey* is worth our consideration before we rejoin the mainstream of epic patterns of order and chaos, since its presentation of the iconic opening moments of comparison is intriguingly different from the *Iliad*'s portrayal of human organisation against a backdrop of natural patterns.

## II. Homer's *Odyssey*

Even allowing for the fact that the *Odyssey* is under four-fifths the length of the *Iliad*, it is still striking that the *Odyssey* has but one-third as many similes as the *Iliad*, and that only one-third of the *Odyssey*'s similes are 'developed', as compared to some three-fifths of the similes in the *Iliad*.[22] There are certainly any number of memorable developed similes in the *Odyssey*, but the difference between the two poems is tangible, and one aspect of this difference is to be seen in the distinctive way in which the later poem sets out to deploy the theme of comparison.

There are a number of half-line similes to begin with in the *Odyssey*, just as there are in the *Iliad*. In response to the kind advice of Athena, disguised as Mentes, the fatherless Telemachus says s/he has spoken 'like a father to his child' (ὥς τε πατὴρ ᾧ παιδί, *Od*. 1.308). This apparently almost throwaway remark will prove to have great programmatic resonance as the poem develops:[23] addressing the assembly in Ithaca, Telemachus once more uses a fatherly analogy, saying that Odysseus was to them 'gentle like a father' (πατὴρ δ' ὣς ἤπιος ἦεν, 2.47); Mentor shortly thereafter uses the same language to describe Odysseus (2.234), as does Athena in the 'second' council of the gods (5.12).[24] Next, Telemachus is 'like a god to look upon' as he goes to the Ithacan assembly (θεῷ ἐναλίγκιος ἄντην, 2.5). This theme, too, will develop as the poem goes on, with repeated formulae tracking each other to link together, above all, the family of Odysseus. Telemachus is once again compared to the immortals (ἐκ ῥ' ἀσαμίνθου βῆ δέμας ἀθανάτοισιν ὁμοῖος, 'he went from the bath like in body to the immortals', 3.468), as are he and Pisistratus, the son of Nestor (γενεῇ δὲ Διὸς μεγάλοιο ἔικτον, 'they were like the offspring of great Zeus', 4.27), then Menelaus

---

[22] Moulton (1977), 117, drawing on D.J.N. Lee (1964), 3.
[23] Podlecki (1971), 81–2; Moulton (1977), 141.
[24] The only other occurrence of ἤπιος in the poem is when Menelaus uses it to describe to Telemachus his relationship with Nestor at Troy (15.152). As with the comparisons with gods, discussed immediately below, Menelaus—Telemachus' surrogate father-figure—is the only character who breaks into the connected similes which create the charmed circle of Laertes, Odysseus and Telemachus.

(4.306–10 = 2.1–5), Odysseus (θεοῖς ἐναλίγκιον, 'similar to the gods', 19.267; ἔκ ῥ' ἀσαμίνθου βῆ δέμας ἀθανάτοισιν ὁμοῖος, 'he went from the bath like in body to the immortals', 23.163 = 3.468, of Telemachus) and, climactically, Laertes, recognised as being θεοῖς ἐναλίγκιον ἄντην ('like the gods to look upon') by his son in the poem's penultimate simile (24.371 = θεῷ ἐναλίγκιος ἄντην, 'like a god to look upon', 2.5 [Telemachus], 4.306 [Menelaus], θεοῖς ἐναλίγκιον, 'like the gods', 19.267 [Odysseus]). Even these brief touches, then, are marking crucial themes—the paternity of Odysseus and the links between the generations of the royal family on Ithaca. Yet by the end of Book 3 we have not yet had a simile of more than half a line.

Book 4 is key to the theme of comparison, although we still have to wait a considerable time to meet the first developed simile. As Telemachus and Pisistratus walk through the palace of Menelaus, 'there was a radiance as of the sun or the moon through the high-roofed house' (ὥς τε γὰρ ἠελίου αἴγλη πέλεν ἠὲ σελήνης/δῶμα καθ' ὑψερεφές, 4.45–6); as Helen enters for the first time, she is 'like Artemis of the golden distaff' ('Ἀρτέμιδι χρυσηλακάτῳ ἐϊκυῖα, 4.122). It is Helen who introduces the crucial theme of likeness and comparison in an extended way with her remarks to Menelaus, when she hazards a guess as to the identity of the still as yet anonymous guest (4.141–5):

> οὐ γάρ πώ τινά φημι ἐοικότα ὧδε ἰδέσθαι
> οὔτ' ἄνδρ' οὔτε γυναῖκα, σέβας μ' ἔχει εἰσορόωσαν,
> ὡς ὅδ' Ὀδυσσῆος μεγαλήτορος υἷϊ ἔοικε,
> Τηλεμάχῳ, τὸν λεῖπε νέον γεγαῶτ' ἐνὶ οἴκῳ
> κεῖνος ἀνήρ... 145

> for I say that I have not seen anyone with such a resemblance, neither man nor woman—wonder holds me as I look at him—as the resemblance that this man has to the son of great-hearted Odysseus, Telemachus, whom that man left, a new-born, in his house...

At this point we see in detail the huge investment that this poem will have in its own area of comparison—the likeness of inheritance, of father and son.

Interestingly, Helen does not straightforwardly say, 'This young man resembles Odysseus.' She says, 'He resembles the son of Odysseus'—in other words, 'He looks the way I would imagine, on the basis of my knowledge of Odysseus, what his son would look like.' And Menelaus agrees. He had already guessed the truth just before Helen entered, when his expression of loss for his dear friend Odysseus had made the young stranger weep, holding up his purple cloak in front of his eyes with both his hands (4.113–19). Now, responding to his wife's prompt, he makes explicit what he had independently been thinking (4.148–54):

> οὕτω νῦν καὶ ἐγὼ νοέω, γύναι, ὡς σὺ ἐΐσκεις·
> κείνου γὰρ τοιοίδε πόδες τοιαίδε τε χεῖρες
> ὀφθαλμῶν τε βολαὶ κεφαλή τ' ἐφύπερθέ τε χαῖται.    150
> καὶ νῦν ἦ τοι ἐγὼ μεμνημένος ἀμφ' Ὀδυσῆϊ
> μυθεόμην, ὅσα κεῖνος ὀϊζύσας ἐμόγησεν
> ἀμφ' ἐμοί, αὐτὰρ ὁ πυκνὸν ὑπ' ὀφρύσι δάκρυον εἶβε,
> χλαῖναν πορφυρέην ἄντ' ὀφθαλμοῖϊν ἀνασχών.

I too now perceive in the same way as you make the comparison, wife. For the feet of that man were like this, and so were his hands, and the glances of his eyes and his hair above. And just now, as I was reminiscing about Odysseus, I was telling how much that man suffered and toiled on my account, and he shed thick tears under his eyebrows, holding up his purple cloak before his eyes.

The two of them are cooperating here in setting up the programmatic comparison between father and son that is going to be so important for the rest of the poem: Menelaus in fact calls attention to her act of comparison-making (ὡς σὺ ἐΐσκεις, 'as you make the comparison', 148).[25]

Telemachus does not just look like his father; he even acts in the way that Homer will later show his father acting at the court of Alcinous, for Odysseus there likewise draws his cloak over his head to hide his tears, when he hears Demodocus sing the tale of the quarrel between Odysseus and Achilles (8.83–5).[26] When we get to Book 8, it will feel as if Odysseus is imitating Telemachus. Actually, in retrospect we are able to see that both father and son are acting in the same way at the same moment, for they are each being entertained by their gracious hosts, Menelaus and Alcinous, on the very same day: they will each have four more nights to pass before they are reunited in Eumaeus' hut in Book 16.[27]

---

[25] Comparisons are a forté of Helen's. Soon after this passage she describes how she saw through Odysseus' attempt to make himself 'like' a beggar (οἰκῆϊ ἐοικώς, 245; ἤϊσκε, 247; τῷ ἴκελος, 249): then Menelaus tells how she tried to trick the men inside the Trojan horse by 'making her voice like the wives of all the Argives' (πάντων Ἀργείων φωνὴν ἴσκους' ἀλόχοισιν, 4.279). Menelaus, in his turn, is good at spotting father–son resemblances: he remarks that Pisistratus' speech shows he is Nestor's son (4.206).

[26] N.J. Richardson (1983), 223–5 adducing the astute remarks of the scholia (MQ *Od.* 4.113) and Eustathius (1489.35–37) on the parallels between the two episodes.

[27] The first night after they try to hide their weeping they sleep at the palaces of their hosts, Telemachus at Menelaus' (4.302–3), Odysseus at Alcinous' (13.17); on the second night Telemachus once more sleeps at Menelaus' (15.4–5) while his father sails overnight to Ithaca, asleep on the Phaeacians' ship (13.93–5); on the third night, Telemachus breaks the journey back to Pylos

In the *Odyssey*, then, comparison, likeness and similarity are going to be exceptionally important, yet in a way that is distinctively different from the strategies of comparison that open the *Iliad*. These two speeches of Helen and Menelaus are, in effect, the programmatic first statement about similarity in the poem.

Soon after this, Menelaus gives the poem's first proper developed simile, comparing Odysseus to a lion, describing the revenge he will inflict on the suitors (*Od.* 4.335–40):

> ὡς δ' ὁπότ' ἐν ξυλόχῳ ἔλαφος κρατεροῖο λέοντος        335
> νεβροὺς κοιμήσασα νεηγενέας γαλαθηνοὺς
> κνημοὺς ἐξερέῃσι καὶ ἄγκεα ποιήεντα
> βοσκομένη, ὁ δ' ἔπειτα ἑὴν εἰσήλυθεν εὐνήν,
> ἀμφοτέροισι δὲ τοῖσιν ἀεικέα πότμον ἐφῆκεν,
> ὣς Ὀδυσεὺς κείνοισιν ἀεικέα πότμον ἐφήσει.        340

> As when a doe beds down her fawns, new-born and still suckling, in the thicket of a mighty lion and then goes grazing over the foothills and grassy glens, and the lion then comes back to his own lair, and unleashes unseemly death on both of them, so Odysseus on them will unleash unseemly death.

On the face of it, this is a profoundly misleading glimpse of what the future holds, although Menelaus may be attempting to reassure his young guest.

At the end of this book there is an answering simile, establishing another crucial area of likeness for the poem, namely, the comparability of Odysseus and Penelope, because Penelope too is compared to a lion—not a lioness (*Od.* 4.791–4):

> ὅσσα δὲ μερμήριξε λέων ἀνδρῶν ἐν ὁμίλῳ
> δείσας, ὁππότε μιν δόλιον περὶ κύκλον ἄγωσι,
> τόσσα μιν ὁρμαίνουσαν ἐπήλυθε νήδυμος ὕπνος·
> εὗδε δ' ἀνακλινθεῖσα, λύθεν δέ οἱ ἅψεα πάντα.

> As a lion anxiously thinks in a group of men, in fear, when they are leading a circle as a trap around him, so was she deliberating as sweet sleep came over her. She lay back in sleep, and all her joints were loosened.

Scholars regularly comment on the incongruity of this likeness between Penelope and a lion, yet the link back to Odysseus, 450 lines earlier, provides the first example of the poem's paradoxical linking of the wife

---

by sleeping at Pherae (15.185–8), while his father sleeps in Eumaeus' hut (14.523–4); on the fourth night, Odysseus once more sleeps at Eumaeus' hut (15.493–5), while his son sails overnight to Ithaca (15.296).

and husband.²⁸ This linking will eventually culminate in the extraordinary reverse simile that crowns Penelope's recognition of Odysseus in Book 23 (233–9). This simile describes the relief of a shipwrecked sailor finally reaching land, and we enter it under the inevitable impression that the simile refers to Odysseus, only to discover when the point of reference is spelled out at the end that the simile refers to *her* (ὣς ἄρα τῇ ἀσπαστὸς ἔην πόσις εἰσοροώσῃ, 'so welcome to *her* was the sight of her husband', 239).²⁹

If the two lion-similes of Book 4, the first developed similes in the poem, ultimately set up this climactic moment of identification in Book 23, then the first lion-simile, delivered by Menelaus to Telemachus (4.335–40), provides another technique of linking family members through simile. This first lion-simile is one of only two repeated similes in the *Odyssey*, and it is very significant that when it is repeated it is in the mouth of Telemachus, who quotes to his mother what he had heard from Menelaus (17.126–31).³⁰ Telemachus shuttles between his mother—the object of a lion-simile herself—and the person who had provided a lion-simile for his father. Cumulatively, these key similes, by pairing up the various focal members of the family and by providing an extended filigree of connection among them throughout the text, are a dynamic element of the larger themes of family likeness that structure the epic as a whole.³¹

### III. Lucretius' *De Rerum Natura*

After the *Odyssey*'s distinctive commitment to its own brand of likeness and similarity, let us return to the mainstream of epic similitude, to follow up the *Iliad*'s deep interest in the paradigms of order and disorder. Virgil's *Aeneid* is our goal, but before arriving there we must consider the first simile of Lucretius' *De Rerum Natura*, which has a great impact on the subsequent epic tradition.³²

---

²⁸ Podlecki (1971), 84; Moulton (1977), 123–4; S. West in Heubeck, West and Hainsworth (1988), 242.
²⁹ On the power of this reverse simile, identifying the experiences of Penelope and Odysseus, see Podlecki (1971), 89–90; Moulton (1977), 129–30; Foley (1978), 24–6; J.J. Winkler (1990), 161.
³⁰ The other repeated simile in the *Odyssey* comes in the repeated passages describing how Athena restores Odysseus to his normal state on the beach in Phaeacia (6.232–5) and after the slaughter of the suitors (23.159–62); see Moulton (1977), 119.
³¹ Ready (2011), 10 acutely observes how different the similes of the *Odyssey* are from those of the *Iliad*, where competitive dynamics are very important: 'many extended similes in the *Odyssey*'s narrator-text rehearse the interconnectedness of the poem's actors'. He attributes this feature to the fact that 'Odysseus has no human competitors in the *Odyssey*', unlike the situation in the *Iliad*, with its many competing peers. Our approaches are complementary, rather than exclusive.
³² I skip over the only surviving first simile in epic between Homer and Lucretius, the fascinating moment in Apollonius' *Argonautica* where Jason's mother Alcimede weeps at his departure like

Lucretius' first simile is part of an extended passage proving the existence of the invisible atoms, with his basic point being that we should not conclude that atoms do not exist just because we cannot see them (1.265–70). There are forces in the world which demonstrably exist even if we cannot see them, and his example is the wind, which can have a visibly catastrophic impact despite being itself invisible. This image of the wind beating the sea and devastating the land parallels Homer's first paired similes of storm on sea and land in *Iliad* 2 (144–9), although in Lucretius the material of the Homeric simile has now become the content of the description of nature (1.271–9):

> Principio uenti uis uerberat incita pontum
> ingentisque ruit nauis et nubila differt,
> interdum rapido percurrens turbine campos
> arboribus magnis sternit montisque supremos
> siluifragis vexat flabris: ita perfurit acri                    275
> cum fremitu saeuitque minaci murmure uentus.
> sunt igitur uenti nimirum corpora caeca,
> quae mare, quae terras, quae denique nubila caeli
> uerrunt ac subito uexantia turbine raptant . . .

> First of all the whipped-up power of the wind whacks the ocean and flattens huge ships and scatters the clouds, and racing over the plains with snatching whirlwind it strews them with great trees and harries the tops of the mountains with wood-smashing blasts: with such keen growling it rages and howls with threatening grumbling, the wind.[33] There exist, therefore, without doubt, invisible bodies of wind, which scour the sea, the lands, even the clouds of the sky and snatch them along, harrying them with sudden whirlwind . . .

At this point he shifts into an analogy, one of his favoured argumentative techniques.[34] The analogy illustrates his argument about the wind by

---

a little girl crying with her arms around the neck of her nurse, victimised by her stepmother (1.269–77). It is as if Apollonius is playing with our expectation that something of more cosmic weight should be presented, which he duly provides just over two-hundred lines later, with Orpheus' cosmogony (1.496–511): in a poem where the serious and the un-serious are so confused, it is piquant that the grand cosmogony is itself a false lead. There are those who think that the first simile that happens to survive from Ennius' *Annales*—comparing the crowd awaiting the twins' augury contest to the later Roman crowd awaiting the start of the chariot races in the Circus Maximus (79–83 Sk.)—may have been the epic's first simile: see P. Hardie (2010), 27, reporting a lecture by A. Barchiesi. It is certainly possible; my own guess would be that Ennius marked the fall of Troy with the poem's first developed simile, one of storm, or fire, or torrent, or falling tree.

[33] The word order is artificial in English but attempts to capture the surprise effect of the postponement of the word *uentus* (276), whose presence is not grammatically necessary: all of this devastation is being done by something apparently insubstantial.

[34] Schrijvers (1978); Schiesaro (1990), 21–5 on this passage.

referring to another natural force which has an analogous impact on the environment, and which can be seen—a river in flood (1.280–2):

> ... nec ratione fluunt alia stragemque propagant        280
> et cum mollis aquae fertur natura repente
> flumine abundanti ...
>
> ... nor do they [the invisible bodies of wind] flow or wreak their havoc in any other way than when the soft nature of water is carried along in a suddenly overflowing stream ...

Lucretius develops the vision of the river in flood with great energy over the next eight lines, describing the devastation it inflicts on woods and bridges and rocks. Once we have this vivid picture in our minds, he returns to the wind, and at this point he finally turns his scientific analogy into the overt form of a simile, which has so far been avoided, and which strictly need never have been used, as he says that the blasts of the invisible wind are *like* a strong stream (1.290–97):[35]

> sic igitur debent uenti quoque flamina ferri,              290
> quae *ueluti ualidum* cum *flumen* procubuere
> quamlibet in partem, trudunt res ante ruuntque
> impetibus crebris, interdum uertice torto
> corripiunt rapideque rotanti turbine portant.
> quare etiam atque etiam sunt uenti corpora caeca,         295
> quandoquidem factis et moribus aemula magnis
> amnibus inueniuntur, aperto corpore qui sunt.
>
> Like this, therefore, must the blasts of wind also be carried, which when *like a powerful stream* they have plunged in whatever direction, they shove things in front and they flatten them with repeated assaults, sometimes they snatch them up in a twisted eddy and rapidly carry them in a whirling spin. Wherefore, there absolutely do exist bodies of wind, invisible, since in their impact and behaviour we find them to rival mighty rivers which have a body openly visible to all.

This is a novel kind of simile, comparing one force of nature to another force of nature, instead of comparing a hero to a force of nature, as Homer had done in his similes of a river in flood in the *Iliad*, the models for Lucretius' river in flood, where Diomedes and Ajax had been compared to raging rivers smashing down bridges and fences (5.87–94; 11.492–6).[36] The

---

[35] D. West (1970), 274 and Schindler (2000), 89 both place the beginning of the simile too early, at *nec ratione alia* (280), at which point the argument is still proceeding by analogy.

[36] On the models, see Schindler (2000), 78–9; P. Hardie (2009), 209.

wind and the water share fundamental natural characteristics, so that both the vehicle and the tenor are having their natures illuminated in the comparison.[37] In fact, in Lucretius we have a case with elements of identity as well as of similarity, since the wind and the river share many bodies. No entity is made up of one single kind of atom, as Lucretius explains in detail later in the first book: the same elements make up sky, sea, land, rivers, sun, fruits, trees and living things, with everything depending on the organisation and arrangement of the *primordia* (1.820–2; cf. 2.581–8). These two forces, then, will even have some *corpora caeca* in common, as Lucretius suggests with characteristic plays on the similarities of the words used to describe the motion both of wind and water: *fluunt* (280), *flumine* (282), *fluctibus* (289), *flamina* (290) and *flumen* (291).[38]

The traditional epic simile is here being harnessed to serve the purpose of a completely different kind of explanatory model. Yet Lucretius is nonetheless fully alive to the Homeric template of a programmatic opening simile sequence, and he emulates Homer by aiming for his own kind of programmatic effect, so that these lines are presented 'as a showpiece, even as a programme, of Lucretian art'.[39] The *Iliad*'s programmatic sequence used similes from nature to chart the fluctuations between order and chaos in the unprecedented social organisation of the Achaean host: Lucretius, at first glance, appears to have pressed down on one side of the balance by using his programmatic sequence of analogy and simile to present a devastating image of chaos and destruction, taking over Homer's similes of chaotic storm in order to do so. Within the larger context of the opening sequence, however, this programmatic image of chaos is the second part of a diptych, for immediately before the wind/water analogy/simile Lucretius has given us an extended description of harmonious growth, with the birth of new vegetation and new animals (1.250–64).[40] The two aspects of nature, the creative and the destructive, complement each other, since to the

---

[37] Important discussions in P. Hardie (1986), 220–1; Schindler (2000), 81–3; cf. Gale (2007), 62. As Gale (1994), 64 points out in connection with the close identity of the wind and water in this passage, it was Empedocles, Lucretius' main poetic model, who pioneered didactic similes which 'point out analogies between processes which are essentially similar': see Sedley (1989), 277 on Lucretius' debt to Empedocles for this aspect of his technique, with reference to our passage.
[38] Friedländer (1941), 18; D. West (1970), 274; P.M. Brown (1984) on 280 and 290–1. For similar identification of wind and water, see 6.142–4, 367.
[39] P. Hardie (2009), 209 n.101, describing 1.265–328; cf. P. Hardie (1986), 182–3 on the programmatic function of 1.271–97.
[40] On the creative/destructive diptych effect in these lines, see P. Hardie (1986), 182–3; Gale (1994), 114 n.61.

Epicurean they are indissolubly part of the same natural processes: without death there can be no new birth (1.262–4; 2.569–80).[41]

It is clearly important, then, that this programmatic image of chaos is counter-balanced by the immediately preceding image of harmony, with the two together giving an overall image of the cycles of nature. Yet there is a strong persistence to the programmatically catastrophic power of the storm of wind and water, as captured in the poem's first simile, and we may observe this persistence at two levels, the microcosmic and the macrocosmic.

At the microcosmic level, the opening evocation of the power of chaotic storm has an enduring effect throughout the poem because the reality of atomic physics means that the order of Lucretius' universe is ultimately grounded in chaos. The emphatic line which concludes the entire proof of the existence of invisible bodies sums up the previous sixty lines with a telling pun, where *caecis* means both 'invisible' and also 'blind, purposeless': *corporibus caecis igitur natura gerit res* ('Nature therefore carries on affairs by means of invisible/blind bodies', 1.328). According to the challenging vision of Epicurean physics, order and predictability at the level of the senses emerge from chaotic unpredictability at the atomic level, where we can imagine nothing but the purposeless and undirected buffetings of the atoms, which are generated ultimately by the randomness of the 'swerve' (*clinamen*).[42] The swerve occurs 'at an uncertain time and in uncertain places' (*incerto tempore ... /incertisque locis*, 2.218–19), 'neither in a certain area of place nor at a certain time' (*nec regione loci certa nec tempore certo*, 2.293). As a result, the atoms are in constantly restless motion (2.95–132), and Lucretius regularly suggests a paradoxical analogy between the atoms' perpetual *error* (2.132) or lack of *quies* (2.95) and the fate awaiting human beings who fail to understand the truth about sub-sensory reality. As student-philosophers we will achieve *quies* only if we acknowledge that there is no *quies* at the atomic level: 'It is the central atomist paradox, that certain knowledge of the endless motion of the atoms brings ἀταραξία.'[43] Like the people who do not understand celestial phenomena at the beginning of Book 6, who 'are carried along wandering

---

[41] On the 'cycle of growth and decay' see Gale (1994), 70–1. From this point of view, the cycle of creation and destruction described in the whole sequence of 1.250–328 is a development of the symbolism evoked in the opening iconic image of Mars and Venus (1.29–40); see Gale (1994), 70–2, 220: '*Venus genetrix* and Mavors/*mors* together represent *natura creatrix et perfica* (cf. 2.1116 f.).'

[42] On the challenge represented by the apparent 'reductionism' of atomic physics, see Wardy (1988); on the *clinamen*, see D. Fowler (2002), 301–10 (on 2.216–93).

[43] D. Fowler (2002), 176.

in their blind way of reasoning' (*errantes caeca ratione feruntur*, 6.67), we will wander in blindness unless we grasp that the constituent elements of matter are always wandering in blindness.[44]

Out of this microcosmic chaos, in a way that Lucretius aims to explain to us over the course of his first two books, fixed patterns of certitude and predictability in the life-cycle do emerge, and at this upper level all the language of un-certainty has its prefix removed. There are, for example, no Centaurs or tree-born men or Chimaeras, Lucretius tells us, and his explanation plays with the common elements of the words for 'certain', 'create', 'mother' and 'grow' (2.707–10):

> ... omnia quando
> seminibus *cert*is *cert*a gene*tric*e *cre*ata
> conseruare genus *cresc*entia posse uidemus.
> scilicet id *cert*a fieri ratione necessust.                   710

> ... since all things, created from certain seeds from a certain mother, we see to be able to preserve their genus as they grow. Definitely it must be that this happens on the basis of a certain rationale.[45]

Again, this certainty of Epicurean physics is based on a fundamental randomness, which is one reason why the first simile is an appropriate programmatic emblem, because here we see the massive uncontrollable power of natural forces, existing in their own realm with no relation to us, as wholly independent entities with their own kind of patterns. If the first simile is an emblem of nature out of control, we are encouraged to reflect that it is natural for nature to be out of control.

At the macrocosmic level, the sheerly destructive impact of the storm-wind also remains a potent image all the way through the poem, for it captures the 'magnificence of the forces of the atomist universe' and also stands for the aspects of the natural world which are most likely to be 'a potential stimulus to superstition': as a result, the opening analogy and simile sequence of chaotic wind and water 'has a programmatic function,

---

[44] So Wardy (1988), 123 on the beginning of Book 2: 'Lucretius' depiction of ordinary, vainly ambitious people from the philosopher's point of view daringly compares them to atoms, as they wander (10 *errare, palantis*; cf. 132) and fight (11 *certare, contendere*; cf. 118–20). From that supreme vantage-point non-Epicureans appear to be caught up in utterly senseless, random turmoil, as purposeless as atomic collisions. *O pectora caeca!* (14)—*o corpora caeca!*'

[45] Cf. 1.167–73 (with another pun, this time on *secreta*, from *secerno*, etymologically linked with *certus*: see P.M. Brown (1984) ad loc.); 3.445–6 (with a pun on *crescere* and *senescere*); 3.547–52, 615–23, 746–7, 787, 794–5; 5.916–24, 1436–9. On these various puns and their import, see Snyder (1980), 38–9, 137–9.

foreshadowing later treatments of natural catastrophe on both the large and the small scale'.[46]

In general terms at the macroscopic level, the universe exhibits a continual state of strife among its constituent members, in such a way that the ultimate destruction of the universe in its currently constituted form is certain (5.380–3):

> Denique tantopere inter se cum maxima mundi 380
> pugnent membra, pio nequaquam concita bello,
> nonne uides aliquam longi certaminis ollis
> posse dari finem?
>
> Finally, since the large-scale components of the world fight among themselves to such an extent, stirred up in a war that is by no means a holy war, don't you see that they can be given some end of their long strife?

The same metaphor of a war between the components of the universe is found elsewhere (2.573–6):

> sic aequo geritur certamine principiorum
> ex infinito contractum tempore bellum.
> nunc hic nunc illic superant uitalia rerum
> et superantur item.
>
> So is war waged on the basis of an equal struggle of the elements, fought from time without beginning. Now here, now there, the life forces of the universe overcome and then in turn are overcome.

In particular, the catastrophic power of wind is consistently Lucretius' favoured possibility for the end of the *mundus* as we know it.[47] This might take the form of a colossal hurricane from outside the *mundus*, which could cause the collapse of this sum of things with a violent whirlwind (*neque autem corpora desunt/ex infinito quae possint forte coorta/corruere hanc rerum uiolento turbine summam*, 5.366–8). More commonly, it might be the winds beneath our feet, in subterranean caverns, which could tear the world apart. If the subterranean winds did not blow back in a different direction in their intermittent rampages, then no power would rein things in and check them from destruction as they moved (*quod nisi respirent uenti, uis nulla refrenet/res neque ab exitio possit reprehendere euntis*, 6.568–9; cf. 5.104–9). A vivid picture of the fear aroused by the rampaging of subterranean winds comes in Book 6 (577–607), a passage culminating

---

[46] P. Hardie (1986), 182, 183.  [47] Ibid., 92–3, 181, 187–9.

in an evocation of the terror felt during an earthquake by people who casually assume the world will last for ever (6.601–7):

> proinde licet quamuis caelum terramque reantur
> incorrupta fore aeternae mandata saluti:
> et tamen interdum praesens uis ipsa pericli
> subdit et hunc stimulum quadam de parte timoris,
> ne pedibus raptim tellus subtracta feratur       605
> in barathrum rerumque sequatur prodita summa
> funditus et fiat mundi confusa ruina.

> So then, they may think as much as they like that the heaven and earth will be indestructible, consigned to safety for ever—still, now and then, the actual present force of danger applies even this goad of fear from one direction or another, lest the earth, suddenly taken away from under their feet, be carried into the abyss, and the sum of things, left in the air from the bottom up, should follow and the world become a jumbled ruin.

The winds, then, will probably overpower our cosmos in the end. For an Epicurean, who can manage a series of perspectival shifts from the infinitesimal to the infinite, the destruction of our universe by colossal storm-winds is no final moment of annihilation. The end of the cosmos may look like a terrifying and conclusive victory for the forces of chaos and destruction, but if you take the long-term Epicurean view, then the end of our universe is only a very large-scale dissolution of a compound body, one that, like all dissolutions of compound bodies, will return the constituent parts to the available sum of matter, ready for new compounds and new forms.[48]

The threat to cosmic order posed by the annihilating power of the storm-wind was, of course, part of Hesiodic myth, embodied in particular in the opponent of Zeus, Typhoeus.[49] In a manner first analysed by the pioneering study of P. Hardie, Lucretius has taken over the prevalent scholarly allegorising readings of such mythic narratives in terms of natural philosophy, but he has 'demythologised' the content completely, retaining the physics and jettisoning the fable.[50] In his turn, Virgil will use his programmatic opening simile sequence to 'remythologise' the power of the catastrophic winds of Lucretius, as we shall now see.[51]

---

[48] Ibid., 189; D. Fowler (2002), 155: 'only the *summa summarum* as τὸ πᾶν, the whole infinite universe, is really immortal'.
[49] Comprehensive discussion in P. Hardie (1986), 95–7.
[50] Ibid., 91, 211–13, with 178 and 181 on Lucretius' 'demythologisation'; Gale (1994), 185–9.
[51] P. Hardie (1986), 178, 182 on 'remythologisation'.

## IV. Virgil's *Aeneid*

Before we enter the *Aeneid*, we note that the first simile in Virgil's poem of nature already shows him engaging with Lucretius' first simile, as he rows hard upstream against the mighty river of Lucretius (*G.* 1.199–203).[52] The blind river of Lucretian nature will sweep Virgil away if he releases his grip, in an image of the constant effort required to create and maintain the human world of the *Georgics*, so distinctively different from that of the *De Rerum Natura*. Virgil's immediate context is the importance of keeping up the relentless work of selecting the right seeds—*semina*, a word regularly used by Lucretius to describe his atoms (e.g., 1.501, 2.773), and explicitly introduced early in his first book as one of a range of terms he will use for the atoms (1.58–61, together with *materiem, genitalia corpora, corpora prima*). In a pointed play on Lucretius' opening proof of the existence of invisible bodies as manifested in the wind, Virgil begins his programmatic simile sequence with an emphatic declaration that the seeds in his poem are ones you can see: *semina uidi equidem* ... ('I have seen seeds ... ', *G.* 1. 193).[53] No matter how much force you exert in this unremitting work of selection, he goes on to say, degeneration is always possible, as he resumes with yet more emphasis on his seeing of the seeds (*G.* 1.197–203):[54]

> uidi lecta diu et multo spectata labore
> degenerare tamen, ni uis humana quotannis
> maxima quaeque manu legeret: sic omnia fatis
> in peius ruere ac retro sublapsa referri,                200
> non aliter quam qui aduerso uix flumine lembum
> remigiis subigit, si bracchia forte remisit,
> atque illum in praeceps prono rapit alueus amni.

I have seen seeds chosen over time and checked with much labour nonetheless degenerate, if human force weren't picking out all the biggest ones by hand every year: in this way all things, by fate, plunge to the worse, slide down and are carried backwards, just as with a person who rows his craft with difficulty upstream, if he happens to relax his effort, and the current snatches him headlong downstream.

---

[52] Note that he has already, before this first simile, treated the *matter* of Homeric simile, but transferred the terms, turning the illustrative everyday vehicle of *Il.* 21.257–62 into the reality of his own poem's tenor (*G.* 1.104–10): Ross (1987), 51; R.F. Thomas (1988), 1.84; Farrell (1991), 211–13. As we have seen, this is exactly what Lucretius had done, turning Homer's opening similes of storm-wind into his own description of storm-wind.

[53] As the sentence continues, it springs a surprise on the reader, demanding a readjustment: *semina uidi equidem multos medicare serentis* ('I have seen *many sowers treating* seeds').

[54] For discussions of the overall context of the simile, see Gale (2000), 81–2; Schindler (2000), 203–4.

Lucretius' programmatic destructive river in spate appears at the end of the first book of the *Georgics* in the guise of the Po, roiling woods in its insane whirl, carrying along flocks, stables and all, all over the plains (*proluit insano contorquens uertice siluas/fluuiorum rex Eridanus camposque per omnis/cum stabulis armenta tulit*, *G.* 1.481–3). There the river in spate is part of a series of natural catastrophes responding to the assassination of Caesar, a graphic portrayal of a world in chaos, culminating in a simile which looks back to the first simile as it conjures up a yet more frightening image of humans' inability to maintain control over their world (*G.* 1.511–14):[55]

> saeuit toto Mars impius orbe,
> ut cum carceribus sese effudere quadrigae,
> addunt in spatia, et frustra retinacula tendens
> fertur equis auriga neque audit currus habenas.

> Unholy Mars goes mad over the whole globe, as when the chariots have poured out of the starting-gates, they speed on the laps, and, hanging uselessly onto the reins, the charioteer is carried along by his horses and the chariot does not respond to his control.

The first simile of the *Georgics*, as part of an overarching pattern within the first book leading up to its final simile, serves to focus the poem's concerns about the limits of human ability to impose order on the world of nature and of politics. These concerns return in the first simile of the *Aeneid*. Here the initial patterns both of Homer and of Lucretius come together to form the *Aeneid*'s opening sequences of similitude and comparison, as Aeneas and the Trojans face the potentially annihilating power of Juno's storm, aroused by the winds unleashed at Aeolus' command (*Aen.* 1.50–156).

Virgil inverts the order of Homer's opening similes. Homer's second, third, fourth and fifth similes, together with their wider context, are amalgamated into Virgil's first simile, while Homer's first simile, comparing men to bees, becomes Virgil's second simile.[56] Virgil's bees are imported from the descriptive reality of his own Fourth *Georgic*, where their applicability to human society had been more oblique; in the *Aeneid*'s second simile they provide a comparison for the sight presented to Aeneas and Achates when they look down on the happy Carthaginians

---

[55] On the responsion between the two similes, see R.F. Thomas (1988), 1.102, 154; Farrell (1991), 167–8. On the many echoes in the *Aeneid* of this mighty storm at the end of *Georgics* 1, see Briggs (1980), 81–91.
[56] Lausberg (1983), 219; Schmit-Neuerburg (1999), 71–2.

working away building their new city (*Aen.* 1.430–6 ≈ *G.* 4.162–9).[57] The order and harmony of the Carthaginians exemplify to perfection the ideal of social cohesion so admired by the ancients in the bees' community, and this order is apparently in strong contrast with the chaotic turmoil of wind and sea in the opening sequence;[58] yet the contrast is ironic, for these Carthaginian bees are very soon to be faced with bee colony collapse disorder following the death of the queen, after sex has been introduced, in the person of Aeneas, into the idealised sex-less life of the bees as represented in the Fourth *Georgic* (4.197–205).[59] As so often, Virgil is reading out of features already detectable in Homer, for Homer's bee-simile, as we have seen, is itself somewhat ironic in its idealising image of the Achaeans' social cohesion.

The storm begun at Juno's initiative unleashes the titanic winds of Lucretius in order to destroy the *cosmos*, the *cosmos* of the Roman *imperium*, before it has even started. As P. Hardie has finely demonstrated, the winds confined in Aeolus' vast cavern evoke at every point the potentially world-destroying winds which, as we saw above, so frequently figure in Lucretius' *De Rerum Natura*: if the winds were not confined by Aeolus under the providential order of Jupiter, we are told, *maria ac terras caelumque profundum/quippe ferant rapidi secum uerrantque per auras* ('they would snatch up and carry off seas and lands and the deep heaven and sweep them through the air', *Aen.* 1.58–9).[60] This was the likely end that Lucretius foresaw awaiting our universe, as the result of entirely natural forces, but Virgil is now restoring the mythic dimension to the paradigm of order and chaos that had been stripped away by Lucretius.[61] Here we see the next turn in the sine-curve pattern of epic literary history charted by Hardie: Homer and Hesiod mythologise, Lucretius demythologises, Virgil remythologises—and, as we shall see, Lucan re-demythologises. It is immensely important to Virgil to capture and then to rewrite Lucretius' vision, in line with the *Aeneid*'s need to assert

---

[57] Briggs (1980), 72 on this switch in perspective, so characteristic—as he shows throughout—of the transposition of narrative and simile world between *Georgics* and *Aeneid*.
[58] Schmit-Neuerburg (1999), 71–2.
[59] Briggs (1980), 72–5; Schmit-Neuerburg (1999), 71; cf. Polleichtner (2005), 138–45, concentrating on the proleptic function of the bee-simile within the whole Carthaginian narrative. On the various theories of bee reproduction, see B. Wilson (2004), chapter 2, 'Sex'. Virgil of course represents the ruler of the bees as a *rex* in the Fourth *Georgic*, even though some ancient opinion had it that the queen was indeed a queen: see M. Davies and Kathirithamby (1986), 62.
[60] P. Hardie (1986), 93, comparing these lines to Lucr. 1.277–9; cf. P. Hardie (1986), 180–3 and 237–40, 'Appendix: Lucretian parallels for Virgil's cave of the winds (*Aeneid* 1. 52–53, 81–83)'.
[61] P. Hardie (1986), 93, 181.

that a providential world-order can be maintained, despite everything that Lucretius claimed.

When Aeolus lets loose the winds in response to Juno's approaches, we meet the poem's first simile, as the winds rush on *uelut agmine facto* ('as if having formed a column', *Aen.* 1.82).[62] Virgil has observed that Homer presents such mini-similes before the first developed one, and he follows suit, characteristically condensing into a single mini-simile the three mini-similes that Homer deploys before his first developed one.[63] Further, even in this short phrase, Virgil is anticipating the reversal of terms that will follow on a much larger scale in the first developed simile, for with this military metaphor for the movement of the winds a natural force is compared to a human one, instead of the other way around, as is regular in epic.

After the storm and its impact on the Trojan fleet have been described (1.84–123), Neptune notices the chaos, and emerges to set things right (124–30). He upbraids the winds, and restores calm (131–47). The whole run of this action of Neptune's is then captured in the poem's first simile, in which the impact of the god upon the natural elements is compared to the impact of a statesman upon a rioting mob (*Aen.* 1.148–56):

> ac ueluti magno in populo cum saepe coorta est
> seditio saeuitque animis ignobile uulgus
> iamque faces et saxa uolant, furor arma ministrat;     150
> tum, pietate grauem ac meritis si forte uirum quem
> conspexere, silent, arrectisque auribus astant;
> ille regit dictis animos et pectora mulcet:
> sic cunctus pelagi cecidit fragor, aequora postquam
> prospiciens genitor caeloque inuectus aperto     155
> flectit equos curruque uolans dat lora secundo.

> And as in a great people when regularly civil discord has broken out and the base mob is going mad with passion, and now torches and rocks are flying—frenzy supplies the weapons; then, if by chance they catch sight of some man, impressive in his pious virtue and his achievements, they are silent, and they stand still with ears pricked; he rules their passions with his words, and strokes their chests/minds: thus did the whole crashing uproar of the sea subside, after the father turned his horses, looking out over the seas and riding under the unclouded heaven, and flying along behind in his chariot gave his horses their head.

---

[62] P. Hardie (2010), 19 notes the military metaphor here, which anticipates the way that the first simile and its context track the martial nature of Homer's assembly in *Iliad* 2.
[63] Hornsby (1970), 20.

Servius already pointed out the connection with Homer's initial similes, in his comment on 1.148:

> iste tempestati populi motum comparat,[64] Tullius populo tempestatem: *pro Milone* [§5] equidem 'ceteras tempestates et procellas in illis dumtaxat fluctibus contionum'. [Servius auctus:] *ita et Homerus seditioni tempestatem* κινήθη δ' ἀγορὴ ὡς κύματα μακρὰ θαλάσσης [*Il.* 2.144].

> *He* compares the turmoil of the people to a storm, Cicero compares the storm to the people: *pro Milone* [§5] 'the other storms and hurricanes just in those waves of the meetings of the people'. [Servius auctus:] *Homer too compares a storm to discord, 'and the meeting was stirred like the great waves of the sea'* [*Il.* 2.144].

Servius also points out the reversal of terms which has so caught the attention of modern critics, even though he initially quotes Cicero, before Homer, to make the point: in Homer (and in Cicero) human action is compared to natural forces, whereas in Virgil natural and divine forces are compared to human action.[65] This reversal of terms is crucial to the programmatic power of the first simile, which, as part of an overall narrative of the restoration of calm after chaos, sets up an ideal template for political action in the poem and its empire.[66] In Homer's case, the concord threatened by disruption is illustrated by reference to the natural world; in the *Aeneid*, the natural world is itself one of the arenas for the establishment of concord, in a hyperbolic vision of a Roman Empire which is fused with the world of nature, overcoming the threats of chaos within a providential order.[67]

The allusions and references in the simile are very dense.[68] J. Henry first pointed to the significance of an iconic moment at the beginning of Hesiod's *Theogony* (81–93), where the good king walks among the quarrelling people and settles their arguments, exemplifying the powers of social concord that are ideally embodied in the Muses, the poet, and the ideal orator.[69] The figure of Augustus is regularly seen as evoked here, not least in light of his self-identification as the favourite of Neptune in his victory

---

[64] The direction of comparison is, interestingly, focalised by Servius in the reverse direction to ours: but the difference between Virgil's and Cicero's (or Homer's) direction is clear.
[65] On this reversal see, e.g., Austin (1971), 68.
[66] Pöschl (1962), 13–24 on how the opening storm sequence (*Aen.* 1.8–296) 'contains in essence all forces which constitute the whole' (24); Otis (1963), 227–35; P. Hardie (1986), 176–83, 204–5; S.J. Harrison (1988), 55; Cairns (1989), 93–4; Beck (2014).
[67] P. Hardie (1986), 223.
[68] Well stressed in Beck (2014), a valuable discussion of the main issues of the simile.
[69] Henry (1873–92), 1.427; fully argued in S.J. Harrison (1988); see Thalmann (1984), 140–1, 179 on the Hesiodic themes.

over Sextus Pompeius in Sicily.⁷⁰ Scholars have suggested various specific historical points of reference, especially a famous moment in Cato's praetorship in 54 BCE, when he stopped the shouting in a riot with his mere appearance and went on to lull the crowd with his speech (Plut. *Cat. Min.* 44.3–4);⁷¹ other candidates for the Republican statesman who soothes the mob with his rhetoric are Menenius Agrippa or M. Popillius Laenas.⁷²

It is in the end misguided to press too hard for an identification with one particular individual or episode, given the generalising and paradigmatic nature of the simile;⁷³ yet the atmosphere of the Roman Republic is unmistakable, picked out with such key items of Republican political discourse as *populo* (148), *seditio* (149) and *uulgus* (149). In general, the first simile 'harks back to the power attributed to the orator in republican culture'.⁷⁴ Cicero's Isocratean descriptions of the ideal power of the orator refer to the historical significance of rhetoric's ability to lift brutish human society above the level of the beasts.⁷⁵ Virgil certainly capitalises on such conceptions in his characterisation of the winds and their human counterparts in the simile as animals, specifically horses: Aeolus controls the winds with reins (*habenas*, 63) and they have their 'ears pricked' in the simile (*arrectis auribus*, 152);⁷⁶ Aeolus has the power to 'stroke' the sea with the wind (*mulcere*, 66), while the statesman in the simile 'strokes the chests/soothes the minds' of the crowd (*pectora mulcet*, 152).⁷⁷ There is an interesting tension generated by the friction between the simile's strong Hesiodic monarchical intertext, channelled through evocations of Augustus, and its strongly Republican atmosphere: is the statesman here walking in the footsteps of a Greek king or is he a Roman *nobilis*?⁷⁸ The simile hovers between Republic and Principate, capturing the interstitial nature of the Roman state at the time of composition.

---

⁷⁰ Galinsky (1996), 21–3.   ⁷¹ Conway (1935), on *Aen.* 1.148–53; S.J. Harrison (1988), 55–6.
⁷² Morwood (1998) (Menenius Agrippa); Galinsky (1996), 21 (Popillius Laenas).
⁷³ Galinsky (1996), 21: 'the simile's applicability is broader than an identification with any specific Roman leader'.
⁷⁴ Spence (2002), 50.
⁷⁵ In particular, Cic. *Inv. rhet.* 1.2, adduced by Spence (1988), 15 and (2002), 50; cf. the praise of the power of the good orator in *De or.* 1.30–5.
⁷⁶ Spence (2002), 49.
⁷⁷ Bartsch (1998), 330, with discussion of the idealised power of oratory to soothe the bestial; cf. Bartsch (1998), 323 on the first simile as raising the question: 'Is it art that soothes the savage beast?' My thanks to Stephen Harrison and Antony Smith for discussion of this imagery, and of the simile in general.
⁷⁸ S.J. Harrison (1988), 58 (a neat and Virgilian irony); P. Hardie (2010), 19 ('Irony, or the deliberate elision of the difference beween Republic and Principate?').

In the context of the simile's interest in the rhetoric of Republican Rome, Servius' mention of Cicero in his initial comment on Virgil's simile turns out not to be the red herring it might initially look like. Servius cites Cicero for his use of imagery of sea storm to describe civic discord, and Cicero's fondness for imagery of civic storm is indeed marked.[79] In more general terms, however, Cicero's wistful conjurings of the power of rhetoric over violence are part of the background noise in this simile. In the *Brutus*, for example, in the aftermath of the victory of Julius Caesar over Pompey the Great, Cicero looks back to the build-up to the war, lamenting the failure of peaceful persuasion by a good citizen to carry the day (*Brut.* 7):[80]

> quod si fuit in re publica tempus ullum, cum extorquere arma posset e manibus iratorum ciuium boni ciuis auctoritas et oratio, tum profecto fuit, cum patrocinium pacis exclusum est aut errore hominum aut timore.
>
> But if there ever was a time in the state, when the authority and speech of a good citizen could have wrested the weapons from the hands of his enraged fellow-citizens, it was then when the advocacy of peaceful measures was ruled out by men's blundering or fear.

The idealised nature of the power of rhetoric in Virgil's simile is rather poignant in this light, given that Cicero is here acknowledging that the power of persuasion that he had celebrated from the beginning of his career did not in the end win out over the madness of armed violence.

Through all of these various echoes, however, Homer remains the crucial intertext, for an entire Homeric episode is being activated here, with the opening similes of the *Iliad* as its armature. We have sea-storm and wind, a gathering in an uproar, with order being provisionally restored by the oratory and authority of an outstanding individual. Virgil is responding to the way Homer has charted out his political coordinates in this single passage, using his similes strategically in order to do so. For him, Homer's epic will be the original political document, and his own epic has to respond by engaging with the patterns of order and the threats to order which this foundational text established. Further, his reworking of Homer

---

[79] Austin (1971), 68 refers to the citation of Cic. *Clu.* 138 in the discussion of Virgil's first simile in Heinze (1915), 206 n.1 (Austin tacitly corrects Heinze's mis-citation of '*Clu.* 130'); cf. e.g. Cic. *Inv. rhet.* 1.4.

[80] Cf. *Off.* 1.77, where Cicero quotes his notorious verse *cedant arma togae, concedat laurea laudi*, and goes on to cite his suppression of the Catilinarian conspiracy: *ita consiliis diligentiaque nostra celeriter de manibus audacissimorum ciuium delapsa arma ipsa ceciderunt* ('in this way, through my planning and care, their very weapons slipped swiftly from the hands of totally reckless citizens and fell to the ground').

has been blended with his reworking of Lucretius, whose patterns of natural chaos are so threatening to the order he wishes to establish in his poem: in the opening sequence of his epic Virgil is building upon his work with Lucretius in the *Georgics*, so as to develop further his conceptions of the peculiar nature of human control over the world.

Virgil will have been reading this opening Homeric sequence in the light of centuries of political theory which regularly took Homer as a starting point in the investigation of the nature of political power;[81] the commentaries which accompanied Virgil's readings of Homer were themselves deeply influenced by such currents of thought.[82] Odysseus' aphorism as he berates the mob and drives them back to the assembly—οὐκ ἀγαθὸν πολυκοιρανίη· εἷς κοίρανος ἔστω,/εἷς βασιλεύς ('it's not a good thing to have lots of leaders; let there be one leader, one king', *Il.* 2.204–5)—became a famous tag: οὐκ ἀγαθὸν πολυκοιρανίη is the only verse of Homer that Theophrastus' character of the Oligarch knows off by heart (*Char.* 26.2); Aristotle read the verse as a condemnation of democracy (*Pol.* 1292a13–15); while a former teacher and confidant of young Caesar, Areius, quoted to him these words with his own twist when Caesar was deliberating what to do with the son of Julius Caesar and Cleopatra: οὐκ ἀγαθὸν πολυκαισαρίη ('it's not a good thing to have lots of Caesars', Plut. *Ant.* 81.2).[83] The scholiasts' comment on Odysseus' aphorism is utterly characteristic of their view of Homer as the original political philosopher: δογματίζει δὲ περὶ πολιτειῶν ('Homer is laying down the law on constitutional theory', bT 2.204).

In general, Homer was claimed as the first writer on political theory (Ps.-Plut., *De Vita et Poesi Homeri*, 176), with a full knowledge of such matters as the 'three-constitution' theory (ibid., 182). Specifically, as Schmit-Neuerburg has demonstrated in convincing detail, ancient commentators and writers on Homer interpreted the sequence of action surrounding the assembly in *Iliad* 2, together with its similes, as illustrating the dangers of disorder, discord and political upheaval: they insistently see Homer as espousing monarchy as the counter-measure to such threatened chaos.[84] Virgil's readings of such sources deeply inform his presentation of the authority of the statesman in his quelling of the riot, even as his whole

---

[81] Murray (1965) re-started the debate; cf. Cairns (1989), 10–11; see S.J. Harrison (1988), 57–8 for similar philosophical interest in the 'good king in Hesiod' passage (*Theog.* 81–93).
[82] Very valuable discussion in Schmit-Neuerburg (1999), 66–74.
[83] My thanks to T.P. Wiseman for the Plutarch reference.   [84] Schmit-Neuerburg (1999), 66–74.

context takes the themes of harmony and discord to a cosmic level.[85] In the light of this pro-monarchical interpretative tradition, the tension with the idealising Republican atmosphere of the simile becomes even more powerful.

If Virgil's first simile, together with its larger context, holds up a programmatic template for the triumph of order over chaos, it remains to ask how far this template is realised in the action of the poem. Similes in general have slippage and lack of precise fit built into their operation, and Virgil's similes 'often juxtapose, undermine, or ironize the surrounding text'.[86] We are prompted to ask, 'When is a statesman *not* like a sea-god?' Just as in the *Iliad*, where the concord emblematised by the bee-simile is called into question by the fact that the Achaeans in Book 2 are manifestly not at that moment a harmonious social order, so too in the *Aeneid* the programmatic power of this opening simile is more fragile than it looks. Even within the immediate context, the idealised power of rhetoric can be read under an ironic guise, for it is not easy to pin down quite how the action of Neptune should be mapped on to the action of the simile.[87] If rhetoric is what achieves the result, then why does Neptune act 'more quickly than speech' (*dicto citius*, 1.142)? Virgil twice calls attention to Neptune's 'savage trident' (*saeuum ... tridentem*, 138; *tridenti*, 145); by reminding us of how Odysseus beat the mob into obedience with Agamemnon's sceptre, and by unveiling the violence that the god can always call upon to back up his words, Virgil may be suggesting that 'words by themselves may not be enough to quell the stormy passions of political life: force will be a necessary part of the equation'.[88]

As scholars have regularly observed, the poem is full of characters who try to live up to the ideal presented in the first simile, but who fail, finding that the quelling of discord through oratory is a lot harder to achieve than the first simile suggests.[89] As the first fighting breaks out in Latium in Book 7, the gradually mounting momentum of the conflict is caught with

---

[85] Well put by Schmit-Neuerburg (1999), 69: 'ἀταξία, die die antiken Erklärer durch das homerische Gleichnis verdeutlichen sahen, erscheint auch in der Aeneis als tiefere Ursache der Ereignisse in Natur- wie Menschenwelt.' See Cairns (1989), 85–7 on the contemporary Hor. *Epist*. 1.2, which has a strong interest in such readings of the politics of the *Iliad*.
[86] Spence (2002), 50.   [87] My thanks to Antony Smith for discussion of this point.
[88] Quint (2011), 291; cf. Spence (2002), 50.
[89] Lapidary formulation in Perret (1977), 11: 'pourtant jamais Énée n'aura occasion de s'imposer de la sorte'. Cf. R.O.A.M. Lyne (1987), 7 n.9, 28 n.55. Hine (1987), 177, citing Lyne, is of course quite right to stress that the ideal espoused in the first simile 'can be regarded as an ideal that must be striven for' even if it cannot be fully achieved. Bartsch (1998) importantly makes oratory, the most prominent Roman *ars*, part of the longstanding debate on the efficacy of art in the *Aeneid*.

a simile of storm, in a passage that inevitably recalls the storm of Book 1, but this time with tenor and vehicle restored to their 'right' relation, with human action compared to the natural world; and we see the failure of one Galaesus to quell the storm, despite his *iustitia* (*Aen.* 7.528–30, 535–7):[90]

> fluctus uti primo coepit cum albescere uento,
> paulatim sese tollit mare et altius undas
> erigit, inde imo consurgit ad aethera fundo ...                   530
> ... corpora multa uirum circa seniorque Galaesus,                 535
> dum paci medium se offert, iustissimus unus
> qui fuit Ausoniisque olim ditissimus aruis.

> As when a wave begins to go white under the first effect of the wind, the sea lifts itself up bit by bit and raises the waves higher, and next surges from the very bottom up to the sky ... There are many bodies of men around, including the elderly Galaesus, as he came forward as an intermediary for peace, who was uniquely just and once the richest in Ausonian plough-lands.

It is important that the conflict here is not one 'within a pre-existing community', as was the case in the simile in Book 1 ('in a great people', *magno in populo*, 1.148), but rather between two different political groups: the template of the poem's first simile is to that extent less applicable.[91] The same point applies in the final book of the poem, when Aeneas is given the chance to live up to the programmatically soothing power of the orator of the first simile, as he tries to calm the *discordia* that erupts over the broken truce (12.311–19); here too we have strife between two opposing sides, Trojans and Latins, rather than within one political entity. Soon after Galaesus is killed in Book 7, however, King Latinus attempts to withstand the storm of war and to be firm against the chaos of his citizenry. At first, his efforts look very promising (7.585–90):

> certatim regis circumstant tecta Latini.                          585
> ille uelut pelagi rupes immota resistit,
> ut pelagi rupes magno ueniente fragore,
> quae sese multis circum latrantibus undis
> mole tenet; scopuli nequiquam et spumea circum
> saxa fremunt laterique inlisa refunditur alga.                    590

---

[90] For the links back to Book 1, see Pöschl (1962), 31–3; Otis (1963), 327; Hornsby (1970), 27–9; the marked language of *primo ... uento* (7.528) may call attention to the reference back to the storm in Book 1. As stressed by S.J. Harrison (1985), 101–2, this simile is part of a chain of similes linking water and war-lust in this second beginning of the epic; note also 7.460–6 and 7.586–90; cf. Horsfall (2000), 381–2 on these links.

[91] I thank Antony Smith for this important observation about whether or not there is a 'pre-existing community' in place.

> They vie with each other to surround the palace of King Latinus. He, like an unmoved cliff of the sea, remained fixed, like a cliff of the sea when a great breaker comes, which maintains itself by its mass with many waves howling around it; in vain the boulders and foamy rocks howl around, and the seaweed dashed on its flank pours back.

But straight after this simile, suddenly he cracks (7.591–4):

> uerum ubi nulla datur caecum exsuperare potestas
> consilium et saeuae nutu Iunonis eunt res,
> multa deos aurasque pater testatus inanis:
> 'frangimur heu fatis' inquit 'ferimurque procella! ... '

> But when no power is granted him to overcome their blind purpose and events go on according to the nod of savage Juno, with many calls to the gods and the empty breezes as witnesses, he says, 'Alas, we are broken by the fates and we are carried along by the storm! ... '

Here the incompatability between simile and context is far more marked than in the case of the ironies that have been detected in the statesman-simile of Book 1. Latinus cannot live up to the role of the cliff in his own simile, any more than he can live up to the role of statesman in the first simile: 'Latinus is not a god of the sea; his people are not sea waves obedient to him.'[92] Nor can Latinus live up to the role of the jutting rock that Agamemnon fulfilled in *Iliad* 2 after the final restoration of order to the assembly of the Achaeans (2.394–7): there the isolated image of the headland surrounded by waves and winds evokes Agamemnon's new-found steadfastness, a steadfastness which Latinus cannot emulate.

If the iconic opening simile in the poem turns out to be a very difficult paradigm to live up to, we observe an actually opposing momentum in play in the poem, as Aeneas is increasingly identified with the titanesque forces of storm and wind that threatened his life and his project at the outset.[93] In his battle rampage after learning of the death of Pallas in Book 10, his frenzy is compared to that of a river in flood or a black whirlwind (*torrentis aquae uel turbinis atri/more furens*, 10.602–4). His climactic attack in Book 12 is like the onrush of a massive storm, bringing devastation from the sea to the trees and crops of the farmers (12.451–7).[94] His final victory over Turnus is achieved by his control of the forces of the storm-winds to which

---

[92] Hornsby (1970), 30.
[93] Important discussions in Hornsby (1970), 124–5; Briggs (1980), 90–1; P. Hardie (1986), 176–80.
[94] R.O.A.M. Lyne (1987), 5–8.

he was helplessly subject at the very beginning of the poem.⁹⁵ The last simile in the poem follows on two 'not-similes', and it loops back to the first simile in the poem, with Aeneas now the agent and not the victim of the storm, as he throws his spear (12.921–4):

> murali concita numquam
> tormento sic saxa fremunt, nec fulmine tanti
> dissultant crepitus. uolat atri turbinis instar
> exitium dirum hasta ferens . . .

> Rocks hurled from a siege catapult do not roar so much, nor do such great cracks flash from a thunderbolt: the spear flies like a black whirlwind bearing dread death . . .⁹⁶

Despite the power and appeal of the programmatic first simile, it turns out to be impossible to keep the categories of order and disorder, chaos and cosmos, tidily separate from each other. Aeneas is at once the victim and the agent of titanic power. Rhetoric is not enough to maintain ultimate control over the forces that threaten the *imperium*, and the forces that have to be mobilised to dominate those threats are going to be very hard to distinguish in kind from the threats themselves.⁹⁷

## V. Sequels

Later Latin epics continue to be enmeshed in this complex of ideas, and they continue to mobilise their first similes in order to set up their terms of debate over the roles and claims of certain kinds of order. Here I do no more than point to a couple of leading instances.

Ovid's *Metamorphoses* has the contest between order and disorder at its artistic and philosophical heart.⁹⁸ One of the first major developments in the poem is therefore Ovid's distinctive solution to the Lucretian and Virgilian titanic winds, showing that there will be control in this poem, but of a very different kind: instead of grouping all the winds together and confining them under a mountain like Virgil's Jupiter (*Aen.* 1.60–2), Ovid's creator-god disperses the winds to the four corners of the world

---

[95] A major theme first fully discussed in Hornsby (1970), 39, 43, 124–5; cf. Briggs (1980), 91; P. Hardie (1986), 176; Tarrant (2012) on *Aen.* 12.951, *soluuntur frigore membra*.
[96] See Tarrant (2012) ad loc. for the echo here of the 'black whirlwind' which Aeneas resembled in 10.603.
[97] Cf. R.O.A.M. Lyne (1983), 202–3 on the 'indivisibility of *uis*'.
[98] A major theme in Ovidian scholarship (see Barchiesi (2005b), CXXVIII–CXXIX); an important early statement in R. Brown (1987).

and then 'puts on top of them aether, clear and lacking in weight' (*haec super imposuit liquidum et grauitate carentem/aethera*, *Met.* 1.67–8).[99] The first simile in the poem builds on Virgil's first simile in order to set up an exaggerated version of the *Aeneid*'s 'statesman-simile'.[100] Virgil had used the realm of human politics to illustrate the providential natural order; now Ovid uses threatened chaos in the realm of human politics to illustrate the threat of chaos to Jupiter's providential dispensation. The first simile comes as Jupiter announces to the assembled gods that Lycaon has attempted to assassinate him, just as Augustus will have announced an unsuccessful assassination attempt on himself to a meeting of the Senate in the temple of Palatine Apollo (*Met.* 1.199–206):[101]

> confremuere omnes studiisque ardentibus ausum
> talia deposcunt. sic, cum manus inpia saeuit        200
> sanguine Caesareo Romanum exstinguere nomen,
> attonitum tanto subitae terrore ruinae
> humanum genus est totusque perhorruit orbis:
> nec tibi grata minus pietas, Auguste, tuorum est,
> quam fuit illa Ioui. qui postquam uoce manuque      205
> murmura conpressit, tenuere silentia cuncti.

They all made a hubbub and with blazing zeal asked for the person who had dared such a thing. Thus, when an impious band had the mad impulse to snuff out the Roman name with the blood of Caesar, the human race was appalled by such a great fear of sudden catastrophe and the whole globe shuddered: nor was the piety of your people, Augustus, less pleasing to you than that display was to Jupiter. And after he checked their murmurs with his voice and hand, all of them held their silence.

Here a new kind of political order is revealed, with the direct power of the autocrat on display in a very different atmosphere from that of the interstitial nature of Virgil's first statesman-simile.[102] Jupiter then goes on (*Met.* 1.253–61) to implement his plan of punishing human beings by returning the world to the state of primeval chaos (*chaos*, *Met.* 1.7) out of

---

[99] Feeney (1991), 191.
[100] See Nicoll (1980), 178–9 for a full account of how closely Ovid's entire opening sequence (*Met.* 1.1–415) is modelled upon Virgil's (*Aen.* 1.1–304), with discussion of the two epics' respective opening similes; cf. Barchiesi (2005b), on *Met.* 1.200–5 for Ovid's treatment of Virgil's first simile.
[101] For this interpretation, as opposed to the still common view that the Ides of March are at issue, see A.G. Lee (1968) on *Met.* 1.200; Due (1974), 71–2; Barchiesi (2005b) on *Met.* 1.200–5. Stephen Harrison points out to me the characteristic ambiguity of the reference in *sanguine Caesareo* (1.201, noted by Barchiesi (2005b) ad loc.): Julius Caesar or Augustus are both initially in view, just as with *Caesar* and *Iulius* in Verg. *Aen.* 1.286, 288 (on which passage see S.J. Harrison (1996)).
[102] Barchiesi (2005b), on *Met.* 1.200–5.

which it has spent the last two-hundred lines trying to struggle. He begins by locking up all the winds in Aeolus' cave (1.262–3), just as his Virgilian predecessor had done—except for the South Wind (*emittitque Notum*, 1.264), which proceeds to run riot. In a surprisingly brief opening sequence Ovid has condensed variations on the universes of Lucretius and Virgil, with different conceptions of divinity, of order, and of control, which are to have their own strange kind of programmatic power for the rest of his epic.

A more abrupt challenge to Virgil's epic world-order is to be found in the first simile in Lucan's *De Bello Ciuili*, where the collapse of the Roman Republic is compared to the Stoic cosmos' return to primeval chaos (1.72–81), culminating in the throwing of all natural laws into confusion: *totaque discors/machina diuulsi turbabit foedera mundi* ('and the whole discordant structure of the convulsed universe will throw its laws into confusion', 1.80–1). Space forbids exploring the strategies of the Flavian epicists in any detail here. Statius has a georgic image of the strife (*discordia*, *Theb.* 1.137) between the brothers, describing two oxen that will not share the yoke (*Theb.* 1.131–6); a second simile brings in the expected storm, comparing the rain-lashed Polynices, journeying to Argos on foot, to a sailor caught in a winter storm (*Theb.* 1.370–5). Silius Italicus and Valerius Flaccus both use sly cunning in their first images, giving misleading initial images of deceit and of trickery: Hannibal is like a Dacian archer using poisoned arrows (*Pun.* 1.324–5); Jason's plot to get Acastus to join the expedition is compared to the wiles of a hunter who has stolen a lioness's cubs (*Arg.* 1.484–93). It is their second similes that shift to the expected register of chaos and allegorised storm: the besieged Saguntines use a catapult that acts like a thunderbolt to shoot at the Gigantesque Carthaginians (*Pun.* 1.356–9); the Argonauts are caught in a storm that is quelled by Neptune (*Arg.* 1.651–4), and their response to Jason's speech of reassurance is compared to that of a group of rustics, terrified by a storm, who have prayers said for them by a priest (*Arg.* 1.682–5).

We close with the first similes in Milton's *Paradise Lost*, where we may see how long-lastingly powerful the appeal is of these epic templates of chaos and cosmos. The poem's first simile illustrates the massive figure of the fallen Satan, lying at the bottom of Hell, and it compares his size to that of various monsters, beginning with the titanic opponents of Jupiter first encountered in Hesiod's *Theogony*. The simile encapsulates the forces of chaos which have threatened divine order since the beginning of the epic tradition (*Paradise Lost* 1.196–202):

> ... in bulk as huge
> As whom the fables name of monstrous size,
> Titanian, or Earth-born, that warred on Jove,
> Briarios or Typhon, whom the den
> By ancient Tarsus held, or that sea-beast          200
> Leviathan, which God of all his works
> Created hugest that swim the ocean stream ...

In the next simile, the place that Satan lands on after he rouses himself is compared to the product of an eruption (1.230–8):

> And such appeared in hue, as when the force       230
> Of subterranean wind transports a hill
> Torn from Pelorus, or the shattered side
> Of thundering Aetna, whose combustible
> And fuelled entrails thence conceiving fire,
> Sublimed with mineral fury, aid the winds,        235
> And leave a singèd bottom all involved
> With stench and smoke: such resting found the sole
> Of unblessed feet.

Here we have an opposite effect from that of the first simile, although Milton is still working within the same epic tradition of interpretation. In the first simile the Titans, Briarios, and Typhon had been presented 'straight', as figures of pagan fable; in the second simile we see instead the violence of a rationalised and demythologised force of subterranean wind. Lucretius' atheistic demolition of pagan religion is very useful to Milton at this point, for he is able to use Lucretian techniques in order to ridicule the truth-claims of the religion of the old epics. Lucretius had argued that there were no Titans fighting Jupiter, and that there was no monster under Etna; the volcanic activity of Etna was simply the action of subterranean wind, exactly as described here by Milton (231).[103] Milton is clearly using those passages here, adapting Lucretius in order to 'demythologise' Virgil's 'remythologisation' of pagan tradition in the aftermath of Lucretius.

Yet Milton is simultaneously 'remythologising' in his own distinctive and Christian way. Virgil's redescription in religious terms of the forces of chaos has also left its impact on Milton, as we see if we compare his first two similes, which polarise out the ancient interpretative options for the mythological forces that embody chaos' threat to the cosmos. The Titans

---

[103] Fundamental discussion in P. Hardie (1986), 91, 181, 211 of such Lucretian passages as 1.722–5, 6.639–702; cf. Gale (1994), 187.

of pagan fable are not simply fictions for Milton, as they had been for Lucretius, but an imperfect memory of the real battle in heaven, between Lucifer and the true God.[104] And Satan is neither a figure of fable nor an allegorised piece of natural history, but a real force in the world, an actual instantiation of chaos and evil of a kind that Lucretius and Virgil could never have imagined.

---

[104] A crucial passage is *PL* 1.738–50, which explicitly says that the pagan fable of Mulciber being flung from heaven by Jove is a false version of the earlier true event, the expulsion of the fallen angels from Heaven by God: on the Lucretian colour of this passage, see Martindale (1986), 72–5. See Carey and A. Fowler (1968) on *PL* 1.50–83 for the importance to Milton of this parallel between the 'false' Titans of fable and the actual devils, 'since it justified treating the brief Biblical references to a war in heaven as more than allegory'.

CHAPTER 16

*Fictions of Citizenship in Livy's* History[1]

I

The starting point of this chapter is the idea that Livy is fascinated by the power of fiction.[2] What fascinates him is not just the power of literary fiction to command an audience's attention through convincing invented versimilitudinous detail—although that is very important[3]—but the power of institutionalised societal fictions to have real sway in the world of politics and of empire, and even to construct those worlds. It is this second kind of fiction that I shall be exploring here: in a range of fields, as we shall see, 'fiction' has become something of a term of art to describe the shared mythologies and invented traditions that are indispensable for the survival of any collective entity. In particular, Livy is intrigued by the fictive dimensions of the Roman citizenship, and his interest in the remarkable nature of the ever-changing *ciuitas* will be the major focus of this chapter.[4] The distinctive Roman *ciuitas* has become very topical in recent years, as globalisation enforces new perspectives on the old questions of belonging and exclusion, with Brexit only the most radical example of a European

---

[1] For their helpful comments I am grateful to Andrew Feldherr, Chris Kraus and Dan-el Padilla Peralta, and to those who heard various early versions of this chapter as lectures at St. Andrews, Stanford, Dartmouth, Princeton's Society of Fellows in the Liberal Arts, Florence, Pisa, and Humboldt-Universität, Berlin; my thanks to Olivia Catanorchi for translating my lecture into Italian for Florence and Pisa. All translations are my own; all dates are BCE.
[2] This is by no means my idea: for recent studies of fiction and Livy to which I am indebted, see Feldherr (1998), 51–72; Sailor (2006); Vasaly (2015a), 17–21.
[3] Woodman (1988), 233 (Index) s.v. 'vivid description' for this aspect of historiography.
[4] It is perhaps worth stating that my object of enquiry is what Livy has to say about the citizenship, and only incidentally what may or may not actually have been the case about the citizenship at any given moment. I am certainly not claiming that it is impossible to use Livy as a historical source; I am only saying that this is not my objective here. On this point see Pellam (2014), 280; cf. Vasaly (2015a), 31–2 on the '"literary school" of Livian studies': a history of the debate in Pausch (2011), 3–8. Similarly, I take it that our object of enquiry is not Livy's own personal belief but what Livy's narrative as a whole is designed to teach us about the Roman experience: this is now the *communis opinio*, and I follow e.g. Levene (1993); Feldherr (1998), 67–8; J.P. Davies (2004).

322

crisis over these issues, and with the United States going through one of its recurrent periods of ricocheting between the foundational myth of the melting pot and the horror of contamination from outside. What are the ties that bind a citizen body? What alternatives are there to 'Blut und Boden' as criteria for belonging? The argument is offered in the same spirit as that of C.J. Smith, which explores the startling modernity and relevance of Roman conceptions of 'citizenship and community'.[5]

In his interest in the fictive underpinnings of the compacts that make a society, Livy may be seen to 'anticipate'—if that term is not too patronising to both parties—contemporary theorists from politics, sociology or economics who describe societies, or indeed any complex organisations, as fundamentally fictions, 'social constructs', 'imagined realities'. As a recent study of American businesses puts it, 'corporations are fictional entities';[6] this is so because corporations are based upon 'the highly abstract concept of a legal personality'.[7] And the Romans invented—or at least anticipated—such corporations, in the form of the *societas publicanorum*, which was 'authorized to own property and form contracts in its own name and did not have to be dissolved if a member died or went bankrupt'.[8] At a still higher level of organisation, societies and nations, likewise, have been analysed as an 'imaginary institution', or 'imagined communities', products of collective acts of will and belief, sharing a 'social imaginary' and a set of 'invented traditions'.[9] Appiah's study of how identities are constructed through 'creed, country, color, class and culture' has a title that says it all—*The Lies that Bind*.[10]

Harari provides an engaging and penetrating example of how far this general approach can take us.[11] He selects the French company Peugeot, a limited liability corporation, as his case of an entity that owes its existence to nothing more nor less than the fact that everyone agrees it exists.[12] More

---

[5] C.J. Smith (2011). Cf. Connolly (2007) and esp. (2014) for sustained arguments about the relevance of Roman political thought to modern concepts of republicanism; note Cornell (1991), 65 on how '[t]he Romans had nothing comparable to the concept of "patriality", a modern British neologism that is as morally odious as it is linguistically uncouth' (dating from the British Nationality Act of 1981).
[6] A. Winkler (2018), 44.   [7] Malmendier (2005), 31.
[8] A. Winkler (2018), 45; see in detail Malmendier (2005) on the emergence of the *societas publicanorum* in the Middle Republic. In general, on 'the intimate interrelationship of beliefs and institutions' in economic activity, see North (2005), 48–50.
[9] Castoriadis (1975) ('l'institution imaginaire'); B. Anderson (1983) ('imagined communities'); Taylor (2004) ('social imaginary'); Hobsbawm and Ranger (1983) ('invention of tradition'). See Hornblower (2018), 170–1 for an account of the different terminologies preferred in different disciplines.
[10] Appiah (2018).   [11] Harari (2014).
[12] Harari (2014), 31–5: 'Peugeot is a figment of our collective imagination. Lawyers call this a "legal fiction". It can't be pointed at; it is not a physical object. But it exists as a legal entity' (32).

profoundly, he describes how *homo sapiens* was eventually able to achieve new levels of social complexity as a result of the cognitive revolution of about 70,000 years ago, when language was harnessed to generate fictions, shared within groups, that could in time be scaled up to make it possible for human beings to live in settled units larger than the hunter-gatherer band.[13] In the end, we have the state, and the state is, as expressed by Runciman in an avowedly Hobbesian account, 'an association that cannot be identified with its members, its constitution, its powers, or its purposes. In law, such associations are known as fictions.'[14]

Roman studies have produced some fascinating work along these lines, pioneered by J.S. Richardson's inspirational account of the Romans' creative powers of fiction, emerging from the law, as seen in their institutions of the proconsulship and of adoption.[15] Y. Thomas has defined the set of legal fictions through which the concept of a *communis patria* evolved to accommodate the far-flung members of the late Republican and early Imperial *ciuitas*.[16] Lavan describes his study of the metaphors of slavery suffusing Roman imperial dominion as 'an exploration of the Roman social imaginary'.[17] Finally, in a study of particular relevance to our topic in this chapter, Ando, on 'Roman social imaginaries', has explored Roman fictions of governance, including the metaphorical contractual underpinnings to the Roman ideas of *ciuitas*.[18]

Approaches of this kind are valuable for an understanding of Livy's presentation of the ever-changing organisms that make up the Roman *res*. Without anachronistically presenting Livy as an early colleague of the scholars cited immediately above, I shall be arguing that Livy's preoccupation with the fictions that sustain his society and empire may be illuminatingly read within the context of these contemporary approaches. As I shall try to demonstrate, Livy keeps reminding us that the institutions of religion and politics cohere through collective acts of will and belief. Since he is an ancient historian and not a modern sociologist or political theorist he proceeds by 'show don't tell', using narrative rather than theorising.[19] He therefore constructs aetiological accounts in which we

---

[13] Summarised at Harari (2014), 22–8.    [14] D. Runciman (2003), 29.    [15] J.S. Richardson (1995).
[16] Y. Thomas (1996).    [17] Lavan (2013), 19.    [18] Ando (2015), 45–51.
[19] Lowrie (2013), 84; Hammer (2014), 230–1. On Livy's dismal modern reception until very recent times as an author with any contribution to make to political theory, see Hammer (2008), 79–81. As Hammer's third chapter shows in detail, Machiavelli knew better: 'We find perhaps the greatest appreciation and fullest elaboration of Livy's contribution to political thought in Machiavelli's *Discourses [on Livy]*' (81); see Coby (1999) for an account of how much Livy's Rome means to Machiavelli, and Kapust (2011) for a history of the role of Livy (together with Sallust and Tacitus) in modern political theory.

see societal institutions coming into being, with their origins revealed as human constructs, and even human fictions. In his narrative, not only the Roman constitution but also Roman religion are presented as nakedly historical products, the result of human actions and decisions taken in identifiable circumstances. Even more than this, as we shall see, in order to make the theme of collective fiction come alive he regularly presents some of these actions and decisions as deliberate acts of masquerade and pretense.

This insight of Livy's does not in any sense result in the demolition of the religious or political traditions of Rome, and it is not necessarily in itself some kind of deconstructive move.[20] If Livy represents human institutions as 'fictive', this does not mean that he sees the institutions of society as necessarily fraudulent, any more than do the modern scholars whose work we have just surveyed. Fiction is not necessarily the same as bad faith. As Runciman says, in establishing a parallelism between the ontological status of money, the state and characters in novels, 'To call these things fictions is not to say that they are lies ... Emma Bovary, after all, is not a lie; she is a fiction.'[21] Rather, we need to concentrate on the fact that the capacity of groups or societies to agree upon fictions and share them is indispensable to their survival. This came home to me when I recently visited Berlin for the first time. As I stood at the Gedenkstätte Berliner Mauer, and in the former headquarters of the Stasi, it was suddenly obvious that the East European dictatorships collapsed because people just stopped believing in them.[22]

Livy, then, is fascinated by the way in which human societies function through strange processes of collective belief; he is intrigued by the way in which these fictive constructs have the capacity to take on a power of their own, to become genuinely 'real' in their own right, commanding adherence, creating affective bonds, and generating profound emotional attachments. The trajectory of the first five books in particular will provide a clear case of Livy's construction of just such a transformation.

This whole project, of showing how historical fictions take root and create lasting bonds, is of course also one that is inextricably bound up with his own historical project. We need to think of fiction in a positive sense also when considering this intimately related issue, of Livy's very form of writing. His *History* is fiction in the sense that Rüpke uses when describing the historiography of religion: historiography, as he argues, is structured,

---

[20] Here I am very much in agreement with, and indebted to, the approach of Feldherr (1998), esp. 51–67, and of Sailor (2006).
[21] D. Runciman (2003), 35; cf. Harari (2014), 35–6.
[22] Not that all dictatorships, unfortunately, end in this way.

rhetorical, figurative, and to use rhetorical tropes 'is to introduce fiction. Yet—and that is most important—it is not fiction for fiction's sake, but fiction for the sake of coherence, of understanding, or explanation, fiction for the sake of orientation with respect to the present and the future.'[23] Accordingly, Livy's own *History* is likewise a human construct, even a fictive construct in certain senses, and one that he hopes will command adherence and become part of the community's tradition and inherited wisdom.[24] As Levene puts it: 'Livy literally has recreated the world of the past, one which may not … mirror consistently the past as it originally occurred, but which partially supersedes that with a reality of its own. Rome's past literally is what Livy has made of it.'[25] This deliberate confusion between Livy's subject matter and his representation of that subject matter is one that we meet very early on, in section 4 of his Preface, where he says that the *res*, the 'thing', the 'matter', is one of enormous effort, *immensi operis*, going back over seven-hundred years, starting from small beginnings and growing to the stage where it is now labouring under its own bulk, *ut iam magnitudine laboret sua*: these words refer both to the Roman Empire and to Livy's own projected *History*.[26]

This chapter will concentrate on Books 1 and 5. The ring-composition that binds these two books, marking off the opening pentad of Books 1–5 as a unified compositional entity, is crucial, as many scholars have noted.[27] At the end of Book 5, after the Gallic sack, the foundational religious and political institutions of Rome are now *re*-founded along with crucial features of the Roman tradition overall, and this refoundation, the responsibility of M. Furius Camillus, happens in such a way as to set up the whole future trajectory of Roman history. In the process Book 5 loops back to the crucial concerns of Book 1 and fulfils them, showing how the early stages of the *ciuitas* have been consummated even as they are transformed. Yet this apparently definitive act of cyclical renewal is already unstable, with less closural force than it appears to

---

[23] Rüpke (2011), 287.
[24] Moles (1993/2009), 71–5; Jaeger (1997), 184; Kraus (1997), 55–6; Feldherr (1998), 77–8; Sailor (2006), 370–83.
[25] Levene (2010), 388.
[26] Moles (1993/2009), 56, on 'the union of theme and writer' as a major general preoccupation in the Preface; 59, '*res* is in the first instance the historian's subject-matter but it then "slides" into being the Roman state itself'; Kraus (1994b), 268–70; Feldherr (1998), 37; Marincola (1997a), 153–4.
[27] Burck (1964), 43–4; Briscoe (1971), 1–2; Stadter (1972/2009), 93–4; Luce (1977), 3–4, 6–7, 25–6; Burck (1992), 8; Levene (1993), 199–201; Kraus (1994b), 283–4; Jaeger (1997), 63; Oakley (1997–2005), 1.122–5; Mineo (2003), 345; Gaertner (2008), 40 n.65, 42; Vasaly (2015b), 218–20; Kraus (2019), 356. As pointed out by Vasaly (2015b), 226–7, Livy's creation of this unit of composition has no apparent parallels in earlier historiography, and is indebted rather to poetic conceptions of creating organic structure through the unit of the book.

have at first. The provisional nature of Camillus' refoundation becomes clear in Book 8, with the constitutional settlement of the year 338 after the final war between Rome and the Latins. The year 338 is a crucial turning point in Roman history, which reconfigures what had looked like a final conclusion in Book 5. In this year, the Romans have another kind of refoundation and rethink their citizenship in the process, in ways that look forward hundreds of years to yet more dramatic reconfigurations of the *ciuitas*.

## II

We begin with some key early passages which help to set up Livy's interest in the power and authority of fiction in history, in both senses of the word 'history'—both 'history' as his subject matter and 'history' as his own project. Already in the Preface we confront this issue, with the famous section on what the right attitude ought to be to the *fabulae* that surround the foundation of the city (*praef.* 6–8):

> quae ante conditam condendamue urbem poeticis magis decora fabulis quam incorruptis rerum gestarum monumentis traduntur, ea nec adfirmare nec refellere in animo est. datur haec uenia antiquitati ut miscendo humana diuinis primordia urbium augustiora faciat; et si cui populo licere oportet consecrare origines suas et ad deos referre auctores, ea belli gloria est populo Romano ut cum suum conditorisque sui parentem Martem potissimum ferat, tam et hoc gentes humanae patiantur aequo animo quam imperium patiuntur. sed haec et his similia, utcumque animaduersa aut existimata erunt, haud in magno equidem ponam discrimine.

> The traditions about the time before the city was founded or about to be founded, which are more appropriate to poets' fables than to the unsullied monuments of history, it is not my intention either to affirm or disprove. Antiquity is granted the indulgence of making the first stages of cities more august by jumbling up the human and divine. And if any people ought to be allowed to hallow their origins and take them back to the gods as a source, then the glory in war of the Roman people is such that when they claim as their father and as the father of their founder none other than Mars, then the races of humankind ought to put up with this with the same resigned frame of mind with which they put up with the Empire. But this and similar material, however it will be noticed or assessed, I'm not going to stake anything on deciding it one way or the other.

What Livy is talking about here with his references to the acceptance of *fabulae* is 'soft' power. There is a belief system in place: the Empire is maintained by the acceptance of a certain frame of mind by the subject peoples. Modern scholars agree that the Roman Empire was a mental construct held together by its inhabitants' various imagined 'grand or metanarratives' about 'a general order of the world'.[28] Livy's word here for the inhabitants of the Empire, *gentes*, is the default term used in Latin to 'represent the Empire as a composite of different peoples, united in their subjection to the *populus Romanus* or *gens Romana*'.[29] Lavan provides an arresting selection of texts from the subject peoples' point of view which in their different ways catch precisely the frame of mind Livy refers to here.[30] Particularly apposite is a passage from Josephus' *Jewish War* (2.358–79), in which the Jewish king Agrippa II recounts to his audience a list of peoples who are slaves to the Romans (δουλεύουσιν Ῥωμαίοις, 358), including the Spartans, who 'put up with the same masters', ἀγαπῶσιν τοὺς αὐτοὺς δεσπότας (359). Here ἀγαπάω is being used in its meaning 'tolerate, put up with' (LSJ s.v. §4), which exactly captures part of Livy's *patiantur aequo animo* (along with—let us not forget—'suffer, undergo', *Oxford Latin Dictionary* s.v. §2a). Remarkably, we have early concrete evidence for this very mindset in the form of an inscription from Chios, probably from the 220s.[31] In paying tribute to the Romans for their assistance to the island, the inscription refers to the birth of Romulus and Remus and to the tradition that their father was Mars, 'which one might well consider to be a true story because of the bravery of the Romans'.[32] In its overlap with Livy's language, this inscription's evidence for the subject peoples' imposed mentality is 'almost too good to be true'.[33]

The projection of this frame of mind onto the subject peoples of course does not mean that Livy himself is vouching for the truth of the *fabulae* about Romulus and Remus, and he distances himself from any such commitment at the beginning and the end of the passage quoted above. When he comes to the narrative of the twins' conception later in Book 1 it is very clear that he does not endorse the idea that the father of the twins was actually Mars. After the Vestal gave birth to twins, he says, 'whether because she actually believed it or because a god looked more respectable as the party to blame, she named Mars as the father of her doubtful offspring' (*seu ita rata, seu quia deus auctor culpae honestior erat, Martem incertae stirpis patrem nuncupat*, 1.4.2). The option that Mars was in fact the father is not

---

[28] J.C. Barrett (1997), 58; cf. Ando (2000), 29: '[P]rovincial obedience to Roman domination was an ideological construct.'
[29] Lavan (2013), 34.    [30] Ibid., 8–9.
[31] *SEG* 16.486 and 30.1073: see Hornblower (2018), 116 for the date, following the view of Forrest in Derow and Forrest (1982).
[32] Translation of Wiseman (1995), 161 for lines 28–9.    [33] Sailor (2006), 350 n.65.

canvassed.³⁴ Similarly, when he comes to narrate the death and 'apotheosis' of Romulus (1.15.6–8), Livy does not give the seal of approval of his narrative authority to the claims that Romulus became a divinity.³⁵

Livy will report the myth of Romulus' divine parentage because it is in the tradition and has immense consequences, but he is not obliged to vouch for it, just as Herodotus does not have to vouch for the stories he tells (1.5.3, 7.152.3).³⁶ Livy acknowledges the force of these myths in bolstering Roman power, and he understands that the way the peoples of the Empire have to acquiesce in the ideology is independent of the truth of the stories. An uncritically proud Roman public might believe these stories, and the subject peoples *have* to believe these stories, but Livy does not want to identify himself with either of these groups: he is the independent historian, with his own *auctoritas*.³⁷

Almost immediately in the narrative of Book 1 we meet another story whose historicity really cannot be established, but which still has the power to matter enormously—the question of who was the mother of Aeneas' son, the founder of the dynasty of the Alban kings. Livy first narrates the marriage of Aeneas to Lavinia (1.1.9) and the foundation of a city named after her, Lavinium, followed by the birth of a son, whom they name Ascanius (10–11). Following a chapter devoted to the wars fought by Aeneas, and his death and burial, Livy returns to young Ascanius and his mother Lavinia. After some very interesting remarks on how Lavinia— thanks to her great natural gifts (*tanta indoles*)—was able to keep the kingdom intact until Ascanius came of age (1.3.1), Livy brings himself up short with a reference to the uncertainty (not previously mentioned) over the identity of this son, and of his mother (1.3.2–3):

> haud ambigam—quis enim rem tam ueterem pro certo adfirmet?—hicine fuerit Ascanius an maior quam hic, Creusa matre Ilio incolumi natus comesque inde

---

³⁴ Levene (1993), 129; Miles (1995), 141; Feldherr (1998), 76; Forsythe (1999), 92; Sailor (2006), 353; Vasaly (2015a), 25–6 in general on the role of *fabulae* and authorial stance in these early sections. Stem (2007), 441–3 argues for the view that Livy's language in the Preface 'is suggestive of why his reader would be wise to indulge in Romulus' purported divinity rather than deny it' (442), but I am persuaded otherwise by the sources just cited.
³⁵ Miles (1995), 139–41; Sailor (2006), 345–8.    ³⁶ Moles (1993/2009), 64.
³⁷ See Chapter 13 above on these passages. Sailor (2006), 351–4 argues that Livy's language in the Preface (6–8) means that all Romans are involved in not believing the Mars/Romulus story, since they are the imperial rulers. I think rather that Livy's language of *si cui populo . . . potissimum ferat* (7) allows for most, not all, Romans to accept this story; note that Cicero could represent Scipio Aemilianus claiming that it was perfectly appropriate and historically justifiable for Romans to believe in the divine parentage of Romulus (*Rep.* 2.4, 17–20, with Zetzel (1995), 161, 174–5). Even in the Preface, then, we have an implied division between elite and mass in Rome of the kind regularly argued for by Sailor in other contexts, with Livy making common cause with his high-status educated readers against the mass: Sailor (2006), 342–3, 355–7.

> paternae fugae, quem Iulum eundem Iulia gens auctorem nominis sui nuncupat. is Ascanius, ubicumque et quacumque matre genitus—certe natum Aenea constat— ...
>
> I shall not argue the question—for who would affirm something so ancient as a certain thing?—over whether this was Ascanius or an older brother, who was born while Troy was still standing with Creusa as his mother, and who accompanied his father from there into exile, the very Iulus whom the *Iulia gens* declare as the source of their name. This Ascanius, wherever he was born and from whatever mother—certainly it is agreed that Aeneas was his father— ...

This raises the key question of whether Ascanius is half-Italian and half-Trojan or else entirely Trojan, and Virgil likewise has both versions of who the mother of Aeneas' son was: in Book 1 of the *Aeneid* Jupiter tells Venus that the Trojan prince Iulus will found Alba Longa (267–71), and in Book 6 Anchises tells Aeneas that it will be his son with Lavinia who will start the line of Alban kings (763–6).[38]

There is a lot at stake in these double myths of origin. Does Aeneas' son emblematise the way that the ur-Romans are already hybridising in the first generation, or is the Trojan strain predominant at first? Are women just vessels, or can they be communicators of culture? For now, we focus only on the fact that Livy told us at the start of this section of narrative that Ascanius is half-Italian and half-Trojan, without introducing any alternatives, but his is not the only voice. The *Iulia gens* have their view of the matter, and the intense interest of the clan in the descent from Iulus is caught in the inversion of the usual word order, with *Iulia gens* instead of *gens Iulia*: this word order highlights the name, and the link implied in the name. It was highly important to Julius Caesar and his heir to claim descent from this Trojan prince: it is noteworthy that on the Ara Pacis and in the Forum Augustum the father, Aeneas, is represented in Roman garb while his son is in Phrygian or Trojan costume.[39] Livy's rhetorical question—'who would affirm something so ancient as a certain thing?'—looks dismissive but in fact reminds the reader of precisely who would affirm this ancient story as a certain thing.[40] From the very beginning of his work, then, Livy is reminding his readers that ancient and unverifiable *fabulae* can have powerful consequences in the real world of empire.

---

[38] See now the full discussion of Rogerson (2017) (18–19 on the Livy passage). Livy maintains the indeterminacy even after this digression. When he resumes the narrative with the resumptive pronoun *is* at the beginning of section 3, he calls Aeneas' son *Ascanius*, not *Iulus*; but then note that he says Ascanius left the city of Lavinium *matri seu nouercae*, 'to his mother or his step-mother' (1.3.3).
[39] Zanker (1988), 202–4.   [40] Miles (1995), 40.

## III

A spectacular example of this insight comes when Romulus founds the city and sets up the asylum, as part of an extended foundation-narrative in which the distinctive nature of the citizen-body of Rome first becomes a major theme.[41] The very foundation of the citizen-body is, according to Livy, an imitation of a famous fiction, a version of Plato's γενναῖον ψεῦδος, 'noble lie'. Yet this apparent 'lie' is going to turn into a kind of 'truth' in due course, as we shall see below in our discussion of the end of the first pentad.

After becoming king, Romulus builds walls of ambitious scope (1.8.4), and then sets his mind to acquiring a population to fill them (1.8.5–6):

> deinde, ne uana urbis magnitudo esset, adiciendae multitudinis causa uetere consilio condentium urbes, qui obscuram atque humilem conciendo ad se multitudinem natam e terra sibi prolem ementiebantur, locum, qui nunc saeptus descendentibus inter duos lucos <ad laeuam>[42] est, asylum aperit. eo ex finitimis populis turba omnis sine discrimine, liber an seruus esset, auida novarum rerum perfugit, idque primum ad coeptam magnitudinem roboris fuit.
>
> Next, so that the size of his city wouldn't be pointless/empty, in order to add population, he used an old stratagem of those founding cities, who by gathering together an obscure and humble population used to lie and say that offspring had been born for them from the earth, and he opened up as an asylum a place, now fenced off, that is on your left as you go down from the Capitol. To that place from the neighbouring peoples a whole mob fled for refuge, without any distinction of status between free or slave, greedy for change, and that was the first element of strength contributing to the size that he had embarked on.

Livy cunningly does not say in as many words that Romulus actually perpetrated this lie. Preserving a sliver of deniability, he says that Romulus in establishing the asylum used the old strategy of those founding cities, who used to tell the lie that their offspring were born from the earth. In his version, the pun on *humilis* is enough to do the work of the myth; the 'humble' population are so called because *humilis* 'is derived from "earth"' (*tractum est ab humo*, Serv. Auct. 4.255).

With the pointed use of the word 'lie' (*ementiebantur*), oddly glossed over in many translations, Livy is no doubt alluding to the 'noble lie' that

---

[41] A theme already anticipated before the foundation of the city in the marriage pact between Aeneas and Latinus (1.1.9) and the amalgamation of Trojans and Latins into one people (1.2.4–5): Gruen (2013), 4. In general, on the Trojan myth as a way of thinking through the issue of the heterogeneous Roman identity, see Reed (2007).

[42] Here following Ogilvie's OCT, which prints the conjecture of H.J. Müller.

Socrates recommends in Plato's *Republic*, where the inhabitants of the ideal city are to be told that they were in fact born from the earth (414b–e). More generally, the passage calls to mind the various Greek states that claimed to be autochthonous, especially Athens, and likewise the Arcadians and Aeginetans.[43] Such comparisons with Greek states, and with Athens in particular, were a crucial part of Roman thinking about the distinctive nature of their citizen-body.[44] In fact, when Cicero mocks Athenian and Arcadian claims to autochthony, he uses the same ironically 'Platonic' language of 'lying' to further his point, saying that 'they told the lie that they had come out of the earth like mice from ploughed land' (*commenti sunt se de terra tamquam hos ex arvis musculos exstitisse*, Rep. 3.25).

In its permeability and comparative openness the Roman *ciuitas* was very different from general Greek concepts of shared ethnic descent as the basis of citizenship, concepts which in their extreme form were encapsulated in the myth of autochthony.[45] This divergence reveals itself incidentally in many contexts, as in the different Greek and Roman nomenclature for civil war. In Latin a 'civil war' is a *bellum ciuile*, a 'war between fellow-citizens', whereas Greek says πόλεμος ἐμφύλιος (Polyb. 1.65.2; Plut. *Pomp.* 24.2), or τὰ ἐμφύλια, as in Appian's title—that is, a war between members of the same φῦλον, people who are related by blood or descent. Even the Latin word for 'citizen', *ciuis*, is not derived from the word for 'city', as πολίτης is derived from πόλις, and nor is the word *Quirites*. As Nicolet puts it, '*Civis* is an associative term: its proper meaning is not "citizen", but "fellow-citizen".'[46] For the Romans, the citizenship results from an association and a partnership, not from shared birth or place of origin, and the beginning of their community is always presented as something generated artificially, the product of human design.[47] Even as Livy is working on his

---

[43] Linderski (1982), 20 n.16; Loraux (1986), 13–27; Dench (2005), 18–19; Gruen (2013), 3–4; Roy (2014); Hornblower (2018), 171–2. As shown by Carlà-Uhink (2017a), 149–64 ('The myth of autochthony'), from the Italians' point of view autochthony was an important part of discourse about 'Italicness', in particular as a way of 'Othering' Greeks, Celts and Etruscans as late arrivals: note his discussion (149–50) of Cato's construction of the Sabines as autochthonous (Dion. Hal. *Ant. Rom.* 2.49–50, Serv. *Aen.* 8.637–8 = *FRHist* F51–2).

[44] On the Romans' use of Greek autochthonous myths as a foil to their own origin myths, see Cornell (1995), 60; Feldherr (1998), 113–14; Lowrie (2005), 959–60; Dench (2005), 96–7; Capogrossi Colognesi (2014), 12–16; Moatti (2015), 272, 281–2, 296–7; Hammer (2014), 240–2; more generally, Dench (2005), 96–117 ('A tale of two cities: Athens and Rome') on the Romans' longstanding use of Athens as a point of comparison in thinking about their own citizenship.

[45] Cornell (1991), 62–3; Giardina (1997), 5–6; Ando (1999), 14–15; Moatti (2015), 270–90; Atkins (2018), 69–71.

[46] Nicolet (1980), 22, with reference to Benveniste (1973), 273–4 and 298–9.

[47] Bonjour (1975a), 12 ('Toujours est-il que, vérité ou légende, les Romains conçoivent l'origine de leur patrie comme une création artificielle, une oeuvre humaine'); Cornell (1997), esp. 10–11; Moatti

version of the quasi-historical origins of such conceptions of citizenship, Virgil is of course creating his own account of the amalgamation of different groups in the process of forming an always changing *populus*.[48] Both authors are intrigued by how the Romans 'created a distinctive theory of citizenship that differentiates Rome from all other political communities and explains why it became the first truly universal state in history'.[49]

Now, some version of shared ethnicity and descent eventually came to be usable within the Roman discourse on their citizenship.[50] By the early Principate, as the result of shifting concepts of 'Italia' and of associated ideas of a shared Italic *consanguinitas*, it would be 'hard to deny that blood and an uncomplicatedly linear idea of descent were *one* available way of thinking about being Roman'.[51] But no one in the Republic ever claims a unified ethnic line of descent for Roman citizens, and all accounts allow for paradigmatic hybridity and assimilation in the early period.[52] Indeed, Farney has documented how Roman nobles of the Republican period regularly advertised their originally non-Roman ancestry (Latin or Sabine in particular), and these claims to glamorous or prestigious outside origins demonstrate that in the Republic the Romans as a group set no store by the idea that they shared a common ethnic identity.[53] In Livy's account we see a prime example of the discourse described by Dench: 'the peculiar permeability of the citizenship was worked out as an essential and permanent feature of Roman identity through the medium of myths of Rome's beginnings'.[54] This permeability no doubt goes back to the monarchical period, with the horizontal mobility across central Italy that has attracted so much attention in recent scholarship.[55] What marks the Romans out is their vaunting of these stories of immigration 'as manifestations of Rome's supposedly essential disposition towards incorporating foreigners':[56] Livy

---

(2015), 287. As Farrell (2001), 27 puts it, 'there are no native Romans'. On Cicero's definition of *res publica* in *Rep.* 1.39, see Zetzel (1995), 128: 'Unlike most ancient theorists . . . C. does not make ethnic or territorial unity of the *populus* an element in the formation of the state.' Padilla Peralta (2019) is a valuable corrective against the common triumphalist readings of the 'inclusive' Roman citizenship as a model for modern empires.

[48] Ando (2002) (on the *Georgics*); Toll (1997); Reed (2007); Barchiesi (2008); Marincola (2010).
[49] Cornell (1991), 62.
[50] Lavan (2013), 34–5; Farney (2014), 439 on the taunts some blue-bloods such as Manlius Torquatus and Sergius Catilina could cast at 'foreigners' such as Cicero.
[51] Dench (2005), 259 (original emphasis); Carlà-Uhink (2017a), 111–49 on 'The *consanguineitas* of the Italic peoples', an idea developing 'with particular intensity from the second half of the 2nd century BCE, and in preparation for the Social War' (113); Moatti (2015), 287–9.
[52] Gruen (2013), 4–5; Moatti (2015), 297–8.    [53] Farney (2007).    [54] Dench (2005), 94.
[55] Ampolo (1988), 172–7; Cornell (1995), 157–8; (2000), 220–1, 224; (2003), 86–8; Bradley (2006), 164–6; Terrenato (2019).
[56] Dench (2005), 121.

contributes substantially to these founding myths, with his regular citations of the movement to Rome of outsiders who become kings or patricians.⁵⁷ Further, this kind of openness to horizontal mobility by individual or clan is very different from the assimilation of entire communities, which we shall soon see the Romans pioneering.

The Greeks, for their part, were intrigued by this unusual form of citizenship. Philip V was already commending the Romans for the openness of their citizenship policy, in contrast to Greek exclusivity, in 215.⁵⁸ Livy's contemporary, Dionysius of Halicarnassus, praises Romulus' asylum policy and his openness with the citizenship (*Ant. Rom.* 2.15.2–4, 2.16–17), and he explicitly declares that Athens, Thebes and Sparta were weak in the long run because they did not share their citizenship as the Romans did (2.17.1–2).⁵⁹ This theme is picked up in Tacitus' report of the speech made by the emperor Claudius on the admission of the elite of Gallia Comata to the citizenship; he too stresses that the main factor behind Athenian and Spartan collapse was the exclusiveness of their citizenship policy (*Ann.* 11.24.4).⁶⁰

One feature of the comparative openness of Roman citizenship which particularly attracted Greek interest as being remarkably different from their own customs was the way that slaves became full citizens upon manumission: Philip V already comments upon this practice.⁶¹ Livy's stress on the fact that the mob who went to Romulus' asylum was 'without any distinction of status between free or slave' must be glancing at the remarkable mixture of descendants of free and slave within the Roman citizen body (1.8.6). In emphasising the lowly status of the first Romans Livy diverges very much from Dionysius of Halicarnassus, who concentrates instead on a stream of high-born political refugees,⁶² and who explicitly

---

⁵⁷ Numa (1.18.5); Tarquinius Priscus (1.34.6: his wife praises this feature of Roman openness); Servius Tullius (1.39.5); Attius Clausus/Appius Claudius (2.16.4–5).
⁵⁸ In his letter to the council of the Thessalian city of Larisa, preserved in a local inscription (*Syll.*³ 543): Dench (2005), 5, 93.
⁵⁹ On Dionysius' deep interest in this distinctive feature of Roman citizenship, see Ando (1999), 21; (2016), 176; Moatti (2015), 286. See Dench (2005), 93 n.2 for Dionysius' positive view of 'Roman success based on incorporation'. Modern scholars have traditionally agreed with Livy and Dionysius: see Cornell (1995), 365–6; Eckstein (2009), 245 on Rome's 'ability to assimilate outsiders' as the key to her success; Woolf (2012), 218–32. For cautions about retrojecting into the Middle Republic later conceptions of the citizenship as a blessing conferred on grateful former enemies, see Cornell (1995), 323–4; Terrenato (2019), 5–6.
⁶⁰ Malloch (2013) ad loc., remarking that the common strategy 'suggests that the comparison was a feature of the historiographical tradition on Romulus'. Claudius does not himself make this point in his original speech (*CIL* 13.1668 = *ILS* 212).
⁶¹ Cornell (1991), 62; Dench (2005), 92. Cicero likewise points out how distinctive a feature of Roman policy it is to extend citizenship even to slaves (*Balb.* 24).
⁶² Dench (2005), 102, referring to *Ant. Rom.* 2.15.3–4 and 3.47.2.

says that slaves were not welcome in the asylum: anyone could come to the asylum 'so long as they were free men' (εἰ μόνον εἶεν ἐλεύθεροι, 2.15.3).[63] At the beginning of his second book Livy is careful to give an *aetion* of this practice of manumitting slaves into citizenship, with the story of the slave who told the consuls about the treachery of Brutus' sons and their aristocratic friends, and was rewarded with citizenship (2.5.9–10).[64] Many features of aetiology are here, with stress on such classic elements as firstness, derived name, and continuance from this point: 'this slave is said to have been the first to be set free by a touch of the rod' (*ille primum dicitur uindicta liberatus*); 'some think the name of the rod as well was derived from that man, and that his name was Vindicius' (*quidam uindictae quoque nomen tractum ab illo putant; Vindicio ipsi nomen fuisse*); 'after that man this custom was preserved' (*post illum hoc seruatum*, 2.5.10).[65]

As Livy presents the theme that the original community founded by Romulus is an amalgam without a natural grounding in any native soil, the idea is planted that the Romans' connection with the soil of Rome is factitious, some kind of ruse or trick, without any necessary affective bond. Livy is emphasising at this early phase of Roman society a theme that became a leitmotif in Roman discourse: 'for Romans, the description of patriotic affection as springing from some biological relationship to the land itself—the description of the soil as maternal or generative—was always self-consciously metaphorical, rather than polemically natural as it was at Athens'.[66] Livy returns to this theme at the beginning of Book 2, saying that liberty would have been premature before Brutus' expulsion of the last king, with a people made up 'of shepherds and immigrants, refugees from their own peoples', 'in a city that didn't belong to them', 'before the guarantees of wives and children, and the love of the soil itself, which takes a long time to become a habit, had brought their minds into an association' (*illa pastorum conuenarumque plebs, transfuga ex suis populis ... in aliena urbe ... priusquam pignora coniugum ac liberorum caritasque ipsius soli, cui longo tempore adsuescitur, animos eorum consociasset*, 2.1.4–5). In a campaign against the Etruscans, twenty-five years after the foundation of the Republic, the Romans are still the butt of 'jibes—some false, some true

---

[63] Moatti (2015), 278. It is interesting that Plutarch's *Life of Romulus* does say that slaves were original recruits to the asylum (9.2–3).
[64] Ogilvie (1965), 241 for this story as 'the aetiological myth of manumission *vindicta*'.
[65] Here following Ogilvie's OCT, which prints Karsten's conjecture of *hoc seruatum*. For these markers of aetiology, with Virgil as a point of reference, see O'Hara (1996), 66–79, esp. 75–9 on aetiologies flagged with *nomen, appello*, as here; on 'continuation from the time of the *aetion*', Myers (1994), 66.
[66] Ando (2015), 50. Hammer (2008), 93–8 offers a fine analysis of 'affection' as part of Livy's founding myths, together with a discussion of Machiavelli's response.

—about the newness of their stock and their origin' (*in nouitatem generis originisque qua falsa, qua uera iacere*, 2.45.4). As we shall see in Section V below, this preoccupation with the Romans' ties to the soil returns very powerfully in Camillus' speech at the end of Book 5.

Events following on from Romulus' establishment of the asylum quickly bring home how far Romulus' new *populus* is from being born of a particular piece of earth, since not only do the first men come from somewhere else but the first women also. Immediately after the establishment of the asylum Romulus attempts to find wives for his new collection of men, and we enter into the story of the 'rape of the Sabine women', which becomes the second exemplary paradigm—after the asylum—of how open the new *ciuitas* is. Spurned by the local communities in their petition for *ius conubii*, the Roman youth invite their neighbours to a festival (1.9.1–7). People come from the nearby Latin towns of Antemnae, Crustumerium, and Caenina, and also from the Sabines (1.9.8–9). The women of marriageable age are seized, their relatives run away (1.9.10–13). The three Latin towns mobilise before the Sabines (1.10.2). The army of Caenina is the first defeated, with Romulus celebrating the first triumph and dedicating a shrine to Jupiter Feretrius, the first temple founded in Rome (1.10.4–7). The army of Antemnae is the next defeated, and it is the new wife of Romulus, Hersilia, worn out by the prayers of the stolen women, who asks Romulus to spare their relatives from this place and admit them into the *ciuitas* (*precibus raptarum fatigata orat ut parentibus earum det ueniam et in ciuitatem accipiat*). She even spells out to Romulus the political advantages of this incorporation—'this way the state could unite in concord' (*ita rem coalescere concordia posse*, 1.11.2). Finally, the army of Crustumerium is defeated: colonies are sent to Antemnae and Crustumerium, with more signing up to go to Crustumerium, and from there many migrate to Rome, especially the parents and relatives of the stolen women (1.11.3–4).

A much more elaborate narrative follows to describe the attack on Rome by the Sabines under their king Titius Tatius. This attack has to be delayed long enough for babies to be born to the new marriages in Rome, so that the mothers can eventually break up the fighting by urging their warring menfolk not to stain their children and grandchildren with parricide (1.13.2). Here too a political settlement follows the end of fighting: 'they do not just make peace but one citizenship/state out of two; they make a partnership of the monarchy and transfer all sovereign authority to Rome' (*nec pacem modo sed ciuitatem unam ex duabus faciunt. regnum consociant: imperium omne Romam conferunt*, 1.13.4).

As Moatti has shown, 'The rape of the Sabine women ... to some extent constituted the paradigm for this Rome that was open to the whole world.'[67] The initial abduction of the Latin and Sabine women is inextricable from the immediate sequel of the reaction of their male relatives and the various political settlements that ensue.[68] The 'rape of the Sabine women' is at once an aetiology for Roman marriage and also a metaphor for Roman dealings with other peoples in general.[69] In both cases we have initial violence, followed by association, *concordia*, and *caritas*.[70] This moment of assimilation is when Romulus' people actually become 'Romans'. The Romans are first called *Romani* in Livy immediately after the first military victory (over Caenina), the first establishment of cult, the first triumph, and also—crucially—after the first marriage (1.11.1).[71] In fact, the word *ciuitas* first appears in Livy when Romulus is winning over the victims of his kidnapping, assuring them that 'they would be members of a partnership in all future outcomes and in the citizenship' (*illas ... in societate fortunarum omnium ciuitatisque ... fore*, 1.9.14); in Livy's text, the women are, literally, the first ones 'invited' to share in the partnership that is the citizenship.[72] As already noted above, it is one of the abducted women, Romulus' wife Hersilia, who is the first advocate of the further extension of citizenship—to the relatives of the women from Antemnae (1.11.2).[73] The second occurrence of the word *ciuitas* comes at the moment of union between Romans and Sabines (1.13.4), yet again expanding the circle of association out from the women to include their male relatives.

---

[67] Moatti (2015), 285; cf. 287 on how the story highlights 'the fact that the city was a *societas* that was based on an alliance, a contract between peoples or families with diverse origins'; cf. Nicolet (1980), 22; Capogrossi Colognesi (2014), 12–16; Atkins (2013), 133–8 on the implications of Cicero's understanding of a *populus* as a *societas*, a 'partnership', as in Roman law (*Rep.* 3.43). For speculation on the historical circumstances that may have generated or crystallised a need to focus on union of Romans and Sabines in particular (the incorporation of the Sabines into the *ciuitas* in 290), see Dench (2005), 14–15 and Carlà-Uhink (2017a), 118–20.

[68] Hallett (1984), 112–13; Stehle (1989), 150; Vandiver (1999), 212–15; Connolly (2007), 81.

[69] Miles (1995), 190–1; Vandiver (1999), 213–14; Gruen (2013), 4–5.

[70] R. Brown (1995), 313–18. As Vandiver (1999), 211 remarks, when stressing the importance of 'consent' in the ideology of Roman marriage (with reference to Treggiari (1991), 54–7, 170–80), 'From a modern point of view, of course, "consent" given under such circumstances hardly qualifies as consent at all': the same could often be said of the incorporation of defeated enemies into the *ciuitas*, as has been noted by Cornell (1995), 323–4. For bibliography on Roman acknowledgement of the elements of *raptus* involved in the wedding ceremony, regularly interpreted as a trace of the very first wedding, see Vol. 2, Chapter 16, 305.

[71] Cf. Vandiver (1999), 209 on 1.9.16 (*uirorum*), where, after earlier being referred to as '*turba omnis* (1.8.6), *Romana pubes* (1.9.6) and *iuuentus Romana* (1.9.10)', 'Romulus' new citizens only become *viri*—in the sense of men as well as of husbands—when they acquire wives.'

[72] Vandiver (1999), 215 on the later intervention of the women into the battle between Romans and Sabines: 'this scene ... forms one of the crucial points at which it can be plausibly argued that Rome truly comes into existence as a *civitas*'.

[73] Well stressed by R. Brown (1995), 302–3.

As Cicero shows (*Balb*. 31), it was possible not to include a reference to the intermarriage between Romans and Sabines when praising Romulus' treaty with the Sabines as a foundational paradigm for the later Roman penchant for expanding the citizenship by assimilation—even if Cicero elsewhere does include such a reference, as in *De Re Publica* 2 (12–13), with explicit stress on the agency of the women (*cum T. Tatio, rege Sabinorum, foedus icit matronis ipsis, quae raptae erant, orantibus*, 13). Livy, however, regularly links marriage with the evolution of the citizenship, as we see, above all, in the speech of C. Canuleius in Book 4: it is no accident that the most eloquent speech Livy presents in praise of admitting foreigners and extending the *ciuitas* to defeated enemies is actually delivered in order to advocate intermarriage between patricians and plebeians and the election of plebeians to the consulate. 'We have given the citizenship', says Canuleius, 'which is more than marriage, even to defeated enemies' (*nos quidem ciuitatem, quae plus quam conubium est, hostibus etiam uictis dedimus*, 4.3.4); as an example of the Roman tradition of admitting talent to the citizen body, he gives the familiar list of foreigners who have moved to Rome to become kings or leading patricians, from Numa to the *gens Claudia* (4.3.10–14), and Alban and Sabine *gentes* (4.4.7).[74] This tactic is part of a general strategy of Livy's, whereby he links important constitutional transformations to moments where women are foregrounded as victims and as agents of change, as we have already seen with the Latin and Sabine women: other prominent examples are Tanaquil at the beginning of the Etruscan monarchy at Rome (1.34.5–8), and Tullia (1.46.2–48.7) and Lucretia at its end (1.58); Verginia at the restoration of the Republic after the tyranny of the Decemvirs (3.44–8); and Fabia, whose humiliation at being married to a plebeian and being upstaged by her sister's marriage to a patrician leads eventually to the Licinio-Sextian rogations of 367 (6.34.5–11).[75]

After the *foedus* with the Sabines, the next great moment of amalgamation comes when Alba Longa is destroyed by Tullus Hostilius and the

---

[74] Moatti (2015), 285 distills the message of Canuleius' speech: 'Not only were the Romans a mixed people from the very start, but they proceeded to welcome numerous foreigners into their city.' Canuleius' speech had a great impact both on the emperor Claudius' speech on the admission to citizenship of the elite of Gallia Comata and on Tacitus' version of it in *Ann*. 11.24: Malloch (2013), 341–2 (and index s.v. 'Canuleius, C. (*tr. pl.* 445 BC)'. Syme (1958), 318 notes that Tacitus includes a reference to the theme of intermarriage, although Claudius' original speech had said nothing of it: Tacitus' Claudius speaks of the leading Gauls, whose admission to the citizenship he is advocating, as 'already mingled with us in custom, culture, and marriage' (*iam moribus artibus adfinitatibus nostris mixti*, 11.24.6).

[75] On Fabia, Kraus (1991); Oakley (1997–2005), 1.646–7. Bibliography on the other women is very large: for an introduction to bibliography on Livy's women, Vandiver (1999), 219 n.2; Hornblower (2019), 71 n.8; see too Keith (2000), 102–3.

entire population is moved to Rome, doubling the number of citizens and bringing key noble families into the Roman story, including the Iulii (1.30.1).⁷⁶ This pattern of destruction followed by incorporation is soon emulated by Ancus Marcius in the case of the Latin city of Politorium (*hostibus in ciuitatem accipiendis*, 1.33.1). Together with more new citizens from Tellenae and Ficana these people are settled on the Aventine, joining the Romans on the Palatine, the Sabines on the Capitoline, and the Albans on the Caelian (1.33.2); later conquests yield another crop of many thousands of new citizens from Latium, who find a home between the Aventine and the Palatine, near the altar of Murcia (1.33.5); yet another *quartier* of the city is given over to outsiders in the next book, when survivors from the defeat of an Etruscan army at Aricia are given a welcome in Rome, and end up in the 'Etruscan district' (*uicus Tuscus*, 2.14.9). We shall return in Section VI to the eventual fate of all these separate and discrete areas of habitation within the city.

Already by the reign of the fourth king, then, Livy has opened up for us a wide range of paradigmatic possibilities for amalgamation after a city's defeat: certain leading members of a defeated city may be awarded citizenship (Antemnae, 1.11.2); there may be extensive migration to Rome (Crustumerium, 1.11.4); a kind of κοινωνία may be set up (Romans and Sabines, 1.1.34); or else a city may be obliterated and its citizens moved to Rome (Alba Longa, 1.30.1, together with Politorium and the other targets of Ancus Marcius' campaigns, 1.33). We still have two-hundred-and-fifty years to wait before the first case of what will become the most distinctive form of incorporation into the Roman *ciuitas*—when a city's population become Romans and remain living in their original site under their own local government (end of Section VI below).

Romulus' 'lie' about the Roman citizen body's relationship to the soil of Rome will be returned to and capped in Book 5 with the refoundation of the city after the Gallic sack. The foundational acts of the other great founder-king, Numa, will also be capped there. The following section is devoted to the fictions of the second king.

## IV

The next crucial moment at which the fictive grounding of Roman institutions comes into view is with the foundational acts of the second

---

[76] On Alba Longa as a key paradigm for Roman assimilation of outsiders into the citizenship, Feldherr (1998), chapter 4.

king, Numa Pompilius. Numa wants to found Rome for a second time. It has already been founded by violence and arms, and now it needs to be founded afresh by laws and customs (*urbem nouam conditam ui et armis, iure eam legibusque ac moribus de integro condere parat*, 1.19.1).[77] Numa has a special plan to make sure that the Romans do not go soft during the period of peace necessary for this work to go ahead (1.19.4–5):

> omnium primum, rem ad multitudinem imperitam et illis saeculis rudem efficacissimam, deorum metum iniciendum ratus est. qui cum descendere ad animos sine aliquo commento miraculi non posset, simulat sibi cum dea Egeria congressus nocturnos esse; eius se monitu quae acceptissima dis essent sacra instituere, sacerdotes suos cuique deorum praeficere.

> First of all, as a thing most effective for targeting a mob that were ignorant and, at that epoch, uncouth, he thought the fear of the gods needed to be injected. Since this could not enter their minds without the fiction of a miraculous event, he pretended that he had meetings at night with the goddess Egeria, and that it was according to her prompting that he set up the rites that were most acceptable to the gods, and put their own priests in charge of each of the gods.

Armed with the authority of this fiction, Numa sets to work, beginning with the calendar, the essential framework for Roman religious activity (1.19.6–7), and then moving on to a whole range of religious institutions and priesthoods, the bedrock of Roman religion down to Livy's day (1.20).

Numa's plan works, and the Romans become deeply pious and true to their word (1.21.1–2). Livy stresses the importance of *fides* in his account at the beginning of this section (1.21.1), and the culminating act of Numa's religious work is to establish the cult of *Fides*, the last cult he is described as instituting: *et Fidei sollemne instituit* (1.21.4). In Dionysius of Halicarnassus the foundation of the cult of *Fides* (Πίστις δημοσία) is also the culmination of the account of Numa's religious reforms (*Ant. Rom.* 2.75), but in Livy's account the establishment of the cult of *Fides* gives the opportunity for another potentially destabilising moment of irony, for it follows immediately upon a second section on Numa's staged meetings with his nymph-wife Egeria (1.21.3–4):

> lucus erat quem medium ex opaco specu fons perenni rigabat aqua. quo quia se persaepe Numa sine arbitris uelut ad congressum deae inferebat, Camenis eum lucum sacrauit, quod earum ibi concilia cum coniuge sua Egeria essent. et Fidei sollemne instituit.

---

[77] On the constant pairing of Romulus and Numa as a 'diptych' of founding figures, see Sailor (2006), 361–2, with reference to earlier studies; see Lowrie (2013), 85 for Numa as the first second founder, after Romulus, beginning a line of refounders of the city. Cf. Verg. *Aen.* 6.810–11, of Numa, *regis Romani primam qui legibus urbem/fundabit.*

> There was a grove, through the middle of which a spring flowed from a dark cave, watering it all year round. Because Numa very often took himself there without eye-witnesses as if for a meeting with the goddess, he dedicated this grove to the Camenae, on the grounds that this is where he had his planning sessions with his wife Egeria. And he set up a rite for Fides.

This second section on Numa's charades concerning his relations with Egeria looks like a closural moment of ring-composition, taking us back to the first section on his fictive meetings at night with Egeria, which opened the whole account of Numa's religious foundations two OCT pages earlier. This closural effect will lead readers to feel that they have come to the end of the account of Numa's religious foundations, but in fact there is one last cult he sets up. Following directly on from more talk of his staged divine meetings, the name of the cult is very telling: *Fides* is not just 'Good faith, honesty, honour' (*Oxford Latin Dictionary* s.v. §6a), but 'the quality of being worthy of belief, credibility' (s.v. §9a). Numa's culminating religious act is to set up a cult to the quality that is going to make people believe in the institutions he has invented on the supposed authority of a water-nymph. It is as if Livy's Numa is saying to himself, 'I've used this cunning fiction about my wife to set up all these cults, now I had better set up an extra cult to make sure people believe in them.'

Now, the idea that religious institutions are the product of the state, that they are in fact *human* institutions, is in itself by no means scandalous. It had recently been given canonical expression by Varro in his *Antiquitates Rerum Humanarum et Diuinarum*, published in 46 BCE. Here Varro declares that he had written about human affairs first, before divine ones, because states come into existence first, and then things relating to the divine are instituted by them; his procedure would have been the reverse, he says, if he had been writing a philosophical account about the general nature of gods and humans (*si de omni natura deorum et hominum scriberemus, prius diuina absoluissemus, quam humana adtigissemus*, Aug. *De civ. D.* 6.4–5 = fr. 5 Cardauns).[78] The further idea that religion in general was invented to instil fear in the ordinary people is likewise not unique. A fragment generally attributed to Critias' drama *Sisyphus* is the most cynical expression of this belief that we know of, with the gods themselves being merely an idea thought up by a wise and clever man to ensure that people behaved properly even in secret out of a fear of divine punishment:[79] religion, according to this

---

[78] Linderski (1982), 17–18.
[79] Critias *TrGF* 43 F19I: see Bremmer (2006), 16–18 for discussion and for problems of attribution.

view, 'is from the start a process of social control'.⁸⁰ Polybius gives a more sober and politically level-headed expression to this fundamental idea, keyed in to the Roman experience in particular: he praises the Romans for their maintenance of religion as a means of holding the state together, instilling a fear of the gods (δεισιδαιμονία) in the common people in order to keep their lawless passions in check (6.56.6–12). Something like this will have been a prevalent view among the *nobilitas* of Livy's day: according to Cicero, for example, augury and all its apparatus is retained 'with a view to the mindset of the common people and the great practical benefits augury gives the state' (*ad opinionem uulgi et magnas utilitates rei publicae*, Div. 2.70).⁸¹

Livy is not very far from Polybius, and in fact what Polybius goes on to say in the following section about the sway of sworn good faith among Roman magistrates (6.56.14) is very close to what Livy has to say about how, as a result of Numa's actions, the Romans came to be governed by 'their sworn good faith' (*fides ac iusiurandum*) rather than by laws and penalties (1.21.1). For all his overt presentation of Rome's religious system as a human construct, Livy is not decrying such an analysis of religious affairs.⁸² As Feldherr puts it, in a discussion of the deceptions perpetrated by Numa and later by Scipio Africanus, with his pretense to the troops of divine visions (26.41.18): 'Livy's exposure of the public statements of Numa and Scipio as false neither in any way discredits either figure nor diminishes the value of the actions endorsed by the fictive claims: Numa's reforms established the religious institutions under which the Roman state achieved its empire, and Scipio's election provides the turning point in the Second Punic War.'⁸³

Nonetheless, Livy's repeated stress on Numa's fictive grounding for his religious lawmaking is distinctive. Numa's fictional work with Egeria is in the tradition, of course, as we see in Dionysius of Halicarnassus and later in Plutarch's *Life of Numa*; but Livy highlights Numa's deliberate acts of imposture more than the other sources.⁸⁴ Livy could easily have given the kind of treatment Cicero provides in the second book of *De Re Publica*

---

⁸⁰ Whitmarsh (2016), 95 (94–6 for discussion of the fragment).
⁸¹ See Pease (1920–3) ad loc. and also Pease (1955–8), on *Nat. D.* 1.118 for a collection of such views. Cf. Döring (1978) (views from Critias to Cicero); Linderski (1982); Kraus (1994a), 93 (on Liv. 6.1.10) for 'religious fear as a form of social control', citing Liebeschuetz (1979), 4–7.
⁸² Levene (1993), 136.   ⁸³ Feldherr (1998), 66–7; cf. Sailor (2006), 342–4.
⁸⁴ Levene (1993), 136. Dionysius has one of his usual 'marvellous vs. rationalising' presentations (2.60.4–61.2), in which Numa's pretense concerning the role of Egeria is one of a number of options (2.61.1); Plutarch certainly mentions the version of Numa's masquerade (4.8, 8.6), but also includes sections where the story of the relationship with Egeria is presented as a fable (4.1–3; 15), distanced through *oratio obliqua* and through reflections on the naivety of that distant time (15.6).

(26–7), where there is nothing of Egeria at all. Numa the showman and spindoctor is peculiarly Livy's choice—not his invention, but his choice. The distinctiveness of Livy's procedure is demonstrated obliquely by the fact that Ovid unerringly homes in on the markedly 'fictive' moments of Livy's Numa-narrative when he adapts it for his *Metamorphoses* and *Fasti*— Ovid's whole focus is on Numa's inspiration by Pythagoras (denounced as false by Livy, 1.18.2–4) and his staged relationship with Egeria.[85] Ovid understood Livy's methods and priorities extremely well.

In the immediate context, Livy is highlighting this aspect of his tradition in order to demonstrate that Varro was right—that religious institutions are human institutions, grounded in particular historical moments. Livy's objective is nothing so trivial as to convince his readers that Numa as a matter of fact lied to the people; rather, this is a narratologically persuasive way of setting out in memorable terms the fact that there are no 'natural' ways for societies' institutions to come into being. But he is also looking much further ahead in time. As we shall see in the next section, Livy is setting up this issue because he is going to return to it in order to demonstrate that these contingently produced human mechanisms—the result of calculated political decisions by a particular historical agent— actually do become and remain sacralised, talismanic, religious. Numa's foundational work is still ongoing in Livy's Rome, as Feldherr makes clear: 'Despite the historian's reference to the "rude and unsophisticated multitude" [1.19.4] of Numa's day, Livy's presentation of the king's reforms also emphasizes both explicitly and implicitly the continuing impact of the institutions, however distant in time, upon contemporary Rome.'[86] Sailor argues that Livy's contemporary reader can see through Numa's stagings: 'The distancing inherent in the project of writing in the present about action in the past is here activated, to considerable effect: at that time and in that circumstance, the multitude believed; now, encountering the story across time and through text, we do not.'[87] Except that, in a certain sense, we do, or Livy's readers do—every time that they view or participate in any of Rome's religious cults they do 'believe'.

Further, Livy's readers are witnesses to a contemporary religious programme of continuity enmeshed in the same processes of innovation, as Livy reminds us at the very beginning of his account of Numa's religious foundations, with his foregrounded reference to Augustus' closing of Janus

---

[85] Aresi (forthcoming), on Ovid's presentation of Numa as being given inspiration by Pythagoras (*Met.* 15.1–8, 479–81), or Egeria (*Met.* 15.482–90; *Fast.* 3.273–6), or either (*Fast.* 3.151–4).
[86] Feldherr (1998), 70.   [87] Sailor (2006), 355.

after the Actium war (1.19.3).[88] Not only Numa but also Romulus is a clear prototype for Augustus in the religious realm.[89] Livy, for example, alludes to the cult of Divus Iulius when he emphasises that the only pre-existing foreign cult on the site of Rome that Romulus took over was that of Hercules, since Romulus was 'even then a fan of the immortality imparted by manly courage towards which his own destiny was leading him' (*iam tum immortalitatis uirtute partae ad quam eum sua fata ducebant fautor*, 1.7.15).[90]

What we see being formed in this early phase of the *History* is what Davies calls Livy's 'reconstructed religious system'. Livy has created a system of representing Roman religion that makes sense in terms of his inherited material but that, more importantly, captures what he sees as distinctive about Rome's progress: 'As was appropriate for historiography, he has created a model that "lies" (or at least, varies events) to tell the truth.'[91] Livy and Numa are collaborating in using their fictions to establish Roman religious practices and to ensure their continuity.

## V

The crucial moment that brings all these issues of foundation and fiction together is the run of action at the end of Book 5—the Gallic sack and its redemption, leading up to the refounding of Rome with Camillus' magnificent speech at the very end of Book 5.[92]

The year before the Gallic sack Camillus had gone into exile in Ardea rather than face indictment on the charge of misuse of the plunder from Veii (5.32.7–9). After he returns from exile to rescue the sacked city from the Gauls, the tribunes suggest, to popular approval, that the population should move from the devastated site to Veii, which had been captured by Camillus six years before (5.49.8). The gravity tugging the Roman people to the site of Veii has been gathering in strength for some time, ever since the end of Book 4, when pay for the legions was introduced for the very first time (4.59.11). At the beginning of Book 5 it turns out, according to the tribunes, that this had been a move designed to make it possible for the legions to remain semi-permanently absent from Rome, encamped over winter in their siege of Veii (5.2.1–3): the siege, with its unprecedented enforcement of absence from Rome, is in itself a variety of migration to

---

[88] Feldherr (1998), 70; Sailor (2006), 365–6 in general on Augustus and Numa. As Chris Kraus points out to me, this is one of only three explicit references to Augustus in the extant *History*.
[89] Miles (1995), 164–6; von Ungern-Sternberg (1998). [90] Sailor (2006), 364.
[91] J.P. Davies (2004), 139.
[92] Ogilvie (1965), 742: 'The speech is ... designed to form a tail-piece to the first five books.'

Veii. Following the capture of Veii there had been repeated proposals by the tribunes to move either half the population to the site (5.24.7–8) or the whole of it (5.29–30). After the catastrophe of the battle of the Allia most of the army had, in effect, 'migrated' to Veii, 'forgetting everything to such an extent that the great majority fled/went into exile to Veii, an enemy city, on the other side of the Tiber from the Gauls, rather than go straight to Rome to their wives and children' (*tanta omnium obliuio, ut multo maior pars Veios in hostium urbem, cum Tiberis arceret, quam recto itinere Romam ad coniuges ac liberos fugerent*, 5.38.5). In the face of the tribunes' proposal actually to migrate to Veii, Camillus makes a long speech to the people in a *contio* arguing against the move (eight OCT pages, 5.51–4). The words of Camillus make a real impact on his audience, even if the decision is still in balance (*rem dubiam*) until a chance event just after his speech is accepted by the Senate as an *omen oblatiuum* directing them to stay on the site of Rome and rebuild the city (5.55.1–2).

Shortly before the speech, as Camillus returns in triumph to the city after defeating the Gauls, Livy has his soldiers hail him as 'Romulus, parent of the fatherland, a second founder of the city' (*Romulus ac parens patriae conditorque alter urbis*, 5.49.7).[93] If Camillus is another Romulus 'having saved the city by war, he saves it a second time in peace by barring the migration to Veii' (*seruatam deinde bello patriam iterum in pace haud dubie seruauit cum prohibuit migrari Veios*, 5.49.8). At this point he becomes another Numa as well as another Romulus, as he proceeds to safeguard the city's religion and ensure the continuance of Numa's institutions (5.50.1–7); the theme is clearly sounded by the significant allusion from this passage back to the passage in which Numa's reforms were introduced in Book 1, where Livy informs us that 'Numa prepared to found afresh by laws and customs the new city that had been founded by violence and arms' (*urbem nouam conditam ui et armis, iure eam legibusque ac moribus de integro condere parat*, 1.19.1).[94] When Camillus comes to itemise key Roman cults in his speech, he begins with the same ones Livy had attributed to Numa in 1.20.1–4 (Jupiter, Vesta, Mars, Quirinus, 5.52.6–7).[95] Camillus, then, is both another Romulus and another Numa.[96]

---

[93] On Camillus as another Romulus in Livy, see Ogilvie (1965) ad loc.; Oakley (1997–2005), 2.37 (on Liv. 7.1.10); Gaertner (2008), 37 n.56. Livy sounds the theme again in his obituary notice of Camillus (7.1.10); in general, see Weinstock (1971), chapter IX ('The Founder', 175–99), on Romulus and his successors (Camillus, Marius, Sulla, Cicero, Julius Caesar).
[94] Levene (1993), 201.
[95] Stübler (1941), 84; cf. Levene (1993), 201; Stevenson (2000), 41–2; Gaertner (2008), 40 n.65.
[96] Burck (1964), 43–4; Levene (1993), 201; Miles (1995), 92; Gaertner (2008), 40 n.65, 42.

The ring-composition inherent in this modelling rounds off the first pentad of the *History*.[97] It also reinforces a major Livian theme—derived more directly from Cicero than from anyone else, but pervasive in the Roman political tradition—that Rome is never just 'founded', but rather perpetuates herself in a continual process of refoundation.[98] This theme is strongly sounded at the beginning of Book 6, when Livy informs us that from now on his narrative will be 'a more clear and definite exposition of the deeds at home and at war of a city reborn from a second origin as if from the roots, more fertile and luxuriant' (*clariora deinceps certioraque ab secunda origine uelut ab stirpibus laetius feraciusque renatae urbis gesta domi militiaeque exponentur*, 6.1.3). Here he gathers the threads together from the previous book, where he had presented a re-run of the whole foundational sequence of Book 1, with a new distinction between *fabula* and *historia* to cap the one introduced in the Preface (6–7); now, as Kraus has shown, the ghost of Troy has finally been laid to rest, Rome's fall has been averted, and a newly definitive foundation may take place in the full light of historical day.[99]

Camillus' refoundation of the city has long been interpreted as not only looking back to the original founder (Romulus) and the first refounder (Numa), but also looking forward to Augustus, who was proclaiming himself as refounding the city yet again even as Livy was composing these books:[100] 'Augustus was both Numa and Romulus.'[101] As Gaertner has demonstrated in detail, Livy certainly did not invent the concept of Camillus as another Romulus (or Numa) and as a model of piety, nor has Livy invented the idea that the 'rebirth' of Rome after the Gallic sack was a second foundation; further, Camillus had been an *exemplum* for nobles to model themselves on long before Augustus, who was continuing a tradition from the Republic in this respect as in so many others.[102] The language of *parens/pater patriae*, applied to Camillus by Livy and regularly interpreted as

---

[97] Above, n.27.
[98] Cic. *Rep.* 2.2, referring to Cato's *Origines* (F131 *FRHist*, where see Cornell's comm. ad loc. for the important parallel passage of Polyb. 6.10.12–14 and discussion of the topos); Serres (1991), 263 ('Foundation is recurrent. It returns like a refrain.'); Kraus (1994b), 284–5; Miles (1995), chapter 2; Mineo (2003), 349–50; Lowrie (2005), 952–3, 968; Feeney (2007), 101–4; Lowrie (2010); (2013) (98–9 on Camillus).
[99] Kraus (1994a), 25–6; (1994b), esp. 269 and 283–4; cf. Kraus (2019), 353–4 on 5.21.7–9, where the *fabula* of the Romans dashing from their mine to grab the entrails of the Etruscan sacrifice is presented in the same manner as the discussion in the Preface (6–7) of Romulus' divine birth.
[100] Burck (1992), 170–6; Miles (1995), 88–94; Edwards (1996), 47–9; Mineo (2003), 346–8.
[101] Galinsky (1996), 84.
[102] Gaertner (2008). Cf. U. Walter (2004), 382–407 for general discussion of Camillus in the Roman exemplary tradition; for Augustus modelling himself on Camillus, see von Ungern-Sternberg (1998); U. Walter (2004), 403 n.122; Gaertner (2008), 52.

a specifically Augustan allusion, had been applied before him to Fabius Cunctator, Marius, Cicero and Caesar.[103] Although Gaertner deploys the earlier traditional material in order to downplay a parallelism in Livy between Camillus and Augustus, the fresh topicality of the old story gives a new charge to the parallels and enforces a contemporary reading.[104] As Uwe Walter has argued, Camillus is a bridge between two epochs, just as Augustus is a bridge between two epochs: there is a structural typology at work here as well as an exemplary moral patterning.[105]

We may add two further considerations to the pattern of a typological relationship between Camillus and Augustus, and between Camillus' contemporaries and Augustus'. The obsession with the danger of moving the city reactivates anxieties going back to the time of Julius Caesar, freshly heightened by the perceived threats of Marcus Antonius and his Egyptian queen.[106] And a crucial extra dimension to the Camillus/Augustus typology is provided by Camillus' use of a newly talismanic number in the middle of his speech. He tells his fellow-citizens that their city is still young, in only its 365th year (5.54.5). This significant number, conjuring the idea of a 'great year', cannot have been in the Camillus-tradition before Livy, since a Roman year had had 365 days only since 1 January 45 BCE, when Julius Caesar's calendar reform came into effect.[107] It is 365 years from the foundation of Rome by Romulus to the refoundation by Camillus, and then—as first argued in detail by Miles—365 years from the refoundation by Camillus to the new refoundation by Augustus.[108] The

---

[103] Gaertner (2008), 38 and n.60.
[104] Ogilvie (1965), 739: 'although the tradition that Camillus was complimented in these terms [as another Romulus] may well be older than L., a Roman reader of the 20's would be bound to feel their contemporary force'.
[105] U. Walter (2004), 402–3; cf. Miles (1995), 89–92. Gaertner (2008), 41–2 has himself clearly shown how Livy has systematically transformed his inherited material in order to put Camillus directly in the spotlight from the beginning to the end of the debate over the fate of the sacked city, and I cannot agree with him that 'Livy's technique of pruning and rearranging the traditional material is obviously determined by literary, not ideological considerations' (42): these are not mutually exclusive terms. Gaertner is very justifiably resisting the scholars who see such typological patterning as inherently and inevitably part of a programme of Livian panegyric of Augustus; but in fact, as Miles (1995), 93 well puts it, 'identification of Camillus and Augustus ... need not preclude a complex attitude toward Augustus on Livy's part'; cf. Stevenson (2000), 37–8 and, already, Ogilvie (1965), 742–3.
[106] Ogilvie (1965), 741–2; Ceausescu (1976); Kraus (1994b), 280–1; Edwards (1996), 47–8; Stevenson (2000), 28, 36; Mineo (2003), 348; Nisbet-Rudd (2004), 36–8; Labate (2013) on Horace *Epodes* 16 and *Odes* 3.3, with 220–2 on Camillus' speech; Isayev (2017), 394; Kraus (forthcoming a).
[107] Feeney (2007), 101–2; cf. Hubaux (1958), 70–88 for the symbolism of the number in Camillus' speech.
[108] Miles (1995), 95; cf. Feeney (2007), 101–2; Mazzarino (1966), 3.44–6 on this cycle of time and the importance of Romulus, Camillus, and Augustus as a sequence in the eyes of Livy.

arithmetic does not work quite as neatly as sometimes claimed by those who are using Varronian dates instead of the basically Polybian chronology Livy is following, but the significance of the numerology is clear.[109] As Livy presents his first pentad to his fellow-citizens sometime between 27 and 25 BCE, he can invite them to see the refoundation by Camillus as the halfway point of Roman history so far, midway between Romulus' foundation and 'now', when the city is undergoing yet another refoundation.[110]

If Camillus, then, is another Romulus and another Numa, what becomes of the two kings' fictions of Roman soil and Roman religion in his great speech? Camillus begins by spelling out the religious lessons of recent events, to conclude that success only returned to the Romans when they returned to proper observance of the gods (5.51.4–10). All the rituals of Roman religion, he goes on to say, are fixed deeply and inextricably in the physical site of the city: the religious rites of the city cannot be performed anywhere but on this site (5.52).[111] After denouncing the idea of abandoning the site for an uncertain future in Veii, Camillus then appeals to the overwhelming emotional importance of the landscape and physical setting of the city, and here he uses remarkable language that takes us back to the very different version of the Romans' relationship to the landscape that we had seen in Book 1 (5.54.2–3):

> adeo nihil tenet solum patriae nec haec terra quam matrem appellamus, sed in superficie tignisque caritas nobis patriae pendet? equidem fatebor uobis, etsi minus iniuriae uestrae quam meae calamitatis meminisse iuuat: cum abessem, quotienscumque patria in mentem ueniret, haec omnia occurrebant, colles campique et Tiberis et adsueta oculis regio et hoc caelum sub quo natus educatusque essem; quae uos, Quirites, nunc moueant potius caritate sua ut maneatis in sede uestra quam postea, cum reliqueritis eam, macerent desiderio.

> Does the soil of the fatherland and this earth which we call mother have so little hold on you? Does our love of the fatherland depend on buildings and

---

[109] E.g. Miles (1995), 95; U. Walter (2004), 402, both arguing that 365 years from the Gallic sack in 391/0 takes us to 27 (with inclusive counting): see Oakley (1998), 284 on how this calculation does not take into account the difference between Varro's and Livy's chronology. Livy is following Polybian, not Varronian, chronology, and Polybius puts the Gallic sack in Ol. 98, 2 = 387/6, not the Varronian 390, as convention now has it (Walbank (1957–79), 1.46–7 [the date is ultimately Timaeus']); the foundation date is therefore Ol. 7, 2 = 751/0 (see Walbank (1957–79), 1.665–9 for Polybius' foundation date). 387/6 minus 365 = 23/2 (counting inclusively): if we want to press for precision (although I do not think we need to), then Livy's first readers can see the 'great year' coming around again in the immediate future.

[110] Miles (1995), 95; cf. Edwards (1996), 48–9; Stevenson (2000), 34. There is no space here to argue in detail for this dating of the first pentad, which is basically the one first set out by Luce (1965/2009), and espoused by Moles (1993/2009), 68, 70 n.56; Kraus (1994a), 5; Scheidel (2009), 656.

[111] Edwards (1996), 46–7.

planks? Indeed I will confess to you, although it is more upsetting to remember the injury you did me than my own disaster: when I was away [in exile], whenever the fatherland came to my mind, all of this appeared to me, the hills and the plains and the Tiber, the region that my eyes were used to, and this sky under which I had been born and raised; it would be better, fellow-citizens, that these things now move you, by the love you feel for them, to remain in your dwelling-place than that later, when you have left it, they make you waste away with nostalgia.

The earth of Rome now really is a 'mother', with a sky under which Camillus was born and raised: these fixed features (in a characteristically Livian pun) should 'move' the citizens (*moueant*) not to move.

We return shortly to examine the full consequences of this language of 'earth as mother' and 'love', and the way in which it rewrites what had happened in Romulus' asylum. First we note the closely related way that the choice of the site of Rome is presented very differently in Book 5 from the way it had been presented in Book 1. Camillus proceeds immediately after the passage just quoted to tell his audience that it was not without good reason gods and men chose this site for founding the city, and he enumerates all the advantages that come from being on healthy hills, in the centre of Italy, by a river not too far from the sea and not too close to it (5.54.4). This version of why the site was chosen for the new city is very different from what Livy had told us in Book 1. There he simply says that 'Romulus and Remus were seized by a desire to found a city in the spot where they had been exposed and brought up' (*in iis locis ubi expositi ubique educati erant*, 1.6.3). These alternative versions go back to Book 2 of Cicero's *De Re Publica*. First, Scipio says that Romulus very cleverly chose this brilliant site for his city, listing all the same advantages that Livy's character Camillus does here (2.5,10, 11).[112] When Laelius later refers back to Scipio's exposition, he speaks differently, pointing out that Scipio attributed to a rational plan those things done by Romulus through accident or necessity (*illa de urbis situ reuoces ad rationem, quae a Romulo casu aut necessitate facta sunt*, 2.22). In Livy, we have Laelius' version in Book 1, where the city is founded where it was just because that is where the boys were exposed and reared; in Book 5 we have Scipio's version, and Romulus' choice now looks providential. The feeling that the site of Rome is divinely chosen is reinforced at the very end of Camillus' speech, where he drives home the point that Rome's religious identity is bound up with

---

[112] Gaertner (2008), 44–5, with details of Livy's debts to Cicero's phrasing and with references to earlier scholarship (n.75); K.F.B. Fletcher (2014), 147–8; Carlà-Uhink (2017a), 165–8; (2017b), 129–30.

rites that are 'here' (*hic*, five times, 5.54.7).[113] Livy repeats his pun on *mouere*, and the first word after the speech ends informs us that Camillus moved his audience (*mouisse eos Camillus . . . dicitur*, 5.55.1).[114]

Since Camillus' whole job is to do repetition, to do things for the second time, it is no accident that this climactic speech of his is a repetition of a much shorter speech that he had already given three years earlier, when the tribunes had also proposed that the whole people migrate to Veii (5.30.1–3).[115] Here for the first time Camillus uses the highly emotive language of 'birth from the soil', as he pleads with the senate to act against this legislation in the spirit of men 'who remembered that the struggle would be on behalf of altars, hearths, the temples of the gods, *and the soil in which they had been born*' (*ut qui meminissent sibi pro aris focisque et deum templis ac solo in quo nati essent dimicandum fore*, 5.30.1). The senators take his advice and plead with the people not to leave the sacred sites (Capitol, temple of Vesta, 5.30.4), and not to live in exile 'away from the soil of the fathers and the household gods of the city' (*ab solo patrio ac dis penatibus*, 5.30.6). It is significant that this emotional language is still not as pointed as Camillus': the senators tone down Camillus' 'soil in which they had been born' to 'soil inherited from one's fathers'. Camillus himself, later in the book, when haranguing his troops before they attack the Gauls, uses this slightly less charged vocabulary, telling his men to have before their eyes 'the shrines of the gods, their wives and children, and the soil of the fatherland' (*fana deum et coniuges et liberos et solum patriae*, 5.49.3). Crucially, in his climactic speech at the end of the book this same phrase *solum patriae* returns, but this time it is immediately followed and capped by *haec terra quam matrem appellamus* ('this earth which we call mother', 5.54.2).

The language of the earth as mother takes us all the way back to the beginning of the city, with a whole lot of men being given asylum on the site of Rome, and with Romulus alluding to the usual city-founders' lie that they were born out of the earth (1.8.5). 365 years later, Romulus' noble

---

[113] Edwards (1996), 45–52.

[114] Henderson (2000), 15 (not referring to a particular passage, but presumably intending 5.55.1). Again, Camillus' speech did not conclusively persuade the people; that required the senate's acceptance of the omen of the centurion's command to his troops to 'stay put' (5.55.1–2).

[115] Ogilvie (1965), 741 (on Camillus' speech at the end of Book 5): 'The proposed removal of the capital from Rome to Veii raises interesting questions. As are many things associated with Camillus, it is reduplicated.' In fact Camillus had already spoken out against a similar idea earlier, when the proposal had been to have two cities, half in Veii and half in Rome (5.24.5): his short speech in *oratio obliqua* concentrates simply on the question of the tithe owed to Apollo from the booty taken at Veii (5.25.4–6).

lie has become a noble truth. The Romans really are born out of this particular soil. To Camillus in exile, as we saw, all his memories were of the hills and the fields and the Tiber and the region familiar to his eyes, and this sky beneath which he had been born and reared: this was *haec terra quam matrem appellamus*, 'this earth which we call mother'. It is a piece of earth for which the Romans now feel 'love', *caritas* (5.54.3)—just as the modern nationalisms studied by Benedict Anderson succeed in generating 'political love' and '"natural ties"' among their citizens.[116]

If Romulus' lie has become a truth, Numa's fictions have also become fully real, with the priesthoods and rites inconceivable in other locales. In the final sentence of his speech, in referring to the very last cult that he mentions, Camillus says that 'here the *ancilia* were sent down from heaven' (*hic ancilia caelo demissa*, 5.54.7). Numa had ordered the Salii to carry these 'heavenly' arms through the city (*caelestia ... arma, quae ancilia appellantur*, 1.20.4). From the same sky under which Camillus had been born and raised were sent down the heavenly shields which Numa had entrusted to the Salii.

At the close of the first pentad we have a very satisfying conclusion. The lie of Romulus and the fictions of Numa have been sacralised and made real on the physical site of Rome.

## VI

But history moves on, as it always does, and there are another 365 years to go, down to Livy's time. Camillus' idealised vision of a Rome where the landscape itself is the natural home of the Roman people is extremely interesting in the light of subsequent Roman history. As the *History* continues, the conclusion of Book 5 loses its apparently satisfying closural power and becomes just one episode in Livy's developing story about that most magnificent of Roman corporate fictions, the citizenship.[117]

Camillus' idea that the Romans have finally managed to become naturalised on the site of Rome after 365 years looks very piquant from the point of view of Livy's immediate readership in the 20s BCE. Livy's readers are

---

[116] B. Anderson (1983), 143; cf. Bonjour (1975a), 469–74 and Ando (2015), 18 on the affective language in Camillus' speech. It is important that Livy implies in his preface to Book 2 that the Romans had developed *caritas ... ipsius soli* by the time of the expulsion of Tarquinius Superbus (2.1.5); this theme lies undeveloped until it is reactivated by Camillus and heightened with reference to this earth as a mother (5.54.2).

[117] Luce (1977), 243–4 on Livy's original insight 'that the Roman national character was a product of the historical process—explicable, in fact, only in terms of that process'.

living with a very different ideology of citizenship, which had developed especially in the aftermath of the Social War (91–88), when everyone in the Italian peninsula south of the plain of the Po became a Roman citizen, while still retaining membership of their own local community (*municipium*).[118] In Livy's time, the body of Roman citizens is living with a new kind of fiction as a result of the fallout from the Social War—a shared citizenship and identity, one that is supposedly anchored in the physical site of the city of Rome, a place that the majority of them never saw in their whole lives.

The aftermath of the Social War is the period which saw the developing ideology of the *duae patriae*, the 'two fatherlands', *unam naturae, alteram ciuitatis*, as Cicero puts it to Atticus at the beginning of Book 2 of the *De Legibus*—'one of nature, the other of citizenship'.[119] In this famous passage (*Leg.* 2.3–6), set in Arpinum where Cicero and his brother were born, Cicero mentions that Arpinum is his and Quintus' 'authentic fatherland' (*germana patria*), and then explains to Atticus how the same dual identity is true for all members of *municipia* in Italy, who likewise have a fatherland of birth and a fatherland of citizenship.

Atticus is the ideal interlocutor for Cicero on this topic, since his own unusual position as citizen and resident helps to throw into relief the intriguing interplay between the natural and the constructed in conceptions of the citizenship. First of all, Atticus needs the ideology of *duae patriae* explained to him because he was born in Rome and therefore has only one *patria*, unlike the majority of Roman citizens.[120] Secondly, Atticus is, after all, called 'Atticus': if he is missing the other dimension to the Roman citizenship that so many of his fellow-citizens have, he has an extra affective allegiance—not to a *municipium* in Italy, but to a city that is altogether foreign.[121] The conversation between Atticus and Cicero, each so differently positioned, enables readers to see from fresh angles the claims to which a Roman citizen was liable and the ties of affection to which he

---

[118] We return at the end of the chapter to the implications of the fact that Livy's *patria*, Patavium, was therefore not included in this citizenship-grant.

[119] Select bibliography on this much-discussed passage: Sherwin-White (1973), 154–5; Bonjour (1975a), 78–86; Y. Thomas (1996), 9–10; Oakley (1997–2005), 2.610; Gasser (1999), 32–49; Farrell (2001), 18–27; Bispham (2007), 441–2; Moatti (2015), 308–10; Isayev (2017), 401–3; Carlà-Uhink (2017c), who shows in detail how Cicero's conception of Italy is behind not only this passage but the whole of his political thinking.

[120] Farrell (2001), 25–6; Carlà-Uhink (2017c), 259–60.

[121] Farrell (2001), 19–20, 25–6. On the importance of the cosmopolitan perspective that was available to Cicero, Livy and their contemporaries, see Carlà-Uhink (2017c), 264–6 and further below, at the end of this section.

could respond. After the Social War, a citizen could feel an allegiance and an affective bond to his natural birthplace—Arpinum in Cicero's case, Padua in Livy's—as well as to Rome, the site and origin of citizenship.[122] It is not a case of 'duty' versus 'affection'. For Cicero at least, it is clear that the larger claims of *caritas* ('love', 'affection') from the *respublica* trump those of the fatherland that gave birth to us (*Leg.* 2.5). In fact, elsewhere he charts the whole range of human association (*societas*) from that shared with all human beings down to the family, and up from there to the *respublica* (*Off.* 1.54–7); none of these associations, he claims, is 'more serious or more dear than that which each of us has with the *respublica*' (*omnium societatum nulla est grauior, nulla carior quam ea quae cum re publica est uni cuique nostrum*, 57).[123] The *caritas* that Camillus wishes the natural landscape of Rome to evoke in his fellow-citizens (5.54.3) anticipates the more abstract *caritas* that future Roman citizens will be able to feel for the *respublica*, even if they have never seen the city itself.

The Social War was of the highest importance in making such issues central to the self-definition of the members of the greatly enlarged Roman citizen body;[124] yet the question of an individual's allegiance both to a native *municipium* and to the Roman *ciuitas* had been potentially in play for centuries before the Social War, ever since Rome had begun the practice of incorporating previously independent states without destroying them.[125] In the *De Legibus* passage we have been considering, after all, Cicero brings forward the elder Cato and his native city of Tusculum as his case study, from a period over a century before the Social War (2.5); such feelings will have been a live possibility among *ciues Romani* well before the Social War, and well before they were given theoretical expression by Cicero.[126] As we shall see at the end of this section, Tusculum is a particularly significant example for Cicero to choose.

An item of granular detail in Livy's adaptation of Cicero for Camillus' speech in Book 5 shows how profoundly Livy has reflected on Cicero's political theory. As Gaertner has shown, when Livy describes Camillus' feelings for the site of Rome he is alluding closely to Cicero's words on his

---

[122] As Feldherr (1998), 112–13 shows, this theme is sounded in the very first sections of the *History*, where Livy dwells on the foundation of his own *patria* of Padua by the Trojan Antenor before narrating the fate of Aeneas (1.1.1–3).
[123] Feldherr (1998), 118–20; cf. Bonjour (1975a), 62–5; Bispham (2007), 440–2; Connolly (2007), 89–95; K.F.B. Fletcher (2014), 6–7; Carlà-Uhink (2017a), 283–4.
[124] Feldherr (1998), 114–15; Carlà-Uhink (2017c), esp. 262–3.
[125] Sherwin-White (1973), 57–8 (concentrating on the *ciuitates sine suffragio*); Y. Thomas (1996), 9–14 (on 'La *communis patria* comme fiction juridique de l'ubiquité de Rome').
[126] Carlà-Uhink (2017a), 284–5.

return from exile in the speech *Post Reditum ad Quirites* (4): both speakers enumerate physical features to which they are responding, and use the key language of *patria* and *caritas*.[127] Crucially, the *patria* whose physical characteristics Cicero responds to in *Post Reditum* is Italy, with 'the beauty of the city' (*pulchritudo urbis*) as just one item in the list of all the features offered by 'the visual impact of Italy' (*species Italiae*); for Camillus, even though he is using very Ciceronian language, the *patria* is not Italy but Rome herself.[128] Livy vaults back to a time before Cicero and imagines a period when the city of Rome and the *patria* or *terra mater* were co-extensive.

Camillus' dream of a *respublica* where all the citizens have a natural grounding in the city of Rome is carried further by the rebuilding of the devastated city at the very end of Book 5. Here we are told that the people 'were in such a rush that they did not bother to lay out the streets/districts in distinct lines, building on vacant land and disregarding any distinction between what was theirs and what was someone else's' (*festinatio curam exemit uicos dirigendi, dum omisso sui alienique discrimine in uacuo aedificant*, 5.55.4). At the end of Section III above we saw how all the incoming groups had taken up discrete areas of residence in the city—Latins on the Aventine and Albans on the Caelian, for example (1.33.2), or Etruscans in the *uicus Tuscus* (2.14.9). These closing sentences of Book 5 are an aetiology not only of the cityscape but of the citizenship, as all these previous *discrimina* are done away with.[129]

In this climactic moment of Book 5 Livy is fantasising about a time 365 years earlier when *natura* and *ciuitas* were fused together in an ideal phase of union, in a unique exception to the general Roman pattern where civic association, not anything natural, is what counts.[130] It is as if the refounding of the city after the sack by the Gauls represents the centre of the hourglass in the history of the citizenship as well as in the history of the city overall. Both at the time of Romulus' foundation and at the time of Livy's writing, in different ways, the *ciuitas* was not grounded in *natura*: in the centre of the hourglass, however, at the time of Camillus, there is no split, there is only one fused concept of *ciuitas* and *patria*.

Camillus, who expounds this fusion of *ciuitas* and *patria* so memorably, is himself a figure who contains latent fissures that gape under closer inspection, already within Book 5 opening up complications for the

---

[127] Gaertner (2008), 43.  [128] As pointed out by Isayev (2017), 399.
[129] A. Walter (forthcoming) for the aetiological power of the phrase *ea est causa* at 5.55.5.
[130] Moatti (2015), 317: 'What in other cities stems from nature—for instance consanguinity and unity—in Rome stems from the civic order.'

assured conclusion he appears to embody. As we have just seen, when Camillus speaks about the emotional power of the earth which he calls mother, he speaks from the perspective of the exile: he is evoking nostalgia, not describing what is in front of his eyes. The very first words of his speech refer to his emotions while in exile (5.51.1).[131] The idea of a lost centre that the absent Roman pines for is already built in to this vision of the city. Camillus enunciates this ideal of Rome-centredness so vividly because he was deprived of it, and in his absence from Rome he anticipates the relationship so many citizens in the future will have with the metropolis.

It is very telling that the only other person before Camillus who is associated with the marked language of being 'born from the earth' is someone who is even more famous as an exile than is Camillus, Marcius Coriolanus.[132] His mother, wife and children confront him as he sits in camp, five miles from the city, preparing to attack it (2.39.5). His mother, Veturia, refers to him as an 'exile' (*exsulem*), and asks him 'Have you been able to devastate this earth which gave birth to you and nourished you?' (*potuisti populari hanc terram quae te genuit atque aluit?*, 2.40.6). As Bonjour has shown, in Livy's presentation it is vital for Coriolanus' mother not simply to appeal to her maternal role as she does in the Greek versions of Dionysius of Halicarnassus (*Ant. Rom.* 8.48–53) and Plutarch (*Cor.* 35–36.3), but to make Coriolanus think of his bond with his maternal soil, and to symbolise with her own body that maternal soil.[133] This scene is replayed in a masculinised version in Book 7, when a Roman army in mutiny marches towards Rome and meets the dictator M. Valerius Corvinus, who recalls them to their duty. In 342 the ambit of the *patria* has extended to eight miles from the city, where the meeting takes place (7.39.16), since Corvinus can appeal to them on the basis of the hills of Rome, just visible from that point ('if you are willing to remember that those hills which you see are the hills of your fatherland', *si meminisse uoltis … illos colles quos cernitis patriae uestrae esse*, 7.40.6); here they are on Roman soil (*in Romano solo*, 7.40.6). It is not women any more who do the pleading, as in the case of Coriolanus (7.40.12); now it is the young dictator, and he talks of the *patria*, the 'fatherland' (7.40.9), not *terra quae genuit*, 'the earth which

---

[131] Isayev (2017), 395.
[132] Bonjour (1975a), 472 remarks that 'entre Romulus et Camille, l'historien n'est parvenu à introduire que peu d'exemples de l'attachement au sol de Rome'. In fact, Coriolanus is the only one who is spoken of in these terms before we get to Camillus.
[133] Bonjour (1975b), 175–6; cf. 180; Cornell (2003), 80.

bore you'. This is now the *respublica* of the *patres*, not the city that Coriolanus had spared, 'la Rome des "mères", la Rome-Mère' of the exile's perspective.[134]

Camillus is always talking about the central importance of the city of Rome, and he eloquently argues that Romanness is tied to this very particular place.[135] But in fact he is a key example of displacement and of de-centring, as Jaeger points out, in contrasting Camillus with Manlius Capitolinus: 'Manlius never leaves the city in Book 6, while Camillus is almost always pictured outside it and seems to be everywhere at once.'[136] Camillus is not just in exile in Ardea: he speaks to the people of Ardea as his fellow-citizens (*ueteres amici, noui etiam ciues mei*, 5.44.1). Rome's inextricable relationship with her allies is emblematised by Ardea's key role in Camillus' victory.[137] Even more, Camillus' sojourn in Ardea became emblematic in the tradition for the fact that legitimacy does not have to be anchored in Rome: Pompey uses this exemplum in Appian, in a scene that is highly likely to derive from Livy (*B Civ.* 2.50).[138] Lucan picks up and exaggerates the theme, with his speaker Lentulus Crus putting Camillus in Veii, not Ardea, when justifying the continued authority of the consuls and senators in Epirus, beyond the consuls' term of office: 'when Camillus was living in Veii, that's where Rome was' (*Veios . . . habitante Camillo, illic Roma fuit*, 5.28–9).[139]

Camillus is the main embodiment of a central theme in Book 5: 'Concomitant with asking, "what makes a Roman?", the book asks, "and where does, or can, Roman-ness happen?" Can Rome be copied? Doubled? Moved? Replaced?'[140] Camillus' mobility and his shifting links with key outside places (Veii, Ardea), together with his passion for the metropolis that is grounded in a sense of loss and nostalgia, anticipate the cosmopolitan atmosphere of the later Republic, the world of Livy and his readership. This was a world where peoples from all over the Mediterranean could find a home in the city of Rome;[141] it was a world where Roman citizens could be found in a diaspora all over the

---

[134] Bonjour (1975b), 178.   [135] Edwards (1996), 47; Oakley (2015), 239.   [136] Jaeger (1997), 88.
[137] Henderson (2000), 15–16 sees Ardea as a 'sideshow', but we could see Ardea foreshadowing the alliance system to come. Tusculum had played a similar role in Book 3 (18–19), helping to liberate the Capitol when it had been captured by Sabines; their commander is rewarded with Roman citizenship (3.29.6).
[138] See Coudry (2001), 59 and Gaertner (2008), 50–1, adducing also Cass. Dio 41.18.5.
[139] Masters (1992), 104–5; Edwards (1996), 66; Gaertner (2008), 50–1.
[140] Kraus (forthcoming b); cf. Stevenson (2000), 35: '"Rome" could in fact exist elsewhere than at the site of Rome.'
[141] Moatti (2015), 47–8; Carlà-Uhink (2017c), 264–6.

Mediterranean.¹⁴² This is the perspective from which to read the idealised vision of Camillus' speech.

In the next book, Camillus will initiate the chain of events that leads, for the very first time, to another community being given the citizenship while still remaining in existence. In the year 381, Camillus moves against the Latin city of Tusculum, much later the *patria* of M. Porcius Cato, who is the *exemplum* of the *duae patriae* mentality for Cicero (*Leg.* 2.5). Tusculum is suspected of planning war against Rome; the citizens defuse the situation by displaying their peaceful intentions and Camillus tells them to go to Rome to plead their case before the Senate (6.25.6–26.2). They succeed in suing for peace and, shortly afterwards, in asking for the citizenship (6.26.8). Unlike Livy's earlier cases of places like Alba Longa or Politorium, where the towns were obliterated and the people were moved to Rome to be incorporated as citizens, Tusculum maintains itself as an entity after being incorporated into the citizenship, becoming 'the first *municipium*'.¹⁴³

The figure who most memorably enunciates the impossibility of being a Roman anywhere else apart from Rome is the figure who not only symbolises that this can in fact be done, but who first makes it possible for another community to live that life.

## VII

With these anticipations of the complex ideologies of citizenship shared by his contemporaries, Livy is clearly writing Book 5 with an eye to his eventual treatment of the enfranchisement of the whole of Italy after the Social War. Like his fellow Transpadane, Virgil, in these very years, Livy is helping his contemporaries process the Social War, 'a traumatic conflict in the collective memory', whose repercussions were still work in progress.¹⁴⁴

---

¹⁴² According to the calculations of population in Scheidel (2004), 9 and 11, something like 20% of Roman citizens were living outside Italy in the year 28, when Livy was writing. On cosmopolitanism in Greek and Roman political thought, see Konstan (2009); on Roman imperial cosmopolitanism in a comparative imperial context, see Lavan, Payne and Weisweiler (2016), 1–24; for a broad survey up to modern times, Busetto (2017). My thanks to Rita Degli-Innocenti Pierini for pointing out to me the importance of the cosmopolitan perspective.

¹⁴³ Cornell (1995), 323; cf. Humbert (1978), 157–9; Salmon (1982), 46; Cornell (1995), 323; Oakley (1997–2005), 1.357–8.

¹⁴⁴ Barchiesi (2008), 251 ('un conflitto traumatico nella memoria collettiva'); cf. Marincola (2010), 186–93 on the importance of the Social War as the backdrop for the second half of the *Aeneid*, thanks to its continuing resonances with Virgil's audience; Carlà-Uhink (2017c), 267–8 on the ongoing traumatic impact of the war. See Levene (2010), 40–1 for a discussion of another moment in the extant *History* where the issues of the future Social War are hinted at (23.22.4–7, with a proposal to make up lost numbers in the Senate by recruiting Latins).

We will never know how Livy treated the citizenship issue in the context of the Social War, but we get some glimpses in his treatment of the year 338—a moment of equal importance to the Social War in the history of the Roman citizenship. The year 338 saw the dissolution of the Latin League after the last Latin War and the establishment of a new understanding of the Roman citizenship and of the Roman alliance system, innovations that were to carry the Romans to the unification of Italy and the conquest of the Mediterranean. According to De Sanctis, this was 'il momento critico della storia romana', 'the turning-point of Roman history'.[145] Occupying 8.13–14, Livy's description of this remarkable watershed is, as Oakley puts it, 'at the heart of the book and the pentad' [i.e., the pentad of Books 6–10].[146]

The crisis is triggered in the year 340 by the Latins' demands for an amalgamation between themselves and Rome, on the basis of their supposedly equal strength. The Latins' demands are delivered to Rome by a certain Lucius Annius, from Setia, a Latin colony to the southeast of Rome. He presents the new arrangement to the Senate in the Temple of Jupiter on the Capitol (8.5.5–6), proposing a Senate chosen from each race (*gente*), 'one people, one republic' (*unum populum, unam rempublicam*), and one consul to be chosen from Rome and one from Latium—the speaker's name, 'Annius' (hinting at 'Mr. Yearly, Mr. Annual'), is a promising one for someone who wants to be a consul. His punchline is remarkable: 'let Rome rather be our *patria*, and let us all be called Romans' (*sit haec sane patria potior, et Romani omnes uocemur*). It is very striking that the Roman consul, T. Manlius Torquatus, in replying to this demand, addresses the Latins in the vocative as *Latini* (8.5.9). This is the only time in the extant books of Livy that *Latini* is used in the vocative. At this moment of crisis, the identity of the Latins as Latins is made very clear by their Roman antagonist.

The Romans reject this demand, and the Latins rise up in revolt. Annius' demand and the Roman response to it are made by Livy to appear close to what will happen some two-hundred-and-fifty years later in the case of the Social War—the Romans will be asked to share the citizenship, they will refuse and there will be a war; after the war the citizenship will be *fully* shared, in the case of the Social War, or reconfigured and *partly* shared, in the case of the Latin War.[147] Here in Book 8 Livy is sowing the seeds for his

---

[145] De Sanctis (1907/1960), 267, in the translation given by Cornell (1995), 348.

[146] Oakley (1997–2005), 2.535. Similarly, at the very centre of the first pentad is the narrative of Appius Claudius and the decemvirate (3.33–54): Vasaly (2015a), 74–5.

[147] Oakley (1997–2005), 2.409–10, 415 for Livy's analogies between the Latin and Social wars. Of course, the causes of the Social War and the nature of the allies' demands and war aims are extremely controversial questions: see Mouritsen (1998).

own depiction of the Social War, which was a crucial part of his overall design.[148] Livy's picture of the causes of the Latin War in the year 340 is distorted by his understanding of the Social War, and by the desire to have the two crises mirror each other: the Latins in 340 were certainly not trying to become Romans.[149] Livy's whole account of the Latin War is coloured by the later perception of citizenship as something of high value, to be keenly sought after, when in fact 'grants' of citizenship in the Middle Republic were regularly coercive, and even resisted:[150] we shall soon see that the people of Tusculum, the first people to be granted citizenship while retaining their status as a self-governing community, appear not to have been very appreciative of the 'gift'.

Livy consistently represents the Latin War as being a kind of civil war, between people who are going to be fellow-citizens;[151] in so doing, he must already be preparing for the theme that the Social War was also very like a civil war. Shortly before the first battle of the Latin War, Livy highlights this point by mentioning how concerned about discipline the Roman consuls were, because they were about to fight against people who were 'like them in language, customs, weaponry, and especially in military institutions' (*lingua, moribus, armorum genere, institutis ante omnia militaribus congruentes*, 8.6.15). The consuls therefore order that no one should step out of the battle line to fight an enemy (8.6.16).

From this setup follows the famous story of how the son of the consul Manlius Torquatus is executed for disobeying these orders by accepting a challenge to single combat from one of the Latins (8.7). Young Manlius leads his cavalry on reconnaissance and meets enemy cavalry, commanded by someone whom he knows (*namque omnes inter se, utique illustres uiri, noti erant*, 8.7.3): this theme of combatants knowing each other is one that played a role in the historiography of the Social War, which contains

---

[148] See Stadter (1972/2009), 100 on how a new decade opened in Book 71, with the tribune M. Livius Drusus' agitation for Italian citizenship—'an excellent choice for the beginning of a unit in Roman history'.

[149] Toynbee (1965), 1.144. Again, see Mouritsen (1998) for arguments against the idea that such was the goal of the Italians in 91.

[150] Oakley (1997–2005), 2.549; on such examples of resentment, Cornell (1995), 323–4; Oakley (1997–2005), 2.549–50; Ando (2016), 177–8; O. Stewart (2017), esp. 190–1.

[151] 8.8.2 is the clearest statement: *ciuili maxime bello pugna similis* (of the battle of Veseris): see Oakley (1997–2005), 426. Livy had already done the same in the case of Alba Longa (1.23.1): Feldherr (1998), 115. This theme is so important to Livy that he suppresses the role of the other combatants in the Latin War: we get the impression from his narrative that the war is between Romans on one side and Latins on the other, but in fact the Romans were fighting a coalition of Latins, Campanians, Volsci, Aurunci, and Sidicini, all of whom were going to receive separate treatment in the settlement of 338. The only mention of any of these other allies is the mention of *Latini sociique* at 8.6.8 and *Campani* at 8.10.9.

famous incidents of antagonists recognising each other.¹⁵² Very significantly, Livy says that young Manlius met not just any Latin cavalry but, specifically, 'cavalry from Tusculum' (*Tusculani ... equites*, 8.7.2). Our other sources for this episode refer simply to 'Latins' (Cass. Dio fr. 35.2 = Zonar. 7.26), without any further specificity. It is very important that Livy makes the Romans' enemies at this moment Tusculans: as we saw at the end of Section VI above, the Latin town of Tusculum had been incorporated into the Roman citizenship in 381, the only time this had ever happened. Unlike any of the other Latins, then, these particular enemies actually are Roman citizens: what we have is a mini civil war at this moment. To drive the point home, Livy gives a speaking name to the commander of the Tusculan cavalry, who is anonymous in our other sources, being referred to by Dio simply as 'the cavalry commander of the Latins' (ὁ ἵππαρχος τῶν Λατίνων, Cass. Dio fr. 35.2 = Zonar. 7.26). Livy calls him *Geminus* Maecius, 'Mr. Twin' (8.7.2). This is a deep civil war theme at Rome, from Romulus and Remus on down.¹⁵³

Sure enough, after the young Manlius has been executed by his father for disobeying orders, the battle of Veseris that immediately follows is described as 'very much similar to a civil war' (*ciuili maxime bello pugna similis*, 8.8.2). This is why Livy puts his famous description of the legion at this exact point (8.8.3–14), immediately after this loaded observation and immediately before the battle: this placement reinforces the communality of Romans and Latins, since this is the fighting machine which they will share in the years ahead, and which will play such a vital role in forging their sense of common identity.¹⁵⁴

Two years later, when the Latin League have been finally defeated, it is no surprise to find that the question of the citizenship for the Latins is raised by someone called Furius Camillus: this one is Lucius, the grandson of the great M. Furius Camillus. After the Gallic sack, it is Marcus Furius Camillus who tries to redefine Roman citizenship as the quintessential blending of nature and culture, a cultural fiction that is so deep it feels grounded in the landscape; now, almost fifty years later, it is his grandson

---

¹⁵² Carlà-Uhink (2017a), 207, citing Diod. Sic. 37.15 for Romans and Marsi knowing each other as their armies come together, and Cic. *Phil.* 12.27 for the Roman commander conversing with his Marsic opposite number, Publius Vettius Scato, a former *hospes*; cf. Barchiesi (2008), 252, citing Plut. *Cat. Min.* 2. At 8.8.17 Livy remarks that the Roman and the Latin *primipili* at the battle of Veseris 'knew each other extremely well' (*notissimi inter se*).

¹⁵³ On the twin/fratricide motif that is pervasive in Roman civil war discourse, see Jal (1963), 393–5, 407–10.

¹⁵⁴ Oakley (1997–2005), 426 on the placement. Joint army service as a crucible for identity-formation is potentially a very large topic: see, for orientation, Carlà-Uhink (2017a), 203–11.

Lucius as consul who makes a speech that begins the process of redefining Roman citizenship yet again, producing a new fiction, with a new relationship to the *patria*. As we have seen, the Camilli are very good at repeating things.

The younger Camillus' speech to the Senate is very short, throwing over to the Senate the question of what to do with the defeated Latins. He frames the issue in stark terms. First of all, he tells the Senate that it is up to them 'whether there should be a Latium from now on or not' (*sit Latium deinde an non sit*, 8.13.14). If there is not going to be a Latium, that could be because the Romans will rub out the whole of Latium (*delere omne Latium*, 8.13.15). Or, as an alternative, the consul asks the Senate, 'Do you want to follow the example of the ancestors and increase the Roman state by taking the conquered into the citizenship?' (*uoltis exemplo maiorum augere rem Romanam uictos in ciuitatem accipiendo?*, 8.13.16). This is a clear reference to his grandfather's role in pioneering such an approach almost forty-five years earlier, since in 381 M. Furius Camillus had initiated the events that led to the first granting of Roman citizenship to a Latin town, Tusculum.

In fact, neither of these stark alternatives is adopted. Instead, the Senate takes each of the individual states one by one (*de singulis nominatim . . . de singulis*, 8.14.1–2), acting on the key political insights arrived at in this extraordinary moment, namely, that the allies of Rome should have no bonds in common except their individual relationship to Rome, and that a variety of different relationships were to be in place.[155] First of all, the Romans broke up the Latin League and dealt with each individual Latin community one by one. They made some of them full Roman citizens, enrolling them in various of the tribes (Lanuvium, Aricia, Nomentum and Pedum, 8.14.2–4), and they left some of them, such as Tibur and Praeneste, in a state of nominal independence, allied only with Rome and with no other community (8.14.9–10). In a remarkable innovation, they also invented the category of the *ciuitas sine suffragio* ('citizenship without the vote'), which was extended to some states in Campania (Capua in particular) and to some Oscan-speaking communities close to the Latin plain (8.14.10–11). Quite what this status was called or what it meant in the 330s, or indeed quite what it meant even in later periods—or even whether *ciuitas sine suffragio* was a 'status'—these are all extremely controversial issues.[156] At the least, we observe a rethinking of what it meant to call

---

[155] On the settlement, Cornell (1995), 348–52; Oakley (1997–2005), 2.538–71.
[156] Sherwin-White (1973), 39–58, 200–14; Humbert (1978); Oakley (1997–2005), 2.544–59; Mouritsen (2007).

a community *ciues Romani*, as the Campanians were called by Ennius when they received *ciuitas sine suffragio*, despite sharing neither language, cult, nor territorial borders with the pre-existing *populus Romanus*: *ciues Romani tunc facti sunt Campani* ('the Campanians were then made Roman citizens', *Annales* fr. 157 Sk.).

The concept of 'Latium' itself was radically redefined. Lucius Camillus told the Senate that the option was whether there should be a Latium or not (8.13.14): what happened was very different. The concept of *Latium* as a political entity disappears with the Latin League.[157] The *nomen Latinum*, however, takes on a new life, above all with the resurrection after almost fifty years of the institution of the Latin colony: these Latin colonies were notionally independent states, with their own citizenship, bound to supply Rome with troops, and composed of a heterogeneous population of Romans, Latins and others, including some local people. As a result, 'Latin status ceased to have a distinct ethnic or linguistic significance, and came instead to depend on possession of legally defined rights and privileges that could be exercised in dealings with Roman citizens.'[158] As Dench puts it, 'This is the sort of conceptual leap upon which changing ideas of the Roman citizenship, and Roman identity itself, will be based.'[159] The status of being a 'Latin' became flexible, exportable and transferable, just as did the status of being a 'Roman' (especially 'without the vote'): it had nothing to do with 'Blut and Boden', nothing to do with soil, or ethnicity, or even language.

The settlement of 338 was a creative moment of great political intelligence—although its development was no doubt spread over a period, and did not spring out of committee on one afternoon. It gave the Romans the supple machinery they needed for the conquest of Italy.[160] Their sense of belonging and of unity was once again radically redefined. Two generations before, in Livy's presentation, the Romans had been bound together as a group of citizens who shared the same soil and the same native land.

---

[157] As acknowledged by Virgil, writing in the same years as Livy. The opening of the *Aeneid*, as pointed out by Barchiesi (2008), 243–4, alludes to the obliterations that Roman expansion will entail (Troy, Lavinium, Latium, Alba Longa, 1.1–7). When Juno itemises her concessions in her final speech to Jupiter (12.826–8), beginning with *sit Latium*, she is returning to this list of entities that will eventually disappear to join the disappeared Troy—Latium and Alba Longa—leaving only 'Roman offspring potent with Italian manliness' (*Romana potens Itala uirtute propago*, 827). My thanks to Gianpiero Rosati for making me think about the links between Livy's and Virgil's *sit Latium*.

[158] Cornell (1995), 351; cf. Nicolet (1980), 30; Kremer (2006); Ando (2015), 46–7; Moatti (2015), 334–5; Carlà-Uhink (2017a), 222–3.

[159] Dench (2005), 123.

[160] Cornell (1995), 365–8, referring to the original insight of Momigliano (1975), 45–6.

Now, their citizenship is redefined, and they have to adopt a new kind of collective sense of belonging, a much more dispersed and variegated one.[161] Marcus Camillus' speech stands as a dominating symbol of the idealised city-state that Rome had anyway already long ceased to be by 386; his speech helps to demarcate the enormous leap that his grandson's generation were to make fifty years later.

## VIII

As remarked above, we will never know how Livy treated the Social War and the eventual extension of Roman citizenship to all the inhabitants of the Italian peninsula. Beyond the Social War, it is particularly frustrating that we do not know how he narrated the destiny of his own native city of Patavium, which he was so clearly anticipating in the very opening of his *History*, where Antenor's foundation of Livy's *patria* precedes Aeneas' arrival in Italy (1.1.1–3).[162] Patavium was not incorporated into the Roman citizenship until the year 49 BCE, when Livy was probably in his early teens. One of Livy's first political memories must have been the extension of the franchise to his community—even if he himself may have been born a *ciuis Romanus*. This moment will have been an opportunity for Livy to return to the hint of the opening of his *History*, and to show how he is not just the chronicler of the growth of Roman citizenship but a participant in the process.[163]

Julius Caesar's extension of the citizenship to Gallia Cisalpina will have been narrated in Book 110. According to the extant Summary, Book 110 also described how Julius Caesar gave the Roman citizenship to the people of Cadiz (*Gaditanis ciuitatem dedit*).[164] Cadiz is a very long way from the soil of Romulus' asylum. It was a citizen of that western-most seat of Roman citizenship, according to Pliny the Younger, who, 'stirred by the name and glory of Livy, came to look at him from the far edge of the world, and then as soon as he had seen him he turned around and went back home' (*Titi Livi nomine gloriaque commotum ad uisendum eum ab ultimo terrarum orbe uenisse, statimque ut uiderat abisse?*, *Ep.* 2.3.8).

---

[161] Of the kind familiar to students of comparative imperialism: see Burbank and Cooper (2010) for the wide variety of models of citizenship and affiliation developed in a range of imperial settings. See Levene (2010), 214–60 for an extended discussion of how Livy's narrative of the Hannibalic War is regularly looking ahead to a time when allies or enemies will themselves one day be Romans.
[162] Feldherr (1998), 112–13.
[163] My thanks to Andrew Feldherr for prompting these closing reflections.
[164] Interestingly, the Periocha does not also mention the enfranchisement of Gallia Cisalpina.

Livy has become his own monument, with an Empire-wide readership, far beyond the city of Rome.[165] His *History* is now one of the elements connecting the far-flung and scattered citizen body whose evolution has been one of his cardinal themes and constructions, with himself as one of its representatives.

---

[165] For the broad readership of historiography in Livy's lifetime, see Pausch (2011), 41–6, 65–70; see Levene (2019), 24 for discussion of the possibility that 'Livy may be primarily writing for an audience outside the city of Rome'.

# *Published Works of Denis Feeney*

(includes books, chapters in books, articles, and reviews: items included in these two volumes are marked with an asterisk)

## 1978

'Wild beasts in the *De Rerum Natura*', *Prudentia* 10 (1978), 15–22

## 1982

*A Commentary on Silius Italicus* Punica *Book 1* (DPhil Diss., Oxford University)

## 1983

'The taciturnity of Aeneas', *CQ* 33 (1983), 204–19; reprinted in S.J. Harrison (ed.), *Oxford Readings in Vergil's Aeneid* (Oxford, 1990), 166–90; P. Hardie (ed.), *Virgil: Critical Assessments of Classical Authors*, 4 vols. (London, 1999), 3.183–203 (= Vol. 1.1)*

Review of J. Volpilhac, P. Miniconi and G. Devallet (eds.), *Silius Italicus. La Guerre Punique. Tome II* (Paris, 1981), in *CR* 33 (1983), 322–3

## 1984

'The reconciliations of Juno', *CQ* 34 (1984), 179–94; reprinted in S.J. Harrison (ed.), *Oxford Readings in Vergil's Aeneid* (Oxford, 1990), 339–62; P. Hardie (ed.), *Virgil: Critical Assessments of Classical Authors*, 4 vols. (London, 1999), 4.392–413 (= Vol. 1.2)*

## 1985

Review of Erich Burck, *Historische und epische Tradition bei Silius Italicus* (Munich, 1984), in *CR* 35 (1985), 390–1

## 1986

'Epic hero and epic fable', *CompLit* 38 (1986), 137–58 (= Vol. 1.3)*
'*Stat magni nominis umbra*: Lucan on the greatness of Pompeius Magnus', *CQ* 36 (1986), 239–43; reprinted in C. Tesoriero (ed.), *Oxford Readings in Classical Studies: Lucan* (Oxford, 2010), 346–54 (= Vol. 1.4)*
'History and revelation in Vergil's underworld', *PCPhS* 32 (1986), 1–24; reprinted in S. Quinn (ed.), *Why Vergil? A Collection of Interpretations* (Wauconda, IL, 2000), 108–22; P. Hardie (ed.), *Virgil: Critical Assessments of Classical Authors*, 4 vols. (London, 1999), 4.221–43 (= Vol. 1.5)*
'Following after Hercules, in Virgil and Apollonius', *PVS* 18 (1986), 47–83 (= Vol. 1.6)*
Review of Werner Schubert, *Jupiter in den Epen der Flavierzeit* (Frankfurt am Main, 1984), in *CR* 36 (1986), 134–5

## 1987

Review of Wendell Clausen, *Virgil's 'Aeneid' and the Traditions of Hellenistic Poetry* (Berkeley and Los Angeles, CA, 1987); Jasper Griffin, *Virgil* (Oxford, 1987); and R.O.A.M. Lyne, *Further Voices in Vergil's 'Aeneid'* (Oxford, 1987), in *TLS* (3 July 1987), 722
Review of A.J. Boyle, *The Chaonian Dove: Studies in the Eclogues, Georgics, and Aeneid of Virgil* (Leiden, 1986), in *CR* 37 (1987), 171–3
Review of Jochem Kuppers, *Tantarum causas irarum: Untersuchungen zur einleitenden Bücherdyade der Punica des Silius Italicus* (Berlin, 1986), in *CR* 37 (1987), 306–7
Review of Cornelia Renger, *Aeneas und Turnus: Analyse einer Feindschaft* (Frankfurt, 1985), in *JRS* 77 (1987), 250–1

## 1988

Review of W.R. Johnson, *Momentary Monsters: Lucan and his Heroes* (Cornell, NY, 1987), in *TLS* (26 February 1988), 227
Review of O. Papanghelis, *Propertius on Love and Death* (Cambridge, 1987), in *TLS* (18 March 1988), 312
Review of D.O. Ross, *Physics and Poetry in Vergil's 'Georgics'* (Princeton, NJ, 1987) and R.D. Williams, *The Aeneid* (London, 1987), in *TLS* (29 April 1988), 476

## 1989

Review of Gian Biagio Conte, *The Rhetoric of Imitation. Genre and Poetic Memory in Virgil and Other Latin Poets* (Ithaca, NY, 1986), in *JRS* 79 (1989), 206–7

## 1991

*The Gods in Epic: Poets and Critics of the Classical Tradition* (Oxford, 1991)
Review of J.B. Hainsworth, *The Idea of Epic* (Berkeley and Los Angeles, CA, 1991), in *The Times Higher Educational Supplement* no. 974 (5 July 1991), 20

## 1992

'*Si licet et fas est*: Ovid's *Fasti* and the problem of free speech under the Principate', in A. Powell (ed.), *Roman Poetry and Propaganda in the Age of Augustus* (London, 1992), 1–25; reprinted in P.E. Knox (ed.), *Oxford Readings in Classical Studies: Ovid* (Oxford, 2006), 464–88 (= Vol. 2.1)*
'"Shall I compare thee ... ?" Catullus 68 and the limits of analogy', in A.J. Woodman and J. Powell (eds.), *Author and Audience in Latin Literature* (Cambridge, 1992), 33–44; reprinted in J.H. Gaisser (ed.), *Oxford Readings in Classical Studies: Catullus* (Oxford, 2007), 429–46 (= Vol. 2.2)*
Review of G.B. Conte, *Generi e lettori: Lucrezio, l'elegia d'amore, l'enciclopedia di Plinio* (Milan, 1991), in *JRS* 82 (1992), 237
Review of D. West, *Virgil: The Aeneid* (London, 1990), in *CR* 42 (1992), 191–2
Review of A.J. Boyle (ed.), *The Imperial Muse: Ramus Essays on Roman Literature of the Empire* (Berwick, Vic., 1990), in *CR* 42 (1992), 323–4

## 1993

'Epilogue: towards an account of the ancient world's concepts of fictive belief', in T.P. Wiseman and C. Gill (eds.), *Lies and Fiction in the Ancient World* (Exeter, 1993), 230–44 (= Vol. 2.3)*
'Horace and the Greek lyric poets', in N. Rudd (ed.), *Horace 2000: A Celebration. Essays for the Bimillennium* (London, 1993), 41–63; reprinted with corrections in M. Lowrie (ed.), *Oxford Readings in Horace: Odes and Epodes* (Oxford, 2009), 202–31 (= Vol. 2.4)*
Review of M. Korn and H.J. Tschiedel, *Ratis omnia vincet: Untersuchungen zu den Argonautica des Valerius Flaccus* (Hildesheim, 1991), in *CR* 43 (1993), 174
Review of Karl Galinsky (ed.), *The Interpretation of Roman Poetry: Empiricism or Hermeneutics?* (Frankfurt am Main, 1992), in *BMCR* 4 (1993), 457–61

## 1994

'Beginning Sallust's *Catiline*', in V.J. Gray (ed.), *Nile, Ilissos and Tiber: Essays in Honour of Walter Kirkpatrick Lacey* (Auckland, 1994), 139–46 (= Vol. 1.7)*
Review of Peter White, *Promised Verse: Poets in the Society of Augustan Rome* (Cambridge, MA, 1993), in *BMCR* 5.4 (1994), 346–9

## 1995

'Criticism ancient and modern', in D. Innes, H. Hine and C. Pelling (eds.), *Ethics and Rhetoric: Classical Essays for Donald Russell on his Seventy-Fifth Birthday* (Oxford, 1995), 301–12; reprinted in A. Laird (ed.), *Oxford Readings in Ancient Literary Criticism* (Oxford, 2006), 440–54 (= Vol. 2.5)*

Review of Geraldine Herbert-Brown, *Ovid and the Fasti: An Historical Study* (Oxford, 1994), in *CO* 72 (1995), 106

Review of T.J. Luce and A.J. Woodman (eds.), *Tacitus and the Tacitean Tradition* (Princeton, NJ, 1992); R. Mellor, *Tacitus* (New York and London, 1992); and P. Sinclair, *Tacitus the Sententious Historian: A Sociology of Rhetoric in Annales 1–6* (University Park, PA, 1995), in *TLS* (10 November 1995), 29

## 1996

Review of R.O.A.M. Lyne, *Horace: Behind the Public Poetry* (New Haven, CT, 1995); R.G.M. Nisbet, *Collected Papers on Latin Literature* (Oxford, 1995); S.J. Harrison (ed.), *Homage to Horace* (Oxford, 1995); D. West, *Horace Odes I: Carpe Diem* (Oxford, 1995); and R. Ancona, *Time and the Erotic in Horace's Odes* (Durham, NC, 1994), in *TLS* (23 February 1996), 9

## 1997

Review of Elaine Fantham, *Roman Literary Culture: From Cicero to Apuleius* (Baltimore, MD, 1997), in *TLS* (1 August 1997), 27

## 1998

*Literature and Religion at Rome: Cultures, Contexts, and Beliefs* (Cambridge, 1998)
*Virgil: Aeneid*, trans. C.H. Sisson, ed. D. Feeney (London, 1998)
'Leaving Dido: the appearance(s) of Mercury and the motivations of Aeneas', in *A Woman Scorn'd: Responses to the Dido Myth*, ed. M. Burden (London, 1998), 105–27 (=Vol. 1.8)*
Review of P.E. Easterling (ed.), *The Cambridge Companion to Greek Tragedy* (Cambridge, 1997) and Charles Martindale (ed.), *The Cambridge Companion to Virgil* (Cambridge, 1997), in *TLS* (29 May 1998), 11
Review of Shadi Bartsch, *Ideology in Cold Blood: A Reading of Lucan's Civil War* (Cambridge, MA, 1997), in *TLS* (24 July 1998), 28

## 1999

'Epic violence, epic order: killings, catalogues, and the role of the reader in *Aeneid* 10', in C. Perkell (ed.), *Reading Vergil's Aeneid: An Interpretive Guide* (Norman, OK, 1999), 178–94 (=Vol. 1.9)*

'*Mea tempora*: patterning of time in Ovid's *Metamorphoses*', in P. Hardie, A. Barchiesi and S. Hinds (eds.), *Ovidian Transformations: Essays on Ovid's Metamorphoses and its Reception* (Cambridge, 1999), 13–30 (=Vol. 1.10)*

Review of Philip Hardie, *Virgil* (Oxford, 1998), in *JACT Review* 25 (1999), 28

Review of Peter Levi, *Virgil: His Life and Times* (London, 1998), in *TLS* (25 June 1999), 38

## 2000

Review of Florence Dupont, *The Invention of Literature: From Greek Intoxication to the Latin Book*, tr. Janet Lloyd (Baltimore, MD, 1999), in *TLS* (28 April 2000), 9

## 2001

Review of Don Fowler, *Roman Constructions: Readings in Postmodern Latin* (Oxford, 2000), in *JRS* 91 (2001) 212–14

## 2002

A.J. Woodman and D. Feeney (eds.), *Traditions and Contexts in the Poetry of Horace* (Cambridge, 2002)

'The odiousness of comparisons: Horace on literary history and the limitations of synkrisis', in M. Paschalis (ed.), *Horace and Greek Lyric Poetry* (Rethymnon, 2002), 7–18 (=Vol. 2.6)*

'*Vna cum scriptore meo*: poetry, principate, and the traditions of literary history in the *Epistle to Augustus*', in A.J. Woodman and D. Feeney (eds.), *Traditions and Contexts in the Poetry of Horace* (Cambridge, 2002), 172–87; reprinted in K. Freudenburg (ed.), *Oxford Readings in Classical Studies: Horace: Satires and Epistles* (Oxford, 2009), 360–85 (=Vol. 2.7)*

Review of John Henderson, *Telling Tales on Caesar: Roman Stories from Phaedrus* (Oxford, 2001), in *TLS* (29 March 2002), 29

Review of Carole Newlands, *Statius' Silvae and the Poetics of Empire* (Cambridge, 2002), in *TLS* (15 November 2002), 29

## 2003

Review of Mary Depew and Dirk Obbink (eds.), *Matrices of Genre: Authors, Canons, and Society* (Cambridge, MA, 2000), in *JRS* 93 (2003), 337–9

## 2004

'Interpreting sacrificial ritual in Roman poetry: disciplines and their models', in A. Barchiesi, J. Rüpke and S. Stephens (eds.), *Rituals in Ink: A Conference on*

*Religion and Literary Production in Ancient Rome Held at Stanford University in February 2002* (Stuttgart, 2004), 9–29 (=Vol. 1.11)*

'*Tenui . . . latens discrimine*: spotting the differences in Statius' *Achilleid*', *MD* 52 (2004) (*Re-Presenting Virgil: Special Issue in Honor of Michael C.J. Putnam*, eds. G.W. Most and S. Spence), 85–105 (=Vol. 1.12)*

'Introduction', in *Ovid: Metamorphoses. A New Verse Translation*, tr. D. Raeburn (London, 2004), xiii–xxxvi

Review of R.G.M. Nisbet and Niall Rudd, *A Commentary on Horace Odes Book 3* (Oxford, 2004), in *TLS* (8 October 2004), 8–9

## 2005

'Two Virgilian acrostics: *certissima signa?*', with Damien Nelis, *CQ* 55 (2005), 644–6 (=Vol. 2.8)*

'The beginnings of a literature in Latin', *JRS* 95 (2005), 226–40: review of W. Suerbaum (ed.), *Handbuch der lateinischen Literatur der Antike. Erster Band: Die archaische Literatur. Von den Anfängen bis zu Sullas Tod. Die vorliterarische Periode und die Zeit von 240 bis 78 v. Chr.*, Handbuch der Altertumswissenschaft VIII.1 (Munich, 2002)

## 2006

Review of Peter Green, *Ovid: The Poems of Exile* (Berkeley and Los Angeles, CA, 2005) and Jan Felix Gaertner, *Ovid: Epistulae ex Ponto, Book I* (Oxford, 2005), in *LRB* (17 August 2006), 13–15

Review of Sander M. Goldberg, *Constructing Literature in the Roman Republic: Poetry and its Reception* (Cambridge, 2005), in *BMCR* 2006.08.45

Review (with Joshua T. Katz) of T. Habinek, *The World of Roman Song: From Ritualized Speech to Social Order* (Baltimore, MD and London, 2005), in *JRS* 96 (2006), 240–2

## 2007

*Caesar's Calendar: Ancient Time and the Beginnings of History* (Berkeley and Los Angeles, CA, 2007)

'On not forgetting the "Literatur" in "Literatur und Religion": Representing the Mythic and the Divine in Roman Historiography', in A. Bierl, R. Lämmle and K. Wesselmann (eds.), *Literatur und Religion: Wege zu einer mythisch-rituellen Poetik bei den Griechen*, vol. 2 (Berlin, 2007), 173–202 (=Vol. 1.13)*

'The history of Roman religion in Roman historiography and epic', in J. Rüpke (ed.), *A Companion to Roman Religion* (Oxford, 2007), 129–42

Review of Peter Fallon, *Virgil: Georgics* (Oxford, 2006) and Robert Fagles, *Virgil: The Aeneid* (London and New York, 2006), in *LRB* (4 January 2007), 37–8

Review of Roy Gibson, Steven Green and Alison Sharrock (eds.), *The Art of Love: Bimillennial Essays on Ovid's Ars Amatoria and Remedia Amoris* (Oxford, 2007), in *TLS* (4 May 2007), 8–9

## 2008

Review of Mary Beard, *The Roman Triumph* (Cambridge, MA, 2007), in *LRB* (21 February 2008), 11–12
Review of Gian Biagio Conte, *The Poetry of Pathos: Studies in Virgilian Epic*, tr. E. Fantham and G. Most, ed. S. Harrison (Oxford, 2007) and Randall T. Ganiban, *Statius and Virgil: The Thebaid and the Reinterpretation of the Aeneid* (Cambridge, 2007), in *TLS* (15 February 2008), 26–7
Review of R.O.A.M. Lyne, *Collected Papers on Latin Poetry* (Oxford, 2007), in *CR* 58 (2008), 459–61
Review of Irene J.F. de Jong and René Nünlist (eds.), *Time in Ancient Greek Literature: Studies in Ancient Greek Narrative, Volume Two* (Leiden, 2007), in *BMCR* 2008.07.24

## 2009

'Virgil's tale of four cities: Troy, Carthage, Alexandria and Rome', The Ninth Syme Memorial Lecture (Victoria University of Wellington, 2009) (=Vol. 1.14)*
'Catullus and the Roman paradox epigram', *Materiali e Discussioni* 61 (2009), 29–39 (=Vol. 2.9)*
'Becoming an authority: Horace on his own reception', in L. Houghton and M. Wyke (eds.), *Perceptions of Horace: A Poet and his Readers* (Cambridge, 2009), 16–38 (=Vol. 2.10)*
'Time', in A. Feldherr (ed.), *The Cambridge Companion to Roman Historiography* (Cambridge, 2009), 139–51
Review of Edith Hall and Rosie Wyles (eds.), *New Directions in Ancient Pantomime* (Oxford, 2009) and Ruth Webb, *Demons and Dancers: Performance in Late Antiquity* (Cambridge, MA, 2009), in *TLS* (2 October 2009), 11–12

## 2010

'Fathers and sons: the Manlii Torquati and family continuity in Catullus and Horace', in C. S. Kraus, J. Marincola and C.B.R. Pelling (eds.), *Ancient Historiography and its Contexts* (Oxford, 2010), 205–23 (=Vol. 2.11)*
'Doing the numbers: the Roman mathematics of civil war in Shakespeare's *Antony and Cleopatra*', in B. Breed, C. Damon, and A. Rossi (eds.), *Citizens of Discord: Rome and its Civil Wars* (Oxford, 2010), 273–92 (=Vol. 2.12)*
'Crediting Pseudolus: trust, belief, and the credit crunch in Plautus' *Pseudolus*', *CPh* 105 (2010), 281–300 (=Vol. 2.13)*

'Time and calendar', in A. Barchiesi and W. Scheidel (eds.), *The Oxford Handbook to Roman Studies* (Oxford, 2010), 882–94

Review of Robert L. O'Connell, *The Ghosts of Cannae: Hannibal and the Darkest Hour of the Roman Republic*, in *The New York Times Book Review* (5 September 2010), 13

Review of Brian McGing, *Polybius' Histories* (Oxford, 2010) and *Polybius: The Histories*, vols. 1–2, Loeb Classical Library (Cambridge, MA, 2010), in *TLS* (1 October 2010), 22

## 2011

'*Hic finis fandi*: on the absence of punctuation for the endings (and beginnings) of speeches in Latin poetic texts', *MD* 66 (2011), 45–91 (=Vol. 2.14)*

Review of Katharina Volk, *Ovid* (Oxford, 2011) and Jennifer Ingleheart, *A Commentary on Ovid, Tristia, Book 2* (Oxford, 2011), in *TLS* (16 September 2011), 26

Review of Peter White, *Cicero in Letters: Epistolary Relations of the Late Republic* (Oxford, 2011), in *LRB* (22 September 2011), 19–20

Review of J. Schwindt (ed.), *La Représentation du temps dans la poésie augustéenne/ Zur Poetik der Zeit in augusteischer Dichtung* (Heidelberg, 2005), in *JRS* 101 (2011), 300–1

## 2012

'Representation and the materiality of the book in the polymetrics', in A.J. Woodman and I.M.LeM. Du Quesnay (eds.), *Perspectives and Contexts in the Interpretation of Catullus* (Cambridge, 2012), 29–47 (=Vol. 2.15)*

Review of Matthew Robinson, *Ovid: Fasti Book 2* (Oxford, 2011), in *Gnomon* 84 (2012), 76–8

## 2013

'Catullus 61: epithalamium and comparison', *CCJ* 59 (2013), 70–97 (=Vol. 2.16)*

Review of Emily Gowers, *Horace: Satires Book 1* (Cambridge, 2012) and R. Tarrant, *Virgil: Aeneid Book 12* (Cambridge, 2012), in *TLS* (5 February 2013), 12–13

Review of Mary Beard, *Confronting the Classics: Traditions, Adventures and Innovations* (London, 2013), in *The Irish Times* (25 May 2013)

## 2014

'First similes in epic', *TAPhA* 144 (2014), 189–228 (=Vol. 1.15)*

## 2015

'Ovid's Ciceronian literary history: end-career chronology and autobiography', Sixth UCL Housman Lecture, pamphlet published by Department of Greek and Latin, University College London (2015) (=Vol. 2.17)*

## 2016

*Beyond Greek: The Beginnings of Latin Literature* (Cambridge, MA, 2016)
'Horace and the literature of the past: lyric, epic, and history in *Odes* 4', in B. Delignon, N. Le Meur and O. Thévenaz (eds.), *La Poésie lyrique dans la cité antique: les Odes d'Horace au miroir de la lyrique grecque archaïque* (Paris and Lyon, 2016), 295–312(=Vol. 2.18)*
Review of Nora Goldschmidt, *Shaggy Crowns: Ennius' Annales and Virgil's Aeneid* (Oxford, 2013), in *Gnomon* 88 (2016), 77–8

## 2017

'Carthage and Rome: Introduction', *CPh* 112.3 (2017), 301–11 (a specially commissioned issue of the journal, edited by D. Feeney)
Review of Pramit Chaudhuri, *The War with God: Theomachy in Roman Imperial Poetry* (Oxford, 2014), in *Mnemosyne* 70 (2017), 173–5
Review of Anne Rogerson, *Virgil's Ascanius: Imagining the Future in the 'Aeneid'*, in *LRB* (15 June 2017), 41–2
Review of T.P. Wiseman, *The Roman Audience: Classical Literature as Social History* (Oxford, 2015), in *Gnomon* 89 (2017), 412–18
Review of David Ferry (tr.), *Virgil: The Aeneid* (Chicago, IL, 2017), *The New York Times Book Review* (10 December 2017), 25

## 2019

Review of A.J. Woodman, *Tacitus: Annals Book IV* (Cambridge, 2018), in *TLS* (16 July 2019), 32

## 2020

'*Forma manet facti* (Ov. *Fast.* 2.379): aetiologies of myth and ritual in Ovid's *Fasti* and *Metamorphoses*', *CJ* 115 (2020), 339–66 (=Vol. 2.19)*

# Bibliography

Acosta-Hughes, B. and Stephens, S.A. 2012. *Callimachus in Context: From Plato to the Augustan Poets*. Cambridge

Adelman, J. 1973. *The Common Liar: An Essay on Antony and Cleopatra*. New Haven, CT and London

Ahl, F.M. 1976. *Lucan: An Introduction*. Ithaca, NY

  1985. *Metaformations: Soundplay and Wordplay in Ovid and Other Classical Poets*. Ithaca, NY

Albrecht, M. von 1964. *Silius Italicus: Freiheit und Gebundenheit römischer Epik*. Amsterdam

  1967. 'Vergils Geschichtsauffassung in der <<Heldenschau>>', *WS* NF 1: 156–82

Alfonsi, L. 1955. 'Precedenti dell'incontro di Enea ed Anchise', *Aevum* 29: 375–6

Allen, D.C. 1970. *Mysteriously Meant: The Rediscovery of Pagan Symbolism and Allegorical Interpretation in the Renaissance*. Baltimore, MD

Ampolo, C. 1988. 'La nascità della città', in A. Momigliano and A. Schiavone (eds.), *Storia di Roma*. Turin. 1.153–80

Anderson, A.R. 1928. 'Heracles and his successors: a study of a heroic ideal and the recurrence of a heroic type', *HSPh* 39: 7–58

Anderson, B. 1983. *Imagined Communities: Reflections on the Origin and Spread of Nationalism*. London and New York

Anderson, W.S. 1957. 'Vergil's second *Iliad*', *TAPhA* 88: 17–30

Ando, C. 1999. 'Was Rome a polis?', *ClAnt* 18: 5–34

  2000. *Imperial Ideology and Provincial Loyalty in the Roman Empire*. Berkeley and Los Angeles, CA

  2002. 'Vergil's Italy: Ethnography and Politics in First-Century Rome', in D.S. Levene and D.P. Nelis (eds.), *Clio and the Poets: Augustan Poetry and the Traditions of Ancient Historiography*. Leiden. 123–42

  2015. *Roman Social Imaginaries: Language and Thought in Contexts of Empire*. Toronto

  2016. 'Making Romans: citizens, subjects, and subjectivity in Republican Empire', in Lavan, Payne and Weisweiler (2016), 169–86

Annas, J. 1981. *An Introduction to Plato's Republic*. Oxford

  1982. 'Plato's myths of judgement', *Phronesis* 27: 119–43

Appiah, K.A. 2018. *The Lies that Bind: Rethinking Identity, Creed, Country, Color, Class, Culture*. New York

Aresi, L. forthcoming. 'Fama storica e fama poetica: Livio e Ovidio alle prese con il mito di Roma', *Rivista di cultura classica e medioevale*
Arnim, H. von. 1898. *Leben und Werke des Dio von Prusa*. Berlin
Ashby, T. 1927. *The Roman Campagna in Classical Times*. New York
Atkins, J.W. 2013. *Cicero on Politics and the Limits of Reason: The Republic and Laws*. Cambridge
  2018. *Roman Political Thought*. Cambridge
Austin, R.G. 1955. *P. Vergilii Maronis Aeneidos Liber Quartus*. Oxford
  1971. *P. Vergilii Maronis Aeneidos Liber Primus*. Oxford
  1977. *P. Vergilii Maronis Aeneidos Liber Sextus*. Oxford
Bailey, C. 1935. *Religion in Virgil*. Oxford
  1947. *T. Lucreti Cari De Rerum Natura Libri Sex*. Oxford
Baker, R.J. 1982. 'Sallustian silence', *Latomus* 41: 801–2
Balsdon, J.P.V.D. 1962. *Roman Women: Their History and Habits*. London
Bannet, E.T. 1993. *Postcultural Theory: Critical Theory after the Marxist Paradigm*. Basingstoke and London
Barchiesi, A. 1984. *La traccia del modello: effetti omerici nella narrazione virgiliana*. Pisa = 2015. *Homeric Effects in Vergil's Narrative*, tr. I. Marchesi and M. Fox. Princeton, NJ
  1989. 'Voci e istanze narrative nelle Metamorfosi di Ovidio', *MD* 23: 55–97
  1991. 'Discordant Muses', *PCPhS* 37: 1–21
  1994. *Il poeta e il principe: Ovidio e il discorso augusteo*. Rome
  1996. 'La guerra di Troia non avrà luogo: il proemio *dell'Achilleide* di Stazio', *AION(filol)* 18: 45–62
  1997a. *The Poet and the Prince: Ovid and Augustan Discourse*. Berkeley, CA. Translation of Barchiesi (1994)
  1997b. 'Endgames: Ovid's *Metamorphoses* 15 and *Fasti* 6', in D.H. Roberts, F.M. Dunn and D. Fowler (eds.), *Classical Closure: Reading the End in Greek and Latin Literature*. Princeton, NJ. 181–208
  1999. 'Venus' masterplot: Ovid and the Homeric Hymns', in Hardie, Barchiesi and Hinds (1999). 112–26
  2000. 'Rituals in ink: Horace on the Greek lyric tradition', in Depew and Obbink (2000). 167–82
  2001a. 'The crossing', in S.J. Harrison (ed.), *Texts, Ideas, and the Classics: Scholarship, Theory, and Classical Literature*. Oxford. 142–63
  2001b. *Speaking Volumes: Narrative and Intertext in Ovid and Other Latin Poets*, tr. M. Fox and S. Marchesi. London
  2002. 'The uniqueness of the *Carmen Saeculare* and its tradition', in A.J. Woodman and D. Feeney (eds.), *Traditions and Contexts in the Poetry of Horace*. Cambridge. 107–23
  2005a. 'Masculinity in the 90's: the education of Achilles in Statius and Quintilian', in M. Paschalis (ed.), *Roman and Greek Imperial Epic*. Rethymnon. 47–75
  2005b. *Ovidio: Metamorfosi Volume I (Libri I–II)*. Rome
  2008. '*Bellum Italicum*: l'unificazione dell'Italia nell'*Eneide*', in G. Urso (ed.), *Patria diversis gentibus una? Unità politica e identità etniche nell'Italia antica*.

*Atti del convegno internazionale, Cividale del Friuli, 20–22 settembre 2007*. Pisa. 243–60
Bardon, H. and Verdière, R. (eds.). 1971. *Vergiliana: Recherches sur Virgile*. Leiden
Barkan, L. 1986. *The Gods Made Flesh: Metamorphosis and the Pursuit of Paganism*. New Haven, CT
Barker, A. 1949. 'Structural pattern in *Paradise Lost*', *PhQ* 28: 17–30
Barker, E. 1946. *The Politics of Aristotle*. Oxford
Barnes, J. 2007. 'The odd couple' (review of Tombs and Tombs (2007)), *The New York Review of Books*, 29 March. 4–9
Barrett, J.C. 1997. 'Romanization: a critical comment', in D.J. Mattingly (ed.), *Dialogues in Roman Imperialism: Power, Discourse, and Discrepant Experiences in the Roman Empire*. Portsmouth, RI. 51–64
Barrett, W.S. 1964. *Euripides: Hippolytus*. Oxford
Barthes, R. 1957. *Mythologies*. Paris
  1972. *Mythologies*, tr. A. Lavers. New York
Bartsch, S. 1998. '*Ars* and the man: the politics of art in Virgil's *Aeneid*', *CPh* 93: 322–42
Basanoff, V. 1947. *Evocatio. Étude d'un rituel militaire romain*. Paris
Bassett, E. 1966. 'Hercules and the hero of the *Punica*', in L. Wallach (ed.), *The Classical Tradition: Literary and Historical Studies in Honor of Harry Caplan*. Ithaca, NY. 258–73
Bayet, J. 1926. *Les Origines de l'Hercule romain*. Paris
Beard, M. 1991. Review of Scheid (1990), *TLS* (25 October 1991), 7
Beard, M., North, J. and Price, S. 1998. *Religions of Rome*, 2 vols. Cambridge
Beaujeu, J. 1954. 'Le mariage d'Énée et de Didon', *RdN* 36: 115–19
Beck, D. 2014. 'The first simile of the *Aeneid*', *Vergilius* 60: 67–83
Bell, C. 1992. *Ritual Theory, Ritual Practice*. Oxford
  1997. *Ritual: Perspectives and Dimensions*. Oxford
Bendlin, A. 2006. 'Nicht der Eine, nicht die Vielen. Zur Pragmatik religiösen Verhaltens in einer polytheistischen Gesellschaft am Beispiel Roms', in R.G. Kratz and H. Spieckermann (eds.), *Götterbilder, Gottesbilder, Weltbilder: Polytheismus and Monotheismus in der Welt der Antike*. Tübingen. 2.279–311
Beni, P. 1607. *Comparatione di Homero, Virgilio e Torquato*. Padua
Benjamin, W. 1968. *Illuminations*, tr. H. Zohn. New York
Bentley, R. 1711. *Q. Horatius Flaccus*. Cambridge
Benveniste, E. 1973. *Indo-European Language and Society*, tr. E. Palmer. London
Bernadete, S. 1963. 'Achilles and the *Iliad*', *Hermes* 91: 1–16
Bethe, E. 1899. 'Choirilos von Samos', *RE* 6: 2359–61
Beye, C.R. 1982. *Epic and Romance in the Argonautica of Apollonius*. Carbondale, IL
Bispham, E. 2007. *From Asculum to Actium: The Municipalization of Italy from the Social War to Augustus*. Oxford
Blessington, F.C. 1979. *'Paradise Lost' and the Classical Epic*. London
Bloch, M. 1989. *Ritual, History and Power: Selected Papers in Anthropology*. London
Bloch, R. 1972. 'Héra, Uni, Junon en Italie centrale', *Comptes Rendus de l'Académie des Inscriptions et Belles Lettres*: 384–95

Block, E. 1981. *The Effects of Divine Manifestation on the Reader's Perspective in Vergil's Aeneid.* New York
Bloomfield, M.W. 1975. 'The problem of the hero in the later medieval period', in Burns and Reagan (1975). 27–48
Bömer, F. 1957–8. *P. Ovidius Naso: Die Fasten,* 2 vols. Heidelberg
  1969–86. *P. Ovidius Naso: Metamorphosen,* 7 vols. Heidelberg
Bond, G.W. 1981. *Euripides: Heracles.* Oxford
Bonjour, M. 1975a. *Terre natale: études sur une composante affective du patriotisme romain.* Paris
  1975b. 'Les personnages féminins et la terre natale dans l'épisode de Coriolan (Liv., 2, 40)', *REL* 53: 157–81
Bowra, C.M. 1945. *From Virgil to Milton.* London
Boyancé, P. 1936. *Études sur le songe de Scipion.* Paris
  1963. *La Religion de Virgile.* Paris
Boyle, A.J. 1972. 'The meaning of the *Aeneid*: a critical inquiry. Part 1: Empire and the individual: an examination of the *Aeneid*'s major theme', *Ramus* 1: 63–90
Bradley, G. 2006. 'Colonization and identity in Republic Italy', in G. Bradley and J.-P. Wilson (eds.), *Greek and Roman Colonization: Origins, Ideologies and Interactions.* Swansea. 161–87
Bramble, J.C. 1982. 'Lucan', in *CHCL* 2: 533–57
Brand, C.P. 1965. *Torquato Tasso: A Study of the Poet and of his Contribution to English Literature.* Cambridge
Braund, D. and Gill, C. (eds.). 2003. *Myth, History and Culture in Republican Rome: Studies in Honour of T.P. Wiseman.* Exeter
Bremmer, J.N. 2006. 'Atheism in antiquity', in M. Martin (ed.), *The Cambridge Companion to Atheism.* Cambridge. 11–26
Briggs, W.W., Jr. 1980. *Narrative and Simile from the Georgics in the Aeneid.* Leiden
Bright, D.F. 1981. 'Aeneas' other Nekuia', *Vergilius* 27: 40–7
Briscoe, J. 1971. 'The first decade', in T.A. Dorey (ed.), *Livy.* London and Toronto. 1–20
  1973. *A Commentary on Livy, Books XXXI–XXXIII.* Oxford
Brooks, P. 1984. *Reading for the Plot: Design and Intention in Narrative.* New York
Brown, P.M. 1984. *Lucretius: De Rerum Natura I.* Bristol
Brown, R. 1987. 'The palace of the sun in Ovid's Metamorphoses', in Whitby, Hardie and Whitby (1987). 211–20
  1995. 'Livy's Sabine women and the ideal of *Concordia*', *TAPhA* 125: 291–319
Brunner, T. 1966. 'The function of the simile in Ovid's *Metamorphoses*', *CJ* 61: 354–63
Bruster, D. 2003. *Shakespeare and the Question of Culture: Early Modern Literature and the Cultural Turn.* New York
Buchheit, V. 1963. *Vergil über die Sendung Roms.* Heidelberg.
  1974. 'Junos Wandel zum Guten', *Gymnasium* 81: 498–503
Büchner, K. 1958. 'P. Vergilius Maro', *RE* 2R 16: 1266–486
Budelmann, F. and Phillips, T. (eds.). 2018. *Textual Events: Performance and the Lyric in Early Greece.* Oxford

Buffière, F. 1956. *Les Mythes d'Homère et la pensée grecque*. Paris
  1962. *Allégories d'Homère: Héraclite*. Paris
Burbank, J. and Cooper, F. 2010. *Empires in World History: Power and the Politics of Difference*. Princeton, NJ
Burck, E. 1964. 'Aktuelle Probleme der Livius-Interpretation', *Gymnasium Beiheft* 4: 21–46
  1992. *Das Geschichtswerk des Titus Livius*. Heidelberg
Burden, M. (ed.) 1998. *A Woman Scorn'd: Responses to the Dido Myth*. London
Burke, P.F. 1979. 'Roman rites for the dead and *Aeneid 6*', *CJ* 74: 220–8
Burkert, W. 1983. *Homo Necans: The Anthropology of Ancient Greek Sacrificial Ritual and Myth*, tr. P. Bing. Berkeley and Los Angeles, CA
  1985. *Greek Religion: Archaic and Classical*, tr. J. Raffan. Oxford
Burns, N.T. and Reagan, C.J. (eds.). 1975. *Concepts of the Hero in the Middle Ages and the Renaissance*. Albany, NY
Busetto, A. 2017. 'The idea of cosmopolitanism from its origins to the 21st century', in Cecchet and Busetto (2017). 302–17
Buxton, R.G.A. 1981. 'Introduction', in R.L. Gordon (ed.), *Myth, Religion and Society: Structuralist Essays by M. Detienne, L. Gernet, J.-P. Vernant & P. Vidal-Naquet*. Cambridge. ix–xvii
Cairns, F. 1989. *Virgil's Augustan Epic*. Cambridge
Calame, C. 2003. *Myth and History in Ancient Greece: The Symbolic Creation of a Colony*, tr. D.W. Berman. Princeton, NJ
Cameron, A. 1970. *Claudian: Poetry and Propaganda at the Court of Honorius*. Oxford
  1995. *Callimachus and his Critics*. Princeton, NJ
Camps, W.A. 1969. *An Introduction to Virgil's Aeneid*. London
Canetti, E. 1962. *Crowds and Power*, tr. C. Stewart. New York
Capogrossi Colognesi, L. 2014. *Law and Power in the Making of the Roman Commonwealth*, tr. L. Kopp. Cambridge
Carey, J. and Fowler, A. 1968. *The Poems of John Milton*. London
Carlà-Uhink, F. 2017a. *The 'Birth' of Italy: The Institutionalization of Italy as a Region, $3^{rd}–1^{st}$ Century BCE*. Berlin
  2017b. '*Caput mundi*: Rome as center in Roman representation and construction of space', *AncSoc* 47: 119–57
  2017c. 'Alteram loci patriam, alteram iuris: "double fatherlands" and the role of Italy in Cicero's political discourse', in Cecchet and Busetto (2017). 259–82
Carspecken, J.F. 1952. 'Apollonius Rhodius and the Homeric epic', *YClS* 13: 33–143
Cartledge, P. and Greenwood, E. 2002. 'Herodotus as a critic: truth, fiction, polarity', in E.J. Bakker, I.J.F. de Jong and H. van Wees (eds.), *Brill's Companion to Herodotus*. Leiden. 351–71
Castelvetro, L. 1570. *Aristoteles: Poetica. Vulgarizzata e sposta per Lodovico Castelvetro*. Venice
Castoriadis, C. 1975. *L'Institution imaginaire de la société*. Paris
Ceausescu, P. 1976. '*Altera Roma*: histoire d'une folie politique', *Historia* 25: 79–108

Cecchet, L. and Busetto, A. (eds.) 2017. *Citizens in the Graeco-Roman World: Aspects of Citizenship from the Archaic Period to AD 212*. Leiden
Chaplin, J. and Kraus, C.S. (eds.). 2009. *Oxford Readings in Classical Studies: Livy*. Oxford
Clark, E.A. 2004. *History, Theory, Text: Historians and the Linguistic Turn*. Cambridge, MA
Clark, R.J. 1979. *Catabasis: Vergil and the Wisdom-Tradition*. Amsterdam
Clarke, M. 1949. 'Rhetorical influences in the *Aeneid*', *G&R* 18: 14–27
Clausen, W.V. 1964. 'An interpretation of the *Aeneid*', *HSPh* 68: 139–47
Clay, J.S. 1983. *The Wrath of Athena: Gods and Men in the Odyssey*. Princeton, NJ
Coby, P. 1999. *Machiavelli's Romans: Liberty and Greatness in the Discourses on Livy*. Oxford
Coleman, R.R. 1982. 'The gods in the *Aeneid*', *G&R* 29: 143–68
Combet-Farnoux, B. 1980. *Mercure romain: le culte public de Mercure et la fonction mercantile à Rome de la République archaïque à l'époque augustéenne*. Rome
Commager, S. 1962. *The Odes of Horace: A Critical Study*. New Haven, CT and London
Conington, J. 1881–4. *The Works of Virgil, with a Commentary*[4], rev. H. Nettleship, 3 vols. London
Connolly, J. 2007. *The State of Speech: Rhetoric and Political Thought in Ancient Rome*. Princeton, NJ
  2014. *The Life of Roman Republicanism*. Princeton, NJ
Conte, G.B. 1986. *The Rhetoric of Imitation: Genre and Poetic Memory in Virgil and Other Latin Poets*, trans. varii, ed. C. Segal. Ithaca, NY
  1994a. *Latin Literature: A History*, tr. J.B. Solodow, rev. D. Fowler and G. Most. Baltimore, MD
  1994b. *Genres and Readers: Lucretius, Love Elegy, Pliny's Encyclopedia*, tr. G.W. Most. Baltimore, MD and London
Conway, R.S. 1935. *P. Vergilii Maronis Aeneidos Liber Primus*. Cambridge
Cornell, T.J. 1978. Review of Wardman (1976), *CR* 28: 110–12
  1991. 'Rome: history of an anachronism', in A. Molho, K. Raaflaub and J. Emlen (eds.), *City-States in Classical Antiquity and Medieval Italy*. Ann Arbor, MI. 53–69
  1995. *The Beginnings of Rome: Italy and Rome from the Bronze Age to the Punic Wars (c. 1000–264 BC)*. London
  1997. 'Ethnicity as a factor in early Roman history', in T. J. Cornell and K. Lomas (eds.), *Gender and Ethnicity in Ancient Italy*. London. 9–21
  2000. 'The city-state in Latium', in M.H. Hansen (ed.), *A Comparative Study of Thirty City-State Cultures*. Copenhagen. 209–28
  2003. 'Coriolanus: myth, history and performance', in Braund and Gill (2003). 73–97
Coudry, M. 2001. 'Camille: construction et fluctuations de la figure d'un grand homme', in Coudry and Späth (2001). 47–81
Coudry, M. and Späth, T. (eds.). 2001. *L'Invention des grands hommes de la Rome antique/Die Konstruktion der großen Männer Altroms*. Paris

Cowan, R.W. 2002. *'In my Beginning is my End': Origins, Cities, and Foundations in Flavian Epic.* Diss. Oxford
Croisille, J.M. 1985. 'Remarques sur l'épisode troyen dans les *Métamorphoses* d'Ovide (*Met.*, XII–XIII, 1–622)', in J.M. Frécaut and D. Porte (eds.), *Journées Ovidiennes de Parménie,* Coll. Latomus vol. 189. Brussels. 57–81
Crusius, O. 1899. 'Choirilos', *RE* 6: 2361–3
Csapo, E. 2000. 'From Aristophanes to Menander? Genre transformation in Greek comedy', in Depew and Obbink (2000). 115–33
Currie, B. 2016. *Homer's Allusive Art.* Oxford
Cyrino, M.S. 1998. 'Heroes in d(u)ress: transvestism and power in the myths of Herakles and Achilles', *Arethusa* 31: 207–41
Dahlmann, H. 1935. 'M. Terentius Varro', *RE Suppl.* 6: 1173–277
 1954. *Der Bienenstaat in Vergils Georgica.* Wiesbaden
Dalrymple, W. 2002. *White Mughals: Love and Betrayal in Eighteenth-Century India.* London
Davies, J.P. 2004. *Rome's Religious History: Livy, Tacitus and Ammianus on their Gods.* Cambridge
Davies, M. 1981. 'The judgement of Paris and *Iliad* Book XXIV', *JHS* 101: 56–62
Davies, M. and Kathirithamby, J. 1986. *Greek Insects.* Oxford
de Beauvoir, S. 1960. *The Mandarins*, tr. L.M. Friedman. London
De Sanctis, G. 1907/1960. *Storia dei Romani I–II: la conquista del primato in Italia.* Turin¹; Florence (1960)²
De Witt, N.W. 1907. *The Dido Episode in the* Aeneid *of Virgil.* Diss. Chicago, IL
 1920. 'An interpretation of Horace *Odes* III.3', *CR* 34: 65–6
Dench, E. 2005. *Romulus' Asylum: Roman Identities from the Age of Alexander to the Age of Hadrian.* Oxford
Depew, M. and Obbink, D. (eds.). 2000. *Matrices of Genre: Authors, Canons, and Society.* Cambridge, MA
Derow, P.S. and Forrest, W.G. 1982. 'An inscription from Chios', *ABSA* 77: 79–92
Desideri, F. 1967. 'Studi di storiografia eracleota', *SCO* 16: 366–416
Diamond, J. 1997. *Guns, Germs and Steel: A Short History of Everybody for the Last 13,000 Years.* London
Dilke, O.A.W. 1954. *Statius: Achilleid.* Cambridge
Dillery, J. 2005. 'Greek sacred history', *AJPh* 126: 505–26
Döring, K. 1978. 'Antike Theorien über die staatspolitische Notwendigkeit der Götterfurcht', *A&A* 24: 43–56
Douglas, A.E. 1961–2. 'The realism of Vergil', *PVS* 1: 15–24
Due, O.S. 1962. 'An essay on Lucan', *C&M* 23: 68–132
 1974. *Changing Forms: Studies in the Metamorphoses of Ovid.* Copenhagen
Dumézil, G. 1974. *La Religion romaine archaïque.* Paris
Dyson, J.T. 1996. '*Caesi iuuenci* and *pietas impia* in Virgil', *CJ* 91: 277–86
Earl, D.C. 1966. *The Political Thought of Sallust.* Amsterdam
 1967. *The Moral and Political Tradition of Rome.* Ithaca, NY
 1972. 'Prologue-form in ancient historiography', *ANRW* 1.2: 842–56

Eckstein, A.M. 2009. *Mediterranean Anarchy, Interstate War, and the Rise of Rome*. Berkeley and Los Angeles, CA
Edelstein, L. and Kidd, I.G. 1972–88. *Posidonius*, 3 vols. Cambridge
Edgeworth, R.J.E. 2001. 'Ascanius' mother', *Hermes* 129: 246–50
Edwards, C. 1996. *Writing Rome: Textual Approaches to the City*. Cambridge
Elftmann, G. 1979. 'Aeneas in his prime: distinctions in age and the loneliness of adulthood in Vergil's *Aeneid*', *Arethusa* 12: 175–202
Elioseff, L.E. 1963. *The Cultural Milieu of Addison's Literary Criticism*. Austin, TX
Eliot, George. 1967. *Daniel Deronda*. Harmondsworth
Elliott, J. 2013. *Ennius and the Architecture of the Annales*. Cambridge
Ellsworth, J.D. 1988. 'The episode of the Sibyl in Ovid's *Metamorphoses* (14.103–56)', in R.L. Hadlich and J.D. Ellsworth (eds.), *East Meets West: Homage to Edgar C. Knowlton, Jr*. Honolulu: 47–55
Elmer, D.F. 2013. *The Poetics of Consent: Collective Decision Making and the Iliad*. Baltimore, MD
Elsner, J. 1991. 'Cult and sculpture: sacrifice in the Ara Pacis Augustae', *JRS* 81: 50–61
Elter, A. 1907. *Donarem Pateras ... Horat. Carm. 4,8*. Bonn
Erskine, A. 2001. *Troy Between Greece and Rome: Local Tradition and Imperial Power*. Oxford
Fanning, M.W. 1933. *Maphei Vegii Laudensis De Educatione Liberorum et Eorum Claris Moribus*. Washington, DC
Fantham, E. 1979. 'Statius' Achilleid and his Trojan model', *CQ* 29: 457–62
  1992. 'Ceres, Liber and Flora: Georgic and anti-georgic elements in Ovid's *Fasti*', *PCPhS* 38: 39–56
  1998. *Ovid: Fasti Book IV*. Cambridge
Farney, G.D. 2007. *Ethnic Identity and Aristocratic Competition in Republican Rome*. Cambridge
  2014. 'Romans and Italians', in McInerney (2014). 437–54
Farrell, J. 1991. *Vergil's Georgics and the Traditions of Ancient Epic: The Art of Allusion in Literary History*. Oxford
  2001. *Latin Language and Latin Culture from Ancient to Modern Times*. Cambridge
Farron, S.G. 1979–80. 'The Roman invention of evil', *Studies in Antiquity* 1: 12–46
Feeney, D. 1991. *The Gods in Epic: Poets and Critics of the Classical Tradition*. Oxford
  1998. *Literature and Religion at Rome: Cultures, Contexts, and Beliefs*. Cambridge
  2003. Review of Depew and Obbink (2000), *JRS* 93: 337–9
  2007. *Caesar's Calendar: Ancient Times and the Beginnings of History*. Berkeley and Los Angeles, CA
  2016. *Beyond Greek: The Beginnings of Latin Literature*. Cambridge, MA
  2017. Review of Wiseman (2015), *Gnomon* 89: 412–18
Feger, R. 1956. 'T. Pomponius Atticus', *RE Suppl*. 8: 503–26
Feldherr, A. 1997. 'Metamorphosis and sacrifice in Ovid's Theban narrative', *MD* 38: 25–55

1998. *Spectacle and Society in Livy's History*. Berkeley and Los Angeles, CA
  2002. 'Stepping out of the ring: repetition and sacrifice in the boxing match in *Aeneid* 5', in D.S. Levene and D.P. Nelis (eds.), *Clio and the Poets: Augustan Poetry and the Traditions of Ancient Historiography*. Leiden. 61–79
Fenik, B.C. 1960. *The influence of Euripides on Vergil's* Aeneid. Diss. Princeton, NJ
Finsler, G. 1912. *Homer in der Neuzeit von Dante bis Goethe*. Leipzig
Flemming, R. 2000. *Medicine and the Making of Roman Women: Gender, Nature, and Authority from Celsus to Galen*. Oxford
Fletcher, F. 1941. *Virgil: Aeneid VI*. Oxford
Fletcher, K.F.B. 2014. *Finding Italy: Travel, Nation and Colonization in Vergil's Aeneid*. Ann Arbor, MI
Flexner, A. 2017. *The Usefulness of Useless Knowledge, with a Companion Essay by Robbert Dijkgraaf*. Princeton, NJ
Flower, M.A. 1994. *Theopompus of Chios: History and Rhetoric in the Fourth Century BC*. Oxford
Flower, M.A. and Marincola, J. 2002. *Herodotus: Histories Book IX*. Cambridge
Foley, H.P. 1978. '"Reverse similes" and sex roles in the *Odyssey*', *Arethusa* 11: 7–26
Foote, S. 1958–74. *The Civil War, a Narrative*, 3 vols. New York
Ford, A. 1992. *Homer: The Poetry of the Past*. Ithaca, NY
Fornara, C.W. 1983. *The Nature of History in Ancient Greece and Rome*. Berkeley and Los Angeles, CA
Forsythe, G. 1999. *Livy and Early Rome: A Study in Historical Method and Judgment*. Stuttgart
Fowler, A. 1982. *Kinds of Literature: An Introduction to the Theory of Genres and Modes*. Cambridge, MA
Fowler, D. 1987. 'Vergil on killing virgins', in Whitby, Hardie and Whitby (1987). 185–98
  2000. *Roman Constructions: Readings in Postmodern Latin*. Oxford
  2002. *Lucretius on Atomic Motion: A Commentary on De Rerum Natura Book Two, Lines 1–332*. Oxford
Fowler, R.L. 2004. 'The Homeric question', in R.L. Fowler (ed.), *The Cambridge Companion to Homer*. Cambridge. 220–32
  2012. 'Written work,' *TLS* (16 March 2012), 28
Fowler, W.W. 1916. *Virgil's 'Gathering of the Clans,' Being Observations on Aeneid VII.601–817*. Oxford
Fraenkel, E. 1949. Review of E.K. Rand et al. (eds.), *Servianorum in Vergilii Carmina Commentariorum Editionis Harvardianae II*, *JRS* 39: 145–54
  1957. *Horace*. Oxford
Fränkel, H. 1968. *Noten zu den Argonautica des Apollonios*. Munich
Frazer, J.G. 1921. *Apollodorus: The Library, Volume I: Books 1–3.9*. Cambridge, MA
Friedlaender, L. 1919. *Darstellungen aus der Sittengeschichte Roms: in der Zeit von August bis zum Ausgang der Antonine⁹*. Leipzig
Friedländer, P. 1941. 'Pattern of sound and atomistic theory in Lucretius', *AJPh* 62: 16–34
Friedrich, Wolf-H. 1941. 'Zur altlateinischen Dichtung', *Hermes* 76: 113–35

Frye, N. 1957. *Anatomy of Criticism; Four Essays*. Princeton, NJ
Fuchs, H. 1938. *Der geistige Widerstand gegen Rom in der antiken Welt*. Berlin
Fürstenau, G. 1916. *De Silii Italici imitatione quae fertur Enniana*. Diss. Berlin
Gabba, E. 1991. *Dionysius and the History of Archaic Rome*. Berkeley and Los Angeles, CA
Gaertner, J.F. 2008. 'Livy's Camillus and the political discourse of the late Republic', *JRS* 98: 27–52
Gale, M. 1994. *Myth and Poetry in Lucretius*. Cambridge
  2000. *Virgil on the Nature of Things: The Georgics, Lucretius and the Didactic Tradition*. Cambridge
  2007. 'Lucretius and previous poetic traditions', in P. Hardie (ed.), *The Cambridge Companion to Lucretius*. Cambridge. 59–75
Galinsky, G.K. 1972. *The Herakles Theme: Adaptations of the Hero in Literature from Homer to the Twentieth Century*. Oxford
  1996. *Augustan Culture: An Interpretive Introduction*. Princeton, NJ
Gallagher, C. and Greenblatt, S. 2000. *Practicing New Historicism*. Chicago, IL
Garner, R. 1990. *From Homer to Tragedy: The Art of Allusion in Greek Poetry*. London and New York
Gasser, F. 1999. *Germana Patria: Die Geburtsheimat in den Werken römischer Autoren der späten Republik und der frühen Kaiserzeit*. Stuttgart
Geiger, J. 1985. *Cornelius Nepos and Ancient Political Biography*. Stuttgart
George, E.V. 1974. *Aeneid VIII and the Aitia of Callimachus*. Leiden
Georgii, H. 1905–6. *Ti. Claudii Donati Interpretationes Vergilianae*, 2 vols. Leipzig
Gerber, D.E. 1982. *Pindar's 'Olympian One': A Commentary*. Toronto
Getty, R. 1940. *Lucan: Pharsalia Book I*. Cambridge
Giardina, A. 1997. 'L'identità incompiuta dell'Italia romana,' in *L'Italia romana. Storie di un'identità incompiuta*. Rome and Bari. 3–116
Gildon, C. 1721. *The Laws of Poetry*. London
Gill, C. and Wiseman, T.P. (eds.). 2003. *Lies and Fiction in the Ancient World*. Exeter
Gillis, D. 1983. *Eros and Death in the Aeneid*. Rome
Giraldi Cinzio, G.B. 1554. *Discorso interno al comporre dei romanzi*. Venice
Gleason, M.W. 1995. *Making Men: Sophists and Self-Presentation in Ancient Rome*. Princeton, NJ
Glinski, M.L. von. 2012. *Simile and Identity in Ovid's 'Metamorphoses'*. Cambridge
Gödde, S. 2007. 'οὔ μοι ὅσιόν ἐστι λέγειν: Zur Poetik der Leerstelle in Herodots Ägypten-Logos', in A. Bierl, R. Lämmle, and K. Wesselmann (eds.), *Literatur und Religion: Wege zu einer mythisch-rituellen Poetik bei den Griechen*, vol. 2. Berlin and New York. 41–90
Goldhill, S. 1986. *Reading Greek Tragedy*. Cambridge.
  2002. *The Invention of Prose*. Oxford
Goodyear, F.R.D. 1972. *The Annals of Tacitus: Volume I (Annals I. 1–54)*. Cambridge
  1982. 'Sallust', in *CHCL* 2: 268–80

Gordon, R.L. 1990. 'The veil of power: emperors, sacrificers and benefactors', in M. Beard and J. North (eds.), *Pagan Priests: Religion and Power in the Ancient World*. Ithaca, NY. 199–231
Gossage, A.J. 1955. 'Two implications of the Trojan legend', *G&R* 2: 72–81
Gould, J. 1989. *Herodotus*. New York
Grafton, A.T. and Swerdlow, N.M. 1985. 'Technical chronology and astrological history in Varro, Censorinus and others', *CQ* 35: 454–65
  1986. 'Greek chronology in Roman epic: the calendrical date of the fall of Troy in the *Aeneid*', *CQ* 36: 212–18
Gransden, K.W. 1976. *Virgil: Aeneid Book 8*. Cambridge
Gratwick, A.S. 1982. 'Ennius' Annales', in *CHCL* 2: 60–76
Greene, T. 1963. *The Descent from Heaven: A Study in Epic Continuity*. New Haven, CT
Griffin, J. 1980. *Homer on Life and Death*. Oxford
  1985. *Latin Poets and Roman Life*. Chapel Hill, NC
Grimm, R.E. 1967. 'Aeneas and Andromache in *Aeneid 3*', *AJPh* 88: 151–62
  1969. 'Point of view in Virgil's Fourth *Aeneid*', *CW* 63: 81–5
Gruen, E.S. 1990. *Studies in Greek Culture and Roman Policy*. Berkeley and Los Angeles, CA
  1992. *Culture and National Identity in Republican Rome*. Ithaca, NY
  2013. 'Did ancient identity depend on ethnicity? A preliminary probe', *Phoenix* 67: 1–22
Gudeman, A. 1912. 'Hellanikos von Lesbos', *RE* 2R 15: 104–55
Guillemin, A. 1951. 'L'Inspiration virgilienne dans la Pharsale', *REL* 29: 214–27
Habinek, T. 1990. 'Sacrifice, society, and Vergil's ox-born bees', in M. Griffith and D.J. Mastronarde (eds.), *Cabinet of the Muses: Essays on Classical and Comparative Literature in Honor of Thomas G. Rosenmeyer*. Atlanta, GA. 209–23
  2005. *The World of Roman Song: From Ritualized Speech to Social Order*. Baltimore, MD and London
Hägin, P. 1964. *The Epic Hero and the Decline of Heroic Poetry*. Bern
Hall, E. 1989. *Inventing the Barbarian: Greek Self-Definition Through Tragedy*. Oxford
Hallett, J.P. 1984. *Fathers and Daughters in Roman Society: Women and the Elite Family*. Princeton, NJ
Halter, T. 1963. *Form und Gehalt in Vergils Aeneis*. Munich
Hammer, D. 2008. *Roman Political Thought and the Modern Theoretical Imagination*. Norman, OK
  2014. *Roman Political Thought: From Cicero to Augustine*. Cambridge
Harari, Y.N. 2014. *Sapiens: A Brief History of Mankind*. New York
Hardie, A. 1983. *Statius and the 'Silvae': Poets, Patrons and Epideixis in the Graeco-Roman World*. Liverpool
Hardie, P. 1986. *Virgil's Aeneid: Cosmos and Imperium*. Oxford
  1990. 'Ovid's Theban history: the first "anti-*Aeneid*"?', *CQ* 40: 224–35
  1991. 'The Janus episode in Ovid's *Fasti*', *MD* 26: 47–64

1993. *The Epic Successors of Virgil: A Study in the Dynamics of a Tradition.* Cambridge
1994. *Virgil: Aeneid Book IX.* Cambridge
1997. 'Questions of authority: the invention of tradition in Ovid *Metamorphoses* 15', in T. Habinek and A. Schiesaro (eds.), *The Roman Cultural Revolution.* Princeton, NJ: 182–98
2009. *Lucretian Receptions: History, the Sublime, Knowledge.* Cambridge
2010. 'Crowds and leaders in Imperial historiography and in epic', in J. Miller and A.J. Woodman (eds.), *Latin Historiography and Poetry in the Early Empire: Generic Interactions.* Leiden. 9–27
2012. *Rumour and Renown: Representations of Fama in Western Literature.* Cambridge
Hardie, P., Barchiesi, A. and Hinds, S. (eds.). 1999. *Ovidian Transformations: Essays on Ovid's Metamorphoses and its Reception.* Cambridge
Harrison, E.L. 1979. 'The Noric plague in Vergil's Third *Georgic*', *PLLS* 2: 1–65
1984. 'Virgil's Mercury', *Vergilius Suppl. Vol.* 2: 1–47
Harrison, G.B. 1966. *Ben Jonson: Discoveries 1641. Conversations with William Drummond of Hawthornden 1619.* Edinburgh
Harrison, S.J. 1985. 'Vergilian similes: some connections', *PLLS* 5: 99–107
1988. 'Vergil on kingship: the first simile of the *Aeneid*', *PCPhS* 34: 55–9
1991. *Vergil, Aeneid 10.* Oxford
1996. '*Aeneid* 1.286: Julius Caesar or Augustus?', *PLLS* 9: 127–33
Harrison, T. 2000. *Divinity and History: The Religion of Herodotus.* Oxford
Häussler, R. 1978. *Das historische Epos von Lucan bis Silius und seine Theorie: Studien zum historischen Epos der Antike.* Heidelberg
Heinze, R. 1915. *Virgils epische Technik³.* Leipzig
1928. *Vom Geist des Römertums.* Leipzig
Hellwig, A. 1973. *Untersuchungen zur Theorie der Rhetorik bei Platon und Aristoteles.* Göttingen
Henderson, J. 1999. *Writing Down Rome: Satire, Comedy, and Other Offences in Latin Poetry.* Oxford
2000. 'The Camillus factory: per astra ad Ardeam', *Ramus* 29: 1–26
Henry, J. 1873–92. *Aeneidea*, 4 vols. Dublin and London
Herrick, M.T. 1946. *The Fusion of Horatian and Aristotelian Literary Criticism, 1531–1555.* Urbana, IL
Hershkowitz, D. 1991. 'The *Aeneid* in *Aeneid 3*', *Vergilius* 37: 69–76
1998. *Valerius Flaccus' Argonautica: Abbreviated Voyages in Silver Latin Epic.* Oxford
Heubeck, A., West, S. and Hainsworth, J.B. (eds.). 1988. *A Commentary on Homer's Odyssey. Volume I.* Cambridge
Heuzé, P. 1985. *L'Image du corps dans l'oeuvre de Virgile.* Rome
Highet, G. 1972. *The Speeches in Vergil's Aeneid.* Princeton, NJ
Hill, G.B. 1905. *Lives of the English Poets, by Samuel Johnson.* Oxford
Hillen, H.J. 2003. *Von Aeneas zu Romulus: Die Legenden von der Gründung Roms.* Düsseldorf

Hinds, S.E. 1985. 'Booking the return trip: Ovid and *Tristia* 1', *PCPhS* 31: 13–32
  1987. *The Metamorphosis of Persephone: Ovid and the Self-Conscious Muse.* Cambridge
  1998. *Allusion and Intertext: Dynamics of Appropriation in Roman Poetry.* Cambridge
  1999. 'After exile: time and teleology from Metamorphoses to Ibis', in Hardie, Barchiesi and Hinds (1999). 48–67
  2000. 'Essential epic: genre and gender from Macer to Statius', in Depew and Obbink (2000). 221–44
  2010. 'Between formalism and historicism', in A. Barchiesi and W. Scheidel (eds.), *The Oxford Handbook of Roman Studies.* Oxford. 369–85
Hine, H. 1987. 'Aeneas and the arts (Vergil, *Aeneid* 6. 847–50)', in Whitby, Hardie and Whitby (1987). 173–83
Hobsbawm, E. and Ranger, T. (eds.). 1983. *The Invention of Tradition.* Cambridge
Höistad, R. 1948. *Cynic Hero and Cynic King: Studies in the Cynic Conception of Man.* Uppsala
Holliday, V.L. 1969. *Pompey in Cicero's Correspondence and Lucan's Civil War.* The Hague
Holzberg, N. 1998. *Ovid: Dichter und Werk.* Munich
Hornblower, S. 2001. 'Epic and epiphanies: Simonides and the "New Simonides"', in D. Boedeker and D. Sider (eds.), *The New Simonides: Contexts of Praise and Desire.* Oxford. 135–47
  2018. *Lykophron's Alexandra, Rome, and the Hellenistic World.* Oxford
  2019. 'Livy, Busa the female benefactor, and the evidence of Delian epigraphy', *ZPE* 210: 71–5
Hornsby, R.A. 1970. *Patterns of Action in the Aeneid: An Interpretation of Vergil's Epic Similes.* Iowa City, IA
Horsfall, N.M. 1971. 'Numanus Remulus: ethnography and propaganda in *Aen.* 9.598ff.', *Latomus* 39: 1108–16
  1973–4. 'Dido in the light of history', *PVS* 12: 1–13
  1976. 'Virgil, history and the Roman tradition', *Prudentia* 8: 73–89
  1980. 'Virgil, Varro's *Imagines* and the Forum of Augustus', *AncSoc* 10: 20–3
  1981. 'Virgil and the conquest of chaos', *Antichthon* 15: 141–50
  1982. 'The structure and purpose of Virgil's parade of heroes', *AncSoc* 12: 12–18
  1989. *Cornelius Nepos: A Selection, Including the Lives of Cato and Atticus.* Oxford
  2000. *Virgil, Aeneid 7: A Commentary.* Leiden
Houston, G.W. 2014. *Inside Roman Libraries: Book Collections and their Management in Antiquity.* Chapel Hill, NC
Hubaux, J. 1958. *Rome et Véies: recherches sur la chronologie légendaire du moyen âge romain.* Paris
Huber, L. 1965. 'Herodots Homerverständnis', in H. Flashar and K. Gaiser (eds.), *Synusia: Festgabe für Wolfgang Schadewaldt.* Pfullingen. 29–52
Hügi, M. 1952. *Vergils Aeneis und die hellenistische Dichtung.* Bern
Humbert, M. 1978. *Municipium et civitas sine suffragio: l'organisation de la conquête jusqu'à la guerre sociale.* Rome

Hunter, R. 1993. *The Argonautica of Apollonius: Literary Studies*. Cambridge
   2006. *The Shadow of Callimachus: Studies in the Reception of Hellenistic Poetry at Rome*. Cambridge
Hunter, R. and Uhlig, A. (eds.). 2017. *Imagining Reperformance in Ancient Culture: Studies in the Traditions of Drama and Lyric*. Cambridge
Hutcheon, L. 1980. *Narcissistic Narrative: The Metafictional Narrative*. Waterloo, Ont.
Hutchinson, G.O. 2008. *Talking Books: Readings in Hellenistic and Roman Books of Poetry*. Oxford
Huxley, G.L. 1969. *Greek Epic Poetry from Eumelos to Panyassis*. Cambridge, MA
Isayev, E. 2017. *Migration, Mobility and Place in Ancient Italy*. Cambridge
Jackson Knight, W.F. 1966. *Roman Vergil$^2$*. London
Jacoby, F. 1902. *Apollodors Chronik: Eine Sammlung der Fragmente*. Berlin
Jaeger, M. 1997. *Livy's Written Rome*. Ann Arbor, MI
Jal, P. 1963. *La Guerre civile à Rome*. Paris
Jansen, L. (ed.). 2014. *The Roman Paratext: Frame, Texts, Readers*. Cambridge
Jocelyn, H.D. 1965. 'Ancient scholarship and Virgil's use of Republican Latin poetry. II (continued)', *CQ* 15: 126–44
Johnson, W.A. and Parker, H.N. (eds.). 2009. *Ancient Literacies: The Culture of Reading in Greece and Rome*. Oxford
Johnson, W.R. 1976. *Darkness Visible. A Study of Vergil's Aeneid*. Berkeley and Los Angeles, CA
Jones, J. 1962. *On Aristotle and Greek Tragedy*. London
Jörgensen, O. 1904. 'Das Auftreten der Götter in den Büchern ι—μ der Odyssee', *Hermes* 39: 357–82
Kapust, D.J. 2011. *Republicanism, Rhetoric, and Roman Political Thought: Sallust, Livy, and Tacitus*. Cambridge
Kates, J.A. 1974. 'The revaluation of the Classical heroic in Tasso and Milton', *CL* 26: 299–317
Keith, A.M. 2000. *Engendering Rome: Women in Latin Epic*. Cambridge
Kelly, A. and Spelman, H. eds. forthcoming. *Texts and Intertexts in Archaic and Classical Greece*. Cambridge
Kennedy, D.F. 1993. *The Arts of Love: Five Studies in the Discourse of Roman Love Elegy*. Cambridge
Kennedy, G.A. 1963. *The Art of Persuasion in Greece*. Princeton, NJ
   1972. *The Art of Rhetoric in the Roman World*. Princeton, NJ
Kenney, E.J. 1958. '*Nequitiae poeta*', in N.I. Herescu (ed.), *Ovidiana: Recherches sur Ovide*. Paris. 201–9
   1971. *Lucretius: De Rerum Natura. Book III*. Cambridge
   1982. 'Ovid', in *CHCL* 2: 420–57
Ker, W.P. (ed.). 1900. *Essays of John Dryden*, 2 vols. Oxford
Kermode, F. 1983. *Essays on Fiction: 1971–82*. London
Kiessling, A. and Heinze, R. 1908–21. *Horaz$^5$*, 3 vols. Berlin
Kirk, G.S. 1985. *The Iliad: A Commentary. Volume I: Books 1–4*. Cambridge
Kirk, G.S., Raven, J.E. and Schofield, M. 1983. *The Presocratic Philosophers$^2$*. Cambridge

Klingner, F. 1967. *Virgil. Bucolica, Georgica, Aeneis (Interpretation der Werke Virgils)*. Zürich

Knauer, G.N. 1964. *Die Aeneis und Homer: Studien zur poetischen Technik Vergils, mit Listen der Homerzitate in der Aeneis*. Göttingen

Köhnken, A. 1974. 'Pindar as innovator: Poseidon Hippios and the relevance of the Pelops story in *Olympian 1*', *CQ* 24: 199–206

König, J., Oikonomopoulou, K. and Woolf, G. (eds.). 2013. *Ancient Libraries*. Cambridge

Konstan, D. 2009. 'Cosmopolitan traditions', in R.K. Balot (ed.), *A Companion to Greek and Roman Political Thought*. Oxford and Malden, MA. 471–84

Koortbojian, M. 2002. 'A painted *exemplum* at Rome's Temple of Liberty', *JRS* 92: 33–48

Koster, S. 1970. *Antike Epostheorien*. Wiesbaden

1979. 'Liebe und Krieg in der "Achilleis" des Statius', *WJA NF* 5: 189–208

Kramer, L.S. 1989. 'Literature, criticism, and historical imagination: the literary challenge of Hayden White and Dominick LaCapra', in L. Hunt (ed.), *The New Cultural History*. Berkeley and Los Angeles, CA. 97–128

Kraus, C.S. 1991. '*Initium turbandi omnia a femina ortum est*: Fabia Minor and the election of 367 B.C.', *Phoenix* 45: 314–25

1994a. *Livy Ab Urbe Condita Book VI*. Cambridge

1994b. '"No second Troy": topoi and refoundation in Livy, Book V', *TAPhA* 124: 267–89

1997. 'Livy', in C.S. Kraus and A.J. Woodman, *Latin Historians*. Oxford. 51–81

2019. '*Fabula* and history in Livy's narrative of the capture of Veii', in J. Baines, H. van der Blom, Y.S. Chen and T. Rood (eds.), *Historical Consciousness and the Use of the Past in the Ancient World*. Sheffield and Bristol. 345–58

forthcominga: 'Urban disasters and other Romes: the case of Veii', in V. Closs and E. Keitel (eds.), *Urban Disasters in the Roman Imagination*

forthcomingb: 'Livy's Faliscan schoolmaster', in A.D. Poulsen and A. Jönssen (eds.), *Usages of the Past in Roman Historiography*. Lund

Kraus, C.S. (ed.). 1999. *The Limits of Historiography: Genre and Narrative in Ancient Texts*. Leiden

Kremer, D. 2006. *Ius Latinum. Le Concept de droit latin sous la république et l'empire*. Paris

Krevans, N. 1993. 'Ilia's dream: Ennius, Virgil, and the mythology of seduction', *HSPh* 95: 257–71

Krischer, T. 1971. *Formale Konventionen der homerischen Epik*. Munich

Kühn, W. 1971. *Götterszenen bei Vergil*. Heidelberg

Kuttner, A.L. 1995. *Dynasty and Empire in the Age of Augustus: The Case of the Boscoreale Cups*. Berkeley and Los Angeles, CA

Labate, M. 2013. 'Constructing the Roman myth: the history of the Republic in Horace's lyric poetry', in J. Farrell and D.P. Nelis (eds.), *Augustan Poetry and the Roman Republic*. Oxford. 205–27

Lamacchia, R. 1964. 'Ciceros Somnium Scipionis und das sechste Buch der Aeneis', *RhM* 107: 261–78

Lamarque, P. and Olsen, S.H. 1994. *Truth, Fiction, and Literature: A Philosophical Perspective*. Oxford
Lane Fox, R. 1986. *Pagans and Christians*. London
Langdon, M.K. 2015. 'Herders' graffiti', in A.P. Matthaiou and N. Papazarkadas (eds.), *AXON: Studies in Honor of Ronald S. Stroud*. Athens. 49–58
Latacz, J. 1975. 'Zur Forschungsarbeit an den direkten Reden bei Homer (1850–1970): Ein kritischer Literatur-Überblick', *GB* 3: 395–422
Lateiner, D. 1989. *The Historical Method of Herodotus*. Toronto
Latte, K. 1960. *Römische Religionsgeschichte*. Munich
Lattimore, R. 1961. *The Iliad of Homer*. Chicago, IL
Lausberg, M. 1983. 'Iliadisches im 1. Buch der Aeneis', *Gymnasium* 90: 203–39
Lavan, M. 2013. *Slaves to Rome: Paradigms of Empire in Roman Culture*. Cambridge
Lavan, M., Payne, R.E. and Weisweiler, J. (eds.). 2016. *Cosmopolitanism and Empire: Universal Rule, Local Elites, and Cultural Integration in the Ancient Near East and Mediterranean*. Oxford
Lawall, G. 1966. 'Apollonius' *Argonautica*: Jason as anti-hero', *YClS* 19: 116–69
Lee, A.G. 1968. *P. Ovidi Nasonis Metamorphoseon Liber I*. Cambridge
Lee, D.J.N. 1964. *The Similes of the Iliad and the Odyssey Compared*. Parkville, Melbourne
Lefèvre, E. 1974. 'Aeneas' Antwort an Dido', *WS NF* 8: 99–115
  1976. 'Die Lehre von der Entstehung der Tieropfer in Ovids Fasten 1, 335–456', *RhM* 119: 39–64
Legras, L. 1905. *Les Légendes thébaines en Grèce et à Rome. Étude sur la Thébaïde de Stace*. Paris
Leinieks, V. 1986. 'The similes of *Iliad* Two', *C&M* 37: 5–20
Lesky, A. 1968. 'Homeros', *RE Suppl.* 11: 687–846
Levene, D.S. 1993. *Religion in Livy*. Leiden
  2010. *Livy on the Hannibalic War*. Oxford
  2019. 'Monumental insignificance: the rhetoric of Roman topography from Livy's Rome', in M.P. Loar, S.C. Murray and S. Rebeggiani (eds.), *The Cultural History of Augustan Rome: Texts, Monuments, and Topography*. Cambridge. 10–26
Levin, D.N. 1971. 'Apollonius' Heracles', *CJ* 67: 22–8
Levin, H. 1977. 'The title as a literary genre', *MLR* 72: xxiii–xxxvi
Lewis, C.S. 1961. *A Preface to Paradise Lost*. Oxford
Lieberg, G. 1966. 'La dea Giunone nell' Eneide di Virgilio', *A&R* 11: 145–65
  1971. 'Vergils Aeneis als Dichtung der Einsamkeit', in Bardon and Verdière (1971). 175–91
Liebeschuetz, J.H.W.G. 1979. *Continuity and Change in Roman Religion*. Oxford
Liebing, H. 1953. *Die Aeneasgestalt bei Vergil*. Diss. Kiel
Linderski, J. 1982. 'Cicero and Roman divination', *PP* 37: 12–38
Lintott, A.W. 1971. 'Lucan and the history of the civil war', *CQ* 21: 488–505
Lipscomb, H.C. 1909. 'Aspects of the speech in Vergil and the later Roman epic', *CW* 2: 114–17
Litchfield, H.W. 1914. 'National *exempla virtutis* in Roman literature', *HSPh* 25: 1–71

Livrea, E. 1973. *Apollonii Rhodii Argonauticon Liber Quartus*. Florence
Lloyd, G.E.R. 1979. *Magic, Reason and Experience: Studies in the Origins and Development of Greek Science*. Cambridge
  1987. *The Revolutions of Wisdom: Studies in the Claims and Practice of Ancient Greek Science*. Berkeley and Los Angeles, CA
  1990. *Demystifying Mentalities*. Cambridge
Lloyd-Jones, H. and Parsons, P. 1983. *Supplementum Hellenisticum*. Berlin and New York
Loraux, N. 1986. *The Invention of Athens: The Funeral Oration in the Classical City*, tr. A. Sheridan. Cambridge, MA
Lowrie, M. 2005. 'Virgil and founding violence', *Cardozo Law Review* 27.2: 945–76
  2009. *Writing, Performance, and Authority in Augustan Rome*. Oxford
  2010. 'Rom immer wieder gegründet', in R. Döring, B. Vinken and G. Zöller (eds.), *Übertragene Anfänge: Imperiale Figurationen um 1800*. Munich. 23–49
  2013. 'Foundation and closure', in F.F. Grewing, B. Acosta-Hughes and A. Kirichenko (eds.), *The Door Ajar: False Closure in Greek and Roman Literature and Art*. Heidelberg. 83–102
Lucas, D.W. 1968. *Aristotle: Poetics*. Oxford
Luce, J.V. 1965/2009. 'The dating of Livy's first Decade', *TAPhA* 96: 209–40 = Chaplin and Kraus (2009). 17–48
  1977. *Livy: The Composition of his History*, Princeton, NJ
Ludwig, W. 1965. *Struktur und Einheit der Metamorphosen Ovids*. Berlin
Lyne, R. 1999. 'Drayton's chorological Ovid', in Hardie, Barchiesi and Hinds (1999). 85–102
Lyne, R.O.A.M. 1983. 'Vergil and the politics of war', *CQ* 33: 188–203
  1987. *Further Voices in Vergil's Aeneid*. Oxford
  1989. *Words and the Poet: Characteristic Techniques of Style in Vergil's Aeneid*. Oxford
McInerney, J. (ed.) 2014. *A Companion to Ethnicity in the Ancient Mediterranean*. Malden, MA
McKay, G.A. 1963. 'Hero and theme in the *Aeneid*', *TAPhA* 94: 157–66
Mackie, C.J. 1990. '*Quisquis in arma vocas*: Turnus and Jupiter in the *Aeneid*', *Antichthon* 24: 79–85
Mackinnon, L. 1982. Review of Shawcross (1982), *TLS* (3 December 1982), 1332
Macleod, C.W. 1982. *Homer. Iliad: Book XXIV*. Cambridge
MacMullen, R. 1966. *Enemies of the Roman Order: Treason, Unrest, and Alienation in the Empire*. Cambridge, MA
Malcovati, H. 1928. *Caesaris Augusti Imperatoris Operum Fragmenta*. Turin
Malloch, S.J.V. 2013. *The Annals of Tacitus: Book 11*. Cambridge
Malmendier, U. 2005. 'Roman shares', in W.N. Goetzmann and K.G. Rouwenhorst (eds.), *The Origins of Value: The Financial Innovations that Created Modern Capital Markets*. Oxford. 31–42
Maltby, R. 1991. *A Lexicon of Ancient Latin Etymologies*. Leeds
Marincola, J. 1997a. *Authority and Tradition in Ancient Historiography*. Cambridge

1997b. 'Odysseus and the historians', *Histos* 1 (www.dur.ac.uk/Classics/histos/1997/marincola.html)
1999. 'Genre, convention, and innovation in Greco-Roman historiography', in Kraus (1999). 281–324
2010. 'Eros and Empire: Virgil and the historians on civil war', in C.S. Kraus, J. Marincola and C. Pelling (eds.), *Ancient Historiography and its Contexts*. Oxford. 183–204

Marti, B. 1945. 'The meaning of the *Pharsalia*', *AJPh* 66: 352–76
Martin, J. 1974. *Antike Rhetorik: Technik und Methode*. Munich
Martindale, C. 1984. 'The politician Lucan', *G&R* 31: 64–79
1986. *John Milton and the Transformations of Ancient Epic*. London
Masters, J. 1992. *Poetry and Civil War in Lucan's Bellum Civile*. Cambridge
Mayer, R. 1981. *Lucan: Civil War VIII*. Liverpool
Mazzarino, S. 1966. *Il pensiero storico classico*, 3 vols. Bari
Michels, A.K. 1981. 'The *insomnium* of Aeneas', *CQ* 31: 140–6
Mikalson, J.D. 1983. *Athenian Popular Religion*. Chapel Hill, NC and London
1991. *Honor Thy Gods: Popular Religion in Greek Tragedy*. Chapel Hill, NC and London
2003. *Herodotus and Religion in the Persian Wars*. Chapel Hill, NC and London
Miles, G.B. 1995. *Livy: Reconstructing Early Rome*. Ithaca, NY
Miller, J.F. 1991. *Ovid's Elegiac Festivals: Studies in the Fasti*. Frankfurt am Main
1993. 'Ovidian allusion and the vocabulary of memory', *MD* 30: 153–64
Mineo, B. 2003. 'Récit d'une crise: la fin du premier cycle historique de Rome, au livre V de l'*Ab Urbe Condita* de Tite-Live', in S. Franchet d'Espèrey et al. (eds.), *Fondements et crises du pouvoir*. Bordeaux. 337–51
Mineo, B. (ed.) 2015. *A Companion to Livy*. Chichester
Minturno, A. 1564. *L'Arte Poetica*. Venice
Moatti, C. 2015. *The Birth of Critical Thinking in Republican Rome*, tr. J. Lloyd. Cambridge
Moles, J.L. 1987. '*The tragedy and guilt of Dido*', in Whitby, Hardie and Whitby (1987). 153–61
1993. 'Truth and untruth in Herodotus and Thucydides', in Gill and Wiseman (2003). 88–121
1993/2009. 'Livy's Preface', *PCPhS* 39: 141–68 = Chaplin and Kraus (2009). 49–87
Momigliano, A. 1987. *On Pagans, Jews, and Christians*. Hanover, NH
1975. *Alien Wisdom: The Limits of Hellenization*. Cambridge
Monti, R.C. 1981. *The Dido Episode and the Aeneid: Roman Social and Political Values in the Epic*. Leiden
Morford, M.P.O. 1967. *The Poet Lucan: Studies in Rhetorical Epic*. Oxford
Morgan, L. 1998. 'Assimilation and civil war: Hercules and Cacus', in H.-P. Stahl (ed.), *Vergil's Aeneid: Augustan Epic and Political Context*. London. 175–97.
1999. *Patterns of Redemption in Virgil's 'Georgics'*. Cambridge
Morwood, J.H.W. 1985. 'Aeneas and Mount Atlas', *JRS* 75: 51–9

1998. 'Virgil's pious man and Menenius Agrippa: a note on *Aeneid* 1.148–53', *G&R* 45: 195–8
Moseley, N. 1926. *Characters and Epithets. A Study in Vergil's Aeneid*. New Haven, CT
Most, G. 2000. 'Generating genres: the idea of the tragic', in Depew and Obbink (2000). 15–35
Moulton, C. 1977. *Similes in the Homeric Poems*. Göttingen
Mouritsen, H. 1998. *Italian Unification: A Study in Ancient and Modern Historiography*. London
  2007. 'The *civitas sine suffragio*: ancient concepts and modern ideology', *Historia* 56: 141–58
Mueller, L. 1884. *Q. Enni Carminum Reliquiae*. St. Petersburg
Mueller, M. 1969. '*Paradise Lost* and the *Iliad*', *CLS* 6: 292–316
Munson, R.V. 2001. *Telling Wonders: Ethnographic and Political Discourse in the Work of Herodotus*. Ann Arbor, MI
Münzer, F. 1921. 'Ti. Sempronius Gracchus', *RE* 2R 4: 1403–9
  1930. 'L. Marcius Philippus', *RE* 28: 1562–8
  1937. 'Die römischen Vestalinnen bis zur Kaiserzeit', *Philologus* 92: 47–67, 199–222
Murray, O. 1965. 'Philodemus on the Good King according to Homer', *JRS* 55: 161–82
Myers, K.S. 1994. *Ovid's Causes: Cosmogony and Aetiology in the Metamorphoses*. Ann Arbor, MI
Mynors, R.A.B. 1990. *Virgil: Georgics*. Oxford
Nagy, G. 1979. *The Best of the Achaeans: Concepts of the Hero in Archaic Greek Poetry*. Baltimore, MD
Narducci, E. 1979. *La provvidenza crudele: Lucano e la distruzione dei miti augustei*. Pisa
Nelis, D. 2001. *Vergil's Aeneid and the Argonautica of Apollonius Rhodius*. Leeds
Newlands, C. 1995. *Playing with Time: Ovid and the Fasti*. Ithaca, NY
Newman, J.K. 1967. *Augustus and the New Poetry*. Brussels
Nicolet, C. 1980. *The World of the Citizen in Republican Rome*, tr. P.S. Falla. London
Nicoll, W.S.M. 1980. 'Cupid, Apollo and Daphne (Ovid, *Met.* 1.452 ff.)', *CQ* 30: 174–82
Nilsson, M.P. 1955. *Geschichte der griechischen Religion*, 2 vols. Munich
Nisbet, R.G.M. 1995. *Collected Papers on Latin Literature*, ed. S.J. Harrison. Oxford
Nisbet, R.G.M. and Hubbard, M. 1970. *A Commentary on Horace: Odes, Book 1*. Oxford
  1978. *A Commentary on Horace: Odes, Book 2*. Oxford
Nisbet, R.G.M. and Rudd, N. 2004. *A Commentary on Horace: Odes, Book 3*. Oxford
Nissen, H. 1883–1902. *Italische Landeskunde*, 2 vols. Berlin
Nissen, T. 1940. 'Historisches Epos und Panegyrikos in der Spätantike', *Hermes* 75: 298–325

Norden, E. 1915. *Ennius und Vergilius. Kriegsbilder aus Roms grosser Zeit*. Leipzig
  1934. *P. Vergilius Maro: Aeneis Buch VI*³. Leipzig
North, D.C. 2005. *Understanding the Process of Economic Change*. Princeton, NJ
Nowotny, H. 1994. *Time: The Modern and Postmodern Experience*, tr. N. Plaice. Cambridge
Nuttall, A.D. 1996. *Why Does Tragedy Give Pleasure?* Oxford
Oakley, S.P. 1997–2005. *A Commentary on Livy, Books VI–X*, 4 vols. Oxford
  1998. Review of Miles (1995), *CPh* 93: 279–86
  2015. 'Reading Livy's Book 5', in B. Mineo (2015). 230–42
Obbink, D. 1993. 'Dionysus poured out: ancient and modern theories of sacrifice and cultural formation', in T.H. Carpenter and C.A. Faraone (eds.), *Masks of Dionysus*. Ithaca, NY. 65–86
Ober, J. 2001. 'Not by a nose: the triumph of Antony and Cleopatra at Actium, 31 B.C.', in R. Cowley (ed.), *What If? 2: Eminent Historians Imagine What Might Have Been*. New York. 23–47
Ogilvie, R.M. 1965. *A Commentary on Livy Books 1–5*. Oxford
O'Hara, J.J. 1996. *True Names: Vergil and the Alexandrian Tradition of Etymological Wordplay*. Ann Arbor, MI
Oksala, T. 1973. *Religion und Mythologie bei Horaz*. Helsinki
Orr, H.A. 2005. 'Vive la Différence!', *NYRB* (12 May 2005), 18–20
Otis, B. 1963. *Virgil: A Study in Civilized Poetry*. Oxford
Padilla Peralta, D. 2019. 'Citizenship's insular cases, from ancient Greece and Rome to Puerto Rico', *Humanities* 8: 134
Page, D.L. 1941. *Select Papyri. III: Poetry*. Cambridge, MA
Page, T.E. 1893. 'Translations of the *Aeneid* by Rhoades and Sergeaunt', *CR* 7: 415–18
  1896. *Q. Horati Flacci Opera: Odes*. London
Paoletti, L. 1963. 'Lucano magico e Virgilio', *A&R* 8: 11–26
Parker, R. 1997. 'Gods cruel and kind: tragic and civic ideology', in C. Pelling (ed.), *Greek Tragedy and the Historian*. Oxford. 143–60
Pasquali, G. 1964. *Orazio Lirico. Studi*². Florence
Pausch, D. 2011. *Livius und der Leser: Narrative Strukturen in ab urbe condita*. Munich
Pavlock, B. 1990. *Eros, Imitation, and the Epic Tradition*. Ithaca, NY
Payne, M. 2018. 'Fidelity and farewell: Pindar's ethics as textual events', in Budelmann and Phillips (2018). 257–74
Pearson, L. 1975. 'Myth and *archaeologia* in Italy and Sicily—Timaeus and his predecessors', *YClS* 24: 171–95
Pease, A.S. 1920–3. *M. Tulli Ciceronis De Divinatione*, 2 vols. Urbana, IL
  1935. *P. Vergilii Maronis Aeneidos Liber Quartus*. Cambridge, MA
  1955–8. *Cicero: De Natura Deorum*, 2 vols. Cambridge, MA
Pellam, G. 2014. 'A peculiar episode from the "struggle of the orders"? Livy and the Licinio-Sextian Rogations', *CQ* 64: 280–92
Pelling, C.B.R. 1988. *Plutarch: Life of Antony*. Cambridge
  1999. 'Epilogue', in Kraus (1999). 325–60

2002. *Plutarch and History: Eighteen Studies*. London
Perkell, C. 1989. *The Poet's Truth: A Study of the Poet in Virgil's Georgics*. Berkeley and Los Angeles, CA
Perkins, D. 1992. *Is Literary History Possible?* Baltimore, MD and London
Perowne, S. 1968. *Roman Mythology*. London
Perret, J. 1977. *Virgile: Énéide I–IV*. Paris
Peter, H. 1902. 'Die Epochen in Varros Werk *De gente populi Romani*', *RhM* 57: 231–51
Pfeiffer, R. 1968. *History of Classical Scholarship: From the Beginnings to the End of the Hellenistic Age*. Oxford
Picard, G.-Ch. 1954. *Les Religions de l'Afrique antique*. Paris
Pietrusinski, D. 1978. 'L'Apothéose d'Auguste par la comparaison avec les héros grecques chez Horace et Virgile', *Eos* 66: 249–66
Pigna, G.B. 1554. *I Romanzi*. Venice
Podlecki, A.J. 1971. 'Some Odyssean similes', *G&R* 18: 81–90
Polleichtner, W. 2005. 'The bee simile: how Vergil emulated Apollonius in his use of Homeric poetry', *GFA* 8: 115–60
Pope, Alexander. 1967. *The Odyssey of Homer: Books I–XII*, ed. M. Mack. London. Originally published 1772
Porte, D. 1985. *L'Étiologie religieuse dans les Fastes d'Ovide*. Paris
Porter, J. 2004. 'Homer: the history of an idea', in R. Fowler (ed.), *The Cambridge Companion to Homer*. Cambridge. 318–37
Pöschl, V. 1962. *The Art of Vergil. Image and Symbol in the Aeneid*, tr. G. Seligson. Ann Arbor, MI
Powell, B.B. 2002. *Writing and the Origins of Greek Literature*. Cambridge
Prag, J.R.W. and Quinn, J.C. (eds.). 2013. *The Hellenistic West: Rethinking the Ancient Mediterranean*. Cambridge
Preisendanz, K. 1932. 'Tanit', *RE* 2R 8: 2178–215
Putnam, M.C.J. 1965. *The Poetry of the Aeneid: Four Studies in Imaginative Unity and Design*. Cambridge, MA
 1979. *Virgil's Poem of the Earth: Studies in the Georgics*. Princeton, NJ
 1985. 'Possessiveness, sexuality, and heroism in the *Aeneid*', *Vergilius* 31: 1–21
 2000. Review of Morgan (1999), *Vergilius* 46: 155–62
Quinn, K. 1963. *Latin Explorations: Critical Studies in Roman Literature*. London
 1968. *Virgil's Aeneid: A Critical Description*. London
Quint, D. 1993. *Epic and Empire: Politics and Generic Form from Virgil to Milton*. Princeton, NJ
 2011. 'Virgil's double cross: chiasmus and the *Aeneid*', *AJPh* 132: 273–300
Rahner, H. 1963. *Greek Myths and Christian Mystery*, tr. B. Battershaw. London
Rawles, R. 2018. *Simonides the Poet: Intertexuality and Reception*. Cambridge
Rawson, E. 1985. *Intellectual Life in the Late Roman Republic*. London
 1991. *Roman Culture and Society: Collected Papers*. Oxford
Ready, J.L. 2011. *Character, Narrator, and Simile in the Iliad*. Cambridge
Redfield, J. 1975. *Nature and Culture in the Iliad: The Tragedy of Hector*. Chicago, IL

1979. 'The proem of the *Iliad*: Homer's art', *CPh* 74: 95–110
Reed, J.D. 2007. *Virgil's Gaze: Nation and Poetry in the Aeneid*. Princeton, NJ
Reeve, M.D. 1995. 'Conclusion', in O. Pecere and M.D. Reeve (eds.), *Formative Stages of Classical Traditions: Latin Texts from Antiquity to the Renaissance*. Spoleto. 497–511
Richards, I.A. 1936. *The Philosophy of Rhetoric*. Oxford
Richardson, J.S. 1995. 'The Roman mind and the power of fiction', in L. Ayres (ed.), *The Passionate Intellect: Essays on the Transformations of Classical Traditions Presented to Professor I. G. Kidd*. New Brunswick, NJ. 117–30
Richardson, N.J. 1983. 'Recognition scenes in the *Odyssey*', *PLLS* 4: 219–35
  1993. *The Iliad: A Commentary. Volume VI: Books 21–24*. Cambridge
Rogerson, A. 2017. *Virgil's Ascanius: Imagining the Future in the Aeneid*. Cambridge
Roman, L. 2001. 'The representation of literary materiality in Martial's *Epigrams*', *JRS* 91: 113–45
  2006. 'A history of lost tablets', *ClAnt* 25: 351–88
Rosati, G. 1994. *Stazio: Achilleide*. Milan
Rosenberg, A. 1914a. 'Romulus', *RE* 2R 1: 1074–104
  1914b. 'Rea Silvia', *RE* 2R 1: 341–5
Ross, D.O., Jr. 1987. *Virgil's Elements: Physics and Poetry in the Georgics*. Princeton, NJ
Roy, J. 2014. 'Autochthony in ancient Greece', in McInerney (2014). 241–55
Runciman, D. 2003. 'The concept of the state. The sovereignty of a fiction', in Q. Skinner and B. Stråth (eds.), *States and Citizens: History, Theory, Prospects*. Cambridge. 28–38
Runciman, S. 1951. *A History of the Crusades. Volume I: The First Crusade and the Foundation of the Kingdom of Jerusalem*. Cambridge
Rüpke, J. 1995. *Kalender und Öffentlichkeit: Die Geschichte der Repräsentation und religiösen Qualifikation von Zeit in Rom*. Berlin
  2001. 'Antike Religionen als Kommunikationssysteme', in K. Brodersen (ed.), *Gebet und Fluch, Zeichen und Traum: Aspekte religiöser Kommunikation in der Antike*. Münster. 13–30
  2008. 'Religion: Rome', *Brill's New Pauly* 12: 489–96
  2011. 'History', in M. Stausberg and S. Engler (eds.), *The Routledge Handbook of Research Methods in the Study of Religion*. London and New York. 285–309
Russell, D.A. 1981. *Criticism in Antiquity*. London
Rütten, F. 1912. *De Vergilii Studiis Apollonianis*. Diss. Münster
Rutz, W. 1984. 'Lucan 1964–1983', *Lustrum* 26: 105–203
Ryberg, I.S. 1955. *Rites of the State Religion in Roman Art*. Rome
Said, E.W. 1978. *Orientalism*. New York
Sailor, D. 2006. 'Dirty linen, fabrication, and the authorities of Livy and Augustus', *TAPhA* 136: 329–88
Salmon, E.T. 1982. *The Making of Roman Italy*. London
Salter, C.H. 1974. 'Dryden and Addison', *MLR* 69: 29–39
Scheid, J. 1990. *Romulus et ses frères: le collège des frères arvales, modèle du culte public dans la Rome des empereurs*. Rome

Scheidel, W. 2004. 'Human mobility in Roman Italy, I: the free population', *JRS* 94: 1–26
    2009. 'When did Livy write Books 1, 3, 28 and 59?', *CQ* 59: 653–8
Schetter, W. 1978. *Das römische Epos*. Wiesbaden
Schiesaro, A. 1990. *Simulacrum et imago. Gli argomenti analogici nel De Rerum Natura*. Pisa
Schindler, C. 2000. *Untersuchungen zu den Gleichnissen im römischen Lehrgedicht: Lukrez, Vergil, Manilius*. Göttingen
Schmidt, P.L. 1973. 'Cicero *De Re Publica*: Die Forschungen der letzten fünf Dezennien', *ANRW* 1.4: 262–333
Schmit-Neuerburg, T. 1999. *Vergils Aeneis und die antike Homerexegese: Untersuchungen zum Einfluß ethischer und kritischer Homerrezeption auf imitatio und aemulatio Vergils*. Berlin
Scholes, R. and Kellogg, R. 1966. *The Nature of Narrative*. New York and Oxford
Schrijvers, P.H. 1978. 'Le regard sur l'invisible: étude sur l'emploi de l'analogie dans l'oeuvre de Lucrèce', in O. Gigon (ed.), *Lucrèce*, Entretiens Fondation Hardt 24. Geneva. 77–114
Schröder, W.A. 1971. *M. Porcius Cato: Das erste Buch der Origines. Ausgabe und Erklärung der Fragmente*. Meisenheim am Glan
Schultze, C.E. 1995. 'Dionysius of Halicarnassus and Roman chronology', *PCPhS* 41: 192–214
Scott, W.C. 2009. *The Artistry of the Homeric Simile*. Hanover, NH
Sedley, D. 1989. 'The proems of Lucretius and Empedocles', *GRBS* 30: 269–96
Seeley, T.D. 2010. *Honeybee Democracy*. Princeton, NJ
Serres, M. 1991. *Rome: The Book of Foundations*, tr. F. McCarren. Stanford, CA
Shackleton Bailey, D.R. 1965–8. *Cicero: Epistulae ad Atticum*, 7 vols. Cambridge
    1977. *Cicero: Epistulae ad Familiares*. Cambridge
Sharrock, A. 1991. 'Womanufacture', *JRS* 81: 36–49
Shawcross, J.T. 1982. *With Mortal Voice: The Creation of 'Paradise Lost'*. Lexington, KY
Shay, J. 1994. *Achilles in Vietnam: Combat Trauma and the Undoing of Character*. New York
Sherwin-White, A.N. 1973. *The Roman Citizenship*². Oxford
Silk, M.S. 1985. 'Heracles and Greek tragedy', *G&R* 32: 1–22
Simpson, V. 1975. 'The annalistic tradition in Vergil's *Aeneid*', *Vergilius* 21: 22–32
Sirluck, E. 1967. *Paradise Lost: A Deliberate Epic*. Cambridge
Skard, O. 1965. 'Die Heldenschau in Vergils Aeneis', *SO* 40: 53–65
Skutsch, O. 1968. *Enniana*. London
    1972. 'Readings and interpretations in the *Annals*', in O. Skutsch (ed.), *Ennius*, Entretiens Fondation Hardt 17. Geneva. 3–37
    1985. *The Annals of Quintus Ennius*. Oxford
Smith, C.J. 2011. 'Citizenship and community: inventing the Roman Republic', in N. Terrenato and D.C. Haggis (eds.), *State Formation in Italy and Greece: Questioning the Neoevolutionist Paradigm*. Oxford and Oakville, CT. 217–30

Smith, J.Z. 1987. 'The domestication of sacrifice', in R.G. Hamerton-Kelly (ed.), *Violent Origins: Walter Burkert, René Girard, and Jonathan Z. Smith on Ritual Killing and Cultural Formation*. Stanford, CA. 191–205
Smith, R.A. 1997. *Poetic Allusion and Poetic Embrace in Ovid and Virgil*. Ann Arbor, MI
Snyder, J.M. 1980. *Puns and Poetry in Lucretius' De Rerum Natura*. Amsterdam
Solmsen, F. 1972. 'The world of the dead in Book 6 of the *Aeneid*', *CPh* 67: 31–41
Sparrow, J. 1973. *Dido v Aeneas, the Case for the Defence: The Sixth Jackson Knight Memorial Lecture*. Abingdon
Speaight, R. 1958. *The Vergilian Res*. London
Spelman, H. 2018. *Pindar and the Poetics of Permanence*. Oxford
  2019. 'Schools, reading and poetry in the early Greek world', *CCJ* 65: 150–72
Spence, S. 1988. *Rhetorics of Reason and Desire: Vergil, Augustine, and the Troubadors*. Ithaca, NY
  2002. '*Pietas* and *Furor*: motivational forces in the *Aeneid*', in W.S. Anderson and L.N. Quartarone (eds.), *Approaches to Teaching Vergil's Aeneid*. New York. 46–52
Spingarn, J.E. 1938. *A History of Literary Criticism in the Renaissance*². New York
  (ed.). 1908. *Critical Essays of the Seventeenth Century*, 3 vols. New York
Stadter, P.A. 1972/2009. 'The structure of Livy's History', *Historia* 21: 287–307 = Chaplin and Kraus (2009). 91–117
Stanford, W.B. 1963. *The Ulysses Theme: A Study in the Adaptability of a Traditional Hero*. Oxford
Steadman, J.M. 1959. *Milton's Epic Characters: Image and Idol*. Chapel Hill, NC
  1967. *Milton and the Renaissance Hero*. Oxford.
  1975. 'The arming of an archetype: heroic virtue and the conventions of literary epic', in Burns and Reagan (1975). 147–96
  1976. *Epic and Tragic Structure in Paradise Lost*. Chicago, IL
Stehle, E. 1989. 'Venus, Cybele, and the Sabine women: the Roman construction of female sexuality', *Helios* 16: 143–64
Stem, R. 2007. 'The exemplary lessons of Livy's Romulus', *TAPhA* 137: 435–71
Stephens, S. 2004. 'Whose rituals in ink?', in A. Barchiesi, J. Rüpke and S. Stephens (eds.), *Rituals in Ink: A Conference on Religion and Literary Production in Ancient Rome*. Munich. 157–60
Steuart, E.M. 1925. *The Annals of Quintus Ennius*. Cambridge
Stevenson, T.R. 2000. '*Parens Patriae* and Livy's Camillus', *Ramus* 29: 27–46
Stewart, D.J. 1972–3. 'Mortality, morality and the public life. Aeneas the politician', *Antioch Review* 32: 649–64
Stewart, O. 2017. 'Citizenship as a reward or punishment? Factoring language into the Latin settlement', *Antichthon* 51: 186–201
Stockton, D. 1979. *The Gracchi*. Oxford
Stübler, G. 1941. *Die Religiosität des Livius*. Stuttgart
Suerbaum, W. 1967. 'Aeneas zwischen Troja und Rom. Zur Funktion der Genealogie und der Ethnographie in Vergils Aeneis', *Poetica* 1: 176–204

Swedenberg, H.T. 1944. *The Theory of the Epic in England, 1650–1800*. Berkeley and Los Angeles, CA
Syed, Y. 2005. *Vergil's Aeneid and the Roman Self: Subject and Nation in Literary Discourse*. Ann Arbor, MI
Syme, R. 1939. *The Roman Revolution*. Oxford
  1958. *Tacitus*. Oxford
  1964. *Sallust*. Berkeley and Los Angeles, CA
  1978. *History in Ovid*. Oxford
Tarrant, R.J. 1982. 'Aeneas and the gates of sleep', *CPh* 77: 51–5
  2012. *Virgil: Aeneid Book XII*. Cambridge
Taussig, M. 1993. *Mimesis and Alterity: A Particular History of the Senses*. New York and London
Taylor, C. 2004. *Modern Social Imaginaries*. Durham, NC
Terrenato, N. 2019. *The Early Roman Expansion into Italy: Elite Negotiation and Family Agendas*. Cambridge
Thalmann, W.G. 1984. *Conventions of Form and Thought in Early Greek Epic Poetry*. Baltimore, MD
Thomas, R. 2000. *Herodotus in Context: Ethnography, Science and the Art of Persuasion*. Cambridge
Thomas, R.F. 1982. *Lands and Peoples in Roman Poetry: The Ethnographical Tradition*. Cambridge
  1988. *Virgil: Georgics*, 2 vols. Cambridge
  1991. 'The "Sacrifice" at the end of the *Georgics*, Aristaeus, and Vergilian closure', *CPh* 86: 211–18
Thomas, Y. 1996. *«Origine» et «Commune Patrie». Étude de droit public romain (89 av. J.C.–212 ap. J.C.)*. Rome
Thornton, A. 1976. *The Living Universe. Gods and Men in Virgil's Aeneid*. Leiden
Tillyard, E.M.W. 1938. 'Milton and the English epic tradition', in *Seventeenth Century Studies Presented to Sir Herbert Grierson*. Oxford. 211–36
  1954. *The English Epic and its Background*. London
Timpanaro, S. 1948. 'Per una nuova edizione critica di Ennio', *SIFC* 23: 5–58
Toll, K. 1997. 'Making Roman-ness and the *Aeneid*', *ClAnt* 16: 34–56
Tolstoy, Leo. 1954. *Anna Karenina*, tr. C. Garnett. Harmondsworth. Originally published 1878
Tombs, R. and Tombs, I. 2007. *That Sweet Enemy: The French and British from the Sun King to the Present*. New York
Toynbee, A.J. 1965. *Hannibal's Legacy: The Hannibalic War's Effect on Roman Life*, 2 vols. Oxford
Tracey, S.V. 1975. 'The Marcellus passage (*Aeneid* 6.860–886) and *Aeneid* 9–12', *CJ* 70: 37–42
Treggiari, S. 1991. *Roman Marriage: Iusti Coniuges from the Time of Cicero to the Time of Ulpian*. Oxford
Trimble, J.F. 2002. 'Greek myth, gender, and social structure in a Roman house: two paintings of Achilles at Pompeii', in E.K. Gazda (ed.), *The Ancient Art of*

Emulation: Studies in Artistic Originality and Tradition from the Present to Classical Antiquity. Ann Arbor, MI. 225–48
Trypanis, C.A. 1981. *Greek Poetry from Homer to Seferis*. London
Ungern-Sternberg, J. von 1998. 'Die Romulusnachfolge des Augustus', in W. Schuller (ed.), *Politische Theorie und Praxis im Altertum*. Darmstadt. 166–82
Vahlen, J. 1928. *Ennianae Poesis Reliquiae*². Leipzig
Valmaggi, L. 1947. *Q. Ennio. I frammenti degli Annali*. Turin
Vandiver, E. 1999. 'The founding mothers of Livy's Rome: the Sabine women and Lucretia', in F.B. Titchener and R.F. Moorton, Jr. (eds.), *The Eye Expanded: Life and the Arts in Greco-Roman Antiquity*. Berkeley and Los Angeles, CA. 206–32
Vasaly, A. 2015a. *Livy's Political Philosophy: Power and Personality in Early Rome*. Cambridge
  2015b. 'The composition of the *Ab Urbe Condita*: the case of the first pentad', in B. Mineo (2015). 217–29
Versnel, H.S. 1987. 'What did ancient man see when he saw a god? Some reflections on Greco-Roman epiphany', in D. Van der Plas (ed.), *Effigies Dei: Essays on the History of Religions*. Leiden. 42–55
  1994. *Inconsistencies in Greek and Roman Religion 2: Transition and Reversal in Myth and Ritual*. Leiden
Vessey, D. 1973. *Statius and the Thebaid*. Cambridge
Veyne, P. 1988. *Did the Greeks Believe in their Myths? An Essay on the Constitutive Imagination*, tr. P. Wissing. Chicago, IL
Vian, F. and Delage, E. 1976. *Apollonios de Rhodes: Argonautiques: tome I*. Paris
Vicaire, P. 1960. *Platon: critique littéraire*. Paris
Vretska, K. 1976. *Sallust: De Catilinae Coniuratione*. Heidelberg
Wagenvoort, H. 1956. *Studies in Roman Literature, Culture, and Religion*. Leiden
Walbank, F.W. 1957–79. *A Historical Commentary on Polybius*, 3 vols. Oxford
Walcot, P. 1977. 'Odysseus and the art of lying', *AncSoc* 8: 1–19
Wallace-Hadrill, A. 1987. 'Time for Augustus: Ovid, Augustus and the Fasti', in Whitby, Hardie and Whitby (1987). 221–30
  1989. 'Rome's cultural revolution', *JRS* 79: 157–64
Walter, A. forthcoming. '*Ever Since Then*': *Time in Ancient Aetiology*, chapter 3
Walter, U. 2004. *Memoria und Respublica: Zur Geschichtskultur im republikanischen Rom*. Frankfurt
Wardman, A.E. 1960. 'Myth in Greek historiography', *Historia* 9: 403–13
  1976. *Rome's Debt to Greece*. London
Wardy, R. 1988. 'Lucretius on what atoms are not', *CPh* 83: 112–28
Warmington, B.H. 1969. *Carthage*². London
Warmington, E.H. 1935. *Remains of Old Latin I: Lucilius and Ennius*. Cambridge, MA
Waszink, J.H. 1957. 'Zur ersten Satire des Lucilius', *WS* 70: 322–8
Watson, G. (ed.). 1962. *John Dryden: Of Dramatic Poesy, and Other Critical Essays*, 2 vols. London and New York

Weicker, G. 1916. 'Iris', *RE* 18: 2037–43.
Weinstock, S. 1971. *Divus Julius*. Oxford
Wender, D. 1978. *The Last Scenes of the Odyssey*. Leiden
West, D. 1970. 'Virgilian multiple-correspondence similes and their antecedents', *Philologus* 114: 262–75
West, G.S. 1979. 'Virgil's helpful sisters. Anna and Juturna in the *Aeneid*', *Vergilius* 25: 10–19
West, M.L. 1971. *Hesiod: Theogony*. Oxford
    1985. *The Hesiodic Catalogue of Women*. Oxford
Whitby, M., Hardie, P. and Whitby, M. (eds.). 1987. *Homo Viator: Classical Essays for John Bramble*. Bristol
White, H. 1978. *Tropics of Discourse: Essays in Cultural Criticism*. Baltimore, MD and London
Whitman, C. 1958. *Homer and the Heroic Tradition*. Cambridge, MA
Whitmarsh, T. 2016. *Battling the Gods: Atheism in the Ancient World*. London
Wigodsky, M. 1972. *Vergil and Early Latin Poetry*. Wiesbaden
Wilamowitz, U. von. 1932. *Der Glaube der Hellenen*, 2 vols. Berlin
Wilders, J. 1995. *The Arden Shakespeare: Antony and Cleopatra*. London
Wilkins, J.B. 1994. 'The Iguvine Tablets: problems in the interpretation of ritual text', in C. Malone and S. Stoddart (eds.), *Territory, Time and State: The Archaeological Development of the Gubbio Basin*. Cambridge. 152–72
Wilkinson, L.P. 1946. *Horace and his Lyric Poetry*. Cambridge
Williams, G.W. 1968. *Tradition and Originality in Roman Poetry*. Oxford
    1969. *The Third Book of Horace's 'Odes'*. Oxford
    1980. *Figures of Thought in Roman Poetry*. New Haven, CT
    1983. *Technique and Ideas in the Aeneid*. New Haven, CT
Williams, R.C. 1917. *The Theory of the Heroic Epic in Italian Criticism of the Sixteenth Century*. Diss. Johns Hopkins
Williams, R.D. 1971. 'Dido's Reply to Aeneas (Aen. 4. 362–387)', in Bardon and Verdière (1971). 422–8
    1972. 'The pageant of Roman heroes: Aeneid 6.756–853', in J.R.C. Martyn (ed.), *Cicero and Virgil: Studies in Honour of Harold Hunt*. Amsterdam. 207–17
Wilson, B. 2004. *The Hive: The Story of the Honeybee and Us*. London
Wilson, C.H. 1979. 'Jupiter and the fates in the *Aeneid*', *CQ* 29: 361–71
Winkler, A. 2018. *We the Corporations: How American Businesses Won their Civil Rights*. New York
Winkler, J.J. 1990. *The Constraints of Desire: The Anthropology of Sex and Gender in Ancient Greece*. New York and London
Winter, J.G. 1910. *The Myth of Hercules at Rome*. New York
Wiseman, T.P. 1974. 'Legendary genealogies in late-republican Rome', *G&R* 21: 153–64
    1979. *Clio's Cosmetics: Three Studies in Greco-Roman Literature*. Leicester
    1984. 'Cybele, Virgil and Augustus', in Woodman and West (1984). 117–28
    1995. *Remus: A Roman Myth*. Cambridge

2002. 'History, poetry and *Annales*', in D.S. Levene and D.P. Nelis (eds.), *Clio and the Poets: Augustan Poetry and the Traditions of Ancient Historiography*. Leiden. 331–62

2015. *The Roman Audience: Classical Literature as Social History*. Oxford

Wissowa, G. 1899. 'Agis', *RE* 1: 821

1900. 'Cornelius Nepos', *RE* 2R 7: 1408–17

1912. *Religion und Kultus der Römer*$^2$. Munich

Wistrand, E.K.H. 1981. *The Policy of Brutus the Tyrannicide*. Göteborg

Wlosok, A. 1967. *Die Göttin Venus in Vergils Aeneis*. Heidelberg

Wofford, S.L. 1992. *The Choice of Achilles: The Ideology of Figure in the Epic*. Stanford, CA

Wolfe, D.M. (ed.). 1953–82. *The Complete Prose Works of John Milton*, 8 vols. New Haven, CT

Woodman, A.J. 1973. 'A note on Sallust, *Catilina* 1.1', *CQ* 23: 310

1988. *Rhetoric in Classical Historiography: Four Studies*. London

2003. 'Poems to historians: Catullus 1 and Horace Odes 2.1', in Braund and Gill (2003). 191–216

Woodman, A.J. and West, D. (eds.). 1984. *Poetry and Politics in the Age of Augustus*. Cambridge

Woodruff, L.B. 1910. *Reminiscences of Ennius in Silius Italicus*. New York

Woolf, G. 2012. *Rome: An Empire's Story*. Oxford

Wyke, M. 2002. *The Roman Mistress: Ancient and Modern Representations*. Oxford

Yonge, L.D. (ed.). 1882. *Essays of John Dryden*. London

Yunis, H. (ed.). 2003. *Written Texts and the Rise of Literate Culture in Ancient Greece*. Cambridge

Zanker, P. 1988: *The Power of Images in the Age of Augustus*, tr. A. Shapiro. Ann Arbor, MI

Zeitlin, F. 1986. 'Theater of self and society in Athenian drama', in J.P. Euben (ed.), *Greek Tragedy and Political Theory*. Berkeley and Los Angeles, CA. 101–41

1996. *Playing the Other: Gender and Society in Classical Greek Culture*. Chicago, IL

Zetzel, J.E.G. 1983. 'Catullus, Ennius and the poetics of allusion', *ICS* 8: 251–66

1989. '*Romane memento*: justice and judgment in *Aeneid 6*', *TAPhA* 119: 263–84

1995. *Cicero: De Re Publica. Selections*. Cambridge

1997. 'Rome and its traditions', in C. Martindale (ed.), *The Cambridge Companion to Virgil*. Cambridge. 188–203

Ziegler, K. 1966. *Das hellenistische Epos: Ein vergessenes Kapitel griechischer Dichtung*$^2$. Leipzig

Zissos, A. and Gildenhard, I. 1999. 'Problems of time in Metamorphoses 2', in Hardie, Barchiesi and Hinds (1999). 31–47

# Index locorum

Apollodorus (mythographer): *Bibliotheca* 2.7.7
    53
Apollonius of Rhodes: *Argonautica*
  1.1 67n
  1.122–3 120–2
  1.130 122
  1.269–77 299n
  1.345–9 122
  1.496–511 299n
  1.532–3 122
  1.544–5 118n
  1.644–5 155n
  1.855–60 123
  1.862–78 123
  1.992 122n
  1.1168 122n
  1.1168–71 122
  1.1212–19 123–4
  1.1261–72 124
  1.1299–1309 124
  1.1315–20 124–5
  2.75 132n
  2.284–300 150–1
  2.700–19 119n
  2.755–8 119
  2.779 119
  2.786–91 119
  2.796–8 119n
  2.806–10 119
  2.1052–8 126
  2.1264–6 118
  3.1232–4 127
  4.125–6 118
  4.551 128
  4.1438–9 129
  4.1477–50 128–9
  4.1487–9 129–30
Aristotle
  *Poetics*
    1451a16–22 64
    1451a16–30 64–5
    1451a18–19 65
    1451a19–22 70
    1451a28–30 68
    1455b16–23 68
    1459a19–22 63
    1459a35–8 64
    1459a37 64
    1459a37-b1 64
    1462b11 64
  *Politics*
    1253a2–4 130
    1253a27–9 130
Catullus
  1.5–7 184
  11.10 83
  64.339 238
Cicero
  *Brutus*
    7 312
  *De divinatione*
    2.70 342
  *De inventione rhetorica*
    1.2 311n
  *De legibus*
    2.3–6 352–3
    2.5 353
  *De natura deorum*
    2.165 108
  *De officiis*
    1.54–7 353
    1.77 312n
  *De oratore*
    2.178 35
    2.188 24
    2.190 23–4
    2.205 23
    2.214 35
    3.106 23
  *De provinciis consularibus*
    18 108
  *De republica*

1.39 333n
2.4 329n
2.5 349
2.10 349
2.11 349
2.12–13 338
2.17–20 329n
2.22 349
2.27–9 194–5
3.25 332
*Epistulae ad Atticum*
  2.19.3 83
*Orator*
  26 23
  132 24n
  213 106–7
*Pro Archia*
  19–21 71
*Pro Balbo* 338
  24 334n
*Somnium Scipionis*
  13–16 95
  14 111n
  20–5 95–6
*Topica*
  86 23
*Tusculan Disputations*
  1.109–11 93
  1.110 109
Diodorus Siculus
  1.2.2 269
  4.26.2 129n
  4.38.4–5 52n
Dionysius of Halicarnassus: *Antiquitates
    Romanae*
  1.2.2 256
  1.39–42 264
  1.67.1–4 264–5
  1.67.4 266
  1.68.1–69.4 266
  1.74.2 187
  2.19.1–2 267
  2.68.1–2 267
  2.75 340
  8.56.1 267
  8.56.4 267
Donatus, Tiberius Claudius: *Interpretationes
    Vergilianae*
  1.2.9–12 72–3
  4.339 16
Ennius: *Annales*
  I.x Sk. 189
  I.xxx–iv Sk. 48–9
  77 Sk. 102
  79–83 Sk. 299n

100 Sk. 53
110–11 Sk. 51–2
154–5 Sk. 188–9
156 Sk. 116
157 Sk. 362
VIII.xv Sk. 43
309 Sk. 43
VIII.xvi Sk. 40, 41
*sed. inc.* lxx Sk. 189
Ephorus: *FGrH* 70
  F 9 256n
  T 8 256n
Florus 1.11.6 100
Herodotus
  1.1.1–5.3 244
  1.5.3 251
  2.65.2 257
  6.105.1–2 253
  9.116–20 244
Hesiod
  [*Scutum*]
    148 136
    178–90 137
    207–15 136
    209 136
  *Theogony*
    81–93 310
    594–601 288
    700–5 288n
    861–4 288n
    954–5 52
    963–8 198–9
    987 288n
  *Works and Days*
    303–6 288
    fr. 25.26–33 52–3
    fr. 25.27–8 52
Homer
  *Iliad*
    1.1 81
    1.2–4 64
    1.47 287
    1.104 287
    1.359 287
    2.87–93 287–91
    2.139–41 290–1
    2.144–50 291
    2.203–5 291–2
    2.204–5 313
    2.207–10 292
    2.394–7 292–3
    2.459–65 290
    2.484–6 251
    3.121–40 149
    3.1–8 281–2

Homer (cont.)
   3.381 48n
   4.13–19 175
   4.51–4 41–2
   4.141–7 171–2
   5.87–94 300
   5.353–69 149n
   6.476–81 31
   11.492–6 300
   12.167–72 290n
   16.431–61 176
   16.439–57 138
   18.117 121
   18.165–202 149
   20.444 48n
   22.166–87 176
   23.192–211 149
   24.628–32 28
  *Odyssey*
   1.77–8 42
   1.308 294
   2.1–5 295
   2.5 294–5
   2.47 294
   2.234 294
   3.468 294, 295
   4.27 294
   4.45–6 295
   4.122 295
   4.141–5 295
   4.148–54 296
   4.306 295
   4.306–10 295
   4.335–40 297, 298
   4.791–4 297–8
   5.12 294
   6.102–9 232
   6.108 234
   6.232–5 298n
   8.83–5 296
   11.121–34 42
   11.601–27 129n
   11.602–3 52
   15.152 294n
   17.126–31 298
   19.267 295
   23.85–240 27
   23.159–62 298n
   23.163 295
   23.233–9 298
   23.300–1 27
   24.371 295
Horace
  *Epistles*
   1.2.17–18 73
   1.11.7–8 100
  *Odes*
   1.12 98
   2.1.25–8 61
   3.3 48, 49–50
   3.3.9–12 54n
   3.3.16 49n
   3.3.17–18 49
   3.3.18–24 58n
   3.3.30–6 54
   3.3.32 55n
   3.3.70–2 49
   4.4.37–8 106n
Isocrates: *Evagoras* 190ab 72
Josephus: *Jewish War* 2.358–79 328
Livy
  *Praef.* 4 326
  *Praef.* 6–8 327–9, 329n
  *Praef.* 7 258–9
  *Praef.* 9–10 259
  *Praef.* 13 257–8
  1.1.1–3 353n, 363
  1.1.9 331n
  1.2.4–5 331n
  1.3.2–3 329–30
  1.3.3 330n
  1.4.1–2 259–60
  1.4.2 328–9
  1.5 338
  1.6.3 349
  1.7 260
  1.7.4–15 260–1
  1.7.15 261n
  1.8.5 350
  1.8.5–6 331–2
  1.8.6 334
  1.9.14 337
  1.11.1 337
  1.11.2 337
  1.13.4 336, 337
  1.15.6–8 329
  1.16.1–3 52n
  1.18.2 194
  1.18.2–4 343
  1.19.1 345
  1.19.4–5 340
  1.20.1–4 345
  1.20.4 351
  1.21.1 342
  1.21.3–4 340–1
  1.23.1 359n
  1.33.2 354
  1.34.5–8 338

# Index locorum 405

1.46.2–48.7 338
2.1.4–5 335
2.1.5 351n
2.5.9–10 335
2.14.9 354
2.45.4 335–6
3.44–8 338
4.3.4 338
4.3.10–14 338
4.4 338
5.24.5 350n
5.25.4–6 350n
5.30.1–3 350
5.30.6 350
5.40.9–10 265n
5.44.1 356
5.49.3 350
5.49.7 345
5.49.8 345
5.50.1–7 345
5.51–4 345
5.52.6–7 345
5.52.8 266
5.54.2 350, 351n
5.54.2–3 348–9
5.54.3 351
5.54.4 349
5.54.5 347–8
5.54.7 350, 351
5.55.1 350
5.55.4 354
6.1.3 346
6.34.5–11 338
7.39–40 355–6
8.6.8 359n
8.6.15 359
8.7 359–60
8.8.2 359n
8.8.17 360n
8.10.9 359n
8.13.14–16 361
8.14.1–4 361
8.14.9–11 361–2
26.41.18 342
29.17.6 42n
31.14.6 84n
30.45.6 42n, 43, 84n
Lucan: *De bello civili*
1.68–9 66
1.72–81 319
1.125–6 83
1.129 83
1.131–3 84
1.135 84

1.143–4 84
1.158–9 66
2.303 89
2.319–20 89
2.320–2 89
5.1–3 83
5.28–9 356
5.46–8 84
5.52 84
6.3 83
6.785–6 106
6.788–9 110
6.788–90 115
6.795–6 107, 108–9
6.805–7 96
7.391–6 101, 115
7.638–41 115
7.686–9 85
7.694–6 85
7.717 85
7.726–7 85
8.19–21 85
8.31–2 87
8.274–6 85–6
8.320–1 86
8.449–50 86
8.551–2 86
8.624 86
8.629–32 87
8.668–71 87–8
8.717–20 87–8
8.759–60 87
9.2 88
9.147 88n
9.190 88
9.202 88
9.204–6 89
9.208–11 89
9.215–17 88
9.593–600 89–90
9.1014 88
10.85 88
Lucretius
1.58–61 306
1.117–19 187–8
1.271–9 299
1.280–2 300
1.290–97 300–2
1.328 302
2.352–9 219–21
2.573–6 304
2.707–10 303
3.833–7 42n
3.834–5 43

Lucretius (cont.)
  3.836 43
  5.366–8 304
  5.380–3 304
  6.67 302–3
  6.568–9 304
  6.577–607 304–5
Maximus of Tyre 26.6b 73
Ovid
  *Amores* 1.1 234
  *Ars amatoria* 1.254–6 19n
  *Fasti*
    1.101 198
    1.103 197
    1.125 197
    1.335–456 216–18
    1.349–52 221
    1.405 238n
    1.408 238n
    1.671–2 218
    1.709–22 218
    2.359–76 224n
    2.481–8 49
    2.485–8 56n
    2.496 49n
    2.643–58 223–4
    2.852–3 224n
    3.177 198
    3.339–40 224
    4.393–620 218–22
    4.401 218
    4.407 219
    4.408 219
    4.413–16 218
    4.414 219
    4.417 219
    4.459–62 220
    4.463–6 221
    4.487 221
    4.559–60 221
    4.617 221
    4.681–712 217
    4.941–2 217
    5.495–536 225
    6.47–8 41n
    6.53–4 55n
    6.99–100 61
  *Heroides*
    7.19 280
    7.51 165
    18.173–5 244
  *Metamorphoses*
    1.4 183, 230
    1.5 196
    1.67–8 317–18
    1.199–206, 318
    1.215 19n
    1.253–64 318–19
    1.438–51 235
    1.452 196
    2.25–30 196–7
    2.31 197
    2.259 199
    2.299 197
    2.365–6 199
    2.538–9 199
    2.642–54 199
    4.284 196
    5.8 196
    5.227 196
    6.419–21 189, 244
    11.194–204 190
    11.194–6 244
    11.199–201 190
    11.215 190
    11.217–20 190
    11.265 236
    11.749–758 191–2
    13.404 192
    14.11 193n
    14.136–53 193
    14.324–5 192–3
    14.772–5 193–4
    14.806–15 49
    14.812 49
    14.818–26 49n
    14.829–31 53–4
    15.1–2 200n
    15.127–39 224n
    15.183–4 201
    15.319 196
    15.365 213n
    15.4 224
    15.5 200n
    15.73–4 224
    15.816–17 202
    15.834–7 200–1
    15.836 200n
    15.870 201
    15.871 203
    15.873–5 202–3
  *Tristia* 2.559–60 183
Plato
  *Hippias Minor* 363b 72
  *Protagoras* 326a 72
  *Respublica* 619c 92
Pliny the Younger: *Epistulae* 2.3.8 363–4
Plutarch
  *Pompey* 13 83

*Romulus* 9.2–3 335n
*Theseus* 1 256
Polybius
  1.3.7 42n
  6.56.6–12 342
  6.56.14 342
Posidonius: fr. 44 Edelstein and Kidd 255
Quintilian: *Institutio oratoria*
  2.16.1–2 34
  3.8.9 141
  6.2.5–6 34–5
Sallust: *Catiline*
  1.3 144n
  2.3 146
  3.1 142, 144n
  3.2 142
  3.3–4.1 142
  4.2 142–3, 144
  4.3 146n
  4.4 144
  6.1 143
  7.7 143, 145
  8.1 145
  8.2–4 145
  22.3 144
  33.2 104
  53.2 144
scholia to *Iliad*
  AbT 2.87 289–90
  b 3.2 289–90
Seneca
  *De beneficiis* 4.30.2 90n
  *De consolatione ad Marciam* 14.3 90n
  *Epistulae* 94.64–5 90n
Servius: *Commentary on the Aeneid of Virgil* (* = S. Auctus)
  *Praef.* 1.4.4–6 255n
  1.1–6* 68
  1.148* 310, 312
  1.281 39–40, 41, 50n
  4.305* 17
  4.335* 18
  4.337 18
  4.362* 24
  4.570* 163n
  4.577 164
  5.606 153
  9.2 153
  10.11 40
  10.467 113
  12.792 47
  12.830–1 45–6
  12.841 39
Silius Italicus: *Punica*
  1.1–4 65
  1.324–5 319
  1.356–9 319
Statius
  *Achilleid*
  1.5 241
  1.7 230n, 246
  1.9 229, 231
  1.11 229–30
  1.14–15 246
  1.28–9 231, 243
  1.34–5 231
  1.81–2 244
  1.159–66 231–2
  1.164–5 233
  1.184 233
  1.204 231n
  1.283–4 235
  1.290 239
  1.293–4 233
  1.294–5 232
  1.304–10 240
  1.313–17 235–6
  1.322 229
  1.336–7 228, 236–7
  1.344–8 233
  1.395 245
  1.398 241
  1.406–11 243
  1.412 241
  1.445–6 231
  1.467–72 230
  1.474–6 230
  1.495–6 241
  1.503–4 241
  1.528 231
  1.567–76 236
  1.583–91 237
  1.642 236
  1.713 238
  1.761–2 238
  1.768–9 238
  1.785–7 245
  1.788 245
  1.790 231
  1.823 234
  1.825–35 234
  1.833 238
  1.848 239
  1.853 240, 241
  1.865 240–1
  1.866 240
  1.868 241
  1.874–5 238
  1.878 238

Statius (cont.)
    1.881–2 241, 242–3
    1.888 241
    1.891 239
    1.947–8 239–40
    2.5–11 239
    2.72–9 244
    2.107 241
  *Thebaid*
    1.1–2 66
    1.131–6 319
    1.370–5 319
    11.28 230n
    12.441 67
    12.442–3 67
    12.588 240n
    12.815 246
Strabo 5.3.2 100
Suetonius
  *Augustus* 84.2 38n
  *Tiberius* 7.3 37
Tacitus: *Annales*
    1.1 143n
    1.4.3 200n
    1.11.1 200n, 201n
    3.27 114n
    11.24 334, 338n
Theocritus
    17.22–7 51
    22 132
    22.85 132n
Theopompus: *FGrH* 115 F 381
        257n
Thucydides
    1.10.2 145
    1.11.3 145
    4.116 253n

Valerius Flaccus: *Argonautica*
    1.1–2 67n
    1.484–93 319
    1.651–4 319
    1.682–5 319
Valerius Maximus
    1.8.7 262
    6.4.5 105
Varro
  *Antiquitates Rerum Humanarum et Diuinarum*
    fr. 5 Cardauns 341
  *De Gente Populi Romani*
    fr. 3 Peter 185
    fr. 14 Peter 190
Virgil
  *Aeneid*

Book 1
    1–7 80–1, 246, 362n
    8 190n
    12–22 45
    14 315
    15–21 42–3
    23–8 45
    58–9 308
    63 311
    66 311
    82 309
    138 314
    142 314
    145 314
    148–53 286
    148–56 309–11
    152 311
    201 35n
    206 274
    265–74 189
    267–71 330
    274–7 102
    279–82 41
    292–3 102–3
    297–304 153
    321–409 25
    406 26
    430–6 307–8
    502 233
    572–4 162
    615–16 160
    715–22 30
    753–4 160
Book 2
    195–8 33n
    255 186
    542 240
    657–70 30
    704 30
    707–20 30
    708 136
    721–3 136
    753–4 30
    789 26
    790–1 25
    1030–42 126
Book 3
    47–8 32
    182–8 30–1
    349–51 274
    372 132n
    443–5 132
    453–60 132
    547 131

*Index locorum* 409

550 131
551–2 131
715 155n, 160
717 160n
Book 4
25 157
102 162
110–11 275n
110–12 162
142 232
149 232n
173–90 155
173–95 174
188 21
197 23
215–17 278
219–78 148
238–9 165
242–4 156
246–53 157
283–4 18n
289–94 20
293–4 18n
294–5 166
305–30 17
305–6 20
333–4 18–19
333–61 15, 17–24
337 17–18
337–9 19–22
338–9 21n
340–1 37
340–4 274
345–59 159
360 22–4
361–2 24
362–87 24
366–7 157
373–5 19
376 24
376–80 160–1
379 24
390–1 25
441–6 157
449 138n
465–70 275n
465–8 30
469–70 161
554–80 148
556–80 162–5
569 169n
571–2 156
577 165–6
579–80 157

595 165
622–9 45
669–70 280
Book 5
45–71 36n
410–14 131
442 132n
519 132n
606–63 154
685–99 154
722–42 26
833–61 126
Book 6
83–94 174
89 229
96–7 283n
129 132
129–31 132
135 132
331–2 32
451–4 129n
466 26
471 157
476 37
689 31
710–11 94
716–18 94
717 19
719–21 94
724–51 91–4
748 189
754–5 97
756–886 91–2, 96–113
756–9 96
763–6 330
767 96
773–6 99–101, 115
777–8 101
780 102
781 101
792–4 189
801–3 132–3
806 138
815–16 103
819 107
823 96, 105
824–5 105–7
834–5 107
836 107
838 107
841 107–8
842 108–9
842–3 109–10
845 97

Virgil (cont.)
    847–53 110–11, 282
    864 97
    868–86 97
    888–9 96
    889 69
    893–8 111–12
  Book 7
    4 112n
    44–5 168
    167–8 278
    223–4 245
    359–72 33
    411–13 100
    438 21
    461 241
    528–30 314–15
    535–7 314–15
    585–94 315–16
    659 133
    733 180n
  Book 8
    86–9 118
    91–2 118
    110–24 31
    185–275 134–5
    200–1 118
    219–20 135
    228–30 135
    230–1 135
    287–302 119n
    290–1 120
    364–5 135–6
    370–415 30
    445–53 174
    477 118
    617–19 32
    622–3 118
    671 136
    671–4 136
    698 272
    702 136
    704–6 272
    729–31 32, 136
  Book 9
    1–24 154
    12–13 168–9
    234–302 33
    614–20 279
    802–5 154
    803–4 153n
  Book 10
    6–14 40–1, 43
    15 169, 175–6
    26–30 277
    58 277
    94–5 23
    132–8 171–2
    175–8 180–1
    185–6 180
    199–203 182
    319–22 137
    345–9 170–1
    406 138
    443 138n
    460–1 137
    464–5 137–8, 176
    467–72 176–7
    467–9 138
    470–1 138
    545 139
    569 139
    572 139
    602–4 316
    603 317n
    604 139
    621–7 138n
    625–32 177–8
    636–42 174–5
    758–9 139, 178–9
    777–82 139
    788 139
    802 139
    813 139
  Book 11
    96–8 31
    225–461 33
    364–5 21
    406–7 22
    618–20 181
    837 178n
  Book 12 317
    10–80 33n
    127–8 181
    190–1 276–7
    238 23
    259–65 33
    311–19 315
    435–40 31
    451–7 316
    548–51 182
    791–842 30, 39, 43–8
    792 47
    793–6 57
    796 47
    819–28 44, 57
    826–8 362n

830–1 45–6
835–6 44, 58–9
838–40 55n
842 47
873–4 173
889 174
921–4 317
*Eclogues*
  4.36 229
  6.3 168
*Georgics*
  1.197–203 306

1.481–3 307
1.490–1 216n
1.501–2 59
1.511 245
1.511–14 307
2.169 99, 105–6
2.172 99
2.395–6 223
4.162–9 307–8
4.197–205 308
4.500–1 25
4.511–15 220

# General Index

For specific authors and works, see also entries in the Index locorum, pp. 402–11

*Achilleid* (Statius), 70, 228–46
    Apollo in, 231–2
    challenge of distinctiveness, 228–9, 230
    Europe and Asia in, 243–6
    and gender transgression, 228, 236–41
    and genre transgression, 240–2
    Ovidian influence, 228, 229–30, 234–6, 243–4
    planned completion, 246
    seascapes in, 230–1
    self-referentiality, 229–31
    Virgilian influence, 228, 232–4, 235–6, 241–3
Achilles (Homer)
    as 'epic hero', 64, 72, 76–7, 79, 81
    and power of speech, 26–8
    shield of, 136–7
Achilles (Statius)
    and Apollo, 231–2
    disguise as girl, 233–4, 236–40
    and eroticisation of war, 240–1
    as lover, 235–6
    uniqueness of, 228–9, 230
Actium, battle of, 271–3, 278
Addison, Joseph, 78, 81
Aeneas
    in Augustan sculpture, 330
    as Easterner, 278–9
    as epic hero, 68–70, 73–4
    as Hercules figure, 118, 119, 126, 131–7, 139–40
    isolation of, 30–2, 37, 135, 140
    in Livy, 329–30
    public speech of, 32–3, 36
    rhetoric and restraint, 17–24, 34, 35–6
    and unity of *Aeneid*, 72–3
    violence of, 139, 173, 316–17
    visitations of Mercury, 16, 148–9, 157–8, 162–6
*Aeneid*
    *Achilleid* and, 228, 232–4, 235–6, 241–3
    and the *Argonautica*, 126, 130–2, 134–5
    battle of Actium in, 272

    Carthage in, 274–7, 279–80
    catalogues in, 180–2
    chronology in, 189
    deferred action in, 168–9, 173–4
    divine-human communication in, 152–8
    doctrine of empire, 110–11
    and the epic hero, 68–70, 73–4
    Greekness in, 281–4
    Hercules in, 124, 130–40, 176
    lament for Marcellus, 91, 97, 111, 200
    love in, 281
    parade of heroes, 91–2, 96–110, 132–3
    philosophy of underworld, 93–6, 111–13
    'Preface', 242
    role of reader, 175–7, 178–9
    Romulus in, 101–3
    self-referentiality in, 168–9, 173–9
    similes in, 171–2, 232, 280, 286, 307–17
    speech in, 15, 17–26, 29–34, 35–8, 94
    violence in, 139, 169–73, 241–2, 314–17
    *see also* Aeneas
aesthetics of violence, 169–73
aetiology, 189, 206, 213–14
    in Livy, 260–1, 324–5, 335
Agonalia, 216, 217
agriculture and aetiology of sacrifice, 217–18, 221, 222
Ahl, F.M., 97
Alba Longa, 264–5, 338–9
Alexandria, 271, 273, 277
Allen, Don Cameron, 73–4
*amor*, in the *Achilleid*, 240–2
Ancus Marcius, 103–4, 339
Anderson, A.R., 51n
Ando, C., 324, 328n
Andromache
    in the *Aeneid*, 29, 277
    in Seneca's *Troades*, 246
Anglo-American relationship, 284–5

412

Anglo-French relationship, 284
Antisthenes, 121
Antonius, Marcus, 271–2, 273
  Aeneas and, 275
*Antony and Cleopatra* (Shakespeare), 275
Apollo
  in the *Achilleid*, 231–3
  in the *Aeneid*, 159–60, 199, 272
  and Augustus, 272
  in *Iliad*'s first simile, 287
  in the *Metamorphoses*, 235
Apollodorus (chronographer), 186, 187
Apollonius of Rhodes
  divine–human communication in, 150–2
  first simile, 298n
  Heracles in, 120–30
  influence on *Aeneid* 8, 117–19
Appiah, K.A., 323
Ara Maxima, 260–1
Ara Pacis, 218, 219, 330
Ardea, 100, 344, 356
Ares *see* Mars
Ariosto: *Orlando Furioso*, 75
Aristotle
  and aesthetic response to epic, 173, 178–9
  on man and god, 130
  on mythological life-stories, 70, 117
  on Homeric structural integrity, 63–5, 67–8
  and *Paradise Lost* as epic, 78
  and Renaissance understanding of epic, 74–7
  teaching, 4
Ascanius
  in the *Aeneid*, 31, 330
  in Livy, 329–30
Asia and Europe, 243–6
  *see also* East–West tension
Athens, 84, 145
  in chronology of *Metamorphoses*, 189
  exclusivity of citizenship, 334
  literature and the divine in, 254
  and myth of autochthony, 332
Atticus, T. Pomponius, 184, 185, 352–3
Augustus
  Aeneas and, 37–8
  in the *Aeneid*, 103, 111, 116, 132–3, 189, 310–11
  and Cybele, 279
  and encomiastic poetry, 71–2
  and Livy, 261, 269
  and the *Metamorphoses*, 199–202
  and Neptune, 310–11
  and re-foundation of Rome, 346–8
  and Romulus, 102, 261, 343–4
  and sacrifice in the *Georgics*, 214
  *see also* Actium, battle of

Austin, R.G., 17, 18, 101n, 102n, 106n
authorial persona in historiography, 252–3, 259
autochthony, 332, 335–6
autonomy of texts, 249–50

Badian, E., 103
Bailey, C., 45n
Barchiesi, Alessandro, 183, 202, 213, 214, 235, 244
Barnes, Julian, 284
Barrett, J.C., 328n
Barthes, Roland, 6, 10, 248
Bartsch, S., 314n
Beauvoir, Simone de, 21n
bee imagery, 287–91, 293, 307–8
Bell, Catherine, 206–7, 216
Beni, Paolo, 75–6
Benjamin, Walter, 173
Bloch, Maurice, 207
Bloch, R., 60n
Bloomfield, Morton W., 62
blushing, 240–1
Bömer, F., 55n
Bonjour, M., 355n, 355
Boyle, A.J., 69–70
Bramble, J.C., 113
Brooks, Peter, 173
Brutus, Lucius Iunius, 95, 104–5, 114
Brutus, Marcus Iunius, 104–5, 114–15
Buchheit, V., 40n, 43n, 60
Büchner, K., 44n, 103n
*bugonia*, 209–10, 213–15, 217
Burkert, Walter, 165n, 172, 206
Byzantium (Constantinople), 273

Caecilius Metellus Pius Scipio, Q., 110
Calame, C., 256n
Callimachus, 213
Camillus, Lucius Furius, 360–2
Camillus, Marcus Furius, 344–51
  and attachment to the *patria*, 348–51, 353–5
  Augustus and, 346–8
  and cyclical refoundations, 326–7, 345–7
  and displacement from Rome, 356–7
  and future development of citizenship, 360–1, 363
  and Roman religion, 266, 348, 349–50
*caritas*, 351, 353
Carlà-Uhink, F., 332n, 333n
Carthage, 59–60, 274–7, 279–80
Cartledge, P. and Greenwood, E., 255n
Castelvetro, Lodovico, 74–5, 76
catalogues, 179–82
Catiline, 114
Cato the Censor
  in the *Aeneid*, 108

Cato the Censor (cont.)
    as chronographer, 187
    in Cicero, 353, 357
    and Ennius, 188
    in Lucan, 115
Cato the younger, 311
    in the *Aeneid*, 108
    in Horace *Odes* 1.12, 98
    in Lucan, 88–90
Cerealia, 212, 218–19, 222
Ceres, 216–17, 218–22
Choerilus of Samos, 71
Christianity
    and the epic 'hero', 73, 79–80
    and the epic simile, 319–21
chronography, 183–9
    *see also Metamorphoses* as chronography
Cicero, 4
    and *Aeneid*'s parade of heroes, 95
    and *Aeneid*'s statesman simile, 310, 311–12
    on the Gracchi, 108
    on inflammatory rhetoric, 23–4
    and Lucan's underworld, 96
    Platonic influence, 92–3, 332
    and Roman Hellenization in Ovid, 194–5
    in Sallust's *Catiline*, 144
    and 'two fatherlands' ideology, 352–4
citizenship, 322–3
    and *Aeneid*'s Asilas, 181–2
    and fiction of autochthony, 331–2, 350–1
    after Gallic sack, 354–5
    in Greek states, 332
    incorporation of Tusculum, 357
    intermingling and, 276–7
    Latin settlement of 338, 360–3
    openness of, 332–9
    after Social War, 352–3, 363–4
*ciuis*, 332
*ciuitas*, 181–2, 337, 354
    *see also* citizenship
*ciuitas sine suffragio*, 361–2
civil war, 215–16, 332
    Latin War as, 359–60
Clarke, M., 17n
Claudian, 71, 72
Claudius, 334, 338n
Coleman, R.R., 45n
colonies
    Carthage as, 276
    Latin, 336, 358, 362
Commager, S., 50, 59n
Constantinople, 273
Conte, G.B., 165n
context, 7, 10, 214–15, 226, 249
    *see also* historicism

Conway, R.S., 45n
Corinth, Isthmus of, 190, 243, 244
Coriolanus, Gn. Marcius, 355–6
Cornelius Nepos, 184, 186–7
Cornelius Scipio *see* Scipio
Cornell, Tim, 13, 283, 323n, 333n
Corvinus, M. Valerius, 355–6
cosmopolitanism, 356–7
Cowan, R.W., 280n
Csapo, E., 249n
Cybele, cult of, 279

Dardanelles *see* Hellespont
Davies, J.P., 268n, 344
Davies, M., 47–8
De Sanctis, G., 265, 358
De Witt, N.W., 57n
Dench, E., 333n, 333, 362
dialogue
    in the *Aeneid*, 25–6, 29–34, 94
    in the *Iliad*, 26–8
    in the *Odyssey*, 27
Diamond, Jared, 206
Diana in epic simile, 232–4
Dickens, Charles: *Our Mutual Friend*, 288
Dido
    Cleopatra and, 275
    death of, 280
    dreams of, 30, 161–2, 275
    *fama* and, 155, 156
    in the *Heroides*, 165, 280
    Mercury's mission and, 153, 154, 156–7, 158, 164–5
    as metaphor for political sacrifice, 36
    and Phoenician exclusivity, 276
    reaction to divine motivation, 159, 160–1, 166
    rhetoric of, 16–17, 19, 24–5
    in the underworld, 157, 275
Dilke, O.A.W., 243, 245
Dionysius of Halicarnassus
    approach to mythic narrative, 263–8, 269
    *Chronica*, 187n
    on Romulus' asylum, 334–5
Dioscuri, 125–6
domesticated animals, 206
Domitian, 229, 246
Douglas, A.E., 17n, 37n, 37
dreams, in the *Aeneid*, 30, 161–4, 166, 275
Drusi, 106–7, 114
Dryden, John, 77–8

Earl, D.C., 146n
East–West tension, 244–6, 273–5
    in the *Aeneid*, 274–5, 277–81
ecphrasis, 174–5

Eliot, George: *Daniel Deronda*, 17n
Ellsworth, J.D., 193n
Elmer, D.F., 291n, 293n
Elsner, J., 214
empire
  as mental construct, 327–8
  *regnum gentibus*, 42–3
  violence and, 172–3
encomiastic epic, 71–3
Ennius
  as chronographer, 187–9
  Juno in, 40, 41, 48–56, 60
  Livy and, 42
  Lucretius and, 42–3, 187–8
  Ovid and, 198, 200
  Romulus in, 133
  Virgil and, 40–1, 43–4, 56–7, 109
*enumerare*, 18–19
epic
  catalogues, 179–82
  conventional features, 169–70, 179–80, 286
  eroticisation of war, 240–2
  and genre shift, 234–6, 240, 242
  gods in, 30, 175–9, 253–4, 255
  in late antiquity, 72
  violence in, 168–73
  *see also* dialogue; 'hero', epic; similes
Epicureanism, 160, 301–5
Erato, 241–2
Eratosthenes, 185–6
eschatology, 91–4
ethnicity and Roman citizenship, 332–4
Etruscans, 335, 339
  in the *Aeneid*, 180–2
*euocationes*, 60
Evander
  in the *Aeneid*, 29n, 118, 134–6, 283
  in Livy, 260
exile, 355–6

*fama*
  Dido and, 155, 156
  Lucan's Pompey and, 83–5, 86–7
  as poet-figure, 155, 174
Fantham, Elaine, 216, 219, 246
Farrell, J., 209n, 333n
*Fasti*
  Juno in, 61
  and *Metamorphoses*, 183, 188, 196–7, 201–2
  sacrifice in, 223–5, 226
  time in, 198–9
feasting, sacrificial, 223–5
Feldherr, Andrew, 215n, 342, 343
Fenik, B.C., 43–4, 46
festivals, Greek, 71

fictions, 322–5
  of historiography, 325–6
  religious, 340–4, 348, 349–51
  *see also* myth and history
*fides*, 340–1, 342
*fingere*, 21–2
Fordicidia, 222
formalism, 6–8, 247–9
foundation of Rome
  appropriate genre for narrative, 258–9
  as chronographic point, 184, 185, 187, 193–4
  and dissociation from Troy, 265
Fowler, Alistair, 79–80
Fowler, Don, 7–8, 11, 152, 165n, 214–15, 240n, 247–8, 302n, 305n
Fowler, Robert, 10
Fowler, W. Warde, 45n, 59
Fraenkel, E., 50n, 57–8
fragmentary authors, 268
Fränkel, H., 130n
Frye, Northrop, 62
Fulvius Nobilior, M., 188
Furius Camillus *see* Camillus

Gabba, E., 263n
Gaertner, J.F., 346–7, 347n, 353–4
Gale, M., 212, 217n, 222n, 286n, 301n, 302n
Galinsky, G.K., 311n
Gallagher, C. and Greenblatt, S., 226, 248n
Geertz, Clifford, 226
genre, 225, 249–50, 261–3, 269–70
  love and epic, 234–6, 240, 281
  and representations of sacrifice, 223–5
  and representations of the divine, 254, 255
*gens*, continuity of, 97–8, 104–5
  *see also* Iulia gens
*gentes*, 328
  *regnum gentibus*, 42–3
  *see also* subject peoples
Georgics
  bee analogy, 288
  sacrifice in, 205, 209–10, 211–16, 223, 226
  similes in book 1, 306–7
  undermining of panegyric in, 99, 106
Getty, R., 63, 64, 65, 68, 84
Gildon, C., 81
Giraldi Cinzio, G.B., 75
Gleason, M.W., 239n
*gloria*
  and the *Aeneid*'s parade of heroes, 96, 112
  in Cicero's *Somnium Scipionis*, 95
  vs. *fama*, 156
  through writing, 142
gods
  demand for sacrifice, 210, 217–18

gods (cont.)
  role in epic, 30, 175–9, 253–4, 255
  role in historiography, 253–5, 266–7
  see also names of individual gods
Golden Age, 218
  end of, 217, 222
Goldhill, Simon, 5, 12
Goodyear, F.R.D., 141
Gordon, Richard, 207, 211, 223
Gracchi, 108–9, 114
Grafton, A.T. and Swerdlow, N.M., 185n
Gratwick, A.S., 188
Greek studies, 9–14, 247–8
Greeks
  concepts of ethnicity and citizenship, 332, 334
  models of sacrifice, 209–11
  Roman attitudes to, 245, 281–5
Greenblatt see Gallagher, C. and Greenblatt, S.
Griffin, J., 27n, 28n, 28, 48n, 110

Habinek, Thomas, 209–10, 214
Hägin, P., 78
Halter, T., 41
Hammer, D., 324n
Hannibal
  and Juno, 59–60
  in Silius' *Punica*, 65–6, 319
Hannibalic (Second Punic) War, 39–41, 55, 59–60, 279, 342
Harari, Y.N., 323–4
Hardie, Philip, 200n, 202, 301n, 304n, 305, 308, 309n
Harpies, 150–1
Harrison, E.L., 149n, 149, 156n, 163, 164, 213, 214
Harrison, S.J., 178–9, 180
Harrison, T., 252
Häussler, R., 44n
Hecataeus, 252, 255
Heinze, Richard, 26, 29, 30n, 50, 68
Hellanicus of Lesbos, 185n
Hellenistic chronology, 185–7
Hellenization in Roman culture, 194–5, 261, 282–4
Hellespont (Dardanelles), 190, 230–1, 243–5
Henderson, John, 5
Henry, J., 310
Hera see Juno/Hera
Hercules/Heracles
  in the *Aeneid*, 124, 130–40, 176
  in Apollonius, 119, 120–30, 157–8
  cult of, 260–1, 344
  in Homer, 121–2
  in the *Metamorphoses*, 190
  portrayals of, 117, 120, 121
  and Romulus, 51–4

'hero', epic
  *Aeneid*, 67–70, 73–4
  Early Modern English critics on, 77
  encomiastic, 71–2
  *Iliad*, 64, 76–7, 79
  late antique, 72
  modern concept, 62–3
  mythological, 70–1
  *Odyssey*, 64, 67–8, 70, 73
  Paradise Lost, 78–82
  Renaissance understanding, 74–7
  Silver Latin, 65–7
  as term, 63, 74, 77
Herodorus, 121
Herodotus, 250–5, 257
ἥρως, 63
Hesiod
  Ovid and, 198–9
  similes in, 288
  storm-wind in, 305
Highet, G., 18, 20, 26, 29, 30n, 33–4, 35n, 36, 37, 140n
Hinds, Stephen, 5, 9, 201, 213n, 229, 236, 239n
Hine, H., 314n
Hippias, 186
historicism, 6–8, 225–6, 247–9
historiography
  as fictive construct, 325–6
  Sallust and the power of the writer, 142–7
  see also myth and history
Hobbes, Thomas, 77
Homer
  desert-island ranking, 13
  divine agency in, 253–4
  divine–human communication in, 149–50
  Heracles in, 121–2
  and historiography, 251
  Nepos' dating of, 184
  as political theorist, 312–14
  speech and dialogue in, 26–9
  Statius and, 246
  violence in, 170, 171–2
  see also *Iliad*; *Odyssey*
Horace
  desert-island ranking, 13
  as evidence for Ennius' Juno, 48, 49–50, 54, 55, 56n
  orientalism in, 272
  Troy in, 58
Hornblower, S., 257n
Hornsby, R.A., 316n
Horsfall, N.M., 41, 45, 91n, 97n, 105, 106, 241n, 241
Hubbard, M., 60, 98
Hutcheon, L., 173n

*Iliad*
  and the *Aeneid*, 307–8, 312–14
  deferral of action in, 168n
  effects of speech in, 26–8
  focus of, 64, 79
  similes in, 171–2, 280, 287–94, 300–1
  Tasso on, 76–7
*incendere*, 23–4
*iners*, 239
intermarriage, 338
intertextuality, 248
Iris, 149–51
  in the *Aeneid*, 152–4
  as the rainbow, 153n
isolation
  of Aeneas, 30–2, 37, 135, 140
  of Heracles, 127, 129–30, 135, 140
Isthmus of Corinth, 190, 243, 244
Italy
  as Roman *patria*, 354
  citizenship rights in, 357–63
  early horizontal mobility in, 333–4
  Italic *consanguinitas*, 333
*Iulia gens*, 97, 330, 339

Jacoby, F., 186
Jaeger, M., 356
Johnson, Samuel, 81n
Johnson, W.R., 30, 44, 46
Jonson, Ben, 77
Julius Caesar
  in the *Aeneid*, 107
  calendar reform, 347
  citizenship extension, 363
  cult of Divus Iulius, 344
  in Lucan, 83, 84, 87–8
Juno/Hera
  and death of Sarpedon, 138, 176
  in Ennius, 40, 41, 48–56, 60
  favour for Rome, 39–40, 41–2
  and Iris, 149, 151, 152–4
  as patron of Dido and Carthage, 42–4, 59, 161–2
  and reprieve of Turnus, 174–5, 177–8
  Roman portrayal as antipathetic, 59, 60–1
  Virgilian reconciliation scene, 39–40, 43–8, 56–8, 61
  worship of, 59–60
Jupiter/Zeus
  in Apollonius, 150–1, 152
  as epic audience, 175–8
  and messenger gods, 149–54, 155

Kellogg. *see* Scholes, R. and Kellogg, R.
Kenney, E.J., 42, 199n
Kermode, Frank, 6n
Knauer, G.N., 117n
κοίρανος, 292
Kühn, W., 39

Lacey, Patrick, 141
Lamarque, P. and Olsen, S.H., 250
Latin War (340–338), 358–60
Latins, 336–7, 358, 360–3
  in the *Aeneid*, 99–101, 115, 180
  and districts of early Rome, 339
  in Lucan, 115
  *see also* Latin War
Latium, concept of, 361, 362
Latte, K., 213n
Lavan, M., 324, 328
legal fiction, 323–4
Levene, D.S., 268n, 326
Levin, D.N., 130n
Lieberg, G., 39
Lintott, A.W., 87n
lion similes, 241, 297–8
literature, models of, 208–9, 227
Livia, 106
Livy
  on Camillus' refoundation, 344–51, 353–5, 356–7
  contemporary citizenship and the Social War, 351–3
  on Coriolanus and Corvinus, 355–6
  genre norms and the divine in, 257–61, 263, 268, 269
  interest in the fictive, 322–3, 324–6, 330–2
  on Latin settlement of 338, 361–3
  on the Latin War, 357–60
  lost books, 363
  on Numa's religious institutions, 340–4, 351
  origin and foundation myths in, 101, 327–32, 333–6
  paradigms of amalgamation in, 337–9
  on Pompeius Magnus, 83
  on the Punic wars, 42–3
  on rape of the Sabine women, 336–7
  readership, 363–4
  ring-composition in, 326–7, 341, 345–6, 350–1
  on site of Rome, 349–50
Lloyd, Geoffrey, 252
Lucan
  on the battle of Pharsalus, 115–16
  'hero' of *Bellum Civile*, 65, 66
  on Latin states, 101
  on Pompey's *nomen* and *fama*, 83–90
  Romulus in, 103, 115

Lucan (cont.)
  underworld in, 91, 106, 107, 108–9, 110, 113–16
Lucas, D.W., 63
Luce, J.V., 351n
Lucretius
  and Ennius, 42–3, 187–8
  Milton and, 320–1
  Ovid and, 219–20
  similes in, 293, 298–305
  Virgil and, 306–7, 308–9, 313
Ludwig, W., 185, 190
Lyne, R.O.A.M., 165

Mackinnon, L., 79
Macleod, Colin, 28n, 48n
Malloch, S.J.V., 334n
Manlius Torquatus, T., 95, 104, 105–6, 107, 358, 359–60
Mantua, 182
Marcellus, Marcus Claudius, 111
Marcii, 103–4
Marcius Philippus, L., 103
Marcius Rex, Q., 103–4
Marincola, J., 257, 263n, 264, 269n
marriage, 15–16
  intermarriage, 338
Mars
  and apotheosis of Romulus, 49, 56
  in imagery of global war, 245, 307
  and reconciliation of Juno to Rome, 55n
  Roman descent from, 328–9
Mayer, R., 87n
Mercury/Hermes
  absence from Apollonius, 150, 151–2
  in the *Aeneid*, 148–9, 152–3, 154, 155–8, 162–7
  etymology of name, 157n
  in Homer, 149–50, 155, 158
*Metamorphoses* as chronography, 183–4, 185, 189–203
  anachronism in, 194–5
  and Augustan teleology, 199–202
  demarcating events, 189–93, 196
  foundation of Rome, 193–4
  and Ovidian time, 183, 196–8, 201–3
  synchronism in, 193, 195
  time-counting schemes, 193
Michels, A.K., 69
Miles, G.B., 347n
*militia amoris* motif, 236, 240
Milton, John: *Paradise Lost*, 78–82, 179, 319–21
mimesis and alterity, 283–5
misogyny, 164–5
Moatti, C., 337, 338n, 354n
models, 204–5
  of literature, 208–9, 227
  of sacrifice, 205–8, 227
Moles, J.L., 251n, 258n, 258, 326n
Momigliano, A., 273–4, 283n
Monti, R.C., 22
Morgan, Llewelyn, 215
Most, Glenn, 250
Moulton, C., 291n
Mynors, R.A.B., 213n
myth and history
  approaches to, 256–7
  chronological demarcation, 189–93, 256
  in Dionysius of Halicarnassus, 263–8
  in Herodotus, 250–5
  inter-generic boundaries, 257–8
  in Livy, 258–61, 327–32
mythological monocentric epics, 70–1
mythologisation and demythologisation, 308–9, 320–1

narrative desire, 173
Neptune, in *Aeneid* statesman simile, 309, 310–11, 314
New Historicism, 8, 225–6, 248
Nicolet, C., 332
Nisbet, Robin, 2–3, 5, 7, 60, 98, 271n
Norden, E., 40n, 99, 101n, 106n
Nowotny, Helga, 197–8, 202
Numa Pompilius, 194–5, 224, 340–4, 351
  Camillus as, 345
Numitor, 101

Oakley, S.P., 348n, 358
Obbink, Dirk, 211
Odysseus
  in the *Iliad*, 291–2, 293
  lion simile, 297
  paternity imagery, 294
  and Penelope, 297–8
  in Plato, 92
  similarity with Telemachus, 294–7
*Odyssey*
  Aristotle on, 64, 67–8
  early similes, 294–8
  effects of speech in, 27
  and idea of the epic hero, 70, 73
Ogilvie, R.M., 60, 260n, 335n, 344n, 347n, 350n
Olympiads in chronography, 185, 186, 187, 190, 192–3
  date of foundation of Rome, 184, 185
oracular dreams, 161
oratory. *see* rhetoric
order through violence, 172–3
orientalism, 272–3, 278–9
  and Roman identity, 279–80

# General Index

Oswald, Alice, 14
Otis, Brooks, 69, 166n
Ovid
  and Lucretius, 219–20
  and Ennius, 188, 200
  and Hesiod, 198–9
  and Livy, 343
  Statius and, 228, 229–30, 234–6, 243–4
  and Virgil, 200, 216–17, 220, 222
  *see also Fasti*; *Metamorphoses* as chronography

Page, T.E., 55n
Pallas
  Aeneas and, 31, 316
  and father-son conversation, 29n
  prayers of, 137–8, 176–7
*parens/pater patriae*, 346–7
Parker, R., 254n, 254
Patavium, 363
*patria*, 350, 354, 355–6, 358
  *duae patriae*, 352–3
*pax deorum*, 210
Payne, Mark, 13–14
Pelling, C.B.R., 254–5, 262n
Penates, 264–5, 266
Perkell, C., 215n
Perkins, David, 8, 226
Pharsalus, battle of, 85, 115
Philip V of Macedon, 334
Phoebus *see* Apollo
Phoenicians, 276
Pigna, Giovan Battista, 75
pity, 178–9
Plato
  and encomia in epic, 72
  and 'noble lie' of autochthony, 331–2
  on soul and afterlife, 92
  and Virgil's underworld, 93–5, 111, 112
poet-figures, 174–5
  Jupiter as, 178
Polleichtner, W., 287n
Polybius
  as chronographer, 184, 194, 348n
  on religion, 342
Pompeius Magnus, Gn., 83–90
Pope, Alexander, 77
Pöschl, V., 45n
Punic wars, 39–41, 42–3, 55, 59–60, 342
puns and wordplay
  in Ennius, 109
  in Livy, 331, 349, 350
  in Lucan, 89n, 101, 115
  in Lucretius, 187–8, 302, 303
  in Statius, 229

  in Virgil, 133
Putnam, M.C.J., 214n, 215n, 242

*querela*, 22–3
Quinn, K., 17n, 32n, 148
Quint, D., 172

rape of the Sabine women, 336–8
Rawson, E., 185
Ready, J.L., 298n
*recusationes*, 71–2
Redfield, James, 64n, 64
Regifugia, 224n
religious institutions, 340–4, 348, 351
  *see also* sacrifice
Remus, 55–6, 101–3, 328–9
  *see also* Romulus
Renaissance views of the 'hero', 73–7
Republican rhetoric in the *Aeneid*, 311
rhetoric
  truth and, 33–6, 326
  violence and, 309–12, 314–16, 317
Richardson, J.S., 324
Richardson, Nicholas, 5, 12, 293n
ring-composition
  in Ennius, 188
  in Livy, 326–7, 341, 345–6, 350–1
Roman identity, 285
  ideas of the East in, 274–5, 279–81
  *see also* citizenship
Roman/Latin vs. Greek studies, 9–14, 247–8
Romanization, 181–2 *see also* citizenship; subject peoples
Rome
  early districts, 339, 354
  as *patria* of all citizens, 354
  re-foundation cycle, 346–8
  site of, 349–50
  Trojan origins, 264–5, 273, 274
  *see also* Ara Pacis
Romulus
  in the *Aeneid*, 101–3, 115
  apotheosis of, 48–9, 51–5
  Camillus as, 345
  in Cicero, 349
  in Dionysius of Halicarnassus, 334
  in Ennius, 55–6, 133, 189n
  in Livy, 258–61, 328–9, 331, 336, 344, 349, 350–1
  in Lucan, 103, 115
Romulus-Remus myth as prototypical, 59, 216
Runciman, D., 324, 325
Runciman, S., 273
Rüpke, J., 207n, 325–6

sacrifice, 226–7
  in Ovid's *Fasti*, 216–25, 226
  in Virgil's *Georgics*, 205, 209–10, 211–16, 223, 226
  models of, 205–8, 227
  non-animal, 222–3
Sailor, D., 329n, 343
Sallust
  criticism of proeemia, 141–2
  historical selectivity, 142–5
  self-referentiality, 142
  on value of deeds vs. writing, 142, 145–7
Schindler, C., 300n
Schlesier, Renate, 249
Schmit-Neuerburg, T., 314n
Scholes, R. and Kellogg, R., 62
Schröder, W.A., 56n
Scipio Aemilianus Africanus (Minor), P. Cornelius, 109
  in Cicero's *De Re Publica*, 95–6, 194–5
Scipio Africanus (Major), P. Cornelius, 109
  in Cicero's *Somnium Scipionis*, 95–6
  in Livy, 342
  in Lucan, 110
Scipio, Q. Caecilius Metellus Pius, 110
Scipiones, 109–10, 115
Scott, W.C., 293n
sea-storm imagery
  in Cicero, 310, 312
  *Iliad*, 291, 292–3
  in Lucretius, 299
Seeley, T.D.: *Honeybee Democracy*, 289
self-referentiality
  in epic, 168–9, 173–9, 229–31, 240–1
  in Sallust, 142
*semina*, 306
Seneca the younger
  on the 'greatness' of Pompey, 90n
  Statius and, 246
Shakespeare: *Antony and Cleopatra*, 275
Shawcross, J.T., 79
shield of Aeneas, 114, 116, 136–7, 278
Silius Italicus: 'hero' of *Punica*, 65–6
Silk, M.S., 120
similes, 286
  *Achilleid*, 231–4
  *Aeneid*, 171–2, 232, 280, 286, 307–17
  *De Bello Civili*, 319
  *De Rerum Natura*, 298–305
  *Fasti*, 220
  Hesiod, 288
  *Iliad*, 171–2, 287–94, 300–1
  *Odyssey*, 294–8
  *Paradise Lost*, 319–21

Silius Italicus, 319
  *Thebaid*, 319
  Valerius Flaccus, 319
Sirluck, E., 78
slaves
  manumission and citizenship, 334–5
  subject people as, 328
Smith, Jonathan Z., 8, 206–7
Social War, 352, 353, 357–9
soil and identity, 348–9, 350–1, 355–6
Sophocles, desert-island ranking, 13
Sparta, 145, 328, 334
Speaight, R., 21n
Spingarn, Joel E., 74
Stanford, W.B., 27
Statius *see Achilleid*; *Thebaid*
Steadman, J.M., 79
Stem, R., 329n
Stephens, S., 213
Steuart, E.M., 55
Stewart, D.J., 36, 37n, 38
structuralism, 207, 225–6, 248–9
subject peoples
  and ideology of empire, 327–8, 329
  and Roman citizenship, 181–2, 338–9, 361–4
symbolic anthropology, 8, 207, 225–6, 248–9
Syme, R., 37n, 141n, 147n

Tarquins, 98, 104
Tarrant, R.J., 111, 112
Tasso, Torquato, 76–7
  *Gerusalemme Liberata*, 76, 80
Taussig, Michael, 283–4
teaching, 3–4
Terminalia, 224
testimonia, evidence of, 268
text and context, 6–8, 10, 214–15, 226, 249
  *see also* historicism
*Thebaid* (Statius), 65, 66–7
Thomas, R.F., 58, 209–12, 214, 223
Thomas, Y., 324
Tiberius, 37
Tillyard, E.M.W., 74, 77
Titius Tatius, 336
Tolstoy, Leo
  *Anna Karenina*, 21
  *War and Peace*, 289
Torquatus. *see* Manlius Torquatus, T.
Troy
  in chronography, 187, 188, 190–2, 256
  date of fall, 185–6
  and Roman origins, 264–5, 273, 274
Tullus Hostilius, 338
Tusculum, 353, 356n, 357, 359, 360

Vahlen, J., 49n, 50n
Valerius Maximus, 262
Vandiver, E., 337n,
Varro
  as antiquarian, 262
  chronology in *De Gente*, 184–5, 190
  as evidence for Ennius, 49
  on religion, 341
Vegius, Mapheus, 74
Veii, 60n, 344–5, 350n, 356
Veseris, battle of, 360
Vessey, D., 66n
violence
  eroticisation of, 240–2
  literary aesthetics of, 169–73
  rhetoric vs., 309–12, 314–16, 317
Virgil
  desert-island ranking, 13
  and Ennius, 40–1, 43–4, 56–7, 109
  Greekness of, 282
  and Homer, 307–8, 312–14
  and Lucretius, 306–7, 308–9
  as Mantuan, 182
  Milton and, 320–1
  Ovid and, 200, 216–17, 220, 222
  Statius' *Achilleid* and, 228, 232–4, 235–6, 241–3

Troy in, 56–9
*see also Aeneid; Georgics*

Wallace-Hadrill, Andrew, 3, 281n
Wardy, R., 303n
Warmington, B.H., 276
West, D., 300n
White, Hayden, 7, 248n, 258n
Wigodsky, M., 45n
Wilkins, J.B., 207
Williams, G.W., 50n, 148
Williams, R.D., 22
Wilson, B., 288–9
wind and water imagery
  *Aeneid*, 308–9
  *Iliad*, 291, 292–3
  in Lucretius, 299–301, 303–5
Winterbottom, Michael, 11–12
Wiseman, Peter, 186–7, 250, 261–3, 262n, 269
Wlosok, A., 25
Wofford, Susanne, 172
Woodman, Tony, 141n, 257–8, 258n
writing, value of, 142

Zetzel, J.E.G., 216–17, 333n
Zeus. *see* Jupiter/Zeus